A New History of Mississippi

Dennis J. Mitchell

A NEW HISTORY OF MISSISSIPPI

University Press of Mississippi / Jackson

www.upress.state.ms.us

The University Press of Mississippi is a member
of the Association of American University Presses.

Manufactured in the United States of America

First printing 2014
∞
Library of Congress Cataloging-in-Publication Data

Mitchell, Dennis J.
A new history of Mississippi / Dennis J. Mitchell.
pages cm
Includes bibliographical references and index.
ISBN 978-1-61703-976-8 (cloth : alk. paper) —
ISBN 978-1-61703-977-5 (ebook) 1. Mississippi—
History. I. Title.
F341.M75 2014
976.2—dc23 2013044104

British Library Cataloging-in-Publication Data available

To my students

Contents

Preface

Mississippi is a place and a state of mind. The name evokes strong reactions from those who live here and from those who do not, but who think they know something about its people and their past. Mississippi is what the American Indians called the river along the state's western border. Only a few Choctaw remain compared to the 30,000 who once dominated the area but shared it with the Chickasaw, Natchez, Tunica, Yazoo, Tiou, Grigra, Koroa, Chakchiuma, and Biloxi. These tribal peoples furnished the romantic labels for cities, counties, and rivers that help to shape the sense of place for the descendants of Africans and Europeans, who displaced Mississippi's indigenous population and struggled to make the state their own. Mississippi's history is a story of violence, endurance, and strained human relationships that have produced America's best music and literature. What has rooted Mississippi's music and literature in a deep sense of place is that, despite their efforts, the human population has never overwhelmed the land. Human beings have abused the land and reshaped it, but Mississippians have never lost their feeling of impermanence, living widely scattered in small communities incapable of even giving the impression of dominating nature. William Faulkner and Eudora Welty conveyed the relationship between fictional characters and their environment in a manner that communicated the haunted, almost Gothic feeling that the blood-stained soil and streams impart today to visitors, to those who live here, and to readers around the world. The cotton planters' antebellum mansions in Natchez, Holly Springs, and Columbus provide a sense that dominance almost happened once in the past, but the current mansions' owners are usually retired professionals who project the image of custodians for the ghosts of the lost era. The slave quarters and sharecropper shacks that housed the majority of Mississippi's population until the Second World War have given way to ranch houses and trailers. Fifteen percent of the state's population lives in trailers, often on a flat, bare piece of earth gouged out of a forest or on a clear-cut lot surrounded by acres of small trees and bushes struggling to replace the forests downed and sold to the paper mills. Those homes provide the clearest indication of the transitory nature of a major portion of the population, who escape the wilderness and the heat in their tin and particleboard havens furnished with the appliances and veneer of twenty-first-century American civilization. But weekends, when there are no college football games, find them, along with the ranch house and apartment dwellers from Jackson, Tupelo, Yazoo City, and Hattiesburg, escaping to the woods, streams, and lakes. Deer camps abound with storytelling, which is probably the most enduring hallmark of Mississippi culture. In the beginning, Indians recounted their war stories and hunting tales, to earn their adult names, and then mingled with Africans and the Irish, who brought their oral traditions of griots and bards to add to the tradition giving birth to Robert Johnson and the blues, to Jimmie Rodgers and country music, to Elvis Presley and rock 'n' roll, to William Faulkner and the Nobel Prize, to Richard Wright and a scream against segregation, to novelist Larry Brown and . . . Living here sucks any half-observant, even dimwitted inhabitant into the mystery of the place.

This book is an interpretative narrative that attempts to tell the story of Mississippi in a readable, straightforward manner unencumbered with notes but based on the most recent scholarship. I shall provide directions to consult two other volumes for greater depth and understanding. One is Bradley Bond's *Mississippi: A Documentary History*, which provides a reader a taste of the most important primary documents. The other is Marion Barnwell's *A Place Called Mississippi: Collected Narratives*, which provides biographical pieces by and about some of the characters from our past.

Acknowledgments

Jim Barnett and Evan Peacock were kind enough to read and offer suggestions for improvements to chapter 1. Lamar Neal and Steven Slimp read most of the manuscript, providing numerous suggestions and improvements. Janet St Lawrence read each chapter as it rolled out of the printer and pronounced it interesting reading, encouraging me to forge ahead. As a massive consumer of fiction and a psychologist who possess no tolerance for the dull or pedestrian, she is skeptical of historians, and provided the sounding board for the general public toward whom this book is aimed. She also made innumerable useful suggestions to better the narrative. Melanie Thomas, the librarian at Mississippi State University (MSU)–Meridian helped me to secure materials and read the manuscript too. The librarians in the interlibrary loan department at Mitchell Library in Starkville worked hard securing, handling, and shipping books. The librarians at Meridian Community College's L. O. Todd (where MSU-Meridian houses its collection) provided assistance and tolerated my demands with great patience. Stephen Cresswell reviewed the manuscript for the University Press of Mississippi and helped greatly with a detailed markup of the manuscript, providing help with revisions. Student workers Shamika Burrage, Alli French, Katie Gough, Miranda Harrison, Sidney McDonald, Tiffany Moss, and Crystel Dorsey helped with the bibliography and a host of other chores. My assistant, Renee Gough, maintained the master copy, made many edits, and read the drafts. Over the years students here and at Jackson State University helped me clarify my understanding of the state's past with questions and discussion, which informed this narrative. Readers will recognize this book's debt to a host of authors whose works I plundered to write this narrative. I appreciate the scholars and writers who created the record and told the stories that I used for this book.

A New History of Mississippi

Geographical Introduction: The Place

Water, flooding, and erosion shaped Mississippi for millions of years. Fifty thousand feet of sedimentary rocks underlie the entire state and crop to the surface in a few places, but most of the state is covered with gravel and sand that washed out of the forming mountains to the north or with soils deposited by periodically advancing ice sheets or seas during warmer periods. The sea covered the whole land area many times and left behind clays, including Yazoo clay, which expands and contacts with its moisture content to crumble roads, interstates, and house foundations in the center of the state.

When the seashore penetrated to near the middle of the state, Basiloscurus and Zagorhiza, early whales, frolicked in the seas, leaving the state rich with deposits of well-preserved fossil specimens. Later humans may have hunted mastodons, horses, and camels along with predators such as saber-toothed cats in forests of spruce, pine, and hardwoods, but as the glaciers retreated north and the temperature rose, the flora and fauna evolved into those living today. The sea level reached its current location about 5,000 years ago when the land and waters began to take on their familiar shapes.

Woodall Mountain, a hill capped with sandstone that prevented its erosion, rises to just over 800 feet above sea level in the northeast corner of Mississippi. From the "mountain," Mississippi slopes south, with most of the state averaging around 500 feet above the Gulf of Mexico. Four of the state's ten landforms crowd into the northeast corner of the state. The Tombigbee Hills surround the "mountain" with sandy loam soil tinged red or orange. To the west of the hills lies a flat narrow Black Prairie with rich dark clay only about twenty miles wide, but inviting to agriculturalists. On the other side of the slightly rolling strip of prairie, the Ponotoc Ridge "soars" occasionally to 600 feet, and the soil returns to a red hue only to be replaced by an even more narrow strip of poorly draining, largely infertile clay called Flatwoods. Between the Flatwoods and the Loess Bluff Hills is wedged the North Central Hills, or Faulkner Country.

One of the three largest landforms in the state stretching in an arc from Tennessee to Alabama in the center of the state, the red clay hills provided the homeland for the Choctaw. The hills disappointed white farmers and eroded when planted with cotton in a manner far different from the

Choctaw's subsistence agricultural system. The river bottoms in the hills supported a few large farms, providing Faulkner with models for the conflict between planters and his poor Snopeses.

West of the red clay hills running the length of the state are the Loess Bluff Hills, consisting of brown loam that had been wind blown into place as the land formed. This narrow strip of rich, easily worked soil provided the ground where slave-owners built most of the antebellum plantations. Below the loam bluffs in the northwest lies the Yazoo Delta, forming a bow from the river marked off by what are now the cities of Memphis and Vicksburg at either end to the Loess Bluff Hills in the east. The Delta flooded for hundreds of years as the Mississippi River deposited much of the North American continent's topsoil into a swampy soup, half land and half water.

Here the Paleoindians settled to feed off of the rich riverine and swamp life living in the soup. Much later they discovered agriculture, and their population multiplied until the diseases brought by Europeans devastated them. The Paleoindian survivors moved into the less fertile hills, taking their agricultural skills with them and leaving the Delta area uninhabited until planters drained the swamps and built levees to protect it after the Civil War.

East of the bluffs in the south, the Piney Woods—or, more properly, the Pine Hills—constitute almost a third of the state but grow pine trees and little else. The area proved so unfit for agriculture and produced such small deer that the Choctaw resisted only halfheartedly when asked by the British to sign it over. Just north of the Pine Hills runs Jackson Prairie, with better soil than the hills on either side but more trees and rolling hills than the flat Black Prairie in the north. South of the Pine Hills, a Coastal Meadow area reaches the Gulf of Mexico. The state extends offshore to barrier islands that block the lapping waves from its beaches.

Streams, ponds, and lakes abound throughout the state. Rock-bottomed streams exist, but most stream bottoms are sand or mud. Rivers drew the first humans to settle and later provided the "highways" for Africans and Europeans to penetrate the wooded, wet land for commercial agriculture. The Tombigbee Hills give birth to the Tombigbee River, which flows into Alabama and directs trade along its banks toward Mobile, where the Tombigbee connects to the Gulf of Mexico. Some of the North Central Hills' rivers drain into the Delta, while others head east to the Tombigbee. The Big Black and Pearl gather the waters from much of the center of the state. The Big Black goes west into the Mississippi River, and the Pearl flows directly to the Gulf. The southeastern section of the state concentrates its rivers and creeks into the Pascagoula River, which holds the distinction of being the longest free-flowing river in the forty-eight contiguous states today. Historically, the rivers provided the only passageways into the state for long-distance trade, but aside from the Mississippi, they did not make it easy. Fallen trees blocked rivers much of the time, and heavy cargoes usually could move only during the rainy season when the rivers rose.

Rain falls throughout the year, but autumns are usually dry. Temperatures vary, but summers are hot, and humidity is often so high that the air seems liquid. Heat, then, is relieved only by thunderstorms, tornadoes, or hurricanes. As bad as those are at times, Mississippians are thankful for the cooler air that follows. Winters are mild, with scattered days of cold and near heat intermingled. Snow falls rarely and melts almost immediately. April and October are glorious with moderate temperatures, blue skies, and color in the plants.

Pine trees dominate the landscape, but hardwoods such as oak, hickory, cypress, magnolia, sweet gum, maple, dogwood, redbud, cherry, cedar, and elm scatter throughout the state in varieties adapted to water and soil conditions. Acorns and nuts played a major role as food sources for Indians and early settlers, as did forgotten foods such as the smilax vine, which provides an asparagus-like vegetable with its early shoots. It is possible to identify 100 different vines in a twenty-acre plot. Any land allowed to grow wild can quickly become an impassable tangle of wild grapevines, honeysuckle, wisteria, or blackberries. Plants provide forage for plentiful wildlife.

Deer flourish; buffalo have disappeared; birds are abundant, but not compared to the days before African and European settlement. Passenger pigeons, Carolina parakeets, and ivory-billed woodpeckers, once important in Mississippi, are extinct. The prairie chicken, or heath hens, have disappeared, and the other populations today are greatly reduced from the 1700s. Turkeys survive, thrive, and still serve as important game. Smaller animals such as rabbits, squirrels, opossums, and raccoons keep the brush alive. Beaver and alligators populate the lakes and streams along with catfish, gar, bass, perch, bream, and crappie. In the distant past, the land and waters teemed with fish, fowl, and animals to supply the needs of humans, and visitors today are amazed at the teeming wildlife in a state that remains 65 percent forest with a population of slightly less than three million people.

Chapter One

RISE AND FALL OF INDIAN CULTURE

As the warm, wet land emerged, the Paleoindians adapted. They continued to hunt deer and bear with an improved spear thrown with an atlatl, a throwing device that increased the distance and force of their weapons, but gradually they came to depend more on the fish, alligators, turtles, snakes, birds, and other small creatures in the swamps and rivers. They ate acorns, hickory nuts, walnuts, pecans, persimmons, wild grapes, hackberries, goosefoot, knotweed, and seeds from honey locust. Although they did not practice agriculture, the plant and animal life in the southeastern portion of the United States grew so densely that humans could concentrate in numbers enough to build impressive mounds. On the west side of the Mississippi River at Poverty Point, these hunters and gatherers built one of the most impressive mound complexes in North America at about the same time Stonehenge went up in England. Some archaeologists believe Jaketown on the Yazoo River to be associated with this culture, along with several other sites.

Not only did some hunters and gatherers build impressive mounds, but they also carried on long-distance trade. Because the area lacked stones, they imported them from as far away as Arkansas and the Appalachian Mountains to craft stone vessels, plummets, atlatl weights, axes, and ornaments. The inhabitants constructed the largest mound at Poverty Point in the shape of a bird, indicating that they found them important and perhaps sacred. They carved stone pipes to smoke tobacco, which again may have involved religious rituals. Their accomplishments indicate a more complicated life than usually ascribed to hunters and gatherers. Even if they only occupied the mounds for portions of the year and had to forage at distances some months, the first complex civilization in Mississippi had long cultural roots that connected them to the historic Indian tribes who inhabited Mississippi.

Mississippi Prehistoric Periods

Paleo-Indian	10,000 B.C.E.–8000 B.C.E. Hunting with spears for large mammals Small nomadic groups

Archaic	8000 B.C.E.–500 B.C.E. Semisedentary with seasonal gathering of groups Gathering wild foods and fishing supplement hunting Atlatl used to throw spears Regional trade begins Ceramic pottery and mounds appear toward end of period
Woodland	500 B.C.E.–1000 C.E. Settled life in permanent villages and tribes develop Agriculture begins while hunting continues Pottery in many shapes for many uses decorated in a variety of patterns Burial mounds become common Bows and arrows and corn adopted toward end of period
Mississippian	1000 C.E.–1500 C.E. Agriculture based on corn, beans, and squash becomes basis for large communities Large temple mounds serve as center of ceremonial sites Chiefs head hierarchical societies Warfare increases Pottery includes crushed shells as tempering substance Widespread trade in rare goods controlled by chiefs

Poverty Point appeared toward the end of the long Archaic period, identified by specialists as lasting from 8000 to 1000 B.C.E. and blended into the Woodland stage, which lasted until 1000 C.E. Life changed because Indians began to gather more seed-bearing plants and to garden them, encouraging the growth of goosefoot, may grass, knotweed, and sunflowers. They settled down into widely dispersed communities, built wood houses, and began to conduct elaborate burial rituals for their dead with prized possessions made of copper, stone, and shells to comfort the dead. Bows provided them a better weapon and improved their hunts. The population probably increased because of a better food supply, and they began to settle into villages before acquiring agriculture.

Around 700 C.E. the Cole's Creek Culture emerged between the Gulf Coast and the Yazoo Basin with distinctive flat-topped, pyramidal mounds usually arranged around an open plaza. Few lived on site, but obviously it provided a civic and ceremonial center. They built the mounds in stages and constructed buildings atop the mounds, which may have been temples, charnel houses, or homes for elite families. Cole's Creek peoples experimented with maize or corn, but the plant served only a supplementary role in their food supply.

In the Mississippian period, from 1000 to 1500 C.E., maize became the main source of food along with squash and beans. In the Mississippian era, corn provided more nutrients than its distant cousin grown today, and Indians made two crops each year. Abundant crops and continued hunting provided food surpluses previously unequaled. Perhaps to protect those surpluses and to store them safely, populations across the Southeast formed chiefdoms. Large populations gathered into villages, and dominant political families emerged. The chiefs lived in houses on top of impressive mounds. The chiefs had access to more meat than the ordinary inhabitants, and claimed burial in or near the "public" buildings with elaborate artifacts, copper jewelry, and ceremonial weapons. "Commoners" buried their dead either in community cemeteries or near their homes with a shell ornament, a tool, or a ceramic vessel.

Evidence indicates that commoners gave food offerings to their ruler, creating a chief of considerable power. The chiefs distributed food to commoners in times of scarcity and controlled rare goods obtained by long-distance trade. Not all peoples formed chiefdoms, and for unknown reasons, in the 1400s chiefdoms suddenly declined, and many Indians scattered into smaller communities again. They continued to farm and hunt, reverting to gathering when crops failed.

In 1539 Hernando de Soto and his expedition stumbled into this world seeking the precious metals that the conquistadores had looted so successfully from the Aztecs and Incas. By the time the Spaniards crossed the Tombigbee in 1540 near what is now Columbus, they had plundered and raped their way across much of the Southeast and had learned about the Mississippian culture without understanding it. The Spaniards lived more in the medieval than the modern European world and never doubted their superiority over the peoples they encountered.

Unfortunately, they provide the only historical record of Mississippian peoples. Mississippian, meaning the culture of corn-growing, mound-building, chief-ruled societies found throughout the Southeast, lived in hierarchal societies and carried their rulers on their shoulders in litters. They spoke a variety of languages as different as Arabic and German, and lived in villages of 300 to 500 people, who might be the only humans they would ever know. They felt surrounded by enemies, who intruded into their hunting grounds. If they lived in a chiefdom with a ruling family, the chiefdom would contain no more than 5,000 inhabitants and extend no more than a day's walk. The family and clan provided the center of their lives and their protection. Injuries to blood relatives required revenge, as clans never forgave and accepted the obligation to kill the killer or, failing that, the killer's relatives. Wearing only a breechcloth, Mississippians fought with war clubs carved from hickory, ironwood, or black locust, unless using a bow from a distance.

If they died in battle, they believed in an afterlife and invested some effort to understand the actions and motives of spiritual beings, whom they knew inhabited the beyond. Omens loomed large to them, and the wrong bird singing could abort a war mission. All societies understood themselves to be at the center of the world; had a special reverence for the four directions, making symbols to illustrate them; and smoked tobacco on special occasions. Their mothers determined their inheritance, and their mother's eldest brother educated and guided their sisters' children through life.

Having fought in what is today Alabama, de Soto continued north. After resting his men for a week and stealing food, he kidnapped a chief from a town on the Black Warrior River, forcing the chief to guide the expedition into the Chicaza (Tombigbee) River valley. December rains and fording swamps, creeks, and rivers made the Spaniards miserable. When they reached the Tombigbee, a large war party assembled on the opposite bank to threaten them if they tried to cross. De Soto sent an Indian to explain he came in peace, but the party seized and executed his emissary as a further warning.

A flanking party of Spaniards swam their horses at a lower, shallow site, and the war party disappeared, allowing de Soto to cross. The Spanish had entered the Black Prairie, where the largest town, Chicaza, contained only twenty homes. When the Spaniards arrived, the chief and all his people had abandoned the town. Yet de Soto decided to winter there. The Chicaza lived in homes scattered about the surrounding countryside, which the Spanish raided for food, even tearing down houses to drag the materials back to construct more lodging for themselves. The Chicaza attacked in small groups at night until the Spanish captured a few men and used them to persuade the chief to visit. He came on a litter bearing gifts and brought his tributary chiefs with him. Eventually, although relations did not improve, de Soto invited the leaders to dine on pork from the pig herd accompanying the expedition. As a result, the Chicaza began to attack the unknown animals, killing and stealing as many as possible.

The chief tried to use the strangers against his enemies, but when the Spanish prepared to leave in March, the Chicaza struck in force by creeping into their occupied town with fire concealed in small pots. They fired flaming arrows onto the roofs of houses containing the sleeping Spaniards. As the Spanish charged out half-dressed, the Indians clubbed them as archers targeted their horses. The Chicaza killed twelve men, fifty-seven horses, and 400 pigs, which burned. They lost one warrior. As the Spanish worked to clothe themselves and refit their armor, de Soto dispatched horsemen in every direction to murder anyone they could find within a circle of fifteen miles. Despite the attempt at cleansing the neighborhood, the Chicaza attacked again, but denied the element of surprise and fighting on open land against horsemen armed with iron weapons, they lost several men and did not return again. De Soto left Mississippi through a wilderness north of Chicaza to wander around what is today Tennessee and Arkansas. When he turned south again, he died, and his men "buried" him in the Mississippi River, hoping the hostile Indians would not learn of his death.

The survivors of the first Spanish incursion did not encourage other Europeans to follow them into the Southeast. Europeans would not appear in the area again until French explorers descended the Mississippi River in the 1680s. Europeans left diseases behind, devastating the Indian populations. Some scholars guess the losses to be as high as 80 percent of the population, but others respond with lower estimates because, they argue, the Indians did not live in densely populated towns. Archaeologists refer to the period between the initial European incursion and sustained contact as protohistoric because written records again vanished, leaving only the physical remains to tell the story. During this era, the historic tribes formed and moved into the territories that we recognize as the Choctaw, Chickasaw, and Natchez nations. The Natchez preserved the chiefdom-type culture encountered by de Soto, while the Choctaw and Chickasaw represented the new confederations of peoples who migrated into the poorer soil areas that had been wilderness in the 1500s.

The Choctaw and Chickasaw understood themselves to be brothers who had chosen to separate. They shared with other southeastern peoples the old memory of traveling from the west following a leaning pole to a new land, sometimes carrying the bones of their ancestors. At some point, the Choctaw abandoned this memory for the story of the earth giving birth to them at Nanih Waiyah mound built by earlier peoples during the Middle Woodland period. In their later creation story, they crawled from the earth at the mound and lay on the grass to be dried by the sun, which became their chief god.

Archaeologists believe the Choctaw shared a prairie culture with the Chakchiuma and Chickasaw, but chose to join with people from the east who traced their ancestry to the devolved Moundville chiefdom in what is today Alabama, and with people from the Southwest related to the Natchez, who may have had a chiefdom in the lower Pearl River valley. The latter group, sometimes referred to as Plaquemine, became the Choctaw of the Six-Towns and the Chickasawhay living on the upper portion of the Pascagoula, speaking with an accent and maintaining distinctive dress and hairstyles. The eastern Choctaw lived on tributaries of the Tombigbee in what is today Kemper County, while the western Choctaw inhabited the upper Pearl. Their confederation evolved as they dealt with the shock and chaos resulting from the spread of disease and death after the European incursion.

The Choctaw lived along streams and farmed corn, squash, sunflowers, and beans on natural levees in soil that could be easily worked with a digging stick or the shoulder blade of a buffalo serving as a hoe. The chiefdoms east and west of them had cultivated floodplains with more extensive fields, but the Choctaw continued to rely more on hunting and gathering to supplement agriculture. Men helped with the heavy work of clearing land and then left food production to women. Corn provided the Choctaw most of their calories, and usually they produced an abundance. They preferred deer meat but consumed a wide variety of small game, including birds and fish. Aside from deer, the Choctaw valued bear the most because bear fat became the most important cooking oil.

A bow made of hickory or black locust with a pull of around fifty pounds served as their main hunting weapon. Arrows armed with stone heads or sometimes with a bird talon or deer antler points provided the ammunition for the hunt. The Choctaw knew how to mix a nonlethal but stunning poison to bring fish to the surface. Boys practiced hunting turkeys and small game with blowpipes fashioned from cane. Mothers also assigned their children to chase away birds from the fields. The women packed their crops close, allowing bean vines to climb the corn stalks and interspersing sunflowers and tobacco among the squash and beans. Using lye, they transformed the dried corn into hominy, and in the process released niacin, which was important to a healthy diet.

In times of drought, the Choctaw reverted to gathering in the river bottoms and extended their deer-hunting season to provide meat. Generally the Choctaw left their towns to hunt when the leaves began to fall. Less foliage made hunting easier, and they practiced game management, allowing the spring-born deer to grow over the summer. During hungry times, women harvested tender young smilax vines as an asparagus-like vegetable and tubers of the vine to pound into flour for bread. Morning glory vine roots provided a sort of wild potato. Nuts and berries remained an important source of food every year, with the Choctaw extracting oil from hickory nuts for a multitude of uses. With more meat from the extended hunting season and the vegetables found in the borderlands, the Choctaw weathered droughts to return to their gardens the next spring.

Animal hides made up most of their clothing and bed covers, but women also wove cloth from fibers obtained from tree trunks. From bird feathers, they manufactured blankets, shawls, and ceremonial garments. European observers compared the process to wig making, as the women attached feathers to a net of strings with feathers on both sides of the "fabric." Some of the bird feather material became a sort of towel used to wipe hands after a meal. Feathers also provided important ornamentation, with eagles' feathers seeming to be the most prestigious.

The Choctaw built their homes of wood and wattle, painting the interior white and thatching the roofs with grasses. Their homes spread along natural levees for considerable distances rather than bunching around a central plaza as some earlier Indian towns had done. Visitors reported winding their way through paths and gardens, giving the impression of rural more than town living even in large population centers. Ball fields brought the entire population together for contests dubbed the "little brother to war." Played with sticks and deer-hide balls, the game created enormous excitement enhanced by the tradition of betting heavily on the outcome. In addition to their private plots, the Choctaw farmed a common field of crops for the town as a whole.

Red and white chiefs led the towns as representatives of the moieties designated by those colors. The white chiefs dominated and controlled the rare trade items such as shell and copper jewelry, which they distributed to members of the tribe to increase and solidify their position and to enhance their ability to negotiate important decisions. The red chiefs led warriors into battle against external enemies. The moieties determined each person's role in life because one could not marry within one's moiety, and certain lifelong obligations stemmed from birth into the red or white group. For example, the Choctaw burial custom required the dead to be exposed on a platform until most of the flesh decayed, and then a bone-picker from the opposite moiety picked off the remaining flesh and placed the bones in a basket for internment in the town's charnel house. A child's moiety depended on his or her mother because the Choctaw's inheritance came from the maternal side. The mother's brother fulfilled the male role for discipline and education. The child's father behaved as a fond, indulgent uncle might in a paternal society.

Women played a more important role in Choctaw life than females did in Western societies at the time. When the Choctaw first met to negotiate with Europeans, the delegation included women. Inheritance depended upon the mother's status, not the father's. Women, as the primary farmers, produced the bulk of the family's food, and the Choctaw had no exclusive male priesthood to inhibit females. The mother mound gave birth to the Choctaw as mothers did to their sons and daughters.

Spirits dominated the Choctaw worldview, which consisted of three levels. The upper level, home of the sun, gave light and order to the middle level where people lived. The underworld, home to the moon, water, and disorder, threatened darkness, disorder, and disaster. The Choctaw tried to balance the forces of the cosmos in order to assure life in the present and beyond, using magic and rituals. Women left their homes during their menstrual period, lived in a house set aside for that purpose, and started a new fire so that they did not pollute the one at home. Outside their towns in the borderland between nations, monsters lurked to snare the unwary traveler. Men who went to war or hunted in dangerous territories cleansed themselves in sweat lodges when they returned home. Choctaw symbols included crosses representing the four directions and circles representing, among other concepts, the perimeter around their land, which kept them safe from the chaos beyond.

Choctaw men judged one another as warriors who tested themselves in battle against other nations. A man did not reach full maturity until he had fought and, if possible, killed another man. They preferred to fight in the woods. If attacked, they abandoned towns to draw the enemy into the surrounding trees, vines, and brush. Most of the fighting traditionally occurred in the borderlands as they competed for hunting lands. An early English visitor judged the Choctaw to be the swiftest, most elusive Indians, outrunning horsemen in wooded areas and firing faster and more accurately with their bows than the Englishman's companions with guns. If captured, a Choctaw reacted with defiance, detailing his battles in a death speech and threatening his captors and all their kin as they tortured him.

The Chickasaw shared many customs with the Choctaw and gained an even more fearsome reputation as warriors. Dominating the Black Prairie area with hunting ground claims stretching far to the north, east, and west, the Chickasaw built more fortified structures in each town, which provided protection from invaders. They buried their dead beneath the floors of their homes unless a man died while away at war or on a hunt. In that case, they used the body exposure and bone-picking method to produce remains to be transported back home. The Chickasaw built summer and winter houses. They constructed the winter house in a circle twenty-five feet in diameter with a dirt floor dug three feet below ground level. They framed the house with pine straight logs and poles, lashing them together with leather thongs. They split hickory, oak, or cane and wove them into material for the walls and roof. A mixture of clay and dry grass served as plaster for the walls. They constructed the summerhouse in a rectangle, with ventilation holes in the mat walls and porches for the two rooms in each house.

Many Indian nations practiced slavery, but the Chickasaw seemed to be more attached to the institution than others. Women urged their warriors on to more raids and enjoyed, by some accounts, the increased status of overseeing slaves.

The Natchez, Mississippi's other large Indian population, grew out of collapsed chiefdoms along the Mississippi and Yazoo Rivers. Peoples such as the Tunica, the Koroa, and the Yazoo drifted south along the river valleys searching for new homes. Perhaps victims of the Little Ice Age or of Old World diseases that spread ahead of direct contact with Africans and Europeans, refugees sought to rebuild as the Choctaw and Chickasaw had. The best guess is that some of the inhabitants of the Natchez bluffs coalesced with wanderers to form the Natchez nation. They constructed Emerald Mound, one of the largest mounds in North America, and then abandoned it during the protohistoric period, relocating to mounds within the current city that now bears their name.

The Natchez held on to more of the Mississippian-era chiefdom's customs, including human sacrifice on the death of the Great Sun who ruled them. Occupying the prime location on the first high ground along the Mississippi River north of the Gulf of Mexico, the Natchez suffered near extermination at the hands of the French allied with the Choctaw. When the French moved into their territory, the Great Sun served as the religious head of the nation, but the chiefs of the individual towns enjoyed near political autonomy.

As the French and English arrived in the Southeast, more than a dozen smaller tribes still lived within the territory that would become the state of Mississippi. In some cases, the French counted only twenty to twenty-five homes for each tribe. Some integrated into the larger confederations during the historic period. Others moved west to escape and find better homes. In legend, the Biloxi defeated the Pascagoula in battle, and the surviving Pascagoula walked into the river singing, giving the river its current name, Singing River. With a population of 30,000, the Choctaw dwarfed all other nations with the manpower to control political power when they desired and organized for war. They dominated the area west of the Creek nation (Alabama) and had the potential to destroy the peoples to their north, east, and south, and, if they chose, they could have closed the Mississippi River and the northern Gulf of Mexico.

The English settled Charles Town (Charleston) in 1670, and by the 1690s they had penetrated into the Chickasaw nation and begun to arm the Chickasaw for the purpose of slave raiding. The French in 1682 descended the Mississippi River bent on a grand scheme of uniting French Canada with the Gulf of Mexico to deter English expansion across the continent. Rene Robert Cavelier, Sieur de LaSalle led an expedition that visited the Natchez and Koroa on the Mississippi River bluffs before battling the Quinipassa near what is today New Orleans. After a threatening group of warriors interrupted their meal at the Koroa town on their return north, the French party bypassed the Natchez and hurried away unsure of their safety. They took along a couple of boy-slaves whom they had traded from the Taensa, and communicated their discovery of a water route linking Canada to the Gulf of Mexico.

Commissioned to find the mouth of the great river from the Gulf, LaSalle explored the coast but missed the river and died in the attempt. As a result, the French chose a hardy Canadian war hero, Pierre LeMoyne, Sieur d'Iberville, for the job of finding the river and establishing an outpost for a new colony. D'Iberville and his younger brother Jean Baptiste LeMoyne, Sieur de Bienville erected the first European settlement in Mississippi at what is today Ocean Springs. After finding the Mississippi River and a letter left behind by another French explorer, d'Iberville returned to his temporary camp on the Gulf Coast, where he encountered two Spanish deserters from Pensacola who were walking to Mexico. Clearly the Indians of the Southeast faced an influx of Europeans, both those sent by their governments to deal with them as foreign powers and stray individuals from Africa and Europe trading or seeking asylum. The stew of complicated cultural, military, trade, and political conflicts brewed a deadly mixture that no government could control.

D'Iberville explored up the Pascagoula and found the Biloxi's town made desolate by European diseases. Most of the people had died, and they had burned many of their homes. The French planted crops around their Gulf side stockade in poor sandy soil, but their seeds failed to grow, and they relied on the Biloxi to feed them. In turn, the Biloxi came to desire French trade goods. Indians had no metal tools or weapons or cloth to match the wool garments of the French. A mutually dependent relationship developed quickly, and the Biloxi relocated to serve the new market for their produce. D'Iberville's brother, Bienville, proved to be a master linguist, learning the Indians' languages and customs in short order. While his older brother returned to France, the second-in-command died, and Bienville assumed control. He would dominate the French colony called Louisiana for decades. D'Iberville returned with orders to move the French from Fort Maurapas, as they had named the Ocean Springs outpost, to Mobile, which had a much better harbor. With that accomplished in 1702, d'Iberville returned to France and severed his ties to the French effort in the Southeast.

Louisiana remained a poor backwater of the French Empire throughout most of its history. Independent of the government-sponsored efforts to head off English expansion out of Carolina and Spanish expansion out of Florida, French missionaries made their way down the Mississippi to take up residence with the Taensa and the Natchez. Coureurs de bois also passed through, enjoying the Natchez women to the consternation of the priest and enslaving Indian women to sell to soldiers in Mobile. The French enslaved relatively few Indians, but the English developed an extensive system, arming their allies and rewarding them handsomely for slaves delivered to Carolina for transshipment to the growing sugar colonies in the Caribbean. The Chickasaw proved to be the best slave catchers of all the tribes. They allied with the eastern portion of the Natchez to war against the small tribes, destroying the population of the Yazoo valley and forcing migration on those who evaded capture. Estimates range that between 2,000 and 5,000 individuals were sold abroad by the English from the smaller tribes alone. The number sold from the whole of the Southeast totaled between 25,000 and 50,000 for the period 1670 to 1715.

Damage to Indian culture started immediately. The white, or civil, chiefs who had predominated in all the nations lost ground to the red, or war, chiefs, who benefited from the European goods supplied to them. What had been the exclusive role of the civil chiefs to distribute rare trade items slipped from their control, and the war chiefs acquired new power, disturbing the balance of the nations' political life. French priests tried to stop human sacrifices and interfered in the chosen sex practices of the women. Most important, Indians continued to die from European diseases.

When the easy prey among the smaller tribes had been exhausted, the Chickasaw turned on the Choctaw, who lost from 1,500 to 2,500 people to the slave trade before 1715. Without European arms to protect themselves, the Choctaw ran the risk of seeing their nation destroyed. For that reason, they welcomed the French, who could arm them to defend themselves. Journeying to Mobile, the Choctaw used their accepted custom of adoption to make the French leaders their brothers, establishing a family relationship between themselves and the French. Having no commercial system, the Choctaw needed a relationship that they understood to facilitate the necessary exchange of arms and goods.

Bienville comprehended that gift giving constituted the heart of the exchange method, and he needed the Choctaw to counter the English-allied Indians. He therefore gladly smoked the calumet and entertained the Choctaw lavishly—the chiefs at his own table. He told the Choctaw the French would be their fathers, which they must have found an odd relationship because the most important male figure to them was their mother's brother. With French guns, the Choctaw fought back against the Chickasaw and tried to adjust to the new neighbors with so many desirable goods.

Unfortunately for the Choctaw, the War of the Spanish Succession shut off the flow of French goods because no supply ships arrived between 1708 and 1711. The French had to look to the Indians to feed them. Of course, the Choctaw would deal with the English too, knowing they needed to balance their allies. Their relationship with the French suffered when, after the war, Louis XIV granted Louisiana to a Canadian businessman, who sent his own governor and demoted Bienville. As a part of the new business venture, the company established a trading post with the Natchez in order to profit from the trade in deer hides that had grown up among the various inhabitants of Louisiana. Cutting prices and declaring a monopoly, the new governor alienated everyone involved.

The Natchez towns split in their allegiances. The Great Sun and his family closest to the river allied against the chiefs near the Natchez Trace, where the English traders worked to make friends. When the English murdered four French traders in Natchez territory, Bienville mounted a military operation to punish the Natchez. Camping on an island below Natchez, Bienville lured the Natchez chiefs from the warring villages to him and then seized and imprisoned them, offering to swap them for the heads of the murderers and the construction of a fort for his troops to occupy the Natchez bluffs overlooking the Mississippi River. He released a minor chief, who returned to Natchez and decapitated all of the killers but one who could not be found. In the missing man's place, he took the head of the man's brother.

Returning to the French island, the chief failed to understand why Bienville insisted that he must produce the additional murderer. To the Natchez, disputes raged between groups, not individuals, and the death had been avenged. The Great Sun and his brother, Tattooed Serpent, acquiesced in the quiet murder of their rival chiefs by the French. The Natchez built Fort Rosalie to French specifications, 150 feet by 90 feet, and the First Natchez War ended with dancing and the calumet ceremony. A new trading post appeared nearby, and the European occupation of Indian lands in the interior began.

After Louis XIV's death in 1715, Louisiana fell into the hands of John Law and his company, which created a financial bubble based on an unrealistic, unworkable plan to establish plantations in Louisiana. The company sent vagrants, deserters, and freed prisoners to the colony, claiming they would carve out prosperous agricultural empires concentrating on tobacco crops. The settlers imported African slaves instead of enslaving the indigenous population, who could escape too easily. The company granted French settlers land along the Mississippi River, but the Natchez already occupied the best, most healthy land. At first the Natchez welcomed the French settlers as they had the tribes for years past.

As it became clear that the French understood land ownership in a different sense than the Natchez and disputes developed over delivery of food and deer hides, tempers flared and violence erupted. The Natchez took gifts and promised to deliver, not understanding that in the French mind a commercial contract had been made. The Natchez fort and trading post constituted the neglected backwater of the French Empire, and the fort quickly decayed while the handful of soldiers stationed in it moved into the Natchez towns to live with Indian women, leaving the French unprepared for any challenge.

The Second Natchez War in 1722 erupted when the Natchez shot a plantation owner who was riding back to his "concession." Because he only had eighteen soldiers in the midst of hundreds of warriors, Fort Rosalie's commander asked Tattooed Serpent to act as intermediary with warriors from the English-allied towns who sniped at settlers. Tattooed Serpent, red chief to the Great Sun's white office, negotiated a settlement and went to New Orleans to be lectured by Bienville, who wanted him to control the English-allied villages. Understanding Tattooed Serpent's need to win friends by distributing scarce goods, Bienville then liberally supplied him with guns, knives, powder, and gunflints.

The peace proved short-lived, and the next year hostilities resumed. Bienville enlisted a coalition of Yazoo, Choctaw, and Tunica along with some passing Canadians to hurry to Natchez. Cutting cloth armbands to distinguish his Indian allies from the Natchez, Bienville conferred with Tattooed Serpent, who informed him that the English-allied towns had slipped completely out of his control. Bienville adopted a scorched earth campaign burning homes, desecrating the sacred temples, having his Indian slaves scalp even an old woman left behind, and enslaving men, women, and children. To call off the killing, he demanded the heads of the leaders and that of a black man who had become influential among the Natchez. The French increased the number of troops at Fort Rosalie to thirty, but settlers and slaves multiplied and ignored the Natchez's complaints about their behavior.

Tattooed Serpent, friend and ally to the French, made this lament to a French settler not long before he died in 1725.

> What need did we have of the French? Before them, didn't we live better than we do now? Because we deprive ourselves of a part of our grain, of game and of fish that we killed to share with them. In what, therefore, did we have need of them? Was it for their guns? We used our bows and arrows which sufficed to make us live well. Was it for their white, blue or red blankets? We did well enough with the skins of buffaloes which are warmer. Our wives worked on these coverlets of feathers for the winter and of the bark of myrtle trees for the summer. It wasn't so beautiful, but our wives were more hard working and less vain than they are now. Finally, before the arrival of the French, we lived like men who know how to do with what they have, whereas today we walk like slaves who do not do what they wish.

The pillars of the Natchez-French alliance system that maintained Natchez tolerance of the French invasion slipped away. Bienville left for Paris in 1726, and in 1728 the Great Sun died. The majority of the French among the Natchez refused to learn their culture as Bienville had, and the growing numbers of African slaves saw Natchez hostility to the French as a boon to them. The French commander at Natchez bullied the Indians and seemed determined to take more land for himself.

Responding with a carefully planned attack, the Natchez used a tobacco smoking ceremony featuring an elaborate pipe called a calumet during a visit by their new Great Sun to the fort. Surrounding the French, the Natchez suddenly shot the commander and the soldiers around him. At the sound of the shots, other warriors fell on unsuspecting settlers throughout the district. The Natchez killed 138 men, thirty-five women, and fifty-six children, losing only twelve of their own. They spared a carter and a tailor—one to haul the loot to their homes in his oxen cart and the other to fit their new stolen clothes for them. The African slaves either joined the Natchez in the massacre or suffered captivity for resale to the English. Captive French women and children served as hostages. A group of visiting Yazoo witnessed the slaughter and set off to rid themselves of the French at Fort St. Pierre, modern-day Vicksburg. They murdered their resident priest and killed the entire garrison of seventeen soldiers.

The obvious goal of ethnic cleansing on the part of the Natchez and Yazoo caused the French to panic. The French governor of Louisiana first armed African slaves and sent them to attack one of the small tribes near New Orleans because he heard a rumor that they might be allied with the Natchez. Then he set the slaves to work constructing defenses around the city. With only sixty soldiers, he had no means of retaliating without allies.

Though he did not fully trust them, he had to turn to the Choctaw who joined him. The French commander sent to punish the Natchez proved hesitant, and the Choctaw lost patience with him. The Natchez moved captured cannons into their own forts and held out while the French in the European fashion of the day dug trenches in an effort to take the forts. The Natchez eventually left in the night with all of their loot, leading the French to suspect that the Choctaw may have colluded in their escape.

The Choctaw took charge at Natchez, keeping rescued hostages in their custody and forcing the French to pay for their release. The governor led a second expedition against the Natchez when he learned that they had crossed the Mississippi and built another fort. Unable to take the fort, the French seized the Great Sun and other chiefs after persuading them to come across the lines for negotiations. Lying to the Natchez and telling them that anyone who surrendered would be protected and spared, the governor got some to surrender while others escaped during a rainy night. The governor shipped those who surrendered to Santo Domingo, where they were sold as slaves to labor on sugarcane plantations. The surviving Natchez fought a guerrilla war against the French, which only gradually decreased in intensity as groups of Natchez dispersed to find new homes among the Chickasaw, Cherokee, and Creek.

The French disaster led the government to reclaim the colony from its private owners and in 1734 to reappoint Bienville, who was living in Paris, as governor. The Natchez plantations did not recover, and the area lingered as a remote military post. Bienville refocused his attention on the Chickasaw, who gave protection to remnants of the Natchez and served as a potent ally to the English. Still lacking enough soldiers, he had to continue to rely on the Choctaw as the most powerful military force in Louisiana.

The Choctaw, unlike the Natchez, did not live on the Mississippi and enjoyed more shelter from contacts with European and African intruders. They shared the same desire to possess European metal tools, weapons, cooking utensils, guns, and cloth, but their distributive chiefs controlled the trade better for a longer period of time. They did not need to replace most of the metal goods frequently. The French respected the chief's role, and in each town traders first went to him. Only after the trader performed the necessary ceremonies and the chief announced his arrival did the trading begin. When the Choctaw received guns, the supply was limited. The chiefs shared the guns and small amounts of powder with hunters, who took turns with the weapon and distributed their kills, too.

The Choctaw benefited from the disease and chaos dating back to the dissolution of the chiefdoms in the river valleys to their west and from the continuing holocaust of disease because the deaths and migrations emptied the prime game land for their primary meat source, the white-tailed deer. The former fields in the river valleys provided ideal habitat for deer and encouraged the migration of small buffalo herds into the area in the 1700s. The Choctaw reversed the more ancient living arrangement by farming the less fertile hills in the east and using the rich river valleys as hunting grounds. They maintained the grounds by burning during their hunts, which not incidentally improved the land's carrying capacity for deer. The Choctaw prospered because they adapted best to their environment and because initially they managed to contain the French and English and all they brought with them within their traditional culture.

The Choctaw adopted chickens, for example, but for many years they did not eat them because chickens consumed dung, so just as they did not eat buzzards, they declined chickens. Later when they did eat them, the Choctaw penned the chickens first and fed them to purge them of impurities.

New food plants posed less of a problem, and the Choctaw readily incorporated sweet potatoes, watermelons, leeks, garlic, and cabbage from Europeans and hyacinth beans and guinea corn from Africans. Pigs slowly became a mainstay, but the Choctaw continued to prefer deer meat. Adjusting to the European/African invasion challenged the Choctaw, but they managed it more successfully than the Natchez.

When the French arrived in the Southeast, the Choctaw were fighting off slave raids from other nations armed by the English. The Choctaw desperately needed firearms to defend themselves, and the French wanted to trade for furs and animal hides as they had long done in Canada, but the Choctaw offered instead a gift-alliance system based on their experience and worldview. They knew reciprocity, gifts, and favors. For example, they left a pot of tan fula, a thick hominy soup, at the door for any visitor, and successful hunters shared their kill with neighbors. They had no market or sense of commerce. Bienville grew to comprehend their view and attempted to be generous with his gifts, but compared to the English, the French were poor, which severely limited what Bienville could provide. The Choctaw, enemies of the Chickasaw because of their competition over deer-hunting lands and then because they enslaved the Choctaw for the English, wanted to be friends with the French but often accused them of being stingy with their gifts.

By 1708 the English had begun to import African slaves and sought to switch from capturing and selling Indian slaves to trade in deerskins, which the Choctaw could supply in great numbers. In 1715 the Yamassee War in South Carolina brought an end to the trade in Indian slaves and removed a major impediment to English-Choctaw relations. The English offered higher quality goods than the French and paid higher prices for skins. The French had an advantage in the better powder and bullets that they offered and in the fact that they would accept the smaller hides from the deer in the pine forests of the southern Choctaw lands.

The French tried to promote an all-powerful chief through whom they would distribute goods to control the nation. This tactic failed because the chiefs maintained their independence and rejected the French attempted revision of their political system. The French had better success offering individual bounties for scalps, but they could not keep up a sufficient volume of gifts to induce the Choctaw to keep fighting, and in 1724 the Chickasaw and Choctaw made peace. Needing Choctaw warriors to survive in Louisiana, the French adopted the ploy of encouraging the war chiefs at the expense of the civil, or white, chiefs.

Shulush Homa, or Red Shoe, developed into the most famous war leader of the period. As a man on the make, he negotiated with the English traders in Chickasaw towns after obtaining his civil chief's permission. Then he helped to lead the large group of warriors who fought with and then dominated the French at Natchez. In 1731, at the instigation of the French, he secretly organized and led a raid into the northern hunting grounds, killing six Chickasaw. His actions outraged the Choctaw civil chiefs, and they grew angrier when the French awarded him a great medal in defiance of all precedents and customs. His rise in the teeth of the civil chiefs' opposition opened two decades of factional strife, war, and murder among the Choctaw.

On his return in 1733, Bienville reversed course as Red Shoe switched back and forth between the French and the English, sometimes arguing for trade with both to "lack nothing." Bienville tried to use the civil chiefs to control Red Shoe, but they failed. Red Shoe invited the English traders into the nation in the mid-1730s. Eventually the competition led to civil war, with Red Shoe challenging the civil chiefs for control of the nation. Factions multiplied and many died, but the conflict always preserved the Choctaw's independence. When the English traders became too aggressive in trying to collect debts, the Choctaw ejected them and repudiated their debts, turning again to the French. If French gifts lagged, the English could be invited back. Warfare in the hunting grounds preserved the deer, ensuring the food supply. Tumultuous times benefited the Choctaw, who, despite the war, remained a dominant military power.

The Chickasaw had treated with the French when they arrived, but by 1711 had committed totally to an English alliance. Fiercely independent, the Chickasaw rejected the French offers of Catholic priests, although they somewhat reluctantly took in a French boy to live with them in order for him to learn their language. They always retained a "French party" who could negotiate and dicker on the nation's behalf with the enemy, but the Chickasaw adopted the more numerous English trade goods readily.

The English trading houses, which the Chickasaw encouraged the English to build in their towns, became the new social centers, replacing the older gathering grounds. The Chickasaw also adopted the horse more actively than most southeastern nations, leading them to produce a recognizable breed popular as the forerunner of the quarter horse. English traders brought their goods on the backs of horses and on the heads of African slaves, the latter of which the Chickasaw also acquired in some numbers.

When the English ceased buying Indian slaves from the Chickasaw, the Chickasaw quickly increased the scale of their fur and hide trading in order to maintain their purchasing power. They had always ranged far and wide on hunts, and with the acquisition of a large number of horses traded for French hostages, purchased from the English or from western tribes, or stolen, they hunted north and west for deer. Competition with the Choctaw to the south in their traditional borderland and attacks on French travelers along the Mississippi led the Chickasaw to seek closer ties with their slave-raiding partners, the Natchez. When the Natchez attempted to wipe out the French and failed, the Chickasaw joined in the guerrilla war that followed and offered refuge to the Natchez.

In retaliation, the French encouraged their Indian allies in the Illinois country to attack Chickasaw hunting parties, costing the Chickasaw thirty to forty people a year. The Chickasaw retaliated with raids on French river commerce. When Bienville returned in 1733, he made the defeat of the Chickasaw his main objective, telling the French government that the Chickasaw had to be eliminated completely for the survival of Louisiana.

While Red Shoe was in Carolina bargaining with the English, Bienville mustered as many Choctaw as possible and ordered Major Pierre D'Artaguette, commander in the Illinois country, to assemble all his French soldiers and Indian allies to attack from the north. D'Artaguette and his forces left in February 1736 to keep their rendezvous in Chickasaw country. Bienville waited until early April for mortars arriving late from France. D'Artaguette arrived at Chickasaw Bluffs, modern-day Memphis, in late February and moved inland to attack a fortified Chickasaw town to capture provisions. While he attacked, Chickasaw from a neighboring town assaulted him, killing or capturing all but twenty of his forces. The Chickasaw burned him and the other prisoners alive in revenge for the Chickasaw who had been burned in a similar manner by the Choctaw at the behest of the French governor after the Natchez destruction of the French settlement. Meanwhile, Bienville made his way up the Tombigbee River with 1,200 French, Swiss, Choctaw, Canadian, and African men, arriving in Chickasaw country in late May.

The Chickasaw waited in their fortifications, encouraged by the capture of powder, bullets, horses, and a written plan of attack taken from D'Artaguette. Bienville assaulted the town of Akia with his Swiss and French troops. They took three fortified compounds but suffered extensive losses in the center of town, where they were caught in crossfire. After reinforcements failed to carry the battle, Bienville retreated to the Tombigbee and attempted to blame the loss on Choctaw troops who, he said, kept their heads down during the battle. The Choctaw did not fight in the European manner and likely thought the French had been insane to attack the fortification as they did. The French disaster imperiled the entire North American empire, and Bienville redoubled his efforts with increased support from the French government.

After three years of preparation, Bienville tried again. Having assembled what was for Louisiana an enormous store of munitions and heavy weapons at Chickasaw Bluffs, he waited because rains made dragging the heavy weapons and stores into Chickasaw country impossible. After one attack using a significant portion of his force against a Chickasaw town failed, Bienville asked the Chickasaw to negotiate a peace, knowing he could not risk another disaster. The embarrassment of the debacle led to his recall. In 1752 the French made a final invasion, but the Chickasaw again remained in their forts, and the French could only burn deserted villages and pillage livestock. No European power ever defeated the Chickasaw. They and the Choctaw endured, but became dependent on their trade with the English, which eventually led them to destroy themselves.

The Seven Years War in Europe sealed the Chickasaw's and Choctaw's fate because the French surrendered the eastern portion of Louisiana to the English and the west to Spain. English traders now enjoyed a monopoly, and they escalated the sale of rum to the Chickasaw and Choctaw. Unlike the other goods the Europeans offered, the Indians had a seemingly limitless appetite for liquor, and they depleted their deer supply almost completely to satisfy their longings. The English tried to end the French/Choctaw custom of gift giving, insisting on individual trade or a pure market system. The English traders used short weights, downgraded hides, insulted women, ignored the chiefs' distributive powers completely, and imported vast amounts of rum.

In 1765 the English held a "congress" at Mobile and offered the customary gifts, but in exchange they asked for title to land along the coast and the southern Tombigbee River. Because the Choctaw had acquired those poor pinelands as they absorbed small tribal groups in recent times and the requested lands did not constitute part of their homeland, the Choctaw agreed, expecting annual congresses and seeing the land as a gift. The English did not call another congress until 1772, and in the interim the Choctaw came to understand that the English refused to recognize the cultural basis of their leadership or the adoptive family/moieties nature of the relationships between peoples.

Without the French to play off against the English and with the introduction of direct trade ignoring the roles of the chiefs, Choctaw society began to unravel. Drinking led to disorder and murder, which led to revenge killings to secure justice. The English promoted a war between the Creek and the Choctaw. The English only paid Choctaw war chiefs for services rendered, promoting them over the traditional leaders. In the 1760s the war went badly, but in the 1770s the Choctaw won more battles; yet in both decades they lost many of their chiefs in battle.

By the time the English held another congress in 1772, the chiefs spoke of their dependence on English trade and dropped the language of adoption and family relationships on which they had always based diplomacy. Tacitly they acknowledged the new world, and the English exploited their weakness by bestowing medals on "chiefs" who no respectable Choctaw would have recognized. The medals granted by the English came in three categories: great, small, and gorge. The last medal introduced a new group into the Choctaw hierarchy commonly called captains. Choctaw leadership had evolved into a competitive system, with the Europeans exercising extensive influence for the first time. In the late 1770s, as the Spanish began to compete for Choctaw support, they spread more confusion.

To participate in the new market economy, the Choctaw and Chickasaw began to hunt deer with an intensity unknown previously. The deer provided their only means of securing trade goods and rum. They depleted the hunting grounds, which had been protected by warfare, and soon had to cross the Mississippi to fight western tribes for access to new areas for the increasingly scarce animals. They hunted to purchase liquor. When they had a heavy load of hides and intended to exchange them for cloth and powder, the traders offered them a drink before the trade, and when they awoke hungover, their hides were gone and they were poor. Faced with the onslaught of more advanced technology and the capitalist-market system, Indian societies entered a crisis that spiraled out of control. Abandoning their old system of farming, hunting, and gathering, the Choctaw and Chickasaw impoverished themselves by overhunting the land until they lost it to the invading descendants of the Europeans and Africans—the Americans.

Chapter Two

FRONTIER AND BORDERLAND

With the end of the Seven Years War in 1763, the French transferred Natchez into the British colony of West Florida, comprised of what today are southern Mississippi, south Alabama, and the panhandle of Florida. France gave western Louisiana, including New Orleans, to the Spanish. The British made Pensacola the capital of West Florida, which removed Natchez farther than it had been under the French from the center of political power. Most of the territory that became the state of Mississippi continued to be ruled by the Choctaw and Chickasaw, who, as we have seen, did not fare well with English traders. In the years between 1763 and the United States assuming control in 1798, the Natchez district traded hands, settlers moved into the deserted outpost to establish commercial plantations, people of African origins increased markedly as a percentage of the immigrant population, and Indians struggled to transform their culture as they destroyed the deer that served as their main food source and whose hides provided their only foreign exchange item.

In 1763 the deerskin trade constituted the bulk of the export economy for Indians and settlers. France had sought and failed to create plantations at Natchez in the mold of successful Caribbean colonies. Failing that, the French rulers tried at various times to manipulate the deerskin business to benefit the various owners of the colony, but to no avail. Until the English flooded the Indians with rum, the Choctaw and Chickasaw held the upper hand. Under Indian domination, the increasingly mixed cultures and diverse human population developed survival skills and incorporated new plants, animals, herding, methods of hunting, agriculture, and commerce into their lives. The French left behind a small but significant population, some of whom had married Choctaw women, producing children who, because of their mother's status, would become leaders in the Choctaw nation. By the same token, English traders who married among the Chickasaw produced heirs who became leaders of that nation.

The Choctaw and Chickasaw continued to farm by girdling trees and burning canebrakes, where they planted corn, squash, and beans in mixed hills. When the soil's fertility declined, they moved to a new location. They left their villages to gather and hunt in the borderlands in the fall and winter and produced deer hides to trade, but gradually, as they became more accustomed to pork and beef, they added herding to the boys' hunting and bird-scaring duties. As some Choctaw crossed the Mississippi River to hunt, they encountered western Indians, who provided them with more horses and cattle, which they began to incorporate into their environment. Aside from traders, few Europeans or Africans penetrated their homeland, but when they did, the Europeans and Africans adopted the Indian style of hunting, gathering, and free-range herding.

Indians, Europeans, and Africans interacted at a personal level, exchanging deer hides and, more often, food, forging personal relationships. Indian enslavement had largely died out, replaced by growing numbers of Africans slaves, but African slaves did a wide variety of tasks in what historians have termed a frontier exchange economy. Africans, who had more experience with cattle than did Indians, served as herders. They worked as lumbermen on early plantations or poled boats. Some fed the other workers as professional hunters, and the French and Spanish even used slaves as soldiers. Before the development of successful commercial plantations, slaves led a life freer of restrictions, rules, and laws and played a more significant, independent role in the economy as traders.

British control had little impact on the economic system for some time. The early governors appointed to oversee West Florida proved to be a sorry lot and rarely left Pensacola and Mobile. The home government removed the first British governor for incompetence, and his replacement found the lieutenant governor, Montfort Browne, who had served as interim governor, charged with embezzlement before the new governor committed suicide. Not until 1770 did the British find a competent governor, Peter Chester (1770–1781). The British occupied Fort Rosalie at Natchez and renamed it Panmure, but since the destruction of the Natchez people, the area had lain largely empty, serving the Choctaw as another hunting ground and inhabited by a few Natchez who kept out of sight. Browne traveled to Natchez and sent back glowing reports of lush, rich farmland, which trees had invaded in the thirty-five years since it had been abandoned. Struck by the emptiness of the site, he found fruit trees left behind by the Natchez and the French, and urged the governor to consider settling colonists again.

Chester took up the challenge, arguing with the home government that its policy of settling along the coast made no sense in West Florida, where the soil was too poor for farming near the Gulf. Instead, he suggested that settlers from the older American colonies be encouraged to take up land grants in Natchez. Because the British government had proclaimed that its seaboard colonies could not move west into Indian nations, land-hungry British subjects needed new frontiers. With few Indians residing on the site, it would be easier for the British than it had been for the French to move into Natchez, but two problems plagued potential colonists. First, the Choctaw might attack, and second, the Spanish held the land across the river, which in the event of another European war would endanger them. Despite Natchez's precarious situation, the British ordered the troops out of Panmure in 1768.

Even without protecting troops, a minor boom ensued in the 1770s as Chester made sizable land grants to veterans of the French and Indian Wars, but most of the grantees never braved the dangers to improve their holding, preferring to speculate from afar. Anthony Hutchins, a former colonel with a pension from the British army, proved the exception. Arriving from South Carolina, where he had been a sheriff until he lost his money by backing a bad debt for a friend, Hutchins found a Natchez, whom he called Tom, to befriend him and to serve as his guide out of antipathy for the French and friendship for the English. With the help of Tom, Hutchins located an abandoned village on St. Catherine's Creek, and, with the assistance of four young apprentices brought along for the purpose, he constructed some log buildings to house his family, cleared a field, and planted corn to feed them.

Returning to South Carolina, Hutchins gathered his family and slaves to make the arduous trip to Natchez. Having made their way overland to the Tennessee River, the party continued in flatboats carrying livestock, the Hutchins family, and slaves. Indians ambushed them at Muscle Shoals, but they fought through and eventually reached Natchez by way of the Ohio and Mississippi Rivers in 1774. The Indians and animals had devoured all of the corn planted in Natchez to feed the immigrants except for seed corn, which Tom had buried in order to preserve enough for a new planting. They lost the boat with their pigs at Muscle Shoals, but they had cattle. Otherwise they lived as the Indians did. Without milk cows or corn, they ate "Indian potatoes" (roots of morning glory vines) mashed or minced with pounded venison baked before the fire with some bear "oil" for seasoning.

In a couple of years they sent word back to South Carolina, and other families joined them, until about fifteen families spread along the creeks. Indians still controlled the area, helping themselves to corn and watermelons in the fields and food from the tables of the settlers' homes when they chose. The settlers dared not protest. Supplies from New Orleans cost too much to purchase. Not one of the families living near Natchez could afford $30 for a barrel of flour or $6 for a blanket. They wore deerskins as the Indians did or homespun clothes made from cotton they grew. They spent evenings and spare moments removing the seeds from the cotton and used homemade spinning wheels and looms to weave their cloth. With nine children, all of whom lived to maturity, Hutchins had adequate labor to assist his slaves. Free men and slaves worked side by side, clearing the giant canebrakes to make fields for corn, vegetables, cotton, indigo, and later tobacco.

John Hutchins, Anthony's fifth child, arrived the first summer the family spent in Natchez, and the boy grew up amid the forests and cane accompanied by Toney, a slave native to Africa whom Anthony inherited from his father. Both Toney's and John Hutchins's memories survive and describe forests rich with game, which they hunted together. In the best winter hunt, they killed 107 bears. They never counted the turkey and deer. Wolves and panthers roamed the land, along with a few buffalo in the beginning. Cats attacked them with some regularity. Hunting for days at a time in the winter, they salted enough meat for a year. Some they cooked in camp, bending large canes over a fire with bear meat impaled on the top cane, and venison and turkey beneath it to absorb the dripping fat. Toney taught the young Hutchins how to read the dogs' barks and backed him up on his first bear kills.

In this frontier, slave and master developed personal relationships at a basic human level. When raiders stole Toney and the other slaves and took Anthony Hutchins captive, John was two years old. Toney landed in Pensacola when he was sold, but hearing from wandering Indians that John's mother had been left alone with the children, Toney escaped with the help of the Indians and made his way back to assist her, earning the Hutchins family's undying gratitude and trust. He remained a slave, but such dedication and sacrifice cemented a strong human relationship within an inhumane institution.

Hutchins and his slaves fought Indians for control of the land. When an Indian shot one of their cattle, Hutchins's men whipped him, and when several hundred warriors came to seek justice or revenge, Hutchins lined up all of his men, including his slaves, in front of his house to meet them. Only luck and gifts avoided bloodshed. Indians stole the few horses owned by the settlers and returned them for a reward, but as the demands escalated, the whites decided to retrieve their animals by force. Killing Indians for their horses led Indians to attack and sent the Hutchinses and other whites fleeing to the fort, which they still called Rosalie, with only their weapons and the clothes on their backs. While the settlers huddled in the fort, Indians looted, burned their homes, and drove off all of their stock. When they made peace, the Hutchinses returned to find no buildings and only three tools left—an ax, a foot adz, and a mattock. They had to use the mattock as a plow and gave the children sticks to beat down the cane and weeds among the corn. Settlement of the area proved difficult, and prosperity seemed elusive for years, but eventually some prospered.

John worked for his father until Anthony became a rich man owning 100 slaves, but when John asked to be released to farm his own land and to marry, his father balked. Only when John left in the face of his father's refusal did his father relent, call him back, and provide farmland. John described his start as spartan. He asked a friend to sell him a slave on credit and made a deal for a runaway, if he could find him. John talked to the slaves on the surrounding plantations to let them know of the deal, and the missing slave came in from the forest to work for him. John bought chickens from his father's slaves and planted crops working beside his one slave, who shared his two-room house with him.

By 1770, 500 whites lived near Natchez. Twenty years later the number of whites had increased to 2,000, and there were 1,000 black slaves. Settlements multiplied along the river. At Bayou Pierre, along the Big Black, and on the Walnut Hills (Vicksburg), refugees from all of the old colonies settled for opportunity and sometimes political reasons—because they were loyal to Britain. The settlers between the Big Black and Walnut Hills came with little except a gun, a few tools, corn seed, and pigs. The hogs fed on the mast in the forest, corn grew well, and the settlers hunted the plentiful game. With game supplying many of their needs, their animals multiplied quickly. Neighbors relied on one another for loan of scarce goods and minimized contact with the outside world. Mostly they traded excess crops and animals with the few general stores located at Natchez, Bayou Pierre, and Walnut Hills, but animal hides remained the currency for foreign trade. Many engaged in the frontier exchange as a necessity, which depleted the deer population as the pig and cattle herds grew.

On the Big Black during this period, the community consisted of about two dozen households containing five or six persons each. Five households owned a slave, with one family holding seven, but by 1790 few families had acquired slaves, and the overwhelming majority remained without slaves. They built no church or public building; only a cabin and the clearing for corn and vegetables separated them from the wilderness. The Mississippi River and other natural landscape features such as an unusual tree provided their landmarks for directions and a sense of place. A few settlers mentioned "Nanchets improvements" as a reference point, but they knew that they inhabited a frontier and that their hold on it was tenuous. They made their mark on the wilderness with their animals, primarily their pigs, which were mostly the Razorback variety that lived on acorns and roots needing little effort from the settler. The corn grew as well for them as it had for the Indians, and game remained abundant at first.

Most settlers prospered, even Matthew Phelps who arrived penniless after losing his entire family to fever and the river. Borrowing tools and livestock from a neighbor, he produced enough in one year to repay his debt and have a decent living. Lack of a cash crop kept most of the families at the subsistence level for many years, and they borrowed and traded with one another to fulfill most of their needs. Phelps chose to abandon his place and return to New England rather than continue a life not too different from the Indians who preceded him on his land.

Pushmataha's life illustrated the fate of the Choctaw in this era. Born around 1764 into the heartland near what is today Macon, probably to parents of low status, he earned the right to leadership as a great hunter and warrior. In an earlier period, he might have won distinction, but he probably would never have become such a dominant man because of his lowly birth. With the destruction of the white, or civil, chiefs' distributive role by English traders who ignored them and with the rise of war leaders such as Red Shoe, Choctaw society suffered turmoil, and it was out of this disorder that Pushmataha rose to fame and a leadership position. He exemplified the link to the Choctaw past because he won his position through prowess demonstrated in the hunt and war, indicating spiritual strength, but ironically he led his people toward expulsion from their homeland because of his adherence to some Choctaw values while disregarding others.

His first appearance in Choctaw memory came in a bear hunt in the canebrakes near the Mississippi River, where he surfaced as a stringy, ill-clad teenager. The large party of over 100 hunters gradually came to realize that no one knew the strange lad, but because the Choctaw deemed it an insult to ask a person's name, they sent an older leader to speak with him in order to learn it. Asked from where he hailed, the lad responded "*luma*," meaning obscure or hidden, and as for his name, he answered "*hohcifoiksho*," or nameless. When the older hunters ignored his possession of a fine bow and knife and urged him to stay and keep the camp, he insisted on hunting. He performed well, and when injured bears attacked, he proved his bravery. He responded to the compliments in camp by bragging that he would do much more earning a name, Ishtilauata (braggart). But he made good his word, killing more game than any other hunter.

At the end of the hunt, when a group of forty warriors among the hunters decided to cross the river to take a few scalps from the Ovashsashi nation, Ishtilauata volunteered first, drawing laughter and derision. As the other warriors gave instructions for the disposition of their share of the hunt should they fail to return, Ishtilauata said that the hunting party should divide his meat and hides as he did not have a family. He attacked an Ovashsashi village with the Choctaw, but his party left him while he was scalping a man he had killed. Separated from the group, he trailed them back toward the Mississippi and mysteriously rejoined them with scalps. Refusing to receive a war name

Pushmataha, renowned Choctaw warrior and leader. Pushmataha's life bridged the Choctaw's decline through the acceptance of American cultural values. Courtesy of the Mississippi Department of Archives and History from the Pushmataha Collection.

for only one kill, he dropped out of sight until a year later when he reemerged in a battle against the Creek.

A large body of warriors observed him kill many Creek with a war club, and as a result he eventually began to lead a band in the continuing war. Questioned by the chiefs after his dramatic appearance in battle, he claimed only the name Ishtilauata, given a year earlier on the hunt. He denied knowing his parents or even his moiety and stated that he had lived in the woods and swamps earning his livelihood from the land. When the high priest performed the ritual of choosing Ishtilauata's war name using a medicine bag, Ishtilauata declined each opportunity until all of the rocks had been emptied from the bag. When he returned to the priest at last asking for a name, the priest said all the rocks were gone, but that Ishtilauata had won the greatest name in history, Apushimataha, or No More Rocks in the Bag. Pushmataha linked the Choctaw to their past, winning his place among them through spiritual power as hunter and warrior, but he defied all the rules of society and became a chief in Six-Towns in the south, not in his birthplace in the east. He led his people in battle allied with Europeans and later with Americans and won respect from all, but despite his bravery and eloquence in negotiations, he could not protect the Choctaw. Although culturally conservative enough to oppose the arrival of missionaries, he had his children educated in English to equip them for the changing world. But they were his sons, not his sister's children, because he had abandoned the Choctaw matrilineal custom.

Had the British been able to retain their American empire and to keep their colonists east of the Appalachians, leaving the land between the mountains and the Mississippi River for Indians as promised, Pushmataha and the Choctaw might have been able to retain their nation, but the colonies revolted. The American Revolution restored European competition for Choctaw support, with the British and the Spanish offering gifts and holding frequent "congresses" to retain their loyalty. The Choctaw again played one foreign power against another for their own advantage, but despite the flow of gifts, the Choctaw continued to lose possessions to traders in exchange for drink. As long as Britain and Spain did not go to war, the Choctaw enjoyed the bounty of gifts painlessly. By the 1770s the Choctaw had played the diplomatic game with European powers for generations, and they expected to carry on indefinitely.

The Europeans and Africans settled on the Natchez's lands and in the borderlands belonging to the Choctaw, who lived in the less fertile eastern heartland but depended upon the lands along the Yazoo and Mississippi Rivers for hunting and gathering. By the mid-1760s the number of deer diminished, and by the 1780s the Choctaw felt a dire shortage. Based on the goods purchased, one historian estimated that the annual deer kill was at least 100,000. With encroaching settlers and Indian overhunting, the game could not reproduce quickly enough. The Choctaw who wanted to maintain their traditional lifestyle began to cross the Mississippi more often to hunt in the Red and Arkansas River valleys. The Spanish government encouraged them, but the Caddo and Osage fought for their hunting grounds. Because of the long distances, some Choctaw began to winter in the west, planting corn and forming temporary villages. Pushmataha and the other war chiefs participated in the western hunting ventures, which proved lucrative in the 1780s, enabling the Choctaw to rebuild their horse herds depleted by the liquor trade, but the western hunting expeditions provided only a temporary solution to the deer shortage. In the early 1790s droughts destroyed the Choctaw crops, and an unknown disease decimated their horse herds. In years past the Choctaw would have relied on gathering in the borderlands, along with extended hunting seasons, to survive, but that system was no longer viable. They turned to the Spanish for food; they killed the settlers' cattle, which roamed free range; and they begged. Settlers for the first time began to describe the Indians not as aggressive threats and proud neighbors but as destitute vagrants. Some Choctaw leaders understood that their traditional hunting lives had ended. In 1792, when Stephen Minor visited Franchimastabe, the chief of the southern towns, to try to purchase grazing land between Natchez and the Pearl River, the chief refused to sell, telling Minor that the days of living by the gun had ended and that in the future the Choctaw would have to live like white men by herding cattle.

Herding as a lifestyle required major adjustments in Choctaw culture. For years the Choctaw preferred to eat horses rather than pigs or chickens. They did not consume animals that ate waste, as pigs and chickens did, because they considered them unclean. Horses ate more like deer and thus seemed more acceptable as a food. Only gradually did the Choctaw overcome their aversion to the Old World animals and adopt them fully into their lives. The leaders in large-scale cattle herding were intermarried couples of Indian, French, English, and American origin or their children. With tribal permission, they moved cattle into the borderlands and began to use the lands left vacant for the hunt as pastures. Full-bloods followed, and the resulting communities became Indian pioneers moving out of their central towns into their former borderlands where they prospered, but at a price. The Choctaw pioneers discontinued the more communal Indian ways, insisting like the white settlers that free-roaming cattle belonged to them and, unlike deer, could not be killed and eaten by anyone else. And they insisted on their children inheriting their wealth, introducing the paternal social system. As a result, rich and poor families emerged, and this innovation destroyed the Choctaw egalitarian tradition. The Six-Towns in the southern core lacked rich borderlands for expansion and turned to strict hunting rules to equalize deer harvesting. As a result, the southern towns resisted the new lifestyle longer and remained dedicated to preserving more of the old ways. As with any society experiencing massive social change, the Choctaw and Chickasaw experimented with various responses to the economic, social, and spiritual assaults on their world. By the end of the 1700s their old world was disappearing quickly, and some recognized the need for change while too many escaped their confusion with alcohol.

As traders subverted Indian culture with "free trade" and rum, the British imperial government encouraged Tories, or loyalists, to settle in West Florida, where many moved to escape the American Revolution in the older colonies. Natchez seemed safe from the war until James Willing persuaded the Americans to make him a naval captain with permission to open the Mississippi River for the Revolution. Willing lived in West Florida for six years, owned property near Natchez, and enjoyed the hospitality of many planters before he returned to Pennsylvania in 1777, a bitter failure. Knowing the loyalist sympathies of most of the planters along the Mississippi, he convinced the rebel government to commission him for an expedition against them. He received enough provisions for thirty men for 180 days, but he accumulated volunteers as he headed west and south until the number reached 100 as he approached the Yazoo River. In Natchez, Willing arrested

Anthony Hutchins and took his slaves, including Toney, to sell in New Orleans. Eighty of the locals at Natchez joined Willing and participated in the looting of farms to the south. Hutchins managed to escape and returned to Natchez, where the locals had broken a neutrality pledge given to Willing by asking Governor Chester to send troops from Pensacola. When Willing learned of the revolt, he dispatched a force to occupy Natchez. Hutchins led an ambush and defeated Willing's forces as they tried to land. The British captured Willing as he fled north, and Natchez appeared to be safely in British hands with river patrols and even a small garrison assigned to Panmure.

Unfortunately, the inhabitants knew Panmure garrison's commander to be a horse thief, and Hutchins led a mutiny against him. Eventually Chester replaced the commander, but the Spanish governor, Bernardo de Galvez, followed all of this with interest as he planned his conquest. In 1779, when Spain joined France and the rebellious colonies in the war against the British Empire, Galvez easily defeated the British on the east bank of the Mississippi and had a letter sent to the garrison at Panmure advising them to surrender without a fight. Fifty-nine of the leading citizens, not including Hutchins, sent a reply that they would welcome an occupying Spanish force. The Spanish found Panmure rotten with leaking roofs and overrun by rats. Someone stole most of their horses, and Captain Juan Delavillebeuvre reported to Galvez that he doubted a loyal subject of the Crown could be found in the entire district. Made aware of the situation, the British sent letters to Natchez appointing several inhabitants to the rank of captain if they would lead an insurrection. Some who had signed the letter welcoming the Spanish joined with loyal British subjects and a few pro-Americans to prepare a ruse to appear stronger than they were and to demand the surrender of the fort. Fooled, Delavillebeuvre agreed to surrender, no doubt relieved to be sent back to Baton Rouge. Suppressing the pro-Americans, Hutchins and the loyal British assumed control, only to hear that the Spanish had taken Pensacola. Hutchins and his compatriots fled through Choctaw and Creek lands to South Carolina, fearing harsh reprisals from the victorious Spanish.

The Spanish returned to Natchez but proved lenient to the rebels, imprisoning a few and inviting the departed to return and take up their farms. Hutchins came back but clashed with the Spanish commander and had to flee again for seven years. Fighting continued to the north of Natchez until 1783, but Natchez settled down under the rule of the dons.

The peace treaties ending the war left Natchez in an ambiguous position. The British treaty with the Americans identified the southern border as the thirty-first parallel, which made Natchez American. The British treaty with the Spanish marked the boundary at the Yazoo River's entrance into the Mississippi, which included Natchez in Spain's holdings. Of course Spain

Manuel Gayoso de Lemos, Spanish governor who presided over the development of Natchez into a successful plantation colony producing cotton for the world market. Courtesy of the Mississippi Department of Archives and History.

had won West Florida by conquest, and the fledgling American government would have been hard-pressed to force the Spanish out; so from the end of the American Revolution to 1798, Natchez remained a border province with an uncertain future.

Because of Natchez's anomalous position, the Spanish took innovative steps to keep the mostly British population intact and to attract more Anglos, hoping to establish a buffer to protect their empire from the expansive American states. Willing's raid did not encourage those in Natchez to relish the thought of joining the Americans. The Spanish only required an oath to support the Crown and allowed freedom of religion as long as Protestant services were conducted in private. To rule Natchez, the Crown called on Manuel Gayoso de Lemos. Born to a Portuguese mother and a Spanish father in Lisbon and educated in England, he spoke a variety of languages. When his wife died at Natchez, he married a planter's daughter. One of Gayoso's assistants, Stephen Minor, emigrated from Pennsylvania to New Orleans during the American Revolution and joined the Spanish army, serving in the campaign to take Pensacola. Gayoso thus integrated into the developing planter community with ease, incorporating the large landowners into his government as members of his council and as the Spanish version of justices of the peace.

His superior in New Orleans allowed him to communicate directly with Spain instead of through the normal channels to Cuba and Mexico and endowed him with freedom to handle most issues locally. He fortified Nogales (present-day Vicksburg) and signed treaties with the Choctaw and Chickasaw to protect Natchez. He organized a militia to apprehend the rustlers and outlaws who plagued the district. Each militiaman received 200 acres of land, a small stipend, and rations on the days they served. Gayoso reported good results with a decline in thefts and vagabonds pilfering. At one point, he outlawed knives and metal weapons in town. He limited some forms of gambling, forbade the sale of liquor to slaves and Indians, and imposed curfews on taverns under-the-hill. By the 1790s, as boating increased, life at the landing below the bluff at Natchez became wild with prostitutes, gamblers, and carousing boatmen working off steam after weeks on the river.

In 1784 the Spanish closed the Mississippi to American commerce in order to fend off encroaching American frontiersmen. In the 1780s fewer than twenty American flatboats made the trip to New Orleans, but in 1788 Spain changed its policy to encourage American trade. As pioneers poured into Kentucky and Tennessee, they needed the river to get their crops and whiskey to market through New Orleans, and hundreds of boats each year stopped off at Natchez on their way to port in New Orleans.

Natchez's economy struggled to find a niche. Lumber and barrel staves proved lucrative, while planters cleared the surrounding land of forests, with sawmills supplying New Orleans. Settlers sold naval products and, as we have seen, grew some tobacco and indigo, but they could not compete with the Caribbean or the American states in quality. Gayoso encouraged hemp as a crop, but that failed. The most important growth came in livestock. In 1784 the area had 3,000 cattle, 1,153 horses, 7,111 pigs, and 117 sheep, but by 1794 those figures had increased to 14,672 cattle, 5,541 horses, 20,106 pigs, and 5,538 sheep. Many of the animals roamed free and required a minimum of care. The cattle descended from the Opelousas breed imported into Louisiana from Spain. The small "cane tackey" horses probably originated from mustangs imported from Texas and sometimes as far away as Santa Fe. Until 1800 purebred stock did not exist. The hogs were small Razorbacks, and the sheep were mongrel and hardy. As the figures above demonstrate, animals provided the first wealth, but reaching a ready market with the surplus proved difficult. The pioneers with large land grants and sizable herds stood poised to make the transition to commercial agriculture as they sold their cattle to New Orleans and markets in the Caribbean.

The Spanish government made planters' fortunes by agreeing to purchase two million pounds of tobacco at a subsidized price even though the quality of the Mississippi product did not match that grown in the United States or the Caribbean. As a result, between 1787 and 1792 the slave population of Natchez tripled. Tobacco required intensive labor to sow the seeds, then to transplant the tiny plants into the field, to hoe around the plants, to top the plants in order to elicit the proper growth, to harvest, to cure, and finally to package the leaves for shipment. As they added slaves quickly, the planters turned to slaves fresh from Africa made available by the Spanish and found they preferred them to American-born slaves. By the early 1790s two out of three Natchez slaves were African-born. Of course the saltwater slaves added to the cultural mix of the area and eventually contributed to changes in the nature of slavery practices.

At this point, the distinctive planter class emerged, led by Gayoso, who acquired a large land grant adjacent to the new city of Natchez, which he laid out in its present form. On his estate, Gayoso built a mansion and stocked its wine cellar with the best bottles available. At his sumptuous home, he entertained and presided over the developing city and commercial farm district that he created. He attracted planters such as William Dunbar, a Scotsman who had owned a plantation in Manchac near Lake Pontchartrain; bought and sold slaves; surveyed land; served as Spanish interpreter in German, English, and French for the authorities; and ran a commercial business in New Orleans before he moved to 5,000 acres near Natchez. Residing in the carriage house with his family for three years, the scientific-minded Dunbar designed a big square white wood frame house that he called Forest. He raised his first floor above the ground on a brick basement story, and his house, surrounded by a deep veranda, was supported by columns made of bricks fired on the site by his slaves. He developed 150 acres of formal gardens, including a park, two orchards, a lake, and an experimental garden as the setting for Forest. He finished the estate in 1795 and amassed the greatest library in the colony, carrying on his scientific experiments and correspondence with Thomas Jefferson. Gayoso also allowed Anthony Hutchins to return despite his efforts against the Spanish and encouraged the immigration of Americans on the make. Gayoso emphasized the creation and enjoyment of wealth. The new planter mansions pushed the wilderness back and both literally and figuratively imposed a new culture on the Mississippi frontier.

By the middle of the 1780s the tobacco boom dwindled as production fell, and in 1790 the Spanish government announced its intention to reduce its support for tobacco. Panic spread among the planters who had borrowed during the flush times to add slaves and land to increase their crops. In desperation, they turned to indigo, which had long been a staple crop in other areas, but the processing of the plant into a dye for the international market required a complicated production process creating a mass of objectionable wastes that polluted the creeks and killed the fish. The harvested plants had to be boiled, drained into a second vat, churned for eight hours with lime, drained again in boxes, dried, and then cut into solid cubes for shipment to market. Planters made quick profits, but flies swarmed around the vats and wastes, which stank badly. Grasshoppers thrived on the plant and destroyed entire crops in the early 1790s.

Cotton came to the planters' rescue. Farmers grew short staple cotton for domestic use because the long staple variety would not survive Mississippi winters. The short staple version required so much labor to remove the seeds that it could not be marketed commercially, but with the invention of a simple, effective gin, the seed removal bottleneck disappeared, and Natchez planters, who had slave labor, land, and the perfect soil, climate, and easy river transport, pounced on the opportunity to supply the growing mills of Lancashire, England. Cotton transformed the struggling frontier outpost into the center of a prosperous commercial agricultural empire. The success of the Natchez cotton planters shaped the culture of the state. What had been a cooperative, subsistence agricultural economy transmogrified into an export-directed economy individualistic and commercial in nature dominated by different goals and values.

The settlement community along the Black River north of Natchez illustrates the transformation from frontier subsistence to cotton kingdom. As described previously, the community on the Big Black lacked ties with the outside world, and although some settlers owned slaves, their community typified the American frontier experience with hides as the only "currency" for purchasing goods not produced at home. Change began when Gayoso ordered the construction of Fort Nogales at what is today Vicksburg and constructed a road from Nogales to the Black River. The troops and workmen building the new fort purchased supplies locally, providing Big Black settlers with a market for their cattle and other excess produce. With the development of a cattle market and opportunities to ship them downriver, some settlers increased their herds of cattle while reducing their swine to the number needed for domestic use. The large herders tended to be the slave owners, and if they did not own slaves, the cattle profits enabled them to buy slaves. The slave owners made the move to cotton planting more quickly, but those subsistence farmers without slaves delayed as a rule. Planting cotton did not require owning slaves. Families with enough children could have maintained their corn, pigs, and gardens and planted a few acres of cotton because the planting and harvesting seasons for the two crops did not overlap, but the subsistence farmers had adopted a slash-and-burn agriculture similar to the Choctaw's along with the Indians' devotion to hunting and fishing. Some rare individuals with extraordinary drive might have spent the extra hours in the fields to plant both corn and cotton, but most chose to continue the frontier lifestyle until the game animals grew scarce, and the reluctant settlers were forced to plant cotton to replace the income no longer available from hides.

Possibly the herders made the move to cotton not so much because they saw the future but because cotton kept their slaves busy throughout the year. Slack times had often been problematic, and slaves had been rented out for their keep in the past. After the Haitian Revolution began in 1791, the Spanish governor of Louisiana suggested assigning slaves fields of their own to work in order to cut down on their free time. For a mixture of reasons, the more prosperous, slave-owning, cattle-herding members of the community began to plant cotton first. All of the settlers knew that alternative lifestyles existed because some came from New York, others from the coast of Carolina, and some from Europe. If they ever ventured to New Orleans, the shops there reminded them of the glittering wealth available beyond the frontier for those with cash. Adopting commercial agriculture and striving for the wealth available to the importer might have been a lifestyle choice that some strove for and few achieved.

The transition from subsistence to wealth through cotton farming came to those able to react to the market first, but persistence and drive played a role, too. For example, Isaac Rapalje descended from a wealthy New York family but lived the subsistence life on the Black River for years. His family came to Louisiana with a 25,000-acre land grant and a shipload of slaves in 1774, but the vicissitudes of war and family disagreements led him to the Black River, where he grew corn and raised hogs as all his neighbors did. When his father gave up and fled back to New York, Isaac stayed, and in 1805 he still labored alongside a slave and a free black man in the field near his small cabin, but he always had pretensions, calling himself Don Rapalje. He planted cotton early, and although he died poor, his son achieved the dream as one of the state's wealthiest cotton planters. The Natchez example inspired the spread of cotton, which inched farther up the river each year as more farmers chose to try the new economy and utilized a growing number of slaves to plant, harvest, gin, and ship the lucrative new cash crop.

Natchez settlers had always wanted to keep slaves. Bernard Romans, a Dutch-born adventurer whom the British government of West Florida employed to survey the colony, wrote, based on his travels, a history and description in which he provided a how-to-settle guide. He heavily advised the need for slaves in West Florida, suggesting that even poor immigrants should sell all they owned and invest in at least one slave to accompany them. Given the heat and humidity of the colony, Romans held the racist assumption, shared by many at the time, that Africans possessed the natural ability to labor in hot, humid conditions that would kill Europeans. The

French had imported Africans from the beginning and supposedly controlled them under a legal system termed the *Code Noir*, though in reality the government allowed owners free rein to discipline and treat slaves as they pleased. In early French Louisiana, the slaveholders treated slaves harshly, but in the period when Natchez lay vacant after the wars, slaves began to work their own plots, sell their own produce and game, and visit other plantations, living a relatively freer existence. After 1763 English settlers either brought slaves from the older British colonies or, if they came without slaves, imported them from back home. In the British/American system, the law considered slaves chattels, and they enjoyed few legal rights. In British West Florida, slavery did not dominate the society, which retained a white majority using slaves in a diversity of occupations in the early years of settlement. Until the growth of intensive commercial agriculture, slaves worked alongside their owners and sometimes hired out to feed themselves when work slackened with their owners.

The Spanish introduced their slave law into Spanish Louisiana in 1769. Their law held that slavery was contrary to natural reason and that slaves possessed certain rights as human beings. Slaves could, for example, hold legal property. If they converted to Christianity, they gained more rights. They could purchase their freedom. They could appeal to the state to protect them from abusive masters. Most of the Spanish governors intermarried with the slaveholders and usually ignored slaves' pleas, but they all occasionally enforced the law and sided with the slaves. When he conquered Pensacola, Governor Bernardo de Galvez employed slaves in combat roles, and he promised freedom along with compensation to any seriously injured slave and the right to purchase freedom to any slave suffering minor wounds. At least half a dozen slaves died on the campaign. Word spread among the slaves that the Spanish government held a different attitude from the British and Americans and emboldened them to seek redress for grievances. The Spanish took Natchez in 1779 and altered the source of slaves for the British/American settlers there. In the 1780s three-quarters of the Natchez slaves came from Africa and others from the West Indies, adding to the mixture of cultures. Gayoso, as governor of Louisiana after his rule in Natchez, freed slaves proving Indian ancestry and protected the property interest of a black mistress from a dead planter's family, indicating more compassion than slaves could expect from a British or American governor.

Despite the inhumanity of the institution, before 1800 slaves and owners shared the experience of shaping a new society on the frontier and managed in some cases to forge human relationships transcending the horror of slavery. Toney's courage and concern for the Hutchins family and his return

Abd al-Rahman Ibrahima, prince of an African ruler, landed in Natchez as a slave, earned his owner's respect, met an English doctor who knew him in Africa, and eventually persuaded his owner to free him so that he could return to Africa. Courtesy of the Manuscripts, Archives, and Rare Books Division, Schomburg Center for Research in Black Culture, New York Public Library, Astor, Lenox, and Tilden Foundations.

to Natchez at the risk of his life to rescue the family demonstrated a strong connection explained only by human bonds and emotions completely foreign to the usual understanding of slavery. Insights into these complex human relationships have proven rare, but the story of Abd al-Rahman Ibrahima, an African slave belonging to Thomas Foster of Natchez, provides a unique window through which to view the Natchez slave world.

Ibrahima, born the son of the king of Fulbe in West Africa, received an extensive Arabic education studying in Timbuktu, which was an important center of Muslim learning. Returning home after school, Ibrahima became a professional soldier and led his father's forces in battle until captured and sold into slavery by his conquerors. An English slave ship captain bought him on the Gambia River and transported him in a ship named *Africa* to Dominica, where an American ship captain purchased him for resale in the Spanish colony of Louisiana. Foster, who worked his mother's land while acquiring adjoining pieces of property to create a plantation, made a down payment and signed notes to pay $930 for Ibrahima and a fellow slave. Foster led the two bound slaves behind his horse up the ancient Indian road to his settlement in an area near Natchez called Pine Ridge. Foster's home was an old blockhouse said to have been built by the French, which appeared to be a shack. Foster had fenced only five acres, and the outbuilding lay amid piles of brush, with stumps dotting the muddy new fields.

At the farm, Ibrahima offered through a Mandinka interpreter to ransom himself out of bondage, but Foster understood nothing of Ibrahima's life story and parentage. As a result of the story, Foster named his new slave Prince and proceeded to try to cut Ibrahima's long hair. When Ibrahima resisted, Foster had him tied to a tree and sheared his hair, humiliating him. Foster then locked him up for three days. When Foster released Ibrahima, he sent him into the field to help harvest tobacco leaves. Such work shamed Ibrahima, who considered himself a warrior and ruler of farmers. Whippings and other punishments only convinced Ibrahima to flee to the forest, where he lived for many weeks. Unable to communicate, ignorant of the geography, and knowing he had no hope of returning home, Ibrahima surrendered in a dramatic fashion. Finding Thomas's wife, Sarah, at home alone, Ibrahima entered the house and startled the woman. Fearing for her life, she offered him her hand, which he touched before laying prostrate on the floor. He took her foot and placed it on his neck, indicating his submission to the intolerable position that he now occupied.

In the years after that symbolic surrender, he completed all tasks assigned to him, but never smiled, never lied, and never drank. Foster acceded to Ibrahima's practice of his Islamic religion and, contrary to the custom of the time, married Ibrahima to Isabella, a Christian American slave purchased by Foster. Ibrahima had a wife and son back home, so his marriage further cemented his acceptance of his new life. Undoubtedly Isabella helped him to assimilate into slave society, although he never learned to speak English well. In spite of his language deficit and the fact that he never made a good farmer, Ibrahima earned his keep as herder and an excellent handler of horses. According to one tale, Andrew Jackson once tried to buy Ibrahima from Foster at a racetrack in Natchez. Foster allowed Ibrahima's family a garden plot of their own, and as he fathered his own family, Ibrahima traded in town for his master and himself. Foster appreciated his absolute trustworthiness and made him the driver, or slave overseer, for the plantation. For this reason, in later years Foster turned down extraordinary sums of money for him.

Foster prospered. He bought Isabella and several children to remove seeds from cotton by hand because he planted the crop ahead of most farmers before the cotton gin brought the rush. Eventually he owned 100 slaves, and they rarely ran away. Foster seemed to typify the slaveholder of the frontier period because he reached an accommodation with his slaves and gave them some freedom within the confines of slavery. Their quarters stood some distance from the house, and Foster did not require strict obedience. He and Ibrahima never developed affection for one another, but they did find respect. When an Irish doctor whom Ibrahima and his father had befriended in Africa appeared in Natchez and recognized Ibrahima, he tried to buy the slave's freedom so that he could return home, but Foster refused, until some years later after Foster's son deserted his wife and family to move to Warren County with a slave named Susy, who was probably Ibrahima's daughter. Foster tried to separate his alcoholic son from Susy, and the affair seemed to cause a break between the two fathers. A newspaper editor had tried for years to get Ibrahima to write a letter in Arabic to gain his freedom, but Ibrahima refused until this incident. When the letter generated publicity and an opportunity for Ibrahima to return home, Foster agreed to give Ibrahima his freedom if he could return to Africa, but insisted that if he remained in America, he reverted to his former status as a slave. Eventually Ibrahima returned to Africa.

Once asked to compare slavery in Natchez with slavery in his native society, Ibrahima insisted that Africa's version seemed much more humane. He attended church with his family and investigated the teaching of his wife's faith, but he could not be convinced to convert. His story became well known in the community, and before he returned to Africa, he became something of a celebrity, enjoying visiting with Natchez residents while selling produce in the city markets.

Not all owners displayed Foster's qualities. William Dunbar ruled his slaves with a whip more often. For getting drunk, Dunbar sentenced a slave to 500 lashes, and when the slave confessed to stealing rum, Dunbar had a heavy chain attached to his leg, only removing it when the leg swelled badly. When one of his slaves killed a white girl, Dunbar ordered the slave's hand cut off before he hung him. Running away called for 500 lashes with a cowhide whip. In his journal, Dunbar referred to slaves as hands and stupid savages, and he never expressed sorrow over a death or compassion for the ill. Dunbar's copious writing made it clear he did not consider his slaves fellow human beings.

By the end of the Spanish period, the number of slaves more than tripled in Natchez, and the frontier period was poised to end with the establishment of the wealthy cotton kingdom. Not surprisingly, the Spanish wanted to hold on to what had become a prosperous buffer outpost for them. They had signed a treaty with the Choctaw to annex Walnut Hills and followed that with a treaty at Nogales in 1793 encompassing peace with the Chickasaw, Choctaw, Cherokee, Creek, Tallapossa, and Alabama. The Spanish employed James Wilkinson of Kentucky, a general in the American army, as their spy and agent. This helped to alleviate their fear of the Kentuckians and Tennesseans allying with the Indians to drive Spanish forces out, but the home government negotiated away Nogales and Natchez in the Treaty of San Lorenzo in 1795. Even after the U.S. Congress ratified the treaty the next year and the Spanish government ordered its administrators in Louisiana to turn over the territory, they delayed for two more years, trying to stave off the transfer and intriguing to separate Kentucky from the United States or to find some means to hold what they had developed.

Some of the American settlers made life difficult. For example, Thomas Green, who served as a colonel under General Washington during the American Revolution, moved to Natchez from Virginia with his family and immediately began to organize a pro-American group to oppose the Minors and Dunbars, who had profited by their association with the Spanish. According to the Spanish lieutenant governor, Green stole slaves for sale and supplied gunpowder to outlaws. In 1785 Green circulated a petition for signatures and sent it to the Georgia legislature asking the state to extend its jurisdiction over Natchez. In response, the Georgia legislature created a huge county including Natchez and sent representatives to investigate the strength of their claim. The Georgians failed to find the support alleged by Green, and their mission ended in farce, but in 1795 the Georgia legislators tried again to annex the land between them and the Mississippi River. The Georgia voters turned out that legislature and elected a new one, which rescinded the land grab. Nevertheless for the next two years speculators prowled Natchez seeking to profit from the scheme.

Descending the river in February 1797, Andrew Ellicott appeared on this complicated scene with orders to survey a borderline that would place Natchez in the United States. Ellicott, a man of science, had lain out the city of Washington and demarcated a number of earlier borders. He had earned the confidence of President George Washington, who instructed him to persuade the Spanish to withdraw from Natchez. Ellicott had never been a diplomat, and when Gayoso offered him rooms at Concord and invited him to dinner with access to his fine wine cellar, Ellicott refused, choosing instead to pitch tents behind a tavern on a knoll overlooking the town. He raised an American flag before his tent and refused all entreaties to remove it. Gayoso responded by reinstalling a cannon that had been removed from the fort and informing Ellicott that he had orders to hold both Nogales and Natchez indefinitely. Ellicott had only a small army escort and two dozen woodsmen with him, but a larger military force occupied Chickasaw Bluffs (what would become Memphis) with orders to support him. The transition from Spanish to U.S. control required a year and generated anxiety and turmoil among the settlers who were concerned about the security of their land titles. They held land granted to them by the British or the Spanish, and the new United States government could question and even invalidate their titles. Indian nations separated Natchez from the United States, and the Spanish, fearing renewed conflicts with Britain and embroiled in the wars of the French Revolution, seemed an unstable colonial master. Rumors circulated constantly and rapidly.

Ellicott landed unprepared in the midst of a morass of intrigues. "Crazy" Percy Pope, the U.S. military commander, descended from Chickasaw Bluffs with his troops, and Captain Isaac Guion replaced him with additional reinforcements at the bluffs. In response, Gayoso appealed to the local people to support him and issued a moratorium on debt collection in order to win support from the debt-ridden planters, justifying continued Spanish governance as the only way to protect lives and property. He had support from the likes of Dunbar, who profited mightily from his Spanish connections. Anthony Hutchins, British though he had been, allied with Green and the indebted planters, while Dunbar and Minor sided with the merchants of the city who owned the planters' debts along with extensive land holdings. Soon Ellicott and Pope split, with Pope calling for the use of force to expel the Spanish while Ellicott continued to counsel persuasion. The rural debtors flocked toward Pope's call for force, and Green organized 200 men along Cole's Creek for an assault on the Spanish. Gayoso arrested Green, but Green escaped from the fort. The merchants and well-connected individuals allied with Ellicott, hoping for a peaceful transition with protection for their property.

In June religion entered the complex mixture when a lay Baptist minister-shoemaker drank too much and began to rail publicly against Catholicism, causing some Irish men to take offense and give him a beating. Gayoso arrested the shoemaker, which set off a series of disturbances. The Spanish soldiers fought off one attack on the fort, and Gayoso had to flee from his home to the safety of the fort. In the middle of the uproar, a band of Choctaw wandered into town, got drunk, and added to the chaos. Gayoso released the shoemaker and agreed to a citizens' meeting to elect a council to restore order, effectively surrendering his control of the district.

Eighty-two-year-old Colonel Hutchins chaired the meeting, which most of the notables in the town attended. The citizens elected Hutchins, who had led the first revolt against the Spanish, to be chair, but he moderated the more violent Americans in order to present Gayoso with resolutions, leaving Gayoso nominally in charge while the committee cooperated with Ellicott and Pope to constitute the new de facto government. The rest of the summer passed peacefully as Gayoso departed for New Orleans and a new post as governor of Louisiana. He left Minor as the temporary Spanish governor in Natchez and sold Concord to him. But the election of a permanent Committee of Safety peopled with merchants loyal to Ellicott led Hutchins to dissent, and a new election in September produced a planter-debtor committee headed by Green, whose son had married one of Hutchins's daughters. Both committees claimed the right to rule, and threats of violence filled public discourse. By November Minor wrote to Gayoso that he could easily procure a majority for a return to Spanish rule if he wished. In early December a large American force occupied the city and assumed command. With the arrival of sufficient forces to impress both the feuding settlers and the Spanish, on March 30, 1798, the Spanish military quietly departed in early-morning darkness. Their retreat left only the drawing of the boundary along the thirty-first latitude between the Mississippi and Pearl Rivers to establish an international border for the two countries.

In the year between his arrival and the Spanish departure, Ellicott made friends with William Dunbar, a fellow scientist. President John Adams appointed Ellicott boundary commissioner and sent a surveyor to serve with him. The Spanish appointed Dunbar and Minor as their representatives on the commission, ensuring a cooperative survey. Surveying the wilderness was an important step in mastering the land, and surveyors played major roles, with many of them turning their skills and their jobs to good account acquiring the best land and becoming wealthy. Surveyors often disputed one another's lines and spent months arguing and debating, making progress slow, but not in this case.

In May 1798, on a high point near the Mississippi River, they chose a spot later named Union Hill, where Ellicott set up his instruments to observe the stars for several nights before declaring his thirty-first parallel. Dunbar made a separate citing and found Ellicott north of the line by six feet, but, he told Gayoso, he made no objection over such a small discrepancy. Gayoso came to the camp to begin the work with a ceremony involving a kiss on a reluctant Ellicott's whiskered cheeks. The commission planned to cut a sixty-foot-wide path to the Mississippi River before turning west toward the Pearl, but spring flooding made working toward the Mississippi impossible, so they went west first instead. Dunbar declared the fifty white workers employed to hack through the nearly impenetrable cane, vines, and brush close to useless and borrowed twenty-two slaves from his nearby plantation for assistance cutting the path. Every two miles they erected square posts, and in August, when the water receded, they made it to the Mississippi River, placing a post ten feet tall surrounded by a mound of earth eight feet high. On the south side, they placed a Spanish crown, and on the north, they inscribed "United States."

The two clearing crews worked seven days a week attacking canes twenty to thirty feet high matted together by vines while mosquitoes, ticks, chiggers, and flies fought back. Dunbar took breaks to go home and supervise work on his plantation, but Ellicott, who reported his eyes almost swollen shut because of the mosquito bites, got no relief. Dunbar left the crew at the end of August on good terms, hoping to win a job as surveyor for his new country—the United States. The rest of the crew soldiered on until November, when Ellicott dismissed his surveyor for verbally attacking Minor. By mid-November they reached the Pearl River, and Ellicott believed they must have been the first white people to traverse the route just completed. After floating down the Pearl to the Gulf of Mexico, they obtained a vessel to take them to New Orleans, where Gayoso and Ellicott signed the official report for their governments in February 1799. The Mississippi Territory, created by Congress the previous April, had its southern boundary, and European settlers had imposed a physical representation of their latitude and longitude on the wilderness. That same month in 1799, the Spanish troops, tired of waiting for American officials to come for a formal surrender, left the keys to Fort St. Stephens on the Tombigbee with a settler and withdrew to Mobile. An American territory awaited creation.

Chapter Three

MISSISSIPPI TERRITORY

In 1798 the newly created Mississippi Territory encompassed the northern portions of the current states of Alabama and Mississippi. The Natchez district consisted of a triangular-shaped piece of land bordered by the thirty-first latitude on the south, the Mississippi River on the west, and a vague line on the east stretching from the southern boundary line northwest to the Walnut Hills at the northern point of the triangle. The Spanish still held all of the outlets to the Gulf of Mexico, including the southern portions of what would become the states of Alabama and Mississippi as well as all of the current state of Florida. The Choctaw wandered through the Natchez district, which sat across their route to the west, where they hunted and warred with their Indian neighbors. The only connections for the Natchez district to its latest mother country required polling or rowing a vessel up the Mississippi, which was almost never attempted, or floating through Spanish territory to take a ship in New Orleans, or alternatively walking or riding Indian trails east to Georgia or north to Tennessee for hundreds of miles. Reaching Georgia meant traversing the Choctaw and Creek nations, while going northeast took a traveler through the Choctaw and Chickasaw countries. Those Indian nations with treaties guaranteeing their sovereignty occupied and controlled almost all the land in the new territory. An unknown number of white squatters and runaway slaves lurked illegally within their lands. The population in the Natchez district numbered 4,500 whites and 2,400 black slaves. Approximately 200 miles east of Natchez, just over 1,000 free and slave inhabitants perched northwest of Spanish Mobile in the Tombigbee settlements accessible only by Indian trails to either Natchez or Georgia overland or down the Tombigbee River through Spanish Florida.

When two land commissioners who were appointed to settle land titles in the eastern portion of the territory tried to reach the Tombigbee settlements in order to hold hearings under congressional legislation of 1803, they left their homes in Connecticut and Kentucky in late September 1803 to take the water route down the Ohio to the Mississippi. Unfortunately, the Ohio River lacked enough water, so they proceeded by horseback to Louisville,

Black workers returning home after picking cotton. Courtesy of the Library of Congress.

Natchez planters built mansions, such as Stanton Hall, as symbols of their wealth and the lifestyle their cotton and slaves enabled them to enjoy. Courtesy of the Library of Congress.

where they sold their horses and bought a flatboat. They reached Natchez in December, two weeks after they were scheduled to be in Fort Stoddert on the Tombigbee, because they experienced a slow float south impeded by many sandbars along their way. They continued by boat to New Orleans on Christmas Eve. From the Crescent City, they took a ship to Mobile and, with the permission of the Spanish governor, ascended the river to their destination, arriving January 24, 1804, two months late.

The year Mississippi became a territory, the Natchez district produced 1,200,000 pounds of cotton, which constituted a harvest thirty-three times its cotton exports four years earlier. One large planter, Stephen Minor, accounted for the lion's share from his plantations alone. Planters had much more in the pipeline. For example, longtime resident Anthony Hutchins had produced his first large cotton crop, but he had been unable to transport it the few miles to the river because he lacked roads and heavy-duty wagons. The next year Hutchins sawed solid wooden wheels out of large trees and had a wagon body woven of canes to transport his accumulated cotton harvests to a gin. Most settlers still herded cattle and grew subsistence fields of corn. The wealth earned from cotton marked it as the future for agriculture in Natchez, but while the large cattle herders adopted it as their new cash crop quickly, many smaller farmers persisted with a mix of planting, herding, and hunting. The nabobs of Natchez, as the rich planters were called, imported wines, silks, playing cards, scientific instruments, books, and more slaves, setting the tone and serving as an inspiration for the ambitious man-on-the-make to emulate, but frontiersmen also criticized the nabobs' lifestyles and challenged their right to leadership. The town of Natchez contained approximately 100 houses in 1798 and a dozen taverns. The nabobs had just begun to build the mansions that later distinguished the city. With the departure of the Spanish, the Catholic church fell into disuse, the priests left with the soldiers, and no other houses of worship existed. The fort did not impress, so in 1798 the town still gave the appearance of a raw frontier outpost.

Natchez under-the-hill enjoyed a separate existence as the second largest port on the Mississippi River and as home to gamblers, prostitutes, musicians, boatmen, and frontier drifters from all corners of the world. French, Spanish, and Choctaw flavored the linguistic soup in the saloons, dancehalls, stores, and whorehouses. A visitor in the early 1800s reported being shocked to observe Americans, French, Spanish, Irish, Dutch, Africans, and mulattoes engaged in all manner of activities together. In the 1790s Natchez under-the-hill extended 800 yards from the base of the cliff to the river's edge, providing room for a racetrack and a jumble of wooden structures to serve the needs of the vast number of frontiersmen who gathered there. Flatboating frontier farmers, generically called Kentuckians, floating their animals, grain, wood products, and barrels of whiskey to market, stopped in Natchez to celebrate the end of the most treacherous stretches of the river with alcohol, music, dance, and female companionship. The rare minister of the gospel who passed through condemned under-the-hill as Satan's capital, professing never to have seen its like. Almost none dared try to preach, and the few who did suffered rude rebuffs from the boatmen, who did not take kindly to having their tension-releasing carousing interrupted.

Travelers sometimes complained about the food in Natchez, where the inhabitants grew their own vegetable gardens and learned to substitute dry-baked turkey meat for bread because of the shortage of wheat flour. Boiled venison still served as a popular meat because the local beef and mutton frequently proved tough and stringy. Passers-through most often praised the fish fried in bear's oil as the one delicacy available.

Outposts existed along the river from Walnut Hills in the far north of the district to Peter Bruin's "Castle" at the mouth of the Bayou Pierre just forty miles above Natchez. Thirty-eight miles to the south of Natchez, Captain Guion occupied Loftus Heights, which had been a French mission establishment for the Tunica, to make it the United States' port of entry from Spanish Louisiana. He called it Fort Adams after President John Adams and completed the construction of fortifications in 1799. Under Spanish rule, the first settlers spread throughout the Natchez district. Peter Bruin held judicial offices under the Spanish and led a militia to control cattle thieves and other outlaws. Daniel Burnett, son of a Spanish army officer living on a Spanish land grant, played a similar role at Grinder's Ford, the last white settlement before travelers entered the Choctaw nation fifty miles north of Natchez. Between Natchez and Grinder's Ford lay Greenville, where Abijah Hunt built the area's first store and cotton gin. Hunt's and Ferdinand Claiborne's lands adjoined the courthouse for Jefferson County, and Cato West, Cowles Mead, and General Thomas Hinds had plantations within two miles of town. Down along the thirty-first latitude, pioneers moved into the Woodville area and even the piney woods of what would become Pike County.

To impose the laws of the United States and to establish a territorial government, the Federalist president Adams selected like-minded Winthrop Sargent. A Natchez wit observed that Natchez did not rate a general to rule it, so the president sent a sergeant. Harvard-educated Sargent went west to make his fortune and won appointment as secretary and sometimes acting governor for the Northwest Territory, where he engaged in the usual land speculation, utilizing his office for profit. His manner ill-suited him for the frontier because he was dignified, laconic, austere, haughty, remote, and suspicious. He disliked the "mob" and immediately attached himself to the ruling elite, turning to the surveyor Andrew Elliott for advice and to planters such as Dunbar and Minor for assistance in governing. Bruin and two outsiders received appointment as judges to assist Sargent, but the outsiders delayed taking up their posts, and Bruin drank far too much to be useful. Territorial legislation required the governor and two judges to constitute a quorum, so Sargent ruled by decree for most of his first year in office. When a second judge arrived, the three men adopted the territorial code cobbled together by Sargent. Punishments included the customary pillory and whipping post, with estate forfeiture for treason, arson, and burglary with violence. The code also required license fees to be paid to the governor for operating taverns and marrying—$8 for a tavern and $10 for a marriage. Given the lack of ministers available, frontier couples often failed to conduct a ceremony to seal their unions, and $10 seemed an exorbitant fee to most.

Anthony Hutchins, Thomas Green, and Cato West, joined together by wedded children, mounted an immediate opposition to Sargent on behalf of the indebted planters and the less-affluent settlers. Sargent insisted on appointing the militia officers, flying in the teeth of the frontier custom that companies elected their leaders. His appointments prompted a flood of resignations from the militia, and opponents began to use grand jury presentments against the governor. Letters to Washington complained that the governor gave office to Spanish collaborators, causing Dunbar to resign in disgust. Petitions for Sargent's resignation or removal went to Secretary of State Timothy Pickering, but Pickering did not forward them to Congress. In order to bypass him, the Natchez opposition sent an agent to Congress requesting that the Mississippi Territory be moved to second-grade status, qualifying it to hold elections for a territorial legislature. W. C. C. Claiborne, a young member from Tennessee, became the Mississippi opposition's advocate in Congress, and in May 1800 Congress passed legislation elevating Mississippi to second-grade territorial rank. Claiborne also joined other congressmen to investigate Sargent's administration. Mississippi held its first election for the territorial legislature on July 4, 1800, with West, Green, and Hutchins winning control. A humiliated Sargent tried to delay the organization of the legislature while his supporters used a grand jury to demand a return to the first level of territorial government. While Sargent prepared to journey to Washington to defend his honor, Thomas Jefferson became president and appointed his supporter Claiborne to succeed Sargent as governor of the Mississippi Territory. Sargent, who had married a wealthy Natchez widow in 1799, retired to his plantation and built a mansion he called Gloucester after his home in Massachusetts.

Claiborne began his career working for the U.S. Congress as a teenage clerk in the 1790s. He attracted the attention of men such as Adams and Jefferson, who loaned him books to educate himself. Going west to make his fortune, he passed the bar, and the governor of Tennessee appointed him to the state supreme court, from which he resigned to be elected to Congress. At age twenty-seven, he became governor of the Mississippi Territory. His youth and frontier experience appealed to Sargent's opponents, who quieted their noisy dissent when he allowed militia units to elect their officers. Determinedly pro-Jefferson, he persuaded a pliable legislature to relabel

Pickering County, named for the Federalist secretary of state, as Jefferson in order to honor the president. For good measure, the legislature organized Claiborne County for the young governor and Wilkinson County for the Spanish spy and U.S. general. At Claiborne's urging, the territorial legislature moved the capital from Natchez to a new town laid out on John Foster's plantation six miles from the city, and with a great lack of imagination, called it Washington. To give the new town (under construction) a boost, Claiborne persuaded the U.S. government to establish Fort Dearborn nearby.

With action by Congress attempting to settle the Georgia claims, Claiborne focused on clearing up the murky land titles caused by the succession of colonial owners of the district. He intended to ease the minds of planters about the security of their property. He had the borders with the Choctaw surveyed for the pockets of white settlers on both the Mississippi and the Tombigbee. He also established Jefferson College at Washington and opened mail service up the Natchez Trace to Tennessee. Nonetheless, fractious politics resumed. Claiborne's brother, Ferdinand, married into the Hutchins family, while a sordid divorce among the Hutchins and Green children engendered hard feelings. Governor Claiborne wanted the land registry job for his brother, and the Greens opposed him. As a result, the Jeffersonian Republicans split into two factions for the 1803 legislative elections, producing a five-to-five split, with four Federalists holding the balance of power. Governor Claiborne left Mississippi in 1803 to oversee the acquisition of the Louisiana Purchase for President Jefferson. West, whom Claiborne had made territorial secretary, became governor and wanted to keep the office, but Jefferson named a North Carolina congressman to the post.

Most historians attribute the divide in early Mississippi politics to economic competition, with wealthy merchants arrayed against debtor planters, and that has some validity, but personal feuds account for much of the political conflict. Family alliances played major roles. Individual friendships were just as important. For example, Dunbar made friends with Ellicott, who introduced him to the scientific-minded Jefferson via long-distance correspondence and to Jefferson's friend Claiborne, who of course favored the old Scotsman/Spanish leader. Some planters preferred to leave politics to the lawyers. For example, Thomas Marston Green, son of the Green patriarch, took the position of delegate to Congress when the first delegate died in office, but gave it up and refused to run for election in order to live on his plantation north of Natchez. An unaristocratic, tavern-frequenting, coarse, and brawling George Poindexter, who emerged as the spokesman of the Green-West faction of the Jeffersonian Republican Party, came to hold most of the high offices in Mississippi and dominated its early politics.

The legislature incorporated the city of Natchez in 1803, giving the municipal government wide powers to create a small site of urban order on the frontier. A mayor's court handled criminal cases calling for no more than a month in jail and less than thirty-nine lashes as well as civil cases involving less than $100. The governor appointed six of the city's leaders, including the mayor and the marshal, while the citizens elected nine, including the tax assessor. By 1809 the legislature allowed the voters to elect a board of selectmen, who chose the mayor from their number. Despite Natchez's reputation as the home of nabobs, middle-class merchants ran the local government and used their taxing authority to make the rich pay for city services. When the nabobs imported fine carriages to ride in opulent style, for example, the city imposed a substantial carriage tax. Planters often went to the board of selectmen seeking relief from their tax burdens, but they almost never got it.

The city imposed licensing requirements and building codes for new construction and even for repairs to structures within the city. They taxed dogs, and the marshal killed strays in large numbers. He also hauled away dead horses for which the city reimbursed him $5 each time. It was not until 1819 that the city forbade water sellers from peddling water taken from the edge of the river, where the docked boats tended to foul it, and chartered the Natchez Water Company to provide running water in the city. The city established a nursery and encouraged property owners to plant chinaberry trees in an effort to improve the denuded city's appearance. It also founded a charity hospital for the indigent boatmen who landed in town, but the institution came to provide health care for the entire population. Most of the cases in the mayor's court involved fighting in the public streets or such infractions as selling liquor to Indians, so quiet and order did not come quickly.

Ruling under-the-hill as well as on the bluff, Natchez maintained cannons in order to repulse any attack from below. The tavern tax contributed mightily to the city coffers, as did a fee for entertainers wanting to display an "invisible lady" or a "Bengal tiger." Under-the-hill inhabitants resented the city's decision to exempt the Natchez Theatrical Association, which presented local and a few visiting professional acting troupes. Some traveling entertainers moved on rather than pay the city tax, thus depriving the under-the-hill folk of diversions. Those below the bluff chafed at the law banning the roulette wheel, especially while the nabobs bet on the horses at their well-kept racetrack. Just as the nabobs and the middle-class merchants feared the under-the-hill mob, the settlers outside Natchez distrusted the city's connections to the sophisticated wider world, and for that reason Claiborne established Washington.

The "Jefferson village" never grew beyond a few hundred people, but it developed from nothing to those few hundred quickly. In 1803, with the

Natchez under-the-hill housed a frontier mixture of races, languages, and classes. The more affluent Natchez on-the-hill kept cannons ready to defend itself from the rough elements below the hill. Courtesy of the Mississippi Department of Archives and History from the Cooper Postcard Collection.

houses only half built, it became the capital, and while the state never constructed a capitol building, thirty homes sprang up along with three hotels, a like number of taverns, a store, an apothecary, and a jail. The Jefferson College faculty and the officers from Fort Dearborn added some variety to the ruling elite of lawyers and politicians. A daily stagecoach operated to Natchez, and by 1806 Thomas Rodney called it the "Versailles" of the territory.

President Jefferson named Rodney, a Revolutionary War veteran, to be one of the western land commissioners and a justice on the territorial supreme court in order to get him out of Delaware and out of his son's career. Caesar Rodney became Jefferson's attorney general. The elder Rodney, at fifty-nine, had a generation on most of the men appointed to office in the new territory and was looked upon as the old man in town, but his Natchez-era biography illustrates the ruling society of the early 1800s. Settled into a hotel, he bought a suit of black cloth—the apparel of the townsman—a sorrel horse, saddle and bridle, and wine and whiskey. While he did not adopt the white, green, or blue blanket coat worn by planters, within a few months he did acquire the planter's broad-brimmed white hat. In Delaware, he had been a broken-down has-been, publishing some idiosyncratic critiques, but in Washington, Mississippi Territory, he reenergized and made a delightful life. He accepted the presidency of the

Washington dancing club and joined Dunbar's Society for the Acquisition and Dissemination of Useful Knowledge.

He reveled in the little ruling society of the town. For example, one evening his special friends Mrs. George Poindexter, Mrs. F. L. Claiborne, and the most eligible young heiress in the territory, Peggy Dunbar, sent for him to join them in games and music, and at the end of the evening the women escorted him home with a lamp. Rodney got on well with the nabobs, calling on Anthony Hutchins often during the last year of Hutchins's life to hear the oral history of the territory. To take one typical outing, to perform a wedding ceremony on a district plantation in May 1804, Rodney paused after a short distance on horseback, as he always did, to drink water and wine with Colonel Benijah Osmun. After another brief ride he stopped with Jessie Greenfield for more wine. He lodged and had dinner in the evening with William Dunbar. The next day he escorted Peggy Dunbar to Captain Jesses Carter's home, where they all dined at around two in the afternoon. After a rest, he performed an early candlelight wedding, and the young people danced until ten o'clock. The next morning he progressed south to the home of a rising politician, where he remained for several days before visiting three more friends during his return to his starting point to eat clabber at Osmun's—no doubt to recover from days of wining and dining. Although Rodney harbored a streak of Puritanism during the Revolution, the famous Mississippi planters' hospitality completely seduced him. While he never acquired a plantation, he bought house slaves for his home in Washington. In fact, he viewed black people as created to be hewers of wood and drawers of water by tracing slavery to biblical ordination, which seemed odd because his religious views comprised an uneasy balance between Deism and Episcopalism, with a period of sun worship mixed in.

Rodney's less than orthodox religious views fit well into the planter society because many planters eschewed religion for indifference, free thought, skepticism, or Deism. An early Methodist itinerant preacher described planters as too rich to need religion. Another doubted that three Christians could be found in the entire Natchez district—a gross exaggeration. As early as 1772 a group of Congregationalists planted a community twenty miles from the city, but they did not prosper. Under Spanish Catholic rule, Samuel Swayze, the group's leader and minister, hid his Bible in a hollow sycamore tree and held "secret" services to avoid repression, but of course the authorities knew and ignored them. After Swayze's death the services petered out.

The Spanish imported Irish priests hoping to convert, over time, the American immigrants to Catholicism. The official religion of the Spanish colony probably played a role in Bruin's decision to transfer there because he was Catholic, but the Irish priests did not win converts, and Bruin took more interest in secular affairs and liquor. Gayoso practiced toleration to the point of attending an Episcopalian service held at Villa Gayoso on Cole's Creek where the Spanish governor kept a summer house, but Gayoso felt pressure from his superiors to tighten control over Protestants, and he encountered a real challenge from the Baptists at Cole's Creek. Baptists embraced an evangelical vision of Christianity, which at its heart accepted the equality of all believers as brothers and sisters united in fellowship. Baptist congregations selected their own preachers, who received a call directly from God, and recognized no governing hierarchy. Any man, white or black, from any class, with or without educational credentials, might get the call and if selected become a minister. Thus the religion contained the seeds of social revolt against any government or religious establishment that might attempt to impose control over the community of believers.

Richard Curtis Jr. crossed the Indian nations from South Carolina in 1780 with his parents, four brothers, three sisters, and a stepbrother to settle on Cole's Creek. His parents and siblings, all committed Baptists, held services in their home, which began to attract their neighbors. The central ritual to signal the spiritual rebirth of a convert was the person's total immersion in water. Curtis had a license to preach but had not been ordained and could not perform baptisms, so he wrote back to his church in South Carolina for guidance, and the church leaders advised him to ask the congregation to elect a member to perform the rite. The incipient congregation elected Curtis, who proceeded to baptize converts in Cole's Creek.

As their numbers grew and the ceremonies attracted larger crowds, Baptists mounted armed guards for their gatherings, and complaints against them to the Catholic authorities gained a public airing. A Presbyterian wrote to the governor condemning the "illiterate" and "ignorant" Baptists, but warned him to be careful because the Baptists would interpret any restriction of their activities as an attack on Christ and his work. When a Spaniard asked Curtis to baptize him, Gayoso wrote to Curtis ordering him to cease his public activities, which Curtis ignored. Arrested and hauled before Gayoso, who threatened to expel him from the colony, Curtis accepted the prohibition on public events, but soon resumed them. When Gayoso again ordered his arrest, Curtis fled to South Carolina in 1795, where his church ordained him. During the transition to American rule, the men on Cole's Creek took up arms to attack Natchez, and it required much effort on the part of the committee overseeing the transition to persuade them to stand down.

Curtis returned to Cole's Creek to find a church building erected, and in 1798 he organized the territory's first Protestant church, calling it Salem, or peace. Other South Carolina Baptists followed him into the territory. One hundred migrated to the southern edge of the Natchez district to found Bethel in 1805, near what would become Woodville. William Foster, brother to Ibrahima's owner, provided the primary support for the organization of the first Methodist church, which began in Washington with a congregation of eight, including two of Foster's slaves, in 1799. Presbyterians with higher educational requirements for ministers lagged in conversions and church founding due to a shortage of missionaries, but James Smylie arrived in 1805 and played a prominent role in establishing churches and an educational institution. Yet none of the churches caught fire in the district. Membership remained small until camp meetings served as the spark that ignited an evangelical revolution among the plain folk of the district.

Adhering to the behavior required of Baptists and Methodists was difficult, but religion played the key role in the struggle for the minds of people in the district. Stark contrasts existed among the planters striving to master the land, their slaves, their families, and the plain folk wedded to subsistence agriculture with a commitment to democracy and sometimes a religious faith that joined them into a community of brothers and sisters recognizing no race or class, not to mention the heedless travelers passing through Natchez under-the-hill. As more planters followed the lead of Gayoso and Dunbar in building impressive houses furnished with imported furniture, drapes, paintings, and wines, the gulf between them and nearby neighbors in dogtrot houses grew into a chasm. The planter class flaunted their wealth and earned the reputation of being the best and most gracious hosts to the likes of Judge Rodney while their neighbors' lives became harder as the wild game that had been an important part of their livelihood disappeared and the price of land and slaves escalated beyond their reach.

The plain folk threw up log homes fast in order to get to their fields quickly. When they had time, they built a second room with a dogtrot between. Children slept upstairs, which really meant climbing a ladder because there were no stairs. Plain folk wore homespun and would never be mistaken for the other classes because of their appearance. Increasingly, their modest homes sat not too far from the planter's mansion. Religion offered the plain folk the means of rejecting the planter's lifestyle while retaining a sense of moral superiority.

Methodists required their preachers to continue wearing the outmoded clothes worn by the first Methodist founders. Women who donned jewelry could expect to be condemned from the pulpit among all evangelicals and arraigned before the congregation to confess their sin. Fancy dresses and other frivolous affectations such as ribbons could trigger censure. Men who drank liquor got the same treatment. The churches forbade dancing and playing cards, and conviction for indulging in those "sinful" activities could lead to expulsion from the brotherhood/sisterhood. Slavery troubled the evangelicals because slaves were baptized and received into the brotherhood/sisterhood with a handshake, just as the white members were. Evangelicals challenged their planter neighbors' worldview directly by their adoption of a simpler lifestyle and a belief in the unity of Christian believers.

As long as they remained a small fringe group, evangelicals did not threaten the ruling class, but camp meetings multiplied their numbers through emotional and physical appeals. Lorenzo Dow, sometimes called Crazy Lorenzo, a wild-haired, disheveled, itinerant preacher, conducted the first camp meeting in the territory in 1805 at Washington. At the meeting, Dow described an old "backslider" coming forward in tears and how his emotion set the audience to weeping and shouting for an extended period of time. During the course of four days, fifty people converted. The camps moved farther into the woods over the years. After clearing the brush, the faithful constructed a preaching stand and spread straw before it for the penitents to fall onto. Later services employed teams of preachers—not necessarily of the same denomination—who adopted a chanting style of delivery, which some scholars attribute to the melding of African and European oral traditions. Certainly intercultural exchange seemed apparent when the camp meetings erupted into physical activity, with people jumping, shaking, dancing, and groaning, giving the appearance of spiritual possession. As the camp meeting evolved, uneducated ministers became performers, relying on messages delivered extemporaneously with maximum emotional import in order to elicit uncontrollable responses from the attendees.

Music aided in the creation of the atmosphere. Services began with a song, continued with a rhythmic sermon, built to a climax with the call to salvation, and concluded with music celebrating the joy of the converts saved during the service. The cultural music exchange between blacks and whites at camp meetings revolutionized music and eventually created many of the modern world's music styles. At the time, the services provided relief to the participants, who were challenged by the vicissitudes of frontier life while facing the cotton revolution and the world of commercial/plantation agriculture with its completely different set of values, its regimentation, and its wealth.

Gender played a major role in the conflicts leading to the creation of a southern culture dominated by plantations and slavery. Women joined churches more often than men and frequently against the wishes of their spouses. In the early Baptist and Methodist churches, women voted as equals with men, and although no denomination would ordain them, women exercised leadership in their congregations. Hannah Swayze, the daughter of Samuel, married Richard Curtis Sr. of Salem Church after the death of her first husband, but she joined the Methodist church, where she became noted for her eloquent prayers and her wise advice on church affairs. Her daughter earned a similar reputation. At camp meetings, women testified to God's work in their lives, and they sometimes called mourners forward into the straw area.

When some members objected to women playing such a prominent role, one Methodist responded that God's ways were not man's ways and that God often chose the weak to do his work in order to "confound" the mighty. Women founded separate religious organizations where they alone exercised authority. In 1816 ninety Protestant women in Natchez founded the Female Charitable Society to provide support for a school and a home for orphans and widows. Women's organizations became the largest donors to the Methodist conference and the Mississippi Baptist Convention. Many observers commented on women's fondness for ministers. The ministers' governing bodies warned them against the dangers of becoming too close to their female followers. Some preachers abused their positions by engaging in sexual relations out of wedlock, while other ministers married well. William Winans, the most famous Methodist minister of the territorial period, married into a slaveholding family and made a comfortable life, while a fellow Methodist preacher married the daughter of Vicksburg's founder and came into a fortune.

Threatened by large female congregations and by husbands and fathers displeased by their wives' and daughters' independence, clergymen by 1800 began to accommodate their fellow white men by limiting women's public role in services and removing their right to vote in some churches. As Winans did, more ministers began to accept and participate in slaveholding. In order to gain access to slaves on plantations, they began to trim their message to suit slaveholding white men. In doing so, they ultimately transformed their teaching to fit the plantation culture, but the transition took time and met some resistance. When the members of the Bayou Pierre Baptist church, who had begun to prosper from cotton planting, asked if the foot-washing ceremony remained a necessary rite of the church, their fellow Baptists assured them that it did. No Baptist church appeared in Natchez until statehood, and only 5 percent of the population belonged to any church in 1817.

By the end of the territorial period, the district's population swelled as migrants from the old states fled their worn-out land and the declining tobacco farms for the Old Southwest, which they viewed, because of cotton, as the "new Canaan." In 1810 the Natchez district supported 16,600 whites and 14,706 blacks. In another decade, the figures grew to 42,176 and 33,272, respectively. A small portion of the black population had their freedom, but most blacks came unwillingly as slaves. The portion of the territory that would become the state of Mississippi was almost half slave (46 percent) in 1810. The white population still contained elements of international, colonial European, and mixed-race individuals recognizing no real nationality, but increasingly the white population came from the older American states. Natchez got settlers from Virginia and northern states, but what became Pike County indicated the future migration pattern, receiving 73 percent of its population from Tennessee, Georgia, and the Carolinas during the territorial period. Planters continued the influx of African slaves despite the territorial ordinance banning the trade, until national law forbade it in 1808. In early 1807 William Dunbar requested a Charleston firm to beat the deadline and supply him with as many African slaves as possible for £3,000, specifying that they be between twelve and twenty-one years of age, two-thirds to three-quarters male, and native to the interior of Africa if possible, but absolutely not Ibo. His instructions indicated his and other planters' extensive experience with slaves imported directly from Africa. The boom in cotton planting starved the district for labor, and when the African supply ended, planters turned exclusively to imports from the older slave states.

The domestic slave migration followed one of three scenarios. In the first scenario, planters went back east and made purchases themselves or employed agents or relative to buy slaves for them. Depending on the number and circumstances, the planters either walked their new slaves overland or shipped them by sea. In the second, slave traders bought slaves and marched them in chained human trains called coffles southwest across the Indian nations to sell or floated them down the Mississippi. In the coffles, women and children might be allowed to walk unchained or in some instances to ride in accompanying wagons. Finally, in the third scenario, entire plantations migrated as plantation owners from southern states sought to maximize profits from their human investments.

The trip from Virginia to Mississippi took seven or eight weeks and usually occurred in the late summer or early fall in order to miss the height of the fever season during the summer heat. If an entire plantation moved, the planters accomplished it in stages, with the hardiest men sent ahead to clear fields and to build housing so that women and children could follow, with fewer casualties caused by the harsh wilderness conditions. Slaves shipped into Natchez before the mid-1830s stood on auction blocks near traders' offices scattered throughout the city. Usually the traders prepared the slaves outside of town by cleaning, oiling, and plucking out gray hair in order to get the best price. Because of the strong demand, unscrupulous traders often purchased and tried to sell human merchandise with flaws such as rebelliousness, alcoholism, or health problems. Buyers shopped with care, but

Mississippi probably received large numbers of troublesome slaves shipped south with considerable relief on the part of their previous owners.

Traders also sold free black people who were kidnapped and mixed into the slave population. In the most famous case, five Delaware men abducted Aaron Cooper from his home as his wife and three daughters pleaded with them. Cooper's neighbors pursued the kidnappers, but they sold Cooper to a trader, who shipped him out of state without leaving a trace. Sold to a Natchez planter, Cooper managed to contact the Mississippi territorial attorney general with his story. He worked for three years as a slave while his new owner and the attorney general made inquiries and then as the suit filed by the attorney general made its way through the court process. In 1814 a jury found him to be a free man, and he returned to Delaware.

The influx of large numbers of slaves and the regimentation of cotton plantations transformed life for Mississippi's slaves. Independence such as that enjoyed by Toney, the herding and hunting slave who belonged to Hutchins, morphed into a more industrial labor system as the proportion of slave to free persons increased and as planters joined in the Industrial Revolution to supply the cotton mills of Manchester by squeezing the maximum amount of labor out of their workers. The cotton gin, which started the cotton boom, proved to be the first of many innovations. Screw presses followed to bale the cotton compactly for shipment. Dunbar added a fan to his gin in order to blow dirt and trash out of the lint. Later he invented another press to extract cottonseed oil as a by-product. Dunbar, Sargent, and many other planters applied the latest science to their farming while engaging in brutal labor practices.

The agricultural routine began in the early spring when women and children beat down the previous year's cotton plants to provide fertilizer for the soil. The men plowed between the previous year's furrows and then went back to break the soil more thoroughly before a one-horse plow created furrows for the new planting. The women sowed the seeds in April or early May, and a man plowed with a harrow to cover them. As the seedlings appeared, gangs of men and women scraped the sides of the ridges with a hoe to destroy weeds and grass. When the cotton plants grew to a few inches, the same gang chopped plants out to leave about a foot between those left to grow. Next, men ran plows with moldboards attached between the rows to toss dirt onto the bottom of the plants and over the grass competing for life there. Scraping might be required a few more times, but by July the crop was "laid by."

Slaves then turned to fields and gardens to feed themselves, their masters, and the plantation animals. Vegetable gardens and corn required much hoeing and harvesting, while hogs, cattle, horses, and mules now fenced demanded attention. Slaves hated pulling and bundling corn leaves in the August heat for fodder, but the corn had to be in the barns before the cotton bolls began to open in September and October. When the bolls opened, slaves extracted the cotton by reaching into the sharp dried bolls with their fingers. The edges of the bolls cut even the most calloused skin, making the task extremely painful. Pickers carried a cloth bag over their shoulders and emptied it into baskets at the end of the rows. Each field required at least three pickings to harvest the entire crop. The slave's day began an hour or two before sunrise and continued until dark to try to get the cotton harvested before the late fall/early winter rains ruined it. The planter or overseer monitored each slave's picked cotton weight, and inadequate levels sometimes led to whipping at the end of the day on some plantations. On rainy days, slaves worked at the gin to separate the seed from the lint and pack the cotton for shipment. If all went well, they transported the bags or bales to the river for shipment to New Orleans and enjoyed a Christmas party with a few days' rest. Before the cycle began again, slaves cleared trees and brush to make new fields or worked to maintain fences and buildings during the short winter months. By 1800 this pattern had emerged, and it changed little over the years.

Early in the life of a plantation, slaves lived in barracks, but as soon as possible the master had them build individual cabins to encourage family formation and the multiplication of his slave property. Some plantation owners continued to set aside garden plots for their slaves and to allow slaves to sell their own produce in the city. Ibrahima was marketing his sweet potatoes in Natchez when he spotted his old friend, the Irish doctor, but Foster, his owner, numbered among the planters urging the tightening of restrictions.

The Haitian Revolution in 1792 worried Natchez, and a few planters from that island took refuge in the district with slaves from their former plantations. When news of an attempted revolt in Virginia reached Sargent, he sent a circular letter blaming the planned uprising on foreign influences. Addressing the Natchez militia, Sargent stated bluntly that owners could not expect slaves deprived of liberty to become reconciled to their condition and that slaves would never forgive those who enslaved them. Seeking vengeance, slaves would always be potential allies for any foreign enemy, and, as a result, Sargent said that Natchez whites could never relax their guard against insurrection.

The expansion of cotton slavery caused deterioration in relations between slave and owner. The Mississippi Territory adopted harsh codes from southern slave states calling for burning hands, nailing ears to the pillory, and then cutting the ear off after an hour, followed by whipping. By

1809 the territory enacted a law to draft militia members below the rank of captain into slave patrols of three men and a leader to ride the roads at night in order to catch any slave without a pass who might be trying to run away or to visit another plantation. Substitutes could be hired for those men choosing not to serve on the patrol, which probably meant the patrols did not attract the best men into service. New provisions forbade slaves owning livestock or obtaining liquor without their owners' permission. The patrollers or any white person gained the authority to kill dogs belonging to slaves. The patrols frequently assaulted slaves and injured them to the point that their owners sued for damages. The newspaper descriptions of runaway slaves listed horrifying descriptions of missing body parts and scars to identify the missing slaves, indicating that owners and overseers did their share of damage, too.

White men sexually exploited female slaves. Often, no doubt, it involved rape, but lasting relationships abounded. Court records document women and children manumitted by their white partners and fathers. White men maintained black and mulatto concubines in Natchez in open defiance of the color line. Some lived openly as husband and wife. Thomas Smith provoked his neighbor by going to bed with his black partner while his neighbors watched through an open window. When patrollers surrounded his house one night and accused him of sleeping with his black partner, Smith responded that he was a free man and no one had any right to question him about his partner. Hauled before a justice of the peace, Smith sued his accuser for slander and won a $50 judgment proving his point.

Sometimes before freeing their black or mulatto companions, slaveholders allowed them to pass as free women of color and supported their businesses. When William Johnson's mother, Amy, had to go to court to defend her operation of a tavern, Johnson's white father testified on her behalf. In the early territorial period, free blacks frequently got access to the courts, where they sued one another and had their testimony accepted. On the other hand, the courts imposed harsh sentences on free blacks. For example, two mulatto women charged with fighting and cursing in the streets received twenty lashes each at the city whipping post. In an effort to end what Sargent referred to as Creole Sunday, the city passed an ordinance empowering the mayor to appoint a man to break up slave assemblies and to ring a bell at three o'clock in the afternoon signaling time for all slaves not residents or on their master's business to exit the city.

In response to the increased regimentation and harshness of their lives, slaves struck back by intentionally breaking tools and machines to slow the work pace whenever they could. Their most destructive weapon proved to be fire. Dunbar lost almost everything on his plantation, except his dwelling, to fire in 1806. After a similar gin fire in 1814, Stephen Minor offered a $2,000 reward for the culprits who set the blaze. Fires grew more frequent, and the government added arson to the list of crimes punishable by death.

Governing the stewing caldron of powerful planters, slaves, Baptist settlers, Indians, grasping lawyers, frontier drifters, and circuit-riding Methodist preachers in an enclave surrounded by the Choctaw and bordered by the Spanish Empire to the south proved to be a tasking business. Sargent just escaped being deposed, and Claiborne rushed on to wider fields in the nearby Louisiana Purchase. President Jefferson appointed Robert Williams, a Republican congressman from North Carolina serving with Rodney as land commissioner, as territorial governor in 1805, but Williams failed to master the unruly Natchez scene.

An incident involving the disgraced former vice president of the United States, Aaron Burr, illuminated the district's politics and served as a last gasp of opposition to inclusion in the United States. Burr killed Alexander Hamilton in a duel and resigned his office, becoming politically powerless and nearly destitute. As with so many other Americans needing a fresh start, he went west, where he received a warm reception in Kentucky, Tennessee, and the Mississippi Territory. Meeting with General Wilkinson, a Spanish spy and governor of the Louisiana Territory (Claiborne became governor of a separate territory that would eventually become the state of Louisiana), Burr hatched a scheme to separate the western territories from the United States and to invade the Spanish lands, making himself king of a new empire. The details of his plan, if it ever existed in coherent form, never became clear. After a visit back east, including an interview with President Jefferson, in the fall of 1806, Burr returned to the Ohio and Mississippi Rivers, gathering boats and men allegedly to settle a new colony, but according to widely circulating rumors, he planned either to break up the Union or invade Spanish territory. Wilkinson, who Burr counted as a co-conspirator, turned on him and went to New Orleans as ordered by the president in order to defeat and arrest Burr.

Burr landed at Bruin's "Castle" on Bayou Pierre on January 10, 1807, hoping to recruit men and to raise money to carry off his empire-building scheme. Bruin met him with an issue of a Natchez newspaper, the *Mississippi Messenger*, containing President Jefferson's public condemnation and a copy of Wilkinson's encoded letter from Burr. Off to a rocky start with the feuding Republican factions fueled by the disappointed West, who had aspired to be governor, Governor Williams had gone back to North Carolina to bring his family out to the territory, leaving Secretary Cowles Mead as acting governor. Mead, the new high-strung young appointee, fell into the Green faction, marrying one of the family. Through his new family connections, Mead no doubt knew that Burr and Wilkinson had visited with Stephen Minor for extended periods of time and that Minor, who had only become an American citizen in 1798, had continued to deal with the Spanish government as he amassed plantations and a fortune from cotton. While Burr did not have the army that Mead feared, the precarious position of the Natchez district caused Mead and other leaders to take Burr's threat seriously because they knew their neighbors' minds.

Wilkinson spent nine days in Natchez on his journey to New Orleans and wrote alarming letters to President Jefferson and to Governor Claiborne as he conferred with Minor and other Natchez leaders. As he progressed through Fort Adams, he ordered its garrison to the Crescent City and then called for the transfer of the men at Fort Stoddert as well, giving every appearance of preparing for a major assault.

Mead did not believe Wilkinson could be trusted. As he readied the Natchez militia, insisting oaths be taken and buying shotguns and fowling pieces to arm as many men as possible, he wrote to Claiborne warning him not to place any faith in Wilkinson and predicting that should Burr get through Natchez with 2,000 men, Wilkinson would be Claiborne's worst enemy. Stunned by Wilkinson's betrayal, Burr tarried at Bayou Pierre drilling the 100 men who joined him there, and then he fled to the Louisiana side of the river to avoid the Natchez militia. Some of his men landed in the Natchez district and assessed the new situation with their friends. Mead prorogued the legislature so that members could carry out their militia obligations, and posted sixty men on the riverbank with orders to stop any boats. One boat slipped through during the night, firing on the militia as it went. Burr left a letter at Bruin's place denying he intended any harm to either the national or the local government. Mead received the letter from the militia, who had sought to take Burr, but dismissed the letter and continued his efforts to capture the intruder. He called Ferdinand Claiborne to him, placing Claiborne in command of the militia with the overly dramatic comment that the fate of the country might depend upon their success. Meanwhile another militia colonel arrived at Bayou Pierre, and Burr sent a skiff across the river with an invitation for the colonel to visit, which he did. He reported to the acting governor, seeing only fifty to sixty men and five barges. The next day sixty dragoons appeared at Bayou Pierre, and again Burr visited with the commander; this time he indicated he would surrender to civil authorities and be tried in a territorial court.

Facing capture by Wilkinson if he continued south, Burr probably decided that he liked his chances in Natchez far better than in any military tribunal Wilkinson might convene. Mead sent two aides, one of whom was George Poindexter, the territorial attorney general, to negotiate Burr's surrender. Mead met with Burr and finalized the agreement for his aides to escort Burr to Washington, which provided relief to the militia mired in an unusual four-inch snowfall. Poindexter got Burr freed on a $10,000 bond and scheduled a February 2 court date.

Planters gave balls in Burr's honor, and he luxuriated in the attention thrust upon him. He went to stay with Benjamin Osmun, a former army officer and old friend who provided a portion of Burr's bail. While visiting a neighboring widow, Burr fell in love and swore his intention to marry her beautiful daughter. Using all his charm, Burr convinced many planters that he had only intended to attack the Spanish, which was a popular notion. Williams returned from North Carolina on December 27 and resumed the office of governor, replacing Mead as the primary agent in Burr's prosecution. Burr continued to confer with friends and possible co-conspirators, including the former Choctaw agent, about possibilities for detaching portions of the territory from the United States. One friend convinced Burr that he could have raised the Tombigbee communities for an attack on Spanish Mobile easily.

Judge Rodney favored trying Burr in his court and threatened insurrection when it was suggested that Burr be transferred, so Burr appeared before Bruin and Rodney on the appointed day. The third judge, Harry Toulmin, resided in the Tombigbee settlement and never attended the Natchez court. Poindexter declined to indict Burr on the technical grounds that the territorial supreme court had only appellate jurisdiction and that Burr had not committed an indictable offense in the territory. Williams shared the attorney general's views, but Rodney summoned a grand jury and proceeded to take depositions. The grand jury absolved Burr and condemned Mead's actions. Bruin wanted to discharge his friend, Burr, but Rodney insisted on releasing him on his own recognizance instead. Wilkinson sent agents in civilian clothes to capture Burr and bring him to New Orleans without arming his agents with warrants. Burr went back to his boats for a day, but no doubt still feared falling into Wilkinson's hands. He told his followers to sell the boats and supplies and disperse. He escaped to the Tombigbee settlements, where the land registrar recognized him despite a disguise and a rainy night arrival. The lieutenant commanding Fort Stoddert arrested Burr and imprisoned him at the fort.

Toulmin began to question Burr's co-conspirators, and Bruin's son-in-law, following Burr to the Tombigbee settlements with Burr's maps and papers, fell into the hands of the militia. Burr seemed set to try for Mobile, having failed to take Baton Rouge from the Spanish. Even in captivity, he tried to corrupt the soldiers guarding him into his scheme. The nervous lieutenant in charge picked eight men and sent Burr through the Indian nations to stand trial back east.

Mead's family knew the men involved in Burr's schemes well and distrusted Wilkinson as the Spanish agent that he was. Some historians have dismissed the Burr affair as a tempest in a teapot, but it seems more likely that Burr did intend to establish an empire and that many Natchez residents may have sympathized with him. Bruin's son-in-law followed Burr to Richmond and lost a good deal of money securing Burr's eventual acquittal. The Burr fiasco in Natchez probably ended whatever hopes some planters harbored for breaking away to join in a slave/plantation empire including some of the bordering Spanish lands. From 1807, the planters faced final incorporation into the United States, and they adjusted their politics accordingly.

Generally the Federalists favored Burr and the Republicans opposed him, but Williams, a Jefferson appointee, revived the Federalists' hopes for a political resurrection. Mead withdrew to the family's estates and let it be known that he no longer considered himself part of the administration. Poindexter allied with Williams's opponents and sought to replace him with either Mead or Claiborne, if the latter could be brought back from Louisiana. Poindexter challenged Williams to a duel, but the governor, citing the responsibilities of office, refused to fight. Williams's crowning mistake proved to be angering Ferdinand L. Claiborne, who commanded the militia, and then dismissing him, which resulted in a flurry of militia officers resigning their commissions. Claiborne joined Mead and Poindexter in opposition, and they garnered a majority in the territorial legislature, which elected young Poindexter to be the territory's delegate to Congress in 1807. This election launched his legislative career, despite reservations about his morals and tavern-frequenting habits. He continued to work with Mead and Claiborne against the governor. Rodney wrote his son, the attorney general, that Williams had gone crazy and allowed the Claiborne brothers to use his house for meetings when the Louisiana governor visited Natchez. The opposition accused Williams of favoring Burr and deserting to the Federalists. In the 1808 elections, the district divided into the country ticket headed by Poindexter and the city ticket made up of the governor's supporters. Ferdinand Claiborne as Speaker of the House got a petition passed asking for Williams's removal. As a result, the president accepted the beleaguered Williams's resignation and appointed David Holmes to replace him. Holmes finally tamed the political system, serving a long tenure as territorial and later state governor because he responded to the Republican base in the outlying counties but looked to the interests of the Federalist planters controlling the economy.

Jefferson's embargo brought on by the raging European wars damaged commerce, causing a depression between 1808 and 1814, with declining cotton and slave prices. As tension between the United States and Great Britain mounted, Natchez planters saw their political control of the territorial government challenged by development in the eastern section of the territory, which would ultimately become Alabama. Between 1809 and 1814 six of the nine new counties created in the territory lay east of the Pearl River, as immigrants poured into the piney woods. Natchez residents paid the greater share of the taxes, but planters began to fear that those in the eastern section might claim most of the public funds for themselves, with Judge Toulmin providing increasingly effective leadership there.

Governor Holmes, a bachelor who had served six terms in Congress representing his Virginia district as a faithful Republican, began life as a bookkeeper in his father's store and then became a competent but not flashy lawyer. He suffered from poor health and proved inept at physical activities. Once while reviewing the militia, his horse ran away with him, and he laughed along with the men at his discomfiture. He had a compromising nature, and even when criticizing a subordinate he took care to preserve the other man's dignity. He lived comfortably on his salary and never used his office for personal gain. As a result of his personal attributes and the revolutions and wars that solved some of the territory's vexing problems, Holmes finally provided the long-missing successful leadership needed in the territory.

Land title questions still troubled the district, and Holmes made certain not to appoint anyone to an office associated with the Yazoo Company's claims and thus protected the large landholders. At the same time, he responded actively to squatters' demands to protect their "rights" to eventually purchase the property on which they settled in the less attractive areas of the territory. He supported the acquisition of Indian land but sought to expel whites who illegally invaded the Chickasaw nation. As he wrestled with those issues, the American settlers in West Florida rebelled against their Spanish rulers.

The United States claimed West Florida under the 1803 purchase of Louisiana, but the Spanish held it and refused to negotiate. Burr's first target, Baton Rouge, fell to American settlers in 1810, and they raised a lone star flag asking for annexation as a state. Holmes called out the territorial militia to patrol the thirty-first parallel boundary and worked with Claiborne to secure West Florida peacefully when President James Madison proclaimed it as American territory. Eventually Poindexter persuaded Congress to divide the acquisition between the Mississippi Territory and the Orleans Territory. Mississippi received the land between the Pearl and Perdido Rivers, rounding out the boundaries of the Mississippi Territory and giving it a coastline for the first time, although Mobile remained in Spanish hands until the War of 1812 forced the United States to occupy the city.

The Mississippi Territory endured most of the fighting during the War of 1812 and the Creek War within the larger conflict, but Andrew Jackson and his Tennesseans hogged the spotlight, keeping the Natchez contingents in a supporting role. Holmes did yeoman's work in settling the West Florida revolt peacefully, and he managed his meager resources well throughout the War of 1812. The 1811 earthquake unsettled Indians throughout the Southwest, and the Creek nation divided into a faction determined to drive the whites out and a party continuing to cooperate and integrate with whites. The war party, the Red Sticks, accepted aid from the British and sought to use it to eliminate the white settlers. Because Jackson had been too close to Burr's scheme, the president and Wilkinson, who still commanded the U.S. forces in the Southwest, kept him out of the war for the first year.

Tennessee's governor ignored their doubts in early 1813 and sent Jackson toward New Orleans with volunteers. Jackson made it only as far as Natchez and camped outside Washington to visit with old friends in the area, where he had married his wife and briefly run a store. The Mississippi militia marched to Baton Rouge and served as a reserve to rush to the defense of New Orleans. As soon as possible, Wilkinson ordered Jackson to disband his men, leaving them to find their way up the Natchez Trace on their own. Jackson defied the order and walked his troops back to Nashville, earning the name Old Hickory.

In the summer of 1813 a group of Creek returning from Pensacola clashed with American forces. The British, invited into Pensacola by the Spanish, had supplied the Creek with arms. Holmes sent the Mississippi militia under General Claiborne, who had been restored to militia leadership, to the eastern portion of the territory to protect settlers. The Choctaw joined him to fight against the Creek, but the regular army imposed a defensive strategy. The Mississippi dragoons assigned to protect the settlers protested and asked to be allowed to attack Creek villages and strongholds. Some of the dragoons, including a young lawyer named Joseph Davis, older brother of Jefferson, wrote to the general in charge of the regular forces questioning his policy, which the general viewed as insubordination. He sent those dragoons home, and Holmes disbanded them before the Creek massacred settlers who had taken shelter in Fort Mims. The resulting outcry unleashed Jackson, who got command of Tennessee volunteers to avenge the white deaths. Combined, the Mississippi militia, volunteers, and Choctaw only numbered around 1,000 men and would only reach approximately 1,500 by the end of the war. Davis, disillusioned by his experience with military life, did not reenlist.

Jackson used his more numerous Tennesseans, friendly Creek, and contingents of the Mississippians, including the Choctaw, to destroy the Creek at Horseshoe Bend. He then double-crossed his Creek allies to force upon them a treaty seizing their land for white settlement. Without orders from the government, he took Pensacola and turned to defend New Orleans. Thomas Hinds's dragoons from Jefferson County aided in all these battles, earning special recognition for their service at New Orleans. Various Mississippi troops scattered throughout the army served in regular army units and with other state militias. Poindexter got himself assigned as an aide to a Tennessee officer, only to be hit by an exploding wall during the battle, leaving him too stunned to participate actively. His inactivity during the fighting initiated accusations of cowardice that continued for years.

Holmes worked from the territorial capital to supply the needs of his troops, even pledging his own money when the national government delayed funds for the effort. He had to resort to a draft, but only the French community in Hancock County resisted, and they relented when he threatened force and gave them a second opportunity to comply. After the Battle of New Orleans, Holmes saw to the needs of the British prisoners quartered at Washington and administered prisoner exchanges with the British. The Natchez district observed the war somewhat removed from the fray, which allowed planters to continue business largely untouched, and no doubt many joined Davis in pursuing their own interests. Holmes's younger brother died in the war, and the Mississippi troops suffered minor causalities, but the planters were poised to resume supplying the British factories cotton as soon as hostilities ceased. The territory prospered as a result of the war. Vast new lands invited settlers into the eastern portion of the territory. Mobile lay open as an American-controlled port. Neither the British nor the Spanish seemed a threat after the war, and New Orleans was secure.

The military activity pointed to the need for better land connections between the older states and the Mississippi Territory. In the territorial period, roads gradually came to link Natchez to other settler populations within the territory and to the older states. What would later be termed the Natchez Trace linked Natchez to Nashville. A shifting group of Indian trails following the ridges north stretched 100 miles through sparsely settled farms and 400 to 500 miles of "wilderness" in the Indian nations.

Two years before the American annexation, Francis Baily made the journey up the path to the Choctaw nation, and then along the Choctaw-Chickasaw Trail to the Chickasaw Trace into Nashville, keeping a journal. He found the trace unmarked, and he often needed Choctaw and Chickasaw to guide him. Expecting little sustenance in the wilderness, his party purchased beef jerky, flour, rice, bacon, coffee, and sugar, and for an emergency food roasted corn ground to a fine powder. The last provision the Choctaw swallowed by the spoonful in the morning to ward off hunger when they lacked other food.

At Grindstone Ford near what is today Port Gibson, his party crossed into the Choctaw nation, where Baily encountered isolated Indians and one war party with recently taken scalps. None of the Choctaw molested his group, except for the theft of two horses. Usually the Choctaw helped the Americans along with accurate information about the trail. Creeks either had to be crossed on downed trees, or they swam across them. Bad drinking water felled three of the party, and the others left them to find healers to send back with herbal remedies. The Chickasaw in the next village sold the Americans roasted corn and went to rescue their ailing companions.

The Americans stumbled upon John McIntosh, son of a British agent to the Chickasaw, who had married a Chickasaw and "gone native." McIntosh farmed with a few black slaves and lived quietly in the Chickasaw nation. He provided the travelers hospitality as required by custom, but expressed no joy at their visit and sent them off with another white man, whom he recommended, as a paid guide. At the Chickasaw big town, Baily had to chase down a Chickasaw who ran away with his hat. He recovered his hat, but had to walk to the next camp because his horse followed his fellow travelers without him. Baily's worst experience came from the swelling of his legs, infected by an allergic reaction to poison oak on the paths. Nearing Nashville, he had to resort to the spoonful of ground corn to stay alive as the group traveled with the Chickasaw and avoided the Creek, who were reported to be lurking along the trail. He reached the outskirts of Nashville after twenty-seven days.

When Sargent arrived in Natchez, letters from the secretary of state took three months to reach him, so he proposed making the trails that Baily traversed into a mail route with "stands" to keep fresh mounts for mail riders, who would meet at a midpoint, six miles from McIntosh's place, to trade pouches. The postmaster awarded Abijah Hunt a contract with the idea that a letter could speed between Nashville and Natchez in two weeks. Despite increased travel by returning boatmen, those involved with the mail complained to General Wilkinson about the trail's condition and asked the army to improve it into a wagon road. The secretary of war commissioned negotiations with the Chickasaw and Choctaw, who agreed in 1801 to allow road improvements but reserved manning the proposed stands for themselves. Wilkinson started his troops working from Nashville, but by 1803 he transferred them to the Natchez section. Two years later the army had only completed the road to Grindstone Ford, with preliminary work done forty miles beyond; meanwhile, undergrowth had reclaimed the original road near Nashville. A new postmaster general hired private contractors and decreed that the road should be twelve feet wide instead of eight as earlier established and that stumps could not stand more than sixteen inches above the ground. Swamps had to be filled with logs and then covered with dirt. Streams less than forty feet wide had to be bridged, he said, and he called for a completion date of 1807. In 1809 a government inspector declared it done.

Other Indian trails linked Natchez to the Tombigbee settlements and along the Mississippi River to New Orleans. The federal government constructed a road, usually called the Federal Road, from Milledgeville, Georgia, to Fort Stoddert, which became a mail route in 1806. The government improved it into a wagon road in 1811. To reach Natchez from the Tombigbee, travelers trod the Choctaw's long-established Six-Towns path and sections of the Trading Path, which the Chickasaw and Choctaw used between what became the cities of Memphis and Mobile. Later they took the new Fort Stoddert and Fort St. Stephens roads cut through the first Choctaw concession ceded at the Treaty of Mount Dexter in 1805. The Fort Stoddert and Fort St. Stephens roads lay outside the Choctaw nation and were shorter than the Six-Town's path, which ran almost entirely within the nation. The dates for completion are vague, but the roads were probably finished by 1811. Many historical accounts over the years have mislabeled these roads and paths the "Three Copped Way," which recent research has shown never existed.

In the far north of the territory, the government initiated what became known as Gaines Trace from Colbert's Ferry on the Tennessee River to the northernmost navigable spot on the Tombigbee River at what became Cotton Gin Port. Edmund Pendleton Gaines surveyed the route after his testimony in the Burr trial on orders from the secretary of war and his brother. George S. Gaines, employed as the government factor at Fort St. Stephens, bargained with the Chickasaw to open the road so that the government could float goods by river to Colbert's Ferry and then transport them by land to Cotton Gin Port to be shipped south on the Tombigbee, avoiding the Spanish duties on goods shipped through Mobile. Obviously the need for this route diminished after the War of 1812 and the occupation of Mobile, but the Gaines Trace merited a mention in the 1816 treaty with the Chickasaw. As the territorial period drew to a close, Captain Hugh Young completed his survey of Jackson's Military Road running from south of Cotton Gin Port where Columbus would develop to Madisonville, Louisiana, across Lake Pontchartrain from New Orleans. All of these roads served military purposes, but they also invited settlers to migrate into the territory.

Roads sped the decline of the Chickasaw and Choctaw nations. Warriors who wanted to maintain an economy based on deerskin trading increasingly crossed the Mississippi River to hunt, and some even settled there, but the majority remained in Mississippi struggling to come to grips with an environment altered by overhunting, cattle, pigs, white settlement, and cotton. By the start of the territorial period, both the Choctaw and Chickasaw had become more herders than hunters. They left their traditional towns, moving into what had been their borderlands reserved for hunting, to herd cattle and raise pigs there. Only the conservative heartland of the southern Choctaw held on to their traditional towns. The families of mixed European and Indian ancestry led this trend toward herding and sometimes commercial farming. Traders such as Louis LeFlore, Nathaniel Folsom, and John Turnbull married well among the Choctaw and produced large families.

Folsom, for example, entered Choctaw country from North Carolina in the 1770s, married two cousins of Mushulatubbe, and fathered twenty-four children, who gained their mothers' status as Choctaw. Folsom operated a tavern on the Natchez Trace and sent his son David to Tennessee briefly for schooling. David fought under Pushmataha with Jackson before he married Rhoda Nail, who was the daughter of Henry Nail, a Revolutionary War hero married to a Choctaw woman. The Nails developed great influence even in the southern, conservative area of the nation. John Pitchlynn's father died in the Choctaw nation while on an errand requested by George Washington, leaving his son to be raised among the Choctaw. Pitchlynn served as interpreter, herded cattle, grew cotton using black slaves, and fathered a son, Peter, who would become leader of the nation after removal. Despite the fact that they benefited from the matrilineal social system, the Europeans refused to adopt it and passed on their inheritance to their children who married one another to produce a ruling elite within the Choctaw and Chickasaw nations, but during the territorial period, the full-bloods remained in control.

Puckshenubbe served as Miko, or chief, of the Western Division, Homastubbe in the east, and Pushmataha in the south. Homastubbe represented his people at Fort Adams in 1801 when Wilkinson led the American delegation seeking approval for the planned Natchez Trace. Agreeing to the road, Homastubbe entered into a series of requests indicating the basic shift that had developed among the Choctaw. He asked for American women to come into the nation in order to teach the mixed-race women how to spin and weave so that they could then spread these skills to the remainder of the nation. He went on to note that the mixed-race among the Choctaw already had proficiency with plows, but that tools such as handsaws, augers, grubbing hoes, and weeding hoes were needed, along with a wheel-maker and blacksmith. Two members of the American delegation who had been at the first negotiation between the United States and the Choctaw in 1785 marveled at the changed nature of Choctaw society reflected in the requests. At the first meeting, the Choctaw, using ceremony and symbols, had drawn on the power of the spirit world to ensure success in their talks, but by comparison, in 1801 they discussed trade and farming, indicating a new appreciation for the material world.

This oil painting from 1848, *Choctaw Village near the Chesuncta* by François Bernard, indicates the extent to which the Choctaw had adopted European clothing, food, animals, and generally the settlers' lifestyle. Courtesy of the Peabody Museum of Archaeology and Ethnology, Harvard University, PM #41-72-10/27 (digital file #60742466).

Even basic Choctaw rituals changed. Sometime around 1800 the Choctaw abandoned the traditional exposure and bone picking for their dead and began burying corpses in a sitting position. Following the burial, they erected seven poles around the grave and painted them red. Decorating the poles with circles of grapevines, the soul of the deceased climbed the vines to the top of the pole and ascended into the spirit world. After thirteen months of mourning, the Choctaw pulled up the poles and held a feast to celebrate the spirit's return to its proper sphere. Though the nature of funerals changed, the ceremonies remained important for family and kin groups to gather and strengthen ties.

Of the three chiefs mentioned above, only Pushmataha gained his position as a result of his mastery of the spirit world as demonstrated in war and the hunt, but even he chose to fight alongside the Americans and served with Jackson. He received and wore proudly the full U.S. military uniform and even once promenaded with his wife at a dress ball. He and the other chiefs, though full-bloods, recognized that adopting the American economy offered their people the only hope for survival.

Nominally, the territorial governor represented the federal government in conducting foreign relations with the Indian nations, but in reality the government also appointed agents who actually conducted the United States' business with the Choctaw and Chickasaw nations outside the governor's direct control. The agents' mission called for the acculturation of the Indians into the American economic and social system. Americans resented the expanses of Indian land required to support a hunting culture and reasoned that turning Indians into farmers would enable the acquisition of much of their land. The unstated governmental goal evolved into one that encouraged indebtedness to the point that the Chickasaw and Choctaw had no means of paying debts except to deed land to the advancing American settlers. The government ended the traditional gift giving and established trade centers, termed factories, at Chickasaw Bluffs and Fort St. Stephens, but the governor also licensed private traders, who took over where the British left off supplying liquor as the most lucrative trade item.

In 1801 and 1803 the Choctaw recognized the loss of Natchez and the Tombigbee settlements to which they had a shaky historic claim, but in 1805 the United States first made a serious attempt to grab a piece of the Choctaw homeland. The British trading firm of Panton, Leslie, and Company had built up such a strong trade with the Choctaw that the Spanish allowed the company to continue its business during the Spanish era. The company floated the idea of accepting a deed to Choctaw land in lieu of payment of the enormous accumulated debt, but President Jefferson proposed instead that the United States take the land and pay off the company in return. At Mount Dexter, the Choctaw refused to cede any prime hunting or herding land along the river and offered only five million acres in the poor Pine Hills, which lay outside their heartland. In return, the United States paid Panton, Leslie, and Company $48,000, John Pitchlynn $2,500 for his "losses," and an annuity of $3,000 to the Choctaw nation. Jefferson disliked the deal because of the poor quality of the land ceded and held up ratification until 1808. The defeat of the Creek with Choctaw assistance led to a massive loss of land for the Creek, and soon after the war in 1816 the United States sent General John Coffee to Fort St. Stephens to distribute presents and promise a twenty-year annuity in return for a concession of the lands that the Choctaw and Creek had disputed for a century in what would become western Alabama and a small piece of eastern Mississippi. As a result, by the end of the territorial period the Choctaw had retreated to their heartland, where they busied themselves learning skills for survival in the new economy.

In 1813–1814 a Presbyterian minister visited the southeastern "Civilized Tribes" to assess the opportunities for missionary work, and he reported back that he found the people spinning, weaving, knitting, and raising great supplies of corn and large numbers of domestic animals such as cattle, pigs, horses, and poultry. He said that the "Civilized Tribes" had abandoned hunting for agriculture and were beginning to live like white people. The Choctaw agent, Silas Dinsmore, assured the minister that the Choctaw "panted for instruction" and requested a school, although he doubted they would welcome religious teaching. Nevertheless, as the territorial period ended, the missionaries poised to enter the Choctaw nation in order to proselytize and educate.

Statehood or continued territorial government: the choice divided the politically conscious after the War of 1812. Governor Holmes worked for a year after the war to secure the money owed militia veterans and stayed above the fray in the disputes over the question of statehood. The quickly growing eastern section, which had demanded separation as a state, switched its position and asked for admission of the whole territory as one state. Natchez had opposed separation but looked over the numbers and opted for division. Adams County paid 74 percent of the territorial taxes, but if the other half of the territory continued to grow while the Choctaw and Chickasaw blocked expansion in the west, the tax funds would be consumed by the more populous east. But neighboring Jefferson County in the Natchez district questioned division. Long-active Cowles Mead, neighbor to Governor Holmes, led a county delegation including Joseph Davis, who had settled in Greenville fairly recently, to the Pearl River Convention, where the eastern section leadership gathered to oppose the Natchez policy. Mead presided and Davis chaired the committee that drafted a memorial to Congress asking for admission of the entire territory as one state, indicating a split among the nabobs. The Pearl River Convention sent Toulmin to Congress to lobby for this policy.

Poindexter had left his post as territorial delegate to accept a territorial judgeship, and William Lattimore, a Natchez physician, had replaced him in Congress. They shared the same political philosophy, so it made little difference because Lattimore easily prevailed over Toulmin. Poindexter continued to play an important political role despite personal problems. His wife had an affair, or at least he was convinced she had, and he failed to provoke her lover into a duel, although he accosted him on the street in Natchez. Her alleged affair, their divorce, and the accusations that Poindexter proved himself a coward in the Battle of New Orleans led him to journey to Kentucky, find a new wife, and remove to Wilkinson County, where he bought a plantation and established a new power base outside the haunt of the nabobs. Popular in the outlying areas of the district, he had enormous influence.

Lattimore persuaded Congress to divide the territory as his Natchez constituents desired, and President James Madison signed the law calling for the election of delegates to a constitutional convention. The law labeled the western portion of the territory Mississippi and created the new territory of

Alabama in the east. Under the property requirements for voters in Mississippi Territory, 70 percent of the delegates came from the Natchez district, giving them control, but the district failed to unite, and at first dissention prevailed. Forty-seven men, including seventeen lawyers, fourteen planters, three farmers, two doctors, two merchants, and a surveyor, met in Washington's tiny Methodist church. Holmes, elected from Adams County, served as president of the convention, but appointed Poindexter to head the committee charged to write the constitution. Cowles and Davis joined delegates from Wilkinson County to oppose the formation of a state, and until a tie vote defeated their motion, they refused to organize a state government. Following their loss, backwoods-minded representatives fought unsuccessfully for more democracy in the shape of elected judges, voting privileges not dependent on property ownership, and an easy constitutional amendment process. Instead, Poindexter and his committee delivered the most conservative constitution of any state admitted after the War of 1812. Voters had to serve in the militia and be taxpayers. To sit in the state house of representatives, a man had to own real estate valued at $150; to serve in the state senate, he had to have 300 acres or have $1,000 interest in land; and to be governor required 600 acres freehold or a $2,000 interest in land. The governor appointed judges. The elite's suspicion of popular religion led them to forbid ministers serving either in the legislature or the governor's office. In the most revealing example of the lasting ambivalence in the attitude toward slavery, the writers gave the legislature the authority to forbid the importation of slaves as merchandise, although they assured an owner's right to bring his or her slave property into the state. Holmes and Poindexter played the deciding hands. Holmes remained above the fray, but favored Natchez in key decisions. Poindexter, long most popular outside the city, delivered a document denying some of his supporters' ardent hopes for a democratic constitution.

The determined planters did entertain doubts about the nature of the state that they established. One of the most striking debates concerned the protection of the slaves who made them rich. Davis and four other members proposed to punish cruel masters by confiscating an abused slave, selling him or her, and giving the proceeds of the sale to the poor instead of to the slave owner. Such a violation of property rights demonstrated strong emotions for a lawyer-planter rising through society and making his fortune in the district. His proposal indicated that Davis's childhood experience of living closely with a family slave in a frontier setting left him with the understanding that slaves were human beings and must be treated as such. His minority view failed to win approval; instead, the constitution obliged "the owners of slaves to treat them with humanity, to provide them necessary clothing and provision, to abstain from all injuries to them extending to life or limb, or in case of their neglect or refusal to comply with the directions of such laws, to have such slave or slaves sold for the benefit of the owner or owners."

After six weeks of summer debate, the delegates signed the constitution on August 15 and declared the document valid without asking voters to approve their work. President Monroe accepted the constitution and signed the resolution admitting Mississippi to the Union on December 10, 1817. At the time of admission, less than a third of the new state's territory lay outside the Indian nations, including the old Natchez district, the Gulf Coast, and the portion of the Pine Hills ceded in the Mount Dexter treaty. Two counties had a slave population under 20 percent, while the river counties had exceeded the 50 percent threshold. Four counties hovered at 40 percent slave populations. The Native American population had dropped, and the number of white settlers in the new Alabama territory soared. The new state government lusted for the land belonging to the Choctaw and Chickasaw. Few believed the Indian nations would long survive, and new state leaders devoted their efforts to seizing their peaceful neighbors' land as soon as possible.

Chapter Four

FRONTIER DEMOCRACY TO SLAVE SOCIETY

Statehood provided Mississippians with the legal means to press for the surrender of the two-thirds of the state occupied by the Choctaw and Chickasaw, but the politicians appeared in many respects to be minor players in the sweep of people and events transforming the land in a quick rush of building, planting, birthing, and dying. In two decades the state forced the two Indian nations to leave for the West; populated most of the state with counties, towns, farms, and plantations; imported slaves in such numbers that they became the majority of the population; and transformed the state from a frontier society based on democracy into a culture dominated by planters consumed by the need to discipline and protect their slaves. Settlers did not intend to found a state dedicated to furthering slavery. They wrote one of the nation's most democratic constitutions in 1832, but seduced by the wealth produced by cotton grown with slave labor, they ignored their laws, altered their ideals, divided their churches from their northern fellow-believers, and isolated themselves from the wider Western world seeking to end slavery. This pivotal period transformed Mississippi and the rest of the South, setting the South apart and propelling it toward the tragedy of the Civil War.

The story of Mississippi's transformation from a democratic frontier society into a culture dedicated to the preservation of slavery is complicated. An unusual starting place, the biography of Gideon Lincecum, provides insight into the mind of an eccentric settler who left a full record of his life in Mississippi, Texas, and Mexico. Lincecum loved nature, never smoked or drank, and always looked for a new land where he could be free. Never typical, Lincecum nevertheless illustrates the pioneer democratic spirit, skills, individualism, and daring. He remained in a place only as long as he sensed that he had the freedom that mattered so much to him. In 1848 he left Mississippi for Texas, and during Reconstruction, at the age of seventy-five, he went to Mexico with a widowed daughter and her family to hack a farm out of the jungle.

Gideon Lincecum, Mississippi pioneer who embodied frontier qualities of independence, appreciation of Native Americans, and love of nature. Courtesy of the Texas A&M University Press.

Leaving Georgia in 1818 with his father, mother, nine brothers and sisters, one brother-in-law, and ten slaves, Linceum entered the new Alabama territory. After a brief stop in Tuscaloosa, the party landed on the east bank of the Tombigbee in what would become Monroe County, Mississippi, when surveyors established the state's eastern boundary in 1820. Traveling along the Tombigbee in November 1818, Lincecum described the Choctaw hunting grounds as near heaven. Nuts, muscadines, and persimmons provided abundant food for the picking, while deer, turkeys, ducks, and pigeons easily made rich meals. Because the Choctaw burned the land in their hunts each year, few logs impeded their wagons, and making a passage among the trees in the pathless wilderness proved relatively easy. Digging down the banks of streams in order to ford them imposed the hardest work on the group, but Lincecum remembered the women and children wallowing in colorful leaf piles, experiencing the journey almost as a joyful party. Choosing a site near a bluff three miles above what became Columbus, Lincecum shot a twenty-nine-pound turkey, and his wife caught a blue catfish weighing twenty-five pounds on the day they arrived. The size and quality of the game induced them to stay. Building their house required six days with family assistance. Clearing six acres of cane, Lincecum burned off the farmland on May 5 and planted corn with a digging stick the next day. Twice during the growing season, he beat down the cane sprouts, and, despite the raccoons and bears, he harvested 150 bushels before the first summer ended.

Hearing that the government was building a road to cross the Tombigbee just south of him in 1819, Lincecum floated down to the site and, judging the bluff a likely town location, he went home, sawed 1,000 boards, built a raft to transport them, and returned. He found an acquaintance from

Tuscaloosa with a boatload of goods looking to trade, and Lincecum entered into a partnership with him, agreeing to pay his partner installments. In three days he knocked together a store building, and the Choctaw flocked to him for sugar, coffee, and whiskey.

Lincecum had blundered into a piece of the 1816 Choctaw cession eighty miles long and twenty miles wide on the Mississippi side of the line. Despite the fact that 200 miles of the Choctaw nation separated the sliver of territory from the next white settlement in the state, the legislature designated it Monroe County in 1821 and named Lincecum "chief justice of the quorum," empowering him to appoint all the other county officers and to lay out the lots for Columbus. Surveyors found the town sat on sixteenth-section land, so Lincecum arranged ninety-nine-year leases and accumulated enough rent money to build a school called Franklin Academy. He founded a Free Mason's lodge in Columbus, and residents talked of sending him to the legislature.

Sensing that such a development would endanger his freedom, Lincecum crossed the river into the Choctaw nation and went into business trading and operating a ferry with the Choctaw interpreter John Pitchlynn's son. Lincecum had visited his Choctaw neighbors as soon as he arrived in the area and had discovered that Pitchlynn was a distant relation. The Choctaw trade continued to be, as it had for decades, in deerskins and fur pelts, but also included a wide variety of nuts, peas, beans, honey, beeswax, cowhides, bacon, blowguns, and game meat. Lincecum made it a point to trade for every item, refusing nothing. At first he had to use the Choctaw's black slaves as interpreters, but he soon began to master the language. He found the Choctaw to be the "most truthful, most reliable, and best people" with whom he ever dealt. When his wife fell ill, the Choctaw came to nurse her back to health. Enjoying their hospitality and company, Lincecum hunted, swam, and fished with the Choctaw.

Pitchlynn had opened another store upriver at Cotton Gin Port, but his new partner there proved unreliable. He asked Lincecum to move north to operate the store, and because his family and slaves seemed to suffer from fevers at the location opposite Columbus, Lincecum agreed. Finding the same fevers in the new location, he moved to higher ground nearby, but the store failed, and Lincecum suffered a heat stroke and heart problems during a bear hunt. Forced to seek medical attention in Columbus, Lincecum looked for a means of supporting his family in his weakened condition. He hit on the idea of touring the country with Choctaw stickball players. Working through Pitchlynn, he assembled two teams that agreed to play for food and fun. He made little money during the eight-month tour in 1829, but with the camping and exercise, his health improved to the point that he gave an injured ballplayer his mount and walked 500 miles back home.

Still without income, he retreated to the woods again to hunt and devise a new career. An ailing neighbor aided by Lincecum suggested that he should become a doctor and insisted on purchasing a supply of medicine to get him started. With only a few months of formal education, Lincecum had already spent a term as a teacher, and on the frontier a man could be whatever he said he was. His medical practice proved highly successful, including his fiddle therapy. Lincecum played well, and sometimes his care took the form of comforting and playing for his patient.

When he lost a patient, he took it hard, and he decided that he needed more education in the healing arts, so he contacted a Choctaw healer from the Six-Towns to teach him plant remedies. Teacher and student lived together in the woods for six weeks, and Lincecum took notes in Choctaw. For his final exam, he read back his notes to his teacher and promised to publish them one day. For years his patients traveled to his home in the woods above Cotton Gin Port, but eventually they persuaded him to move back to Columbus, which had grown by the 1830s into a substantial town. Probably sensing his restlessness, his neighbors financed an exploratory expedition to Texas with Lincecum as the physician for the group. Even as Columbus prospered, the city's citizens began to look farther afield for new frontiers.

During the 1820s and 1830s thousands of settlers strained around the Indian nations yearning for the Indians' land, and some entered the nations, as Lincecum did, illegally. He contributed to the decline of the people whom he admired so much by selling whiskey to them, but given his independent nature, prohibition probably never appealed to him. He had his own idea of God, did not attend church, and when he sent his children to an academy run by a minister in Columbus, their education in biblical "facts" appalled him. After examining them in selected subjects on his first visit, he withdrew them the next morning.

In 1848, disturbed by what he considered the decadent lifestyle that had developed in Columbus as the center of the plantation Black Belt where his children attended balls and drank, Lincecum gathered his family and moved to Texas, hoping to recapture the frontier spirit and raise his family in a more constructive setting. He owned slaves and accepted slavery as natural, but the grasping, clawing plantation world did not appeal to him. It took away freedom, which to Lincecum could only be enjoyed in a state of nature not overwhelmed by man's rape of the land or man's imposition of laws, rules, and bureaucracy on his own kind. As a founder of Columbus, Lincecum had the opportunity to acquire land and more slaves in order to enter into the prosperity of the era. Certainly he demonstrated his entrepreneurial bent, but he disliked the plantation world and escaped from it.

As Lincecum had entered Mississippi, the politicians struggled to establish a state government. They annexed Monroe County as soon as they discovered its existence and added it to their argument for building roads across the Indian nations. Their purpose was to provide settlers easier access to the Indian lands and to drive the Indians out. General Andrew Jackson lobbied for a more direct route between Nashville and New Orleans at the end of the War of 1812. As soon as the federal government granted the funds, upward of 300 workmen toiled through 1819 and early 1820 to build bridges and causeways through the swamps, with the heaviest construction in what would become Noxubee County, the heart of the Choctaw domain. Thanks to Monroe County's demands, the settlers gained a more direct route to the capital when Robinson Road connected Jackson Military Highway to the Natchez Trace. With this network of roads crisscrossing eastern Mississippi linking the white citizens of Tennessee and Alabama to Mississippians, the pressure for annexing more Indian land became irresistible.

Governor Holmes carried on as the elected governor of Mississippi rather than the appointed territorial one, which eased Mississippi's transition to statehood. He negotiated with the Alabama Territory to disentangle the budgets of the two new entities, vetoed the legislature's efforts to sell sixteenth-section land set aside by the federal government for education, and battled those who stole timber from the sixteenth sections. He endorsed the legislature's bills to provide funds for clearing some of the state's rivers for navigation, but practiced strict economy, which limited the work actually accomplished. Above all, he voiced the citizens' demands for more land. Poindexter, who had been elected to the represent the new state in the U.S. House of Representatives, chaired the committee on public lands and used his position to issue a report accusing the Choctaw of trespassing on western lands purchased in 1803 by the United States in an effort to prod them toward negotiations. In 1818 the United States sent low-level negotiators to ask for land and for the removal of the nation to the west. The Choctaw rejected both ideas out of hand.

The next year, the secretary of war designated Jackson and Hinds, whose Mississippi cavalry had been so helpful to Old Hickory in the recent war, to negotiate with the Choctaw for a land concession. Building on Poindexter's ploy, Jackson sought to divide the Six-Towns, whose many hunters moved freely across the Mississippi River to maintain their hunting culture, against the Choctaw's Eastern and Western Divisions, where the mixed-bloods had built up their cattle herds and begun to shift the population out of their old towns into the old borderlands. Pushmataha, chief of the Six-Towns, responded cannily to Jackson's ploy by disowning the trans-Mississippi hunters. Speaking at a general council held in preparation for the treaty conference, Pushmataha called the wayward Choctaw "wolves" and invited the U.S. government to round them up and send them home. Pushmataha knew some of his warriors would be impressed with Jackson's claims to have the interest of the poor full-bloods at heart, so he discouraged them from going to Jackson's meeting. Jackson countered by using paid mixed-blood agents to solicit their participation and by providing plentiful food and whiskey at Doak's Stand on the Natchez Trace where the negotiations were scheduled.

Jackson intended to secure what the Mount Dexter negotiators failed to obtain in 1805, the land along the Mississippi and Yazoo Rivers. He offered a parcel of land in Arkansas much larger than what he asked the Choctaw to give up, but Pushmataha told Jackson that he had hunted the land and knew it to be infertile and, besides, whites had already settled on portions of it. Puckshenubbee, who governed the Western Division, which included the land demanded from the nation, and who owned cattle herds using the land for pastures, met separately with the commissioners, protesting that they asked for too much. Jackson replied that if he did not get what he wanted, he would go to the Choctaw living west of the Mississippi and make a deal with them to give up all of the nation's Mississippi holdings. He insinuated that the trans-Mississippi Choctaw might be determined to be a majority of the nation. Frustrated, Puckshenubbee left the meeting, and Jackson made a deal with the remaining leaders, being careful to designate a private grant within the ceded area to Puckshenubbee. The Choctaw ceded between five and six million acres, a concession far larger than the original Natchez district, and the United States agreed to fund the Choctaw Lighthorse, a police force, to maintain order and to see that debts were paid. The treaty forbade the liquor trade and encouraged Christian mission schools, continuing the government's efforts to foster sobriety, education in American values, and the sanctity of property.

The Choctaw resented the deal forced upon them, and the mixed-bloods capitalized on the unrest in the nation. Because the mixed-bloods not in the U.S. pay opposed the treaty, they emerged as patriots. Espousing modernization and calling for an end to the old ways, they adopted white farming methods, herding, and weaving in order to resist the onslaught of whites. They also made up the leadership of the new Lighthorse.

In 1818 the Choctaw chiefs had invited Protestant missionaries into the nation in order to secure schools. The Presbyterian mission board responded by sending Cyrus Kingsbury to lead a group, which established Eliot Mission on the Yalobusha River. The missionaries wanted to convert the Indians to Christianity while the Choctaw wanted secular education to prepare their children to better resist the advance of the whites into Choctaw lands. At enormous cost in lives—especially of their wives' lives—the missionaries built schools complete with farms and blacksmith shops, mostly in the borderlands near mixed-bloods' farms. The Choctaw resisted conversion while their leaders struggled to open and control more schools. The missionaries tried to do both the physical and intellectual work themselves because they condemned slavery as immoral, but eventually they employed slave labor for the physical tasks. Slaves proved to be an important source of converts in the Choctaw nation, which provided some solace to the men engaged in tough and frustrating work showing but little progress among the Choctaw. On occasion, the missionaries demonstrated their inability to remain aloof from the culture that they tried to "improve." One missionary with an ailing wife succumbed to temptation and impregnated one of his Choctaw students, leading to recriminations and negotiations over the financial responsibility for the child. The Presbyterians, who insisted on sustained evidence of conversions from their converts, felt stymied by intruding Methodists, who accepted immediate displays of emotion or physical transformation as adequate evidence of religious conversion. The full-blood Mushulatubbee, threatened by the mixed-bloods and their alliances with the missionaries, seized the annuity provided from the Doak's Stand concession to found a school in Kentucky run by the Baptists along secular lines as a finishing school for the leaderships' children.

In a striking move demonstrating the cultural change afoot in the nation, the leadership of the Six-Towns, normally the most conservative region, inaugurated a new law code banishing whiskey and forbidding the stealing of hogs and cattle. Then intruding into the personal lives of the residents in an unprecedented fashion, they outlawed infanticide, polygamy, and adultery. When the missionaries failed to follow up with a school to reward them for their efforts, the Six-towns leaders wrote to Kingsbury that they wanted to "follow the ways of the white people" and needed the school denied them.

As the full-blood and mixed-blood leaders battled for control in the nation, the president called the leaders to Washington to renegotiate the Doak's Stand treaty deemed too favorable to the Choctaw. Pushmataha had been right; whites had already claimed some of the territory deeded to the Choctaw. Puckshenubbee, Pushmataha, and Mushulatubbee journeyed to Washington as members of the Choctaw delegation, but Puckshenubbee fell off a cliff en route, and Pushmataha died of pneumonia and received a military funeral in the capital, leaving Mushulatubbee to face the disgruntled Choctaw stirred by David Folsom, a mixed-blood member of the group, who condemned the full-bloods for drinking during the negotiations and for giving up too much land. Riding a wave of discontent over the treaty revision, the mixed-bloods deposed the full-bloods and replaced them with Folsom, Greenwood LeFlore, and John Garland. The new chiefs stood firm when another American delegation came to ask for more land and Choctaw

Greenwood LeFlore, controversial mixed-blood Choctaw leader who embraced assimilation into American society as the only means of survival. Courtesy of the Mississippi Department of Archives and History from the Greenwood LeFlore Collection.

resettlement, and, as a result, their prestige soared. This popularity encouraged them to attempt to remake the Choctaw nation into an American-style state with a constitution, inheritance through the male line, and enclosed fields with trespass prohibited. LeFlore banned Choctaw burial customs to answer missionary complaints about the ball games, drinking, and "unseemly" conduct surrounding funerals. The mixed-bloods aimed for full Americanization of the nation, hoping to contain the advance of the white settlers and to prevent the Indian removal from Mississippi.

As the Choctaw and Chickasaw wrestled with economic, social, and political alterations, Americanized Mississippi evolved from a frontier to a plantation society. Warren County, at the northern tip of the old Natchez district, probably illustrates the process best. Cotton transformed the close-knit, interdependent settlers, who owned few slaves, into a patriarchal-dominated land of plantations with slaves outnumbering whites. Clusters of families on adjoining farms came under the control of a male family member who emerged as the patriarch. Women, who in frontier families enjoyed more autonomy because of the importance of their labor, lost independence as slaves replaced them at most of their former tasks. By the same token, children's labor became less significant with increased slave ownership, and the father, who owned the land and slaves, grew independent of his family because he had slaves to perform work that his family had done in the past.

One man usually emerged as dominant in the family clusters, controlling and overseeing land left to widowed relatives or orphaned children.

Joseph Davis left his successful law practice to build a model plantation on a peninsula south of Vicksburg, where he adopted work incentives and a court system for his slaves. Courtesy of the Beacroft Foundation at Rosemont Plantation.

Formal government structures played an insignificant role in such communities where the patriarch controlled so much wealth and labor. Counties wanting to build a road, for example, probably had to ask for right-of-way across his land and even for slaves to build the road in many cases. Such powerful men developed a code of honor, which imposed limits on their behavior and fostered a sense of noblesse oblige in many, but far from all, cases. Violations of the code called for ritualized violence in the form of a duel. Frontiersmen who failed to acquire land and slaves did not have the right to challenge a patriarch to a duel. The patriarch could take his cane to them, but he would not stoop to a duel with one he considered to be his inferior. Clearly the rough equality of the frontier vanished as class emerged as an important aspect of plantation society. Other Mississippi men, women, and especially slaves had no recourse against the wealth and power amassed by cotton planters, who dominated Mississippi society, even though they frequently chose not to enter into its political frays.

Joseph Davis, for example, having made his fortune in Jefferson County and Natchez, chose in 1827 to abandon the Natchez nabobs, among whom he moved, to make a new life on 5,000 acres of rich bottomland just fifteen miles south of Vicksburg. Although he had never married, he had three daughters whom he openly claimed—a sign of his frontier-nourished disdain for convention. He married a girl the age of his eldest daughter—sixteen—when he was forty-three and took the four of them—wife and daughters—with him upriver to Hurricane Plantation. A brother had managed the place for him until a tornado destroyed his home and gave the plantation its name. The setting appeared tropical with blue and white cranes, large alligators, and cane intermingled with briers too thick to uproot. Slaves burned the tangled mass of vegetation and dug small holes to plant the first cotton.

As the slaves cleared more land and Davis prospered, he designed a mansion of three stories with broad, two-story galleries around the entire structure. He built the walls thick enough and the windows small enough to give the house a cavelike coolness, and he installed a bathroom with flush toilet supplied from a water tank installed in the attic, which a slave filled with water from a pump from his well. All twelve rooms contained fireplaces. The circular drive in front of the house, he lined with live oak trees, but most visitors arrived by steamboat at his private landing located on his fifteen miles of river frontage. Outbuildings became wings of the house, with a dining hall and a music room. The kitchen stood separately along with storerooms and the overseer's office. Just off his master bedroom, Davis maintained his private storeroom from which he drew gifts—dresses for female slaves, tools for male slaves, a bridle for a friend, or musical instruments. He delighted in the role of patriarch. In the quarter of a mile between the house and the river, he planted a mixture of native and exotic plants. The back garden surrounded by hedges of roses, jasmine, and honeysuckle contained acres planned by a hired English gardener. Beyond the flowers, acres of fruit trees and vegetables stretched toward the stables where purebred horses were housed. In the 1830s Davis added a steam engine to power his gin, sawmill, and gristmill.

Eventually owning in excess of 300 slaves, Davis made his plantation self-sufficient growing corn, sweet potatoes, buckwheat, peas, and beans, in addition to cotton. He produced 500 pounds of butter from his dairy herd and sold enough beef cattle to net $1,000 most years. Extra fruit and vegetables supplied the passing riverboats.

Having rescued his father from debt and provided for his siblings, Davis became guardian and father figure to his brother, Jefferson Davis, twenty years his junior. Joseph made the arrangements for Jefferson to attend West Point and made a trip to visit him there in 1825. Joseph eventually provided Jefferson Davis a plantation, but apparently retained title in his own name.

Joseph Davis epitomized the successful planter transforming the wilderness into an economically productive business by applying the best science of the age to production and utilizing the latest equipment such as the steam engine. With his wealth, he built a palace and ruled his plantation with wisdom, a sense of honor, and justice. Of course, his slaves did the necessary labor under his management, and his method of ruling his slaves set Davis apart from the norm.

Influenced by the ideas of Robert Owen, the British industrialist turned socialist and philanthropist, Davis adopted a benevolent attitude toward his slaves, recognizing their humanity and encouraging them with incentives. He established a court over which he presided on Sunday with a jury of slaves to hear and rule on disputes. Even overseers had to bring their complaints to this court, and no punishment could be administered without a court decision. Davis provided good housing and clothing and allowed his slaves to work for profit when their field duties had been completed. He encouraged them to learn new skills and provided training.

The most outstanding example of success with his policies proved to be Ben Montgomery, whom Davis bought at the age of seventeen. Montgomery had learned to read from his master's son in Virginia, and he was dismayed to find himself in the wilds of Mississippi. When he ran away only to be quickly recaptured, Davis asked him why he ran and listened to his complaints. Instead of physical punishment, Davis explained the discipline system and the advantages to be had on the plantation, including the use of his own library. They came to an understanding, and Montgomery made the most of Davis's system, eventually opening a successful store on the plantation and becoming Davis's business manager. As Davis guided him through his reading, ignoring the law that forbade slaves to read and write, they ultimately began to hold late night discussions of philosophy and current affairs. Davis respected his slaves as fellow human beings, which was not the norm among plantation patriarchs.

Davis's system was unusual, but all Warren County slaves' lives underwent a revolution in the early years of statehood. In 1800 slaves made up only slightly over 25 percent of the county's population. Most of the slaves were older women and children because the strongest and more valuable young women and men had been sold to Natchez, where plantations developed first. In Warren County, as on most of the frontier, many slaves worked for hire under rental agreements that they could influence by discussion with their owners and their temporary employer. The system enabled slaves to feel more independent and in control of their lives, but as plantations appeared the renting-out system became more formalized and then declined after 1830. Plantations brought more young men and women into the county, and by 1820 slaves made up the majority of the county's population, with more of them working for large slaveholding plantations.

Slaves began to form more families, encouraged by their owners, who provided separate cabins for couples and oftentimes wedding clothing, food, and drink for a ceremony. Plantation owners knew that slave couples increased their wealth by having children, and good managers reduced workloads for mothers, understanding that a woman driven too hard in the field could not successfully raise her children. Warren County planters discussed raising slaves just as they did raising corn and cotton, but they did not sell slaves as a rule. More slaves added value to the plantation. More labor meant larger crops, and more slaves could be used as collateral to borrow money for expansion. Procreation and importation increased the slave population in Warren County to almost three times the white population by 1840.

Slavery rested on a foundation of violence, which meant that the white minority lived in a state of fear and dread. Three of Joel Cameron's slaves beat him to death and dumped his body in a Warren County lake. When the county court freed an overseer who killed two slaves, reasoning that he acted in self-defense, the other slaves on the plantation burned the corncribs and the crop in the field to protest his acquittal. The causes of violence sometimes proved more convoluted. For example, when Henry Jones's master sold him to a distant owner, Jones asked his wife to run away with him, and when she refused, he killed her and not his master. Violence often appeared when masters asserted their control in ways affecting the slave's family relationships, shattering the illusion of familial independence for slaves.

White rapists who sexually assaulted their slaves committed arguably the worst offences and precipitated discord for multiple families. In one instance that went to court in Bolivar County, Lafayette Jones's slave-lover murdered his young wife. Jones squelched the investigation of his wife's death and kept the murderess in his household and continued having sex with her as he raped another slave's daughter. Bringing in yet another slave-lover from New Orleans provoked a second poisoning incident that killed his daughter and sickened him and his second wife. The courts convicted two slaves, the new slave-lover and a poor man who had the misfortune to find a bottle of poison, and sentenced them to death for the murders while Jones doubtlessly continued his life of debauchery. No record of his wife's reaction to events exists, but if she remained with him, his black child, born to his youngest victim, had to be a constant reminder of his crimes.

White society enmeshed in a large slave population depended upon the nature and whims of the patriarch. If he ruled wisely and with moderation as Joseph Davis did, the white family and the slaves benefited and could possibly lead relatively good lives. But if men such as Jones ran a plantation, no one would feel secure, and the potential for violence escalated. Of course not all areas of the state developed slave majorities. In the piney woods where the soil was poor and suitable more for sweet potatoes rather than cotton, white frontiersmen continued in the majority.

Some of the trees in the piney woods of south Mississippi required six men to wrap their arms around a trunk. Scattered among the forest, streams flowed out of swamps, which provided habitat for bears and panthers. Canebrakes and meadows, in clearings, provided deer and free-ranging cattle pastures. Pigs, fattened on nuts and roots, provided the most abundant meat for settlers.

Originally from North Carolina, Jackie Knight arrived in the piney woods with his wife, a wagonload of children, and his slaves from Georgia in 1815 or 1816. A man of some wealth, he owned books, velvet and silk tablecloths, china, and silverware. He had some education, and his children all learned to read and write, which distinguished them from many of their neighbors. He built a substantial log home with two parlors near the Leaf River, claiming land on both sides of the stream. Bottomland allowed him to raise cotton for the market in Mobile, which most of his fellow settlers in the piney woods could not do.

As patriarch, he gave each of his children a pair of slaves as a wedding gift, helping them to prosper and claim additional farmland. The families supported one another, raising homes and barns with log rollings. They turned corn shucking into a community event, and quilt-making became a group project shared by the women. The Knights attended Leaf River Baptist Church, practiced foot washing, and held baptisms in the river. Twice each year the Knights drove wagons down a faintly distinguishable trail along the river 125 miles to Mobile. The boys herded livestock with cowhide whips or urged flocks of turkeys and chickens more gently while the men drove teams of oxen pulling wagons loaded with melons, bushels of corn, and bales of cotton. Camping along the route, the trip took ten days. They returned with whiskey, calico, a little flour, syrup, salt, and iron bars to be shaped into tools back home.

For some reason, only one of Jackie Knight's sons, Albert, never received a slave from his father and chose not to own one. In the manner of most settlers, he remained a small farmer, and added to his income by shoemaking. He and his family lived from what he could grow and the sale of shoes made from the leather he tanned. He owned only fifty acres of land, raising sweet potatoes, corn, hogs, greens, and peas, which the family consumed. He grew only enough cotton for his wife, Mason, to make homespun clothes for the family. She served as healer to the neighborhood and taught her children to read. They donated the land for the first school in the area and took pride in their independence. Eventually the Leaf River Baptist Church ejected Albert for repeated intoxication, which did not set him apart from many in the community. All of his family drank hard, and most left the church when a new pastor began to meddle in their behavior.

George Poindexter, planter who garnered support from ordinary farmers to hold most of the state's important political offices while opposing Andrew Jackson's democratic policies. Courtesy of the Mississippi Department of Archives and History from the George Poindexter Collection.

The piney woods settlers tolerated little interference in their lives. They worshipped an egalitarian God and viewed the planters as lazy and in violation of Christ's teaching about rich men entering into heaven. Perversely, they took pride in their simple lives. Travelers reported a lifestyle dependent on sweet potatoes as the table's mainstay, including both beer and tea made from the plant, but observers also noted the cleanliness and order of their homes as well as their hospitality.

Although Natchez planters dominated the politics of the new state, non-slave-owning whites such as Albert Knight rapidly came to make up the majority of voters. These voters presented a challenge to the wealthy Natchez planters who controlled both the territorial and state governments. In Governor Holmes, the planters had found an astute politician capable of looking after their interests without angering the piney woodsmen to the east, but holding on to power proved tricky. When Holmes chose not to run for reelection in 1819, Poindexter left the House of Representatives in Washington to campaign for governor. Poindexter's relocation to Wilkinson County gave him an advantage with voters, who resented the Natchez nabobs. Poindexter was a planter, but his crude, tavern-bred style set him apart. In the wake of Jackson's military victories and his treaty dispossessing the Creek, all candidates ran as Jacksonian Democrats, making the only issues personal ones. The voters seemed not to care about the old charges of misconduct in the Hunt-Poindexter duel or alleged cowardice during the Battle of New Orleans. Poindexter triumphed easily over the battle's hero, Hinds.

As governor, Poindexter urged and supported the federal government's efforts to secure land concessions from the Choctaw. When Jackson and Hinds succeeded in the negotiations, Poindexter went along with the legislature's determination to move the capital to a new location at the center of the state and to name the new capital Jackson. Poindexter played a small part in those changes, but his major goals were to overhaul the state law code and to create an educational system. He described the lack of any existing schools as deplorable, noting that Mississippi's schools consisted of a few private institutions distributed unevenly across the state and often conducted by incompetent teachers. Reluctantly, the legislature established a "Literary Fund" without providing adequate money to build any schools. As for the law code, the legislature provided Poindexter funds to hire an assistant and told him to revise it, which he did, leaving it for his successor to ask the legislature to enact it.

Poindexter tried to return to Congress rather than seek reelection as governor, but the incumbent, Christopher Rankin, defeated him largely because of the new code that Poindexter had authored. Rankin and others enraged the churches against a provision making it illegal for six or more slaves to assemble and conduct a worship service. Interestingly, the white churches revolted against a law forbidding slaves to worship separately without supervision. In this instance Poindexter's representation of the planters' interest in controlling the slaves' gatherings on plantations clashed with the white churchgoers who desired that slaves have freedom of worship. In addition to his political woes, Poindexter's second wife and their only child died, he developed crippling rheumatism, and he took up his law practice again as a bitter, sour man. His health removed him from politics for eight years.

The old Natchez ruling elite found a formula to retain political control by denying Natchez's aristocratic reputation, stressing their Jacksonian sympathies, and finding candidates acceptable to voters in the piney woods and the new counties created from the 1820 concession. Known as the Junto and funded by wealthy planters such as Stephen Duncan, the Natchez cabal sponsored four of the first five U.S. senators, five of the first seven members of the U.S. House of Representatives, five of the attorneys general, five of the seven Speakers of the Mississippi House of Representatives before 1830, and two of the first four governors. From 1820, the Junto worked on the defensive. After moving the state capital, the legislature tried to close Jefferson College, which folks in the piney woods saw as an aristocratic institution. Although saved from closure, the legislature never provided enough funding to make the school a success.

Creation of more counties such as Jones in 1822 (where eighty-nine petitioners, including Jackie and Albert Knight, asked for "Recognition and

Representation") left the nabobs reeling from the onslaught of democracy as counties ruled by small farmers multiplied. By 1827 Powhatan Ellis of Wayne County, a friend of Jackson and champion of the piney woods folks, defeated Thomas Reed, the Junto's long-serving senator. The Junto rallied to elect Reed to the other Senate seat, but he died soon after his election. Again the Junto placed their candidate, but he too died, and Poindexter returned to politics when Governor Brandon appointed him to fill the vacancy in the Senate.

In 1830 Franklin E. Plummer finished off the state's first political machine by defeating its candidate for Congress. Far from being a nabob, Plummer worked his way from Massachusetts to Pearlington at the mouth of the Pearl River on a sailing ship. He claimed to have driven the first wagonload of supplies to construct the original house in Jackson. Moving to Copiah County, he quickly advanced from schoolteacher to sheriff, clerk, and judge. Elected to the legislature before the legal age, he resigned to run for Congress under the slogan "the People for Plummer and Plummer for the People." He mastered the backwoodsman's vocabulary and not only kissed their babies but picked red bugs from their bodies while he had them in his arms. He won by a landslide, the Junto's effectiveness ended, and the Junto's nightmare came true. With only about a third of the state's white population in 1830, the Natchez district paid 70 percent of the state's taxes to fund a government for the other two-thirds of the state.

Plummer's election followed Jackson's overwhelming victory in the 1828 presidential race, when Jackson carried every county in the state—most of them by 80 percent or more. With Jackson in the White House, Mississippians raged for the removal of the Choctaw and Chickasaw in order to make more land available to settlers. The legislature addressed a memorial to Congress demanding removal. Before the election, Mississippians supported Georgia's attempt to assume control over the Creek and Cherokee within their borders. When President Adams admonished Georgia to respect the existing treaties protecting Georgia Indians, William Haile, Mississippi's congressman, asserted that Mississippi would spring to the defense of Georgia should the federal government employ force to protect the Indians. He claimed that Mississippi could no longer tolerate its "Indian encumbrance." Certain that Jackson would support them, Mississippi legislators held off claiming jurisdiction over the Choctaw and Chickasaw in 1828, giving the federal government time to dispossess Mississippi's Indian population. Despite all federal threats and promises, the mixed-blood chiefs declined to sell or move.

Faced with the prospect of removal, a massive Christian revival swept the Choctaw nation in 1828. Beginning in the Western Division at a Methodist camp meeting, the desperate Choctaw groped for protection from a higher spiritual authority. The captains led the way, reacting to the enormous pressure exerted upon them to adopt new lives and to save their homeland. During the winter, the movement entered the northeastern district, and by 1830 the missionaries estimated that a quarter of the nation, including many captains and chiefs, had converted to Christianity. This conversion came as the federal government persuaded an exploratory Choctaw expedition to go west and examine the proposed new homeland. Skeptics favoring removal such as John Pitchlynn scoffed at the conversions, describing them with the slogan "Join the church and keep your country." The deposed Mushulatubbee promoted removal, refused conversion, and while visiting his school in Kentucky talked the students into drafting a letter demanding the Choctaw be admitted as an American state. Returning home, Mushulatubbee set out to depose Folsom, the mixed-blood who unseated him. As they battled, the Mississippi legislature voted to force the issue by passing a law extending the state's jurisdiction over all the inhabitants of the state. The act declared tribal government abolished and made it a crime for anyone to claim a leadership position among the Choctaw.

Mushulatubbee secretly bargained with the government for a deal to remove west. LeFlore visited the Cherokee nation and became convinced that removal offered the only viable course. On his return, he invited Folsom and Garland to a council mostly attended by his own western supporters. Facing possible prosecution from the state, Folsom and Garland resigned, and LeFlore carried out a coup, claiming to represent the entire nation by his council's action. LeFlore prepared a removal treaty and asked Mushulatubbee to sign it, which he did, but Mushulatubbee immediately attacked LeFlore for the coup, denied his legitimacy, and condemned the just-signed treaty. Tapping into the deep resentment the full-bloods held for the mixed-bloods, Mushulatubbee urged an uprising. The Choctaw deserted the churches, burned some of them, deposed their captains, repealed Sabbath laws, promoted ball playing, and revived old ceremonies. LeFlore and Folsom gathered an armed force to retaliate, but a confrontation dissolved into a council, and the federal officials called for treaty negotiations at Dancing Rabbit Creek.

In white society, only church leaders protested Mississippi's dissolution of the Choctaw nation. Methodist bishop William Winans denounced the action in strong language as a miscarriage of justice, a violation of human rights, a breach of treaty obligations, and "a display of ingratitude rarely equaled in the annals of human depravity." Kingsbury called the law unjust and wicked, commenting that he "blushed" for his country. He argued that the Choctaw had begun to live as whites did and that their removal was unnecessary. Other white Mississippians ignored the churchmen and celebrated the impending seizure of Indian lands. Governor Gerard Brandon told the legislature that the Choctaw had made progress toward "civilization" and had become attached to the soil. As a result, he said, they must be removed quickly, while they still could be, in order to free their rich farmland for white settlement.

Jackson sent his trusted cavalry leader John Coffee, along with a Tennessee friend, John Eaton, to conduct the negotiations. After making certain annuity payments had been delayed to step up pressure, they provisioned the site with the usual large supply of food and whiskey. Prostitutes and gamblers followed closely behind the commissioners in large numbers to prepare Dancing Rabbit Creek. The commissioners denied Kingsbury and the Presbyterians admission to the site because of their opposition to removal, but Alexander Talley, a Methodist missionary, appeared at Dancing Rabbit and announced that the commissioners would have to tie him up and carry him away, so he remained.

Despite LeFlore's threat to boycott, he came along with all the other leaders, both mixed-bloods and full-bloods. Physically the Choctaw groups separated themselves into two camps, and they emphasized their division by dressing differently. Mushulatubbee donned a military uniform while most of his allies chose traditional dress. LeFlore and Folsom wore the white townsman's suits, raising suspicion among the 6,000 Choctaw gathered along the creek. Despite their attire, the mixed-bloods argued against concessions and removal in public while admitting in private that both were inevitable. After two weeks of argument and threats from the commissioners, the mass of Choctaw departed thinking that the treaty had been rejected, but the leaders remained behind and all signed an agreement, which gave those Choctaw who chose to remain in Mississippi the right to a section of land with a provision to claim more for their children. The chiefs received four sections each, and those who chose to go west were promised supplies of food, tools, iron, and blacksmiths to continue their assimilation into the American economy. The market economy had brought the Choctaw to this sad end. Their entrance into the deerskin trade for European goods had eventually destroyed their main source of food. Alcohol addiction sped the process as many Choctaw squandered their wealth on drink and weakened their productive lives.

Their misery increased after the signing. As the poor Choctaw learned what their leadership had done, they deposed LeFlore and the others, desperately seeking leaders who could reverse the removal. A drought caused their crops to fail in 1830. The old subsistence cycle called for them to take to the borderlands to forage and hunt, but most of those lands had been ceded to the whites in 1816 and 1820. Faced with the choice of starvation in Mississippi where they would be marginalized and subject to the white man's state, the majority of the Choctaw chose exile in the West. LeFlore remained to become a rich, successful planter, but most who chose to stay in Mississippi either failed to have their land deeds recorded by the government-appointed agent, who made it extremely difficult for them, or lost their claims to unscrupulous whites eager to swindle them. The Mississippi Choctaw lived in the swamps and on the poorest lands selling baskets and their labor as cotton pickers to the white farmers and planters who displaced them.

The Choctaw's fate left the Chickasaw little hope. With a much smaller population than the Choctaw, they had followed the same pattern as their more numerous neighbors. They had conceded their vast holdings to the north, concentrating in their heartland in north Mississippi. The mixed-bloods, especially Levi Colbert and his brothers, controlled the nation through a front of tradition. Levi practiced polygamy, scattering wives and estates from Colbert's Ferry just across the state line in Alabama to "French Farm" located near what is today Okolona. Admitting missionaries, the mixed-bloods led the Americanization of the nation, adopting farming and herding with notable success. They owned far more African slaves than the Choctaw—almost 5,000 Chickasaw owned just over 1,000 black slaves along with vast herds of horses, cattle, pigs, goats, and sheep.

Colbert delayed the inevitable as long as possible, absolutely refusing demands for removal, but by 1828 he agreed to an exploratory western visit. He returned adamant as ever against concession, but the passage of Jackson's removal act and Mississippi's extension of its laws over the Indians persuaded the Chickasaw to accept Jackson's invitation to treat with him in Franklin, Tennessee, where they accepted a removal treaty with the provision that they must find a suitable new home in the West. When they failed to find one, the Chickasaw negated the treaty. A second treaty followed, which the leadership signed at the council house on Pontotoc Creek. Levi died in 1834 on the verge of another trip to Washington, and the process dragged out until 1837. During the last three years of the removal process, surveyors, land speculators, auctioneers, and lawyers swarmed over the Chickasaw cession. Although the Chickasaw made more money than the Choctaw from their land sale, exploitation and cheating washed over the land on a whiskey tide separating the Chickasaw from their new allotments and enriching devious entrepreneurs.

John Bell operated one of the companies acquiring land from the Chickasaw. His father, a Baptist minister, founded Charity Hall as a mission school at Cotton Gin Port in 1820 and also owned the river ferry. Obviously not wishing to follow his father's profession in the ministry, John Bell bought Cotton Gin Land Company in 1824 and laid out a town on the east side of the river where eight to ten families settled, but his aim was to move into the Indian land on the west side of the river. As a means to that end, he got elected to the Mississippi legislature in 1829. After the legislature passed the law extending its legal control over the Chickasaw, Monroe County people invaded the Chickasaw nation to stake out claims for prime real estate. As their representative, Bell argued against a proposed state "no trespass" law to protect the Chickasaw and sought to sponsor the construction of roads through the cession from Bolivar, Tennessee, to Manchester (Yazoo City). He formed a partnership with Robert Gordon, an Indian trader in Cotton Gin Port, to locate the best plots for settlement. After the Treaty of Pontotoc, Bell wrangled the appointment as U.S. surveyor-general of the Chickasaw cession. He sold his company in Cotton Gin Port and moved to Pontotoc, where the land office opened. He and his partner acquired more than 600, 640-acre sections at an average price of less than $10 per section.

A flood of young men on the make invaded the newly opened lands brimming with ambition and driven to gamble that they could emulate the success of Joseph Davis, whose wealth and power they sought to replicate. Often they went about armed with pistols and bowie knives. They drank too much and took refusal to advance credit as a personal insult. Cotton had made Natchez wealthy and inspired their dreams. President Jackson had been one of them. He had defeated the Indians and the British and chased the Indians west so that these young men could have opportunity on new land in Mississippi. These settlers did not have to fight the Indians or even the panthers that greeted the early settlers in eighteenth-century Natchez. They dreamed of railroads and immediate founding of towns complete with hotels, newspapers, and the amenities of civilization. In order to establish cotton plantations, they needed credit to buy slaves, equipment, and land. From the highest level of politics to the dirt farmers who left the piney woods to move into the Indian lands to their north, everyone wanted money to make their dreams come true. The majority of settlers were yeomen farmers, but they did not intend to remain so. Credit, banks, and lack of hard coins dominated the lives of Mississippians from 1830 to 1840 as they populated another half of the state establishing farms, plantations, and towns with amazing speed.

Poindexter, or Old Pons as his few friends knew him, had been sent to the Senate as a Jacksonian, but he soon clashed with Jackson over the spoils of office made available by the Indian treaties. Jackson appointed a Tennessean, Samuel Gwin, to register land in the Clinton office. Old Pons blocked the appointment and waged a long, losing contest for Mississippians to get federal jobs in their state. Gwin and his brother William, appointed U.S. marshal, held a variety of posts and operated the Regency, a new governing cabal, out of Vicksburg. Acting as Jackson's agents, they controlled federal patronage, ignored Mississippi's elected representatives, printed and distributed tracts, and manipulated state politics to build up the Democratic Party in Mississippi as a support for Jackson's men and policies. The Regency replaced the Junto as the central power in Mississippi politics during the Jacksonian period. Old Pons fought it and emerged as a leading figure in the new Whig Party.

Too weak to walk when he arrived in Washington, Poindexter had to be carried into the Senate by a servant, but the battle with Jackson seemed to invigorate him, and his health improved during his years in the Senate. He made an immediate splash in the capital with his carriage drawn by matched horses and slave servants arrayed in elaborate costumes. When Jackson chose to destroy the United States Bank, Old Pons, who benefited from friendly loans from the institution, emerged as the bank's strong defender. The Whigs elected Old Pons president pro tempore in the Senate, and passions rose so high between the president and Pons that when an insane man tried to kill Jackson, the president accused Pons of being involved. Pons demanded and got a Senate investigation to clear him of the charge. Back in Mississippi, the Jacksonian legislature passed resolutions asking Poindexter to resign because of his betrayal of the president.

Jacksonian democracy reigned, and Natchez nabobs, fearing further loss of power as representatives of the new counties carved out of the Indian lands joined the legislature, agreed to a referendum for a constitutional convention. Elected by popular vote, lawyers predominated in the convention, but on the whole, the delegates lacked the experience of the aristocratic group that had authored the 1817 document. The most controversial argument at the convention concerned the election of judges, and the Jacksonian democrats triumphed. The only eligibility requirement established for a judge was a minimum age. Neither voters nor officeholders had to meet any property ownership requirement under the new constitution, and ministers could hold office after 1832. Slavery remained legal, of course, but after 1833 importation of slaves for sale was to end. The convention gave Mississippi the most democratic constitution in the South, meaning blacks and women had no vote, but all white men could. The convention saw no need to submit the document to the people and ordered elections to implement the new constitution.

Jackson's Democratic control of Mississippi suffered because of South Carolina's challenge to the president over the protective tariff. Mississippi did not support South Carolina's threat to nullify the tariffs, but some Mississippi Democrats questioned the president's assertion of national power, favoring states' rights instead. They became known as Nullifiers, and if they cooperated with the Whigs, they could sometimes win Mississippi elections.

John A. Quitman emigrated to the Natchez area as an ambitious young lawyer, won fame in the Mexican War, rose to the governorship, and resigned because of filibustering dealing with a conspirator's proposal to annex Cuba.

John A. Quitman, a Natchez lawyer turned plantation owner, became the most prominent Nullifier.

Born to a Lutheran minister father who tried to educate him for the ministry, the tall, handsome Quitman escaped to the West. Landing in Ohio, he attended church only to seek female companions and studied law. An aunt recommended Natchez as a less competitive site to practice and earn high fees. Taking her advice, in 1821 he migrated to Natchez with the intention of practicing law and making his fortune. Disguising his poverty with a good suit of clothes and genteel manners, he made his way in the profession and married a wealthy planter's daughter after agreeing to a prenuptial document that promised him none of her inheritance. Quitman took readily to the nabobs, enjoying the flow of port, Madeira, and sherry in the mansions of the city. Land disputes and quarrelsome neighbors made the district a lawyer's paradise, and he made money to invest in land and slaves. Having been raised in part by a black servant, Quitman adjusted easily to Natchez's slave society. By 1826 he purchased Monmouth near Natchez and a quarter of a mile from Woodlands. He had already organized the Fencibles, a volunteer militia unit, and joined the Masons, rising to be Grand Master, while playing an active role in Trinity Episcopal Church, which served the city's elite.

Although he initially worked for the Adams wing of the Republican Party, he arrived late enough to see that the political winds blew toward the Democrats. He entered the legislature in 1828 at the height of Jacksonian fever and made himself a workhorse ably defending the interests of his beleaguered constituency and earning an appointment as chancellor of the equity courts for the state. His position handily removed him from the center of the vicious political fray while garnering a statewide reputation for him at the same time. As with most men with any money or credit, Quitman joined in real estate speculation. By 1829 he joined with Democrats William Gwin and Robert Walker in buying the Choctaw lands ceded at Dancing Rabbit Creek. He added lands in Louisiana and Texas eventually.

Visiting New England and his home in New York in 1831, Quitman recoiled from evangelical revival meetings where preachers solicited funds for the poor Indians and slaves of the South while endorsing temperance. Denouncing the land of his birth, Quitman headed south and encountered Poindexter in Charlottesville, where they held extended political discussions. Back home mulling over the threats in the making from abolitionists, the protective tariff politicians, and Poindexter's advice, Quitman began to speak publicly of a state's right to defy the national government in order to protect slavery and the cotton-made prosperity he had just begun to enjoy.

By contrast, Quitman's partner in the Choctaw lands, Walker, never fully adopted Mississippians' belief in slavery and eventually sided with the Union, but he nevertheless made a successful Mississippi political career, which catapulted him to the national level. The diminutive, curly haired Walker came to Natchez well connected and immediately became a nabob. He joined his brother's established law practice and had a cousin who headed the state bank. He eased into the society of transplanted Natchez district Pennsylvanians who began with Stephen Minor. Joining the Junto, he operated in the political shadows for many years. Despite his place among the elite, he had supported Jackson back in Pennsylvania and made the most of his Jacksonian credentials with the Mississippi Democratic Party. When Jackson visited Natchez and New Orleans in 1828, Walker shone among the speechmakers, and he became the leading orator protecting Jackson's policies.

Despite having held no office, Walker stood as a leader among the Democrats. Much of his energy went into land acquisition not only in Mississippi but also in Louisiana, Arkansas, and Texas. Perhaps what made his political career was his service to squatters who had jumped the gun and occupied Chickasaw lands ahead of the legal deadline. Walker formed a company of speculators and made his way to Chocchuma (near today's Grenada), being careful to have a presale survey done to identify the most promising sites. Arriving, he found two problems: first, a group from Alabama had made a similar plan, and second, the squatters threatened violence if their claims were sold from under them. Walker persuaded the Alabamians to merge with his company and forged an agreement to buy and then sell the squatters' plots back to them at cost. Those squatters voted for Walker when their new counties joined the legislature. Deciding to offer himself for election, he disguised his Natchez connections by buying a plantation in Madison County and advertising himself as a planter. The Democratic Party, a letter of support from Jackson, and the voters of the new counties allowed him to defeat Old Pons for a seat in the U.S. Senate. A rich lawyer and businessman, he proved a strange choice for the new democracy.

Plummer, by contrast more representative of the farmers, ran for the Senate against Walker and Old Pons, but Plummer went down to defeat because the farmers outside his Pearl River area did not know or appreciate him. The new Whig Party that coalesced out of Jackson's opponents used Plummer as a diversion, and Jackson's letter supporting Walker sealed Plummer's fate. Plummer, in spite of his democratic rhetoric and folksy style, took a loan from Natchez bankers for his campaign and speculated in what became Yalobusha County. Only in his early thirties, Plummer vanished from the political scene, incongruously trying banking during the flush times and dying poverty stricken in Jackson.

Not many Mississippians concerned themselves with politics because opening north Mississippi brought a flood of migrants into the state. Offering the Choctaw lands in 1833, the federal government set records for land sales. At Columbus and Chocchuma, the auctioneers sold 1,121,455 acres, doubling sales in the next highest state. Two years later Mississippians purchased 2,931,181 acres. From 1833 to 1835 the state had the busiest land offices in the country.

Money was scarce, but credit was easy. Farmers had not participated much in the money economy because they grew and produced everything that they needed, but eyeing the spreading success of the cotton barons, they wanted to replicate the plantations of the river counties in north Mississippi. To assist them with easy money, Jackson determined to destroy the national bank and to allow state institutions to replace it in order to provide the funds needed by the entrepreneurial frontiersmen. Two "pet banks" in Natchez received the federal deposits from the enormous land sales under way in the state. Planters' Bank, chartered by the state with bonds insured by the legislature, loaned enormous sums, including most of the sinking fund set aside to pay the interest on planters' state-sponsored bonds, but that proved insufficient for the speculators.

In response to their demands, the legislature, over the governor's objections, granted banking privileges to corporations promising to build railroads in the state. They built no railroads but made the most of their banking rights, issuing paper currency without a trace of gold or silver to back up their bills. Prospective planters used those bills to buy land, and those funds made their way into the pet banks to fuel further larger loans. The spiraling surge of paper money led men with no collateral to demand and receive thousands of dollars in loans. All that they needed were endorsements from friends, neighbors, or acquaintances. Refusal, they considered a slight on their honor, which they sometimes avenged in a knife fight or a duel, depending on their class.

Though he never became a planter, Seargent S. Prentiss's career illustrates the tenor of the times. A graduate of Bowdoin College without money, he went west in 1827, and after a chance meeting with two Natchez nabobs in Ohio, he proceeded to their city seeking employment as a teacher. Checking into his hotel, he spent the last $5 of his borrowed travel money to have wine and cigars delivered to his room, establishing, he said, his credit. He found a position and tutored before opening an academy, which he abandoned to study law in Robert Walker's office for just less than a year when he passed the exam for admission to the bar. Seeing greater opportunities in Vicksburg, he moved there and immediately established his reputation as good lawyer. He had an amazing mind, quoting pages of Lord Byron's poetry to amuse fellow travelers. His partially crippled legs did not deter his spending weeks in the saddle as he rode the court circuit or keep him from engaging in his favorite pastime, fishing. He drank and loved to gamble. In one nightlong game, he lost all his money and repeatedly sent messengers to the lawyer-companion with whom he was sharing a hotel room asking for loans and eventually for his companion's watch. Rising in the morning, the companion found Prentiss in the bar still at the poker table with a pile of watches and money entertaining the crowd. He good-naturedly told his friend to retrieve his watch and whatever funds he had loaned him during the night. In another instance, having lost all of his money, Prentiss returned to the tables as an observer the next night and proceeded to deliver a lecture on the evils of gambling to the crowded saloon.

Usually an agreeable companion and kind to fault—once giving a diamond pen to children playing in his hotel—he adopted the code of honor current in his adopted state. He fought two duels with Henry S. Foote, another Vicksburg lawyer, who opposed him in court frequently. Foote made the mistake of using abusive language to Prentiss in court once, and Prentiss struck Foote in the heat of the moment. Foote issued a challenge to a duel, which Prentiss accepted. As was the custom, they met on the Louisiana side

Seargent S. Prentiss, Mississippi lawyer who provided leadership to the Whig Party before losing his fortune and rejecting his adopted state. Courtesy of the Mississippi Department of Archives and History from the Seargent S. Prentiss Collection.

of the Mississippi and fired from ten paces. Prentiss grazed Foote's shoulder and emerged unscathed, but rumors circulated that Prentiss, who leaned on his cane, had an unfair advantage. Enraged by the reference to his disability, Prentiss issued a second challenge, which Foote accepted. In the second duel, Foote missed and Prentiss's pistol failed to fire, requiring them to face one another a third time. Prentiss wounded Foote, satisfying the code and bringing the incident to an end. Years later a story circulated that Prentiss had warned some boys who had climbed trees near the "field of honor" to observe the duels that they should beware of his opponent's wild aim. To his brother in Maine, Prentiss insisted that he had a moral obligation to fight and could not have lived with the shame of not taking up the challenge, but at the same time he urged his brother not to tell his mother about the duels knowing, he said, that New Englanders would not understand the custom.

Choosing to invest in Vicksburg town lots instead of plantation acres, Prentiss prospered in the flush times and entered the legislature, rising to be a star in the emerging Whig Party. In 1837, as Martin Van Buren succeeded Jackson as president, the banks collapsed across the country and nowhere more spectacularly than in Mississippi. Prentiss, as an opponent of Van Buren's subtreasury plan, ran for a special election called in the summer of 1837 to fill Mississippi's House of Representative's seats for a special congressional session called by the president. Because of Democratic domination in Mississippi, Prentiss did not take the election seriously, spending much of the summer in Maine instead of campaigning. Two Democrats won, but as the financial panic sank the state into depression, the Whigs' prospects improved. Prentiss ran again in the regular November election, defeating a Democrat. Elevated to the national scene, Prentiss challenged the Democrats, who claimed their special summer election entitled them to the seats that the Whigs won in the fall. The twenty-nine-year-old Prentiss's oratory held the nation in its grip as all of Washington came to hear him claim his seat. Congress sent the decision back to Mississippi for a third election, which Prentiss won along with a national reputation.

As an answer to the banking crisis, the Mississippi legislature created more banks, pledging the state's credit for the new Union Bank. The bonds sold amounted to more than the total capital of the combined banks in all but three or four states in the nation at the time. Mississippians gone bust moved on to Texas and left notes penned to the doors of deserted houses reading "G.T.T." (Gone to Texas). Banks experimented with accepting cotton in lieu of specie or bank notes, but the price of the commodity plummeted, deepening their debts. The Democrats swept state elections for the next two years by turning on the banks and voicing the anger of the confused, indebted farmers and planters.

At the same time the white population struggled with political and economic problems, their religious view of slavery underwent a revolutionary transformation. Respect for the slave as a fellow child of God predominated in the territorial period, but by the 1830s the majority began to use religion to justify the inhumanity of the slave system. Frontier society engaged in a shared struggle against nature fostered master/slave relations such as those between Toney and Hutchins or Foster and Ibrahima based on a mutual respect for one another's humanity. The ideals of the American and French Revolutions had caused the educated to question slavery. In an 1818 ruling, the Mississippi Supreme Court voiced the prevailing sentiment, writing, "Slavery is condemned by reason and the laws of nature." While rejecting the Age of Reason, evangelical religion condemned slavery as a necessary evil and recognized slaves as fellow children of God. Until the 1830s evangelicals favored future emancipation of slaves. Some of the largest, wealthiest slaveholders joined the Mississippi Colonization Society and supported its goal of repatriating slaves to their continent of origin. Cowles Mead, Governor Gerard C. Brandon, and Stephen Duncan, a physician, planter, and banker, joined with ministers such as Methodist bishop Winans to raise funds to send free blacks to settle in West Africa, but they soon turned to emancipating slaves for settlement. By the mid-1830s they established a separate colony in Liberia named Mississippi and settled over 500 freed slaves there. Mississippi's Methodist Church founder, William Foster, freed his twenty-one slaves in his will and paid for their transportation to Africa. As late as 1832 Edward Brett Randolph, a descendent of the famous Virginia family who moved to northeast Mississippi in 1824, freed the slaves on his plantation near Columbus when he had a religious conversion and joined the Methodist Episcopal Church. Though not an extremely wealthy man, he paid passage for his former slaves to Liberia in hopes that they would spread Christianity in Africa, but in a farewell speech, after warning them of the harsh conditions they would encounter, he noted the greatest advantage for them would be that they and their children would enjoy freedom and equal rights.

The first minutes of the Mississippi Baptist Association in 1808 expressed concern over how the church should handle members whose treatment of their slaves was "unscriptural," and the association recommended using the accepted process of investigation and disciplinary action for slaveholding members, if required. In 1821 the Baptist Association published instructions to both masters and slaves outlining each party's obligations, admonishing slaves to accept their fate as God's wisdom. Without defending slavery as good, the document warned owners not to oppress their slaves in such a manner as to offend God. In 1827 the Pisgah Presbyterian Church called an owner before the conference for cruelly whipping a slave. The Methodists and Baptists rose up against Poindexter's code for curtailing a slave's right to worship and got the law revised to allow blacks to worship with a white minister or a black one if observed by two respectable whites appointed by some church. The law and slave conversions brought more blacks into white churches, and whites grew uncomfortable with large numbers of slaves sitting in the back of the church as had been the custom. Most churches began to segregate blacks into areas of the building such as balconies or side additions. As time passed and the number of black worshippers increased, more churches provided separate services, which appealed to slaves because they gained some control and more participation in the services.

As church membership exploded and church buildings began to replace brush arbors, divisions appeared among the faithful. Baptists divided into Missionary, Primitive, and Campbellites. Missionary members tended to be townsmen, and Primitives mostly lived in the country. Missionary Baptists ceased foot-washing ceremonies and led the crusade to hire educated ministers, while Primitives insisted that being called by God served as the only credential needed for a minister. Campbellites rejected any form of worship not found in the New Testament, including organs and other musical instruments. The Methodist Protestant Church challenged the Methodist Episcopal Church over the same sort of issues. Churchgoers changed their clothes. Planters' wives began to wear hoop skirts that barely fit through the sanctuary doors, sleeveless silk gowns, and jewelry, while their farmer neighbors continued with homespun or calico in dark colors. Many ministers began to claim professional status because of their education and the journals they founded. Such ministers discouraged emotional demonstrations by those attending services, organized choirs to do the singing, and introduced musical instruments in some churches. The Episcopal Church, with its English ceremony, attracted the wealthiest planters and professionals. The more sophisticated churches existed alongside the older, simpler communities, and by the 1830s they provided their adherents different messages.

Churches in the North continued to develop the theme of slavery as evil, and some churchgoers turned into abolitionists, seeking to end the practice. Wounded by the accusation of sinfulness, southerners began to seek religious justification for the "necessary evil" that many saw as the basis of their economy. James Smylie, a Presbyterian minister who graduated from the "Log College" in North Carolina before migrating to the Mississippi Territory in 1806, provided the needed defense of slavery in the late 1820s. He owned 1,000 acres and worked a prosperous plantation in addition to preaching. Studying the Bible and probably lost tracts, he settled on the old curse of Ham as the basis of his assertion that God created blacks to be slaves and that slave owners did God's work by keeping slaves. He adopted the story that Noah's curse on Ham and Ham's on his son, Canaan, condemned Africans to perpetual servitude by God's will. He first delivered this doctrine as a sermon not in the rural churches where he normally spoke but in the elite Port Gibson Presbyterian Church. Eventually he engaged in a lengthy newspaper battle on the topic with ministers in the North and later wrote a pamphlet that was widely distributed throughout the South. Even men such as John G. Jones, who had offered to free his slaves and crusaded against slavery as an evil after his conversion, wrote by 1840 that further study of Smylie's arguments had modified his views. Mississippians embraced Smylie's justification of what some called their "peculiar institution."

Unfavorable publicity and threats to the institution of slavery multiplied in the 1820s and 1830s. Thomas Foster gave in to requests to free Ibrahima in 1828 with the stipulation that Ibrahima must go back to Africa or return to slavery if he remained in America. Helped by the newspaper editor Marschalk, Ibrahima traveled north and became a celebrity, meeting with Secretary of State Henry Clay, who had appealed for his freedom, and with groups opposed to slavery, who gave him donations to buy his family from Foster. Ibrahima wrote letters to his family promising to free them, which enraged Foster, who insisted that Marschalk, the deal's broker, get Ibrahima out of the country quickly. Newspapers reported toasts hostile to slavery at banquets for Ibrahima in Boston, and rumor had Ibrahima returning to Natchez. Foster threatened to reenslave him if he did. Every mail delivery bought more news of Ibrahima's triumphant tour of the North, and Foster's threats grew more vociferous, causing fear of his intentions toward Ibrahima's family, who remained his slaves. Marschalk, a Jackson supporter, saw an opportunity to embarrass the administration, quiet Foster, and get himself off the hook. He published his correspondence with Clay and accused Clay of breaking a legal contract in a handbill distributed up and down the Mississippi River. He charged those feting Ibrahima with inviting slaves to revolt, to murder their masters, and to revel in whites' blood. At the end of his attack, he connected the threat to the Adams administration. Newspapers reprinted the text frequently and kept the furor going throughout the 1828 election. In early 1829 Ibrahima returned to Africa but died before he could reach home.

Nat Turner's rebellion in Virginia in 1831 and the murder of slave owners caused whites throughout the South to reassess their relationships with their slaves, but the immediate fear quieted until abolitionists stepped up their attacks on slavery. Mississippi's panic over insurrection came not in the old plantation area but in the new Choctaw cession district, where some new slave owners represented a new breed. In Aberdeen, one slave owner delighted in having his slaves pull him around town in a carriage. Such behavior on the part of Hutchins or Foster would have been unimaginable. By 1835 Madison County erupted in a hysterical outburst of lynch law brought on by the increasing fear of rebellious slaves. The county consisted of a small white minority and a large majority slave population at work clearing vast tracts of land to create plantations—often for absentee landlords. Communities had not yet formed. Governments and legal systems were not well established. All emerged newly out of the wilderness, and outlaws still roamed the quickly developing land.

Virgil A. Stewart, an ambitious Georgian, passed through the Madison area promoting his new pamphlet on the career and conspiracy of Tennessee-born outlaw John A. Murrell. In the publication, Stewart described how Murrell lured slaves into his plan to initiate a slave rebellion, to kill the masters and their families (except for the best-looking women, whom they would make sex slaves), and to plunder the wealth of the South. Murrell treated slaves as equals, according to Stewart, and violated all the accepted norms of white society. A widow overheard a portion of a conversation between two of her slaves, and her female servant reported a plot to kill the family as a part of a Murrell-like uprising. The widow lived at Beatty's Bluff on the Yazoo River near Livingston, a new town recently established to handle cotton sales and shipment. Using the whip freely, the Livingston lynch committee, established in reaction to the perceived threat, extracted the answers desired based on Stewart's fantastical story.

The slaves, encouraged by the whip, implicated whites, including two "steam doctors" engaged in practicing a new healing method employing steam baths and cayenne pepper. The enraged whites hanged the slaves on July 4, the expected date of the insurrection, and the two steam doctors shortly thereafter. White families gathered together for protection, and armed vigilantes rode about seeking more victims. The spirit spread to Vicksburg, where five gamblers who refused to leave town paid with their lives. The Madison County "posse" raided into Hinds County, attacking a prominent planter who harbored and released suspected conspirators. Governor Hiram Runnels responded to appeals from Hinds County neighbors of the planter by offering arms to the Madison County committee. Only in mid-July, when the hysteria had subsided, did the governor issue a proclamation calling on the state's population to leave justice to the proper authorities. Twelve white men and an unknown number of slaves died in the emotional outbreak of lynch law.

Politicians dared not condemn the unlawful violence. Prentiss proclaimed that everyone approved of the actions taken by the irregular committees. Foote endorsed Stewart's version of the plot in the heat of the moment, but later noted that doing otherwise made one a suspect during the frenzy. Only in retrospect did he question his approval of the lynchings. Walker sensed an opportunity, which, as already noted, led him to capture a Senate seat. In the aftermath of the panic, he accused the Whigs of fostering slave rebellion and used the theme effectively to boost his campaign. His correspondence made clear that he exploited white fears, which he knew to be exaggerated, for political purposes.

The Regency, which backed Walker, elected Alexander G. McNutt governor in 1837. McNutt practiced law and operated plantations in Warren County. When his partner, Joel Cameron, was murdered by slaves, McNutt married Cameron's beautiful young wife and gained control of his dead partner's land. Foote charged in the heat of a political campaign that McNutt had instigated Cameron's death. Though never proven, the charges dogged McNutt, who nevertheless won the governorship. A humorist, not a proud aristocrat, McNutt once replied to the news that Quitman intended to physically attack him over campaign rhetoric with the quip that Quitman would have to catch him first. In the legislature, McNutt opposed the creation of the Union Bank, but then, as governor, signed the legislation authorizing it. When the depression worsened, McNutt wrestled with various schemes to bring the banks under control without success. The legislature continued to place its faith in the Union Bank, electing former governor Runnels as president and Samuel Gwin as cashier at annual salaries of $10,000 and $8,000, respectively. In the 1839 election, the voters handed McNutt a decisive reelection victory and elected a legislature that overwhelmingly chose Walker over Prentiss as senator because the Democrats ran on an anti-bank/hard money platform, ignoring the fact that their policies had created the panic and resulting depression. Following his reelection, McNutt escalated his attacks on the Union Bank, and Runnells caned the governor on a Jackson street. McNutt began to advocate the repudiation of the state's obligation to redeem the bank's bonds.

The 1830s ended with a Mississippi transformed. The Choctaw and Chickasaw had lost their lands to invading entrepreneurs, who spread plantations around the state and peopled them with slaves. Mississippi's population had tripled, and half lived in what had been the Indian nations. Church membership, which had been low in 1817, had soared for both blacks and whites. Whites were adopting a new view of slavery as a labor system ordained by God, which they believed would remain forever as the basis of the state's economy. The slaves had learned the biblical stories and treasured the message of a loving God who would lead them out of bondage as Moses had led his people out of Egyptian slavery. The democratic constitution of 1832, which had foreseen the end of slave importation for sale, had been forgotten. The Democrats dominated the state's politics, with Gwin manufacturing public opinion using the media of the age and recruiting the likes of Walker to represent the democratic masses.

In January 1840 Andrew Jackson visited Mississippi for the last time, returning from New Orleans where he celebrated the twenty-fifth anniversary of his victory over the British. He was ill, broke, and splendid in the glory of what he had helped to create. Suffering a lung hemorrhage during the speechmaking and hand shaking in Natchez and bleeding internally, he took refuge in Gwin's Vicksburg home, where he ordered a doctor to bleed him as treatment. Despite the doctor's care, two days later he took the new Vicksburg-Jackson train to its terminus fifteen miles short of the capital named for him. The city's' largest-ever crowd greeted him, with planters' carriages mingling alongside yeomanry's wagons and even Choctaw on horseback decked out in new shirts and moccasins joined by crowds of slaves granted a holiday. The Speaker of the Mississippi House of Representatives delivered the welcoming address, but Jackson's adopted son, Andrew Jackson Donelson, had to read his father's response because Old Hickory was too weak to answer. Enduring the festive events proved worth it because Gwin and former governor Runnels delivered $15,000 in loans for Donelson as a parting gift for the former president, who provided surety. His last visit to the state must have been gratifying because of the progress made in building and economic development, but surely the grubby money raising had to temper his enjoyment of the triumphant parade through the burgeoning plantations and cities.

Seeking to explain the essence of the new southern society birthed by the events of two eventful decades, Bertram Wyatt-Brown, in his conclusion to *Southern Honor*, turns to the murder of Susan Foster near Natchez in March 1834. Susan married James Foster Jr., son of Thomas Foster, owner of 16,000 acres and, at one time, Ibrahima. Thomas fathered thirteen children and amassed great wealth, which he used to purchase carriages and other accoutrements of the nabobs. Unlike his brother, who helped to found the Methodist Church in the state and supported Jefferson College, Thomas never took an interest in such institutions, never acquired a library, and never educated his children beyond the basics. When he died, none of his children rose to claim the patriarchal position necessary to control a plantation. His widow, Sarah, proved incapable of filling his place, and the family went into decline. James had joined an older brother in Louisiana, where he became a planter and addicted gambler who was arrested and jailed for swindling his business associates. He married Susan, an unknown girl of fifteen, and returned to Foster Fields to await the outcome of a court suit claiming a dead sister's share of the family's wealth from a divorced husband. James took Susan on a walk along St Catherine's Creek near his mother's home on the evening of March 14, 1834. At some point between seven and ten o'clock, he strangled her, and after taking her body to the home of Prince, Ibrahima's son, he awakened some female relatives to ask them to revive her. Faced with the death of this young woman and James's confused behavior, the family hastily buried her, but rumor spread. The next week Ferdinand L. Claiborne, the man who arrested Burr, presided over an inquest, and eventually the family's protection failed to save James from arrest and jail. The family lawyer got the charges dismissed on a technicality after several months, but as James emerged from the courthouse at noon on January 2, 1835, his lawyer and the prosecutor, Spence Monroe Grayson, a young descendent of a notable Virginia family and rising star in Natchez, allowed the holiday mob assembled around the courthouse to seize James. The community avengers whipped James to a bloody pulp and tarred and feathered him. Transporting him back to the courthouse, many wanted to mutilate or hang him, but Grayson sent them home with a short speech saving James's life. With help from distant relatives from another county, he escaped Natchez and disappeared, probably to Texas.

Wyatt-Brown's analysis of Mississippi society reflected in the incident was one held together by the planters' domination lacking adherence to formal governmental institutions. In a manner to be repeated frequently, the elite absented themselves from James's punishment, allowing the lesser members of white society to express righteous, violent community sentiment overseen by younger, rising members of the planter class, who controlled the mob before it completely violated social norms. The planter's code of honor motivated and restrained planters, who manipulated the masses by using them to exact vengeance but stopping them short of executing one of the planter class. Death, they reserved for slaves and the lower classes. Such a society was flawed because it excluded the mass of the population from the code of honor and risked its existence by relying on the honor of a class espousing chivalrous ideals while grasping to build their plantations.

The early years of statehood failed to produce either a political system or leaders capable of shaping events or building a healthy society. After Holmes, Poindexter possessed the most obvious talent, but he failed in his efforts to introduce a public education system and ended his career utterly rejected by voters because of his clash with Jackson over the spoils of office. Walker, who defeated Poindexter for the Senate, represented some of the worst traits of the era, operating in the shadowy world of banking, speculation, and finance. His talent landed him in the president's cabinet, but as governor of Kansas Territory, he refused to carry out the South's program to make it a slave state and went on to work for Lincoln during the Civil War, claiming falsely to have freed his slaves in the 1830s. The Whig Prentiss, though a magnificent orator, never liked Mississippi much, as he made clear in his letters to his family in Maine. He drank too much and ended his career cursing his adopted state as he left it to end his life in New Orleans. Quitman emerged in this era as the most admired leader. He reflected the values of Mississippi plantation society, but his militant states' rights views and propensity for military expansionism propelled the state toward disaster.

It might be that the majority of early settlers shared Lincecum's love of the land, enjoyed its natural bounty, and could appreciate the Indians' adaptation to its rhythms as he did. Though the first Mississippi settlers shared his indifference to organized religion, the second wave adopted an emotional faith in the brush arbors, anchoring their belief in humility and a loving God who required them to respect the humanity of all men, including slaves. They lost the love of nature and their fellow man in the pursuit of wealth to be gained by planting cotton. The desire to replicate the achievements of the wealthy planters drove the majority to exile the Choctaw and Chickasaw so that they could develop the Indians' land into plantations and to transform their religion into a justification for never-ending slavery endorsed by a God who created black people to be a servant class. This worldview placed Mississippians and their fellow southerners in opposition to trends in the remainder of the Western world and set the stage for a tragic dedication to King Cotton.

Chapter Five

COTTON KINGDOM

In the late 1830s and early 1840s American surveyors imposed imaginary lines on the Choctaw and Chickasaw homelands, continuing Elliott's mission begun with the thirty-first parallel dividing American from Spanish territories. Between 1840 and 1860 Mississippi's population increased from 375,651 to 791,305 as settlers raced to buy the quarter sections identified by the surveyors' lines. They subdued the land, turning it into towns and farms dedicated to producing cotton extracted from the recent wilderness by teams of oxen hauling heavy wagons across rutted muddy roads, by steamboats navigating unlikely snag-filled shallow streams, and by railroads penetrating the streamless forest areas. In the 1830s new counties placed bounties on wolves to protect farmers, but by the 1840s the wolves had vanished. Only the Delta still harbored the type of abundant wildlife Lincecum described along the Tombigbee when he entered the state twenty years earlier. Delta residents still harvested carrier pigeons with night raids on their roosting trees and killed multiple bears in a morning's hunt, but Natchez district farmers battled erosion as their light loess soil washed away, leaving enormous gullies in their fields.

Buffeted by the depression, which was triggered by the Panic of 1837, planters revolutionized agriculture by adopting new techniques and continuing old practices learned from American Indians to keep their land producing. Squatters and pioneers who relied on the natural abundance of wildlife, edible wild fruits, a cornfield, a small vegetable garden, and half-wild pig herds for their livelihood had to replace their reliance on deerskins and pelts with a cotton patch as their only source of cash. They, like the Choctaw and Chickasaw in some instances, joined the world's market economy with reluctance and equally little success. This era's settlers brought churches with them, and their ministers adapted theology to a society with a slave majority. Ministers also furnished the backbone of the education available to most of the population by founding academies and colleges, but the leaders of the new Mississippi society were lawyers. Land disputes, trespass, assaults, and debt collection created a lawyer wonderland, which they exploited in

Steamboat loaded with cotton, illustrating the productivity of Mississippi's farms and plantations. Courtesy of the Mississippi Department of Archives and History from the Cooper Postcard Collection.

order to buy land and slaves to escape into the more appealing life of the patriarchal planter and political leader. Power shifted quickly from Natchez to the newly settled north, where the ambitious lawyer-planters seized control and generated an aggressive ideology identified as "fire-eating" southern nationalism, which depended on slaves, whose lives deteriorated during this period because of more restrictive laws and regulations.

Cotton made Mississippi, dominated its economy, and dictated the development of its culture. In the first half of the nineteenth century, cotton constituted over half of all American exports. The American South supplied much of Great Britain's industrial expansion in textiles and purchased both agricultural and industrial supplies from the North. Cotton fueled the American nation's expansion and made a few of the most successful planters the richest elite in America. Slaves produced the cotton. In 1840 slaves outnumbered free Mississippians by about 15,000 and in 1860 by over 80,000. Being a minority altered the white population's psychology by immersing whites in African American culture. The mass of the whites reacted aggressively and fearfully to their new status as a racial minority, enacting increasing controls over the majority while asserting their determination to extend their domination and exploitation forever. In the late 1850s many fire-eating secessionists began to demand reopening the African slave trade in order to provide a cheaper, more plentiful supply of labor. The more moderate fire-eaters advised against advertising their ambition, but nevertheless led Mississippi to secede from the United States, seeking to preserve slavery and expand its cotton economy either westward across the continent or into Latin America.

In nineteenth-century terms, Mississippians enjoyed a democratic government in that all white men could vote. Such was not the norm in much of the world. Even in Great Britain at the time, all men did not have the right to vote. The 1832 Mississippi Constitution removed property qualifications, and white men elected all their leaders, including judges. Therefore the mystery of Mississippi's history in this period is why did the majority of white men, who did not own slaves, choose to follow leaders who did and to leave the Union and fight a war in order to preserve slavery?

First, one must understand the cotton economy and what planters accomplished in the twenty years before the Civil War. Mississippi cotton planters faced three major hurdles in the 1840s. First, the depression that began with the Panic of 1837 dried up credit and left them with paper money that depreciated in value or sometimes became worthless. Second, the price of cotton dropped to such low levels that they could not count on even a good crop allowing them to buy necessities for their families and their slaves. Third, the established farmers who had been growing cotton since the late 1790s had worn out the land's productivity, and they began to face erosion problems that would force them to abandon their farms. Planters surmounted the crisis by developing new farming techniques and diversifying their crops so well that they revolutionized cotton farming and made it profitable even with low prices. Mississippi never solved its banking problems before the war and cotton prices did not hit bottom until the mid-1840s, so survival called for change.

Some planters escaped their debts by leaving for Texas—then another country. In some instances, they made night moves. A plantation appeared normal at sundown with animals in their pens, smoke from the chimneys, and slaves loitering outside their quarters, but in the night everyone departed, riding all of the plantation's animals west. If the planter, his family, slaves, and livestock could make it over the county line, chances were that they could make it to the Mississippi River and the Texas border, because law enforcement was usually limited to the county sheriff.

Those who chose to stay adopted a new self-sufficient strategy. Before the depression, farmers made so much money growing cotton that they bought food and clothing for their slaves in order to optimize the amount of time and land dedicated to their cash crop. In the 1840s planters raised more corn, sweet potatoes, and pigs to supply food; developed better varieties of cotton; improved their herds; cut down on hoe work by using more animals to pull the harrows; and invented farm implements. Dr. Rush Nutt, a Jefferson County planter, probably implemented one of the most important reforms by adopting the Indian habit of planting Indian peas or cowpeas in his cornfields. Nutt traveled widely in Europe and North Africa, returning with seeds and ideas to try on his plantation, and adopted the habit of observation and experimentation. He also introduced the custom of plowing cotton and corn stalks back into the soil to nurture his fields rather than burning them as was the established procedure. The peas, although he did not know it, captured nitrogen from the air and fertilized the soil. In the 1830s farmers typically planted cornrows five and a half or six feet apart and the "hills" in the rows two feet apart. Nutt began to plant peas between the cornrows after the last pass through the corn with the harrow to destroy the grass. The peas matured after the corn had been harvested, and in the fall, when grazing grass petered out, farmers turned stock into the fields to eat the peas. Planters rotated cotton into the field the next year and found the land produced significantly better.

In 1839 Martin W. Philips of Edwards, who read agricultural journals with enthusiasm, began to ask his neighbors why they planted their corn so far apart. None of them had a good answer because it apparently developed as an imitation of cotton planting, but cotton plants needed more space than corn. When Philips planted corn more thickly, he increased his yield per acre, and the practice spread. Several planters developed and marketed improved varieties of cottonseed, but the most successful was Henry W. Vick, son of the Methodist minister who married into a fortune. After growing the ubiquitous Petit Gulf Mexican cotton for seven years, Vick began to try selecting the best-looking seeds in an effort to improve his crops, but not until 1843 did he try selecting the hardiest, largest plants with the best cotton as the source for his seed. Spending a summer at Nita Yuma on Deer Creek in Yazoo County, he personally selected the plants and harvested the seeds by hand. He called the resulting superior cotton Hundred Seed. Marketing Hundred Seed well by sending samples to cotton men up and down the Mississippi, he commanded a premium price and helped planters boost production.

Agricultural societies formed at Jefferson College and in Raymond. Agricultural innovators used them to promote new techniques, and they established farm journals. New breeds of cattle, pigs, and sheep drew a great deal of attention at their agricultural fairs. First rich planters and then their poorer neighbors bought Durham cattle, Berkshire pigs, and Merino sheep. After some experience with the less hardy breeds in the Mississippi environment, most interbred the new specimens with the Creole types that fared better in the heat and rough pastures. A few planters began to produce wool for the first time. Creole sheep had been raised only for mutton, so the new hybrids provided major improvements with wool and better meat. For some unfathomable reason, Mississippians never bred mules or workhorses and continued to import those from Kentucky and Tennessee.

Mississippi planters did adapt and invent new plows and harrows to cut down on hoe work, enabling a slave using these horse-drawn tools to do the work of many men. Plows cut the roots of maturing cotton plants so they developed harrows to drag grass away from the plants and to throw dirt at the plant's base to further inhibit weed growth. They experimented with ditching to drain fields, contour plowing to retain water, and creating horizontal planes with their rows to hold water on hillsides. Not until 1857 did Joseph Gray of Raymond patent a "Grade and Horizontal Level," which enabled him to eliminate erosion on his hilly fields by creating furrows capable of retaining heavy rains.

By using the new techniques and diversifying their crops, planters survived even as cotton declined below five cents a pound in 1845. They planted sweet potatoes to feed themselves, their slaves, and their pigs. A half an acre of potatoes fed most plantations. Planters grew oats, barley, yellow clover, grasses, peanuts, and millet. Some planted Egyptian oats in their cotton fields during the winter for use as spring pasture. In 1854 the U.S. Patent Office introduced Asian sorghum cane into the South, and north Mississippi planters raced to embrace it because sugarcane failed to grow there. Molasses made from the new cane added a vital source of sweet taste and essential vitamins to the diet. Planters adopted cutting machines to prepare fodder to feed the increased number of oxen and horses used in their new operations. In north Mississippi, they successfully grew wheat for much-desired white bread, reducing dependence on the Midwest. They began to weave both cotton and wool cloth to clothe their slaves, and some tanned leather and made shoes on the farm.

By the end of the 1840s planters fed and clothed their slaves and stood ready to reap enormous profits when the price of cotton recovered. The spread of improved, more easily picked cotton eliminated the last bottleneck for cotton planters who had often planted more than they could pick. The older varieties limited pickers to an average of around 50 pounds per day, whereas the improved cotton developed by Vick enabled a picker to harvest 200 pounds per day. The sum total of all their innovations meant that by the 1850s, Mississippi planters temporarily triumphed in the market and enjoyed unparalleled prosperity, which they and their slaveless neighbors expected to continue indefinitely.

The addition of the Indian lands made Mississippi not only larger by half but also more complex. Natchez, having lost its political dominance, held on to its economic power and acquired the patina of age. Jefferson College remained the leading intellectual center of the state until the University of Mississippi opened in 1848, and the old village of Washington became a pleasant abode for a forgotten society. Vicksburg in this era attracted the leading lawyers, furnished political leaders, and grew to be the state's largest city. Columbus had grown to become the capital of the black prairie because of its head start in the Monroe County enclave and its location on the Tombigbee. Holly Springs in the hills of the far north blossomed into the capital of the north hills. Along the Gulf Coast, summer residents from New Orleans and the interior gave birth to tourism, and a string of communities along the length of the state's coastline were served regularly by steamboats plying between Mobile and New Orleans. The piney woods gradually destroyed its free range grazing by overstocking and had to turn to lumber, forest products, and increased farming during the 1850s. Immigrants seeking cheap land made it the fastest-growing section of the state in the last decade before the war. Floods kept the Delta's settlements sparse, but hardy planters began to try fending off the rivers with private levees. By 1860 only Natchez, Vicksburg, and Columbus had a population density of over thirty persons per square mile, so despite the influx of settlers, a great deal of wilderness remained among the small towns and farms.

Stephen Duncan, the leader of the nabobs, epitomized Natchez in this era as its richest planter-banker. He emigrated from Pennsylvania, where he attended college and studied medicine with the famous Benjamin Rush. Unlike many migrants, he came to Mississippi in 1808 with money, connections, and influence. He, like many professional men, abandoned his medical career for planting cotton and sugar on his Louisiana holdings. After his first wife died, he married Catherine Bingman, who was related to the Minor, Surget, and Lintot families constituting the inner core of the wealthy Natchez elite. Involved with the Bank of the State of Mississippi, which his uncle headed, Duncan got preferential loans and in turn made private loans within the family circle, but always making certain the loans were secured by property and slaves as collateral. With cash on hand, he bought land cheap during low cotton prices in the 1820s and became president of the bank when his uncle died of yellow fever in 1825. He bought his own steamboat to control shipping costs and advocated plantation "self-sufficiency" early. A Whig, Duncan thought Jackson weak-minded and too ambitious, and before the election, he dismissed the possibility of a Jackson victory as an absurdity. But faced with Jackson's win, he decided that as long as his bank's stock rose and his cotton grew, he could accept Jacksonian democracy.

Spending his summers in Pennsylvania and northern resorts to escape the heat, Duncan took a long view, advocating the diversification of the southern economy and building slave-staffed mills to produce rough cloth to clothe slaves. Recognizing the growing antislavery sentiment in the rest of the world, he accepted the presidency of the Mississippi Colonization Society, seeking an answer to ending gradually the very institution responsible for making his fortune. Seeing the opportunities that former Indian lands made available, he invested $2,700 there, and thirty years later his acquisitions were worth $1.4 million in what became Issaquena County. When the state took the banking monopoly away from the Bank of the State of Mississippi to found the Planter's Bank, Duncan got a charter for a private institution, the Agricultural Bank of Mississippi. He did well in the flush times, but sold his shares in 1839 before the complete collapse of the banking system. Having cash, he continued to make private loans and to buy land and slaves at bargain prices. In 1840 he owned 18,600 acres and 440 slaves in Mississippi and Louisiana. A decade later he had added 1,000 acres and doubled the number of slaves who worked his land. The Jacksonian Democrats railed against Duncan and the Natchez elite, but he and his relatives prospered most from Mississippi's growth.

On the periphery of the elite lived men such as Benjamin L. C. Wailes, who descended from a Georgia family who immigrated into the Natchez territory and worked in minor government jobs such as land office administrators. Wailes grew up in Washington when it served as the capital of the Mississippi Territory, doing the same sort of work as his father and getting an informal education. He traveled a great deal when young, overseeing land sales, and learned to love the state's woods and streams, seeking refuge in nature when ill or troubled. He visited with General Jackson and Pushmataha at the Doak Stand negotiations on one trip up the Natchez Trace, so he got to meet almost all the major figures in the state. Inheritance brought a plantation, but Wailes chose to live at the end of Washington's only mile-long street, which was lined by oaks and cypress drooping Spanish moss. His home, named Meadvilla, had previously been the home of Cowles Mead and was once the Washington Hotel. From his front porch, he looked at the main street, which was part of the Natchez Trace, and across to the grounds of Jefferson College. Just to the west stood the Methodist church where the state's first constitution had been written. Behind his house lay forty acres of gardens, orchards, pastures, and fields. He kept eighteen of his youngest and oldest slaves at his town home to care for his gardens, fields, horses, cows, hogs, and sheep. He and the slaves grew an amazing variety of vegetables and eighteen different fruit trees, which he improved by grafting and pruning regularly. Wailes won prizes for both his pigs and sheep at the local agricultural fair, and his wife took ribbons for her flowers. The yard contained roses and other flowers, shrubs, and a variety of ornamental trees. Aside from beauty and the joy of gardening, the establishment provided much

Benjamin L. C. Wailes, representative of the smaller Natchez planters, collector of natural and political history, and savant. Courtesy of the Mississippi Department of Archives and History from the Benjamin L. C. Wailes Collection.

of the family's food, supplemented by corn and other basics from the two plantations that he owned and managed.

Employed by banks and railroads at different times, Wailes hired overseers to run the plantations. Like most absentee owners, he complained about the results and accused one overseer of killing two of his slaves through neglect of their health. He speculated in land but never bought new slaves or sold any of his own. He had to assume the duties of a master and deal with slave violence. For example, when one of his slaves knifed a neighbor's slave, Wailes visited the neighbor to settle the matter. They decided in essence that it had been a fair fight instigated by the neighbor's slave, so they dropped it without punishment. In another instance, when several young female slaves returning from a religious service got into a fight with slaves from his second plantation and behaved insolently toward a member of his family, he flogged five of the young slaves.

Comfortable but not wealthy compared to Duncan, Wailes used the leisure provided by slave ownership to dabble in intellectual affairs. Aside from agricultural research, he participated in the Lyceum's exploration of Indian mounds around Natchez and developed a passion for natural history, collecting rocks, petrified wood, fossils, and Indian relics. He stuffed and mounted snakes, wild cats, and all manner of animals, although he failed to master bird preservation. His collection of mastodon bones and jars of specimens grew too large for his home, and Jefferson College donated space until he outgrew that and filled two small houses that he owned in Washington. He also kept a pond at his home for his live turtles—numbering fifty different specimens at one time. Naturally when the state authorized and funded a natural history survey in 1850, Wailes got the contract for the fieldwork from the professor paid to do the report.

Despite his intellectual curiosity, Wailes could not function equally well in the North as Duncan did. Living in Mississippi his entire life, he felt uncomfortable outside the South. In New York, what he described as a "low order" of whites on the waterfront made him uneasy. Sea bathing in Atlantic City by both sexes disturbed him. He found being served by young white females in an Illinois restaurant revolting because slaves did those tasks in Mississippi. Slaves who knifed one another did not concern him. Overseers and other rough southerners did not disturb him because they made up his world, but Wailes saw and understood himself as fundamentally different from Americans in the North.

Both Wailes and Duncan followed the Whig Party and lacked sympathy for democracy. Duncan participated in the Natchez Junto, manipulating elections behind the scenes, while Wailes served a term in the legislature before withdrawing to his retreat in the old capital to ignore the rough-and-tumble political world in Jackson. The majority of Mississippians despised Duncan, who stood for everything they felt held them back. Men such as these had no hope of providing leadership for the state in the Jacksonian era as they held to the old notion that the aristocracy should run the government without having to consult the common man.

In the 1839 elections, the candidates receiving the highest vote totals were Governor McNutt for reelection and two new congressmen, Albert Gallatin Brown and Jacob Thompson. Brown, one of the most popular antebellum politicians in the state, considered himself the champion of the common man. He emigrated from South Carolina to Mississippi in 1823 at the age of ten with his family, settling in Copiah County. He spent his youth deadening trees—girdling them to kill them—clearing brush, planting, chopping, and picking cotton. Motivated to escape the fields, he studied hard and persuaded his father to send him to Mississippi College at sixteen, where he entered the preparatory program. After four years he went to Jefferson College, then in a phase as a military school, but he could not endure the planter/Whig institution and returned home after six months, pleading with his father to send him to Yale or Princeton. His father lacked the money, so Brown went to the county seat and read law with a local attorney. Handsome and well built, with a fine sense of how to identify with and please his neighbors, he never

Albert Gallatin Brown, Mississippi's most successful antebellum politician. Brown represented the fire-eaters but ended his career suggesting Mississippians accept black voting rights. Courtesy of the Mississippi Department of Archives and History from the Albert Gallatin Brown Collection.

practiced much law, preferring political office to the courts. Barely twenty-one, his militia unit elected him colonel and, before long, general.

In 1835 he ran for the legislature supporting Jackson's campaign against the national bank but decrying the president's nationalist opposition to South Carolina's attempt to nullify the tariff law. Perhaps because his father was known to be an old Federalist turned Whig, he won with only the second highest vote total among the nine candidates. He never finished out of first place again in the many races of his career. The Mississippi House of Representatives elected him speaker pro-tem during his first term. In 1838 the Whigs in his district circulated a letter of instruction requiring him to vote for the Bank of the United States, acquiring the signatures of 750 of the 900 voters in his district. Such political ploys were common in this era when voters often insisted that their representatives had to take public advice. Brown returned to the district, resigned, and then ran for reelection with opposition to the bank as the sole issue, and he won back his seat with a 150-vote majority. Back in the House of Representatives, he voted to allow the Union Bank to issue post-notes in an effort to keep it afloat—the bank promised to pay the notes with interest in a year—and meantime the notes served as money with which planters could pay their debts. Brown owed the Union Bank $16,000 and had endorsed $50,647.05 for others. His father and brother owed similar amounts and had also endorsed additional debts. Of course, he backed McNutt's repudiation of the state's bond for the Union Bank when it failed.

The Democratic Party nominated McNutt for reelection in 1839 and Brown for Congress. Brown attacked the national Whigs as abolitionists because Clay had supported the Colonization Society and declared himself to be a strong states' rights man loyal to the Democratic Party, willing to follow its leaders obediently. In Congress, he quietly supported his party until the run—up to the presidential election of 1840 when he unleashed a masterful campaign speech against William Henry Harrison as the tool of the nabobs who lived in marble palaces and drank French wines. Democrats outside the state pleaded with him to speak for them against the Whigs, but he returned to campaign in Mississippi.

Thompson, his new congressional colleague, did the same. Thompson's father, a North Carolina Presbyterian, wanted him to become a minister for the church and sent him to the University of North Carolina to prepare for the ministry while keeping him in near poverty as befitted a clergyman. Thompson rebelled after graduating with honors and read law instead. Heading for Natchez to establish a practice, he stopped over in Columbus and altered his plan, settling instead in Pontotoc, headquarters for the land office where the Chickasaw lands were being sold and litigated. Flourishing in the dispute-rich environment, Thompson prospered and watched the north develop as he rode the circuit helping to organize it while practicing in the new county courts throughout the region. He had the opportunity to oppose the creation of the Union Bank in public meetings and used his foresight to run for state attorney general. Though defeated, he won heavily in north Mississippi, and for that reason the party nominated him for Congress in 1839. Winning easily, he transferred his headquarters to Oxford, where he wooed the fourteen-year-old daughter of the region's pioneer founder, who looked kindly on Thompson's marriage proposal and gave him a chest of gold as a wedding gift. Understanding that his beautiful but uneducated young bride would not be suited to life in Washington, Thompson took her to France for an education and polish before they began to live together as husband and wife. Meanwhile, he invested in land and slaves, established a plantation, and built a mansion in Oxford. On visits to Europe, he and his young wife bought furniture, crystal, china, and silverware to furnish their future home. Thompson supported McNutt's decision not to pay bondholders and defended the state from detractors in Congress over the embarrassment of not meeting its obligations. Strong on states' rights, he condemned the growth of abolitionist sentiments, advocated annexation of Texas, and favored secession early. With his young wife, his Washington home became a social success and enhanced his career in the capital.

Forty-six of the fifty-two antebellum Mississippi congressmen earned a living as lawyers or lawyer-planters. Many of them came to Mississippi—only three were born in the state—broke and taught school before becoming lawyers. Two edited newspapers. Fifty percent had college training, and nineteen held degrees, with more having a degree during the last two decades before the war. Thompson, Walker, and William S. Barry were the only three who earned honors for college work. As a group, they were not notably religious. Neither Poindexter nor Walker professed any religion. Quitman, who attended an Episcopal church, was never confirmed, according to his daughter. Jefferson Davis joined the Episcopal Church after he turned fifty. Congressmen who served after 1839 owned twice as many slaves as earlier members. Brown, who claimed to represent the common man, had one slave when elected in 1839, but held sixty-one in his last term in the U.S. Senate. Only John J. McRae owned fewer than fifteen slaves. Thirty-four of the fifty-two served in the military as officers because it was a rare man of any note who did not hold the title of at least major. Units elected officers, and once a man held a rank, no matter how briefly, he might be called captain or colonel for the rest of his life.

As Brown's and Thompson's biographies indicate, Mississippi's politicians consisted of men on the make. Although remaining Whigs, the nabobs withdrew from state politics in this period, depriving the state of some of its best-educated and wealthiest men as leaders. The clever lawyer Prentiss continued to lead Mississippi's Whigs in the 1840s, though he suffered financial losses in the depression following the Panic of 1837 and did not hold office again. He served as a presidential elector in 1840 and crossed the state and nation extolling the Harrison-Tyler ticket and explaining how the log cabin and hard cider image reflected the party leadership's western virtues. The Whigs energized the state with campaign stunts such as raising log cabins and providing a huge ball decorated with slogans to roll through the streets of Natchez. Despite the fact that the new Whig administration, which had won Mississippi, offered him no post in the new government, Prentiss returned to the fray with more enthusiasm in the 1844 election when his friend Clay ran for president, but Clay failed to carry Mississippi or the country. At about the same time, Prentiss lost a major case in the U.S. Supreme Court, affecting his already battered finances. As a result, in 1845 he relocated to New Orleans, and in a parting shot at his state for repudiating its debts in the Union Bank case, he called Mississippi "disgraced and degraded," declaring that he would not bring up his children in such an environment.

In 1841 Brown declined to run for reelection to Congress in order to avoid having to take a stand on repudiation. Instead he chose to stand for district judge as a safe cellar until the storm cleared. The Democrats had some difficulty finding a candidate to take the nomination for governor, knowing that he must repudiate the debt. The first nominee for governor left the state, and eventually Gwin, still operating the party from Vicksburg, found Tilghman M. Tucker, a state senator from Columbus who began life in Mississippi as a blacksmith before reading law. With the Democratic Party divided and many threatening to back the Whigs because they favored honoring the debt, the contest looked hopeless, but Tucker carried thirty-six counties to his opponent's twenty-one. Tucker's counties paid only $82,025 in taxes in 1841, whereas his opponent's counties paid $189,559. Clearly the mass of the poor wanted no part of the debt that the legislature created. With the party divided, Tucker endured a miserable administration. His state treasurer embezzled a large sum and escaped to Canada after his arrest. Tucker was the first governor to live in the new official mansion, but he and his wife disliked ceremony and high society so they disappointed the political class by rarely entertaining in it. The legislature passed a resolution inviting Union Bank bondholders to sue the bank and any responsible individuals, but denying the state's responsibility for the bonds, and Tucker signed it. Having determined the direction of the political wind, Brown set out to win the governor's office in 1843.

He began by manipulating Tucker to prevent the governor from announcing his intention to seek reelection while Brown organized his support. He hinted to J. F. H. Claiborne that he might expect a congressional appointment. He enlisted Thompson, who disliked Gwin heartily, and he won over McNutt, who, next to Gwin, was the most powerful leader in the party. McNutt angled for a Senate seat and wanted a governor who supported him, especially because the convention declined to name a candidate so far in advance of the election. The Tucker-Walker-Gwin wing of the Democrats renounced the work of the convention and called on Brown to withdraw, but Brown refused until newspapers built up pressure. A second convention obviously implemented backroom deals made by the feuding leaders. Brown got the governor's nomination and Tucker went to Congress, while the bond-payers headed by Quitman were ignored. The Whigs ran again on a platform committed to paying off the bonds and attacked Brown and his family for indebtedness and land speculation. Brown ignored the bond issue and declared a hard money policy while concentrating on national and international affairs, warning the British out of Oregon and the Mexicans out of Texas. Forced to take a stand on bonds, he called the Union bonds unconstitutional and the Planter's bonds legal, but declared that he would only pay the Planter's bonds from a surplus and would never raise taxes for that purpose. His middle stand won party support because it obscured the issue and meant the Democrats did not have to raise taxes to pay the bonds. Jefferson Davis, who entered politics during this period, adopted a similar tactic, calling on the courts to settle the debate without endorsing repudiation. Brown won the governor's race by the same margin as Tucker had.

In his inaugural address, Brown confined himself to state affairs such as public schools, but he advocated annexation of Texas and called on Mississippians to aid that cause vigorously. During his first term, Brown managed to terminate the Planter's Bank and get physical possession of the Union bonds to cancel them. The legislature denied his appeals for a state system of free schools and substituted local options for counties to create their own, but in playing the political game, he checked the Gwin-Walker element to create his own political machine. He favored the nomination of Jefferson Davis for a seat in the U.S. House of Representatives to keep Gwin out of that office and thwarted Gwin's and Walker's plans to move Gwin into Walker's Senate seat when Walker entered James K. Polk's cabinet as secretary of the treasury. Thompson defeated Gwin's campaign in the House of Representatives to have the national government take control over the debt owed the Chickasaw from the sale of their lands. After challenging Thompson to a duel, which was avoided through the work of Davis and others, Gwin moved to California and won his Senate seat there.

President Polk resided in Tennessee but owned a second plantation in Mississippi and fully sympathized with Mississippians' desires to expand slavery by annexing Texas. For that purpose, he led the United States into a war with Mexico. Mississippians volunteered in such numbers that the military could not accommodate them. Davis left Congress to serve, and the first Mississippi regiment elected him colonel. Quitman, who led volunteers to assist in the Texas revolution, received a commission as a general. When Brown initially could not get the U.S. Army to take more than one regiment from Mississippi, angry citizens burned him in effigy in front of the governor's mansion. All the aspiring lawyer-politicians desperately needed to serve, knowing it would make their political careers. Davis left his letter of resignation from Congress with his brother Joseph at Davis Bend to be sent to Governor Brown if the war went on long enough that it became necessary.

Davis had an advantage because his first father-in-law, Zachary Taylor, commanded the invasion. Taylor made certain that Davis and the Mississippi Rifles, as they were known, accompanied him and got into battle. In the initial fighting, Davis and his regiment performed well under Quitman's command. Davis rushed home as Taylor signed a temporary armistice that was later overturned by Washington. Davis had to settle his wife's unhappiness over his absence and ownership of their plantation (Joseph still held title to the land), but he also got a hero's welcome and boosted his political standing. Quitman seethed because Davis failed to mention him in his

Alexander M. Jackson, north Mississippi lawyer whose career demonstrated the ambitions and foibles of his class in the Mexican War and the politics afterward. From the Jackson (Alexander M.) Papers. Courtesy of the Dolph Briscoe Center for American History at the University of Texas at Austin.

Vicksburg speech or to visit the general's family in Natchez. Davis returned to the renewed war and again covered himself in glory. Appointed military governor of Mexico City, Quitman again lost the advantage of an early return to Davis. Polk offered Davis a promotion to general, but he chose the Senate seat offered by Brown instead.

Davis enjoyed more wealth and connections than most of the young men on the make. Alexander M. Jackson's experiences might have been more typical. Jackson came from an Alabama family, but after his father's death, he lived with relatives and did college work in Ohio. His sister in Holly Springs got him into a Whig congressman's office to read law. After he passed the bar, the short, gray-eyed, red-haired twenty-two-year-old moved to Ripley, the seat of nine-year-old Tippah County's government. He coedited a Democratic newspaper as he sought to establish a law practice. In the paper, he called Polk's election a triumph of democratic principles, opposed Tucker for Congress, supported Davis over Gwin, and urged the legislature to provide funds to clear the Tallahatchie for better cotton shipment.

As soon as the Mexican War began, Jackson organized the Tippah Guards, whose members elected him captain. At the same time, they chose as his first lieutenant William C. Falkner, another young Ripley lawyer whose great-great-grandson would change the spelling to Faulkner. The Tippah Guards did not get to Vicksburg in time to be included in the Mississippi Rifles and so had to wait for Brown to convince the military to authorize a second Mississippi regiment. Brown did, and the Tippah Guards left Ripley on Christmas of 1846. After an eighty-mile march, they reached Memphis New Year's Day 1847 to board a steamboat for Vicksburg, where they camped in cold, windy conditions to elect Reuben Davis as their colonel. Shipped to New Orleans, they camped on the site of the War of 1812 battle. At that point, Jackson and seven other captains had caught colds and/or pneumonia. The unit's soldiers gained a bad reputation in the city, where citizens accused them of disorderly behavior and crimes including rape and murder. The city assembled troops to protect itself from the Mississippians. Governor Brown came to review them, but probably did little to raise spirits because they boarded their transport vessels soaked to the bone and did not receive their uniforms and overcoats until January 29.

Twenty-five percent of the men were too sick to function when they reached Mexico. Assigned to occupation duties, the colonel had to order the Guards to fire on one of their units because they refused to drill after their captain had been arrested. They fought no battles, but smallpox broke out, and Jackson suffered from diarrhea so badly he was incapacitated. Falkner left camp against orders and was wounded. Despite his illness, Jackson hunted Falkner's attackers without success. Because of Falkner's wounds, Jackson allowed him to return to Ripley to heal, and Jackson later went to a New Orleans hotel to recover. Jackson's colonel resigned, and under the temporary command of another captain, the regiment lost all discipline with liquor in camp and regular brothel runs. Falkner returned from Ripley with another Guards member, and Jackson learned that a whispering campaign had been launched against him back home. After a disagreement with his superiors, Jackson avoided discipline by agreeing to resign. Ordered back home, he traveled back to the Guards and enlisted as private in defiance of the order, and his men reelected him captain. No doubt he and his men rejoiced to be able to march back into Ripley and out of the military.

In 1848 Ripley had a population of about 150 people, six of whom were lawyers. Jackson established a practice with Nathaniel S. Price, who had served in the state senate and became a judge. Most of their work consisted of suing people who failed to pay their notes, but it could be a rough life. Jackson had to pay a fine for fighting in court with another lawyer in Tishomingo County. Judges sometimes descended from the bench to join in the fistfights. Falkner killed the son of one of the older attorneys on the town square and did not go to trial because it seemed a fair fight. In 1851, when he killed a second man in an argument over a rental house, Falkner went to trial but was acquitted. In 1854 another lawyer barged into the Price/Jackson office and shot Price dead. Jackson found another partner, but never made as much money again. He bought and sold small pieces of land and occasionally slaves at small profits, but his real hope for success was in politics.

Jefferson Davis, Mississippi Democrat, senator, U.S. secretary of war, and president of the Confederate States of America. Courtesy of the Mississippi Department of Archives and History from the Jefferson Davis Collection.

Jackson assisted Jacob Thompson with his campaigns and supported Jefferson Davis in a run for governor, but Jackson became identified with the Brown machine. Jackson served in the State Rights Democratic Party and went to the national convention. Locally, he played a sizable role in the effort to get a railroad to Ripley. In 1852 he campaigned as an elector for Pierce, making a good showing with his campaign speeches. In 1854 the congressional delegation and Senator Brown put him up to be appointed consul in Cuba. Davis, who was growing more powerful and estranged from Brown, blocked it. In 1855, while on the central committee of the state party, he was nominated for a lucrative post as clerk for the Mississippi Superior Court of Chancery, but lost again. He received the appointment as consul to Constantinople, but turned it down. He tried to secure the nomination for Thompson's seat in Congress when Thompson retired, but L. Q. C. Lamar defeated him on the sixtieth ballot at the district convention. As a consolation, Thompson got Buchanan to appoint Jackson as secretary in the territorial government of New Mexico at $2,000 per year. He borrowed $500 from his new partner to finance the move.

Moving through Mississippi to points west persisted during the disappointment of the depression years and through the 1850s. Warren County even lost population in the 1850s as farms grew larger and those who failed to

Steamboats provided essential transportation for plantation development in antebellum Mississippi. Courtesy of the Mississippi Department of Archives and History from the Cooper Postcard Collection.

grow cotton moved west. Most farmers began to grow cotton. Even farmers with only fifty acres of improved land produced at least one bale of cotton each year. In 1850 slightly less than half made a bale, but by 1860 almost 70 percent did, while 91 percent of those with 100 improved acres made a bale or more. The spread of cotton to smaller farms boosted Mississippi's production to 20 percent of the world's total in 1860. Planters, who gained that status by owning around thirty slaves, made up only 20 percent of the white population. The remaining 80 percent mostly farmed, but of course there existed in that generalization a complexity difficult for a historian to convey.

The overseer worked for the plantation owners and filled a key position managing slaves, caring for their health, adjudicating disputes, and ordering the daily work schedule to make the crop. The typical overseer came from a yeoman family, had limited education, and had almost no personal property or a wife. Many migrated into the cotton region intending to work as an overseer only long enough to earn the money to buy their own land and slaves. Planters usually did not respect their overseers and certainly did not treat them as social equals; in fact, they looked down on them for the close association with slaves required by their occupation.

Rural whites made a living at a variety of nonfarm occupations. Even though Mississippians continued to press heavily on wildlife, enough game survived for hunting and freshwater fishing to persist as a livelihood for some. More herders took advantage of open range, which continued into the twentieth century in some parts of the state. Woodsmen could scrape out a living making charcoal or cutting wood to fuel the steamboats that operated on even some of the small streams of the state by the 1850s. The census records reveal a substantial landless white population in Mississippi. For example, in 1860, 39 percent of white families owned no land in Pontotoc County. Eighty percent of the landless had given up property in other states to move to Mississippi in order to join the scramble to become cotton farmers, but most of the landless moved on, looking elsewhere for an opportunity. Approximately two-thirds of the landless immigrants failed to improve their economic status by coming to Mississippi.

Land speculators often funded by money from New York or Boston impeded landownership in north Mississippi. The speculators bought the best land early and held on to their purchases through the depression, determined to make a profit. On the poorest land in the northeast corner of the state, squatters ignored legal title until the companies began to use local land owners to move the squatters out and lease the land to more reputable tenants. Tishomingo County had 40 percent landless farmers in 1850 and 30 percent in 1860. The myth was untrue that all whites owned land in antebellum Mississippi, but if whites became paupers, county governments cared for them relatively well compared to other states at the time. The state made poor relief a county responsibility, and counties adopted a system not unlike the one in England with poorhouses and what was referred to as "outdoor relief." Each county district or beat had a representative in the county's overseers of the poor who built a poorhouse if they wished to have one, provided medical care, buried dead paupers, and set the tax for the county. The poor consumed 30 percent of the county's taxes even though the legally poor only represented 0.1 percent of the population. Individuals cared for most paupers and then sought reimbursement from the overseers monthly, and they almost always paid. Perhaps their generosity grew out of the desire not to have whites utterly destitute in a society with a black slave majority.

Urban whites tended to be professionals such as lawyers, teachers, and doctors. It took little formal education to claim to be any of those. Local lawyers admitted applicants to the profession after a brief oral exam. The state had no effectual law to regulate the practice of medicine, and, as with Gideon Lincecum, individuals just declared themselves doctors, and their success depended on customer or patient satisfaction. The boundaries among the professions remained fluid. Reuben Davis tried doctoring but decided lawyers had an easier route to success. Stephen Duncan came to Natchez to practice medicine and became a planter and banker, which was common. Doctors and lawyers only wanted to practice long enough to buy land and slaves so that they could become planters. Ministers made the leap more rarely, but some such as James Smylie and William Winans did. Towns for the most part only existed in Mississippi to serve the countryside. Almost all of the clients for the professionals lived in the country, and a doctor spent much of time on the road to visit the ill on farms. Perhaps the most important town dweller was the commission agent. Agents in Mississippi generally worked for a house in New Orleans, Memphis, or Mobile, the three cities where all of Mississippi's cotton made its way for shipment. Plantation owners and farmers relied on agents to handle the shipment, insurance, warehousing, and sale of their crops. Without banks after the depression, the majority of cotton growers depended on agents to order the tools, furniture, and general supplies needed on the farm and to advance credit until growers made a crop. In essence, commission agents became the state's bankers, handling all the credit available.

Generalizations, such as those as attempted above, never give the full flavor needed to depict a society. For example, describing the entrance of settlers into the vacated Chickasaw land and the quick growth of Holly Springs ignores the story of Henry and Benjamin Love, who were brothers from a Tory family that took refuge among the Chickasaw to escape the American Revolution. Their father took three Chickasaw wives, but the sons invited Presbyterian missionaries to educate their children, converted, and limited themselves to one Chickasaw wife each. Allied with the Colberts, they helped negotiate the treaty giving up the Chickasaw land and then claimed the best sites such as Wyatt, the northernmost navigable point on the Tallahatchie River, and the site of Holly Springs for themselves and their children. They sold those sites for good profit and settled down on what became known as the Indian Reserve a short distance from Holly Springs. Henry's daughter married a white man, and with Henry's assistance they formed a real estate company to lay out the city and sell lots. Henry served on local government committees, and another daughter married a director of the new town's bank. But Henry's oldest son married his brother's daughter in Benjamin's home decorated with French wallpaper depicting Indians with bows and arrows in a forest surrounded by wild animals. When the U.S. Army built a fort on the Washita River to provide enough protection from the Kiowa, the Loves sold out their Mississippi holdings and took their families, including the new white members, to Indian Territory, where they built a small empire. Their story illuminated the complexity of antebellum Mississippi, which did not become solely a land of plantations and white farmers overnight. More than a few reminders of the past lingered. In his life of Sam Dale, a famous Indian fighter, J. F. H. Claiborne recalled Dale harboring and feeding Choctaw who gathered around his farm in Lauderdale County in 1841. He said that Dale admired the Choctaw and sympathized with their landless plight.

In his famous book *Flush Times of Alabama and Mississippi*, Joseph Glover Baldwin, who practiced law in both states before leaving for California, remembered Old Uncle John Olive, who loved to sit in the Kemper County courthouse listening to lawyers try cases understanding, Baldwin felt sure, almost none of what he heard. The seventy-five-year-old Olive stood about four-and-a-half-feet tall and had a gray, grizzled look. He claimed to be a "Hardshell" Baptist, but spent his life drinking enormous amounts of cheap whiskey. He lived in a shack in the woods indistinguishable from an earlier Indian house without another white person on his place. He owned fifteen slaves and worked six or seven hands growing cotton, but he was too ignorant to do it well. He made only a bale per hand, but had accumulated a fortune by refusing to spend any money. He and his slaves dressed in the same homespun cloth, and he hid his fortune in a chest under the floorboards of his shack. Statistics might make Olive a yeoman farmer marching toward becoming a planter, but his story was more complex.

Penetrating the void left by the lack of documents to tell the slaves' stories is the most frustrating aspect of antebellum Mississippi history, but the glimpses left reveal a more human story than the surviving documents predict. In the 1840s and 1850s more slaves worked on larger plantations, but that did not mean they all worked as field hands. Some large planters had steam engines running their gins and presses, and they trained slaves to operate them. Although white mechanics sometimes refused to train slaves to protect their own livelihoods, town slaves could be found doing every conceivable type of work. Railroads and steamboat companies employed slaves in transportation. The majority worked on plantations, but even there jobs changed over the seasons, and some slaves worked in the owners' homes.

The field slaves received their clothing between September and February, and most of it was rough, sturdy material either imported from England or the North or manufactured on the plantation. In the summer slaves went barefoot, but each fall the owner issued a sturdy pair of leather shoes but no socks. Slave children got a single garment resembling a long shirt. House slaves wore clothes handed down from the owners' family. Slaves ate corn and pork, as did all southerners. Most slaves received between three and four pounds of pork each week. Most owners allowed slaves to grow gardens and raise chickens to supplement their diet. Children had to make do with meat gravy, vegetables, and bread, leaving the meat for the men and women doing hard labor. Thompson's Lafayette County in-laws fed their slaves originally in a trough made from a hollowed-out tree. By the 1850s the grown slaves got metal plates, but the trough was still used for the children. Slave housing sometimes drew the most criticism from Yankee visitors, with poorer plantations still relying on log cabins, but more substantial planters built finished houses for their slaves, in some cases even brick structures. The furnishings consisted of beds, chairs, and boxes in all the houses. Plantation slave society developed a hierarchy with house servants at the top. Drivers, as the name suggests, oversaw the gangs in the fields setting the pace for hands.

As always, anomalies existed. In Amite County, James Brown fell in love with his slave Harriet and fathered four children by her. Such relationships happened because both slaves and masters were human beings, but in this case Brown lived with Harriet as his wife and invited white neighbors to dine with the family. He made his two sons, Francis and Jerome, masters of the plantation, and the slaves accepted them as required. The sons conducted business for Brown in Liberty, and, as they grew older, Brown took them to Ohio to free them and enrolled them in school in Indiana. He visited them there, and when he aged too much to make the journey, Francis and Jerome returned to Mississippi to visit their parents. Brown registered his will at the courthouse, leaving his property to be divided among Harriet and their children, but when he died, James's brother, John, filed for an injunction against the sale of the property and the distribution of the assets. The court found for the brother, making his sister-in-law and his brother's offspring John's slaves.

James Green Carson decided to free his slaves out of religious conviction, but needed a profession to support his family, so he went to Pennsylvania to obtain medical training. Finding that he could not legally free his slaves in Mississippi, he sent one to Liberia at the cost of $5,000. Deciding that he could not afford to free them in that manner, he surrendered his ambition to the law and moved his plantation to new land in Louisiana to continue planting. It is difficult to believe that such an owner treated his slaves in the usual manner of other slaveholders.

The lives of slaves continued to depend on the patriarch. Lewis Weathersby, also of Amite County, left a will dividing his slaves between his sons with provisions that land and animals be provided for certain slaves to farm independently and that the adult children of one couple be allowed to purchase their freedom in order to care for their parents in their old age. The sons tried to carry out their father's wishes, but other family members went to court to break the will. When one son died they got control of the slaves, and after long litigation the slaves became the property of minor children. The guardians hired out the slaves and kept careful records of the purchases and of the education of these slaveholders-in-training, who were supported from the income generated by their slave property. Weathersby was born in 1762 and died in 1843, so it would appear that he may have held more of a frontier attitude. As a rule, the further removed from the frontier owners were, the less they perceived slaves as fellow human beings. In Weathersby's case, there may have been a family relationship because some of the slaves were described as "yellow." Yet Joseph and Jefferson Davis, separated by only twenty years in age but having different childhood experiences, developed different attitudes about slavery. Joseph remembered facing the Indians in Georgia with their few slaves carving a living out of the wilderness, while Jefferson grew up on an early plantation in Mississippi with no Indian threat and more slaves about him, but with a slave relationship that was less personal.

Generalizations prove dangerous. General Hinds left his sons plantations in Jefferson County and among the slaves, a family named Collier. Holt Collier grew up caring for the family's hunting hounds and watching his father and Howell Hinds drink themselves insensible on night hunts, which convinced Collier never to drink. When the Hinds brothers moved to the Delta to start a new plantation in 1856, they took Collier with them and made him responsible for feeding the plantation from the game he killed. Given a pony and a twelve-gauge shotgun, he shot until one shoulder became too sore, then switched to the other. He learned to be such a marksman that Hinds took him to quail matches between Mississippi and Kentucky, winning large bets by pitting Collier against the rich sportsmen along the way—once $1,000 in gold. Hinds tried to enroll Collier in a Kentucky school once with some relatives caring for him, but Collier slipped off to the woods and refused to attend. Hinds traveled the country with Collier throughout the North, visiting the leading vacation spots of the age. Northerners often tried to induce Collier to leave his owner, and once he became so disturbed by their taunts that he told Hinds about it. Hinds told him that he was in a free state and he could stay if he wished, but Collier responded that he had no desire to leave his life with Hinds. In this instance, Collier led a relatively comfortable life as a slave, and one suspects that he had formed the sort of the personal bond that Toney developed with the Hutchins family in the frontier era. Collier did similar work as a hunter, and it would be difficult to equate his life to that of a cottonfield hand.

Mississippi passed increasingly restrictive laws to control the always growing population of slaves. In 1831 the legislature decreed that all free blacks, who seemed to be more feared than slaves, had to leave the state except for those licensed by counties to remain because respectable whites vouched for them. Of course, some wealthy free blacks understood the direction, sold out, and left Mississippi. One Natchez widow took her family to Peru. The laws expressed the growing fear of the white community, which held the laws in reserve in case they needed them but rarely enforced them. Woodville, for example, passed a law that no black residing in town or country could be on the streets of the city on Sunday for worship or visiting purposes without written permission from their owner. The city government decreed that the slave patrol or town constable would administer twenty lashes to those breaking the law. Slave owners protected their slaves, and any such harm to one of their slaves would have brought the owner's wrath down on the city. Three years later the city enacted the same law, but threatened to fine the owners of those slaves who violated it.

In 1841 the city confirmed the law and empowered the town constable to summon four citizens for up to twelve-hour patrols, but four years later the government issued a plea for cooperation, noting that the streets filled with trading carts and drunken slaves every Sunday. In 1847 the newspaper published a protest against Sunday trading and gambling by blacks and noted a noisy Jewish wedding that attracted the participation of a large group of slaves who disturbed the leading citizen with loud partying in the streets at midnight. The newspaper's protest concluded with a rhetorical question: why tax for a patrol when it did no good? Vicksburg had the same problem and built a workhouse in 1851, threatening to lock up any slave found on the streets after nine o'clock in the evening and then to charge owners a fine to retrieve them. That may have been somewhat more successful, but illicit black trading, gambling, and drinking continued until, in 1854, Vicksburg closed all city shops on Sunday. Slaves crowded establishments outside the city limits in response. Nothing seemed to change the strong tradition that Sunday served as the slave population's one day for rest, relaxation, and trade for their own profit. One suspects that owners tacitly approved their slaves' defiance of the law in order to have a more satisfied and pliable workforce on Monday mornings.

Free blacks in Mississippi enjoyed a precarious independence. By 1840 the Mississippi Supreme Court had ruled that a slave had no inherent rights, only those granted to him or her by the legislature. All that differentiated a slave from a free black in the eyes of the law was the free black's ability to own property. Free blacks could not testify against whites in court, vote, hold office, serve in the militia, or violate the unwritten social code that relegated them to an inferior position. Most free blacks in Mississippi lived in and around Natchez. Vicksburg only had 29 free blacks in 1860, while Natchez had 208. As Natchez's economic role declined and it became politically impotent, both the slave and free black population of the city increased. Some free "blacks" inherited wealth and slaves from their white fathers, while others earned their fortunes by skill and hard work in order to buy slaves, but most free blacks remained poor, working as peddlers, prostitutes, unskilled laborers, fishermen, or woodcutters. In the summer of 1841 the lower- and middle-class white citizens of Natchez opened what was called locally the "Inquisition" against the free black population. Vigilante committees accused free blacks of harboring abolitionist ideas and "deported"

The preservation of the William Johnson house in Natchez symbolized the recognition of a more complex history than the one generated by the original Natchez pilgrimage. Courtesy of the National Park Service.

considerable numbers. The nabobs supported the free blacks by signing statements of good character for them and moderated the damage to the free black community, but manumission of slaves, which had been over 100 between 1824 and 1840, dropped to under 10 for the next decade.

The most famous free black person in Natchez was William Johnson, who left a diary. Johnson operated a barbershop in the heart of the city and served the elite both in the shop and in their homes by appointment. Johnson adopted the code of honor that his clients lived by as his own. He did business with them, making handshake deals, loaning whites as well as blacks money, and he eventually bought his own plantation. He owned slaves, whipped them as whites did, and frowned on the entertainments such as "darkie" balls presented by whites for blacks in hotels and other venues. Johnson lived a lonely life as a result, but helped to found an elite "black" society in the city. His favorite pastimes were riding each afternoon and less frequently hunting and fishing. In 1851 Baylor Winn, a mulatto, murdered Johnson as he rode back to town from his plantation. Winn owned a small farm adjoining Johnson's property, and they had been involved in a long boundary dispute. A black companion riding with Johnson saw the crime, but Winn claimed to be white and thus protected from the companion's testimony. Winn's claim rested on the fact that he had voted and held some minor county office. Johnson's family hired researchers to prove Winn's racial status, but eventually the court chose not to admit that evidence and concluded that he was white based on his claims and set him

Alexander Keith McClung, Whig politician, Mexican War hero, and professional duelist who took his own life in a Jackson hotel. Courtesy of the Mississippi Department of Archives and History.

free. Thus Johnson died at the hands of a "white" man, and because he was black, neither the white legal system nor the men he had known and done business with all his life saw any need to demand justice for his murder.

The elite male honor code proved a flimsy reed to lean on when a poorly developed legal system failed to protect Tippah County lawyers or Natchez barbers, and it harbored some disturbed individuals. Alexander Keith McClung may be the best example. Originally from Kentucky, McClung served in the U.S. Navy briefly, but the navy discharged him for dueling. In his twenties, he emerged as a not too successful lawyer in Jackson who seemed to be acquainted with most of the leading lawyers and politicians. He served as Foote's second in Foote's duel with Prentiss. McClung killed General Augustus Albert Allen on the banks of the Pearl River in a fight in which they used several pistols and large knives. He killed John Menefee, the brother of a Kentucky congressman, in Vicksburg after an incident during a swimming outing in the Pearl and a fight in a Jackson pool hall. He shot Menefee with a rifle, which was probably not a duel. McClung was described as cold-blooded. Active in politics, he served as a Whig elector for Harrison, and, as a result, the president appointed him U.S. marshal for north Mississippi. He resigned when Polk won the presidency and at this point had probably killed ten men.

Reuben Davis described blundering into a Jackson restaurant one evening with two other politicians known not to be McClung's friends. McClung had already cleared the room and sat drinking wine with a pistol on the table. The waiters had gathered in the street outside. Davis described

Reuben Davis commanded the second Mississippi regiment in the Mexican War, went on to serve in Congress as a fire-eater and, after Reconstruction, to challenge the Democratic Party establishment.

being afraid to leave because McClung would have considered their departure an insult. After a drink, the three men backed carefully out of the restaurant, eyeing the waiters who had allowed them to fall into a deadly situation. The Mississippi Rifles elected McClung lieutenant colonel, second in command to Jefferson Davis. McClung served gallantly, suffering severe wounds, and was awarded a sword for bravery in battle. In 1849 President Taylor sent McClung to Bolivia as an American diplomat. He returned to Jackson in 1851 followed by a rumor that he had killed two men in Bolivia. The next year the Whig Party chose him to deliver the eulogy when Clay died, marking him as one of the leading men of the party. In 1855 he dressed well, set his polished boots at his bedside, lay in his hotel bed, and shot himself in the head.

With such players, Mississippi politics called for men with nerve. As the leading Mississippi heroes of the Mexican War, Davis and Quitman held a strong claim for advancement. Brown recognized the inevitable when he appointed Davis to the Senate, as we have already seen. Davis's colleague in the Senate was Henry S. Foote. Foote, aside from dueling with Prentiss and others, wrote a history of Texas, published newspaper articles, and served as a presidential elector with Davis in 1844. The legislature had to pass special legislation to exempt Foote, who came from Alabama after being disbarred for fighting a duel, from the prohibition against duelists holding office. Foote had just been elected in 1847 to a full term in the Senate before Brown appointed Davis to serve two years of a deceased senator's term. Brown, having no Senate seat available, went back to the House of Representatives for the southern district. Quitman would have to content himself with the governor's office in 1849.

Southern politics had been transformed by a little known Pennsylvania congressman, David Wilmot, in 1846 when he proposed the admission of Texas as a slave state, but asked to exclude slavery from any other territory acquired from Mexico. His proposal caught fire and eventually passed the House, but not the Senate, and yet it would not die because of opposition to the war and growing abolitionist sentiment in the North. Before leaving the governor's office, Brown condemned any interference with slaveholders' rights to extend slavery and like John C. Calhoun claimed extension to the territories as a constitutional right. After taking his seat in Washington, he continued a vociferous defense of the South, its recent conquests, and states' rights. Davis, while shoring up his chances to win a full term in two years, launched a spirited defense of slavery as the only means of allowing whites and blacks to live peacefully together, claiming southern slaves were better cared for than free blacks in the North or freed British slaves in the Caribbean. He argued for a compromise, but not one that sacrificed the territory recently won by the blood of southern heroes. Davis and Foote, who campaigned together for Polk in 1844, who traveled to Washington on the same steamboat, and who lodged together in the same rooming house, suddenly came to blows on Christmas morning 1847 during an argument in the sitting room of their boardinghouse.

Such a break proved serious. Men dueled and died over less. Foote further enraged Davis, who chaired the committee required to report on the president's nomination of Quitman for major general. A West Point graduate, Davis believed giving a militiaman such a promotion was wrong. Foote forced the nomination out of committee, and the Senate confirmed Quitman over Davis's objections. Despite the break between the senators and the fact that north Mississippi wanted a senator and opposed Davis to get one, Davis easily won a full term in January 1848 because the Whigs supported him. Quitman wanted the presidency or at least the vice presidency in 1848, but got neither. Back at Monmouth, he had to prove his Democratic Party credentials by serving as an elector for Lewis Cass instead. Cass failed to win, and the South quickly lost any hope for Whig president Taylor, who seemed to be implementing the never-passed Wilmot Proviso by admitting California as a free state.

In running unopposed for reelection to the House, Brown warned his constituents of an impending crisis brought on by denying southerners the new territories, by abolishing slavery in the District of Columbia, and ultimately by the abolition of slavery. He asked for instruction because he thought that "unsheathing the sword in defense" would be the only option other than abject surrender. Quitman joined him and other southern congressmen in issuing an appeal to both parties to unite as representatives of the South against the national government. Quitman attended a states' rights convention in Jackson led by his old nullifier friends and launched his campaign for governor. The Whigs backed him as an old probond man, and he carried forty-six of the fifty-eight counties.

Quitman, looking beyond his state, delivered an inaugural speech addressing the North's attempt to dominate the South. He likened the impending subjection of the South to Ireland's position in the British Empire or Poland's in the Russian state and found it intolerable to accept an inferior status. An unusually young and receptive legislature referred his concerns to committee and endorsed his analysis, offering $250,000 to preserve the state's constitutional rights and suggested that he call a convention to consider the state's course should an impending meeting of southern representatives in Nashville advise action against northern aggression. The congressional delegation contacted Quitman and asked him to confer with the legislature on the course to be taken. Quitman and the legislature responded by choosing delegates to go to Nashville, where they hoped the southern states would map a plan for concerted action against the federal government. Quitman became a veto governor and quickly tired of administration, packed his family off to Natchez, and went to New Orleans to help organize a Cuban expedition dedicated to seizing the island for unification with the United States as a slave state.

Quitman had met with Narcisco Lopez at the Mississippi governor's mansion as Lopez made his way south, and Lopez offered Quitman the leadership of a filibustering expedition to invade Cuba. Quitman considered it, contacting some fellow veterans from the Mexican War, but eventually turned it down. He did, however, provide Lopez contacts and stayed in touch with him through Louisiana senator James Henderson, an old friend. Quitman probably agreed to lead a reinforcing expedition if Lopez could pull off a landing and rally the Cubans to him. The secret leaked as Quitman's friends began to contact him for a place in his new command, and newspapers spread the tale across the country. As Lopez left for Cuba, Quitman returned to Jackson and went over to the Yazoo River to survey a site for a new plantation. When he returned from the wilderness, he learned Lopez's expedition had been a complete disaster. Quitman wined, dined, and boarded some of the filibusters at the mansion again, but still declined to take command of the project. Lopez had escaped Cuba and returned to New Orleans, where the government arrested him for violating U.S. neutrality laws. His legal defense team, including Henderson and Prentiss, developed a strategy to have Lopez incriminate so many prominent Americans that the government would abandon the case. Thus a grand jury indicated Governor Quitman, who reacted angrily because he thought there was nothing wrong with what he did. He believed that the nation stood on the precipice and thought that he could lead it back from the edge by some dramatic adventure abroad or at home. If the invasion of Cuba failed, he hoped to lead a force into New Mexico in cooperation with Texas, which was threatening to annex a portion of the new territory. As Quitman tried to delay his trial to be able to lead southern resistance, President Taylor died, and Millard Fillmore became president, helping to further a series of compromises worked out in Congress. Furious at what he considered a betrayal of southern interests, Quitman convened the Mississippi legislature and asked it to consider withdrawal from the Union. Quitman took to the stump to convince Mississippians to support him.

In Vicksburg, he encountered Senator Foote, one of the prime movers in crafting the Compromise of 1850. Bald and five feet seven inches tall, the boisterous Foote challenged the distinguished-looking, tall, gray-haired Quitman to a debate in Jackson before the legislature arrived. Quitman agreed, but a malaria attack sent him to bed for weeks. Foote launched a speaking tour for the compromise and called for a Union Party to support the legislation and avoid secession. Quitman's hometown, a reservoir of Whig sentiment, supported Foote, and a convention of unionists in Jackson urged Foote to run for governor to eliminate Quitman's control of state government. Large crowds greeted Foote as he made a swing around the state. Back on his feet, Quitman sent the legislature a message that stopped just short of calling for secession, and he corresponded with South Carolina's governor to coordinate a joint secession of the two states. The legislature craftily passed legislation to convene a convention, but not until a year later. At this juncture, a Mississippi district judge issued a warrant for Quitman's arrest on the filibustering charge. Quitman agonized over his course of action. Should he bow to federal power or fight on as governor of his sovereign state? He was always inclined to fight, but advisers convinced him that the legal complications would do much harm, so he resigned, knowing his replacement would be another fire-eater. His resignation made him a martyr for the fire-eater cause. Jefferson Davis praised Quitman in the

Senate and criticized his prosecution, wondering why the federal government could not show the same diligence in returning runaway slaves. While Quitman journeyed to New Orleans to be feted and tried, Foote continued to organize the Union Party in Mississippi. Thus the campaigning for the elections of 1851 began in the fall of 1850. The legislature set up two elections. The first, for the convention, would be in September, and the second, for the governor's office and other state offices, would be in November.

Brown opposed the Compromise of 1850, but said that he opposed it to save the Union. He reasoned that the compromise would destroy the Union and argued for the South to demand equality in the territories and for the federal government to change its policy to protect slavery. He too crisscrossed the state during the congressional recess in the fall of 1850, adding his third way to the turbulent babble of discontent.

Foote spoke widely across the North and became the southern champion of the compromise. Taking leave without resigning from the Senate, he returned to Mississippi to accept the governor's nomination from a coalition of Whig and Democratic supporters called Unionists. They presented him with a bay horse and buggy to use in his travels around the state, and he toured the state from April to November.

Back in Natchez, Quitman organized county states' rights groups and corresponded with allies in South Carolina, urging them to secede first. Worried by Brown's talk of saving the Union and noticing that other politicians adopted safer language, Quitman returned to Jackson in May for a massive barbecue, where speakers praised him for winning an empire only to be persecuted by the federal government from which he would save the South. The barbecue concluded with a torchlight parade and a glittering ball. Quitman stayed over another day to debate Foote in the capitol's House of Representatives chamber.

Davis traveled from Washington to Brierfield, but paused only briefly, despite his wife's pleas, before leaving for Jackson and his speaking tour. Davis, elevated to leader of the Mississippi States' Rights Democrats (as they now labeled themselves), took the position that Mississippi should boycott northern goods and build up its industry so as to become more economically independent. While he recognized the right of secession, he never advocated it, stressing instead that it was not yet justified. He traveled and spoke with Brown and other congressmen for five weeks before returning to Jackson for the state convention of the States' Rights Democrats. Davis strove to dismiss the impression that the party stood for secession, and the nominations committee wanted him to accept their nomination for governor. He agreed if Quitman would consent. Quitman absolutely refused and Davis conceded the nomination to him, but wrote a platform denying the party's intention to secede. Returning to the speaking trail with Brown until mid-July, when he collapsed from exhaustion, Davis returned to Brierfield and suffered a severe eye infection.

Quitman tried, on the advice of his friends, to moderate his rhetoric as Brown had, but he could not maintain any subterfuge. The Union Party press got hold of some of his South Carolina correspondence and laid out his secessionist views in print. In June and July Foote and Quitman launched a traveling series of forty-eight debates across the state. Foote adopted a slash-and-burn style, mocking the ineptness of Quitman's speaking style and even criticizing Quitman's sore throat at one stop. Foote told the crowds that there had been threats on his life and insinuated that Quitman was behind them. Violence threatened their debates, with guns drawn by their supporters in Holmes County. It degenerated with Foote accusing Quitman of providing the Cuban filibusters with arms from the state militia supplies, which Quitman denied. At a later appearance when Foote repeated the charge, Quitman labeled the statement scandalous, false, and ungentlemanly. Foote lunged at Quitman and struck a glancing blow while the general landed a punch and kicked his opponent. Foote carried a black and blue bruise on his forehead for a month. Quitman took this as an opportunity to abandon his losing debate series and undertook a grueling tour of the state through all but his home base around Natchez. He usually rode into town on a white charger, and supporters engineered cannon salutes to whip up crowds, but friends began to warn him that he had forged too far ahead of public opinion on secession.

The Union Party carried the convention election by 57 percent and a 7,000-vote majority. The convention would have two unionists for every secessionist selected. Quitman did best in the piney woods, where farmers held the fewest slaves in the state, and worst in the river counties, where the wealthiest slaveholders believed his southern nationalism to be a danger to their extensive property. Quitman finally understood that the people opposed secession and that he would not win the election for governor. He sent a note to the *Natchez Free Trader* respectfully recognizing the "will of the people" and announcing his departure from the governor's race. The party turned to Davis, still recuperating at home, to challenge Foote, and he accepted, resigning his Senate seat and blasting Foote for keeping his.

Davis hated and despised Foote. He had contemplated challenging him to a duel when he heard reports that Foote had bragged about striking him in their Christmas Day fight in the boardinghouse. Only the mediation of Brown and Walker prevented the duel. They probably convinced Davis that killing Foote would sully his reputation because Foote was a notoriously bad shot. From Brierfield, Davis issued campaign material stressing his loyalty to the Union but condemning the Compromise of 1850. Still not well, he took to the stump in October and spoke throughout the northern counties. He closed the gap to 999 votes, but Foote won the governor's office and control of the Mississippi House of Representatives.

Foote returned to the Senate to spread the word of his victory and Mississippi's loyalty to the Union. Davis went back to his plantation and continued to enlarge and improve it. In an unusual event in 1851, he and Joseph armed their slaves and led them to stop construction of a cutoff that would have turned Davis Bend into Davis Island. The Davis-Foote battle continued by proxy in the state's newspapers and in the legislature, with Foote controlling the House and Davis the Senate. Foote proved to be an inept governor and alienated many. He intended to return to the Senate, but the legislature elected nonentities—one Whig and one Unionist. Unionist representatives elected along with Brown helped to moderate his opposition to the compromise in Washington, but the unionists failed to create a viable party, and the Democrats quickly returned to power.

Davis remained active in the party and backed Pierce for president, earning an appointment to the cabinet as secretary of war in 1853. Foote, having failed to persuade the legislature to elect him senator, ran for governor again and lost to John J. McRae, a States' Rights Democrat from east-central Mississippi. Enraged by Davis's advancement and his rejection, Foote resigned before the end of his term and migrated to California, where he would later come within one vote of winning back a Senate seat. The 1853 election also saw William Barksdale, who had campaigned for the compromise and gone to the convention as a pro-Union representative, nominated by the Democrats on an appeal to forget the split and reunite the party. Barksdale survived Reuben Davis who, while attempting to split the party again, knifed Barksdale in a fight at one of their debates. Reuben Davis ran as an independent but withdrew to take a lucrative job as a railroad lawyer. Mississippi's Whigs ceased to offer any opposition to the Democrats and the Know-Nothing, or American, Party replaced the Whigs briefly as the main opposition to the Democrats. Oddly in 1855, the party nominated a Pontotoc lawyer, who ran as a fire-eater for the convention and lost. His main qualification seemed to be that his family descended from Huguenots, who did not like Catholics. McRae won reelection overwhelmingly.

The new divide in the Mississippi Democratic Party developed between Brown and Davis. Brown resented Davis getting all the credit for the revival of the party, claiming that the party rallied around his lone States' Rights Democratic district in 1853. Davis, he said, got his easy chair, champagne, and $8,000 a year in Washington while he rode the piney woods in ninety-degree heat, ate miserable food, and drank rotgut. Davis wanted to go back to the Senate in 1854, but Brown's miles in the woods paid off, and he defeated Davis in the Democratic caucus by two votes. Brown and Davis nurtured a disdain for one another, with Brown complaining to his friends of Davis's condescension. They did not speak to one another for some time but gradually did reach at least that level of civility. In 1855 Quitman won a seat in the U.S. House of Representatives, and while he did not like Davis, he did not view Brown as an equal either. In 1856 Brown and Thompson tried to deny Davis the Senate seat again, but Davis had made good use of the patronage available through the war office and he, like Brown earlier, won by two votes in the caucus. The next year Brown got sixty-eight of the eighty caucus votes to ensure his reelection to the Senate. Brown had reached the peak of his career with a good friend as adviser to the new president and Thompson in the cabinet as secretary of the interior.

Brown represented the common white man throughout his career. He favored a homestead bill, and at the end of the Mexican War he held that the government should offer land grants to the citizens who won its empires. He believed in American acquisition of Cuba, of additional Mexican land, and of Central America in order to spread the blessings of slavery and religion. Unlike radical fire-eaters, Brown opposed reopening the African slave trade because to do so would stop white immigration and crowd out whites already in the South. In Senate debates, he denounced Davis for being too moderate on slavery in the territories and grew more radical after his second election to the Senate when he felt safe to espouse his views more openly. After Quitman's death, Brown became the most radical fire-eater in the Mississippi congressional delegation, and eventually he reduced his appeals to race, warning his Mississippi audiences that the North would not stop short of abolition and that abolition would lead to blacks murdering whites and raping their women.

In the 1850s a series of national issues inflamed animosities between the North and South. In the early 1850s the debate over the Kansas-Nebraska Act renewed the territorial slavery question and northern opinion hardened against slavery, while in the South the public felt further alienated. The Republican Party gained ground with the demise of the Whigs and frightened southerners with its militant antislavery message. As settlers fought to make it either slave or free, "Bleeding Kansas" kept the rhetoric at a boil. Preston Brooks's severe caning of Charles Sumner on the floor of the Senate and the outpouring of southern support for Brooks by 1856 indicated a nation divided and drifting toward increasing violence.

Mississippians heard only one side of the debate because all of the state's newspapers, Whig or Democrat, made no attempt at independent reporting and agreed in supporting slavery and condemning the abolitionists. Foote had left the state, and other Unionists returned to the Democratic Party as the only viable pathway to public office. Mississippi ministers preached that God ordained slavery as the natural and proper status for black people and that slave owners did God's work in owning slaves. Bishop William Winans, a slaveholder, ran against Brown for Congress as a Whig in 1849 and dared to say, as he had been saying for decades, that slavery was a moral evil, to which Brown retorted that Winans was an abolitionist.

Believing that God created black people to be slaves did not mean to antebellum Christians that God had abandoned blacks. On the contrary, the Methodists and Baptists, which were the largest denominations, held that converting slaves and seeing to their needs constituted their most important missions. Compared to the frontier era, more Mississippians belonged to churches—in 1860 one out of three—and three-fourths were Methodist or Baptist. By 1860 Mississippians had built 1,441 churches—a quarter of those in the 1850s. Churches and churchgoing existed less in the southeastern part of the state and only a few Methodist missions to slaves had made it into the Delta, but in the rest of the state, church members no longer separated themselves from mainstream society, primarily because of increased economic prosperity and a decline of church discipline on their white members. Camp meetings still existed, but most people worshipped in church buildings in the 1850s. Remaining camp services usually had eliminated the bodily manifestations of spiritual possession common in earlier times. Larger churches had established libraries and operated Sunday schools. Church groups organized temperance societies, sewing societies, and fairs to raise money for the church and mission work.

In 1856 the Mississippi Baptist Convention passed a resolution stating that, wherever enough slaves lived to justify it, a full-time missionary should be hired to serve them. Many Baptist churches reported large slave majorities. In 1846 the Natchez Baptist church reported sixty-two whites in a congregation of 442. In Columbus, four-fifths of the members were slaves. The Baptist had to admonish their white members not to trade on Sunday as the black members mixed their church attendance with sales of foodstuffs and handicrafts. Church records filled with accounts of slaves repenting of their sins and repeatedly being readmitted to the fellowship. In some instances, the white members refused to pass judgment and turned the repenting member over to his or her fellow slave members for a verdict. In 1861 the Mississippi Baptist Convention described its missionary work with slaves as its most important mission. Slaves too sought to spread the gospel. When a Methodist minister appealed to the Yazoo Methodist congregation to assist his brother in China, the black members contributed $21 to support him. In 1858 the Mississippi Methodist Conference urged plantation owners to build churches instead of using the floors of their cotton gins for services and to attend along with their families and overseers. Baptists married slave members in church and admonished slave owners that it was a sin to separate husbands and wives. Living with slaves, worshipping with them, and being concerned for their welfare convinced Mississippi church people that northerners failed to understand either them or their slaves. In the minds of Mississippians, they had rescued slaves from paganism and were caring for them as God intended they should.

Churches also created academies and colleges such as Oakland and Mississippi College. In this period, churches played a major role in what was taught in all schools. Ministers often also worked as teachers. The state had no system of public schools, but counties provided mostly ungraded schools to teach the basics of reading, writing, and arithmetic. When the state opened the University of Mississippi in 1848, the board argued over whether to hire a secular scholar or a religious chancellor. The secularists won and hired an Englishman, who tried to introduce a progressive honors code instead of the normal rigid discipline. He quickly left to be replaced by a Methodist minister-planter chancellor, who brought his fire-eating son-in-law, L. Q. C. Lamar, to Oxford as a professor. His replacement as chancellor faced an uproar for dismissing a student who attacked his female slave in his home. The contention came from his acceptance of the slave's testimony over the word of a white student.

In 1851, as the debate over secession raged, a man, upset about the accusation that Oakland College's president had dismissed a student for favoring secession, attacked the president outside his home with a whip and then stabbed him to death. By the late 1850s school boards began to declare they would refuse to hire Yankee teachers. Mississippians sought to ban or destroy books and pamphlets advocating abolition as seditious materials. Newspapers reported *Appleton Cyclopedia* sales agents being threatened and barred from selling their books because the townspeople feared they might contain offensive material. Newspapers in this period called for the adoption of southern textbooks to protect students. Nothing existed in the educational institutions of the state to challenge the worldview of the fire-eaters.

The fire-eaters made up the progressive, forward-looking element of the community. They embraced the development of the state's rail system and proved to be its major promoters. Some plantation owners even built sections of the track across their land. The extension of the Jackson-Vicksburg railroad east to Brandon, for example, showed dramatic results. In 1851, before the railroad reached the area, farmers shipped 7,500 bales of cotton, but in 1853 with the rails, they made 12,000 bales. Mississippians saw railroads as the means to spread cotton and slavery into the areas of the state still untouched by cotton culture. Even as they worried about the North's assault on slavery, they sought to continue the phenomenal expansion of their economy.

In 1859 John Jones Pettus of Scooba, who hovered on the borderline of planter and farmer with twenty-four slaves and who had almost no formal education, ran for governor as a devoted fire-eater. Like Brown, he used images of slave rebellion—he referred to the Jamaica riots to impress his audiences with the need to resist northern aggression—leading to abolition. He left no doubt that he intended secession as the ultimate cure for the crisis facing the South. He won all but three counties in the state. A month before Pettus's inauguration, John Brown raided the federal arsenal at Harper's Ferry as a prelude to arming slaves for a rebellion against their southern masters. In his inaugural address, Pettus spoke of the impending armed conflict and assured the capitol audience that the South would win because it possessed double the population and twenty times the resources of the original thirteen colonies, neglecting to mention the vastly superior men and resources of the North. The Christmas season abounded with rumors of John Brown's agents and of planned uprisings.

In response, Pettus asked the legislature to pass a law ordering the arrest of all free blacks who did not leave the state by July 1 of the following year. The legislature complied and furthermore removed the right of free blacks to own property. If they remained in the state, they would be reenslaved. Pettus inventoried the state's supply of arms and munitions, asked the legislature for more, and with its approval ordered 4,000 muskets. Unknown outside the state before his election as governor, Pettus quickly established correspondence with other southern governors in order to organize resistance. In Washington, Lamar charged in the House of Representatives that Republicans had conspired with John Brown to carry out his raid. When the southern delegations walked out of the national Democratic nominating convention, Pettus ordered several thousand rifles with bayonets attached. Militia units called for arms faster than he could deliver them. During the presidential election, Pettus called for abandoning the celebration of July 4, which had been declining in significance throughout Mississippi during the 1850s.

The entire congressional delegation campaigned for the sectional, secessionist candidate for president and agreed that Abraham Lincoln's victory would be cause for secession. Foote returned from California to practice law in Vicksburg again, but devoted himself to campaigning for the Union candidate for president, challenging any opponents to debate. Every other politician stayed well clear of him, only following in his wake to repudiate his views. Brown said the Union was dead and all that remained was to bury the carcass, which Pettus proceeded to try to do by calling the legislature into session and sending delegates to other southern states to coordinate secession. Pettus dismissed Davis's, Brown's, and Thompson's suggestion to slow the process and await developments. The Whigs proposed a giant opposition rally in Vicksburg, but only four counties sent representatives, and the Whig demonstration ended with a whimper. In Washington, Mississippi, Walies wrote that Pettus was a "miserable demagogue" and despaired for his state. Cooperationists did emerge from both parties, and one of them penned a brief play depicting Pettus in an insane asylum quoting the Bible and raving about secession. The play's conclusion described the governor's mental disease as an epidemic raging through the state's population. Learning that President Buchanan had ordered the completion of a fort on Ship Island and realizing that the fort would threaten Mississippi's commerce and its coastline, Pettus seemed to pause as if the enormity of what he was doing had sunk in. He asked Jefferson Davis if he should postpone action on "disunion." Davis replied: "We should not halt, least of all hesitate; the moral power of steady progress must not be impaired."

The Mississippi secession convention met on January 7, 1861, and the lawyer-planters who had led the state to this point dominated the body. Only 15 percent of the men owned no slaves, but none owned over 300 either. Extensive analysis reveals few patterns among the members of the convention. The largest slave owners opposed secession, but they had been excluded from office long before. William S. Barry defeated James L. Alcorn, a larger slave owner, to preside over the convention. Barry grew up in Columbus, where his father helped Gideon Lincecum lay out the town lots and later operated the Eagle Hotel and Tavern renowned for its fried chicken. Barry graduated from Yale with distinction, returned to Columbus to practice law, and later took up land belonging to his father in order to establish a plantation in Oktibbeha County before striking out for the Delta. Active in states' rights groups, he served in the legislature and one term in Congress. At the time of the convention, he had just bought a substantial home in Columbus and taken up the practice of law again. His income made him typical of the other members.

Lamar wrote the Ordinance of Secession, which passed by a vote of eighty-four to fifteen. The ordinance makes clear that the action was taken to protect slavery as the basis of the state's economy. Barry signed the ordinance and saved the pen for his son. The majority of men responsible for secession had no doubt concerning the justness of their cause or regrets about defending the society they had forged. They considered Lincoln's election an insult to their personal honor, and the devout Christians among them called Republicans heathen infidels. Senator Brown noted God's ordination of slavery, calling it a blessing for both master and slave.

Chapter Six

CIVIL WAR: DISASTER AND FREEDOM

In congressional debates, Reuben Davis warned his colleagues that failing to protect slavery and denying slaveholders their right to expand into the territories would lead to war and that southerners would resist coercion even if it meant devastating their homeland and making it a wasteland. Yet despite his prophesy, he supported secession. A decade of rhetoric since a majority of white Mississippians supported the Compromise of 1850 boxed the Democratic lawyer-planters into an inescapable position. Secession became a matter of honor because political leaders gave their word over and over throughout the decade as they escalated the debate to eliminate their political rivals and to convince the electorate that further compromise would violate the voters' honor. Mississippi's leaders knew what they had done and understood the price that the South would pay for secession. Prosperity based on high cotton prices and slavery deluded the lawyer-planters and most southerners into believing that their economy and their social system pointed to the future both for themselves and the world. Events of the 1850s persuaded them that the North intended to force an end to slavery. For slaveholders, that meant economic ruin. For nonslaveholders, a free society placed them on par with the black population, which they viewed as unacceptable. As a minority, white Mississippians felt the need to keep the black majority enslaved in order to protect themselves from demands for equality. The Civil War initiated a century of racial conflict in Mississippi pitting blacks against whites—first to end slavery and then to achieve racial equality.

Few, aside from the leading political leaders, foresaw where secession would lead. The Mississippi legislature, meeting alongside the secession convention, refused to vote adequate funds to permit the hard-charging Pettus to prepare the state's defenses. Instead, the convention created a military commission to rein in the governor lest he involve the state in unnecessary conflict. In Oxford, the chancellor of the university tendered his resignation after all the students abandoned their studies and enlisted for the war, but the board persuaded him to withdraw it and encouraged him to plan for the fall session on the assumption that war could be avoided. In Vicksburg, the female academy announced its fall schedule. Excitement ran high. The returning congressional members described passing through towns illuminated by thousands of candles, with crowds singing and cannons booming salutes. Secession released a decade of tension, and Mississippians celebrated the end of the Union and the bright prospect of increasing prosperity. Based on recent memories of the Mexican War, they assumed any fighting would be brief and that because of their military prowess, southerners would triumph easily. As with the Mexican War, Mississippians volunteered in such numbers that Pettus could not begin to handle the influx of heady men ready to whip the Yankees.

The state lacked the means of equipping any of the units, but local communities often saw to their volunteer company's needs. Local leaders paid to arm and clothe a company, and the grateful company often elected their patron to lead them into battle. Pettus exerted himself by asking for militia arms early from the U.S. arsenal in Louisiana and buying shotguns with the little funds that he possessed. He appointed Jefferson Davis to lead Mississippi's armed forces, but when the Montgomery convention asked Davis to become president of the new Confederate States of America (CSA), Davis resigned. Pettus next turned to Bolivar County planter Charles Clark to head the military. Clark toured the state to inspect the units springing up in almost every community and bluntly told a hostile crowd in Vicksburg that they must look to the governor for leadership and that they could not determine policies themselves. In Natchez, he observed that the militia reminded him of "women with broom handles." The new CSA army offered Clark a commission, and he escaped the messy Mississippi military situation in June 1861. James L. Alcorn, the Whig Coahoma lawyer-planter who opposed secession until the final vote, stood next in line on the military commission to get the appointment, but Pettus refused to give it to him and turned to Reuben Davis, another member of the commission who had commanded the second Mississippi regiment in the Mexican War. Trying to manage the horde of volunteers, Pettus sent troops to Alabama and Florida to assist in assaulting U.S. facilities and halted accepting any more companies. His decision angered the populous, and the military commission reversed the governor's decree, reopening the floodgates of volunteers, who numbered 125 companies by the summer of 1861. Pettus urged passage of a "stay law" to prevent the collection of debts from those in military service, and he favored cooperation with Alabama and Louisiana to procure steamers to patrol the Gulf of Mexico. Thinking that the first battle of Manassas meant the end of the war, the legislature ignored the governor's pleas for that legislation and his warning that Mississippi faced an invasion. Instead of addressing the military situation, the legislators passed two laws of their own design. One provided harsher penalties for tampering with slaves, and the second sought to prevent cohabitation and fornication between whites and blacks.

During this period, William Howard Russell, a reporter for the *London Times*, interviewed Pettus in his capitol office, which Russell described as mildewed with ragged carpets and broken windows and filled with tobacco-spitting, grimed-faced men going and coming as if it were a public house or tavern. He quoted Pettus as declaring that the sovereign state of Mississippi could do better without England than England could do without Mississippi's cotton.

Pettus's brave words belied the fact that Mississippi possessed no banks or medium of exchange. In an attempt to provide money and enable an economy to function, the legislature, in December 1861, enacted the Mississippi Cotton Loan Act, authorizing the issue of $5 million in treasury notes in denominations from $1 to $100. Planters obtained the notes as an advance on cotton at a rate not to exceed five cents per pound. They were to hold the cotton until the governor called for its delivery. In addition, the legislature granted county boards of police the power to issue notes in order to provide relief for needy soldiers' families. The legislature also allowed Delta levee boards, mercantile houses, railroads, and insurance companies to create similar notes. These instruments and currency from the CSA filling the need for a medium of exchange immediately depreciated in value, leading to runaway inflation. The legislature later chartered banks, but they did not help.

Despite such problems, enthusiasm among the volunteers remained high. Russell described a train journey between Holly Springs and Corinth in the summer of 1861. Flags flew from the train windows, attracting crowds in every hamlet. At Holly Springs, while passengers ate corn bread, rancid butter, and "dubious meats," soldiers danced wildly atop the train to the music of their band while knots of slaves admired their antics. Back on the train suffering from the heat and odors, Russell watched the stump-filled fields out his window and marveled at soldiers with bowie knives and pistols calling themselves "The Toothpick Company" with a coffin labeled "Abe Lincoln died" in their laps. The soldiers assured him that they would bring Lincoln's body back having defeated the Yankees with their knives and six-shooters alone. In Corinth, which served as a staging center for volunteers, Russell saw rows of soldiers suffering from fever and dysentery left on the depot platform to roll about and groan on stretchers unattended. Feeling sorry for the men, he shared quinine, calomel, and opium from his medicine chest. Back on the train, he chanced to meet General Charles Clark and asked him about the lack of medical services. Clark explained that the army lacked doctors because all the doctors wanted to be at least a colonel, and as educated, influential men they insisted on enlisting to fight. While recognizing his army's lack of transport and quartermaster services, Clark hoped to whip the army into shape with courts-martial and severe punishments.

Given the confusion and obvious incompetence of governmental authorities to organize the army, why did Mississippians rush to fight, and what were they fighting for? They went to fight for their families, their friends, and their women. They enlisted in companies with brothers, or sometimes with their fathers, neighbors, and friends. In Lafayette County, for example, the Guards, Farmers, and Rebels all adopted Lafayette in naming their units, while the Paris Rebels honored their community within the county. Former congressmen Thompson and Lamar both sponsored companies—Thompson Cavalry and Lamar Rifles. Planters Avant, Southrons, and Pegues each raised a company providing the uniforms, weapons, and other supplies.

Their women sewed the uniforms and took pride in the number and quality of men they sent off to war. In a public ritual, each unit formed across the state received a flag made by the women of the community. Women transformed the war into a crusade, asking their "knights" to do battle to protect their women's honor, their homes, and their families. Thompson's daughter, Macon, led the elite women of Oxford and set the standard for county rituals in February 1861 when, wearing a white dress that emphasized her dark hair and eyes, she marched up the aisle of the Presbyterian church bathed in candlelight and presented the banner sewn by her own hand to the Lafayette Guards with the admonition to guard it well and to bring it back with honor or not at all. The flag depicted a cotton plant and a Latin motto, which translated, "For altars and hearths." In an age when women rarely spoke in public, such rituals engendered powerful emotions, including, no doubt, sexual desire. As the year progressed, the rituals grew more elaborate. One woman referred in her flag presentation speech to Mississippi as "she" and indicated that the North threatened "her" honor, challenging the young men of the Lamar Rifles to protect "her." Given the code of honor that so often led to violence in Mississippi and a young man's desire to impress and hopefully win these young women's love, the Lafayette companies, and all the other units across the state, marched to war motivated by powerful rituals and by the knowledge that, serving with family and friends, everyone would know how they performed. The social pressures overwhelmed most men in the early months of the war, and few young men could resist the rush to enlist.

Even in the Natchez district where the Whig population opposed secession and war, the Hinds family participated fully in parties, the excitement of enlistment, flag rituals, and nervous gaiety. Their slave, fourteen-year-old Holt Collier, watched the riding to and fro, the barbecues, and the drilling and worried that he might be left behind. Descended from General Hinds, the hero of the Battle of New Orleans, with plantations near old Greenville in Jefferson County and Plum Ridge near new Greenville in Washington County, Howell Hinds epitomized the old planter lifestyle, but split his time between the old district and the new frontier in the Delta. He joined an artillery unit in Jefferson County, and his son Thomas, who had been sent to take day-to-day responsibilities of the Delta operation, joined there. Howell's unit went to the Gulf Coast, where state forces occupied the federal fort on Ship Island only to abandon it when Union naval forces threatened. Howell's company saw no action, and he soon wrote to his old friend President Davis, demanding to be sent north to Virginia. Developments in Kentucky and Tennessee, where Union forces collapsed CSA defenses, led the army to order him north. Howell united with his family and Collier at Plum Ridge on their way to Memphis. Collier begged to be allowed to go to war with Howell and Thomas, but they refused, telling him that he could be killed, which did not concern the teenager. Despite the excitement, Collier sensed the danger and noticed the worry beneath the high spirits of the planters, recalling that when no one was watching the older men looked "kinder solemn."

Aside from the danger of invasion, they worried about a slave rebellion. Howell Hinds wrote to Pettus in the summer of 1861 to tell him that, expecting Lincoln's troops to grant them freedom, Natchez district slaves were plotting an insurrection to kill their masters, take the plantations, and seize the white women. Hinds questioned the wisdom of sending units out of the district given the threat. "Vigilance committees" formed in the district and across the South to deal with the danger of slave revolts. Wailes served on one in Washington and recorded the news of plots in Natchez, Adams, and Jefferson Counties. Nothing appeared in the newspapers because the planters wanted desperately to keep word of the plot from spreading among the slaves while the vigilantes did their work. Using the whip, planters extracted confessions and details. The plot began in May 1861 during a fishing outing among the slaves of an economically stressed school owner who sold some of his slaves and thus separated families. He housed his remaining slaves badly while applying the whip regularly. The plotters had unusually specific goals, having identified which of their owner's teenage daughters would become their partners. The plot spread to the slaves of some of the richest, oldest plantation owners in the area. In May committees hanged half a dozen blacks and whites in Jefferson County and in September perhaps dozens of slaves on Cherry Grove plantation along Second Creek. The committees held other slaves in irons as they assured themselves that they had eradicated the plotters.

Despite the efforts at secrecy, Collier probably knew the fate of the plotters and understood the furtive, solemn looks of his owners, but he wanted to go to war with them so he ignored their command to stay home, followed them to their steamboat, and stowed away in the hold. In Memphis, Hinds relented and allowed Collier to accompany him as his body servant. Collier labored in a camp outside Nashville until their unit rushed by rail into Kentucky. Their train derailed near the Green River Bridge, where Union forces had damaged the tracks. Collier, working as an orderly tending a wounded man, took up his rifle and joined Confederate forces fighting their ambushers. According to Collier, the soldiers accepted him as one of them because of his performance in that fight, which he admitted made him proud. Collier and his owners fell back with the CSA forces into Mississippi and then participated in the attack on General Ulysses S. Grant's army at Shiloh just north of Corinth. With over 10,000 causalities on each side during the first day of the battle, the war came home to Mississippi in April 1862. Reinforced during the night, Grant pushed the South's army across the border into Corinth.

North Mississippi descended into a nightmare trying to care for the thousands of wounded and bracing itself for invasion. The Confederate army suffered a causality rate of 25 percent at Shiloh. Every sizable building in Corinth became a hospital, and the wounded paid the price for their new country's failure to organize and equip its army adequately. The women of Corinth turned out to nurse the wounded, but the men lay shoulder to shoulder covering the floors and porches of the hotel and college. The wounded soldiers' groans and cries filled the air, and the stench from the thousands of bodies sickened the nurses. The steps of the buildings ran red with blood, and amputated limbs filled buckets in the improvised surgery suites. Relatives rushed to Corinth if they could and sometimes found their men lying on bare earth suffering from exposure and lack of water. A town of 2,500, Corinth could not supply drinking water for the army of thousands. Authorities sought to disperse the wounded across north Mississippi, where the civilian population cared for them. The University of Mississippi became a hospital, and local physicians along with the women of Oxford labored mightily to save the wounded and comfort them when it proved impossible. The women who had presented the flags with such strong words of encouragement for their men to go to war looked into the eyes of men racked with pain and dying in despair and must have wondered what they had done. Okolona took in 2,000 wounded. The hotel resort at Lauderdale Springs became a hospital, and citizens took the wounded into their homes for extended recovery across the state.

More men died at Corinth from poor food, lack of sanitation, and wretched drinking water than were killed in the battle of Shiloh. Yet desperate to fend off the federals and protect the rail junction at Corinth, the CSA ordered in more troops, bringing the number around the town to 80,000. Even those numbers proved inadequate as the new Union commander massed 120,000 around Pittsburg Landing and slowly moved south. The best that the CSA could do was to evacuate using a clever ruse. As the trains shuttled the southern army out of town, the men cheered each arrival of empty cars as if they were being reinforced.

Collier migrated to a Texas cavalry unit during his time at Corinth because he admired their horsemanship and spirit, and they in turn liked his marksmanship. Both Thomas and Howell Hinds requested to leave the army in order to organize new units back home. When permission did not come, Thomas resigned his commission that summer, claiming ill health, and never returned. Howell interpreted a confused response from Jefferson Davis as granting him the right to go home. Enjoying army life and his new freedom as a soldier, Collier wanted to stay with the Texans. Howell gave him an iron-gray racehorse and purchased Collier a uniform. Nathan Bedford Forrest asked Howell Hinds for Collier, but Hinds gave Collier his choice of staying with the Texans or going with Forrest. Collier chose the Texans, becoming the only black combatant soldier in the southern army.

The battle of Shiloh and the fall of Corinth transformed the war for Mississippians because it became obvious that Yankees could fight and that war was hell in so many ways. The naive volunteers hardened by battle and the terrors of hospitals had become veterans who knew the price it would cost them to continue the war. Some thought the price too high and deserted. Others went on without the romance with which they started the war. The CSA government altered the soldier's contract made at the beginning of the war by passing a conscription act lengthening their period of service and exempting the owners of twenty or more slaves from conscription. The enlisted men translated the latter provision to mean that it was a rich man's war and a poor man's fight. Reorganizations in the army placed more and more men under commanders they had not elected, eroding the community nature of their units and bringing home to many that they were in the type of central-dominated government that they thought they were fighting to prevent.

Between March and April 1862 Union forces raided along the Gulf Coast from their base on Ship Island. They occupied Corinth on May 30, 1862, and roamed south to Booneville and Guntown, skirmishing with Confederate forces. On May 13 Natchez surrendered without resistance to Union naval forces steaming toward Vicksburg after taking New Orleans. By the summer of 1862 Mississippians began to rally around their homes and communities and to abandon the CSA. Former carpenter Solomon G. Street, for example, hired a substitute, which he was allowed to do by the conscription act, and returned to Tippah County. He had enlisted in the Magnolia Guards in Ripley in late 1860 and fought loyally across Virginia until he heard that north Mississippi had been invaded. William C. Falkner left ahead of Street when he lost his command in a unit election and reshuffle. Falkner returned to Ripley and organized a 750-man cavalry unit known as the Mississippi Partisan Rangers, but the CSA conscription bureau broke it up and drafted its members. Street, a giant of a man with a booming voice, arrived back home at this point in August 1862 and responded to Pettus's call for minutemen to protect their local communities.

Pettus had been rescued by the CSA, which called up the restive Mississippi companies in 1861 just before the fall election, enabling Pettus to win all but four counties in his reelection contest. Pettus repaid the CSA by refusing to support fully its draft efforts. Deserters infested the state, and law and order disintegrated. Howell Hinds, who could only find eight men for the new company that he proposed to start as an excuse for leaving the Confederate army, accepted office as provost of Jefferson County, and a host of others took similar state offices to avoid the draft. Pettus tried to organize state armed forces to restore security and ordered sheriffs to seize firearms for the use of the government, but the sheriffs defied him. As a solution to his inability to provide protection from the state level, Pettus called on minutemen to operate as free agents to respond quickly to whatever threatened their communities. Former third sergeant Street became captain of the Citizens Guards of Tippah County, which the state mustered into the army of Mississippi.

Street's Citizens Guards had no hope of stopping Grant's army, which drove into Mississippi headed for Vicksburg in early November 1862. While Grant's army occupied Ripley and rolled on to Holly Springs and Oxford, Street hid with thirty men in the all-but-impenetrable "bottom" near his boyhood home, waiting to do what he could.

Shiloh convinced Grant that defeating the South required total war. Earlier he and his subordinate, William T. Sherman, had assumed, along with most northerners, that the slave-owning elite were to blame for the war and that ordinary southerners would not fight and devastate their country as the fire-eaters had predicted. In north Mississippi, Grant and Sherman struggled toward a new policy of using pillage and destruction to collapse the social system that had not crumbled as they anticipated. The Confederate army conceded Holly Springs to Grant and established defenses just south of the Tallahatchie River near Abbeville, but frightened by a raid to his south at Coffeeville, General John C. Pemberton ordered a retreat by his army of 40,000. They paused in Oxford as cold December rains soaked both armies, but quickly resumed their retreat, leaving the distressed women of Oxford to the mercies of Grant's army. One of those women, Taylor Cook, ran to the front porch of her house and with the wind blowing her hair about gave voice to the town's distress, calling the retreating soldiers miserable cowards. Large numbers of civilians followed the army with all the livestock they could herd ahead of them, clogging the road to Okolona with a mass of people and animals. Confederate leaders fearing arrest left their women in some cases and escaped beyond the Yankees' reach. Mud slowed the armies and the refugees. Grant thought it prudent to halt just below the Yoknapatawpha River before his army outran its supply lines and bogged down in the Mississippi mud. He intended to make Oxford his winter camp and held parades through town complete with bands. No longer fighting, his soldiers scoured the planters' homes for alcohol to take some rest and relaxation. They took special pleasure in destroying Thompson's impressive home and its European-purchased contents. Grant personally examined Thompson's abandoned correspondence, seeking proof of his disloyalty to the Union.

A Confederate cavalry attack on Grant's supply base at Holly Springs disrupted his plan to winter in Oxford and forced him to pull back to Memphis in order to regroup. As he withdrew, Grant carried a new sense of bitterness toward the Mississippi population who celebrated his discomfiture openly. Holly Springs women shocked his wife, a southern woman accompanied by her slave, by lecturing Mrs. Grant on the rightness of their cause and serenading her with defiant music. Asked by gloating Mississippians what he would eat with his Holly Springs warehouses burned, Grant responded that he would take what he needed.

December marked the high point for Mississippi defenders despite their loss in an assault on Corinth. Earl Van Dorn failed there, but redeemed himself with his victory capturing Grant's supply base at Holly Springs. Vicksburg turned back Sherman's attempt to capture that city at Chickasaw Bluffs and forced the federals to devise a new plan centered on Vicksburg, which Lincoln called the key because it represented the last impediment to complete control of the Mississippi and because its capture would bring about the division of the Confederacy.

Grant went north with renewed determination and ordered his men to confiscate all of the food available along with the animals and wagons to transport it. For fifteen miles on either side of the railroad, his men took everything edible and movable. The Yankees also plundered all manner of booty, including silverware, jewelry, china, crystal, clothing, and even an occasional church Bible. Victims of this robbery saw a new level of viciousness in the war. The federals issued vouchers for some property, but the victims had to prove their loyalty in order to collect compensation. Trying to claim reimbursement meant suffering contempt and sometimes violence from their neighbors.

Lincoln had signed the Emancipation Proclamation on September 22, 1862, just before Grant invaded Mississippi, and as Grant retreated, much of the slave population followed his army seeking the freedom that the army told them would be granted in January—just days away. Slaves drove overseers from plantations in Lafayette County and made clear they intended to claim their freedom. Slave owners reported that slaves refused to obey and that they feared violence. The chaplain, who Grant appointed to deal with the contraband, as they called the fleeing slaves, described the hordes as "oncoming cities." The camps the army prepared for them proved entirely inadequate, and many of the Union soldiers treated the black refugees worse than southerners ever had. Often those slaves choosing to stay on farms refused to work and treated their owners with insolence, taking what they wanted from the smokehouse and corncrib. College Hill Presbyterian Church tried one of its members who murdered his mother's female slave, and he cited as his defense the current slave rebellion. The church session chose to forgive the murderer and allowed him to remain a member.

Some Union sympathizers took the loyalty oath and earned privileges from the federal forces, introducing an element of civil war among Mississippians. Many Mississippians began to run the blockade to sell cotton in Memphis, where it brought $2.50 a pound. Colonel Falkner made his fortune in this period selling cotton to Yankee traders.

Street emerged from the bottoms and began to ambush Union patrols, sometimes wearing a Union uniform to gain an edge. His attempts to capture a payroll train and success in capturing the paymaster led the Union to send a Tennessee Union freebooter and his irregulars looking for Street. After Street captured some of the freebooter's men, the Tennessee freebooter announced that Street and his men would not be treated as soldiers in the future. The threat sent Street to the CSA seeking authorization and legitimacy. The regular Union army accused Street of killing two of their captured soldiers in cold blood and announced that they would execute four of Street's men in their custody. The CSA commander protected Street's men by reminding the Union commander that he held four Union prisoners. Street found a CSA kindred spirit in Nathan Bedford Forest and brought his men under the loose control of the Confederate army, cooperating profitably with Forrest raiding into west Tennessee and Kentucky for the southern cause. Street's exploits ended when a sixteen-year-old Confederate soldier shot Street in their camp to revenge the murder of his father by Street's unit. This type of violent vendetta characterized life in Mississippi for the remainder of the war. Armies contended and killed large numbers in the name of two nations, but individuals allied themselves with the state of Mississippi, which operated independently of the CSA sometimes, or with the Union government when it proved convenient, or with a local warlord who might, or might not, have cover from one of the governments.

Governor Pettus knew that courts had ceased to function, federal troops roamed fifty miles inland from the coast, and deserters defied law enforcement officials, particularly in the northeast corner of the state and the piney woods. He tried without much success to support the CSA in its enforcement of the draft, but for once the legislature responded readily to some of his suggestions for remedial legislation in 1862. They empowered sheriffs to enforce the draft and offered them a $5 fee for each deserter apprehended and returned. To further strengthen the war effort, legislators passed a law to draft any slave between eighteen and fifty along with animals and wagons needed for the "public safety." This law responded to complaints that planters refused to loan their slaves for public service. Carried away, the legislators outlawed the manufacture of alcohol, imposing a six-month jail sentence and a $5,000 fine. They refused to impose price regulations to fight inflation, and they restricted Pettus's power to send state troops to assist the CSA. State forces could only serve outside the state for limited periods, the legislators decreed, and they granted Pettus the unwanted privilege of granting exemptions from the draft. Even in the face of invasion, the legislature as well as the governor favored local control and resisted CSA efforts to maximize military resources for the war.

Letters from this period provide a clear idea of how the planter class coped with the war in 1861–1862. Dr. Thomas Watkins, one of many doctors who gave up his practice of medicine to run his plantation, owned 1,500 acres in Carroll County. He lived with his wife, two daughters, and fifty productive slaves. After hearing of slave insurrections nearby in the summer of 1861, he joined the "Home Guard" and drilled with them. His wife and a daughter, who still lived at home, joined in a sewing circle to support the Winona Stars. Much of family life remained mundane, with the mother drying peaches and damsons and the daughter conducting a long-distance romance with a soldier away in the army. They suffered from a lack of salt and coffee as all did, but they made a coffee substitute from sweet potatoes and dug salt out of the floor of the smokehouse. With the men gone, the Watkins women took over school teaching. When they lost their overseer, Watkins appointed a slave named Prince to oversee the daily work on the plantation. His wife told her daughter in Texas that she considered Prince "a black grand devil" and that his promotion made her blood boil, but that she had to resign herself to it. She complained about the high cost of provisions because of inflation and worried about the war while consoling herself that their slaves remained obedient even if the South was "whipped."

When the wounded came to their community from the fighting in the north, Watkins allowed his daughter to take buttermilk, boiled chicken, biscuits, and preserves to them, but forbade her entering the improvised hospital. He did send slave women to Grenada to care for the wounded. One slave died as a result and another returned home sick. With a good corn crop at the end of the summer in 1862, they and the slaves would not go hungry, but they did not have enough hogs for the next year because two per week were required for the family and slaves. Mother speculated to her daughter that the chickens and turkeys would tide them over for a brief period, but they could see want ahead. In December Dr. Watkins heard that Yankees had reached Grenada and moved his most productive slaves to Alabama, leasing them to a railroad company. His wife reported that the war had affected his mind by this point and that on the evening he prepared the slaves for their journey, his eyes took on a "very unnatural expression." All of the slaves, even the strong men, cried. Dr. Watkins admitted to his wife that separating the slaves from the family—his and their own—"liked to have killed him." Clearly by December 1862 planters could see the end of their world approaching, and as the wife of this one reported, the patriarch suffered deeply when he lost the ability to nurture and protect all those dependent upon him.

Other classes left scant information to describe their daily lives, and the best information usually comes from more literate observers. A British diarist who traveled through Mississippi during this period observed that the lives of poor women with husbands away fighting haunted him. They possessed little clothing, little to eat, and worried themselves sick about the welfare of their absent partners, who rarely wrote. A Delta lawyer wrote his wife unflattering word pictures of poor women clothed in dirty rags and heavy work-boots with tobacco stains dribbling down their chins from the chewing tobacco or snuff in their mouths. They possessed, he said, hordes of dirty children and lived packed into log cabins with only a ten-acre cornfield, sharp-nosed pigs, and a few chickens to sustain the family. He marveled that most of the South's soldiers came from just such homes. One correspondent wrote to Pettus complaining that wealthy planters worked slaves in cotton fields within sight of soldiers' wives plowing their own fields trying to raise enough corn to feed their families, and the planters, he wrote, refused to even loan the poor wives a slave to assist. Without male relatives to work farms, the women had to care for the children and do all the man's work on their farms. Unaccustomed to such labor and lacking a man's upper-body strength, a woman could not split rails to mend a fence or repair a plow if it broke. Church would have provided such women the most comfort, but with the number of animals reduced and considering the need to rest them on Sunday, church attendance dropped. Soldiers at war at least had camaraderie in the ranks, but their wives at home lacked even that. The British diarist met with President Davis and recalled to Davis his admiration for the quiet, calm manner in which most women bore their desperation. Davis responded enigmatically that he always thought silent despair the most painful sort of misery just as he considered mute insanity the worst sort of madness. Perhaps Davis wondered why such women did not scream outside his office seeking an end to the war and the return of their husbands.

Though not typical, Serena Knight of Jones County suffered as did many women left alone. Related to wealthy slave-owning kin who rose to fill county offices, she married Newton Knight in 1858. His relatives owned slaves, but Newt's father, Albert, chose not to. Despite his opposition to secession, Newt volunteered for the army, becoming a fourth sergeant. He got discharged within a year because of his father's death. When he returned home, he learned that his brother-in-law had abused his children, and he probably murdered his younger sister's husband for that abuse. He had only four months to work his farm before faced with conscription; he reenlisted and went to north Mississippi to face the Union invaders. He deserted after Corinth, and when the authorities captured him back in Jones County, they had to tie him and haul him to prison in a wagon. He reenlisted rather than die, which left Serena to provide for her entire family alone after the murder of the brother-in-law. Newt may have rejoined the Seventh Mississippi Battalion at Vicksburg, but clearly his loyalty to the CSA no longer existed.

In December 1862 a member of the elite ruling class announced his preference for a Union victory to the federal commander in New Orleans. J. F. H. Claiborne, descended from a territorial governor, served as a congressman from Mississippi and played an active role in politics, including acting as an elector for Douglas in the 1860 election. Using a sinecure from his friend President Pierce, Claiborne retired to a plantation that he called Laurel Wood near the mouth of the Pearl River before the war and wrote history and biographies covering the political history of Mississippi. From his isolated position on the Gulf Coast, Claiborne grew more disillusioned about the course of the war. He wrote to Pettus asking permission to trade with the enemy in order to provide food for the hungry women and children of the piney woods whose husbands manned the Confederate army, but did not get it. In the summer of 1862 he told his old political ally Brown, then serving in the CSA Senate, that he had witnessed companies of state troops being formed in Hancock County for the purpose of avoiding the draft. The company commander took bribes for slots in the outfit and furloughed its members soon after enlistment so that the members could resume their normal lives. He reported another artillery unit was in the offing for the same purpose. His observations of the reaction to the course of the war along the Gulf Coast and in the piney woods convinced him that the southern cause was lost by the end of 1862. Claiborne assured the Union commander that the people of the piney woods lacked any convictions or sense of duty. They had joined the CSA army, he said, in hopes of plunder, but death and suffering had "disgusted" them with service, and their essentially "animal" nature compelled them to turn toward the Union for relief. He suggested that in three months the whole coast at least would be ready to declare its allegiance to the United States. Although he remained outwardly loyal to the CSA and lost a son fighting for it, he spent the rest of the war writing intelligence to the Yankees and selling them the Sea Island cotton grown on his plantation.

Also in December 1862 at Pettus's urging, President Davis made his only wartime appearance in Jackson to attempt to rally the distressed population of Mississippi. On December 26 he spoke for ninety minutes to a packed House of Representatives chamber. He emphasized his attachment to the state and urged his listeners to remember that they fought for liberty and their inheritance. He reminded them that the only other choice was slavery imposed upon them. He praised those fighting and called for others to devote themselves to the "noblest cause." He assured his audience that the CSA had enhanced its ability to wage war over the last year and that Generals Pemberton and Joseph E. Johnston made up the best team to protect the state. He concluded by stating his belief that the people of Mississippi would win their independence.

Alienated by Davis's refusal to give him a CSA commission and disgusted with the failure of Mississippi to adequately equip, supply, and train the troops that he had led to Kentucky, Alcorn returned to his plantation and grew cotton. By the fall of 1862 he wrote to his wife ensconced with her family in Alabama for safety, denouncing Davis as a tyrant who was losing the "jewel" entrusted to his care. Alcorn hid his cotton from Confederate forces, which would burn it to prevent the federals acquiring it, and loaded it onto smugglers' boats to sell in Memphis. He assured her that he would earn $20,000 in gold and greenbacks in order to preserve their lifestyle. In 1862 Mississippians still produced 1,597,000 bales of cotton despite growing hunger among the state's population, so Alcorn was one among many.

Pettus heard complaints of trading with the enemy from Iuka to Natchez, and Pemberton condemned disloyalty among those he fought to protect, musing that the enemy seemed to be making friends of "nearly all the citizens." In the debate preceding the passage of the conscription act revision exempting slave overseers in August 1862, both Mississippi senators warned of the damage the act would do. James Phelan called on the Senate to let the poor man stay home to protect his family from the slaves of the rich, and Brown, opposing an amendment to exempt college students, observed that exemptions favoring one class were wrong. The act passed nonetheless and further embittered the yeomanry.

Preparation for the defense of Vicksburg led the army to impress slaves to do the digging and construction. Slave owners resisted even when threatened with arrest. They sent their slaves to hide in the bottoms or ignored it if slaves went away on their own. Johnston said that he never knew of one master who returned a slave who ran back home to escape the labor detail. Planters complained to the governor that impressment officers did not administer the law equably because they took too few slaves from the largest plantations. In Holmes County, officers encountered what they described as "armed mobs" refusing to allow their slaves to be taken. Even as the state faced renewed invasion to take Vicksburg, governmental power to resist evaporated in the face of low morale borne of racial and class divisions.

Pettus knew that he had lost control of the state, but he continued to send speakers out around the state to deliver messages similar to Davis's. Pettus urged Jacksonians to donate their slaves' labor to build defenses around the capital city, but owners wanted to be paid for their slaves' work. A British observer passing through the city found the resulting trenches laughable. Pettus's brother, Edmund, stationed at Vicksburg, gave the governor intimate reports of the situation there. He found the population of the city dispirited, more ready to "exercise their patriotism at home," and prepared to trade with the Yankees whenever they had an opportunity. Visiting Vicksburg, Pettus happened to be on the bluff when a Union gunboat tried to run past the city. The brazen boat captain yelled up demanding the surrender of the city, to which Pettus shouted back that he would defend Vicksburg until it lay in ruins and continue to fight among the ruins.

Many still shared Pettus's defiant attitude. One of the women called to nurse the wounded in Corinth recorded that the horrible experience caused her to redouble her determination to resist the Yankees to her last breath. In Meridian, a young woman spat in the face of a wounded Union soldier being treated there to demonstrate her hatred. Dr. Watkins parted willingly with his slaves as the state or army demanded and never trafficked with the enemy, considering it dishonorable as well as illegal. Most soldiers continued to obey orders and remained with their units.

Grant relentlessly probed at Mississippi's defenses during the winter of 1862–1863 as he continued work on a canal to bypass Vicksburg, but meanwhile he developed a number of plans to take the city. He destroyed levees along the river and reached the Yazoo with boats loaded with soldiers hoping to float to Vicksburg through the Delta. Pemberton ordered a temporary fort, dubbed Fort Pemberton, built by slaves out of dirt and cotton bales at the confluence of the Tallahatchie and the Yazoo, which turned back the invading Union flotilla. Grant moved his headquarters to Milliken's Bend on the Louisiana side of the river opposite Vicksburg and decided to march his army south of Vicksburg and ferry it across to approach the city from the east. As diversions, he sent a force into the Delta to raid and then a cavalry troop the length of the state entering north of Ripley and exiting south of Summit. The cavalry did not do heavy damage, but in plundering stores in towns such as Starkville along the way, they kept Pemberton busy rushing troops from place to place. At Newton, the Union cavalry captured a rail shipment of provisions and ammunition, but they accomplished their larger mission as Grant marched south unnoticed. His gunboats successfully made the run past Vicksburg despite fires lit to illuminate them during the night passage and the efforts of the Confederate batteries. Linking up with his gunboats, Grant tried to cross at Grand Gulf but could not take the gun emplacements there. At undefended Bruinsburg, he conducted the largest amphibious operation in history to that date. Sherman attacked Vicksburg from the north again just to ensure Grant got established to the south unmolested. Grant took Port Gibson, overwhelming the 6,000 defenders with his larger force. Calling Sherman to join him raised the federals to 40,000 men against Pemberton's much more scattered 30,000 men. Pemberton misjudged that Grant would attack Vicksburg first. Pemberton sent a small force to Raymond, where they faced impossible odds. Davis sent Johnston from Tennessee to take personal charge of the battle for Vicksburg. When Johnston arrived in Jackson, he found Pettus had escaped to Enterprise, where he had earlier sent his family. Pettus announced that he had relocated the capital for safety's sake. His action sparked a mass exodus by all classes from the capital city. Johnston possessed too few troops to stand up to Grant, so he ordered the destruction of the city's cotton and rail cars before retreating north to Canton. Poor whites, liberated slaves, and the prisoners released from the penitentiary were looting when Grant's army reached the city. Grant and Sherman strolled into a textile factory busy rolling out tent material labeled CSA. Telling the young women to grab all they could carry and leave, they ordered the factory and many others burned.

Pemberton moved east, and portions of the two armies met at Champion Hill, where the outnumbered Confederates fought hard but retreated west toward Vicksburg at the end of the day. The federal army abandoned Jackson and moved on Vicksburg. Pemberton reached the city well ahead of Grant, but his troops limped back in bad condition. Bands assembled at the courthouse and played "Dixie" and "Bonnie Blue Flag" in an effort to boost morale. Davis told Pemberton to stay, while Johnston ordered him to evacuate and save his army. Pemberton stayed, and Grant tried to break through the defenses and failed. Grant laid siege and bombarded the city from land and river. The population dug caves in the hills and gradually starved until Pemberton surrendered on July 4, 1863. Grant's men took pity on the emaciated survivors and shared their food with their defeated enemy. Grant paroled the surrendered soldiers, hoping they would add to the already lawless situation within the state. Pemberton tried to keep the paroled force together, but his men ignored him and simply went home. The CSA did not have enough Union prisoners to exchange for Pemberton's men, so eventually they broke the agreement with the Union and ordered the men back into service without the necessary exchange.

While Grant waited for Vicksburg to fall, the Union army began to train and arm freedmen. The army now encouraged slaves to leave the plantations they passed, or looted, and enrolled the able-bodied freedmen in their ranks. Freedmen had been used as laborers to build the defenses around Corinth, but none had been employed as fighting men. The federal ranks expressed skepticism couched in racist stereotypes and predicted that blacks would not fight. Some threatened to change sides if blacks were enlisted to fight. Just over 1,200 new black soldiers—some with only three weeks' training—had been left to garrison Milliken's Bend, which Texas troops attacked hoping to shut off some of Grant's supplies and distract him from the siege. Despite a determined assault, the black soldiers, fresh out of the cotton fields of Mississippi and Louisiana, stood their ground and fought hand to hand until gunboats appeared to pound the Texans. The black soldiers' bravery revolutionized attitudes toward them and convinced many commanders to give them a chance. Sherman refused to use them in combat, but many others did. During the remainder of the war, former slaves fought former masters across the state, and former slaves occupied cities and demanded to see the passes of their former mistresses passing through the lines. The slaveholders' worst nightmare arrived in the summer of 1863: the slaves who had been held in check by whips had guns.

Freedwomen presented a problem for the military, which wanted freedmen but struggled to find a role for women. As the former slaves battled to maintain their family in the confusion of war and relocation, Union army policy required a legal marriage before husband and wife were allowed to cohabit. This regulation kept army chaplains busy marrying couples, who referred to the service as marrying again. The army's first experience had been at Corinth, where the freedmen eventually built log cabins in their camp, turning it into a village larger than Corinth. The men enlisted first as laborers and then as soldiers while the women worked as laundresses and cooks. Those not employed by the military were encouraged to enter into agricultural wage labor for white employers, who sometimes failed to pay them. With the pattern established in Corinth, the same policies applied at Vicksburg and later in Natchez and Meridian. The freedmen flocked to cities, and the army built camps on the city's outskirts. The freedmen resisted the military's efforts to separate families, and the military usually compromised, allowing wives who worked for them to live in the barracks with their husbands. Some freedwomen also formed temporary unions with federal soldiers who used them to satisfy their sexual needs with no intention of keeping the promises made to the women. A few freedwomen became prostitutes. The "colored troops'" camps did not conform to the model of military order because they were filled with women and children. Most of the occupation forces for Mississippi's cities consisted of black soldiers, but some black cavalry fought through the entire state.

Pettus did not fight among the ruins of either Vicksburg or Jackson. His hasty departure when the federals first took Jackson precipitated a massive evacuation by the population, and after the Union troops pulled out, Pettus could not be convinced to spend the night in the city. He came back while they laid siege to Vicksburg but left each evening to camp on the east side of the Pearl, fearing arrest and prison if captured. The state's archives remained scattered about cities in Alabama because much of Jackson lay in ruins. In July after the surrender of Vicksburg, the Union army headed back to Jackson. Johnston had waited out the siege west of the Big Black River with 23,000 men, but withdrew in the face of superior numbers skirmishing as he retreated. The federals did not occupy the city the second time either, but retreated to Vicksburg and undertook the full occupation of Natchez. Pettus established a temporary capital at Enterprise again and then moved to Meridian and later Macon, with some parts of the government housed in Columbus. In his last address to the legislature, Pettus recognized the value of black soldiers to the enemy and urged that a policy of removing slaves from the reach of the enemy be adopted to prevent more slaves from falling into their hands. Limited to two terms, Pettus had to leave office at this low point of the war. He enlisted in a state unit as a private but was elected a colonel and served out the remainder of the war.

The 1863 elections brought more moderate men into office. General Charles Clark, who used crutches because of his wounds suffered in battle, beat Reuben Davis and other fire-eater politicians. James L. Alcorn, despite his refusal to run, won a seat in the legislature and played a role in defeating Phelan, a supporter of President Davis. The legislature elected J. W. C. Watson, a former Whig, as senator. Both Reuben Davis and President Davis's brother told the CSA president that the conscription law caused the defeat. Joseph Davis advised his brother to repeal the law as soon as possible.

Inaugurated in Columbus with Colonel Barry, the former president of the secession convention, looking on with his company, Clark warned any who wished to reconstruct the Union that they should wake from such dreams because it was better to die in battle than to surrender. He suggested that Mississippians might wish to emulate the Pascagoula who marched into the river and drowned when their braves had been slain. Then as Pettus had been doing, he commended the state to God's care. Meeting in the courthouse in Columbus from early November until December 9, the legislature passed a number of bills authorizing more aid for soldiers' destitute families, funding railroad repairs, and calling for a day of prayer and fasting. None of their actions had any impact. The state had no money, and church attendance had dropped off because there was so much disorder around the state that not many churches were able to hold regular services. Clark called the legislature in to subsequent sessions, and it continued to pass laws that no one enforced. The courts no longer operated, so the only effective government within the state consisted of the federal military-run enclaves.

Johnston's army dispersed as Union forces roamed at will across the state, fighting skirmishes until Sherman returned to the state. Called away to Chattanooga, Sherman returned to Vicksburg determined to wage total war in order to force the South into destitution so severe that the population could not continue the war. Meridian, with the crossing of east-west and north-south rail lines, constituted the only important transportation hub in the state still controlled by the CSA, and he determined to take it while feeding his army completely off the civilian population as he marched back and forth across the state. Leaving Vicksburg on February 3, 1864, Sherman once again marched east, reaching Jackson in two days. He crossed the Pearl without bothering to stop because nothing remained worth destroying. At Morton, he paused long enough to tear up some rail tracks and raze a few buildings. In Decatur, he encountered the only important obstacle along his route when a CSA cavalry force struck, destroying forty wagons and almost capturing Sherman. The federals quickly recovered and chased the cavalry off. Leonidas Polk, the former Episcopal minister turned Confederate general responsible for Meridian, decamped well ahead of Sherman, leaving the rail center to the enemy. Sherman's men spent five days with axes, crowbars, and fire trying to make the city useless to the CSA. The wounded soldier who was spat on in Meridian found the young woman who did it, burned her home, the next one that she had fled to, and ignored her pleas for mercy. Sherman expected to be joined in Meridian by cavalry dispatched out of Memphis to link up with him, but they did not come.

The Union cavalry left Memphis on February 11, several days late. Making their way through New Albany, Pontotoc, and Houston, they encountered militia along the way, slowing their progress, and by the time they reached the Mobile and Ohio rail track to follow it to Meridian, they had accumulated 1,000 freedmen and a sizable herd of livestock. At Prairie Station and Aberdeen, they began to skirmish with Nathan Bedford Forrest's cavalry. Forrest, a self-made man lacking any military training, rose to command the only effective resistance in north Mississippi for the rest of the war. He lost his brother in one of the early skirmishes and enraged by the loss pursued his opponents hard. Losing a sizable engagement in Okolona, the federals retreated to Memphis, leaving Sherman to return to Vicksburg without his cavalry. Sherman's return trip proved largely uneventful, but he reported taking 500 prisoners and being followed by a line of freedmen ten miles long.

Sherman left the state to march through Georgia using the same tactics that he perfected in Mississippi, and for the remainder of the war Mississippi became a sideshow. Vicksburg and Natchez continued to be occupied by mostly black soldiers. Vicksburg never recovered the economic dynamism of its prewar years. It became a military enclave and refugee haven. The army established a program to feed the hungry, and long lines seeking relief stretched through the rubble. Adventurers seeking to profit waded through the desperate crowds to lease seized and abandoned plantations in order to raise cotton. As early as the summer of 1862 the federal government began to lease land and to encourage freed people to work it for wages. The government got half the crop, but the contractor stood to make sixty times what he paid the freedwoman or freedman per pound. His workers had a difficult time distinguishing their new wage job from their old role in slavery. Some workers returned to their former owners seeking a better life. Guerrilla activity continued until the end of the war, and some contractors changed occupations from farmer to smuggler, serving as middlemen to supply guerrillas and the Confederate population with goods from Vicksburg.

Holt Collier and his former owner, Howell Hinds, morphed into Delta guerrillas during the war. Typically, Hinds returned to the fight when Grant crossed the Mississippi and landed near his home. Joining a cavalry outfit, he was gut shot and was left to die, but locals rescued him. While north of Vicksburg with his Texas unit, Collier heard about Hinds's condition, took leave, and went to visit him in Jefferson County, sleeping in Hinds's room for several nights before he had to leave ahead of the federals. Hinds mended and moved to his Delta plantation to try to protect it from seizure by the federals. Collier and a small group of Texans had been placed on permanent "detached duty" raiding the Yankee contractors and trying to protect the Confederate planters. The lines between just who was what often got blurred. In one operation, Hinds joined forces with Collier and the Texans to destroy a successful thief named Milford Coe. Before the war, Coe worked as an overseer. He joined a local company but deserted to become an outlaw, making his headquarters on Island 76, also known as Goat Island, in the Mississippi. His lieutenant was a tall, powerful former slave named Tom, also well known to locals as a bad man. Coe kept a small army of runaway slaves and a few white cohorts on the island from which he raided the mainland for livestock and loot. Collier went to the island as a spy and returned with Hinds and three of his friends on the evening of January 19, 1864. In a daring raid they captured Coe and his leadership. After returning the livestock to its owners, they killed Coe, Tom, and one other of the outlaws. Vigilante justice became the norm in the last two years of the war because there was no legal system outside the federal enclaves.

Newt Knight provides another, more famous example of a man trying to protect his home and family, in his case from CSA authorities. Forced back into the army before Vicksburg, Knight may have been there during the siege. After Vicksburg, he had deserted for the last time and turned against the Confederacy. Hiding out in the swamps near his home protected by his friends, relatives, and their slaves, he connected with other deserters, and they cooperated to work one another's fields in groups with lookouts to avoid capture. The Confederates of the county may have been in the minority from the beginning of the war because the voters elected a representative to the secession convention with the understanding that he would vote against secession. When he voted for it, some of the nonslaveholders harshly criticized him and accused him of selling out for a post in state government. By 1863 the Confederate army and civil authorities had grown unpopular for drafting unwilling soldiers, collecting taxes in the form of food, and seizing horses for military use. On August 5, 1863, President Davis announced a twenty-day amnesty for deserters to return without penalty, but by the fall the army began shooting deserters to retain their manpower. Clearly the Confederate government had grown desperate, and Jones and the surrounding counties held large numbers of men needed by the army. The general in charge of conscription sent Major Amos McLemore, a battle-tested officer who was a native of Jones County, to flush out the deserters and return them to service. The McLemore family were well-off merchants before the war and strong supporters of secession. One of McLemore's in-laws held the despised post of tax-in-kind collector. Acquiring a large pack of hounds and the cooperation of local officials, in five weeks McLemore reported netting 119 men for the army, but he failed to find Knight, who sent messages warning McLemore to desist.

On October 5, 1863, McLemore and some of his troops stopped at the home of a state legislator in Ellisville to dry out after a rainstorm and to have dinner. An unidentified man burst into the room and shot McLemore through the chest, killing him. Everyone in the county assumed it was Knight. According to Reconstruction-era depositions from Knight and Jasper Collins, a group of deserters met a week later to form a company and to pledge their loyalty to the Union as a way to protect themselves from Confederate forces. The men communicated by signals from cow horns and armed themselves mostly with double-barreled shotguns loaded with heavy lead pieces. Their women and children smuggled them food out in the swamps, and the men had to cease sleeping at home. Elected captain, Knight led his company on some daring raids on Confederate wagon supply trains and storage facilities. For example, he led 200 men to Paulding and looted a CSA warehouse of corn, hauling it way in wagons commandeered for the purpose. Complaints from Confederates that Knight and his men had taken control of the county prompted the army in Mobile to send 500 men into the county in March 1864. After some battles, the commander reported that he had restored order and that only a few more deserters needed to be hunted out of the swamps with dogs.

He proved to be badly mistaken. Reports of pro-Union public meetings and Yankee agents in the area disturbed the Richmond government. Knight claimed after the war that he sent men to both Memphis and New Orleans seeking assistance from the Union army. Some of his men did travel to New Orleans to enlist in the Union army. In mid-April the Confederate government dispatched Colonel Robert Lowry (governor-to-be of Mississippi) with an infantry force to put down what appeared to be a rebellion against the state and central government. Lowry ruthlessly hanged and shot men and children and then used large packs of dogs to flush men from the swamps. His tactics eliminated all but the hard core of Knight's company, which Lowry failed to dislodge from the swamps. The majority of the Knight company either joined the Confederate army again or fled to New Orleans to become federals. Some of those in the Confederate army surrendered at the first opportunity. Despite the sweep of the county, it remained lawless, and the *Natchez Courier* reported in the summer of 1864 that the county had seceded from the state and formed its own government.

Knight's affair with Rachel Knight added spice to his story because she was first his grandfather's and then his uncle's slave. She assisted him as he hid and eluded the Confederate army, and eventually they had a number of children together. Knight continued to live with his wife, Serena, while carrying on an affair openly with Rachel. Eventually he maintained black and white families living side by side and working their fields together. More

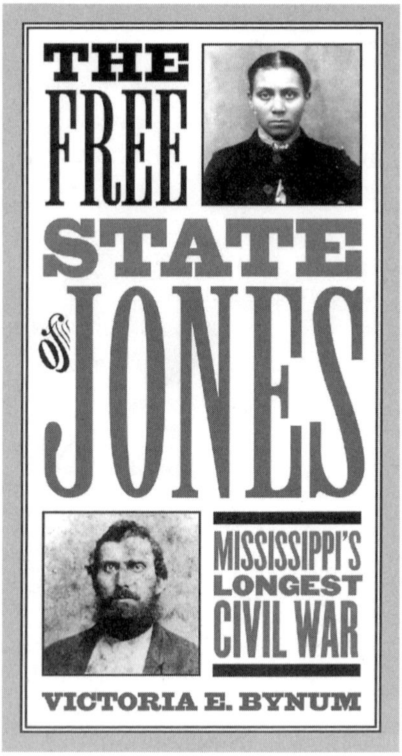

The Jones County revolt against the Confederate States of America and the lives of Newt, Serena, and Rachel Knight demonstrate the complexity of Mississippi society behind the facade where human relationships defied the stereotypes.

than a few aristocrats had kept black mistresses and recognized children from their relationships, but yeoman rarely accomplished such a socially unacceptable lifestyle.

Working out new relationships especially between blacks and whites challenged Mississippians during the war. Just prior to the federals taking Jackson, a city resident complained to the *Daily Mississippian* about the behavior of black men on the streets. Walking through the city with a friend from South Carolina, he saw well dressed "negroes" striding arm and arm smoking cigars and swearing loudly, ignoring his and his friend's presence and affecting the air of "foppish whites." On other occasions he had observed blacks failing to give way on sidewalks, hardly touching their hats in deference, and only reluctantly giving way to women when told to do so. He called for action to require respectful behavior and a proper dress code for slaves before such behavior led to a loss of restraint among "negroes." If he remained in the city, he must have truly been offended at the presence of black soldiers during the second occupation.

The developing relationships proved varied and complex, as demonstrated in Mary Knox Gales's account of her journey between Meridian and

Vicksburg in February 1864. Her grandfather lay seriously ill in Nashville, and because of the war, she and her aunt had to travel a circuitous route through Mississippi. Her description of riding in boxcars and having to be carried over streams to change trains where bridges had been destroyed paints a picture of the destitution left by the Union armies. In Clinton, a relative suggested that they take his wagon manned by "Old Bart," who would be taking a load of cotton to sell in Vicksburg. An ebony black man, Old Bart, wrapped in a Union overcoat and well armed, drove a covered wagon filled with four bales of cotton, food for the journey, and utensils such as a coffeepot and cups. The women negotiated passage through the Confederate lines at the Big Black in return for carrying letters to be mailed to relatives around the country. At noon, they stopped for coffee, with Old Bart sharing his cup at a respectful distance. At another stop, the three of them shared their food with a white woman, whose man had been killed in a robbery on the road, and her children. That night the only lodging available was a slave cottage owned by a white family. Old Bart woke the women early and urged them to leave quickly because the owners of the cottage "dey ain't our folks." Gale knew what he meant and trusted the black giant of a man unquestioningly with her life, knowing his assessment of the white family whose "hospitality" they had enjoyed could be trusted.

Passing through the desolation on the outskirts of Vicksburg, they began to encounter black soldiers, and Old Bart demonstrated his disapproval of them through grunts of anger and disgust. He refused to speak to the soldiers even though Gale sensed that they knew one another. Taken to headquarters, a "sassy negro woman" searched Gale, jerking her around and causing Gale to wish to "slap her jaws." Having passed inspection, the soldiers turned her over to a southern "Union man" whom the women's relatives had contacted to assist with the remainder of their journey. In her trip across the state, Gale met all the actors in society at the time, and she expressed most appreciation for Old Bart. There were blacks who chose to align themselves with whites and to maintain personal relationships that developed during slavery but evolved into more complex ties as time passed.

Meanwhile the war continued. Forrest and his superiors treated the affair at Okolona as if it were a major victory in order to boost morale. As the war shifted to Georgia, the CSA assigned Mississippi to General Stephen D. Lee. A graduate of West Point and a professional soldier, Lee gave Forrest free rein in north Mississippi to harass the federals who lightened their grip to transfer men east. Corinth had been abandoned, and Sherman worried that Forrest would drive north into middle Tennessee to threaten his supply lines, so he ordered 8,000 men to keep Forrest in Mississippi and destroy him. Forrest had begun to march toward Tennessee when Lee called him back to confront the force seeking him.

Forrest learned the whereabouts of the rain-soaked, slow-moving column, and knowing the land well, he chose Brice's Crossroads as the battleground. His plan was to defeat the column's cavalry first and count on the water-logged terrain to slow infantry, who would tire themselves running through the muck to reach the sound of the firing. Forrest engaged before all of his troops and artillery had arrived in order to have the ground that he wanted. When a part of his force managed to get around the enemy's left flank and attack them from behind, the Union forces panicked and fled, leaving behind their artillery, wagons, and wounded. Forrest sent cavalry after them and after a short rest had his full force on the road by 1:00 A.M. hoping to finish off the federals. He caught them at 8:00 A.M. at Ripley, where they stood and fought until their ammunition ran low and they broke and ran, losing any semblance of an organized army. Forrest's generalship was masterful, and the tactics are still studied in military schools today. Brice's Crossroads earned Forrest and Lee, who had little to do with it, plaudits. The CSA promoted Lee to lieutenant general—the youngest officer in the army to attain that rank—and used the victory to buoy flagging spirits. Given the long string of defeats, the victory provided a late bright spot in the dark military record in Mississippi.

The only flaw was that the Union army commander charged that Forrest had repeated the atrocity of murdering captured black soldiers after they surrendered. Forrest had been accused of murdering black troops at Fort Pillow after they surrendered, and the story had been widely publicized in the North. In this instance, both Lee and Forrest denied the allegation, and both repeated the South's policy of treating captured blacks as property, not as soldiers. They insisted that captured blacks would be forced into service, returned to their owners, or sold to a new one.

Furious, Sherman ordered another expedition of 14,000 men to find Forrest and kill him if it took 10,000 lives and bankrupted the treasury. Perhaps jealous of sharing acclaim with Lee, Forrest suggested that Lee take command to meet this incursion into north Mississippi. Lee declined, but Forrest's heart did not seem to be in this fight. Andrew Jackson Smith, the Union general, moved slowly, determined not to be lured onto a field selected by his opponent. He outmaneuvered Forrest by disguising his movements and not taking the usual routes. Lee and Forrest tried to entice Smith to Okolona, where they had concentrated Confederate forces, but he turned to Tupelo. Forrest pursued him, but cavalry and two black infantry regiments kept Forrest off balance by hiding well and then rising up to fire when Forrest and his men got close. Smith chose a high ridge near Tupelo to make his stand. After Lee and Forrest talked about attacking, Forrest and an aide rode into the Union lines at night, bluffing their way along and estimating the Union strength. He judged it a mistake to make the head-on attack the next morning, July 14, 1864, but followed Lee's orders. The attacks cost the Confederates 1,300 causalities to Smith's 700, but water had ruined the federal unit's bread supply, and Smith had only one day's rations left, so he withdrew instead of attacking. Lee could claim a technical victory because he held the field.

Not pleased, Sherman ordered Smith back to Mississippi the next month to find Forrest. Smith headed to Oxford, where Forrest liked to quarter, and in a repeat of the first invasion two years earlier, the Confederates occupied a line south of the Tallahatchie, abandoned it, and retreated south of Oxford. Smith occupied the town and seemed to be respecting and preserving property until news came that Forrest had ridden to Memphis and into the lobby of the Gayoso Hotel, sending at least one Union general fleeing in his nightshirt. Smith turned his troops, including black units, loose on the town. He chose the homes of known Confederates to be looted and razed, especially that of former congressman Thompson. Many homes, the courthouse, and the buildings around the square all went up in flames. The army ran wild, plundering homes, invading churches, and stealing at will. Finally the war ended for Oxford because it contained too little to interest anyone. Having destroyed the town, the federals marched north toward Memphis, again leaving the people of Lafayette County to try and survive in the burned town and on devastated farms.

For the next year of the war, survival possessed the population's mind. In Mississippi, the conflict degenerated into a struggle for life and food. An inhabitant in Abbeville chose not to join the army but developed a technique to make Union scavengers pay for their looting. Hiding near chicken houses, he crowed like a rooster, and when a soldier came looking for chickens, he shot the looter. He claimed to have killed eleven men using that trick.

Joseph Davis spent the last years of the war seeking a safe haven from the invaders. As Grant closed in on Vicksburg, he relocated to Hinds County with some of his slaves, his wines, books, and furniture. Approaching eighty and suffering from rheumatism, he nevertheless insisted on continuing to protect his family and slaves. When Grant and the federals entered Hinds County, Davis escaped in an oxcart and, after wandering from one Confederate camp to another, took refuge at Lauderdale Springs, where one of the doctors assigned to the resort turned hospital befriended him. His wife died there, and he tried to return to his plantation in order to find more of his slaves. He was enraged to hear of a Confederate raiding party shooting and hanging some of his slaves because they were armed, and he lost hope when he learned that Ben Montgomery had fled to Ohio with his family. Forced to flee again with only forty of his hundreds of slaves and a granddaughter for comfort, he followed his doctor friend to Tuscaloosa and lived in fair comfort among the wealthy population there until the end of the war.

Alcorn refused to take the Union oath, but kept smuggling cotton and developed an informal understanding with the local Union commander. Alcorn told his wife that his residence on their plantation depended on the commander's judgment of his behavior as a "good boy" and the "witness" of the "negroes of the neighborhood." Crossing the river to visit with the commander, he watched black troops drill and described them to his wife as a fine, proud-looking group of soldiers. He also visited a school for black children, and after being introduced as a "rebel gentleman," he said that the children smiled at him as if to say, "How do you like us Mr. Secesh?" Intending not only to survive but to prosper in the new society, Alcorn began to resurrect his legal career in the federal courts beginning to function again. He ceased attending the useless Mississippi legislature, but while in Columbus, he did make a speech advising that the legislature declare an end to slavery in twenty years and endorsing the proposal to enlist black troops for the CSA.

Howell Hinds was still serving as provost marshal of Jefferson County, and on September 30, 1864, as a Union force on a foraging mission entered Fayette, a single shot was fired at them. The lieutenant in command of the unit could not identify the shooter, but while searching for him, the lieutenant shot Hinds and reported killing him. Again Hinds recovered, and two months later an unidentified "soldier" shot the lieutenant dead from forty yards away as he again rode into Fayette. Hinds survived, but his health was broken, and he failed to preserve much of his prewar wealth.

Newt Knight continued to battle the Confederates in Jones County, but the army sent cavalry to guard the voting stations during the local elections of October 1864, preventing the pro-Union voters from casting ballots. In November Knight's band captured and paroled twenty Confederate cavalry along the Leaf River. The conflict grew meaner. For example, one member of the band was either shot or hanged (accounts differ) in front of his wife, who was then forced to kill all of her chickens and cook them to feed her husband's Confederate murderers. The most famous incident in the last months of the Jones County war involved an attack on a Knight wedding party. A neighbor, who knew the Confederates were coming, sent a note by her slave to Knight. It arrived just in time for him to run carrying a baby in one hand and his gun in the other. From the edge of the woods, he bellowed orders to his "battalion," bluffing the attackers into believing they and been lured into a trap and thereby escaping. Shortly after this incident, Knight's cousin was caught at home with his wife when a group of Confederates came searching for him. With no time to bolt, he climbed up the chimney and had her build up the fire and put on a kettle for cooking. They did not find him, but his rear was scorched before they left. A diarist visiting the region on January 21, 1864, recorded the gossip highlights of a typical day: a widow's house burned because she was accused of poisoning dogs belonging to the cavalry, a doctor was shot to pieces because he had guided cavalry through the county, a woman had stampeded a deserter by drawing a gun, a deserter named Warren Waters was killed by the cavalry, and some of the cavalry had been killed and wounded.

In December 1864 the federals sent the state a Christmas greeting, the last major Mississippi operation consisting of 3,500 men on an extended raid through Ripley and Booneville stealing food and burning any building that could be of any use to the CSA. They destroyed the recently repaired tracks of the Mobile and Ohio Railroad and burned the Choctaw County courthouse before discovering a real target at Bankston. Tucked away in a remote location, James M. Wesson established a steam-powered textile mill on a tributary of the Big Black in 1848 and turned it into a highly profitable mill to weave both wool and cotton cloth as well as milling flour and corn. Wesson added a tannery and a shoe factory and built a model mill town to house his 500 workers. When the federals arrived, the mill turned out 1,000 yards of cloth and 2,000 pairs of shoes each day. The federals burned it all, destroying the last large mill in the state. Turning west toward the Mississippi Central Railroad, they found, killed, and burned 800 hogs destined for the Confederate army and destroyed rail tracks. Near Vaiden, they stopped at the home of Margaret Virginia Whitehead Kennedy, who described the raid. She had sent off and hidden everything of value, and dressed in her best silk concealing valuables on her person, she met the raiders at the door, asking only that they not let the black soldiers into her house. Granting that request, some of the white officers and men entered and rummaged through all of her trunks and clothing. They took what they wanted of the clothing and destroyed much of what they did not care to take. They stole the horses, mules, bedding, and food. At her seventy-year-old grandmother's, they repeated the process, with the added twist of throwing the chickens in the air to cut off their heads with sabers as they fell. She noted that a "negro" soldier killed a neighbor and registered the "passionate rebellion" in her heart resulting from the raid. Brushing aside a few Confederate cavalry, the federals rode into the Vicksburg enclave on January 4, 1865.

Retreating after the disastrous defeat at Franklin, Tennessee, the last large Confederate army rested at Tupelo before being ordered to the Carolinas to try to confront Sherman, who was still marching through the South.

Lee had been transferred earlier, leaving Richard Taylor, son of President Taylor, as the Confederate general commanding the few remaining CSA forces in the state.

The hapless Governor Clark met the legislature on February 20, 1865, and recommended the enlistment of slaves as Confederate soldiers. Introduced by Ethelbert Barksdale, past editor of the *Mississippian* who served as Confederate congressman from Mississippi, the "Negro Soldier Law" would not have offered freedom for service, only equal pay. Clark recommended it as "an experiment," as if the South had time to see how it worked for a few years. He ventured that with firm discipline, slaves could make good soldiers, but that they should continue to be slaves because that status best suited them. The members of the legislature scattered, and Clark made some effort to enlist blacks, but a federal officer heard some of them say that if they were to fight they would prefer to fight for the Union. From Virginia came the news that the Confederate capital had fallen and Robert E. Lee had surrendered. Clark waited until Taylor surrendered outside Mobile to issue an appeal to Mississippians on May 6, 1865, asking them to maintain law and order and practice common sense. He sent William Sharkey, a Whig who opposed secession, to meet with President Andrew Johnson to discuss terms for rejoining the Union. He called the legislature to meet in Jackson and it did, empowering the governor to negotiate a return to the Union. They met for only an hour before leaving town assuming they might be arrested. The federal district commander told the governor to turn over the state's public documents and Clark did, with the understanding that he did so "under protest." The commander arrested Clark and sent him to a federal fort in Savannah, but released him on parole in a few weeks.

Pettus so feared federal punishment that when President Andrew Johnson did not immediately grant his request for a pardon, he fled Kemper County to a relative's farm in Arkansas. He hid in the swamps near the farm, sometimes without even a tent. He died on the farm, and his relatives buried him in a cornfield.

The Civil War proved a victory for the majority of Mississippians who won their freedom from slavery. About 17,000 fought for it alongside federal troops, while others remained on plantations loyal to the elite white minority of the population who gradually and reluctantly recognized the emancipation of their human property. Around 80,000 white Mississippians fought in the Confederate army, while about 500 chose to serve in the Union forces. At the beginning of the war, the white population overwhelmingly supported the war and coerced doubters such as James L. Alcorn either to support the "revolution" or be excluded from white society. Slaves demonstrated by their behavior during the conflict that most of them longed for an opportunity to gain their freedom. As the Confederate army suffered an almost unbroken string of defeats in Mississippi and impoverished families suffered from the absence of their men, large numbers of soldiers voted with their feet by deserting in order to return home to provide for and protect their loved ones. The conscription law, by exempting large slaveholders, contributed to yeomen's dissatisfaction with their leaders, who brought their body servants to camp and reinforced the gulf between classes by eating better and leaving camp to party with other elites along the campaign trails. By late 1862 large numbers of Mississippians had begun to lose confidence in the leadership and to believe that the war was lost. After the fall of Vicksburg in 1863, probably the majority were ready for an end to the war as the state and local governments had collapsed. Much of the real history of Mississippi during the war is not the list of battles fought within the state but the disintegration of the government, churches, schools, society, and economy.

At the outset of the war, Mississippi's churches flourished, with large increases in both black and white membership, growth in the number of physical structures, development of Sunday schools, and the creation of institutions of higher learning. For the first two years of the war, churches held their own, with women using them as the center of activities to support the war, but as the war wore on, churches could no longer pay their ministers, travel even to church became unsafe, and church activities to support the war declined. In addition, ministers who endorsed the secessionist cause as the will of God fumbled for an explanation of God giving victory to the North. Their solution was to blame southerners for some undefined sin for which God was punishing them—not nearly so appealing as the prewar sermons. But the decline at home was offset by revivals that swept the Confederate armies, producing mass conversions among men who traditionally had been much less supportive of church membership than women. Blacks joined wartime churches in large numbers as ministers and slaveholders continued to target slaves for conversion, but as freedmen obtained independence, both races gradually divided their worship services into separate, racially distinct churches.

Although the legislature always refused to create a state public school system, the counties, towns, and churches had established a substantial number of schools by 1861, which suffered badly. The university and all of the colleges except Mississippi College closed during the war, and Mississippi College limped weakly along. Most of the high school education had been provided by private church academies, and they closed. Women took over teaching some of the elementary schools, but many of those closed as well.

The enemy destroyed all of the state's factories, leaving only sawmills in operation. Much of the planters' wealth had been in slave property, which the nation abolished without compensation. War-making had badly damaged the rail system and destroyed incalculable numbers of animals, crops, and stored cotton. Untended fields had gone back to brush and would require years to restore. Inflation and investments in CSA bonds wiped out accumulated savings, making investment capital scarce. The most experienced banker in the state, Stephen Duncan, left Natchez in 1863, moved to New York, and lived there the rest of his life.

Mississippi's old social system based on slavery ended with emancipation and the Union's decision to arm the freedmen. Given the option, white Mississippians would have restored slavery, but submission to the federal government made that impossible. The human suffering resulting from the war is hard to grasp. Thirty percent of the white men who went to war died. The University Greys suffered 100 percent casualties at Gettysburg, and only a handful of the Greys lived to see Appomattox. Visitors to the state after the war expressed shock at the number of men missing arms and legs, and in 1865 the largest item in the state budget was the purchase of artificial limbs. But the physical suffering paled compared to the psychic pain. Like Margaret Virginia Whitehead Kennedy, the majority of white Mississippians retained in their hearts "passionate rebellion." The white minority refused to accept black Mississippians' freedom, making it impossible to construct a healthy new society to replace slavery.

Despite the fact that most whites refused to accept black equality, human relationships that had developed among slaves and owners continued sometimes to bridge the racial divide. Holt Collier maintained his relationship with the Hinds family. Thomas Hinds lived openly with Collier's sister as if married. In defiance of all conventions, Newt Knight merged his white and black families in Jones County. As time passed after the war, former slave owners regretted that their children lacked the same personal and human relationships with black people that they had enjoyed. It was impossible for human beings to have their lives so closely intertwined as Mississippians did and always maintain the divisions imposed by social conventions. Inevitably blacks and whites recognized one another's humanity and behaved accordingly.

Chapter Seven

RECONSTRUCTION: WAR BY OTHER MEANS

The war between the North and South ended in May 1865, but the fighting continued for another decade. Initially, President Johnson, a fellow southerner, encouraged the old planter class to resume their rule of Mississippi with minimal interference from the federal government, but Mississippi's attempt to limit the freedmen to an inferior caste led congressional Republicans to initiate military rule as a means of guaranteeing the former slaves' citizenship. The overwhelming majority of white Mississippians rejected the free society embodied in the Thirteenth, Fourteenth, and Fifteenth Amendments to the Constitution and resisted black equality using political maneuvering and ultimately violent oppression. By 1875 voters in the North tired of occupying the South and acquiesced when Mississippians first used violent methods to keep the black majority from the polls and then ousted the Republican government to institute Democratic white rule. Behind the politics and constitutional debates lurked one basic question: how would black and white Mississippians live together? By establishing separate churches and schools, blacks demonstrated that they desired their own institutions free of white control or supervision. By voting and engaging in political activities in impressive numbers, they announced their intention of using the government to secure legal equality, educational opportunities, and decent treatment in public transportation. Rare white individuals, both southern and northern, supported and assisted blacks in their efforts, but most whites insisted that slavery be replaced with a caste system denying blacks legal equality, recognition of social standing due a fellow citizen, or economic opportunities to earn those rights.

President Johnson met informally with the emissaries Governor Clark sent to Washington before the war's end and selected one of them, William L. Sharkey, an old Whig who had never supported the Confederate States of America (CSA), as governor of the state. The Democratic fire-eaters such as Lamar, Barry, and McRae retired to their farms or private law practices and kept quiet at war's end. Thompson hid out in Europe and Pettus in the Arkansas swamps. Nathan Bedford Forrest got a crop planted on his Coahoma plantation. Former senator Brown admitted that they (the fire-eaters) had played "hell" and advised Mississippians to renew their allegiance to the United States. Sharkey tried to appoint Whigs who had opposed secession to help him govern, but many of his appointees had served the CSA, and bad press required him to defend his record to Johnson. Claiborne wrote to warn Johnson that Mississippians did not comprehend the new society created by the war and suggested a military occupation government to give Mississippians time to adjust. A few planters still held blacks in slavery and refused to accept emancipation in 1865. Some who recognized emancipation still deluded themselves that the nation would compensate them for the slave property taken from them to win the war, and almost none even dreamed of accepting blacks as citizens. By stretching their collective imagination, they could begin to grasp the idea that freedmen might attain the status held by free blacks in antebellum society, meaning they could hold property but not testify in court and certainly not vote. Sharkey nevertheless forged ahead to reconstruct a government composed of the same men who led the state before the war.

Sharkey's call to elect representatives to a constitutional convention produced light voting. Many prewar voters died fighting, others failed to take the loyalty oath in time to be eligible, and the secessionists wanted to be left alone. Seventy-one Whigs and eighteen Democrats assembled in Jackson in August 1865 to prepare a constitution that would enable the state's readmission to the Union. Johnson telegraphed advice to Sharkey. First, the convention should abolish slavery. Second, adopt the Thirteenth Amendment to the national Constitution outlawing slavery. Third, extend the right to vote to literate and property-holding black men. He made plain that the last point would squelch the growing clamor in the North for a black franchise because it would bring Mississippi in line with voting laws in the North. Sharkey responded that black voting stood no chance of passing because Mississippi intended to keep that privilege for whites only. The convention members debated long and hard the abolition of slavery, but could not bring themselves to abolish it. Instead, they compromised on wording indicating that it had been destroyed and would no longer exist. They took no action on the Thirteenth Amendment and left the freedman's status to the legislature soon to be elected. A few mentioned submitting the constitution to a vote of the people, but the convention decided that it was unnecessary and declared it valid.

Their arrogance in the midst of a ruined capital city and a destroyed state set the stage for continued resistance. The federal army still occupied the state, while U.S. treasury agents scoured the countryside seeking CSA cotton for confiscation. Such cotton proved hard to identify, and some Union officers and treasury agents used their power to enrich themselves by "legal" plunder. The army tried not to interfere with local authorities who proved incapable of reestablishing law and order. Seemingly random violence dominated the newspapers, shocking visitors. One New Yorker reported seeing news stories of more knifings and shootings in a few days in Mississippi than he had witnessed in six years in New York. As white federal troops mustered out, the military moved black soldiers from the river counties into the center of the state, where people were not accustomed to them. Confrontations between black troops and the white population soured the relationship between civil and military authorities, and sheriffs declined to call on the army for assistance any longer. Planters complained that the arrival of black soldiers inspired their black workers into restlessness. Rumors of an impending black uprising against whites circulated constantly through the white population, keeping many in a state of apprehension, especially around the holidays. Sharkey responded by organizing a militia in each county. Naturally the federal commander, not willing to see the recently defeated Confederates rearmed, ordered him to dismantle the militia. President Johnson overrode his general and allowed Sharkey to proceed, enraging northerners already critical of the Sharkey-Johnson alliance. Reports multiplied that militia were abusing freedmen, but the military hesitated to intervene given Johnson's actions. In late 1865 the army sent a Kentuckian to command the occupation, and he mustered out almost all the black regiments in order to establish better relations with Mississippi's civilian government.

Mississippi held an election on October 2, 1865, to choose a new state government. Three men ran for governor—a Union Democrat from the piney woods, a Whig judge endorsed by Sharkey, and a planter who served as a general in the CSA army. General Benjamin G. Humphreys won. He had opposed secession, but of the three, he had rendered the greatest support to the rebellion, and, though not wounded, he had three bullet holes in his coat worn in battle. He had not received his pardon, and Johnson had to issue one before he could take office. The Whigs won control of both the House of Representatives and the Senate, but with smaller majorities than they enjoyed in the convention. The five congressmen elected had all opposed secession, but one was a former CSA general and two others were colonels. The only known secessionists elected went to the courts, with the chief justice being one of the leading fire-eaters in the state. As soon as the legislature met, it moved to elect two senators. Sharkey and Alcorn stood to win the seats, but a movement against them arose because both had indicated a willingness to allow freedmen the right to testify in court. A Mississippi Senate resolution aimed to bar any candidate from a seat if he favored "any rights, civil, political, or social," for freedmen greater than those granted to free blacks before the war. The Whigs tabled the resolution and elected their candidates despite the protest.

Governor Humphreys addressed the legislature and plainly stated the state's position. Mississippians, he said, accepted the verdict of the war and recognized that they could not secede, but he affirmed that a state enjoyed all of the powers not explicitly granted to the national government. Although he recognized the end of slavery, he asserted the state's right to determine the status of freedmen. He stated that Mississippi would protect the person and property of freedmen, "but they cannot be admitted to political or social equality with the white race . . . ours is and ever shall ever be a government of white men. The purity and progress of both races require that caste must be maintained."

The legislature proceeded to reenact the slave code forbidding freedmen to own weapons, preach without a license, or drink liquor unless it was provided by an employer. Laws forbade (among a long list of behaviors) insulting language and gestures as well as seditious speeches. In order to prevent freedmen gaining economic independence, they were forbidden to lease farmland. They could sue and be sued in state court, but could only testify in cases involving fellow freedmen and not in cases involving white persons. Former masters, having lost the right to administer the lash, intended to use the state as the means of disciplining the freedmen. While they did not legislate public floggings, they did provide for freedmen to be hung by their thumbs in front of the state's jails and courthouses. The black code, as these laws were called, required each freedman to have a labor contract by the second Monday of January 1866 or be arrested as a vagrant. If arrested, they would be auctioned off to the highest bidder to work as a prisoner for no wage. The most egregious provision declared that orphans or children whose parents could not support them would be apprenticed to employers to work without pay until their eighteenth birthday for females and the twenty-first for males. Former owners received preference under the law to apprentice the children whose parents they had owned. Former slave owners continued to hold their former slaves' children against their will across the state, leading to innumerable individual struggles for freedom.

Laura Taylor complained to an agent of the Freedmen's Bureau that when she left her former owner's plantation after Christmas 1865, he refused to allow her to take her two children, Mary and Joseph, with her, claiming that they had been bound to him by a county judge as apprentices. When she protested, the planter drove her off his farm. She returned and took them away, but the planter sent the sheriff after her, and he seized the children and returned them to the plantation. Taylor went to the judge and begged for her children, but the judge refused to listen, insisted the children had to remain with the planter, and threatened to jail her for contempt if she complained. The Freedmen's Bureau agent could only sympathize because the apprentice law was valid until the legislature repealed it in 1867.

Silas Clear mustered out of the "Colored Infantry" in 1866 and walked to Vicksburg to claim Mary Jane Kelley as his wife. Kelley worked for a white family named Fisher, who told him that he could not have her. He went home to Washington County, saved some money, and sent for her the next spring. She came, adopted the name Clear, and, according to Silas, "has been owned by me as a wife" since her arrival. Freedom had many meanings for people during Reconstruction. Silas thought his freedom gave him ownership of his wife, but she had other ideas. As a slave, she married twice before marrying him. Her first husband left her for another woman, so she took up with Ed Kelley and escaped slavery with him on a federal gunboat. The navy separated her from Kelley, but she made her way to a Louisiana plantation across from Vicksburg so that she could visit Kelley until he was killed in Yazoo City. Then she moved to the Davis Bend community, where the federals were experimenting with a freedman-run plantation. She returned to Vicksburg to care for Ed Kelley's mother, who had a terminal illness. She went to Clear only after her mother-in-law died. One suspects she may have engineered the Fisher refusal to let her go. To her mind, neither the Fishers nor Clear owned her because freedom to Mary Jane meant moving where she pleased, to care for members of an extended family. As with most freed people, she maintained an extended family network forged in slavery.

War and emancipation produced fluidity in all relationships, destroying the patriarchal society known to southerners before 1861. Silas Clear, the black veteran, wanted to claim his own version of a patriarchal family. Planters wanted to reclaim what they had lost. Observers noticed that older Mississippi men seemed to adjust more readily to their new world than younger ones. Older men could recall the frontier when they had battled to establish themselves, but younger men had only known the matured slave society and, as a result, suffered severe disorientation. L. Q. C. Lamar, for example, spent the war in lackluster assignments on missions abroad or in the military's judicial wing and returned to Lafayette County to fail at farming during Reconstruction. Forced to deed his plantation back to his father-in-law and to try to earn a living as a lawyer, he suffered from depression and near mental breakdowns. Stephen D. Lee, the youngest lieutenant general in the CSA, received a Noxubee County plantation from his wife's grandfather at the end of the war, but he never enjoyed farming, spent nights patrolling to keep down any black rebellion, moved to Columbus to escape the plantation, and sought a life in the business world. Having served four years away in the war, young Clay Sharkey returned to his Hinds County plantation in June 1865 wearing threadbare clothes, a straw hat, and Yankee boots four sizes too big. Although he had only four of his prewar eighty-five mules left, many of the former slaves remained working the place. Together they made seven bales of cotton in 1865 and he owed no debts, but he made no effort to rebuild the plantation, returning instead to his antebellum pastimes of hunting and fishing. He restored his pack of hunting dogs and enjoyed pursuing the animals grown more numerous during the war. Good-hearted, he helped a one-legged veteran with his farm, enduring the ribbing that he took because he did not know how to plow. He considered a move to Mexico but joined the Ku Klux Klan instead. He married and left his wife to manage the plantation. Finally, he moved to Leake County, where he established good relations with the Choctaw and acted as sort of an agent for them with planters seeking to hire Choctaw workers. He owned a mill on Cobb Creek, hunted with the Choctaw, and led the local opposition to Republican rule. Restlessness and dissatisfaction plagued many young men of the elite seeking to reestablish a society based on their will to rule. Clay mixed the joy of hunting and Indian companionship with local politics and never made much of a mark in history, but Lee and Lamar turned their restlessness into successful careers.

Postwar society satisfied few. Freedmen hoped to be given land and a mule. Rumors of an impending distribution encouraged hope and discouraged them from signing labor contracts during the winter of 1865. Planters raged because only about a third of the people living on their farms actually worked their fields in many cases. During the war, slaves had enlarged their gardens and flocks of chickens, which they sold for profit, and freedmen continued to expand their personal sphere of operations. Freedmen resisted planters' attempts to reintroduce the gang labor system and went on pilfering the smokehouses and corncribs as they had as slaves. Urged on by the Freedmen's Bureau established by Congress to assist in the transition from slavery to freedom, freedmen and freedwomen negotiated individual deals with planters. Sometimes they agreed to gang work but stipulated no white overseers. At other times they asked for a church building or a school as part of the contract. Forrest contracted with workers on his Coahoma plantation not to hire white overseers in 1866 and then violated the agreement two months later by hiring two former federal army officers for those jobs. Tom Edwards, one of Forrest's freedmen workers, led a protest and called on the Freedmen's Bureau to send an investigator. The next Sunday Forrest marched down to the quarters and ordered his workers to use their day of rest to clean up his property, telling them that they might be free but that they lived on his land and in his houses. Following Forrest's visit to the quarters, Edwards went directly into his house and demanded that his wife fix him something to eat. When she refused, he screamed at her and began to beat her. Hearing her cries, Forrest rushed into the house with a stick and beat Edwards to death. Edwards paid with his life for his desire to hold Forrest to his word and to dominate his wife as Forrest tried to dominate him.

Planters began to manipulate labor contracts to their advantage, and they and the freedmen reached a compromise at the expense of the freedwomen. Planters forced the nonworkers off their farms and stipulated that only cotton could be grown on their land in order to eliminate the independence earned by gardening and keeping animals. These tasks had been the work primarily of women and children. Freedmen insisted on controlling their wives' and children's labor and standing as a buffer between their family and the white landowner to provide the freedman a patriarchal sphere that had not existed in slavery. Freedmen desired to have their own space too, so they moved houses from the quarters or built their own log cabins on individual pieces of land that they worked on shares with their families. This labor arrangement eliminated the gang system employed by all the cotton plantations and gave the freedman the independence to order his own schedule. Planters eliminated contracts with women and began contracting only with freedmen, who took responsibility for their families and thereby gained more control over them. From this struggle for gender, racial, and economic dominance emerged the sharecropping system. For all of its faults, it represented a compromise solution to the labor problem faced by the planter deprived of his slaves and to the landless freedman determined not to continue living in the quarters or working in gangs alongside his wife and children driven by an overseer.

As they struggled to devise a labor system, blacks also quickly established separate churches. Usually their separation from white churches proved amicable as whites often no longer felt comfortable worshipping with them as free people, but generalizations are dangerous because biracial churches continued to exist for decades. In independent black institutions, the secret churches hidden from white view during slavery emerged from the night and the woods. Dismayed whites encountered the body movements and shouting retained from the brush arbor experiences of the early evangelicals. To those traditions, shared with some white churches, the freedmen added African experiences of visions, trances, and "traveling." Oxford's freed slaves returned to a brush arbor for their first free church meeting in the woods back of the Old Pegues estate. Later they pitched tents on the site and then met in the back of the First Baptist Church before finally building the Second Baptist Church. By the end of Reconstruction, Lafayette County alone had fifty black churches. As early as 1866 what became the Second Baptist Church formed the Freedmen's Benevolent Aid Society to dispense charity and provide burials. Just after Christmas, 150 members paraded through town and concluded at the white Methodist church for singing, praying, and speech making. Two white ministers and the university chancellor praised the black congregation for their efforts at self-help and expressed the community's respect and sympathy. In parallel with the worst conflicts between the races, such demonstrations and expressions of Christian brotherhood coexisted.

Northern missionaries came to Mississippi during the war to spread their version of Protestantism and to establish schools. Impressed by black people's deep religiosity, they tried to convert them, but made no progress in getting freedmen and freedwomen to adopt their more staid versions of Protestantism because freed people loved their churches. Churches became the centers of black life, serving often as schools and community centers as well as religious institutions.

The American Missionary Association (AMA) became the most active missionary organization in Mississippi. With a long commitment to abolition, the AMA responded to the need to establish schools for freed people and cooperated with the Freedmen's Bureau to create schools in camps and occupied towns during the war and later across the state. The paternalistic organization encountered black people starved for education and taught huge classes of all ages and both sexes. One "scholar" called education the next best thing to liberty. The AMA learned in Natchez that blacks had already established six schools in the city taught by black teachers. Holly Springs, Meridian, Raymond, and Aberdeen also had created their own schools, and as early as 1865 Mississippi had ten black schools outside Natchez and Vicksburg. Until creation of the public school system, the majority of black schools drew their financial support from their students and their families and not from the AMA or the Freedmen's Bureau. Between 1863 and 1870 Mississippi averaged only eighty-two northern teachers, but they had an impact. Many of the teachers were young white women, which created a number of problems. In Natchez, the white AMA teachers refused to live with the young black teachers sent south by their organization. In other locations, the white teachers had to board with black families as no white family would have them because whites opposed the black schools and especially the idea of Yankees teaching in them. A white woman living in a black household outraged the racist sensibilities of the local population. Blacks preferred teachers of their own race and resisted AMA efforts to displace black teachers with white ones or to play any role in their churches, which often housed schools.

Black teachers played a variety of roles beyond the classroom, helping blacks with their labor contracts and sometimes mediating disputes. All the teachers endured harassment from the local population, ranging from rowdy boys tagging along calling the teacher names to murder. Four men tarred and feathered an AMA teacher in Natchez. In Grenada, someone nearly beat J. P. Bradwell to death for teaching an AMA school, and when the local bureau agent protested, another unidentified person shot him in the chest three times. He died three days later. When the federal troops pulled out of Meridian in 1866, whites terrorized the AMA teachers, and they all left town except for Addie Warren, who stayed and lived to continue her teaching, demonstrating that the terrorists drew the line at killing white women. Whites did burn many black schools, some repeatedly when they were rebuilt. Whites made war on black education, rightly seeing it as a threat to the caste system they intended to maintain.

Mississippi was the first among the southern states to pass a black code, which provided a model for others, setting off a firestorm of criticism in the North and among more thoughtful and politic Mississippians. In October 1866 Humphreys called a special session of the legislature, asking it to reconsider the black codes and relax their provisions. The legislature refused. After the national elections went against the president, more Radical Republicans won office, and Major General Edward O. C. Ord came to oversee the occupation forces, the legislators changed their minds and in the 1867 session repealed most of the black codes, save the vagrancy laws. But they compromised far too slowly. The governor reacted more quickly than the legislature, and by January 1867, when the legislators convened, he advised them to approve the Fourteenth Amendment, which conferred citizenship on freedmen. The legislature would not, but in March the Republican Congress passed the first Reconstruction act, making the black franchise inevitable. Suddenly state leaders discovered the wisdom of Alcorn, who had been watching Washington political maneuvering while he waited hoping to be allowed to take a seat in the Senate. Alcorn advised acceptance of full black citizenship and the creation of a new party to lead blacks, with himself at its head. Given that blacks would constitute a majority of voters in Mississippi, even former secessionists did an amazingly rapid about-face, urging Mississippians to embrace black voting. Letters to the editor made the case. Alcorn circulated a pamphlet arguing that Mississippi leaders had to rush to appeal to the new black voters whom the Republicans hoped to capture in order to cement their radical control of Congress. Brown, the former fire-eater, addressed a mixed-race crowd in Copiah County and expressed his willingness to serve as a guide to freedmen as they entered the political fray.

Brown and other secessionists such as McRae decided to reenter the political process, urging acceptance of black voting as a means of winning readmission to the Union. To attract black voters, they offered the franchise and support for their schools. A younger man, Lamar kept silent and attended to his classes at the University of Mississippi, where he had rejoined the faculty. In the spring of 1867 newspapers and older politicians urged cooperation. Meanwhile the Republicans organized their Union Leagues and easily convinced blacks that they represented black interests far better than the Mississippi Whigs or Democrats. By the summer of 1867 some of the old Whigs floated a new Constitutional Union Party dedicated to defeating the franchise for blacks, and they criticized the turnabout on the part of the older Democrats. Brown's sensitive political nose let him down in his last try at following public opinion. The fleeting moment for white acceptance passed, and the overwhelming majority of whites rejected cooperation. Of the major figures, only Alcorn agreed to join with Republicans and try to shape the new emerging majority of voters in the state.

Ord had the task of implementing congressional or radical Reconstruction, and he began by registering the new electorate and eliminating those who had supported the rebellion from the voter rolls. Because he came from Maryland, some Mississippians hoped for his sympathy, but what they got was conscientious efficiency. He removed only twenty-five men from state office; he stayed court-ordered evictions for debt, winning some poor white support; and he mollified planters by ordering his officers to tell freedmen that they must sign their labor contracts or he would allow the sheriffs to enforce the vagrancy laws. He tried not to choose Republican organizers as registrars, but in the poorer interior counties his choices proved limited. Claiborne was his most prominent registrar. Ord used carpetbaggers, but there were never more than 200 politically active Yankees in the state. He found the few white Mississippians willing to support black rights—scalawags—and used them. For convenience sake, he used counties as registration districts and appointed three-man teams for each district. Henry Warren served in Leake County, where he and his brother owned a plantation.

Originally from Massachusetts, Warren was teaching school in Nashville when the war ended. Relatives who had served in the army in Mississippi convinced him that growing cotton would be a way to make his fortune. As with most of those from the North, he and his brother invested a substantial sum in their enterprise. They bought a 1,200-acre farm and its livestock from a planter who returned after Shiloh and spent the rest of the war protecting his home. Warren's farm straddled Cobb Creek, so he was neighbor to Clay Sharkey. Rustlers broke into his pen and stole horses and took all the plantation's colts while they were free on his land. Two white men burned his gin house and his supply of cottonseed with it. He read a couple of law books and bought the two Leake County lawyers who examined him a quart of champagne to obtain a law license. His friend, a Vermont native who spent the war in Carthage as postmaster, urged him to start a Union League and then recommended him as a registrar. He served with an old Whig, Walter C. Brewer, who could take the oath because he never supported the rebellion, and with a former federal soldier. They traveled the county in Brewer's lumber wagon drawn by two mules. No one of "their class" would board them, so Brewer cooked over campfires to feed them as they went about their work. No one threatened him with physical violence during the registration, and he felt a good deal of sympathy from the poor whites.

Some of the scalawags based their support for black rights on religious teaching. Alston Mygatt moved from New York to Vicksburg in 1837 and always held abolitionist views, but stayed quiet about his beliefs until the Union victory in his city. In the 1860s, as a tall bent man in his fifties, Mygatt spoke of having a sacred responsibility to deliver freedom and equal rights to former slaves, depicting himself as something akin to an Old Testament prophet. Robert Worth Flournoy, a slave-owning planter who moved from Georgia to Pontotoc County, described his conversion to a Reconstruction civil rights advocate as purely New Testament Christian humanitarianism. These two represented a rare group of Mississippians who dedicated themselves to delivering justice to freedmen.

Alcorn did not share their idealism, but from shrewd political analysis he decided to throw in with Republicans and became the first beneficiary of the Reconstruction political upheaval in Mississippi. The new electorate chose ninety-seven delegates to another constitutional convention that met in a cold capitol in January 1869. The outlook was grim, with many observers predicting starvation in the state before spring vegetables could be gathered. Two bad crop years added to the woes of disorder and social upheaval. Forty-one of the delegates were white southern Republicans, and only eighteen were black, and one of those blacks voted with the seventeen conservative delegates. Some delegates were cynical political bosses who had hoodwinked black voters. Meridian's boss, R. C. Merryman, fit the carpetbagger stereotype well except that he hailed from Virginia. Edward J. Castello, who was accused of embezzlement in Missouri when he migrated to Natchez in 1867, obviously simply saw an opportunity because he had opposed equal rights for blacks until he moved into the Republican Party. Called the Black and Tan Convention, the delegates wrote a constitution doing all the things that the first Confederate convention refused to do, such as abolishing slavery. They extended the governor's term to four years and restored the office of lieutenant governor, which had been abolished in 1832. Most significant, they created a state-funded public school system, and though they did not write it explicitly into the constitution, they allowed a dual system for blacks and whites. They added a new oath requiring voters to affirm the political and civil equality of all men.

Unlike the first convention, members of the Black and Tan Convention submitted their work to the voters in the spring of 1868. White voters crowded into the polls in several counties and assaulted blacks trying to vote. In many other counties whites ostentatiously wrote down the names of the blacks waiting in line to vote in order to frighten them away from the polls. Whites supplied liquor to groups of blacks to keep them from voting or to have them vote differently. Humphreys, who began to campaign against ratification, finally was removed by the military authorities, but ratification failed.

In Lafayette County, the 1868 vote provided a dress rehearsal for white tactics that would spread statewide to control black voters, and Lamar chose the vote as his time to reenter politics in order to condemn the "Mongrel Constitution." Democrats treated their faithful black voters to dinners, provided them "democratic stars" to wear, and praised them in speeches. On the other hand, one planter had three graves dug on his place the day before the election to insinuate that they would soon be filled by Republican voters. A band of outlaws shot at Republican election commissioners on the way to the polls and stole their horses. Prior to the election, horsemen rode into a black church during a political meeting and ordered speakers to cease. At Taylor's Depot, a planter told black voters at the poll that he would take away their jobs, houses, and land if they voted. A physician added for good measure that black voters would receive no medicine from him. In Abbeville, whites threatened to burn the black voters' houses and shoot them in the fields. As a result, Lafayette County voted 1,895 to 298 against the ratification of the constitution in a county with over 40 percent black voters. In the national elections in November, Grant won the presidency and on his first day in office sent General Adelbert Ames to Mississippi to take over the administration of state government. Grant persuaded Congress to separate the text of the constitution from the oath and the proscriptive clauses excluding former Confederates from voting and holding office. The revised document went to the voters again, and in April 1869 they approved the constitution but not the separate clauses. With Humphreys gone, Ames became the military governor and appointed a new set of rulers across the state from the county and city to the state level, filling 2,000 offices.

Albert T. Morgan, a carpetbagger who had established himself in Yazoo City, became a supervisor for Yazoo County. Morgan, a wounded Union veteran, came to Yazoo with his brother after the war and bought a plantation, where they raised cotton and established a sawmill. Initially, the white planters welcomed the brothers, but when the brothers built a church/school on their plantation for their workers and contributed to a school in town for the freedmen, their neighbors ostracized them, and the family from whom they bought the plantation went to court to reclaim the property. Morgan served as a registrar and then ran successfully as a delegate to the Black and Tan Convention. Appointed supervisor, he became the political boss of the county protected by his black followers, abused in the streets by boys calling him names, and threatened by violence constantly. Dividing his time between the legislature in Jackson and his duties in the county, the Yazoo Reconstruction government built 100 schools, a courthouse, and a jail; improved the poor farm; and constructed roads and bridges. While serving in the legislature in Jackson, he met and married a mixed-race teacher, which further alienated him from whites. Morgan, although he provided a good, efficient government, represented the worst nightmare of the racist planter class, who owned 60 percent of the county though they only made up 3 percent of the population.

Republicans sensed the opportunity to entrench themselves and establish permanent control of Mississippi based on the majority of black voters in the state, but they divided their forces. One branch nominated Grant's brother-in-law, Louis Dent, for governor, but Alcorn challenged him along with a ticket including one black as candidate for secretary of state. Truly a carpetbagger, Dent claimed Mississippi citizenship based on some rented land on which he had not paid any taxes. Alcorn used the money that he made selling cotton during the war to increase his land holdings and continued to play the role of grand planter, still dressing impeccably and confident of having a destiny to lead. He despised the white lower class and simply looked upon blacks as one more group in need of his direction. He tried to form a new party to be his vehicle for leadership, but when that failed, he moved into the Republican Party. Sharkey's and Alcorn's old political associates in the Whig Party dropped away from him and gravitated toward the Democrats reluctantly as the whites' party. Claiborne warned Alcorn that he would be killed if he ran as a Republican, but Alcorn proved fearless. He debated Dent in venues around the state and destroyed him with humor, bombast, and courage. In Aberdeen, Alcorn calmly drew a pistol from his satchel after he heard guns cocked in the audience standing before him. By facing down those who wanted to shoot him, Alcorn won over the crowd. At Winona, local Democrats dissuaded whites who wanted to assassinate him from afar with a rifle. Both Grant and Ames supported Alcorn, as did some Democrats, and he won easily, with most Democrats refusing to participate under the Black and Tan constitution. Dent left the state before the ballots had been counted. Ames offered to appoint Alcorn governor immediately, but Alcorn was too proud to accept and insisted on waiting for his scheduled inauguration date.

The new legislature met in January and quickly ratified the U.S. Constitution's Fourteenth and Fifteenth Amendments, earning Mississippi readmission to the Union. The legislature elected Ames to the Senate along with Hiram Revels, a black minister, for the one year remaining of Jefferson Davis's term. Alcorn took the governor's oath on March 10, 1870, and immediately began to try to build a political machine. He ousted Ames's appointees and installed his men—many of them Democrats. He issued $500,000 in state warrants scheduled to pay 8 percent interest in order to provide liquidity to the economy. On the whole, he followed a conservative spending policy, and the economy revived. Mississippi did not issue railroad bonds as many southern states did, and it is a myth that the Republicans bankrupted the state and looted it through graft. To restore law and order, Alcorn persuaded the legislature to authorize $50,000 for a secret service, which Alcorn used to hire a director and seven detectives—five white and two black. One of the detectives infiltrated the Klan in Oxford and reported that every young white man in the county either belonged to the Klan or sympathized with it. Several of the members of the secret service went to Winona after Alcorn's appointee as mayor was assassinated at a church concert, but they found no one would talk about the murder. Alcorn, not surprisingly, failed to restore law and order.

Education proved to be the most divisive issue of Alcorn's administration. Henry R. Pease, the Freedmen's Bureau's director of education, ran for state superintendent of education along with Alcorn and won. He followed a policy of establishing a New England–style system, with a superintendent in each county and with teachers paid well enough to attract qualified applicants, both of which proved expensive. Having to construct separate black and white schools doubled the cost. County supervisors appointed the local school boards, and many of those failed to cooperate. White taxpayers complained about the high taxes needed for the schools and especially about being taxed to support black schools, which whites continued to burn in some areas. Alcorn did not support Pease and responded to criticism by calling for economies in education and the election of county superintendents. He issued a pamphlet extolling his "separate but equal" policy in education, and when criticized for his rejection of social equality, he warned that a revolution had been made and that stirring "old prejudices" would endanger the gains made. In higher education, he recommended the purchase of Oakland College and the establishment of a black college there. To gain political support, he hired Senator Revels to head the institution, which came to bear Alcorn's name. Lamar resigned from the University of Mississippi when Alcorn became governor, fearing that he would be fired. When a rumor circulated that a black student might attend the university, the entire faculty threatened to quit. Alcorn attempted to finesse the race issue but failed. In his governmental appointments, he never named a majority of blacks to a board of supervisors, and as judges, he appointed blacks to nothing higher than a justice of the peace.

Blacks began to appeal to Senator Ames for relief. Revels's term expired in 1871, and Alcorn took the vacant Senate seat but then lingered in Mississippi, refusing to resign as governor until after the fall elections. Alcorn launched a speaking tour, where the Democratic Party opposed him with Lamar, Robert Lowry, and Ethelbert Barksdale, the newspaperman. Ames returned from Washington to lead the Radical Republicans, and he bristled at what Alcorn had done, accusing him of selling out blacks and conducting an "Andrew Johnson policy." In the Senate, Ames supported sending troops to Meridian where a white riot killed a number of blacks and ran the Republican mayor out of town. Alcorn sent state forces, but did not reinstate the mayor and insisted that violence would abate without outside interference. For the first time Ames, the soldier, entered into political speaking and found himself flattered by and engaged with the largely black audiences that attended his events. He began to commit to their cause, and the black audiences responded in turn to him. Alcorn left the governorship to R. C. Powers, a carpetbagger who shared his political ideas, and the Radicals asked Ames to leave the Senate to run for governor in 1873. Alcorn refused to treat Ames as an equal when he joined him in the Senate, and they argued openly in Senate debates about the policy to be followed in their state. Ames had supported the antiterrorism legislation aimed at the Klan, while Alcorn opposed it.

In north Mississippi, a brave U.S. attorney general, G. Wiley Wells, took on the Klan in the summer of 1871, winning 200 indictments from federal grand juries that were drawn from widely dispersed communities. Twenty of the men indicted for killing a black man in Monroe County appeared in the federal court in Oxford. Lamar served as co-counsel with their attorney, who was the Klan leader in his county. Lamar interrupted the court to complain that a man in the courtroom had been stalking and threatening him. The judge ordered Lamar to come to order, but he refused and continued to talk. When a court deputy approached him, Lamar picked up a chair and threatened the deputy. The judge grabbed the chair, and when a U.S. marshal came to calm Lamar down, Lamar struck him, fracturing his cheekbone. Lamar defied the court to arrest him, and some university students and the

L. Q. C. Lamar, fire-eater member of the antebellum House of Representatives who returned to Congress as the spokesman for whites during Reconstruction and later served in Grover Cleveland's cabinet and on the U.S. Supreme Court. Courtesy of the Mississippi Department of Archives and History from the Mrs. W. H. McCardle Collection.

Klansmen began to cheer, stomp their feet, and give rebel yells. The soldiers guarding the Klansmen drew their weapons, and one raised his rifle to fire. At that point, the room got still. This small incident illustrates the atmosphere of the times, with a former and future congressman, cabinet member, and Supreme Court justice shaking his fist at the national government, earning cheers from students and Klansmen who responded to his defiance, which most of the white population of the state shared.

White resistance remained strong, but change came to much of the state. Forrest announced that the Klan had disbanded, and it did cease to be a regional force. It never overthrew a government, and the anti-Klan laws and congressional investigations against it had an effect. In Vicksburg, the legal system changed, with blacks comprising from a third to a half of jurors. By the early 1870s, 85 percent of the black jurors could read and write, and they convicted three-quarters of the black defendants between 1868 and 1873. The all-white court system disappeared, and the integrated replacement seemed to work well. The Klan never had much presence in the Delta, and Morgan reported that rising cotton prices in the late 1860s led to prosperity among black farmers who had begun to rent and even buy land. Yazoo City swelled with small merchants seeking the business of black customers with cash to spend. Freedmen now referred to their boss and not their master.

Increasingly, black farmers could sign bonds for elected officeholders, allowing them to take office, which they could not do without adequate bond. By the early 1870s Morgan hoped that endurance would stabilize the new biracial society. This mattered to Morgan and his wife, who were producing a steadily increasing number of children.

Yazoo County sat on the edge of the Delta, which served as Mississippi's new frontier during Reconstruction. Forest covered 90 percent of the Delta at the outset of the Civil War. The land flooded regularly as it had for hundreds of years, leaving the richest soil in the world, which grew an almost impenetrable jungle of cane, vines, cypress, oak, and sweet gum. Settlement was limited to ridges providing some high ground safe from most floods, but only ridges near rivers were suitable because rivers offered the only transportation. Many big Delta landowners were land poor. Increased taxes led some to sell land in order to divest themselves of a liability. To attract workers to the swamps where malaria and yellow fever lurked, more Delta planters than in the rest of the state rented land at fixed, cheaper prices to earn a dependable income. Experiments with Chinese coolie labor did not prosper, so planters had to fall back on attracting freedmen. Credit for the planters and their workers came not from factors as before the war, but from storekeepers extended credit by Yankee businessmen who flooded into the South to profit in the war's wake. The successful Delta planter wore several hats—farmer, lawyer, and merchant. Alcorn and his family sometimes worked behind the counter of his store at his massive plantation. "Furnishing merchants" was the name given to operators who concentrated in the trade. Foreign-born peddlers—about half of them Jewish—worked the Delta as small traders, and after they mastered the market, they settled in towns and opened substantial stores.

Even illiterate freedmen sometimes built fortunes in the Reconstruction Delta. Bohlen Lucas, as a slave, worked as a driver, but he rented land along Deer Creek after the war until he saved $1,000 to pay down on 200 acres. When he had enough sharecroppers for that land, he rented land from the widow of his former owner and filled it with sharecroppers. Eventually he went back to the widow and took over the entire plantation where he had once been a slave. He went into partnership with a white man, and when his partner died, Lucas, with the assistance of white patrons, convinced the court to make him executor of the partner's estate. Unfortunately, a long-abandoned wife from New York demanded the partner's property, and after an extended court battle she got it, costing Lucas dearly. Lucas survived the setback and continued to manage reduced acreage, but then his white patrons needed him when blacks gained the franchise because he could march all of his tenants to vote Democratic. They elected him county treasurer as a reward for his service, and he hired white literates as his assistants.

Edmund Richardson made himself king of the Delta planters during Reconstruction by using prison labor on a massive scale and developing industry as well as agriculture. Before the war, he established a successful string of stores in Mississippi and then became a factor in New Orleans. At the end of the war, he purchased many plantations. In Washington County, his largest plantation, Refuge, measured ten square miles of improved land. At first he purchased prisoners by bidding at jails as many planters did, but then in 1868 he convinced the federal authorities in Mississippi to pay him $18,000 per year to take the entire Mississippi prison population to Refuge, where he maintained and guarded the inmates. When he became governor, Alcorn ordered an investigation of the agreement, but the legislature found that the lease was working well, and Alcorn agreed to renew it. Richardson built mills to process cottonseed and a private railroad on Refuge as well as establishing other larger railroad companies around the South. He bought the mill at Wesson in 1873 and served as president of the company until his death. A ruthless agribusinessman, Richardson scorned planters who spoke of being concerned for "their people." He eschewed politics and built an unmatched private empire, earning the title of King Cotton.

Alcorn resigned as governor on Thanksgiving Day 1871, leaving Powers to carry on his policies as Alcorn made his way to Washington, where he and Ames confronted one another in the Senate. Ames considered the white violence in Mississippi as a continuation of the Civil War—he told Sherman that it still raged in Mississippi—and he made his first speech in the Senate to seek congressional intervention. He told the Senate that unless the black people of the state retained their voting privileges, they would be worse off than they had been as slaves because as free men subject to whites they had no value—their death meant nothing to the whites. He reminded the Senate that as the majority of the state's population, black Mississippians deserved to control the government. After some efforts to coexist, Alcorn and Ames clashed on May 20, 1872, over the extension of the expiring Ku Klux Klan act. Alcorn told the Senate that Ames did not represent Mississippi, was not a citizen, and never paid a dollar of taxes there. He only came to be in the Senate because of the war. By contrast, Alcorn bragged about his plantation and how he had rescued the Republican Party after its defeat in the 1868 vote against the Black and Tan constitution. He claimed that blacks and whites lived peacefully together until the Freedmen's Bureau and the military drove a wedge between the races.

Ames replied that Alcorn likewise would not be in the Senate except for the war, which he had sat out on his plantation relying on the Union

Adelbert Ames won the Congressional Medal of Honor as a Union general and governed Mississippi during its military occupation. Elected governor by black Mississippi voters, Ames resigned to avoid impeachment by white Democrats after Reconstruction. Courtesy of the Mississippi Department of Archives and History.

victory for his opportunity. A winner of the Congressional Medal of Honor, Ames said that he won his place through blood and battles and that he, not Alcorn, spoke for the Mississippi Republican Party. The state, he assured the Senate, needed the act. The Senate approved, but the House of Representatives did not vote to extend the act. Stripping away the personal arguments, the division between the two men and their followers concerned the role of black Mississippians in the government. Would blacks be allowed to control the government with the help of the carpetbaggers and use it to protect themselves, or would they follow Alcorn and the scalawags, allowing them to retain white control with token black participation?

When Mississippians once again elected county and city leaders in 1871, no city and almost no counties had a black majority. James D. Lynch was the only black elected to statewide office in Mississippi before 1873. He came to Mississippi in 1868 to work for the Methodist Episcopal Church and earned the respect of even the Democrats, who called him the most popular carpetbagger in the state. Widely admired for his educated oratorical skills, most considered him a black gentleman who represented his race admirably. In 1872 John R. Lynch, a black man in his early twenties, won the speakership of the Mississippi House of Representatives with Alcorn's backing. Lynch was born to a slave mother who lived with a white man. His father tried to free them, only to have a friend sell them into Mississippi after the father's death. Lynch became the favored body servant to a leading Natchez man, and after the city's occupation, he worked for a photographer and attended night school. Blacks held only thirty-two seats in the House of Representatives when the House elected Lynch, making his advancement all the more remarkable. Alcorn backed him to satisfy black Republicans who disliked being overlooked for appointment and pressed for a larger role in the government.

Ames sympathized with their point of view. In the Senate, he introduced a bill to integrate the army, and in a letter to his wife, he spoke of the respect he had for the quiet, "moral nobility" of black people in Mississippi. His wife hated Mississippi and did not care for mixing with black people, but Ames came to believe that he had a mission—with a capital M, he said later in life—to work for black Mississippians' equality and citizenship. On the practical side, he wanted to win a state election to answer Alcorn's criticism of his being an outsider. He decided to run for governor in 1873, intending to return to the Senate after he had taken control of the party from Alcorn and the white scalawags. He brought his wife, Blanche, to Natchez, which was the only place in the state that she considered habitable. She did not enjoy her residence, reporting how women on the street admired her baby until they learned Ames was the father, and then they turned up their noses and stalked away. As summer approached, she fled north, but Ames still campaigned, alone, attending balls, dinners, and speeches with thousands of black Republicans who responded enthusiastically to his speeches. After he defeated Powers for the Republican nomination, Alcorn came back to run against him as an independent candidate. They debated around the state, and the once inarticulate Ames held his own, winning the election with 20,000 more votes than Alcorn.

Seeing the loss coming, Alcorn tried to have the legislature postpone the election for a year. He got a bill passed in the House of Representatives, but Ames took the Senate. Both sides bribed senators freely. Ames at one point had to send for a senator who had been spirited off to New Orleans for debauchery by Alcorn's minions. When they got him back to Jackson, two of Ames's people slept on either side of the senator until they got him to the capitol to vote. After the election, Powers and Alcorn tried to get the Mississippi Supreme Court to invalidate the election, but it refused. Ames and the Radical or black Republicans had control of the state government. Fifty-five of the 115 members of the House of Representatives were black as were nine of the thirty-seven senators. Ames's lieutenant governor was black, as was most of the rest of his ticket. Blacks won a few counties with overwhelmingly black populations, but probably only about 5 percent of the local officeholders in the state were black. Even this small percentage taxed the pool of literate blacks in the state, and many elected officials who were literate could barely read, while others could neither read nor write.

Before the 1873 election, the Republican legislature redistricted the state to lump all of the white northern counties into one district, which they conceded to the Democrats, as a means of ensuring the other districts for their party. Lamar gradually stepped up his political activities, beginning with Jacob Thompson's triumphal welcome back to Oxford in 1869 on his return from Europe. Lamar demurely denied he was a candidate, citing his exclusion by the Fourteenth Amendment, but then he decided that he could not miss the golden opportunity to reenter politics and won the Democratic nomination. The Republicans ran Flournoy, and when two independents got into the race, it threw a scare into the Democrats before the independents withdrew. Lamar lost his home county but won the district by a two-to-one vote. He went to Washington and got Congress to remove his banishment, clearing the way for him to take his seat. Thus Lamar became de facto leader of the Democratic Party, but in the governor's race he backed Alcorn against Ames, reasoning that Alcorn, despite his history, had become the leader of conservative elements in the state.

During his first months back in Congress, Lamar kept quiet, waiting for an opportunity to establish himself as spokesman for reconciliation between the South and North that would persuade the North to abandon its protection of the freedmen in Mississippi. Charles Sumner's death provided the perfect occasion. Before his death, Sumner had called for amnesty and forgiveness for the South, and Lamar used that as a springboard to praise Sumner and make his appeal for reconciliation between northerners and southerners, concluding: "My countrymen know one another and you will love one another." The timing and tone proved to be perfect, winning the former fire-eater the reputation of peacemaker and conciliator and gaining lavish praise from the press. In the next Congress, Democrats elected him chairman of their caucus, further enhancing his status. As the face of the Mississippi Democratic Party, Lamar practiced the big lie technique as his allies back home brutally wrestled control away from Ames and his black majority. Lamar and his fellow Democrats adopted the face of reasonableness and conciliation to the white North while their allies employed violence to eliminate blacks from the political process in Mississippi. Confronted with accounts of murder and white intimidation of voters, they simply lied and denied the evidence.

Ames and his family moved into the governor's mansion in January 1874, and while Blanche tried to convince the cook not to use lard in every dish and to call her madame and not "Ole Gal," Ames wrestled with the legislature. He asked for steps to reduce black illiteracy and to increase black land ownership, but instead he found himself vetoing railroad subsidies. As a teetotaler, he wanted statewide prohibition, but he settled for local

Blanche Ames, wife of Governor Adelbert Ames. She despised Mississippi and spent as little time as possible in the state. Courtesy of the Mississippi Department of Archives and History.

option. As a fiscal conservative, he tried to adjust taxes for more equity, but his administration fell victim to sensational events and to the corrupt colleagues around him. His lieutenant governor, A. K. Davis, an obscure black Republican from Noxubee County, became acting governor each time Ames left the state, issuing pardons and appointing inappropriate people to office. Albert Morgan, who had been a close adviser to Ames, caused a scandal when he attempted to take the sheriff's position in Yazoo City. After serving well as supervisor and boss of the Republican Party, he ran in 1873 against the man whom he had installed as sheriff, probably because he needed the money for his rapidly growing family. His brother had taken a sheriff's office in Washington County, and because sheriffs also served as fee-paid tax collectors, he made $10,000 a year. Morgan could have had the sheriff's office at any point but seemed content dividing his time administering the county and serving in the legislature. Being sheriff meant he would have to drop out of the legislature. Morgan defeated his former friend, who ran against him with Democratic support, by a vote of 2,365 to 431, but the defeated sheriff refused to vacate the office.

Morgan and his deputies chased away a guard and took over the courthouse office only to be attacked by the former sheriff and his deputies. In the resulting gunfight, the former sheriff died. Morgan surrendered to the Yazoo City mayor, who released him until he appeared before a judge. The county judge ordered Morgan to jail for his protection and later moved him to Jackson about the time of Ames's inauguration. The judge without any authority appointed a Democrat to be sheriff. Ames visited Morgan in jail and later removed the judge, whose appointment had not been confirmed by the Senate, and replaced him with a University of Mississippi law professor. The new judge released Morgan on bail. The evidence from witnesses to the gun battle could not assign blame for the shot that killed the former sheriff (it could have been one of his own men), and as a result the grand jury declined to indict Morgan, who returned to take up his duties as sheriff. Democrats used this incident to brand Morgan a murderer and Ames as his accessory.

In June 1874 Ames took his wife north to escape the southern heat, leaving the lieutenant governor in charge—not a good decision. On July 4 a group of white men attacked a black holiday crowd in Vicksburg, killing and wounding several people. Peter Crosby, a black Union veteran serving as sheriff of Warren County since January, reported to acting governor Davis that armed whites controlled the city and talked of "doing a Meridian" to rid the state's largest city of Republican rule. He requested Union troops to restore order, and Davis passed on the request to Grant. Surely the irony did not escape the president—an attack on black Republican rule on the same day he had accepted surrender of the city eleven years earlier. An inspector sent to the city did not raise alarm, and Grant declined to send troops. Ames rushed back to Jackson, and repeated Davis's appeal, but again Grant said no. City elections were scheduled for August 5, and armed whites continued to control the city, patrolling at night, mounting guards, screening those entering the city by land and riverboat, and monitoring voter registration while fully armed. The Democrats had a white slate, and the Republicans had a white mayoral candidate with a black slate supporting him. On election day, blacks feared to attend the polls, and the Democrats swept to victory.

Reports of incidents from smaller hamlets in the state in which whites simply murdered blacks without consequence reached Ames at the governor's mansion, but he now had no troops at his command. His wife discovered that she was pregnant again and remained with her parents, but shipped Ames a pistol. Ames probably saw the end of his Mississippi political career because at about this time he contacted Frederick Douglass about becoming president of Alcorn College. Appointing the renowned abolitionist to the post would most certainly have enraged the Democrats.

Whites had gathered into three groups, which overlapped in membership and communicated with one another easily, for the purpose of retaking control and eliminating black domination of state and local government:

first, members of the Democratic Party, which had absorbed most of the Whigs who, unlike Alcorn, could not bring themselves to cooperate with blacks; second, the taxpayer leagues, which spread the message that carpetbaggers and blacks were looting the state and stealing tax money; and third, the more amorphous "white liners," who advocated using violence, fraudulent elections, and any means necessary to reestablish white rule. The label "white liner" derived from their slogan to vote the white line, admitting no blacks to office. In the 1874 national election, the Democrats won control of the U.S. House of Representatives for the first time since the war, encouraging Mississippi whites to believe that the time for overthrowing the Republicans was at hand.

On November 17, 1874, a grand jury indicted three black officeholders, including Thomas W. Cordozo, the state superintendent of education, for embezzling public funds. Cordozo came to Mississippi after ethical failings in other states and with an unsavory reputation, so he was probably guilty, but the indictment inflamed the white population, confirming their worst suspicions about all Republican officeholders. On the day of the indictment the Vicksburg taxpayers league called a mass meeting for December 2, the day they were to pay Crosby their taxes. Five hundred Warren County whites turned out for the meeting and decided to send a representative to the impressive courthouse, which dominates the city from the highest hill, to demand the sheriff's resignation. He refused, so the 500 white men marched on the courthouse with the same demand, and Crosby resigned and left immediately for Jackson, being careful to ride to a remote stop to catch the train.

He met with Ames at the governor's mansion in a room filled with men coming and going as they talked. Ames did not want the humiliation of having Grant refuse him federal troops again, and he knew if he sent white militia, they would probably defect and join the white Vicksburgers. If he sent black militia and they killed the whites occupying the courthouse, a race war would spread through the state. He told Crosby to raise a posse and retake the courthouse and his office. One witness to the meeting claimed Ames responded to Crosby's protest that his posse would be slaughtered with: "The blood of the martyrs was the seed of the church." That was the story that circulated throughout Mississippi and convinced whites that Ames intentionally engineered the deaths that followed. Crosby played out the governor's plan, hired a writer to produce a proclamation calling for volunteers, had it read in the black churches on Sunday, and eventually got a supporter to lead 400 armed black men on the city. The mayor declared martial law, and 500 whites, who had gathered in Vicksburg to await the attack, arrested Crosby and went out to confront the posse. Crosby's friend, the posse's leader, asked to see the sheriff, while the black posse faced the white defenders of the city. The posse leader went to the jail, where Crosby advised his friend to disperse their supporters. Returning to the bridge where the two groups faced off, their leader ordered the black men to go home. As they reluctantly turned to go, the whites began to shoot them. One witness told a government investigator that it had been like shooting rabbits. Whites hunted posse members for days, killing blacks found with guns as their screaming families watched. Ames called the legislature into special session and got it to pass a resolution requesting troops from the president. Grant sent the army, which restored Crosby to his office, and Grant assured Ames's father-in-law that he would sustain the governor.

Lamar decided to remain in Washington over the congressional Christmas break to manage damage control and get the white version of events accepted. Lamar had been handling a similar task for whites in neighboring Louisiana as the Vicksburg crisis unfolded. His former law partner, Edward Clark, had helped to engineer the Vicksburg coup, and Lamar shared with Clark his vision to combat the investigations and arguments to shape the reaction. First, whites would claim that most blacks died at the hands of other blacks. Second, they would point out that whites in New York killed more blacks than Mississippians did. Third, they would admit the southern propensity for violence, but they could justify it by the depiction of the corrupt, rapacious nature of Republican rule while assuring the country that whites had no intention of using violence as a means of establishing political or racial supremacy. Lamar recommended the Democrats for the resulting investigating committee, but they could only issue a minority report. The Republican majority denied white claims and in stark terms said that either the national government had to use force or Mississippi whites would use violence to suppress black voting in order to seize control of state and local government.

Ames shared that analysis, but seemed to have lost his fire for the revolution that he had initiated. While his wife's family pushed him to have the Republican legislature send him back to the Senate, Ames wrote to Blanche that they could not live among Mississippians. His first such statement came after he encountered a white youth crying near the mansion. When he asked why, the youth said that he had been kicked in the stomach by a bigger black boy, and he assured the governor that it was common for blacks to beat whites found on Jackson's streets after dark. On his visit to see Blanche, Ames visited with President Grant, who reassured Ames that he would support him, but Ames saw no evidence of it on the ground as the rising tide of violence continued unchecked. When the legislature convened for its regular session in January 1875, Ames got authorization for three companies of militia, one white and two black, and he got them organized, but he still faced the real possibility of a statewide race war if he used them. The all-white taxpayers' convention came to Jackson too and demanded relief and an end to Republican corruption.

While Ames dithered, Lamar spent the summer campaigning for Democrats. Beginning at a small rail depot operated by Colonel Falkner, who was bringing a railroad to Tippah County, he covered the state. Lamar told his audiences that blacks were unfit to vote and failed to mention the violence endemic to the state. He insisted that he had no objection to "negroes" voting as long as there were no federal troops to oversee elections. Ames heard Lamar's message and knew that he was losing the propaganda war in the northern newspapers, which reported Lamar's request to withdraw federal troops favorably. When the Democratic convention met, Ames told Blanche that the Democrats designed their platform for northern consumption while the dedication to the "color line," which was the real policy, went unstated. Ames read Anthony Trollope's and Sherman's war memoirs and wrote Blanche that he had decided not to seek the Senate seat. She tried to sway him from afar, but he seemed sickened by what he described as depravity and fraud in the election campaign. By contrast, Lamar knew that a Democratic legislature would give him the place in the Senate that Ames rejected.

In Yazoo County, Henry M. Dixon, a planter, organized an armed white force called Dixon's Scouts for the purpose, he claimed, of protecting whites from a black insurrection. At the same time as whites won control of the city government in Vicksburg, they took control in Yazoo City, while leaving Morgan in control of the county government. Morgan conferred with Ames about the white extralegal military force, but Ames had no means of fighting them. In the summer of 1875, Morgan invited everyone to a community meeting at a black church, where he advised his followers to adopt passive resistance and predicted that, if a race war came, it would be a slaughter that would cause the white people of "Christendom" to revolt, ensuring blacks' peace and a bright future. But he sent his wife and children out of the troubled county to Holly Springs in order to escape the "heat and humidity" of the Delta. On September 1 Morgan held a Republican campaign rally in Yazoo City. His followers suggested that he arm several black deputies, but Morgan declined, insisting that weakness provided their strength. Into the meeting hall, Dixon ushered one of Morgan's few black opponents, who shouted down Morgan's speech, before gunfire erupted, leaving a white Republican dead and several blacks wounded. Dixon's Scouts took control of Yazoo City's streets, and Morgan hid out until he could make his way to Jackson and the governor's mansion.

Meanwhile, fifteen miles west of Jackson some drunken whites disrupted a large Republican political rally to which Democrats had been invited as guests; shooting broke out, and the rumor spread that blacks had murdered and mutilated whites. Armed whites arrived by train the next morning and undertook a Warren County–style attack, indiscriminately killing between twenty and thirty black people. Blacks began to seek safety around the governor's mansion and the federal courthouse in Jackson. Ames asked for troops, and the attorney general telegraphed Grant's refusal, quoting him as explaining that the northerners had tired of the regular fall outbreaks across the South and were ready to condemn outside interference. Grant had his eye on the Ohio elections, which his advisers told him the Republicans would lose if he sent troops to Mississippi again.

Lamar continued to provide a face of reason and reconciliation, while James Z. George, the chairman of the Democratic Central Committee and the man coordinating the white line extralegal forces, telegraphed the attorney general, with the backing of the leading Democrats, claiming that peace and order prevailed throughout the state. A delegation of the Alcorn Republicans went to Washington, minus Alcorn, who maintained complete silence during this tumultuous period, and gave the same assurance of peacefulness. The *New York Tribune* as a result opined that Ames created the turmoil and that without him, Mississippi's black and white population would get along well. Alcorn, at home in Coahoma County, accused the black sheriff of plundering the county and participated with a group of armed whites who interrupted the sheriff's political meeting, killing six blacks and a couple of white followers while chasing the sheriff out of state.

Ames offered the militia companies that he had organized to Morgan so that he could return to Yazoo County and take back his office, but Morgan declined, telling the governor that the whites would defect to Dixon and the black companies would be destroyed. When a rumor spread that he was returning, Dixon and almost 1,000 men met the train. Grant's attorney general sent C. K. Chase as a personal emissary to try to reach a peaceful settlement. Chase brought George and a Democratic delegation to the mansion on October 13 to negotiate a truce. George promised to call off the extralegal whites terrorizing Republicans and to allow a peaceful vote if Ames did not use the militia. Two weeks later, when violence increased again, Chase went to George to complain. Using the big lie tactic, George denied any of the outrages ever took place. Chase and the governor relied on George's word as a gentleman, and George obviously assumed that the normal rules of gentlemanly behavior did not apply to blacks and those who associated with them. Morgan could not return to Yazoo City for fear of his life, so he tried to organize a Republican slate via the mail, but several of his Republicans had

Blanche K. Bruce, son of a white Virginia planter and a slave. He moved to Mississippi during Reconstruction, established a large Delta plantation, and won the state's U.S. Senate seat, where he served amiably alongside L. Q. C. Lamar. Courtesy of the Mississippi Department of Archives and History.

been killed, and the rest decided to keep their heads down. By election day 1875, Republicans in the embattled counties hid to save their lives. Morgan, who won by 2,000 votes in 1873, lost by a count of 4,000 to 2 in 1875.

As election day neared, Ames wrote to Blanche correctly predicting the outcome. Chase stayed in the mansion with Ames and, having been disillusioned by George breaking his word, informed the attorney general that troops were needed, but it was too late. Three weeks before the election, Ames told Blanche that the national government had abandoned Mississippi's black population and that the whites had made an armed revolution with the intention of consigning blacks to serfdom—"an era of second slavery." Chase and the governor huddled inside the mansion, as whites, displaying a cannon loaned to them by a Union officer, paraded out front jeering and gesturing at them. Well liquored up, the group returned after midnight by torchlight, firing their pistols at the mansion. With the election over, Ames went north to visit his parents and his wife while his father-in-law tried to get Grant to act. Ames harbored no illusions; he knew the Democratic legislature would impeach him.

The Democrats had chosen their battles to have the maximum effect, and in some counties the Republican votes actually increased in 1875. The Democrats targeted majority-black counties for massive intimidation and left a third of the state's counties alone. Consequently the Republicans still had significant representation in the legislature. They captured two of the six seats in the national House of Representatives and installed Blanche K. Bruce, Mississippi's second black senator, in Washington to join Alcorn, but neither of them would speak out for Ames. Alcorn had long ago broken with Bruce, and Bruce proved to be a survivor. Ames's father-in-law went to Lamar seeking help to stop Ames's impeachment, but despite soothing words soon learned of Lamar's true alliance with the white liners. The Democrats charged only political offenses against Ames, who was scrupulously honest, and Bruce actually suggested the compromise that culminated in Ames's resignation. Because the Democrats had already disposed of the lieutenant governor, the Democratic president of the Senate would take over when Ames resigned. Therefore the Democrats withdrew the impeachment charges and allowed Ames to resign without official accusations of wrongdoing. After he resigned, they again violated the gentleman's agreement and published the charges they had withdrawn. That same year Ames testified in secret to a Senate investigating committee that he had been forced out not because he was an outsider but because he had advocated black citizenship.

The Redeemers, as the new white rulers called themselves, moved slowly to accomplish their goal of completely eliminating blacks from public life, still fearing federal intervention until the national crisis in the presidential election of 1877 guaranteed complete removal of federal forces. In 1875 Grant moved more soldiers into the state, giving himself the option of using force, but he decided not to intervene. Newt Knight, who had become a deputy U.S. marshal during the Ames administration, lost his job when the Redeemers took control. He broke off with many of his neighbors when they refused to allow his "black" children to attend a school that he helped build. The school then burned to the ground, and the neighbors said that he did it. After the end of Reconstruction, he retired to his farm and dropped out of politics.

Howell Hinds lost his life when he tried to prevent a Washington County doctor from killing a friend after an argument in a bar. The doctor killed Hinds in the struggle over the knife that he was trying to use on Hinds's friend. Collier continued his life with the Hinds family despite harassment from freedmen and federals about his war service with the CSA. Accused of killing a Freedmen's Bureau agent who tried to use his position to the detriment of the Hinds family, Collier won an acquittal with the help of a lawyer provided by the family. In order to escape harassment, he was spending some time in Texas working as a cowboy with veterans of his Texas unit when Hinds died. He returned to the Delta to earn a living as a hunter and lived near Thomas Hinds and his sister.

Bohlen Lucas, the illiterate planter, lost his white patrons when they did not need him anymore and ended his life working twenty acres of land for subsistence. Richardson grew more and more wealthy, expanding his land and industrial holdings. Lamar got his Senate seat in 1875, and Alcorn had to return to his private empire, where he eventually constructed a railroad that meandered from plantation to plantation through the Delta without making any money. Morgan moved to Washington and descended into poverty, eventually abandoning his family to become a prospector in Colorado. Bruce and Lynch married light-skinned wives and maintained successful careers in the Senate and House of Representatives, respectively. Lynch consulted with Republican presidents. Bruce's wife, from a wealthy Cleveland family, broke the color barrier for some time, exchanging visits with white wives of leading politicians and entertaining successfully in their Washington home. Bruce continued to own his Delta plantation and served alongside Lamar until his term expired. Black newspapers criticized Lynch and Bruce for their choice of wives, perhaps implying that they were not committed enough to their black constituents. The sharecropping Clears dropped out of the historical records.

Reconstruction became one of the most controversial periods in state history because white Mississippians forced the black majority into an inferior caste. Whites denied blacks the vote, relegated them to an inferior social status, separated them into underfunded schools, and exploited them as agricultural and domestic workers. Recent accounts of the period seek to make heroes of Ames, Knight, or Morgan, but Morgan wrote a memoir and rejected that designation. Ames harbored heroic ambitions, but he lacked the will and daring to carry through on his intentions and accepted that he failed badly. At least he had the decency to admit the damage done to the black population he tried to lead. Although interesting and suggestive, too little information exists about Knight to judge his life, and some of what does exist is not heroic.

The old heroes—George and Lamar—have lost their luster in an age accepting racial equality as a given. Collier has appeal living by his personal code of justice. Mrs. Howell Hinds had to go and plead with Collier not to kill the doctor who murdered her husband when the doctor's mother secured him a pardon and he returned to the Delta. One assumes that she did it to protect Collier, who otherwise would have felt honor bound to revenge Hinds's death, but he probably did murder that Freedmen's Bureau agent out of the same loyalty. The only persons mentioned in this account whose lives might appeal to modern appraisers of Mississippi Reconstruction would be Flournoy and Mary Jane Clear, both of whom seemed to act selflessly. Flournoy owned sixty-six slaves before the war, reluctantly voted for secession, helped organize a company for service in the CSA, but resigned his commission in 1861 and declared his neutrality for the remainder of the war. During Reconstruction, he worked with the Methodist Church to care for freed people, raising money to assist with their education and religious development and establishing a mutual aid society. Joining the Republican Party and opening a newspaper entitled *Equal Rights*, he dedicated his Reconstruction years to securing citizenship and a good education for freedmen. He took the job of county school superintendent and became the local political boss for the Republicans, but his administration centered on appointing only the best-qualified people in education and government, even Democrats. As a result, he earned respect and support in the community. When the Klan made a raid to capture him, a friend forewarned him, and he fought off the raiders, killing one of them. He ran for Congress against Lamar in 1873, stayed with the Republican Party through its radical phase, and was identified as a black Republican. Though ousted from local office, he continued to live in Pontotoc and remained active in Republican Party politics on the state and national levels until his death in 1894.

Just as the majority of the white population made a poor choice by following the fire-eaters into the war, they made an equally bad decision by following the Redeemers out of Reconstruction. In the Civil War, Mississippians paid an incredible price, suffering massive deaths and destruction of their cities, homes, and fields. By choosing the Redeemers, Mississippians destined themselves to stagnation with an inferior school system, continued dedication to cotton agriculture, and sharecropping, which eventually sucked in many white farmers who fared no better than the black farmers who helped the planters to design it. Admittedly it would have been difficult to move from slavery to a free society, and condemning past people and ages is problematic, but a few people such as Flournoy did see a better path to a more productive future, and they were ignored and swept aside largely because of racial prejudice. He is not well known, and there were probably more like him who have been lost to history. The depth of suffering endured by Mississippians was not inevitable. Shared poverty and religious beliefs sometimes bridged the racial divide, and the population, which had been so mobile in the decades leading up to the war, put down deep roots during Reconstruction and was little disturbed by immigration so that Mississippians for generations lived together within their Magnolia curtain forging personal relationships that could transcend caste and class, forcing them to appreciate their common humanity even as owners and slaves did before the Civil War.

Sorting out the truth about the Reconstruction era is made extremely difficult by mythmaking, particularly of the planter-class women of the

South. For example, Susan Dabney Smedes's memoir sanctifies her father, owner of the magnificent Burleigh plantation in Hinds County. During Reconstruction, she has him washing the family clothes so that Sherman's alleged wish to drive every southern woman to the washboard would not be true for his daughters. According to her, the poverty-stricken Thomas Dabney fed the family from a three-quarter-acre garden, and the daughters did all the other housework as they paid off prewar debts surrounded by former slaves who kindly bestowed needed food on the family out of loyalty resulting from Dabney's kindly care for his slaves and later freedmen. She records their efforts to build a small church and how they successfully persuaded her father to be confirmed in the church as an old man. She paints a picture of true sainthood, but in the same chapter she also has Dabney spending much of the summer in Pass Christian fishing, and has a cook sheltered in their home when white terrorists raided the neighborhood. Neither her memoir nor the thousands of accounts attributing high ideals to either the Redeemers or the carpetbaggers can be accepted as the truth about Mississippi's past. Those who made the war and imposed white rule on the state afterward acted out of greed, fear, ambition, and what they considered high ideals just as their opponents did.

Chapter Eight

REDEMPTION AND BLACK SUBJECTION

Too often the period of Redemption (1876–1903) has been misunderstood as a return to absolute white control; instead, historians have come to view these years as a contentious time when Republicans continued to share power and a variety of political parties challenged the Bourbons, as the Democratic elite became known, for control of state and local government. Intertwined with the political conflict, a racially segregated society emerged with customs designed to remind black Mississippians daily of their status as an inferior caste. White Mississippians bolstered their new political and social system with a civic religion that held the "War Between the States" to have been a holy crusade fought by saintly men defending a righteous cause. J. William Jones, Virginian prophet of the creed, routinely invoked the secular saints Jefferson Davis, Robert E. Lee, and Thomas Jonathan "Stonewall" Jackson along with Abraham, Isaac, and Jacob in his public prayers. By the end of this period, white Mississippians had incorporated segregation into their worldview based on evangelical religion and deemed a violation of the informal segregation code a sin. On the other hand, maintaining white control justified lying, theft of ballot boxes, stuffing them if necessary, or violence against political opponents when required. The political conflict and growth of a new social system took place in a declining cotton economy in which furnishing merchants used legislature-provided lien laws to exploit and essentially enslave a growing sharecropping population whose economic desperation grew with the fall of cotton prices.

When Ames resigned on March 28, 1876, John M. Stone, president pro tempore of the Mississippi Senate, became governor and certified Lamar's election to the U.S. Senate. Lamar left for Washington, and while he initially offered Stone advice, he quickly became absorbed in congressional work, leaving Stone unhindered to handle Redemption in Mississippi. Stone had been a railroad station agent in Tishomingo County before the war, but during the war he rose to the rank of colonel in the Confederate States of America (CSA), indicating drive and talent for man from humble origins. Educated in the common or field schools of Tennessee, he worked as a teacher and clerk on Tennessee River boats before settling in Mississippi. He earned his Senate position by leading the Democratic opposition during Reconstruction, but he also learned to respect some of the Republican members of the legislature. Unconnected to the prewar aristocracy, Stone represented the rising democratic agrarian spirit that made the 1875 revolution, but he carried out the elimination of Republican officeholders gradually and with tact. On the supreme court, for example, he replaced a carpetbagger and a scalawag with two moderate Democrats who proceeded to elect the remaining Republican on the court as chief justice. His other judicial appointments were equally moderate but always Democrats.

In other areas of administration, he did not demonstrate as much care, appointing, for example, the defecting Republican who had headed the corrupt Vicksburg ring as commander of the state militia because the Democratic Party planned to use the former Republican to defeat John R. Lynch. Stone reappointed Hiram Revels as president of Alcorn University and left five Republicans on the University of Mississippi's board of trustees. He worked with the legislature to lay the basis for permanent Democratic domination of the state by redistricting the congressional districts to reverse the Republican pattern giving them one seat in the shoestring district running along the Mississippi River. He allowed a bipartisan majority in the Senate to retain the state legislative apportionment, which heavily favored the black plantation counties to the detriment of the white hill counties—a costly error in judgment. Stone headed the new board of registration created by the Redeemer legislature and appointed three-member election boards for each county with the power to establish election districts and register voters. Seen as correcting the lax Republican registration, these powers enabled Democrats to begin eliminating Republican voters and paved the way for blatant fraud schemes to regularly steal elections.

Agrarian outrage over high taxes swept Stone and the Redeemer legislature into office, and they had to respond quickly or face continuing revolt. They slashed salaries in all departments and reorganized the judiciary to eliminate courts in order to save money. They gutted the new public education system, leaving only a facade. Superintendents received only 20 percent of their previous salaries, and teachers likewise were reduced to a fraction of what Republicans paid them. Expecting a backlash from parents who had grown to appreciate the schools, James Z. George, speaking for the Democratic Party, again employed the big lie technique, denying that large cuts had been made and declaring the Democrats' commitment to providing education for Mississippi citizens. He disingenuously alleged that $40 per month for a teacher amounted to $2 a day for only five to six hours of work and assured farmers education would not suffer.

Aware of Mississippi's reputation as a bond defaulter, the Redeemers, despite tax cuts, moved aggressively to pay off the state debt and earned a strong reputation for fiscal responsibility. Both Alcorn and Ames had been careful stewards of public money and thus bequeathed the Redeemers a relatively small debt. Some counties, such as Warren, faced more daunting debts, but the Redeemers added to their woes by shifting expenses from the state to the county level. Government at the local level did not improve under the Democrats. Supervisors reigned supreme in each of their districts and tolerated no oversight, making continued Democratic mismanagement and fraud widespread.

Law enforcement failed to improve, and violence remained a common fact of life. Mississippians frequently armed themselves with guns and knives. Minor disputes escalated into matters of "honor," and sheriffs usually understood murder committed in the heat of such arguments to be justifiable homicide. Most violence occurred between members of the same race, though less often, usually over economic questions, blacks and whites clashed in what was almost always an uneven contest. White planters considered themselves above the law while black men, with justification, saw themselves outside the law. Both views contributed to a lawless atmosphere. The Delta earned the reputation of being the most violent section of the state. The Greenville newspaper once described the Delta as combining the worst vices of the South and West, where men resorted to their pistols and bowie knives at the drop of a hat.

Precisely because they recognized the potential for violence, Democrats and black Republicans worked out fusion agreements to share offices and eliminate election contests that could produce violence. Before the Democratic victory in 1875, black and white Republicans had parted ways. White Republicans wanted to respond to the taxpayer revolt by reducing salaries, but only one black Republican joined the party's white members in voting for reductions. Even Flournoy criticized black Republicans in their caucus for rejecting biennial legislative sessions—another demand of the taxpayer movement. In secret, Lamar set the tone for cooperation by inviting Bruce to his Washington home to discuss and arrange patronage matters. Bruce welcomed Lamar cordially to the Senate, and both men treated one another as gentlemen. Because they voted differently on most issues, they often paired for votes, being careful to respect one another's positions. Their cooperation grew into a secret deal between the Mississippi Democrats and the state's black Republicans.

Bruce enjoyed a close relationship with J. R Lynch and James Hill; Hill had been secretary of state in Ames's administration. The triumvirate of Bruce, Lynch, and Hill battled white Republicans for control of the

Mississippi Republican Party between 1875 and 1878 and probably had a closer relationship with the Redeemer Democrats than any historian will be able to document because neither side wished to reveal their activities. Bruce played the Lamar-like role of distinguished, reasonable front man, while Lynch chaired the Republican executive committee and provided energetic organizing skills in the state when necessary. Hill did the detailed county-level maneuvering to ensure majorities in conventions up to and including the state level. Hill was something of a mystery man, and though never accused of any dishonesty, he operated in the shadows at times. Educated as a slave by his owner's daughters on a plantation outside Holly Springs, he repaid the family by quietly helping relieve their distress after the war. In the 1880s, after serving as a federal tax collector, he became a businessman, working as a land agent for a railroad, among other interests, and accumulating a modest fortune.

All of the leading political figures shared the need for political office to support themselves and their families. Both Republicans and Democrats—black and white—sought government employment for the income and security it provided them. Lamar failed as a farmer, suffered on the low pay of a university professor, and struggled to exist on meager earnings as a lawyer. Stone spent two-and-a-half terms as governor: in between terms, he served on the railway commission, and after his last governorship, he took the presidency of the agricultural and mechanical college. Understanding the politics of this period requires acknowledgment of the fact that place-seeking dominated or played a significant role in the motives of all the political players at all levels of government.

At the county level, cooperation between the Democrats and Republicans reflected the deals made by the state leaders. Democrats liked to include a cooperative black member on the voter registration committee as a reminder to the white minority of voters that whites faced the danger of renewed black rule. The common practice placed a minority of blacks on the board of supervisors and blacks in subordinate county offices while whites kept control of the sheriff and tax collector offices and judgeships. White Republicans sometimes after 1875 confessed their political sins and renounced their former allegiances in order to be accepted into the Democratic fold. But these arrangements were not static. Ambitious men could upset even long-standing agreements, and blacks did not always accept powerless positions. For example, in Bolivar County with a large black majority, fusion left blacks in control of the county's senate seat for much of the period and with at least one member of the House of Representatives. Blacks controlled the sheriff's office throughout the 1870s and the county treasurer's post during the 1870s and 1880s.

By the 1880s Bolivar Democrats decided to enhance their control of the county, so they devised more devious methods of stealing elections. The distance between the voting precincts and the county courthouse at Rosedale on the Mississippi River allowed for mislabeling boxes of ballots to go to St. Louis while a coil of rope reached the courthouse instead of the ballots. Boxes sometimes disappeared out the train window into a swamp to be replaced with a Democratic box. In one instance, when suspicious black election officials hovered too closely over a box so that the Democrats could not substitute their fraudulent one, a Democratic physician among the group went out for food. Coming back with sardines and crackers, he announced that, on this special occasion, blacks and whites could eat together in violation of custom. He had injected croton oil into the black men's sardines with a hypodermic needle, and when the sick black men rushed from the room, the Democrats switched ballot boxes. Such tactics over the course of the 1870s and 1880s gradually eroded the status of black voters and gave more offices to Democrats.

Violent revolutions between Democrats and Republicans did occur. One of the most famous incidents took place in Kemper County, where a scalawag named William Wallace Chisholm organized the Republican Party and refused to relinquish control during the Redemption. Chisholm lived in the county before the war as a small planter and officeholder and during the war served in the state militia. As a Republican after the war, he became sheriff and a colonel in the militia. Former CSA officer John Gully, a hairy-chested Democrat who sported an open shirt, as a rule led the opposition during Reconstruction with widespread violence. His failed attempt to oust Chisholm in 1875 led to the indictment of several Gully relatives by the U.S. government. Then in December 1875 an unknown person shot Gully twice with a double-barreled shotgun, but he survived, only to be murdered by ambush between his home and Dekalb in April 1877. Chisholm had lost the last election, and when two black men swore out an affidavit against him for the crime, the new Democratic sheriff placed Chisholm under house arrest.

When 200 Democrats surrounded the house, the sheriff removed him and his family, armed with two pistols, to the jail. The mob hung two of Chisholm's black servants using bridle reins and attempted to extort incriminating evidence, but the servants declined to oblige, were lowered before they expired, and escaped. Then the mob surrounded the jail, and when two fellow Republicans from Scooba arrived in answer to Chisholm's appeal for help, the mob shot one of them to death, but allowed some mob members to rescue the second. All of the guards left the jail except one who was a Chisholm friend. Chisholm sent his daughter home for food and powder and shot for the jail's shotguns, reasoning that the mob would not harm a woman. She completed her mission, and in the late afternoon Chisholm's wife, Emily, went to feed the horses. While she was out the mob rushed the jail. When she returned, she found the mob hacking at the door leading to the cells upstairs with an ax and firing through the door. Both her son and daughter were wounded, and as the door broke down a physician at the head of the mob killed her son. Chisholm blew the doctor's brains out, and the mob retreated back down the stairs with his body, crying "Fire the jail." The smoke from all the guns convinced Chisholm that the jail was burning, so he came out with his daughter clinging to him hoping to save his life. The mob shot them both, killing the daughter and wounding Chisholm eleven times. Emily Chisholm killed Gully's son in the melee. Governor Stone came to assess the situation several days later, but failed to convince Chisholm to leave. Stone called for federal troops, which did not come, and instructed the sheriff to protect Chisholm. Ten days later Chisholm died of his wounds.

The southern press called it a personal feud, while the northern papers termed it a slaughter of Republicans and condemned Mississippians as savages with the "morals of Sioux." Mrs. Chisholm authorized a book detailing the events, which portrayed her family as the only civilized beings in Kemper County with a nice house and piano among unpainted churches and sandy fields surrounded by scrub oaks. In the book her daughter became "a refined young lady" sacrificed to the ruthless barbarians. Mrs. Chisholm went on a Republican speaking tour across the country after the book came out, and the Democrats hired an author to pen an alternative version of events.

Many black deaths went unrecorded as whites reasserted their control by lynch law. Port Gibson residents hanged one black man within 200 yards of a U.S. Army post. Wilkinson County witnessed one of the largest outbreaks of interracial violence. Early in 1875 "Honest Men's clubs" formed to suppress what they called widespread thefts. In May a three-man group, including a Jewish shopkeeper, whipped a black man accused of stealing and killing another black man's steer. The following night, thirty black men went to the merchant's store and killed him in revenge. Immediately a band of whites pursued the blacks and lynched two of them. News of the lynching prompted 150 black men to gather for protection. Whites saw their action as a revolt, and white families sought refuge in Woodville while blacks took to the woods and swamps. The scalawag sheriff who had been a CSA officer organized a "military force" of whites from both Mississippi and Louisiana to put down the blacks. The two groups met near Fort Adams, and after prominent black leaders brought along by the sheriff failed to convince the black men to disarm, shooting broke out. The white "military force" killed fifty blacks without suffering any casualties. In the northern part of the county an even larger force of black men barricaded themselves on an island in the backwaters of the Mississippi River to await an assault. The sheriff turned down offers of white assistance from Natchez and Baton Rouge, went to the island, and persuaded the men to disarm and return home. With calm restored, Wilkinson County planters gathered in Woodville with black leaders to assure them of their safety and fair treatment in the future. Given the state's lack of any police force, Redeemers had to work out county-by-county settlements to realign the new power structure.

At the state level, the Redeemers practiced care not to bring the national government's military force back. Lamar failed to head off a Senate investigation of the tactics used in the 1875 elections, so the legislature left the Republican civil rights laws on the books. Aside from adopting biennial legislatures, they left the 1868 constitution in place. As one of the new Democratic supreme court justices observed, not much altered in the law despite the fiery rhetoric leading up to the elections, but the men administering the laws changed, which made everything different.

Jefferson Davis, for example, got back his prewar plantation, Brierfield. Joseph Davis never deeded the land to his brother, causing hard feelings between Joseph and Jefferson's wife, Varina, but that fact had allowed Joseph to reclaim all of the plantations after the war. He sold them to Montgomery, his former slave-manager, but when Joseph died in 1870, Montgomery had fallen behind on the mortgage, and Joseph left the bulk of the estate to his niece, Lise Mitchell, who had been his constant companion in his old age. Jefferson's children received bequests, but Jefferson only served as executor of the estate according to the will. After three years of serving, Davis, needing the money, sued the estate to regain the plantation that he had built but never received a deed. His suit required him to violate his brother's wishes to continue lenient mortgage terms for Montgomery and to break with Lise, who claimed Joseph never intended to give Brierfield to his brother. His suit languished in the Republican courts, but the redeemed Mississippi Supreme Court overturned the lower courts in 1878, awarding him Brierfield. By that date, Davis had ended his failed insurance careers and European wanderings to settle at the home of a wealthy widow on the Mississippi Gulf Coast.

Beauvoir was where he wrote his two-volume justification of the CSA, and the widow left the home to him when she died of breast cancer. As was the case with many planters, Davis never made Brierfield profitable again, but as the years passed, Mississippians and other southerners made Davis a secular saint in the "Lost Cause" civic religion. His youngest daughter, Winnie, became the "queen" of the United Daughters of the Confederacy and a temporary member of hosts of Confederate veterans' "camps." With her European education and literary interests, she became a professional writer. The Davises attracted all manner of important and famous visitors to Beauvoir. Surely the strangest had to be Oscar Wilde, who came on Winnie's eighteenth birthday. Wilde, touring the United States giving lectures, stopped in Vicksburg and New Orleans, and Davis invited him at the behest of his women. Finding something vaguely objectionable about Wilde, Davis retired early on the night Wilde spent at Beauvoir and left Wilde to entertain the women. During his years at Beauvoir, Davis maintained a sphinxlike silence and played no political role in either Mississippi or the nation.

In 1876 the Democrats repeated their night riding and cannon firing during the congressional elections. They claimed to have won all the House of Representative seats, but Lynch contested the results in his district and eventually unseated his Democratic opponent a year into his term. White Republicans dismantled their party organization the next year, and some carpetbaggers began leaving the state for minor appointments in Washington or the West. Few scalawags left the state. The most famous one, Alcorn, lived like a prince on his extensive plantation. Others made peace with their neighbors. Some, such as Flournoy, went on supporting the Republican Party and retained the respect and admiration of their neighbors. Enclaves of former Mississippi carpetbaggers settled in Kansas and Colorado, where some of the former Mississippi Republicans made outstanding careers. A considerable number of carpetbaggers continued in federal positions around the state until the Democrats won the White House in 1885. At least twenty-five carpetbaggers joined the Mississippi ruling elite as successful planters-lawyers. Only one significant carpetbagger was convicted of embezzlement—William H. Gibbs, who stole from the mail while serving as postmaster in Jackson.

In the state elections of 1877, discontented farmers expressed their dismay at eleven-cent cotton—it had been nineteen cents a pound in 1873—and threatened to run independent candidates who would be more responsive to farmers' needs than the Democrats. The most important Democratic newspaper, the *Weekly Clarion*, warned that splitting the Democratic Party endangered white rule and claimed that one black independent candidate had said that he wanted the white men in his county killed so that black men could have a white wives. Such less-than-subtle appeals to racism kept the agrarians in line. Only Marshall County elected an entire independent slate of county officers, and the Democrats won all but eleven seats in the new legislature. Seven independents and four Republicans offered little opposition to the Democratic Party.

Yet as they achieved near complete control, a natural disaster and a new political party challenged the Democrats. Yellow fever struck the state with a vengeance in 1878. Holly Springs, which had been a healthy haven with a population of 2,300, suffered 114 deaths. The banks and the post office closed while the town's newspaper ceased to publish. The largest city, Vicksburg, lost 1,100 people, and the small city of Grenada suffered 127 deaths. No one knew that mosquitoes spread the disease, and most blamed vapors or contaminated water. Towns tried to close their borders to visitors and shut down public events to stymie the spread of the disease. Whites more often had the means to flee to the countryside, leaving large black populations in towns with a skeleton crew of white volunteers. Fear of the disease created some strange incidents. In Columbus, a horse thief died of the fever, and for three days no one would remove his body from the jail. An elderly fisherman died in his seaside hut, and neighbors burned the hut with his body inside. State government lacked any funds or adequate personnel to offer any assistance, but the national government did organize relief by the fall.

A federal steamboat brought supplies and ice to relieve the suffering. In most cases the river towns had been out of touch for three months, and the government armed the boat well, fearing mob assaults. None occurred, but officials had to negotiate food distribution with black and white representatives in Vicksburg. Planters who had retreated to the north for protection from the disease worried that free food would weaken their control over their sharecroppers and compete with their plantation stores. Some whites rejected any aid for blacks because it was October and cotton needed to be picked. They feared aid distribution might allow blacks to stay away from the fields. On the whole, Mississippians drew three lessons from the worst yellow fever epidemic in history. First, they realized that action by the federal government seemed necessary and desirable in some cases. Second, they learned that all northerners did not hate and despise them because northern sympathizers sent aid and prayers while expressing sympathy for Mississippians' suffering. Third, Mississippians confirmed their traditional values and portrayed the heroes who risked their lives rendering assistance as akin to the heroes of the war. From Memphis to New Orleans 15,000 died, but the death of Jefferson Davis Jr., a bank clerk in Memphis, received the greatest attention, and southerners mourned him as a Confederate martyr. Historians estimate that the epidemic cost Mississippi $40 million in lost economic activity and reduced income.

Added to the epidemic and the economic depression, Mississippians struggled with tax burdens that the Redeemer legislature had shifted to the counties. Farmers faced increased land taxes to pay for education and the lean government services provided to them by counties. Prior to the war, planters paid a slave tax, but with the end of slavery, counties taxed land more heavily, and the state reduced the exemptions that had formerly been granted for personal property such as mules and horses, shifting yet more taxes to small farmers. As a result, county taxes increased six or eight times.

Taxes required cash money, which farmers lacked. The nation's money supply had shrunk as the national government withdrew greenback bills, considered an emergency war measure, from circulation, causing advocates to demand that the currency be brought back. They founded a national party in 1875. Mississippians responded avidly to this new party, with Greenback clubs forming in communities across the state. Most of the Greenback leaders switched from the Democratic Party, but a few old Whigs joined as well. Blacks provided the largest bloc of voters but played few leadership roles. The Greenback Party earned black votes by insisting on an honest vote count and by not being Democrats. White Greenback members insisted that their only chance to win in Mississippi required avoiding the Democrats' charge of renewed "Negro rule." The Mississippi Greenback Party represented the views of small farmers squeezed by the depression. Its platform advocated reducing the number of state employees, ending the prison lease system, and passage of a graduated income tax as well as increasing the money supply. The Grange, a farmer organization dedicated to bettering farmers' lives through education and cooperative marketing, backed the Greenback Party, which mounted its first serious campaign in 1878 by nominating Reuben Davis for Congress in the northeast Mississippi district where the party enjoyed particular strength.

Davis, the sixty-five-year-old former fire-eater, had been shunted aside by the postwar Democratic Party, so the irrepressible, successful lawyer assented to run as the Greenback candidate. As had been the custom in past Mississippi elections, he traveled with his Democratic opponent for "joint speaking." But Democrats used the same tactics against him that they had developed for Republicans. Ten minutes into his speeches, Democrats began to cheer for Davis's opponent, drowning out his words, or Democratic plants yelled out so many hostile questions that he could not speak. At Mayhew, the meeting disbanded because of the noise and gunfire from Democrats surrounding the school. Both Davis and his campaign manager received constant death threats. On election eve, Columbus Democrats hung Davis in effigy, and the next morning they burned his effigy. To keep black voters from the polls, Lowndes County Democrats fired a cannon each half hour of election day. Clay County Democrats spread a rumor that Davis had withdrawn for a Republican and then printed Republican ballots to be distributed to blacks. The Democratic election officials threw out a Monroe County box where Davis had won ten to one because, they said, there had been irregularities at the precinct. The Democratic secretary of state declared victory by 59 percent.

Davis wanted to contest the election, which he believed that he would have won with a fair count of the votes, but he could find no one brave enough to help him gather the necessary evidence. In 1879 the Greenback Party defied the death threats and the dirty tricks to win control in a handful of northern Mississippi counties. The party also took seventeen seats in the legislature, demonstrating growing resistance to the Bourbon elite.

Farmers hurt because overproduction of cotton depressed their income, and the value of their farms dropped precipitously. Between 1860 and 1870 the average farm value declined from $5,169 to $1,203, or 77 percent. Values varied around the state, but for the next two decades on average they continued to fall, so that by 1890, the value of an average farm had declined another 1.5 percent. Farms shrank in size. Grain production fell, and cotton planting increased in the teeth of declining prices. More yeomen farmers lost their land and became sharecroppers. Almost all farmers lived on credit, and furnishing merchants would only advance credit to those who grew cotton because only it served as the single cash crop. The merchants charged at least 10 percent interest and hiked the price of goods purchased on credit as much 25 or sometimes 100 percent. The railroads, built with incentives from the state, counties, and cities, charged discriminatory rates for shipping cotton and goods within the state.

By the 1880s, even the farmers on rich Delta land could not make a living by raising cotton. Even assuming that the farmer owned the land unencumbered by a mortgage or a lien, which the majority did not, the price fell below subsistence levels. Doing all the labor with family members did not produce enough profit for existence, oftentimes because the farmer still had to pay gin fees to produce a saleable bale, a commodity agent charged fees for selling the bale, and the bale had to be transported at the farmer's expense. The production cost for a pound of cotton in the late 1880s totaled 4.57 cents, and the cotton sold for 6 to 8 cents. The margin of profit fell too low for survival, but for years the farmers' creditors continued to demand more cotton, adding to the oversupply and further reducing the price.

As leader of the Democratic Party, Lamar refused to respond to the farmers' distress and ignored their pleas for monetary assistance. In 1877 he attended the state Democratic convention and tried to win the governor's nomination for his friend Edward C. Walthall. Walthall, an aristocratic Civil War general from Holly Springs, had taken Lamar into legal practice in Coffeeville during Lamar's darkest despondent period after Lamar had lost his plantation. To reward his friend for that old favor, Lamar ignored the political currents. The convention ignored Lamar and nominated Stone for a full term. The press roundly criticized Lamar for his lack of political insight, and the effort brought his leadership of the party into question. In 1878 the legislature responded to farmers' demands for relief by passing a resolution instructing Lamar to vote for a bill to increase the coinage of silver as money. Lamar refused to follow instructions and opposed the measure, announcing that he doubted the connection between the money supply and the economic depression. He associated himself with the conservative northeastern wing of the Democratic Party and the Republican's hard money men. He haughtily told the state that he preferred to deserve their approval rather than to have it. The *Jackson Clarion*, edited by his chief critic, Ethelbert Barksdale, denounced the vote and gave voice to agrarian discontent. The legislature, as a rebuke to Lamar, passed a resolution commending Bruce for his vote in favor of the bill. Lamar continued his defiant attitude and spent much of his time working for aid to construct a southern transcontinental railroad, which did not earn him much credit back home.

He did not campaign in Mississippi's 1878 congressional elections because of the yellow fever epidemic, but he gave a newspaper interview in which he denied that Mississippi had disfranchised any black voters. Ignoring Reuben Davis's Greenback campaign, he claimed that no "human being" had been molested or "made afraid." The story went national, and Senator James G. Blaine attacked Lamar in the Senate for obviously lying. Lamar lost his temper when Blaine ridiculed him and lost the debate, which continued with articles by each man in the *North American Review*. He followed up the debate by voting against federal protection for black voters and warded off efforts to empower the federal government to police congressional elections. He grew verbally violent again in the Senate over an attempt to deny Jefferson Davis a Mexican War pension, which undoubtedly did play well at home. In 1879 he returned to north Mississippi to combat the Greenback Party, obscure his vote against coining silver, and trumpet his work for Mississippi River levees.

Lamar skipped the beginning of a Senate session to attend the state Democratic caucus to nominate a senator to replace Bruce, whose term expired in 1880. Lamar again tried to install his friend, Walthall. Ethelbert Barksdale, editor of the leading Democratic newspaper, former CSA congressman, and brother to General William Barksdale, hero of Gettysburg, wanted the nomination and led the anti-Lamar wing of the party. Lamar almost carried it off on the first day of the caucus, falling short by only two votes of winning Walthall the nomination. The tension and mental strain brought Lamar down with a paralysis attack, and doctors applied leeches to his head as treatment. Walthall, who, according to accepted custom, did not attend the caucus, rushed to Jackson with Lamar's wife. The caucus compromised and chose James Z. George for the office. Lamar took his defeat badly and limped home on crutches.

As the architect of Redemption, George must have felt that he deserved the reward because his Mississippi Supreme Court seat did not seem

James Z. George, known as the Great Commoner because of his humble origins and his success as a lawyer. Engineer of Reconstruction, George replaced Bruce in the U.S. Senate. Courtesy of the Mississippi Department of Archives and History.

adequate compensation. Known as the Great Commoner, George had the advantage of understanding small farmers. His father died when he was a year old, and he enjoyed none of Lamar's advantages. He grew up in poverty, attending field schools when he could. At age eighteen, George moved to Carrollton and read law with a local judge, who took him into partnership at age twenty. He served in the Mexican War in Jefferson Davis's regiment and returned to enter into Democratic politics. At age twenty-eight, the party made him reporter for the high court of errors and appeals, and George served on the committee in the secession convention that drew up the ordinance to secede. Elected captain of a company, George served in the army until Union forces captured him at Fort Donelson. Exchanged, he became a general in the Mississippi militia, but refused orders to lead his troops away from their homes because he told his commander they would all desert. Joining the CSA again, he was captured once more.

Following the war, George formed a partnership with Wiley P. Harris, one of the most outstanding lawyers in the state. George dressed poorly, spoke bluntly, and, despite his legal career, appeared to be somewhat uneducated. When he was a young man, his religious wife asked a Baptist preacher to convert him. The preacher hounded George for an extended period of time until one day, as he rode home from Carrollton, the preacher appeared out of the woods and followed George, urging baptism. They had to cross a swollen creek, and even though it was midwinter, George demanded that the minister dismount and baptize him immediately, which he did. Climbing back in the saddle, George told the preacher to go home and stay there because he was finished with his damned foolishness. Lamar seemed to have preferred dealing with Bruce, because he disparaged George to others. George became known in the Senate for his hair, which he wore long. If it was parted and slicked back, George would listen to the debates and remain quiet. If George came to the floor with his hair disheveled, he had been thinking through an argument and would have a good deal to say. Although he had a larger corporate clientele than Lamar or Walthall, George was not as closely identified with the railroads and corporations as they were. Probably because of his origins, George managed to identify closely with the small farmers, and he did more in their interest. With George's elevation to the Senate, Lamar had a rival instead of a friend serving with him.

Democrats conscientiously guarded their circle of "elite" allowed to hold office and insisted on strict adherence to the color line. Emmett L. Ross's career demonstrates how admission to the elite worked. Ross served in the CSA army until released because of a wound, and after the war he worked in a host of clerk's posts in Canton to support his growing family. Interested in politics, he ran for mayor in 1873, lost, bought the *Canton Mail*, and won the position of secretary to the Madison County Democratic convention. As editor, he encouraged the party not to adopt a whites-only organization and instead to recognize "Negroes" as citizens and rescue them from the carpetbaggers. The county convention did not send him to the state convention in 1875. He defended the party's "military" efforts in 1875, but after the victory he urged moderation and protection for blacks. The Democratic city government gave the city's printing contract to his Republican rival when he underbid the *Mail*. The county sent Ross to the state convention in 1876 and nominated him for the House of Representatives, but he withdrew in favor of a black Democrat. In 1877 Ross tried to win the nomination for secretary of state but lost. Following his rejection, he toyed with switching the *Mail* to the Independent Party and castigated Democrats for failing to keep their promises to blacks. Ross lost his paper because of debts and had to work for a New Orleans newspaper. Returning to Canton in the mid-1880s, Ross supported white supremacy down the line and referred to Canton as a white man's city. In 1891 the party nominated him to the state senate, and he defeated two other candidates by just over 100 votes, fulfilling his lifelong ambition to hold public office. Unfortunately, Ross died of a spider bite before the Senate met, but clearly he had to have the party's approval to get political office, and he did not win party sanction until he accepted the color line.

Benjamin King mounted a populist challenge to the Democrat establishment, appearing in brogans and sometimes topless to impress audiences with his affinity for the common man. Courtesy of the Mississippi Department of Archives and History.

Mississippi Democrats practiced hard politics, won elections, and kept the white minority in power by ruthless measures, but their hold on the state's offices was more tenuous than it appeared from the massive majorities. Whites were a minority, and the unsatisfied agrarians constantly threatened to bolt from the party. If the agrarians joined with the blacks allowed to vote, they could defeat the Democrats. Democratic opponents understood the corrupt system that the Redeemers had created and sometimes manipulated it. In his congressional race, Lynch knew that in some counties all of his votes would be misreported as Democratic votes, so his solution was to discourage his supporters in those counties from voting, which in the final count kept his opponent's numbers down because the Democrats could not misreport more votes than had been cast—if they used their usual reporting system. In 1881 Lynch hatched the scheme to unite the Republicans, Independents, and Greenbacks behind the candidacy of a popular Democratic state senator from Copiah County. Benjamin King had been a Whig before the war and a Democrat since. He gained notoriety for wearing brogans while giving political speeches and sometimes appearing shirtless. King was unconventional enough to listen attentively to Lynch's proposal. He refused to join either the Republican or the Greenback Party, but he agreed to accept the endorsement of all the Democrats' opponents in an effort to break the Bourbons' hold on office.

The Democrats appeared vulnerable because of dissension within the party. Barksdale and his faction continued to oppose Lamar's followers for every office, and Lamar's perceived greed in promoting his friend Walthall caused unfavorable comment. One Democrat in Lamar's old congressional district wrote a friend in 1881 that Lamar had done less and gotten more credit than any other man he had ever seen. He said that Lamar, who attended Senate sessions irregularly, only gave two speeches a year and voted with Wall Street more than he did for Mississippi. Congressman James R. Chalmers, who edited the *Vicksburg Daily Commercial*, brought up Lamar's failure to support coinage of silver and suggested that Lamar should divide the spoils of office more equitably, giving up either a Senate seat or the governor's office. Lamar remained aloof but secretly fed information through backstairs sources to editors favoring his faction. In the summer of 1881 Lamar quietly secured the county conventions' support for his reelection to the Senate, knowing that once the delegates to the state convention pledged to him, his seat was safe. He did not repeat his mistake of attending the state convention again; instead, he directed his faction to back Governor Stone for reelection. Stone had forgiven Lamar's opposition in the last convention and joined Lamar's group during his first full term in office. Barksdale's faction raised the cry of a third term against Stone and kept the convention deadlocked for thirty ballots before Barksdale dropped out in favor of a compromise candidate, Robert Lowry.

Lowry, another corporate lawyer, had been promoted to general after he tried to hunt down Newt Knight in Jones County during the war. Elected to the state senate in 1865, he played an active role in politics throughout Reconstruction, including the revolutionary overthrow of the Republicans in 1875. Active in the United Confederate Veterans, he used those ties for political purposes. Lamar knew little of him and told friends that the selection confused him, but he embarked on a vigorous campaign in his favor to defeat King.

King possessed a galvanizing issue in Campbell's Code. Passed by the 1880 legislature to codify the state's laws, it contained a provision in the crop lien section allowing landlords to seize a farmer's crop to collect rent owed. Given low cotton prices and the precarious state of most farmers' finances, this law frightened many farmers who desired a government willing to protect their interests. King promised to be that governor, and he decried the corruption in Mississippi's elections, promising to root out illegal voting practices. He listed specific cases of missing and altered ballot boxes in past elections, and Lowry answered with a twinkle that King seemed to have been oblivious to how he won office as a Democrat. Lowry brushed aside the charges of fraud with the comment that boys will be boys. Lowry constantly drummed on race, accusing King of being a radical—a word connoting Republican, black rule, and corruption in the context of the times. King countered with the fact that Democrats entered into fusion agreements with blacks in many counties, to which Lowry did not answer directly because those alliances remained a discreet compromise necessary but not open to discussion. Lamar, Mississippi's face of moderation, had to compromise his public persona to keep the farmers in line. Lamar, who had always publicly condemned depriving blacks of the franchise, covered the entire state, not just his usual ground in north Mississippi, with the message that a King victory would be a return to black rule. In letters to Democratic editors, Lamar urged whites to unite to prevent "the negro from grasping the power of the State." And he explicitly supported Lowry, he said, not knowing if Lowry supported him, because it was necessary for white solidarity.

The Democrats claimed that Lowry won the election with 60 percent of the votes, but only fraud, intimidation, and theft produced those figures, and King may have won an honest election. Stone carefully appointed only trusted Democrats to the election boards in the counties where they were most needed. When the Greenback Party came to him asking for appointments to ensure a fair election, Stone appointed some of their approved men in counties that Democrats could afford to sacrifice, but in counties Democrats had to carry, he appointed only Democrats and Republican stooges previously corrupted and known to be safe. King tried to nullify Democratic intimidation by bragging that his followers intended to rely on "six-barreled" law for their protection, and some on his ticket went armed to their political meetings, but violence and the threat of it influenced the outcome despite his tough talk. In Sharkey County, someone ambushed a crowd of blacks walking to a political meeting killing three and wounding two others. Lowry ominously predicted that if violence marred the polls, everyone knew who would suffer. In Winston County, the Democrats ran one of the leaders of the Kemper County mob that murdered Chisholm and his family for the legislature. In Marion, black supporters of King and the Anti-Monopoly Party angered an old white man with their enthusiasm, and he hit a black man in the head with a stick, prompting gunfire and a race riot. Initially, whites suffered more casualties, but a white posse from Meridian reversed the numbers. Democratic newspapers blamed King for inciting the riot with his comments. Computer analysis of voting patterns and the returns indicate that King might have won if votes had been honestly reported, but the Democratic secretary of state reported Lowry's victory and the loss of fifteen Greenback seats in the House of Representatives. The election proved to be a disaster for the opposition.

Despite the 1881 disaster, Chalmers gave new life to the opposition in the congressional election the next year by deserting the Democrats and allying with the Greenback and Republican Parties in Lamar's old House district. Chalmers served with Forrest and commanded George in north Mississippi during the war. Aside from being a newspaper editor and initially defeating Lynch for Congress, Chalmers had led the white forces that restored white rule in Austin, a rundown Mississippi River town, in 1874. His opponent, the sitting congressman Vannoy Manning, had been sheriff of Tunica County at the time and had fled the town in the face of an angry black mob that insisted on keeping a white physician in jail after the physician accidentally shot a black girl to death while pistol-whipping a black man. The Democratic Party's lukewarm support for Chalmers in his contest with Lynch enraged the editor and prompted him to move back to Panola County, a center of Greenback power, and challenge Manning and indirectly Lamar. Lynch had unseated Chalmers halfway through his term in the House of Representatives by winning a challenge in the House. Chalmers enjoyed enormous popularity among white voters, and the Democrats would have difficulty labeling him a radical. From Washington, Bruce pronounced his blessing to giving Chalmers a shot at the Democrats. President Chester Arthur had adopted a policy of encouraging independent groups outside the Republican Party to challenge southern Democrats, and so he provided some financial support and encouraged federal law enforcement officials to aid Chalmers in preventing election fraud. Both Republicans and Greenbacks supported Chalmers, who drafted a platform to appeal to farmers. Ham Carter, a black independent Republican, entered the race with Lamar's secret support, but Lamar laid low, making no public statement on the contest.

Carter aired Chalmers's war record, which included being at Fort Pillow, where Forrest was accused of massacring black Union soldiers, but black voters ignored him and Chalmers's record in order to defeat the Democrats. On election day thirty-eight deputy U.S. marshals watched the polls, recording the names of all those denied the right to vote and keeping an eye on the boxes to prevent tampering. As a result, Chalmers won with 52 percent of the vote; however, when the Mississippi secretary of state issued the official returns, Manning won by a few votes. In Tate County, Chalmers's name had been misspelled, and the secretary of state threw out Tate County's entire vote. Chalmers got an appointment as an assistant U.S. district attorney to prosecute the Democrats for fraud in his election, but he failed to make much headway. He finally got his seat in Congress in June 1884 just in time to face a new election campaign.

Lynch also ran for Congress again in 1882, but the Democrats had redistricted him into a constituency including many eastern majority-white counties such as Jones and Covington. Lynch had to tour his new district by wagon because the counties lacked rail lines, but to his surprise, he found his white constituents hospitable. In Greene County, the white hotel owner rented him a room and the county judge adjourned court for his campaign speech. He attended an all-white camp meeting in Covington County.

Knowing that he could not win enough white votes to take the election, the Democrats did not rig the polls, and Lynch won 47 percent of the votes in his losing effort. Lynch's campaign illustrated how the complex Democratic political machine operated. When they did not need violence and fraud, they simply relied on racial division, but they could be ruthless.

In the 1883 county and state elections, the Democrats went after King's home county, Copiah. The Democrats formed a mounted paramilitary force of 150 men for the purpose of eliminating the black voters who aided the opposition. The night riders whipped and assaulted blacks, warning them not to vote against the Democratic Party. They shot one black leader and his wife to death. A Democrat shot a white Independent leader in the groin. The Independent white candidate for sheriff defied a Democratic order not to vote, and when he appeared to cast his ballot, Erastus Wheeler told him again not to vote. As he continued to prepare his ballot, Wheeler shot him dead in front of the ballot box. Hazlehurst named Wheeler town marshal three weeks later, and the local paper proclaimed "No more nigger domination."

In 1884 Lamar entered fully into the campaign in his congressional district as he also stumped for Grover Cleveland for president. Lamar kicked off the campaign with Governor Lowry, Manning, Walthall, and the new candidate, James Morgan, in Holly Springs, where Lamar delivered a major speech accusing the Republicans of illegal campaign tactics and declaring that the Democrats intended to clean up elections. As a sop to the farmers he attacked high protective tariffs and accused monopolies of oppressing the "masses." He concluded with an appeal for white men to unite to protect "civilization." Chalmers carried only one county in 1884, and for the first time since 1875, Mississippi sent only Democrats to Congress. Cleveland named Lamar secretary of the interior as the symbol of southern Democrats in his administration, and Lowry appointed Walthall to fill his friend's seat in the Senate. With a Democrat in the White House, Mississippi Republicans lost the valuable patronage that had helped to keep their party alive in Mississippi, and the Democrats no longer had to be concerned that the national government might investigate misconduct or post deputy U.S. marshals to oversee congressional elections. By 1885 most farmers accepted that they would have to work within the Democratic Party to get any relief from their misery.

During the decade dominated by political struggle and agrarian decline, Mississippians engaged in a host of diversionary activities. For example, in the 1880s marriage insurance enjoyed a brief but hectic popularity. A number of companies such as the Blue and Gray or the Climax Day Marriage of Grenada offered to pay couples a generous sum on the day of their wedding. One ad promised $600 in five months for $23.30. Insurance advertisements flooded the newspapers, and one letter to the editor complained that the writer's daughter had subscribed to fourteen companies while her "bow" had sold his roan horse to buy policies in eighteen. The editor of the *Raymond Gazette* proved to be one of the few voices of reason, warning the companies had no sinking fund and observing that southerners should have learned from the insurance failures that followed the war not to be taken in. After the initiation fee, the policies called for annual dues and periodic assessments, which participants resisted paying. Policy holders began to employ lawyers and attach funds, leading to a speculator collapse.

Mississippians also accomplished much of a more permanent nature, founding several institutions of higher learning, for example. Missionaries aided blacks to establish Tougaloo, Rust College (started as Shaw), and Natchez Seminary, the last of which moved and turned into Jackson State. The state established Alcorn with federal funds provided to develop agricultural education. Although called colleges, these institutions mainly provided secondary education in preparatory schools. Alcorn graduated its first student with a college degree in 1882 and Tougaloo did so in 1901. At the same time the state bought Oakland College to begin Alcorn College, it funded an agricultural and mechanical department at the University of Mississippi. Few students enrolled in the land grant program, and the university abandoned the department in 1876. The Grange, on behalf of its 30,000 Mississippi members, demanded the establishment of a proper land grant institution to provide education and leadership for Mississippi farmers. After the Grange unseated legislature members for opposing the bill to establish a school in 1877, the next legislature authorized Mississippi A&M. Governor Stone appointed a board to chose a site for the school and to hire a president. The board selected Starkville as the site and state senator and former general Stephen D. Lee as president. Lee gave Mississippi A&M a military air, with all students required to wear uniforms and with a drill field at the center of the institution. Lee was a long-standing member of the Grange and shared the Grangers' philosophy that farmer-owners should operate farms to make them successful. He advocated breaking up plantations and persuading northern immigrants to fill up Mississippi's surplus land in order to improve the state. He also shared the new south philosophy seeking modernization and industry.

Railroads provided the impetus for modernization in nineteenth-century America, and Mississippi had been moving quickly to build railroads before the war, but in the first decade after the war the state added only 120 miles of track. The state constitution prohibited the use of state credit for such purposes, and other states offered better incentives, causing Mississippi to lag behind. Former general P. G. T. Beauregard, as president of the

New Orleans, Jackson, and Great Northern, restored service to the Mississippi capital, but Colonel Henry S. McComb bought up state and city stock in the firm, displaced Beauregard, and consolidated the Southern Railroad Association. Bringing in northern men and investment capital, he ran the first train from New Orleans to Chicago, using a ferry across the Ohio River. But then the Illinois Central swallowed the company and made Mississippi part of one of the nation's largest rail systems, with no local participation in management. Between 1880 and 1890 the state rails increased by 119 percent.

Railroads opened up the Delta frontier, but the most dramatic growth in Mississippi during Reconstruction and Redemption occurred in Meridian, which had been not much more than an outpost and small rail stop when the war began. Growth came after the war because the wartime government completed the east-west line and used Meridian as a military post during the war. Sherman destroyed what little existed, but Meridian sprang back quickly. A number of Jewish merchants such as I. Marks, who had worked as a peddler before and after the war, spotted Meridian's potential as a distribution center for retail goods and established stores and warehouse establishments to service the crossroad stores in Alabama and Mississippi. By working the rural clientele, the merchants learned their customers' psychology and developed contacts in markets in New Orleans and New York to buy low and sell high. The railroads allowed farmers who had practiced subsistence agriculture raising grains and herding animals before the war to switch to cotton in order to earn cash. Never mind that the soil of east Mississippi was ill suited to cotton, the peddlers had learned how the farmers craved the small baubles and pretties in their packs. Farmers planted cotton, and store owners also served as cotton agents. The merchants built gins and fertilizer factories to sell the farmers the remedy for their cotton-impoverished soil. Merchants organized the Meridian Cotton Exchange in 1873, which shipped its first compressed cotton bales in 1875.

Marks brought in his three half-brothers, Levi, Marks, and Sam Rothenberg, from New York, and their store prospered. They built large, substantial Victorian homes furnished with the best, and Levi operated an opera house. Traveling salesmen filled new hotels and needed diversions. Entertainers passed through, riding the rails between New York and New Orleans. Levi put the two together and learned the entertainment business on the job. He offered Mississippi operas such as *Fra Diavola*, the Al G. Fields minstrels, Shakespeare's *Richard III*, and the all-American *Be Sure You're Right Then Go Ahead*, the dramatization of Davy Crockett's life. Meridian got its telephone system in 1882, by which time it was one of the fastest-growing cities in the South. E. H. Dial, one of the city's progressive mayors, wrote a play, *The Queen of the East or The March of Progress*, in which he chronicled the city's history and presented its moneymaking attitude. In the play, presented at the opera house, he played the character Eli, who was the irrepressible promoter. Eli dismissed questions about a mayoral candidate's war record with "It makes no difference." He tells the townspeople that they need to capture a capitalist. Asked how, he responds: put salt on his tail, meet him at the station, write flattering resolutions, or give him a banquet. He probably wants to build a factory, Eli assured the town, and it was his capital that they wanted. As it attracted industry and serviced the railroads, Meridian's population grew 165 percent between 1880 and 1890, when Marks and Rothenberg opened a five-story shopping palace and a grand opera house. Meridian had become the most dynamic city in Mississippi, which had always lacked such urban centers.

The urban places providing services to Mississippi's population had always been New Orleans and Memphis. Meridian became the largest city in a state that failed to produce any other cities. In 1880 Mississippi employed only 5,805 industrial workers because industrialists had built only eight mills, most of which wove both cotton and wool cloth. The mills were scattered from Corinth to Natchez. The largest, in Wesson, had been founded by Colonel J. M. Wesson, who had operated in isolated Choctaw County until discovered by Union raiders. He sold his mill to New Orleans businessmen in 1871, and William Oliver ran the plant for the Cotton King Edmund Richardson when he bought it. The steam boilers consumed fifty cords of wood per day, and the carding room alone comprised five acres. Oliver brought Edison's lightbulbs to the factory the year after their invention, and Mississippians would travel miles to marvel at the light in a bottle illuminating the thousands of windows of the five-story brick buildings constructed to resist fire. Oliver worked 99 percent whites in the mill and 64 percent females. Children went into the mills after a year or two of schooling and worked twelve-hour days, never seeing the sun except through the factory windows much of the year. Wesson was atypical for Mississippi industry, which primarily consisted of cottonseed mills or wood-processing shops employing fewer than ten people in each one. Some Mississippians escaped the drudgery of the farm to work in factories, but most farmers viewed the regimentation of a factory with horror, preferring their relative freedom in the fields.

Some farmers tried to leave the state. In the mid-1870s a group of blacks inspired by the prewar efforts of the American Colonization Society asked Senator Bruce to introduce a bill to provide $100,000 to finance black migration to Liberia. Bruce did as they asked, making clear that he did not support the idea because he believed that he and they were African Americans and should remain so. He had more sympathy for the Exoduster movement, which spread "Kansas fever" among Mississippi's black population in 1877.

A few prominent blacks moved to Kansas and wrote back home of the rich land and the lack of social/political oppression in the state. By March 1879 crowds of black Mississippians—many lacking the money for transport and sustenance—appeared on the banks of the Mississippi trying to hail passing steamboats. Chalmers, among others, interceded to convince captains not to stop because planters feared losing their labor supply. Isaiah T. Montgomery made an inspection trip and purchased land in Kansas, but decided to make another effort in the Mississippi Delta. As a black planter, he worried about his labor supply and reported back to Mississippians the suffering among the migrants unprepared for a new life. White planters employed lien laws and intimidation to end the exodus that saw the departure of around 3,000 black Mississippians over a two-year period.

Approached by representatives of the Louisville, New Orleans, and Texas Railroad about becoming an agent for them and convincing blacks to settle on company-owned Delta land, Montgomery conceived the idea of building a community to provide blacks a haven from white oppression and violence. He and a cousin purchased 840 acres of land in Bolivar County and recruited settlers, who began to arrive in early 1887. Establishing farms required privation and hard work. Former slave Simon Gaither typified their experience, buying forty acres, building a log cabin, and clearing an acre the first year. He planted corn, cane, rice, and garden vegetables on his first acre, cut firewood to sell for $6 a cord, and hired out to clear more prosperous settlers' land for $4 an acre. His wife and children also hired out to work other farmers' cotton while he gradually cleared more of his forty acres. Twelve years later he had saved enough to buy another forty acres. Gradually the surrounding farms developed enough to support the town of Mound Bayou, where Montgomery became mayor and built a twenty-seven-room mansion. Northern philanthropists invested in the experiment. Andrew Carnegie built a library, but the town never purchased any books for it, so while Montgomery's idea of separate black economic development offered hope and promise, he failed to execute the idea well.

Farmers—both black and white—tried several methods of self-help and individual betterment schemes. In 1889 Oliver Cromwell, an agent for the Colored Farmers' Alliance and the Durant Commercial Company, a cooperative store established by the Alliance, appeared in Leflore County trying to enlist farmers in his organization and soliciting business for the store. He preached the liberating advantages of the Durant cooperative and generated some enthusiasm. White planters soon heard of his success and began to fear trouble with their sharecroppers. White merchants spread the rumor that Cromwell was a con man who had once been the leader of a gang of horse thieves. They told their black neighbors that Cromwell just wanted their money. Called before the new chapter of the Alliance to refute the rumors, Cromwell mounted a good defense, and the majority voted to support him and passed a resolution announcing their decision signed by "Three Thousand Armed Men."

The white minority reacted with alarm, and whites in the neighboring counties spread rumors that the Colored Farmers' Alliance had stockpiled weapons for a black uprising. Armed whites gathered in Greenwood, while blacks concentrated in Minter City. The sheriff rode up to parley with the blacks, but when his speech convinced some to leave, one of their leaders shot a "deserter." At that point, the sheriff retreated and telegraphed Governor Lowry for troops. Lowry accompanied three companies of the Mississippi National Guard to Greenwood, where he found a large white mob that had descended from the nearby hills. He spoke to the mob and persuaded them to leave the blacks to the National Guard, and then he forbade any of them to follow the troops. The sheriff guided the National Guard to the black camp, but the black Alliance men had vanished. The troops arrested forty blacks and confiscated 220 rifles from black farmers in the area. A number of blacks were reported killed, but no accurate count was made. Cromwell escaped to Jackson and never returned. Cromwell's assistant, whom the sheriff identified as the camp killer, was executed for burning a store while searching for more ammunition. Local whites lynched at least five other leaders after the troops left and sent warnings to the Colored Farmers' Alliance and the Durant cooperative to cease activities in the county or face united white hostility.

In Webster County, where whites outnumbered blacks over three to one and where 70 percent of the farmers owned their land in 1880, farmers still felt the agricultural depression and mounted strong opposition to Democratic domination of the county. Split off from Choctaw County and called Sumner by Radical Republicans, the Redeemers changed the name to a more acceptable Webster, identifying their local party with the Bourbons at the state level. By 1883 the leader of the Greenback Party, John. E. Gore, sought to unite all Webster's opposition elements—Independents and Republicans included—against the Democrats. The Gore family, which included ministers and doctors, had been brought in to oppose the Bourbon establishment by their experiences working to serve the impoverished farm population. An Anti-Monopoly Party bolted from Gore's coalition, but Gore won a seat in the legislature. In 1885 the opposition carried the county for the Grange candidate for governor over Lowry, but Gore lost his seat in the legislature by a slim margin.

The next year even the Democratic organ the *Walthall Warden* took up harsh criticism of the Democratic government for allowing legislators to take excursions to Ship Island while working men drove themselves and their mules to death making seven-cent cotton to pay the taxes to foot the bills for them. The opposition rallied around a new organization, the Great Agricultural Relief, which allied with the National Union Party, a creation of the Grange and the Knights of Labor. Although the new organization insisted that membership be limited to manual laborers and explicitly excluded lawyers, doctors, officeholders, and literary men, Gore, who was a minister, continued to be a leader. Some "reliefs" or units within the county, presumably led by Democrats, balked at the unification with the Union Party and tried to expel Dr. A. C. Gore for violation of the rule against professional men joining the organization. In 1887 the Democrats won every office by stuffing the ballot boxes, according to the opposition, and the opposition shifted to a new organization, the Farmers' Alliance. Although the Farmers' Alliance tried to work within the Democratic establishment, it demanded the radical overhaul of the party. The Farmers' Alliance condemned the idea of donating toward the construction of a Jefferson Davis monument in Richmond and demanded the reduction of all governmental salaries, from the governor to the county supervisors. The neighboring *Starkville Times* condemned the Webster radicals for breaching the civic religion by criticizing Davis and called the Webster Farmers' Alliance men "savages" for attacking the American flag and the public schools. The newspaper recommended that the state Farmers' Alliance send a "missionary" to deal with the savages.

As in Webster County, the Democrats' opponents statewide had been eliminated by the late 1880s, but the mass of the white population desired change. Frustrated by complete Democratic domination, prohibition emerged as the strongest political reform movement and drained off some of the political rebellion. Flournoy, for example, became a prohibitionist. Efforts to restrict the manufacture and sale of alcohol dated to before the Civil War, but during the war the legislature, at Pettus's urging, outlawed the distillation of spirits in an effort to conserve grain for the troops and to depress drunkenness. Sheriffs refused to enforce the law, and Governor Clark got a stronger measure, but on the run from the U.S. forces, Clark had no power to implement the statute. The Reconstruction legislature quickly repealed the law, and saloons and crossroad grog shops reopened. By 1873 the temperance crusade persuaded the legislature to pass a law holding saloonkeepers liable for damage done by drunks who left their saloon and caused harm, but not until 1879 did the crusade begin in earnest.

John B. Gambrell, a Baptist minister and editor of the *Baptist Record*, published a series of articles urging statewide prohibition. The next year Kansas passed such a law, and Gambrell's young son undertook speaking and organizing duties in the small towns and hamlets across Mississippi, meeting with racially mixed groups combining religious intensity and the crusading fervor for reform. Antiprohibition spokesmen warned that the prohibitionists endangered white rule with their appeals to black voters and declared drinking to be a southern tradition, hinting, in effect, that it might be a part of the civic religion of the South. In 1880 the chancellor of the University of Mississippi, former CSA general Alexander P. Stewart, sent a letter to state religious leaders suggesting that they organize to lobby the legislature for prohibition. By 1882 the prohibition leaders had secured resolutions from all of the state's black and white Protestant churches endorsing the crusade for state prohibition.

Frances Willard, national leader of the Woman's Christian Temperance Union (WCTU), visited the state at the invitation of the prohibition leaders and addressed a joint session of the Mississippi legislature before touring the state to speak against liquor. She met with Chancellor Stewart's wife to organize the state's first WCTU chapter, and then the chapters rose quickly around the state, providing women with an important outlet for their political energies. By 1885 the movement appeared unstoppable. Governor Lowry refused to endorse it and ignored it in his messages to the legislature, but he told the prohibitionist leaders that he had never vetoed a local prohibition law and would not begin to do so if reelected. Charles Galloway, the leading Methodist minister and soon-to-be bishop, derailed the push for statewide prohibition and accepted a local option law allowing county and municipal elections to decide the issue in each community as the best compromise. The legislature enacted the law in 1886, and the most spirited election contests of the period followed in communities throughout the state, often including considerable violence.

For example, in Montgomery County, prohibitionists riddled the homes of eleven antiprohibitionist blacks with gunfire and killed one black "anti" leader with several loads of buckshot while tying a less important "anti" to a tree until he promised to vote right. But the most dramatic events occurred in Hinds County, where Jones S. Hamilton, Bourbon state senator, businessman, holder of the prisoner lease contract, and outspoken opponent of prohibition, gunned down the younger Gambrell, whose father was out of state attending the Southern Baptist convention. The young Gambrell wounded Hamilton, who claimed self-defense. Prohibitionists saw Hamilton as the poster image of all Bourbon evils in the ruling elite because in addition to his obvious flaws, it was known that he won his election through fraud. His trial for murder consumed months of public attention. Hamilton got it moved to Rankin County and enlisted a dozen of the leading lawyer/Bourbon politicians for his defense, and a mixed-race jury found him not guilty. The WCTU meeting in a Presbyterian church in Columbus hung Gambrell's photograph from the altar with "Hero and Martyr" printed underneath. In a coda to the trial, former CSA general Wirt Adams, who testified for Hamilton at the trial, challenged a prohibitionist editor whom he heard intended to criticize him in print, and they shot one another to death on a Jackson street.

In the fall of 1887 Galloway, head of the prohibitionist executive committee, clashed with Jefferson Davis. Galloway, who attended the University of Mississippi with CSA veterans and became the spokesman of the "Lost Cause" religion in Mississippi, criticized Davis for a letter that Davis wrote to the governor of Texas opposing passage of a prohibition amendment to the constitution there. Davis only uttered his condemnation of the amendment in response to a question from the Texas governor and certainly had no desire to enter the debate in his home state, but Galloway pressed the issue after the *Clarion* obtained a copy of the letter and printed it. Hedging his remarks with the usual praise for the secular saint, Galloway regretted that Davis endorsed saloons. Davis took umbrage, and when Galloway declined to apologize, Davis responded in a public letter, which concluded that "prohibition did not prohibit," which boosted the antiprohibition elements in the state. Many papers dared to suggest as a result of the exchange that many "good and pure Christians" opposed prohibition, demonstrating the power of the civic religion to counter the political weight of the churches.

The prohibitionists joined in demands for a new constitution to replace the Black and Tan 1868 document, hoping to get statewide prohibition. The agrarians had been demanding a convention for a decade to clean up the corrupt Democratic system in place since 1875. State politics split between the white counties and the black counties. The small white population in the black counties controlled the legislature representing blacks, who were either not allowed to vote or who were made to vote Democratic. In Yazoo County, 300 voters elected four legislators, while in Tishomingo County 1,600 elected one legislator. The whites of the hills and piney woods hoped to reapportion the legislature, get elected judges, and create a whites-only democracy. Lowry vetoed a constitutional convention bill passed by both houses in 1888, but with Stone back in the governor's office the next year, a new bill became law. Senator George broke the Bourbon blockade by endorsing the convention, followed quickly by Walthall. National politics may have influenced the Bourbons' decision because the Republicans had retaken control of both houses and the presidency, and a bill had been introduced to use federal powers to protect southern black voters. Almost no white Mississippian wanted that to happen.

The Democrats had such a tight hold on the Mississippi electorate by 1889 that only 15 percent of the voters turned out to elect delegates to write the new constitution. Webster County proved the exception, because Gore united the opposition and defeated the Democrat 697 to 621. Gore served as the lone Greenback delegate along with two Republicans from Bolivar County, including Montgomery, who was the lone black delegate. Only seven non-Democrats served in the convention. Solomon S. Calhoun, the lead lawyer for Hamilton in his murder case, won election as presiding officer and opened the convention after Galloway's prayer with the declaration that the purpose of the convention was for the dominant race to ensure the continuation of white rule. He contended that rule by dark-skinned people led inevitably to "economic and moral ruin." His remarks addressed no other theme.

Calhoun appointed George to the franchise committee and provided it with the only staff assistance at the convention in order to have the committee devise a means of disenfranchising blacks without violating the Fifteenth Amendment. He naturally appointed antiprohibitionists to the committee to consider that question. The Bourbons had the convention in hand from the outset. The white counties gained a few seats in the legislature, but the Bourbons perpetuated their control of the party and state government through the continued domination of the black counties. The new constitution continued the appointment of judges, and many whites got excluded along with blacks by the new voter restrictions. First, the Bourbons imposed a poll tax of $2, which had to be paid for two years before a voter qualified to vote in any given election. Aimed at blacks, it affected white farmers who might see only $50 a year in cash if they were lucky. Second, the literacy test meant to exclude blacks would also take the vote from a substantial portion of the white farmers, but a clever ruse eliminated this objection. The circuit clerk could read a clause from the constitution to the potential voter and then determine if the prospective voter understood it, leaving it to the discretion of the Democratic circuit clerk to admit whites and exclude blacks. Third, the constitution imposed strict residence requirements aimed at blacks who changed plantations, often seeking a better landlord. Wiley P. Harris, George's old law partner, investigated the constitutionality of the new requirements and assured the convention that they did not violate the Fifteenth Amendment. Montgomery addressed the convention and as the sole black delegate acquiesced in the work of the convention, telling the white delegates that he hoped blacks would earn the franchise in the future and that he hoped they would be admitted as voters when they did. The Bourbons emerged from the convention with their power intact. Gore and a few others voted against the document for what it did to poor whites, but their protests were futile. The small white farmers would have to find another means of reforming the political system.

The delegates decided not to submit the constitution to the voters for ratification and extended officeholders' terms of office for two years in order to synchronize state and county elections. The Bourbons' arrogance was breathtaking, but they clothed themselves in the civic religion and relied on the corrupt system built up during the fifteen years since they took power to perpetuate their rule forever. Jefferson Davis died just before the constitutional convention met. While on his fall visit to Brierfield, he fell ill and died after making his way to New Orleans. His funeral surpassed any spectacle ever witnessed in the South. His body lay in state for five days while thousands filed passed. Varina and the family saw the funeral ceremony from their carriage as ministers preached the funeral sermon on the steps of city hall because no structure in the city could accommodate such a large crowd. Thousands of veterans followed the elaborate caisson to Metairie cemetery, where Davis's body was temporarily placed in a vault. Three years later Varina decided to move him to Richmond, and the train transporting his body across the South resulted in another outpouring of public affection. The train paused at special places such as Beauvoir, and along the rails fires burned and old Confederate soldiers lined the route in formation. In the 1880s Davis told the Southern Historical Association in New Orleans that the southern cause was sacred and that had he known the future in 1861, he would have pursued the same course. White Mississippians along with other white southerners desperately wanted to believe that the war had not been a mistake, that their family members had not died for an ignoble cause, and that the Bourbons represented the extension of that cause transformed into a white man's government necessary for the protection of the white population. The history of the Redeemer period called their interpretation into question because the black majority of Mississippians always had a portion of the white minority willing to work with them to oppose the Bourbons, whose rule rested on a weak foundation of violence and lies despite the legitimacy claimed from the South's civic religion.

Chapter Nine

ATTEMPTED REVOLT OF THE REDNECKS

The corrupt political and economic system imposed on Mississippi by the Bourbons produced indescribable suffering for the vast majority of the state's people. Conditions in the state were so bad that northern life insurance companies refused to write policies for Mississippians, and some required their northern policyholders to get permission to visit the state in order to maintain their coverage. Pellagra, a disease caused by inadequate diets, weakened a significant portion of the population who were restricted to eating fatback, corn bread, and molasses by the sharecropping system. Denied opportunities for education, the population endured the nation's highest illiteracy rates, with the black majority's rate approaching 50 percent. The restive white small farmers seethed with resentment against the oligarchy that controlled their lives and ignored their clamor for change. When the hoped-for relief did not appear in a political system little altered by the 1890 constitution, farmers forced the adoption of the all-white primary for the Democratic Party and turned to two demagogues—James K. Vardaman and Theodore G. Bilbo—to reform the political system. Their elections demonstrated the wide class divisions between the white farmers and the Bourbons and gave poor whites hope. The farmers' "saviors" proved to be flawed individuals, and the reforms they generated fell short of producing the miracles dreamed of by their followers. Yet change did begin. For example, the legislature in 1908 authorized the establishment of agricultural high schools, regional institutions that enabled rural students to continue beyond elementary education. Two years later the legislature established a normal school at Hattiesburg to improve the quality of teachers in the state. Progress came slowly, but unseating the Bourbons began to make a difference.

To understand where Mississippi stood at the end of the nineteenth and the beginning of the twentieth centuries, consider Matt Brown, who worked as a sharecropper near Black Hawk, Mississippi, from 1884 until he died in 1905. He bought his goods from the "Jones store," and we have the store's

Sharecroppers came to make up the overwhelming majority of the state's population, and declining cotton prices drove them deeper into poverty, lowering their standard of living to a nadir of disease and ignorance in the twentieth century. Courtesy of the Mississippi Department of Archives and History from the Allen (Leigh Briscoe) Collection.

books detailing his expenditures and debts. Brown was black and owned next to nothing, selling his labor for the credit advanced to him by the Jones store. When he settled with the store at the end of each year, he owed on average $450. In 1892 he began the year obligated to $226.84 and ended owing $452.41. During the year, he earned credits from the sale of his cotton, cutting wood, clearing land for others, and hauling goods for the store, accumulating credit amounting to $171.12, but he bought $54.45 more than he earned. He spent $35.15 for food, $29.45 for clothing, $173.64 for farming expenses, $.55 for drugs, and $112.81 for miscellaneous items, including $9.75 for chewing tobacco and snuff. He also borrowed $4.00 cash. Four years later Brown brought forward a debt of $387.16. During the year, he purchased food worth $8.42, clothing costing $27.25, farm and household supplies amounting to $38.30, drugs for $.95, and miscellaneous items totaling $12.08. And he borrowed $2.35. That year his cotton sold for enough to clear his accumulated debts, leaving a credit of $58.76, but he slipped back into debt. The last charge in 1905 was for a coffin and burial supplies. The storekeeper marked off the remainder owed, indicating that Brown escaped the cycle only by dying.

Details of exactly how planters and storekeepers kept farmers in peonage were understandably not well documented because of the fraud and usury involved in the transactions, but the investigation of Italian immigrants' complaints by the U.S. attorney general's office provided a glimpse into some of the methods used by planters. In 1907, 180 Italian families worked on cotton plantations in the Delta region. Leroy Percy and other large planters violated the federal alien contract labor law to import the Italians with the idea that they might be able to replace their overwhelmingly black labor force with immigrants. The planters sent tickets for ship transport to labor agents in Italy, allegedly from relatives in the United States, in order to get families to immigrate to the Delta. Of course, the planters charged the price of the tickets to the new employees' accounts so that they arrived indebted. Percy and a partner, O. B. Crittenden, ran Sunnyside plantation across the Mississippi River from Greenville in Arkansas. By the summer of 1907 they had 160 Italian families on the place. The plantation managers charged each family for mules, cottonseed, tools, and living provisions at high company-store prices plus a flat 10 percent annual interest fee. The company claimed a monopoly on the families' cotton crops, buying them cheap at Sunnyside and selling them for 40 percent more in Greenville. The customary broker fee should have been 2.5 percent. The families ended the year in the same manner as Brown, owing the store, but unlike Brown, the Italians had an ambassador to whom they complained. Letters prompted questions to the American government, and that initiated the U.S. Justice Department's investigation.

The families alleged, aside from the financial fraud, that the managers abused them, that the living conditions were unhealthy, and that they could not leave if they chose. The government sent Mary Grace Quackenbos, a rare female lawyer from New York who had recently been investigating labor camps in other southern states, to determine the facts about Sunnyside. She tried to infiltrate the plantation as she had labor camps, but Percy's managers detected her interpreters/assistants and had them arrested and jailed. Securing a letter from the acting governor of Arkansas, she forced her way onto the plantation and tried living with the Italian immigrants. Percy and Crittenden decreed that she had to spend her nights in Greenville and insisted on accompanying her as she did her daytime interviews with the Italians. Despite heated verbal clashes with their bosses, the Italians bravely voiced their complaints, and Quackenbos secured access to the company books, where she discovered that Sunnyside used a clause in the tenant's contract to assign day laborers to a tenant's field at harvest time and then charged the day-labor to the tenant's account.

Summing up her findings, Quackenbos admitted that Sunnyside did not fit the classic description of peonage, but believed that it constituted a more subtle form of intimidation and oppression. She negotiated an end to the 40 percent marketing fee and got the standard 2.5 percent for the Italians. But she learned that after she left, thirty families fled Sunnyside, some owing debts. Managers pursued the tenants and forced them back under threat of imprisonment and the chain gang if they refused. When two men tried to leave their families on the plantation while they moved to Birmingham to work as miners in order to escape their indebtedness, Crittenden summoned the sheriff, removed them from a train, and used force to return them to Sunnyside. A month later managers evicted tenants with a small child from the plantation, leaving them on a levee overnight with no shelter while they waited for transport to Greenville. Quackenbos decided that this constituted peonage and indicted Crittenden. The Delta press undertook a campaign against Quackenbos, and her legal files disappeared from her Greenville hotel room, turning up in the hands of former congressman Thomas C. Catchings, who was a good friend of Percy's. Witnesses on Sunnyside ceased cooperating with her because of intimidation by the managers. The U.S. attorney in Jackson, another friend of Percy's, began to express doubts about the case. Percy went to Washington to meet with yet another friend—President Theodore Roosevelt. Percy convinced the president that a woman could not possibly understand the southern labor situation and that she should be recalled. The man sent to replace her dropped Crittenden's prosecution and decided not to challenge the Mississippi lien statute that facilitated peonage. No more Italians immigrated to Sunnyside, and the company went back to using African Americans because neither the United States nor any foreign government took any interest in the tactics used to keep them in peonage.

Planters used all of the tactics employed against the Italians, and more, against both black and white sharecroppers. Poor white farmers believed that their state government had abandoned them as they slid into the cycle of sharecropping or teetered on the edge of it. By 1890, 90 percent of Mississippi's farmers had been trapped by the lien system. Even those who still owned their land felt themselves being sucked in. Faced with cotton prices so low that they could not recoup their costs, much less make a profit, farmers feared having to take out an "ironclad or anaconda" mortgage, which provided that the merchant's account book would be "incontestable" in court. Having watched their black neighbors' economic decline, white farmers knew the fate awaiting them.

In the years after the adoption of the 1890 constitution and before the First World War, Mississippi experienced a boom in the piney woods. Because of the region's poor soil, overgrazing of the open range, and increasing population, the inhabitants had turned to the forests to support themselves. Turpentine and resin gathering played a small part, but lumbering became a major industry. During Reconstruction, loggers cut the convenient

Railroads provided the means of extracting Mississippi's most valuable natural resource from the land. Courtesy of the Mississippi Department of Archives and History.

trees near sizable streams and floated them as rafts down the Pearl and Pascagoula Rivers to the Gulf Coast. Loggers placed dirt on the rafts and built fires on top of the earth in order to float overnight. Some loggers remembered fires on the water as far as they could see in both directions. In the 1880s crosscut saws replaced axes and sped felling the trees. Pushed back from major streams, loggers had to resort to waiting for flooding rains to get their logs into the waterways and to hauling some timber out using massive wagons pulled by long teams of oxen.

Railroads opened the new logging frontier. Fifty to sixty mills located, for example, along the 300 miles of the Gulf and Ship Island Railroad. By 1902 the seventy-four miles of track between Hattiesburg and Gulfport supported a turpentine distillery or a lumber mill every three miles on average. Heavy use of the line for export led to the digging of a deep-water channel to Gulfport, and as a result, in 1907 the Gulf and Ship Island carried 10 percent of the yellow pine lumber produced in the entire South–800 million board feet. By 1900 eleven lumber companies operated rail logging lines, called tap lines, into the forests from five to twenty-five miles in length. Operations of increasing magnitude required increased capital and investment. As the Midwest's white pines disappeared, big lumber companies moved in and bought Mississippi mills and forest acreage. A few local operators, such as L. O. Crosby, survived the influx of out-of-state giants to build Mississippi fortunes, but by the 1890s the dissatisfied small farmers had been joined by the lumber industry workers in opposing the railroads and lumber corporations, who failed to compensate them adequately for their work.

Logging with oxen proved to be a hard life for loggers, who often camped in the wilderness and worked long hours harvesting the state's most valuable asset. Courtesy of the Mississippi Department of Archives and History from the Stanton College Photographs Collection.

Just as there had been a labor shortage in the Delta after the Civil War, the piney woods experienced a similar dearth of workers. Skilled saw-men at the mills got $2.50 per day, but the companies imported many highly paid workers from their older mills out of state. The usual pay by the 1890s was $1 per day—sometimes in script redeemable only at the company store. Loggers worked in isolated camps, living in temporary log structures thrown up quickly. A normal workday lasted fourteen hours, beginning with rounding up the oxen left to graze overnight. Then each worker prepared breakfast and something to eat in the woods for lunch. At the end of the day, they faced preparation of another meal unless they lived close enough to return home, which grew more rare over time as the lines drove farther away from the main railroads. The companies employed both blacks and whites on their crews, but they did not integrate. In the mill towns, sometimes run as open towns with drinking, gambling, and pool halls to placate workers, blacks and whites segregated into separate communities, often divided by the railroad track if the town had one.

By the early 1890s whites began to organize "bulldozing" organizations in the southwestern part of the state to drive black workers out of the camps and off the companies' payrolls. Whitecappers, as they called themselves, visited black loggers and mill workers at night, threatening blacks' lives unless they departed. For five years between 1893 and 1898, the whitecappers

At the beginning of the Great Depression, the *Clarion-Ledger* estimated that nineteen million of the state's thirty million acres had been clear-cut. Lumbermen left treetops piled among the stumps, which fueled fires and left a wasteland where a forest had once stood. Courtesy of the U.S. Forest Service of Mississippi.

burned company buildings, beat black workers, and frightened them into leaving the piney woods.

Just as with cotton agriculture, lumbering exploited Mississippi resources and placed the state in a colonial relationship to northern companies. The companies often owned the railroads and most of the timber resources, so that profits flowed out of state. They clear-cut the forests, and when they could not sell the cleared land to farmers, they abandoned it without replanting. Hundreds of square miles of Mississippi forests disappeared each year in an orgy of greed, and most Mississippians benefited little from the devastation of their greatest natural resource.

The Bourbons, or as their opponents called them, "the system," presided over the state undisturbed by the poverty or complaints from either the black population excluded from participation in the political system except as pawns or the white voters. Stone reclaimed the governor's office in 1889 and had his term extended by the 1890 constitution. George and Walthall reluctantly agreed to the 1890 convention, but made certain little change resulted from it. They gladly assented to the poll tax and other measures certain to exclude many poor white voters as well as blacks. The two senators and the governor announced their conversion to silver coinage and took the stance that being silver advocates made them champions of the poor farmers. Back in the Democratic Party, poor farmers tried to take control away from the Bourbons by following Barksdale, the unhappy outsider kept out of office by Lamar and then George.

Frank Burkitt, the Farmers' Alliance leader, acted as the farmers' spokesman and chief advocate. A captain in the Confederate States of America (CSA), Burkitt practiced law briefly, but spent much of his life editing the Okalona *Chickasaw Messenger*, which served as the voice of the agrarians. He published a pamphlet entitled *The Wool Hat*, outlining agrarian discontent and demanding redress by the government. He wore a wool hat as a symbol of his solidarity with poor farmers, who could afford no better headgear, during his many years in the legislature and a brief stint in Congress. He could be something of a crank, making life miserable for the president of Mississippi A&M, for example, because Stephen D. Lee had belonged to the Grange and did not immediately warm up to Burkitt's Farmers' Alliance. Nevertheless, he served as the voice of the alliance, and was selected as "State Lecturer" to travel throughout Mississippi spreading the organization's ideas. He linked with Barksdale when the dissident Democrat endorsed the "sub-treasury" plan. Under this scheme the government would establish warehouses where farmers stored their crops until prices in the market improved enough to make them profitable. Meanwhile the "sub-treasury" would issue the farmer a receipt, which he could spend as legal tender.

All of the Bourbons condemned the plan as economic heresy and rejected it. George ran for reelection in 1891 against Barksdale, with Burkitt providing vociferous support to his opponent. Pro-Barksdale and pro-George Democrats opposed one another statewide, each claiming to be the true Democratic Party member. In Chickasaw County, Burkitt won the county party's endorsement only to face an independent or pro-George opponent in the general election. Burkitt's newspaper building burned in the middle of the night, and his opponent shot Burkitt in the head, but the bullet only grazed him and he recovered. Governor Stone appointed no Barksdale men to the county election commissions, so the George Democrats could count the votes as they pleased. In agrarian Pontotoc County, George's supporters stole the voter registration books from the courthouse in an attempt to prevent an election from being held. George agreed to meet Barksdale in a series of debates, but they had to be called off to prevent riots breaking out at each stop. The last campaign held before the new voter registration procedures (ordered by the 1890 constitution) proved to be an exciting contest, with Burkitt and Barksdale covering most of the state and rousing the farmers with the promise of the "sub-treasury" to provide some relief from their suffering. But "the system" ultimately prevailed as always. The legislature elected George by 101 votes to Barksdale's 53. Walthall, who announced that he declined to serve again and then changed his mind before the legislature met, also won reelection for a new term beginning in 1895 by a much larger margin.

The disappointment Farmers' Alliance's members felt led some of them to consider joining a new political party forming across the South and West, the People's Party, or as it was widely known, the Populist Party. The Populists gave voice to disgruntled farmers, demanding direct election of senators and ultimately government ownership of the railroads. Burkitt played a major role in the national party, and the Mississippi Farmers' Alliance elected two congressmen in 1890 as members of the Democratic Party. Those gains, and the creditable showing in the senatorial contest against George, encouraged them to continue challenging the Bourbons. As Burkitt and the Farmers' Alliance moved toward the Populists, a division appeared among the organization's members. W. S. McAllister replaced Burkitt as the "State Lecturer" and opposed the "sub-treasury" plan. At a state Farmers' Alliance meeting in Starkville, McAllister challenged the national president, engaged in a fistfight with him, and drew his pistol offering a duel. Burkitt then expelled McAllister from the Mississippi Farmers' Alliance. The organization's records burned in the fire that destroyed Burkitt's newspaper office, and many Alliance members rejoined the older Grange, rejecting populism before Burkitt chose to break with the Democrats.

Many Mississippi farmers believed in Stone's and George's conversions to their cause. Stone sent delegates to the National Farmers' Congress in 1893, and George strongly supported the establishment of the U.S. Department of Agriculture. Along with their adoption of free silver, the Mississippi Democrats—on the surface at least—measured up to farmers' demands. Six of Mississippi's seven congressmen passed the test established by the Farmers' Alliance. The less politically aggressive Grange welcomed back errant members by waiving membership fees for those wishing to return. The new voter registration completed in 1892 eliminated thousands of poorer farmers, and because of the extension in office granted by the 1890 constitution, Mississippi Democrats did not have to run for election in 1894. Beginning in 1892, the Democrats adopted the Australian ballot as provided by the new constitution, and the ballot made it almost impossible to identify Populists because it listed candidates without party labels.

Grover Cleveland's election as president again in 1894 buoyed the Democrats and detracted from the Populists' victory in having twenty-two Democrats in Mississippi bolt from the party in the legislature to declare themselves Populists. The Democrats got a glimpse of their future in 1894 when Walthall, suffering from ill health, resigned for a year to recover before taking up his next six-year term. Many Democrats aspired to the one-year replacement duty in the Senate, but Stone and other recent converts to free silver withdrew when it became clear that only a strong free silver candidate had any chance of winning the Democratic legislative caucus. A. J. McLaurin, an outsider who shared the farmers' attitude of being disinherited and believed the old guard was too close to northern moneymen, shouted loudest for silver to win the place of temporary senator. McLaurin, a lawyer from Brandon, cast himself as a plainspoken farmer who rose from poverty to fight "the system." Cotton sold for five cents a pound that year, and hog cholera killed thousands of swine, meaning that farmers faced hunger and a lack of cash. Conditions encouraged Burkitt and the Populists, but the 1895 state elections wiped out the Populist threat to the Democratic Party.

Burkitt ran for governor in 1895 as a Populist, and in his convention speech, he converted dollars to cotton bales, charging that using his measure, the Democrats spent three to four times more than the Republican Reconstruction government had. To protect farmers from "the system," he called for an elected judiciary, and to better their children's lives, he called for more money for elementary and secondary education. His theme remained the Mississippi Democrats' connection with "money powers in the East." The Democrats adopted a platform similar to the Populists and nominated their strongest free silver man, McLaurin, who had to leave the Senate for the returning Walthall. McLaurin and Burkitt spoke at several joint appearances, and McLaurin questioned Burkitt's competence while touting his own experience and swearing his loyalty to farmers. In Webster County, the Populist heartland, the contest grew into one of the most colorful and hard-fought elections in the county's history. Songs provided an entertaining element. "Populism Is Mississippi" contained a line to the effect that the ship of state had been sold to "thieving pirates" who pocketed the gold and ran the state with the courts at their command, saying, "Thy people may be damned." A second song's chorus advised voters to "join" the Democrats if they wanted to loot the treasury, stuff ballot boxes, or have hard times. The star of the electoral speakers in 1895 was Thomas Pryor Gore, the blind son of one of the long-standing opposition family. McLaurin encountered Gore in Calhoun County, where the papers said the young Cumberland Law School graduate "scalped" the would-be governor so badly that McLaurin left cursing Calhoun as the worst Populist county in the state. In the Gore family's Webster County, the Democrats defeated the entire slate. While admitting that some former friends deserted them, the Webster Populists blamed the loss on the voters dropped from the rolls under the 1890 constitution. White voters declined from 1,438 to 1,077, and black voters dropped from 206 to 38.

The Democrats sent all of their heavy guns to battle Burkitt and the Gores, including future governors Earl Brewer and James K. Vardaman. Populism, the last challenger to total Democratic domination in Mississippi, died in the 1895 election because the Populists went into the race divided, and the Democrats turned to a new-style candidate in McLaurin and continued to commit widespread fraud. In Burkitt's home county, Populists found their potential voters dropped from the registration books while Democrats who failed to pay their poll taxes or who had moved away remained on the books. In a Kemper County Populist precinct, the Democrats had a "drunk" charge into the polling area and grab some ballots, which provided them an excuse to throw out the box without counting it. Sensing the futility of continuing to battle "the system" in Mississippi, the young Gore soon left for Texas and later moved to Oklahoma, which elected him to the U.S. Senate.

Overly fond of his whiskey and inclined to appoint his numerous brothers and other relatives to office, McLaurin failed to provide much for the farmers. He no doubt impressed them by attempting to collect back taxes that he said the Illinois Central Railroad owed as a result of its acquisition of a rival line. He used appointments and his pardoning power to build a personal machine outside "the system." In a classic letter during the Spanish-American War, one of McLaurin's cousins wrote to the governor asking to be given a quartermaster's post or some other lucrative spot where he could "get some money or stealings." There was no record of the governor's response, but the letter indicated the spirit of the times because the cousin stated his desire so bluntly. McLaurin's brothers did benefit from the prisoner lease system for many years. In the spring of 1895 Senator George announced that he would retire when his term ended because of ill health. This announcement poisoned the political atmosphere because McLaurin, who had already declared for governor, fumed over the timing as a plot by "the system" to keep him from returning to the Senate. He and his machine plotted to get him the seat, but he failed in his maneuvering, and the legislature selected Congressman Hernando Desoto Money. When George died in office, a second round of plotting ensued, but finding no way to ensure his own election to the Senate, McLaurin reluctantly appointed Money to fill the vacancy in the office that Money had already been elected to fill when George retired. Walthall died the next year, and in the resulting scramble for office, former governor Lowry's opponent accused him of abducting a young woman for immoral purposes, further degrading the political atmosphere. The strategy worked, and the legislature elected Lowry's opponent, indicating the end of the small ring that had run the state since 1875.

McLaurin ran for the longer-term Senate vacancy against "Private" John Allen, a congressman renowned for his wit and humorous speeches. He earned his title "Private" during his initial run for Congress. After listening to a former Confederate general who was running against him describe his troubled night in a tent before the battle of Shiloh, Allen rose and claimed to have been the private outside the tent guarding the general. Then he asked all of the former generals to vote for his opponent and all of the former privates to vote for him. Much in demand as a speaker around the country, newspapers often referred to Allen as the "ablest" man in Mississippi "public life." McLaurin labeled Allen a Bourbon and attacked him as one whose economic, legal, and political system kept down the common man. During a joint appearance in Winona in their 1899 race, Allen used all his oratorical skills, along with his keen sense of humor, to attack McLaurin's message. He derided McLaurin for claiming that the rich opposed him because he ate greens with a knife or because he had split rails and driven oxen to make a living. Allen called such talk demagoguery and accused McLaurin of trying to establish one-man rule with his personal machine of hirelings.

McLaurin refused to respond directly and, claiming to be ill, sat in a chair to speak. He said the rich opposed him because he wanted to make them pay taxes and that he was an honest man who stood by the poor. He called Allen a vulture ready to prey on him—the wounded lion. Allen responded that if he were a vulture, he would choose better meat. Allen's wit did not win the same response that McLaurin gained with his open pleas for sympathy. Frustrated by his opponent's success with the poor simple-man theme, Allen hit back harder with less humor, accusing McLaurin of neglecting his duties, using free railroad passes, and being drunk in office. When evidence piled up substantiating the last charge, McLaurin admitted his drinking and begged forgiveness. As Allen began to make progress in the race, his mother fell ill, and he abandoned the stump to be with her until she died. McLaurin continued his appeal to the sympathy vote and readied his followers to pay poll taxes for voters where needed, to stuff ballot boxes, and to move voters across precinct lines where required. Allen lost because he did not understand the increasing need to fan the flames of class hatred, whereas McLaurin was the first post-Bourbon to use the tactic effectively.

McLaurin recognized a dangerous opponent in James K. Vardaman, a newspaper editor from Greenwood who battered McLaurin for the corruption in his administration. When Vardaman sought a commission in the Mississippi armed forces headed for Cuba, McLaurin denied it to him, knowing a veteran had appeal with the voters. Vardaman had to secure an appointment in the regular U.S. Army. His experiences in Cuba seemed to alter Vardaman's attitude on race and perhaps led him to become Mississippi's worst raving racist. Prior to serving in Cuba, Vardaman's views on race seemed typical, but in Cuba, he encountered people of all colors sitting alongside one another in church and even marrying one another. He said that the Mississippi "nigger"—he began to always use that word—was a scholar and gentleman compared to black Cubans. A poor relation of H. D. Money, Vardaman read law and passed the bar, but spent his career as a newspaper editor, first in Winona, where he participated in the battle over passage of a local option law, killing a man who attacked him in the street over one of his editorials. He married an older widow with a son and 3,000 acres near Greenwood, so he relocated there and bought a newspaper. Entering politics, he quickly rose to be Speaker in the Mississippi House of Representatives and earned a record indistinguishable from other Delta politicians. He wore his hair shoulder length in the older fashion and spent an inordinate amount of time brushing it to a high sheen. Although a prohibitionist, he enjoyed wine with his meals at home and a sherry in the evenings. He claimed to be a Methodist but did not attend church.

Back from Cuba, where he served in a noncombat role, Vardaman's newspaper writing expressed admiration for Ben Tillman, a South Carolina demagogue who ruled his state with the same sort of racist and class-dividing rhetoric that Vardaman adopted. Vardaman sounded new themes of anti-imperialism (condemning the annexation of the Philippines), opposition to "money power" (criticizing the Robber Barons such as John D. Rockefeller), and the loss of agrarian and Christian values to the desire for money. But his most consistent issue became virulent, vicious racism. He compared black people to animals, denying they possessed full human qualities, and advocated lynching any black who committed a crime against a white person. "Black beasts" raping white women proved to be one of the most popular subjects in his political speeches.

Within days of returning from Cuba, Vardaman hit the speaking trail running for governor. At the county level, the Democratic Party mixed primaries with conventions, depending upon the choice of the county executive committee, but "the system" still functioned. McLaurin threw his support to A. H. Longino, a former legislator and congressional candidate whom McLaurin had appointed a judge. The state convention of 1899 went as such conventions usually did, and Longino easily won the nomination. The previous year, newspaper editors began to ignore the Populists and Republicans because they offered no creditable threat to the Democrats. The Republicans split into Hill and Lynch factions, reducing their effectiveness to a nadir. Only twenty delegates attended the Populist state convention in 1900. But the Democratic state executive committee in its arrogance aroused opposition within the party by refusing to schedule elections for its members. The committee scheduled primary elections for the presidential nomination, which was a formality because everyone knew that the candidate would be

William Jennings Bryan, but then the members simply continued themselves in office. Vardaman, using his paper as a platform, seized leadership of the Democrats, demanding the adoption of party primaries to choose all candidates and party functionaries by popular vote. Calling for Democrats to hold a state convention in defiance of the executive committee, Vardaman garnered wide support from leaders such as Percy and John Sharp Williams, who was making an outstanding record in the U.S. House of Representatives. Vardaman positioned himself as the reform candidate to oppose the disreputable personal machine created by McLaurin.

A. H. Longino, the first non-Confederate veteran elected governor since the war, demonstrated independence from McLaurin and called for industrialization as the means to transform the state. Vardaman did not assail Longino as he had McLaurin, only criticizing Longino's plan to lure industrialists with tax exemptions. Longino took on the long-simmering question of building a new capitol building and managed to construct an impressive structure on the grounds of the old prison. During Longino's administration, Vardaman's demands for primaries to govern the Democratic Party grew to become a groundswell as fraudulent primaries made headlines. Journalists proved in one instance that the votes reported from Coahoma County were for an election that was never held. In a Warren County district, ballots showed long lists of supposed voters voting identically for the machine's delegates to the national convention. Issaquena County reported more votes than it had registered voters. After revealing the frauds, newspapers took up the cry for reform. Longino endorsed primaries in his message to the legislature in 1900 and again 1902. The Delta Bourbons naturally opposed the adoption of primaries, knowing that the white counties with more voters would gain power by abolishing the old county conventions; nevertheless, the act passed in March 1902.

Democratic primaries transformed the state's political process, but they did not create a truly democratic system. Only those who had paid their poll tax and met the other stipulations of the 1890 constitution could run for office or vote in primaries, and the number of voters dropped to half the number who were eligible before 1890. Because the primary was not an election, but only a party selection of candidates, the whites-only rule could legally apply and did. This provision eliminated any black participation in Mississippi politics. County executive committees replaced the election commissioners as the managers of the polls, which put an end to the old system of having blacks and Republican stooges involved in the process. The election commissioners still kept the voting registration books to turn over to the executive committee for each primary. The primaries called for runoffs when candidates in crowded fields failed to receive a majority of

Serving as a major rail center, Meridian grew to be the largest city in the state, and a major influx of Jewish businessmen fostered big city connections to New York and even Europe. Courtesy of the Mississippi Department of Archives and History from the Meridian, Mississippi, Collection.

the votes. The state executive committee lost most of its power, and the county executive committees gave up some of their functions. "The system" ceased to exist, and white Democrats gained the right to choose their leaders in statewide primaries. Candidates had to pay for the elections through fees assessed by the party so that candidates for state offices paid sums in each county. Increased costs for candidates required large organizations and more fund-raising. Appealing to the masses gave an edge to the orator who could move large audiences by emotional appeals. The resulting primaries gave Mississippi new leaders who battled the wealthy Bourbons and tried to use the government for the benefit of the white masses rather than the small circle of planters and professionals who had held a monopoly of power since 1875.

In the quarter century of Bourbon rule, Mississippi changed. Railroads made Meridian the state's largest city, with a population of 14,050. Jackson gained industry to supplement government in its economy and grew significantly. Instead of five towns with populations in excess of 2,500, by 1900 Mississippi had twenty-two. In Meridian and other rail towns, restaurants stayed open around the clock. Department stores displayed a wide array of merchandise in palatial buildings designed to match the stores in Europe and the North. I. Marks, owner of one store, imported a Swiss architect to design a streetcar park on the edge of Meridian, and all of Mississippi's larger towns had such public transportation. Smaller towns such as Newton and Port Gibson built opera houses and hosted traveling entertainers of all types. Mississippians brought another three million acres of land under cultivation. They saw many of their forests cut. Some listened to agricultural reformers and began to diversify with dairy and beef cattle herds. In Crystal Springs, a few farmers began to raise tomatoes and beans to be shipped by rail to cities such as Chicago. A man with a half an acre of tomatoes who made a good crop earned more than a sharecropper with ten acres of cotton or a lumberjack.

In their memoirs, men who were ten years old in 1900 remembered trips to towns such as Laurel or Oxford as eye-opening, life-changing experiences. Some of them still lived in log cabins, and the roads between them and town consisted of dirt tracks that converted to mud when it rained. Mississippi still maintained its roads by requiring men to work on them or pay a fine. When reluctant laborers convened with their hand tools and perhaps a few mules to attempt any grading or filling, they sometimes did more damage than good. Lacking gravel or certainly paving as well as any central planning, Mississippi roads meant that a journey of ten miles to town took hours under optimal, dry conditions, but became impossible after a rain. Most ten-year-olds would only go to town once a year after the cotton had been gathered. They remembered excitement so great they could not eat breakfast, and they hurried to gather chickens, butter, and eggs to sell in town. Approaching Oxford in 1900, they saw the new water tank towering over the town and wondered about having water piped into a house. They drove under an archway of trees shading a street lined with what seemed to them immense Victorian homes set back in lawns with flowering plants surrounding them. If they had been able to go inside, they would have seen wonders such as gas, electricity, telephones, indoor toilets, and bathtubs. Hanging in front of the stores on the square were bananas—a fruit never available at the country store. After selling their chickens and other produce, they might be granted fifteen cents for a café meal of three vegetables and a meat. They might wander into Neilson's to gasp at the racks of ready-made dresses, shirts, and pants in a bewildering number of colors. If their timing was right, they could go to watch a train come into the station or a visiting circus could be in town. Before the end of the day, the boys returned to their family's log cabin or substantial plantation house, longing for the next trip to town. Although Mississippi possessed few urban centers and no city to match Memphis or New Orleans, its small outposts of urbanism affected its people in ways exceeding their size and numbers.

Vardaman appealed to Mississippi's rural population starved for entertainment and flattery. When he made his next run for governor in the first statewide primary, he sometimes arrived on a lumber wagon pulled by several yokes of white oxen. He wore white suits, shoes, and a cowboy hat, which contrasted with his long black hair. In his speeches, he extolled the virtues of southern womanhood, lauded the cult of the Confederate civic religion, exploited the fear of blacks, and occasionally sanctioned the growing ferocity of lynching blacks. If he needed an especially high level of response, he described a black man—although he never used either of those words to describe the person—raping a white woman. Listeners frequently swept him off the stage or wagon and carried him to his train or carriage on their shoulders. In one instance they seized his hat as they carried him away and cut it into pieces for souvenirs of the event. Vardaman never pretended to be one of the people. He cultivated an aristocratic air, but he gave voice to the poor's resentment against blacks and the Bourbons, and many loved him for it.

Vardaman ran as the opponent of the Bourbons and President Theodore Roosevelt. Not only had Roosevelt invited Booker T. Washington to the White House for a meal, but he came to the Delta and hunted bear with Holt Collier as his guide. Longino invited the president to a large hunt, but Roosevelt declined. He had appointed Longino's brother-in-law, Edgar Wilson, as his sole adviser on Mississippi federal patronage matters, despite the fact that Wilson refused to leave the Democratic Party and recommended mostly Democrats to the Republican president. The politics of hunting with Longino might have been too tricky. Roosevelt accepted an invitation to a smaller affair from the president of the Illinois Central Railroad, and local organizers asked Collier to organize and guide the hunting party. After the war, Collier hunted bear commercially and infrequently worked as a deputy—killing a white outlaw once. When game grew too scarce, he became a hunting guide to wealthy clients. Nationally, the hunt made headlines because the president disobeyed Collier's instructions and left his stand, forcing Collier to lasso the bear that he had driven toward the president. When the president refused to shoot the large bear tied to a tree, a cartoonist misrepresented the bear as a cub, giving birth to the teddy bear as a children's toy. In Mississippi, the hunt made news because the president's party chose a black guide and because Collier placed armed black men on the road to their camp in order to protect the president's privacy. In his newspaper, Vardaman resorted to racist verse to link Roosevelt to a belief in racial equality and to criticize his hunt.

Holt Collier, slave, accomplished hunter, Confederate soldier, and professional hunting guide to Theodore Roosevelt, who gave birth to the teddy bear. Courtesy of the Mississippi Department of Archives and History.

In Indianola, Vardaman found another issue with Roosevelt and the postmistress. Appointed by Benjamin Harrison, Minnie Cox, a well-educated black woman, had done a good job for many years, but Roosevelt's appointment of Wilson to handle patronage raised the hopes of some whites that they could rid the state of black appointees, so they raised objections to her continuing to hold the office and began to threaten her safety. Wilson secretly endorsed her to the president, but protests continued. Perhaps because it was only thirty miles from Greenwood, Vardaman began to visit Indianola to make speeches supporting whites in their efforts to oust Cox. In 1903 Longino ran for the Senate against Vardaman's cousin, H. D. Money, the incumbent senator. Money used the Roosevelt/Cox issue and racist rhetoric similar to that employed by Vardaman to win. As Vardaman escalated his attacks on Cox and Roosevelt, Cox resigned and left town, fearing for her life. Roosevelt closed the Indianola post office in retaliation, handing Vardaman a golden political opportunity.

Because of Vardaman's showmanship and speaking ability, large audiences assembled for him. Local businesses closed, courts adjourned, and farm families made a rare trip to town. His supporters organized parades and displays. In Chickasaw County, Burkitt led hundreds of horsemen flying banners to Vardaman's event. In other areas, cannons greeted the speaker along with band music. His familiar themes delivered with passion and intensity brought him in first, but left him with a runoff. Vardaman's most

James K. Vardaman, known as the Great White Chief because he adopted virulent, populist racism as his theme to win the governorship and a U.S. Senate seat. His opposition to World War I ended his career. Courtesy of the Mississippi Department of Archives and History from the Governors of Mississippi Collection.

substantive campaign promise was to distribute school funds according to the race of those paying the tax. For years the Delta received more than its share of funds from the state to support public schools because the Delta counties had the largest number of children to educate, but most of those children were black, and the Deltans spent the bulk of the money to educate their relatively few white children. Vardaman called for ending the pitifully poor support of black schools altogether because, he said, education ruined a good field hand and that was all blacks would be allowed to be. His call for changes in education funding played well in the hills, but his opponent in the second primary, Frank Critz, hailed from northeast Mississippi and commanded support in the hills. Critz got help from McLaurin in the second primary, which caused important Delta figures to swing behind Vardaman. John Sharp Williams and Percy both spoke out for Vardaman, as did former congressman Allen. Along with the poor white farmers, they swept Vardaman into office, making Vardaman's initial victory as much about intraparty politics as it was a revolt of the rednecks. But some observers worried about his prospects as a leader. Roosevelt's patronage adviser, Wilson, thought the primary system elevated cheap men to office. James Garner, a new Ph.D. visiting his home state fresh from Columbia University, credited Vardaman's election to race baiting and predicted dire consequences for the state. Vardaman meant to govern well and told the press that he intended to suppress lynching if necessary.

Confronted with a lynching in Sunflower County in which a white mob mutilated two blacks and burned them alive and a renewed upswing in Whitecapping in southwest Mississippi, Vardaman acted vigorously to restore law and order. He took a personal interest in law enforcement, riding over to the Rankin County prison farm frequently to help train the bloodhounds used to track down escapees and criminals. When the second lynching during his administration threatened in Batesville, Vardaman took an overnight train along with National Guardsmen and brought the prisoner to Jackson. He hired a Pinkerton detective to investigate the Whitecappers, formed an alliance with local businessmen against members of the organization who had been elected to county offices, sent several Whitecappers guilty of murdering a black man to prison, and then broke up the secret society. He kept his promise and asked the legislature to eliminate funding for black education, but legislators ignored him. He increased funding for education and raised teacher salaries. He battled the state's corrupt prison system and finally ended prisoner leasing by establishing Parchman for the incarceration of almost all state inmates. He ended a textbook monopoly that had swindled poor parents by keeping the cost of schoolbooks artificially high, and he endorsed the passage of laws regulating insurance companies, utilities, banks, and trusts.

When the legislature passed a law limiting timber companies' land ownership to $10 million, Vardaman vetoed it because he believed it too high, and when the legislature approved a railroad merger, he vetoed that as well. He advocated limiting the interest rate in Mississippi to 8 percent, but the legislature refused to pass his bill. He asked for a state highway commission, a school for those who were deaf, and limits on child labor, but the legislature refused. Relying on two of his brothers and an old friend from Winona as personal advisers, he ran a tightly controlled administration, which journalists declared the most honest and efficient in state history. An out-of-state journalist touring Mississippi at the end of his administration could not find a single critic, and no one accused Vardaman of graft or corruption.

Vardaman had not made the full transition from Delta Bourbon to Populist by the end of his administration as governor, but his defeat in the senatorial election pushed him farther in that direction. His choice of a successor as governor was a Delta planter who donned a Confederate uniform and rode the length of the state, but lost to another progressive. Vardaman's cousin, Senator Money, announced his intended retirement, opening Vardaman's path to the Senate by the 1907 primaries. John Sharp Williams, Delta Bourbon, Democratic minority leader in the U.S. House of Representatives, and Vardaman supporter for governor, opposed him. Brought up at Cedar Grove, his mother's family's plantation before and after the Civil War,

John Sharp Williams, Mississippi lawyer, planter, and senator who was a friend of President Woodrow Wilson. Courtesy of the Mississippi Department of Archives and History.

Williams lived a life of privilege compared to Vardaman. His father died at Shiloh, but his mother's family sent him to Sewanee, Europe, and law school at the University of Virginia. Abandoning his law practice in Memphis, he returned to the plantation and by hard work made it profitable while he learned to navigate within the Mississippi political culture. He entered politics to oppose the "sub-treasury" plan, was well known to love his whiskey, and once initiated a fistfight with the much larger Edgar Wilson because of Wilson's association with the Republican Party and because of words from Wilson that Williams took as an insult. In their most famous joint appearance in Meridian during the campaign, Williams and Vardaman defined their positions well. Williams invoked the memory of Lamar and George and noted that, as gentlemen, they did not mention the race issue. When Vardaman repeated his frequent demand to repeal the Fourteenth and Fifteenth Amendments to the Constitution, Williams offered his opponent a pencil to edit the document, but warned that repeal could not be achieved and that trying it would open the South to northern meddling.

Williams advised leaving blacks to destroy themselves by moving to cities, which, he said, they were already doing. Vardaman responded with his rape description and a diatribe against blacks, engendering an outpouring of emotional responses from the audience. Vardaman avoided many joint appearances because he could not match Williams as a debater and stuck to his strength as a demagogue. Ben Tillman and Georgia Populist Tom

Edmund Noel, progressive governor who oversaw the adoption of statewide prohibition and suffered Bilbo's ridicule as "Granny" Noel. Courtesy of the Mississippi Department of Archives and History.

Watson endorsed Vardaman, and the remnants of the McLaurin machine lined up behind Williams. Williams won by 648 votes in a primary marred by the old tactics, which saw more votes cast than there were registered voters. Acting as a Bourbon "gentleman" did, Vardaman made no public protest, but in private he seethed at William's refusal to join with his voters to celebrate because, Williams said, the victory was too small to warrant cheering. Vardaman remained in Jackson, started a new paper, and prepared for the next senatorial election.

Edmund Noel, who had been defeated by Vardaman, authored the primary election law and won a close race to take the governor's mansion in 1907. He continued Vardaman's progressive legislative initiative, but his administration was overshadowed by the contest for McLaurin's Senate seat when McLaurin died in 1909.

Despite the fact that Vardaman supported him in the runoff primary, Noel refused to appoint the former governor to the Senate pending an election by the legislature. Noel left the office vacant until the legislature met. When the legislature convened, Vardaman joined a long list of applicants for the job, including Percy, who had determined to "save" the state from Vardaman because he considered Vardaman a dangerous demagogue. The legislature met as the Democratic caucus to choose a candidate by secret ballot, whom they would then, as the legislature, elect to be senator. All of the other candidates agreed to cooperate to deny Vardaman the nomination.

The public and reporters attended all of the caucus debates—only the votes were secret. This had been normal procedure, but the cabal to defeat Vardaman differed in the scale of corruption employed. Lobbyists for railroads and big business offered legislators whiskey, women, and bribes. Some of the candidates did the same. In session as the legislature, the caucus members passed a law creating the office of county attorney, which gave the governor seventy-nine patronage slots that could be used to influence caucus members. Vardaman cried foul, and the battling candidates grew more and more bitter along with their partisans, who reported instances of being bribed, seduced, and induced to overindulgence in alcohol. This took place in an atmosphere of intolerance for alcohol and in a state supposedly made dry by the adoption of statewide prohibition in 1908. After six weeks of balloting, Percy won the Senate seat.

Vardaman held a rally of his supporters in Jackson, and charges of corruption flooded the state. A Hinds County grand jury returned an indictment against L. C. Dulaney, a levee contractor and Percy supporter, because an heretofore unknown Pearl River County state senator named Theodore G. Bilbo accused Dulaney of paying him $645 to vote for Percy. Bilbo claimed to have been part of a group investigating rumors of illegal activity during the secret caucus and swore that he voted for Vardaman. The Senate launched an investigation of Bilbo, bringing former employers and acquaintances from Pearl River County to testify.

Although he served as a lay Baptist preacher, Bilbo had a checkered past. His father worked as vice president of a bank and was one of the more substantial inhabitants of the county, and he supported Bilbo's efforts to obtain an education. Bilbo attended the University of Nashville, but did not graduate. Returning to Mississippi, he taught school and tried for a county office in 1903 but lost the race to a one-armed Confederate veteran who taught Bilbo the importance of the sympathy vote. After Bilbo returned to teaching at Wiggins, the superintendent fired him because of accusations of impropriety with an orphan girl living in the same dormitory where he resided. With a loan from his father, he purchased a half interest in a Wiggins's drugstore and returned to Nashville to attend Vanderbilt. Having overdrawn his investment in the drugstore, he again failed to earn a degree. From Nashville, he filed to run for the Senate and returned home. Riding a borrowed horse around the district, Bilbo won his second political race for the state senate in 1907 and passed the bar at the same time. Often wearing his roommate and fellow senator's Palm Beach suits, Bilbo earned a reputation among his colleagues for womanizing and boozing, but in an effort, he claimed, to make Mississippi completely dry, he introduced legislation to prohibit federal facilitation of importing liquor. His knack for publicity led him to introduce specious bills to build a railroad track to the capitol so that the lobbyists could more easily bribe legislators or one to prohibit the sale, barter, or donation of a new soft drink that he did not like—"coke-o-cola." The *Clarion Ledger* predicted a successful career for him.

The Senate investigation laid out his past for public scrutiny, including his spotty school record and a cheating incident. On the charge of receiving a bribe, prosecutors found that some of the bills that Bilbo turned in as the bribe money had been issued after the date of the bribe. Bilbo explained that he had given the money to his wife for safekeeping, and she had deposited it in the bank. Other creditable witnesses supported parts of his story, and the Senate failed by one vote to expel him, but the senators asked him to resign. He refused, and the Senate passed a resolution stating that Bilbo was unfit to serve in the Senate. Later a Yazoo County jury found Dulaney innocent of bribing Bilbo, but kept unseemly testimony before the public. Bilbo reacted by announcing his intention to run for lieutenant governor.

Lost amid the uproar, Governor Edmond Noel carried out an effective reform administration. At age sixteen, Noel moved to live with his uncle in Louisville, Kentucky, in order to get a high school education. His family was too poor to afford a boarding school, and Holmes County had no institution to provide an education for him. His uncle was a lawyer, so Noel read law and returned to Holmes County to practice and enter politics. After one term in the House of Representatives, an Independent defeated him in 1883, giving rise perhaps to Noel's penchant for reform. He volunteered for the Spanish-American War, and his company elected him captain, but they only made it to Florida before the war ended. He adopted a strict prohibitionist stance and earned a reputation for his "Christian manhood." Bilbo and others in the legislature called him "Granny" Noel.

Elected to the Senate, Noel introduced the primary law that revolutionized Mississippi's political system and got a constitutional amendment passed to elect judges. The courts invalidated the judicial amendment because of a technical problem with its adoption by the voters, so as governor, he got the legislature to adopt it again, ending the appointment of judges. He asked the legislature for over 100 reform measures, and a large number were passed, including the establishment of agricultural high schools, a child labor law to limit children's employment in cotton mills, and statewide prohibition. At his urging, the legislature gave unpaid lumber workers a lien on the assets of companies and mills that closed and made it illegal for companies to blacklist workers because of union activity. As an administrator, Noel worked conscientiously to appoint good men to office down to and including notaries and to make informed decisions exercising his pardon power. He persuaded the legislature to authorize cities to bid for the establishment of a normal college so that Mississippi would no longer be the only state without a teacher-training institution. "Granny" Noel made a start toward undoing the Bourbon-style government of the state, but the Vardaman/Bilbo campaigns overshadowed his accomplishments.

Vardaman had announced for the Senate primary to take the Senate seat from Percy in 1911, but he had to be absent from the state much of the time leading up to the contest in order to deliver his Chautauqua lecture, "The Impending Crisis." A popular nationwide lecture series, Chautauqua provided Vardaman's income during this period of his life, and he was forced to leave an opening for Bilbo, who traveled the state telling his bribery story, condemning the Bourbons, and soliciting sympathy for the "Man," as the five foot two inch politician liked to call himself. Bilbo's notoriety drew an audience, and his listeners came away believing that the Bourbons and the old "system" had robbed the Great White Chief of his seat and slandered the Man in the process. Bilbo targeted the white upper class and not blacks, redirecting the poor farmers' anger and resentment away from blacks to the planters, lawyers, and store owners. Vardaman appreciated the power of Bilbo's appeal, even though he belonged to that class, and supported Bilbo's campaign despite criticism from Vardaman's more affluent and respectable supporters.

Senator Percy, the epitome of a Bourbon, mistakenly added to the class warfare of the campaign when he lost his temper while attempting to speak at a July 4th gathering in 1910. As Vardaman supporters continued to interrupt his talk with cheers for the Great White Chief, Percy called them cattle and rednecks. Vardaman/Bilbo supporters began to wear red neckties and promoted the stunt of bringing Vardaman to an event on an ox wagon. Bilbo adopted red ties, suspenders, and sometimes socks. One of Bilbo's favorite lines described the contest as a "fight between the classes and the masses." On April 4, 1911, Bilbo gave an example of how low he would sink with his rhetoric at Blue Mountain College when he attacked John J. Henry, who had testified against him, as "a cross between a hyena and a mongrel dog . . . begotten in a nigger graveyard at midnight . . . suckled by a sow and educated by a fool." The president of Blue Mountain opined that any father, brother, or husband would have been justified in shooting Bilbo to protect his women from such foul language and that no jury would convict the shooter.

Former governor Longino wrote to Henry asking him not to soil his hands with such a depraved and unworthy foe, but he concluded that if Henry had to kill Bilbo, he should wait until after the election. Henry sent friends asking Bilbo to retract his words, but instead Bilbo repeated them to followers in New Albany. Percy refused to share a platform with the Man, whom he considered a degenerate, but devious promoters invited both Percy and Bilbo to appear at the July 4th celebration at Lauderdale Springs. Percy considered

Theodore G. Bilbo, a corrupt but accomplished politician, dominated state politics for decades as governor and senator. He served as the champion of poor white sharecroppers. Courtesy of the Mississippi Department of Archives and History from the Governors of Mississippi Collection.

leaving, but was persuaded to stay and speak. Percy's son stayed up the night of July 3 to practice drawing and firing his pistol. Percy's brother, Walker, decided someone needed to kill Bilbo, walked into the hotel dining room the morning before the speech, spotted Bilbo eating oatmeal, and announced to the room that he intended to kill that little son of a bitch. Bilbo ignored the insult sure to provoke a "gentleman" and concentrated on his cereal.

Speaking from the porch of the hotel, Percy had to silence the pro-Vardaman/Bilbo crowd in order to be heard. After condemning Vardaman, Percy turned toward Bilbo and called him a "vile degenerate" and a "moral leper." Comparing him to a three-headed calf in a freak show, Percy said that viewing him degraded his audience because of his lying and consorting with lewd women. At the end of his long denunciation, Percy told the audience that he felt like a man who picked up and swallowed a yellow-striped caterpillar. It was not his regular diet, but he wanted to know if his stomach could take it. On July 6 Henry, then working as a railroad claims agent, boarded a train carrying Bilbo through Starkville and pistol-whipped Bilbo. Despite the fact that two doctors declared his injuries minor, Bilbo spent weeks in a Jackson sanatorium milking the public's sympathy.

Although he spent less than 10 percent as much money as his opponents and he had almost all of the newspapers against him, Vardaman took an overwhelming victory, and Bilbo won with just slightly fewer votes. A week after the election, thousands gathered to celebrate their victory. Six thousand people slept in Jackson's streets the day before the event. Men on horseback dressed in white with red neckties paraded with the men of honor from

Earl Brewer, lawyer who rose from poverty to own large Delta plantations. His one term as governor fell victim to a campaign to convict Bilbo of corruption. Courtesy of the Mississippi Department of Archives and History.

Vardaman's campaign headquarters on Capitol Street to the capitol building to hear Vardaman say that government had been returned to the people and that he would go to Washington in order to "strike at predatory wealth." Horrified by the prospect of a Vardaman/Bilbo government, Governor Noel called a special legislative session and sought to discover crimes committed by both Vardaman and Bilbo as a means of keeping them from taking office, but his efforts failed. A dedicated reformer, Noel acted not for the Bourbon establishment but out of fear of Bilbo's corrupting influence.

Senator Williams formed a close relationship with President Woodrow Wilson and effectively froze Vardaman out of contact with the administration, making Vardaman an ineffective senator. Vardaman's followers packed the Mississippi legislature, but running the state from Washington would not work. Bilbo adroitly appointed his state senate enemies to good committee assignments, earning their support, and within sixty days the Senate passed a resolution of thanks to Bilbo for his fairness and dedication to duty. For the only time in history, the Democrats nominated a governor unopposed. Earl Brewer slipped unnoticed into the governor's office as the Vardaman/Bilbo ticket dominated the headlines.

A lawyer who migrated from the hills into the Delta, Brewer lost to Noel in the previous election, but through persistence and good fortune won the office in the exciting 1911 contest. His hallmark was a speech entitled "Patriotic Citizenship," which he bragged contained no politics but leaned heavily on mom, apple pie, and patriotism. Brewer paid for private detectives to delve into corruption in the legislature and state agencies. He discovered the theft of cotton on a massive scale from the prison farm, and personally accompanied his detectives to the farm to conduct inquiries. When told to appear with his records, one sergeant among the guards committed suicide. Brewer even made a mysterious trip to Liverpool on the trail of the stolen cotton trying to discover to whom the money went in Mississippi. According to his unpublished memoir, Brewer spent much of his time in office trying to expose Bilbo's corruption. The state librarian got involved taping secret meetings. Detectives bugged hotel rooms and shadowed members of the Senate. In December 1913 the attorney general indicted Bilbo and one of his senator friends for soliciting bribes. Bilbo kept the Senate in session to delay his trial, and information that the governor promoted the indictment against Bilbo led to another acquittal. Bilbo announced that he would run for governor.

Unable to convict Bilbo, perhaps the most important contribution that Brewer made to the state had little to do with politics. In his memoir, he acknowledged that supporting the research of Joseph Goldberger, a Public Health Service (PHS) officer, into the causes and cure for pellagra was his most outstanding accomplishment. No doubt pellagra existed for many years, but doctors began to diagnosis it only in 1908. Victims developed rashes and butterfly splotches across their noses. They often went insane and eventually died. Mississippi suffered so many cases in 1913 that the state board of health asked the PHS for help. Cooperating, the state board and the PHS counted 1,313 cases and 268 deaths in the first six months of the year, and they knew that this represented only the tip of the iceberg. The heaviest concentration was in the Delta, with more blacks than whites affected. No one had any idea what caused the disease, but they guessed mosquitoes or germ transmission. Fearing for their lives, nurses often refused to care for pellagra patients. Goldberger, a Hungarian Jewish immigrant, brought a new perspective to the search when the PHS assigned him to investigate the disease. He traveled the South looking, listening, and asking questions. He noticed that the poor consistently ate salted pork, corn bread, and molasses to the exclusion of just about all other foods. With the development of sharecropping, the gardens, chickens, and wild game that had provided a more varied diet to frontiersmen disappeared, leaving the three Ms—meat, meal, and molasses. He guessed that the limited diet caused pellagra. In Jackson, he located two orphanages—one Baptist and one Methodist—and he found in 1914 that 60 percent of the children in the Baptist orphanage had pellagra. With funds from the PHS, he provided milk, meat, eggs, and beans for the orphans. After a year, the diet banished the disease. Mississippi officials believed Goldberger's analysis, but many of their public health colleagues refused to accept his findings. Meanwhile the number of deaths increased.

Joseph Goldberger, a public health service officer, proved that the inadequate diet available to much of Mississippi's population by the early twentieth century caused the disease labeled pellagra.

In order to convince the professional community of his diagnosis, Goldberger conceived of a plan to produce the disease by feeding volunteering prisoners the three-M diet. Briefed by Mississippi health professionals, Governor Brewer hesitated to authorize the experiment, declaring that he knew a state senator who died of pellagra. Goldberger interviewed the waiter who served the senator in his favorite Jackson restaurant and found the deceased senator limited his diet by choice. Satisfied, Brewer authorized Goldberger to use volunteers at the Rankin County prison farm. Brewer offered the participants pardons for their service. Having built a new clean cage with screens to keep out the mosquitoes, Goldberger placed the men on the three-M diet. At first the men thought it an easy assignment, eating what many had always eaten for a pardon, but they began to grow weak, some developed mental problems, and at the end of a year the diet had given the prisoners pellagra. Word leaked out before the end of the year, and Brewer had to weather a great deal of criticism before the results made him and Goldberger heroes.

What Goldberger did not say to the press or the governor was that poverty caused pellagra and that the political/economic system creating the poverty horrified him. When he later broadcast his suppressed thesis that the political, economic, and agricultural systems of the South were killing the poor, it caused a firestorm of criticism from southern spokesmen. While

Mississippians were not starving, the diets of the poor (and others such as the state senator who chose the three Ms as their only foods) were so inadequate that pellagra made them listless, disfigured their bodies, drove them insane, and eventually killed them in steadily increasing numbers.

In 1915 Brewer campaigned against Bilbo and Lee Russell, who was running for lieutenant governor in tandem with Bilbo. Having decided to return to his Delta plantation, Brewer sought no office but charged the pair with planning massive corruption. Brewer cited a host of illegal acts stretching back to the secret caucus. In a platform confrontation, Russell accused Brewer of stealing a pending bill from the legislative hopper, and Brewer threatened to cut Russell's throat from ear to ear if he ever repeated the story again. Russell shot back that Brewer conducted an affair with an actress. Despite the accusations and Brewer's personal appeals to the senator to abandon the pair, Vardaman stood by the Bilbo/Russell ticket.

Russell came from the lawless, poor-farmer region at the south end of Lafayette County, from which he walked the rutted roads to the University of Mississippi, where he worked his way through law school waiting tables. Because the university was dominated by planters' sons ensconced in fraternities, Russell failed to be admitted to university "society" or a fraternity, but after graduation, Colonel John W. T. Falkner invited him to join the family law practice. As a student, Russell made a name by leading nonfraternity student protests on campus and to the state capital in an effort to have fraternities banned. Russell made the point that fraternities represented the Bourbon element being challenged by Vardaman. Falkner, after having served for years in the legislature, had recently been defeated for reelection and chose Russell for his firm as a representative of the rising power in the state. Russell repaid his patron well, winning office in the legislature and making money in multiple business ventures in Oxford. In Jackson, Russell allied himself with Bilbo, which opened the door to the lieutenant governor's office.

Bilbo and Russell won handily, with the usual charges of illegalities at the polls. Disgusted by the prospect of Bilbo as governor, newspaper editor Fred Sullens wrote that the golden eagle atop the capitol should be removed and replaced by a "puking buzzard." Based on Bilbo's previous record, well-informed politicians and newspaper reporters held low expectations for the new administration. Brewer refused to escort the incoming governor to his inauguration. After the ceremony, Bilbo and his wife skipped the inaugural ball because, as a Baptist, Bilbo could not endorse dancing.

Bilbo confounded his detractors by asking the legislature for the usual reform measures circulating at the time, but then spending hours on the floor of the legislative chambers lobbying for the resulting bills. He increased funding for education, started night schools to lower the state's rate of illiteracy, established a state highway commission, and opened a state tuberculosis sanatorium, but his greatest accomplishment was revamping the state's tax system. Since Reconstruction, the state had relied on property taxes for which the legislature set the rate, but the county supervisors established land values. Over the years, the counties had competed to lower land values in order to avoid taxes, with the rich Delta counties often winning and the poorer counties paying more taxes. Bilbo got the legislature to establish a commission to accurately assess land values and thus equalize taxes, thereby revolutionizing the state's tax structure. Bilbo also did better with his appointments than expected. Most of his scandals involved sexual escapades at a state hospital, but the state had become accustomed to such stories surrounding Bilbo. Sullens admitted that Bilbo administered the state well and produced a wealth of needed reform.

Provision of government services improved life for Mississippians. For example, scientists discovered the hookworm around the turn of the century, and Mississippians turned out to be heavily infected. Africans brought the worm in their intestines, and because of the state's sandy soil, rainfall, and temperatures, it thrived. Excreted by humans, the worms infect barefoot people, usually entering between the toes and making their way to the intestinal tract. Infected people developed bloated bellies, coughed, suffered fever, and lacked energy. The cure only required one dose of thymol and an Epsom salts enema, but to prevent reinfection, Mississippians had to build better outhouses to keep worms from returning to the soil. Dr. Waller S. Leathers, head of the Mississippi public health department launched a public education campaign displaying worms and their life cycle at the state fair in Jackson and at the Harrison County Fair. The same type of exhibits appeared across the South, and stories abounded of people traveling long distances to see the worms and learn how to protect themselves. In 1910 Leathers received a $1 million grant from the Rockefeller Sanitation Commission to fight hookworms. The state board of health tested students, found heavy infestations, distributed prevention instructions, and sent parents information by their children. Health officers found that school "facilities" often consisted of the woods on opposite sides of the school being designated male and female, so they helped construct school privies. Plans for better outhouses went out to the public, and dispensaries opened around the state treating patients. Infections declined, and thousands of lives improved as a result.

The founding of Mississippi Normal College demonstrated how Mississippians struggled to educate their way to better lives. If teachers had any professional training before 1912, it consisted of a one- to four-week summer institute held primarily to prepare attendees to take the examination for a teaching license. Teachers were not college educated. They got their education in rural schools, and if they passed the rudimentary state exam, they went back to one-room schools teaching all eight grades whatever they had learned. The pay was too low to keep teachers employed for long. Sixty percent of them moved on each year looking for something better. As with physicians and other professionals, teachers organized the Mississippi Teachers Association, which lobbied for a normal college to provide better training. When the legislature acted, it asked for cities to bid for the right to host the school, stipulating that nothing less than $100,000 and land for construction would be considered. Riding high on the timber boom, Laurel and Hattiesburg submitted competitive bids more than doubling the minimum, but Hattiesburg, as the fastest-growing city in the state, won the school. The selected site west of town was cutover timberland with pine stumps as far as the eye could see in three directions. East two miles lay Hattiesburg, which ran a streetcar to campus along with electric, water, and sewer lines. Rain and mud hampered construction, while cattle and pigs roamed the campus. Forrest County still had an open range law. In 1914 the school fenced 200 acres with pine posts and barbed wire, which, though it was said to be hog-proof, never kept the pigs out. Students could work for fifteen cents per hour digging stumps or sweeping the mud off of the wooden walkways constructed between the five brick buildings built to house the 500-book library, dormitories, classrooms, and dining hall. A bell awakened students at 6:30 in the morning and everyone ate in a 500-seat dining hall family-style, with a faculty member presiding at assigned tables to offer thanks and make announcements. Classes met from 8:30 A.M. until 4:00 P.M. with mandatory "chapel" at 11:00 A.M.

The president, Joseph A. Cook, formerly superintendent of schools in Columbus, presided. An extremely frugal man, Cook sometimes lectured students on practicing strict economy or whatever subject he felt needed airing. He refused to allow students to smoke not because he opposed tobacco on moral grounds—he chewed tobacco constantly—but he told students that no school would hire a teacher who smoked cigarettes. The only social time allowed students was half an hour after dinner and on Sunday afternoons between 2:00 and 5:30. A bell each day at 6:30 P.M. sent students to their rooms for study time, ending at 10:15 P.M. At 10:30 a bell signaled lights out. Cook suspended those caught kissing. He forbade dancing or females younger than twenty-one riding in automobiles. Religion played a major role on campus, with prayer services and Bible teaching scattered over the weekly activities. Each semester also included revival meetings. The YMCA and the YWCA provided the main opportunities for social outlets.

Cook hired seventeen faculty members, and all but four were Mississippians. The school offered a two-year certificate for a four-year teaching license and a four-year degree for a lifetime license. The early curriculum included a great deal of high school work because it was impractical to do otherwise. The first bulletin stressed the democratic nature of the institution, and the faculty emphasized the institution's connection to the community. Many of the students came from poor families, and in general treasured the opportunity to earn a better life with their training. Cook kept the costs low in order to attract students with limited means. The school waived the $4 per month tuition fee for students who agreed to teach in rural public schools. During the first years, Cook planted chinaberrys, oaks, pecans, and Bermuda grass to improve the campus's appearance and to remove the raw edge. By 1917 the school raised its entrance requirement to admit only those students who had graduated from high school, marking the institution's move toward real college status.

The normal college (which became the University of Southern Mississippi) illustrated how Mississippians began to pull their state out of the mire created by destructive Bourbon policies. Agricultural high schools and new city schools raised the education level of the state. Teachers from the normal college staffed the high schools, so that students like Noel did not have to seek education in other states. The public's health began to improve. The Bourbons still held enormous power at the beginning of World War I, but the populist, redneck, and progressive movements had forced them to share power. Many imitated Colonel Falkner and brought some of the new men into their law offices, businesses, or governmental operations. The Bourbons lost some political offices, but Williams continued in the Senate and possessed far more influence on the national level than Vardaman. Percy lost his Senate seat, but he vacationed in the Mediterranean to recover from his encounters with the rednecks and went on running his plantations and enjoying his private empire. Presidents, bankers, and governors still took his calls and heeded his advice. Bilbo continued on the political scene, but his productive or creative days were past when he ended his first term as governor.

In the end, all of the noise and excitement of the redneck revolt produced far less than the white farmers wanted. The political culture based on fraud and violence endured, marring Mississippi politics for generations. The flawed political system, poverty, and deep racial divisions made progress difficult. The normal college students graduated to work for the lowest salaries in the nation and to teach students from impoverished families who still kept their children home from school when they were needed to plant or harvest crops. Many blacks did not send their children to school, and those blacks who did attend schools endured institutions that whites intentionally designed to be inferior. Progressive accomplishments in Mississippi did not match those in the rest of the country because none of the leaders made any effort to extend reform to include race relations. Vardaman made it his mission to destroy the few educational opportunities blacks had, and while other leaders did not match his virulent racism, they all endorsed it more sedately. Not one Mississippi leader challenged black oppression, and it never seemed to occur to them that social and economic improvement required raising living standards for the majority of the population. Ironically, Vardaman improved life for some blacks because his reforms, though he might not have desired it, helped blacks along with poor whites because it proved impossible to segregate the benefits.

Chapter Ten

SEGREGATION: RED, YELLOW, BLACK, AND WHITE

White Mississippians fought to establish their racial superiority after seizing control of the government in 1876. In order to achieve total dominance and feel secure as a ruling minority, whites created a segregation system designed to humiliate blacks as a means of social control. Ultimately the social customs required by whites as daily reminders denied blacks basic human dignity and degraded whites to the point that some performed unspeakable acts of barbarism in ritualistic lynchings designed to shore up the segregation system at the turn of the century. The Mississippi legislature did not pass the first law to enforce the separation of the races until 1888, but by that time customs had developed to the point that few laws were necessary. Segregation customs grew out of violent conflict and were designed to avoid further violence by forcing blacks to adopt a subservient attitude and manner, enforcing their deference to the ruling white minority.

Customs varied from county to county and from town to town. Any black person traveling around the state had to seek guidance from a local black resident concerning the rules of the area. Some towns, such as Clinton, had a policy that no black man could remain inside the city limits after dark. A stranger unaware of the rule could place himself in extreme danger unintentionally. Whites created the segregated society through an evolutionary process, pressing for ever more stringent controls as they gained more political and economic power over blacks. As slavery gradually ended during the war and blacks joined the Union army occupying parts of the state, whites adjusted to being ordered about by their former slaves. One southern woman writing her memoirs at the turn of the century remembered being forced off of a Jackson sidewalk by a black man and her father's resignation at the affront and his dire prediction of worse to come. During Reconstruction, whites never accepted freedmen as equals, but they had to recognize the power and position of black officeholders. Newspapers wrote of black leaders with titles such as "Mr." The black elite lived in the best neighborhoods along with wealthy whites. When black leaders died, they were buried alongside whites in Jackson's Greenwood cemetery. Blacks, and their white Republican allies, consented to segregate the new public schools, but they allowed interracial marriages and passed acts against discrimination in public transportation, even though they never tried to enforce the laws. In the 1880s whites gradually removed black officeholders and stepped up the rigidity of segregation. After the adoption of the 1890 constitution and the elimination of any black participation in the whites-only Democratic primary, whites imposed the harshest regime and practiced the most violent attacks on blacks by the turn of the century.

Allowing for only two racial categories, Mississippi whites classed the Choctaw and the Delta Chinese as "colored." The state established a separate, third school system for the Choctaw before the second Choctaw removal in 1903 and sometimes forced Chinese children to go to black schools. Mississippi law designated any person with one-eighth African heritage as colored, but in practice, Mississippians adopted the one-drop policy, meaning that any African ancestry made a person black and thus subject to the sanctions imposed on "colored people."

According to racial customs, a white Mississippian refused to call a colored person by his or her last name, addressing them by their first name or as "boy"—never "man." A black person, on the other hand, had to use a title of respect when speaking to any white. Boss, Captain, Mam, or Miss and the child's first name for a white child were acceptable. A white man never removed his hat or touched it on the street for a black woman, but he always made those signs of deference to a white woman. Blacks did not sit in the presence of whites and always removed any headgear when a white man entered their vicinity. If whites approached blacks on a sidewalk, blacks had to step into the street for the whites to pass. A black driver dared not pass a white driver on any road. In some towns, blacks could not drive on certain streets—Capitol Street in Jackson, for example. Blacks never approached the front door of a white residence because they could only use the back door. Some whites adopted the habit of locking the back door when they were out, but not the front so strong was their confidence that even a black thief would not enter by the front door. In a store, blacks stood in line to be waited on only after every white person had been served, including those whites entering the store during their wait. Custom forbade any interracial dining. In the early days of Reconstruction, blacks and whites ate in the same restaurant at separate tables on occasion, but by the 1880s such anomalies had ended, and blacks and whites patronized separate establishments. Whites could violate the rule by going to a black restaurant, but of course blacks could enter a white establishment only as servants. Blacks knew not to smoke cigars in front of whites and that it was prudent not to wear dress clothes on a weekday. If blacks had money, they took care to deposit it in a number of institutions in order to conceal their wealth. They learned not to make their dwellings too attractive to avoid arousing the envy and wrath of whites. Sullenly performing segregation's customary rituals did not satisfy some whites. Smooth functioning with whites required blacks to adopt a mask of submissiveness agreeing and playing the Sambo. Probably everyone knew the pretense involved, but all played their part in a society not unlike the caste system in India.

Whites treated blacks as unclean in the same way a Brahmin understood an untouchable. If a black woman wanted to buy a hat or shoes, she had to guess at the fit as the clerk displayed the item for her. If she tried on any apparel item, it could never be sold to a white woman. Some white physicians adopted the practice of refusing to touch a black patient, relying on sight and a description of symptoms to prescribe a treatment. The psychological costs of suffering white oppression were enormous, but blacks never believed they were less than whites. Former slaves told Works Progress Administration (WPA) interviewers during the Great Depression that their parents always told them that they were as good as anyone. Even as they trained their children to adopt the "white manner," they conveyed the message not to believe in the inferiority that the segregation customs were intended to symbolize. They imposed the training on their children to keep them alive.

William H. Foote, a black Mississippi native, studied at Oberlin College before he returned to represent Yazoo County in the legislature during Reconstruction. After whites redeemed the state, the Republicans made him a deputy federal revenue collector, and Foote refused to adopt the "white manner." Strangers who spotted him walking the streets of Yazoo City with his head erect and a confident stride asked, "Who was the black with the 'audacity' of a white man?" Whites feared that they could not keep the large black Yazoo majority in "their place" with such a role model in the community. The opportunity to make an example of Foote came when he defended another black man from a white mob wielding whips. In the melee, three whites died and two more received wounds, and yet Foote refused to flee the county. Instead, he went to jail with ten other black men, and when a white mob broke into his cell, he dropped the first white man and fought until shot to death.

Despite the violence and the heartlessness of segregation customs, blacks knew the difference between the mean racists and the kinder, gentler whites who could be counted on to demonstrate compassion. Such whites instructed their children to show respect for favored black people and granted them the titles of aunt and uncle. They might refer to a black teacher as professor even though he lacked an elementary education. As the system matured, most blacks developed a special relationship with a white person who acted as their spokesman and representative in legal and economic difficulties. The white patron represented a remnant of the noblesse oblige to be found among some slave owners, but in most cases the patron was an employer with an economic interest in keeping his employee out of jail and at work.

The story of Napoleon Carter illustrated the dicey nature of white compassion for blacks. The sixty-year-old Carter worked as a railroad depot night watchman in Water Valley. One evening in 1908 while on duty, he exchanged blows with a white conductor known to be a troublemaker. Tried for assault, the jury sentenced Carter to ten years in prison even though many in the community believed that Carter had been provoked. The consensus seemed to be that because Carter was black, he and his community needed to be taught a lesson about striking any white man. In 1910 Carter's white "friends" asked Governor Noel to pardon him, reasoning that he was an old man and sorry for his offense. The "friends" pointed out that if Carter had struck a black man or if he had been white, he would have never gone to jail in the first place. Using all necessary code words describing Carter as "humble" and "chastened," Carter's "friends" brought him home with a pardon.

A few ministers spoke out against lynching, took an interest in black educational efforts, and decried the denial of all rights of citizenship to blacks. Charles Galloway proved to be the most consistent in his sermons and speeches, but he endorsed segregation and simply tempered racism with a little Christian kindness. The Episcopal bishop Theodore DuBose Bratton continued Galloway's theme, justifying his ideas with a modified version of the argument used to rationalize slavery. God, he said in one speech, put blacks in the South with Anglo-Saxons in order for whites to raise the level of black civilization, and he called on whites to respond to their God-given challenge. He assured whites that blacks possessed the capacity for development, but cautioned that blacks had the intellect of children and the morals of savages. He found white/black relationships "estranged" in theory but "affectionate" in practice, and he urged the development of enlightened, responsible character based on Christian teaching as the way forward. He saw the establishment of rural "industrial" plants with either white ministers or devout white men to govern black workers and guide their improvement. Bratton closed his speech with the admonition that blacks had to learn first that there would never be "race equality." Bratton went on to found biracial committees to work for better race relations, and as limited as his sympathies were, his help was the best black leaders got from Mississippi whites during the depths of segregation.

Overwhelmingly the Anglo-Saxon peoples of the world shared Bratton's racist assumptions about black people. The zenith of segregation coincided with the growth of social Darwinism, scientific racism, and European imperialists dividing Africa. Social Darwinists held that societies evolved in the same manner that Charles Darwin described in his theory of biological evolution, and just as the strongest animals survived, reproduced, and dominated, the best societies would do the same. Linking themselves to Anglo-Saxon countries, which the Industrial Revolution had made the wealthiest in the world, Mississippians claimed the right to dominate non-Anglo-Saxons. Fake science reinforced such ideas with books and articles demonstrating white superiority while news of European conquests and colonial annexation in Africa reinforced the theories on the ground. Mississippians sought to discipline their colored neighbors because they believed, as the state's leading historian, Dunbar Rowland, said, that emancipation had unleashed the "defective moral nature of the negro" and a crime wave that had to be contained.

In 1876 the "redeemed" legislature passed what became known as the "pig law" defining the theft of any item worth $10 or more as grand larceny. A short time later the legislature broadened the state's prisoner lease laws, allowing all state and county prisoners to be leased to work on private land at any sort of labor. Between 1874 and 1877 the number of state prisoners more than tripled, and under the pig law prisoners received sentences of ten years for stealing a pig or a suit of clothes. As the state created the opportunity to fill its prisons with black men, whites set about reducing black participation in the legal system. Blacks gradually disappeared from juries, and if they served, courts excluded them more often from cases involving whites. By the 1890s the courts eliminated black jurors altogether, leaving blacks completely at the mercy of a white justice system. A few black lawyers still tried to practice in majority-black counties, but with increasing difficulty. In Yazoo and Greenwood, the court denied black lawyers entrance inside the railing of courtrooms. In Columbus, faced with a black attorney, the court adjourned, and courthouse officials told the black lawyer that court would not resume until he left the city. They did not want to kill him, they said, but if he persisted in trying to enter "their" court, they would. At West Point, the sheriff drew his gun to shoot a black lawyer trying to practice, but white attorneys surrounded him and saved his life.

The only black lawyer who attempted to practice in a white county, John C. Hill, sought to take the bar exam in Meridian. The court informed him that it did not matter whether he passed because he would not be allowed to practice. When he appeared in court, whites sprinkled a mixture of horsehair and cayenne pepper down his back, and after years of persistence, Hill left the city. With complete control of the legal system, whites used it to reduce a segment of the black population to a condition worse than slavery.

A sentence to state prison for black prisoners meant being leased to a contractor who became analogous to a slave trader, subleasing men to employers. But state prisoners served as only the tip of the iceberg. Towns and counties could sentence blacks to a year or less for breaches of local ordinances and lease them as prisoners. Sentencing involved fines and court costs, which most prisoners had to work off. Arrested for shooting dice, Walter Blake received a fine of $50 and court costs of $132 and worked for a year to earn his freedom again. The judge, mayor, sheriff, and jailer split the court cost, which a lessee paid for Blake. The lessee then subleased Blake to a planter or a contractor who did as he pleased with Blake. Few records exist documenting the fate of local prisoners, but a great deal is known about the state system

In the 1860s Edmund Richardson worked the entire state prison population on his giant Delta farm, but by the 1880s Jones S. Hamilton operated a sublease system, supplying black prisoners to railroad builders, levee contractors, and all types of construction projects for monthly, weekly or daily fees. White prisoners remained in the "walls," as the state prison in Jackson was called, while blacks went to the chain gangs. With no investment in the prisoners or motivation to provide food, clothing, and medical attention for them, sublessees worked men to death and rented a replacement. Sublessees beat prisoners to make them work or to increase the speed of their work. They chained them together and provided no remedy for the raw sores caused by the chains. They sometimes failed to feed prisoners enough to sustain them or to provide any shelter at night. One sublessee chopped off the frostbitten fingers of a convict with an ax. The state occasionally sent doctors to inspect prisoners, and the honest ones decried the filthy cages filled with excrement, blood, and dirt or, perhaps worse, the lack of a roof at all and prisoners sleeping on the bare ground. When the New Orleans and Northeastern Railroad needed to clear a swamp south of Hattiesburg, the company leased convicts at the high rate of $1.75 per day, sent them into the malarial waters, and left them there for days, knee-deep in mud, water, and muck, forcing them to drink the same water in which they deposited their waste. When the rail boom ended, most of the prisoners went to Delta plantations, allowing planters to revive the gang labor system used to work slaves.

When the deplorable conditions came to light, some newspaper editors crusaded for reform, pointing out the shocking death rates for Mississippi prisoners compared to other states and the lack of any provision for incarcerated children who served alongside adults on chain gangs. As a result, the 1890 constitution provided that no prisoners would be leased after 1894, but the system had become so ingrained and lucrative for the state that Governor Vardaman had to devote much of his energy to forcing the prison board to adhere to the constitutional mandate ending the lease system and establishing state responsibility for its prisoners.

With great effort, Vardaman established Parchman on 20,000 acres purchased by the state to create a state-run plantation to feed, house, and discipline black criminals and those violating the segregation customs. Under Vardaman's watchful eye, prisoners cleared and drained the land, built a sawmill, constructed cages and a superintendent's house, planted cotton, and raised hogs, cattle, and a dairy herd. In one year Parchman made a profit of $185,000 in addition to supplying the needs of the prisoners. Just as with the antebellum plantation, slavery proved profitable.

Vardaman hired farmers as Parchman's superintendents because he saw the prison as the instrument to properly socialize blacks. As he often said in his campaign speeches, blacks could only work as field hands and at no other occupation. He did not believe with Bratton that blacks could improve either morally or intellectually, and so he designed Parchman to teach blacks discipline, strong work habits, and respect for white authority. The Parchman system consisted of a number of cages scattered about the plantation containing inmates segregated by sex and race. White prisoners often worked at skilled jobs as carpenters or mechanics and not in the fields. Those who were insane mixed in the general population, which included murderers, thieves, and rapists. A sergeant, who was usually a rural, uneducated white man, oversaw each camp with two white assistants known as drivers or "captain" to the prisoners. The sergeant's word was law, and he brooked no appeal as a rule. The sergeants determined a prisoner's life—what he ate, if he got free time, or if he was a trustee or a gunman. Sergeants chose trustees and armed them with either a rifle or a shotgun. Parchman had no walls, but if a prisoner tried to escape, the trustee with the shotgun would shoot for the prisoner's legs. If he missed, the trustee with the rifle would aim to kill. Killing a runner earned the trustee a governor's pardon. A sergeant usually chose the meanest, scariest murderers as his trustees, and he had to make the right choices because his and his family's lives depended on the man's loyalty and obedience.

Ordinary prisoners were called gunmen because they toiled under the gun. They worked in a line through the fields from dawn to dusk, eating their midday meal in the field or in the shade at the side if the driver allowed. "Callers" created a work rhythm, singing about life at Parchman using the African-derived call and response. The caller sang a verse, and the line of men responded with a chorus that visitors reported almost swept them off their feet with its power. Sergeants imposed discipline with a leather strap

Parchman developed to spare Mississippi prisoners from the horrors of the convict lease system and to discipline troublesome blacks with hard agriculture labor, the only role allotted to them by the segregation system. Courtesy of the Mississippi Department of Archives and History from the Parchman Collection.

called "Black Annie." The state refused to build a church, so prisoners worshipped on Sunday mornings in the open. In the afternoon, women arrived for conjugal visitation. To satisfy the Baptists, one sergeant said, they called them the men's wives, although they might often be a group of prostitutes from Delta towns. Wives and families came on the Midnight Special, a train that departed Jackson at midnight on Saturday to arrive at Parchman Sunday morning. Parchman won worldwide fame for its brutality, its music, and its ability to terrorize Mississippians by its reputation.

Early release from Parchman required the approval of white society, beginning with the sergeant and the superintendent. Having secured those men's approval, the prisoner then published a petition for a pardon in his hometown paper, which triggered letters to the governor expressing the opinion of the "best" white men in the area—judges, sheriffs, ministers, attorneys, and planters. If they proved persuasive, the governor issued a pardon. Most prisoners lacked the writing skills to apply, and so they engaged lawyers, who portrayed their clients as "good" and "humble" members of their race. One murderer who shot his wife's college-educated lover got his pardon for being an honest field hand. Sometimes the governor had to be careful of his white advisers. One white group intervened for a one-legged black barber whom they claimed accidentally killed a woman while firing at a man during a fight. The governor found that the white petitioners were a group of bootleggers trying to free one of their best customers who owned a barbershop as a cover for an illegal drinking place. In another instance, with a black accused of raping a white girl, the governor acted only after the sheriff tracked down the girl's brother and had him write a letter to the governor giving his consent to the pardon. The governor issued the pardon thirty years after the accused rapist went to prison for what the community knew to be a false accusation. Justice for Mississippi's black population was neither fair nor swift. Whites controlled it and administered it to compel black submission. Plantation owners often dispensed with the formal system and hired enforcers to do their bidding outside the state apparatus. One Parchman prisoner told the governor that he had held such a job and killed twelve people in his line of duty, but when he killed his wife, the planter turned him over to the courts, which sent him to Parchman. He did not understand why.

Whites did not treat black-on-black crime seriously because they expected such behavior and failed to value blacks' lives as they did whites'. Their assumption, and the failure to punish blacks for assaults and even murders, led to widespread crime among blacks. A Delta newspaper expressed how lightly whites took black crime by entitling its Monday morning crime report "Good Mawnin Judge." If a black person went to jail, his or her white patron, without much investigation, interceded, and in many cases got the guilty black freed.

Until the 1920s white men went to jail rarely and only for really brutal crimes or for violating social norms in the conduct of their crimes. For example, Dabney Marshall and his friends shot R. F. Dinkins to death in a train station after Dinkins accused Marshall of making a homosexual advance. Marshall might have gotten away with murder except that he employed helpers and shot Dinkins between the eyes as he lay dying on the platform. In prison, Marshall got a safe, comfortable job as a bookkeeper. White women did not go to jail even for murder. Marion Drew of Ashland accused her father-in-law of murdering her husband, but after her father-in-law went to prison, she confessed to the murder in a rambling poem. Despite her confession, the judge released her without bond and ordered her to behave in the future. In Jones County, a judge sentenced a murderess to house arrest. In a famous Greenwood case in which an affair between two doctors went bad and the woman physician poisoned her lover, the convicted woman got a pardon from the governor after all her appeals failed. Mississippi courts clearly dispensed justice based on a person's gender and race.

One small group, the Choctaw, continued for the most part to exist in a no-man's-land between black and white. When most of the Choctaw went west, 2,000 to 3,000 remained in Mississippi. The Six-Towns group fled to Louisiana, and a Kemper County community moved to Harrison County, where they found refuge with a Catholic landowner. Most Choctaw scattered about their old Mississippi homeland, worked as cotton pickers, hunted, farmed, sold baskets and firewood, but left few records of their activities. Having lost their land and the promised legal equality to whites, they distrusted whites and kept their distance from them as much as possible. The Mississippi Choctaw, unlike their western brothers and sisters, retained their matrilineal family structure, polygamy, and other aspects of their culture such as ball games and funeral rites. Gradually the Choctaw joined in the sharecropping system and suffered from extreme poverty. In the 1880s the Mississippi Catholic Church bought around 1,500 acres of land and established a mission at Tucker. Some Choctaw gathered on church land and attended services, but then played ball on the church grounds afterward and accompanied the game with their usual drinking and gambling, distressing the priest. The most isolated community, the Bok Chito Choctaw, remembered that an earlier conversion led to the loss of their land and remained aloof. The Methodists established a circuit in an attempt to reach the Choctaw, but the Baptist religion grew to be the largest denomination among the Choctaw not through the efforts of white Mississippi Baptists but after some Choctaw attended a black Baptist church near Carthage and learned to appreciate Baptist independence and autonomy.

In 1888 the Baptists ordained a Choctaw minister, and the religion spread quickly. By 1891 nine churches were scattered around the old homeland, and the Choctaw ministers formed the Choctaw Baptist Association. The Baptists mingled Christian hymns sung in Choctaw with traditional songs and passed around a tobacco pipe during the service. After the service, they enjoyed a meal on the lawn with men and women seated separately and followed it with a ball game. They used all of the churches as their new social centers without abandoning their traditional culture. In 1882 the state recognized their community by establishing a separate Indian school office with a superintendent paid with Bureau of Indian Affairs funds. In the 1890s the superintendent reported a mixture of seven public and private schools.

The Mississippi Choctaw got caught up in the national government's effort to destroy tribal governments and integrate Indians into American society as independent farmers. In 1898, with Congressman John Sharp Williams's urging, the Dawes Commission decided that Mississippi Choctaw qualified for individual claims in Indian Territory if they moved west.

The Dawes Commission enrolled 2,240 Choctaw, and lawyers pressed their services on Choctaw families seeking to profit out of the land deals. The Bok Chito ignored everyone. In 1903 a second removal took hundreds of Mississippi Choctaw west, leaving, according to the 1910 census, only 1,253 Choctaw in Mississippi. The state closed its Indian schools, and the many churches vanished. Catholics maintained two churches—one at Tucker and the other at Forest. One Methodist church survived, and the year after the second removal a Choctaw Baptist minister, Scott York, preached at twenty different sites to hundreds of Choctaw.

By 1914 the Choctaw Baptist Association revived with 144 church members conducting six Sunday schools with eighty-five pupils. A St. Louis law firm seeking to profit from the unsettled land claims of the Mississippi Choctaw prodded Mississippi representative Pat Harrison to investigate the question, and Harrison introduced legislation to reopen the Dawes rolls in order to get adequate compensation for the Mississippi Choctaw. The possibility of compensation brought out a host of claimants, but the Dawes Commission denied all except 1,640. A Baptist minister, J. E. Arnold, helped to arrange a meeting of the "full-blood" Choctaw first in Carthage and then with Choctaw from neighboring states in Meridian's Great Southern Hotel. At the Meridian meeting, they organized a council of Mississippi, Alabama, and Louisiana Choctaw to look after their interests. The full-bloods fell out with Arnold, who tried to represent them as their sole lawyer, and some unrecognized "Choctaw" from Harrison County formed a society that also petitioned Congress and muddied the waters.

Harrison's pressure enlisted the help of Mississippi senators Williams and Vardaman. By blocking the settlement with the western Choctaw, they got money to carry out an investigation of Choctaw life in Mississippi. Vardaman held hearings around the state and found that Choctaw children were not allowed in white schools and would not attend black ones. Neshoba and Leake Counties provided some inadequate elementary schools, but many Choctaw did not attend those, depending on Sunday schools for the little education they received. The Choctaw, Vardaman found, lived largely by wage labor, with only forty-one owning any land, and most of it was heavily mortgaged. Most Choctaw resided in shacks and verged on starvation much of the time.

In the petitioning and maneuvering to achieve recognition and obtain compensation from the federal government, the Mississippi Choctaw defined who was a Choctaw. Operating in the racist climate of the period, the Choctaw used the term "full-blood" to eliminate over 20,000 claimants who rushed to ask for compensation as Choctaw. Race had been a foreign concept to the Choctaw who, in the past, had adopted persons into the tribe regardless of race, but at the turn of the century they adopted the language of race to press their demands and protect themselves. They denied any intermingling with blacks, and, in fact, the Mississippi Choctaw mingled little with whites either.

The Choctaw government in Indian Territory with more mixed-bloods adopted the one-eighth rule for enrolling tribal members. The Mississippi Choctaw insisted on using cultural distinctions as well as blood—dress, language, keeping traditional customs, and cultural characteristics. Archibald McKennon, who enrolled the Mississippi Choctaw for the Dawes Commission, relied on appearance, clothing, language, and, in a strange way, silence. He reported that African Americans who tried to enroll talked too much, while a real Choctaw would only speak if questioned repeatedly and almost forced to reply. Many Mississippi Choctaw resisted the government's efforts to move them west and by adhering to their customs, retaining their language, and remaining in their homeland, persuaded Congress to appropriate $75,000 to purchase land and establish schools, allowing them to settle on the land and make the schools the centers of Choctaw communities. In using the language of race, the Choctaw did not become racist. They adapted to the racist culture of the period, but clung to their language and a separate culture to define themselves. Eventually they achieved their goal of being recognized as a distinct legal entity—neither black nor white.

The Delta Chinese made up another such group occupying a middle ground between the two more numerous Mississippi races. Planters talked of importing coolie labor after the Civil War because the Chinese would not be able to vote and planters dreamed of reinstituting the gang labor system with them. Not much came of the talk, although the British Empire, among others, employed Chinese laborers extensively at the time. Many early Chinese settlers drifted into the Delta after working on railroad construction, looking for work picking cotton or other wage labor. Most came from the Canton area in China and had a rural but not impoverished background. Wong On fit this profile and came up the Mississippi River in 1875 with a dozen other men to pick cotton. Quickly seeing no future in cotton picking, Wong began to look for a means of making a living. In Greenville, Wong found two other Chinese running a grocery store, but he attempted farming as a renter. When he tried to sell his cotton independently, the planter made trouble for him, so he transported his cotton to New Orleans and sold it. He moved to Stoneville in 1881; married a black woman, Emma Clay; and opened a grocery store. Local whites accepted his store, which catered to blacks, and Wong prospered, raising a family of twelve mixed-race children. Referred to as "Captain" in the community, he attracted Chinese bachelors to his store, where they smoked opium to ease their loneliness for their homeland and to escape the harsh Delta climate.

Chinese-owned groceries attracted black customers with better treatment and provided a place where all three races might have a beer together. Courtesy of the Mississippi Department of Archives and History from the Farm Security Administration Collection.

Later Chinese immigrants found operating small grocery stores for mostly black patrons to be the best occupation for them because the Chinese could make a profit and provide a middle ground acceptable to the three races. They lived in back of the store, saved their money, and gradually grew prosperous. Men found ways to send for their wives, and fewer followed Wong's course of marrying a black wife. The Chinese store owners did not require blacks to use titles in speaking with them, and they treated blacks better than white merchants did. Good salesmen, the Chinese mastered their customers' buying habits and squeezed every possible penny out of them by keeping inexpensive items at the register so that no change left the store. They provided a racial middle ground where poor whites and blacks could sit around the store and drink a beer together. Given the ancient history of China, the store owners brought with them the assumption that, as inhabitants of the Middle Kingdom, they possessed a superior culture, but when they tried to send their children to white schools, the whites demurred. Some white schools admitted Chinese, but because of mixed-race children such as Wong's, whites began to resist, fearing they might admit a Chinese person with a drop of black blood.

In order to gain admission for their children to white schools, the Chinese grocery owners began to move out of the back of their stores in black

Gong Lum, a Rosedale businessman, fought in the courts to keep his Chinese American daughter enrolled in the white schools when Mississippi classified her as "colored." Courtesy of the Delta State University Archives.

neighborhoods and established their own Baptist church. They shunned Wong, the 20 percent of men like him, and the children of interracial marriages as the price whites demanded for acceptance. Through social pressure, refusing loans, and boycotts, they rid their small society of its racially mixed members by encouraging them to move out of the Delta. At the same time, the Chinese ingratiated themselves with whites. In the midst of this process in 1924, Gong Lum, a successful Chinese merchant in Rosedale, sued when his daughter, Martha, was asked by the Rosedale school board to leave the white school she attended. He claimed that his daughter was not "colored" or of mixed ancestry, but "pure Chinese" and therefore should not attend the black school. The Mississippi district court ordered the school board to readmit Martha, but the Mississippi Supreme Court overturned the ruling on the grounds that Mississippi had divided the state's pupils into Caucasian and colored categories and since Martha was "yellow," she rated colored status. In 1927 Lum's wife continued the appeals process to the U.S. Supreme Court, which upheld the Mississippi decision on the rationale argued by the Mississippi Supreme Court.

Charles Banks was a Mound Bayou businessman who amassed a fortune, represented Booker T. Washington in Mississippi, and tried to lead blacks to become successful businessmen. Courtesy of the General Research and Reference Division, Schomburg Center for Research in Black Culture, New York Public Library, Astor, Lenox, and Tilden Foundations.

By the 1940s, with the Chinese purge of mixed-race members and with China fighting Japan as a U.S. ally, whites reversed themselves and admitted Chinese to white schools, often praising their ability as students. The Chinese campaign to disengage from the black community and gain acceptance in spite of the fact that they were not Caucasians proved a success. They, like the Choctaw, resisted being labeled colored and categorized with blacks. Both the Chinese and the Choctaw proclaimed themselves full-blooded representatives of their "race" and defeated white attempts to class them as colored alongside black Mississippians.

The Choctaw and Chinese avoided the colored designation adroitly, but black Mississippians had to focus on the long-term goal of making their race acceptable to the ruling whites. Charles Banks did not achieve his goal of making his race acceptable to whites through economic development, but he earned a fortune and wielded great influence during the worst years of segregation. Born the son of poor ex-slaves in Clarksdale, he excelled in the Coahoma County public schools and studied at Rust College before opening a store at age sixteen, which he made successful by sheer hard work and determination. A joiner, he played a leadership role in the African Methodist Episcopal Church, Republican Party, Masons, Knights of Pythias, Odd Fellows, National Negro Bankers Association, and Negro Bankers Association of Mississippi. When he sought appointment as a census enumerator in his Clarksdale district in 1890, he got every white man in town to endorse his application. After achieving success in Clarksdale, he sold his business and moved to Mound Bayou in 1903, establishing the Bank of Mound Bayou in 1904 and quickly surpassing the town's founder, Isaiah Montgomery, as the town's most influential citizen. He married a suitable Natchez bride and built a palatial residence with wraparound porches and a gazebo.

As with many such couples, the Bankses had no children and devoted themselves to advising others on how to succeed. He spoke to farmers, advising them to diversify by raising their own meat and grain. He asked them to subscribe to at least one farm journal to keep up on scientific farming advances. Advocating pride and confidence building, he told them to straighten their fences and whitewash their homes and farm structures. Booker T. Washington made Banks his man in Mississippi. Banks organized Washington's speaking tour of the state and made certain that requests for anything from Washington went through him. Using those connections, Banks obtained funding from northern philanthropists for Mound Bayou projects. Courting whites, Banks laid on the compliments heavily, crediting his success to the aid and help of white friends. Dealing with Mississippi whites, he wore the mask carefully, spelling "negro" in lowercase, which he did not otherwise do. He served in national offices of the Republican Party and other organizations and became a director of educational institutions across the country. He added real estate, insurance companies, an undertaking establishment, and lumber to his empire, accumulating in modern terms millions of dollars. His wealth and influence declined after Washington died, but his life illustrated the path taken by the most successful Mississippi African American of the period.

Arguably the best-educated black man in Mississippi during this period might have been Dr. John A. Miller of Vicksburg. He attended Howard University Preparatory School, graduated from Williams College, and got his medical degree from the University of Michigan. During twenty years in Vicksburg, he kept out of controversy except for two incidents when he opposed the appointment of white men's black mistresses as teachers. In a letter to a white lawyer during the second flare-up over an appointment, Miller explained that he and his fellow petitioners wanted to disprove the frequent charge that blacks were too sexual and immoral. Obviously he was a "race man," a term used to designate a person who cared for his larger community. Miller cared deeply about bettering his people's lives because he joined the state's first chapter of the National Association for the Advancement of Colored People (NAACP) in 1918. When a white representative of the war bond drive called on him to make a sale, Miller gave the salesman a lecture on how Mississippi "crushed" black people and told the salesman to think over his comments and come back to ask the question again. Rumors of his audacity spread, and another member of the bond drive committee called Miller and threatened to have him arrested for sedition unless he bought $1,000 worth of bonds. He did not buy the bonds, and almost a month later a white mob tarred and feathered him along with a white man who lived openly with a black woman. The mob brought the white man to the front of city hall first and hung a sign around his neck reading "I am disloyal to the United States Government." After whisking him away, a second car brought Miller to the courthouse to wear the same sign. Mississippi whites usually reserved tarring and feathering for whites, making Miller's case unusual. Miller knew lynching blacks in his situation to be more the norm, so he left the state.

Over the decades after Redemption, whites consistently drove members of the black middle class out of either their professions or the state. Even skilled tradesmen were pressured out of their jobs. The most precipitous decline came among black barbers. In 1890 seventy-four black barbers worked in Mississippi, but by 1940 the number dropped to twenty-five. Antebellum whites preferred close, personal association with a black barber, but prejudice and negative attitudes erased that preference during the development of segregation. White Mississippians in low-level, constant racial warfare degraded the opportunities available to blacks working toward Vardaman's often-repeated goal of limiting blacks to field work.

Peonage grew to replace slavery, with an estimated one-third of the majority-black county sharecroppers in 1907 held in that state of servitude. Journalists described instances when debt holders sold families and imposed physical punishment on the father/husband who resisted. In 1915 Governor Brewer wrote to inform the Tallahatchie County sheriff that "negroes" from plantations in his county had been fleeing to Jackson bearing physical scars of abuse and talking to federal authorities about being held in peonage. Brewer advised the sheriff to have the planters mend their ways or federal prosecution would result. The sheriff replied that he would like to enforce the laws against such behavior, but he reminded the governor, who had been a prosecutor in a neighboring county, that enforcing the law without being "backed up by at least some of the people" was impossible. To remedy a specific case, Brewer wrote to one of his friends, Selwyn Jones, to inform him that one of his workers, Eva Blackburn, had escaped to Jackson bearing evidence of a whipping and claiming to have been held against her will. Brewer said that he had treated her story lightly at first as just an example of a cropper leaving after credit had been advanced and before making a crop, but, he told Jones, many such stories had interested federal justice officials. To avoid complications, he asked Jones, as a friend, to send Blackburn's two young daughters, whom she had been forced to leave behind while making her escape. Jones sent the girls and Blackburn's few possessions by train two days later. No charges were ever filed against Jones.

Neither governor nor sheriff could defend against united white determination to dominate the black population. Law, as the Tallahatchie County sheriff pointed out to Governor Brewer, meant nothing without the support of at least some of the people. The most notorious examples of white direct action to suppress blacks came in instances of "lynch law." Mississippians lynched people more than did the citizens of any other state. Existing numbers are guesses based on newspaper reports starting in the 1880s. Many lynchings never got reported, and if they did, they often only rated a line giving the number of persons lynched and the location. The best estimate reported 476 people lynched between 1889 and 1945. Prior to the Civil War, most lynch victims were white, but during Reconstruction blacks became the targets, and there were no records kept of the numbers who died in that era. Until about 1890, whites shot or hanged blacks as whites fought to establish white rule, but after 1890 lynching took on ritualistic qualities and grew increasingly perverted, with victims tortured, mutilated, and burned alive. Lynching occurred in all but eight counties in the state with the largest numbers in the Delta and four counties along the east-central area bordering Alabama. Hinds County, home of the state capital, led the state with twenty lynchings.

The peak in numbers took place between 1889 and 1908 when white control became absolute under the new constitution and again from 1918 to 1922 when whites feared the First World War had introduced challenges to white domination. In common perception, lower-class whites made up the lynch mobs, but even when they did, they acted with the tacit consent of the ruling elite. And they often did not act as mobs. In what newspaper accounts described as a good lynching, the executioners proceeded in an orderly manner without drinking or unnecessary shooting to carry out the will of the white community. In Oxford, former U.S. senator William V. Sullivan led a mob in 1908 to lynch a black jail trustee who killed a white woman. Sullivan even boasted about his accomplishment to a newspaper reporter.

In a rare instance, Pass Christian involved the black men of the town to punish a rapist. The lynch "mob" housed the accused in the jail while they assembled both black and white men at the Woodman Hall, where the victim identified her attacker and submitted to questioning. After hearing the evidence, the crowd agreed that the "defendant" had committed the crime and should hang. They took him to a grove of trees, where the "defendant" spoke the ritualistic confession, and they hanged him, with physicians and the county coroner present to pronounce him dead. A grand jury quickly assembled and absolved those involved of any crime. The local paper praised the process and said that the lynching would effectively quiet any ill feeling between the races.

While not typical, the 1904 Sunflower County lynching of Luther Holbert and Mary, often reported to be his wife, illustrated how whites used lynching to terrorize the black community. As with most lynchings, it involved murder, not rape. Holbert worked for the Eastland family for many years. Hiriam Eastland owned a prosperous drugstore in Scott County and used his profits to invest in cheap land in Sunflower County during the 1880s. He sent two of his sons to oversee the clearing of the land and the development of a cotton plantation. On February 3, 1904, James Eastland was mending fences with Albert Carr, one of his black employees, when Carr complained about a dispute with Holbert over a woman. James had dismissed Holbert and ordered him off the plantation. Upset that Holbert remained on his property, James and Carr armed themselves and rode over to Holbert's cabin, expecting a confrontation. When they burst through the door, Holbert met them with gunfire, killing Carr on the veranda and putting a bullet through James's head as he entered the cabin. Hearing the shots, other workers rushed to the cabin, and, discovering the dead men, they sent for Woods Eastland, James's older brother and the plantation manager. As the oldest white male, the responsibility for exacting revenge fell to him, but Holbert and his woman had fled into the junglelike countryside. Within the hour, white neighbors assembled to assist in the manhunt. Woods requisitioned bloodhounds from neighbors and the new prison at Parchman, and offered $1,200 to the public as a reward for the couple's capture.

By the time the pack of dogs reached the plantation, the fugitives had a ten-hour head start, but Woods and fifty armed men set off. For four days, Holbert eluded the dogs, possibly helped by black lodge members along his route toward the Yazoo River, where he hoped to get out of the Delta on a boat. Newspapers followed the chase and reported the lack of progress. On the third day of the hunt, members of the "posse" spotted two men in a field fitting Holbert's description and when the two black men ran, the mob members shot them down. A black woman also died when one of the guns wielded by the hunters discharged accidentally. The mob swelled to several hundred men riding and walking through the rain following the dogs. When they guessed that Holbert was headed for the Yazoo River, part of the group hopped a train in an effort to cut him off. They did not find Holbert, but a teenager spotted him at the edge of a swamp twelve miles south of Greenwood and informed two men at a nearby store. They captured Holbert as he slept and turned him and Mary over to the Sunflower County sheriff. The sheriff made no pretense of holding the prisoners and gave them to Woods, whom the newspapers had announced, planned to burn them.

Woods retained Holbert and Mary Saturday night and Sunday morning before choosing the grounds of Doddsville's black Baptist church as the site for the "negro barbecue," as such lynchings were called. Sometimes mobs chose the scene of the crime for the death venue, but in this case Woods made the selection to provide the clearest possible message to the black population—no lodge or even a church offered any protection. Well publicized, the lynching could have been stopped, and newly inaugurated Governor Vardaman dispatched troops north by train, but they mysteriously vanished along the way. More than 1,000 people of both races gathered at the church for the lynching. The deputy sheriff who had accompanied the doomed couple spoke out against lynching, but the crowd drowned him out with shouts of "kill them." With the pyres prepared, the mob tied Holbert and Mary to separate trees and cut off their ears and fingers, passing them out to mob members as souvenirs. The mob beat the couple leaving Holbert's eye hanging by a shred from a socket, and then tortured them with a large corkscrew, twisting the tool into their flesh and withdrawing it with quivering flesh hanging on. The mob forced two black men to drag the still-breathing bodies to the pyres. Holbert watched his wife burn before suffering the same fate.

Mississippi newspapers condemned the brutality of the lynching, and Booker T. Washington denounced it as destructive of good race relations. Black journalists reported that the fight leading to the two murders involved a runaway worker whom Holbert tried to protect from James Eastland and declared that the methods used were too barbarous even for Mississippi. Occurring days after the murder and not in the white heat of passion, the lynching sent the intended message to the overwhelmingly black majority in the Delta through calculated terror.

In this case, the mob dispensed with ritualistic confession, which always played a role in a "well-ordered" lynching, but lynching took place in all manner of settings. In Vicksburg a year after the tarred-and-feathered Miller left town, a young white woman reported being attacked in her apartment by a black man, and police used bloodhounds to capture Lloyd Clay. The victim of the attack, Mattie Hudson, refused to identify Clay in two lineups as the man who attacked her, but a mob of 1,000 men tore Clay from the jail and terrorized Hudson into accusing him in the street as they screamed at her. The mob stripped Clay, covered him with oil, hanged him from a tree on the side of the street, and built a fire beneath his feet. Members of the mob, including some women among the drunken crowd, began to fire guns into his body. In the days following the incident, men referred to the hanging tree as a symbol of white manhood, but the woman who lived next to the tree asked the city to cut it down. By all accounts, Clay was innocent and his lynching was called a bad one, but as always no mob member was indicted.

Ida B. Wells, a black woman who grew up in Holly Springs and edited a paper in Memphis, crusaded against lynching and collected information

Leroy Percy, Greenville lawyer and planter who fought the Klan and Vardaman for a Senate seat, winning in the secret caucus but losing the popular vote. Courtesy of the Mississippi Department of Archives and History.

to disprove the frequent charges of attempted rape by black men. With the support of men such as Charles Banks, she sold and distributed her paper to black readers in Mississippi, but her effectiveness was limited. Not until the 1930s did an effective Mississippi voice emerge to oppose lynch law. Organized in Atlanta in 1930, the Association of Southern Women for the Prevention of Lynching included two white Mississippians among its founders, Bessie C. Alford of McComb and Ethel Featherstone Stevens of Jackson. They established a model state organization using women's groups to destroy the myth that lynchers acted to protect southern womanhood. They asked for and collected statements from sheriffs that they would not allow lynching and established a list of county contacts to spread the word when a lynching appeared imminent. They attempted to organize opposition in the press and solicited political support for sheriffs who thwarted lynching. Although she failed to obtain Baptist support, Alford secured a resolution from the Mississippi Conference of the Methodist Church condemning lynching in 1935. Alford's and Stevens's work helped to diminish Mississippians' acceptance of lynching, and by the 1940s it almost disappeared, although a suspicious number of black men still died while trying to escape police custody. As bad as that was, it eliminated the public spectacle of barbaric, ritualistic, illegal executions.

Despite lynching and other violent oppression, some whites continued to believe that Mississippi planters carried on the noblesse oblige tradition of some antebellum slave owners. LeRoy Percy, laid claim to such a

William Alexander Percy, poet, hero of World War I, and lawyer-planter whose idealistic concepts of noblesse oblige fell victim to the realities of the 1927 flood. Courtesy of the Mississippi Department of Archives and History.

reputation by opposing Vardaman and his racist rhetoric, by running the Klan out of Greenville, by favoring education facilities for blacks, and by treating blacks respectfully and allowing them to retain their dignity. His son, William (Will) Alexander Percy, worshipped his father in part because of that reputation and in part because they were so different. Will grew up rebelling against the rough, masculine lifestyle expected of white males in the Delta and epitomized by LeRoy. Will wrote poetry, and loved books, art, and flowers. Educated at Sewanee and Harvard and well traveled in Europe, he took up the family work as a lawyer and plantation owner only because his younger, more boyish brother died in a shooting accident as a youth. Will tested himself by fighting in the First World War and earned his father's respect for his heroism. In 1927, when the levees broke and the Mississippi River flooded the Delta for months, LeRoy forced Will to come face to face with the ugly truth about their relationship with their black tenants, stripping away the myth of noblesse oblige and embittering blacks held prisoner on the levees.

The 1927 flood devastated the Delta, leaving Indian mounds, levees, and the second stories of some buildings as the only dry places remaining for human and animal refugees. The narrow tops of the levee at Greenville quickly filled with cattle, mules, hogs, dogs, and people. Will, who had worked with Herbert Hoover as a Red Cross administrator in Belgium before America entered the war, headed the Washington County Red Cross committee when the flood struck, and because of that position and the fact

Nineteen twenty-seven saw the greatest river flood in American history. Whites fled the Delta, but planters kept black sharecroppers imprisoned on the levees in order to preserve their labor supply for rebuilding. Courtesy of the Mississippi Department of Archives and History from the Mississippi Flood of 1927 Collection.

that he was LeRoy's son, he commanded relief efforts. He called for barges to evacuate refugees to Vicksburg. White women and children went first, but Will intended to ship everyone away. Some of his relief committee members objected because they knew that the black sharecroppers had nothing to return to the Delta for, if they left. All the sharecroppers owned were the debts owed to planters, and they would be happy to escape those. The committee voted to adopt Will's evacuation plan because they believed he spoke for his father too. But LeRoy had been occupied with calls to the governor and bankers across the nation, raising the donations and loans needed to survive and rebuild. When planters came to him protesting Will's decision, LeRoy agreed to talk with Will. Taking his motor launch and dressed in a suit with hunting boots, he found Will on the levee directing the rescue. Pulling Will aside, they trod the muddy levee caking mud on their boots in the cold rain as LeRoy tried to reason with his son against denuding the Delta of its black labor force. Will would not relent, but he agreed to take another vote of his committee. LeRoy contacted all of the members and, pledging them to secrecy about his call, got them to agree to keep the black population on the levee. Will reconvened his committee and argued vehemently with its members, who refused to support his evacuation plan. After the conversation with his father, Will ordered the barges to cease loading and after the meeting he sent them away empty except for a few white women and children. He claimed to have only learned of his father's actions years later, but he had to have known, even if he did not admit it to himself. He turned mean and abused blacks in his frustration.

Black families lived with the animals on the levee. At first they had no shelter, forcing them to sleep in the mud. Even after tents arrived, there were no cots or flooring for some time. They had no utensils, so they ate the Red Cross food with their hands, squatting in the mud. Among the canned items provided by the Red Cross were tins of peaches, but Will did not distribute those because his committee feared it would "spoil" the blacks. Will required blacks to work for Red Cross food and paid no wages, unlike other relief camps. In order to be fed, a man had to wear a tag provided by the Red Cross indicating that he had been unloading supply barges or working to build a bridge from the levee to the city's two-story buildings. Will and LeRoy continued to live in the upper story of their home. Hotels and restaurants opened again minus their ground floors. Whites could dine on steak and buy their cigars as always. Boats delivered a reduced-sized newspaper to their homes by boat with Will's orders printed on the front page. Will called for more national guardsmen who policed the camp. Planters supplied lists of their tenants, who could not leave the camp without written permission from the Red Cross. Guardsmen removed their leather rifle straps and used them to whip the black men who left the levee camp without permission. Will had transformed the refugee camp into a concentration camp.

Will had wanted to do the honorable thing and save blacks from the horror that the camp became, but his father committed several dishonorable acts in order to stop him. The mask of noblesse oblige fell away, revealing the ugly truth of economic exploitation to the sensitive poet. Will turned his anger not against his father but toward the helpless blacks, but he hated himself for what he did and why he did it.

Two years after the flood, LeRoy died, and Will continued the fiction of his father's nobility by placing a statue of an armored knight over his grave. Holt Collier, who had hunted with LeRoy, came to Will's office to express his condolences. According to Will's description, Collier sat in a chair across from his father's old desk resting his hands on a heavy walking cane, but still impressed Will as having massive shoulders and a noble head. Struggling with his emotions, Collier, who was going blind, openly cried and said, "I am out in the dark and the cold alone. I want to go where he is." With that, Collier rose and left. LeRoy's father saved Collier from the noose with a good legal defense, and Collier knew LeRoy from their hunts, but his tears must have signified more than affection for the planter. Surely he must have been moved in part by the utter destruction of the type of personal relationship that once existed between him and a few white men—a remnant of the frontier that bound even slave and owner together as human beings battling nature to survive. Collier's connection to whites seemed to be like that of Toney with the Hutchinses, and it all but died out in the early twentieth century.

Newt Knight, who died early in 1922, lived to see his and Rachel's children begin to suffer for their black ancestry as the outside world impinged on their Jasper County homes. In 1920 Stewart Knight, one of Rachel's sons and probably Newt's, died at the hands of a white neighbor jealous over Stewart's prosperity, which the neighbor thought no black man should enjoy. In 1914 Fannie Knight went to court to claim an inheritance, but her opponent's lawyer focused on her race. She claimed to be Choctaw and French, to which the lawyer countered that she lived with "niggers." Fannie admitted that she "stayed" on that side, which in the parlance of the time determined her to be black despite her white skin. Fannie's sister had two daughters who also had white skin. One remained in Mississippi, never married, and lived in a black community. The other daughter married a white man, moved to Texas, and joined a white community.

In Jones County, Newt and Rachel's descendants became known as the "white Negro" community, and local town residents pointed them out as oddities when they ventured away from their rural homes. The state tried Davis Knight, a great-great-grandson of Newt and Rachel, for miscegenation in 1948. Davis served in the navy during World War II as a white man and returned to marry a Jones County white woman in 1946. His marriage angered some Jones County residents enough that the state indicted him. The trial led to an airing of Rachel's identity and attempts to reconstruct complicated genealogies with the Knights' white family members and old friends choosing sides either condemning Rachael's "stain" or trying to somewhat defend her as a mixed-race Choctaw. The county court convicted Davis, but released him on bond while he appealed. The Mississippi Supreme Court reversed the lower court's decision because the county court had not proven Davis to be one-eighth black as the constitution required. The county did not try the case again, leaving Davis as a legal white man. He lived as such until he died accidentally in Houston, Texas, in 1959. His cousins chose one side or the other—white or black. His sister fought successfully to have her sons admitted to white Mississippi schools.

As a custom, Mississippians continued to adhere to the one-drop rule and to segregate all "blacks" into an inferior caste, but the Delta Chinese, Choctaw, and some mixed-race Mississippians challenged the custom successfully even during the harshest segregation period. Whites excluded black Mississippians from citizenship and enforced caste-type rules of behavior with extreme violence, economic oppression, and daily reminders of "inferiority" through rules governing interracial encounters, but blacks maintained a purely defensive mask of deference, never accepting that they were inferior. As Miller demonstrated by joining the NAACP in Vicksburg, they bided their time and looked for an opportunity to challenge white authority and to reclaim the rights provided to them in the Fourteenth and Fifteenth Amendments to the Constitution.

Chapter Eleven

WAR, DEPRESSION, AND ENVIRONMENTAL RESTORATION

In the period spanning the First World War and the Great Depression, Mississippi struggled with modernity and the destruction of its natural resources. Lumber companies finished clear-cutting the state's forests without replanting trees on land unsuitable for any other crop and left wastelands of stumps. The state's denuded hills eroded into its streams and rivers leaving gullies, streams choked by mud, infertile land, and deepening poverty among small farmers who sought admission to the world market and the money economy by raising cotton. Delta planters presided over a precarious cotton kingdom inadequately protected from the rivers' floods that for centuries provided the topsoil that made planters rich. They benefited from the vicious exploitation of a black caste, which they held in virtual peonage. Beginning during the First World War, black Mississippians remade Mississippi and American culture by escaping to the North for better lives, leaving whites in 1940 as the majority of the state's population for the first time in 100 years.

Most Mississippians failed to notice or understand the changes shaping the birth of their new society because they lived as tenant farmers in the manner of their parents at the end of the Civil War. Electricity, indoor flush toilets, automobiles, and telephones had not penetrated Mississippi's rural world of sharecroppers. As Mississippians struggled to comprehend their lives, more of them turned to evangelical religions. The Presbyterians and Methodists, with higher education requirements for ministers, lost ground to churches offering ecstatic, emotional services akin to those of the frontier era. Political leaders groped toward a path to a modern economy and an altered society, calling for education, agricultural diversification, and industrial development. But they spent most of their energy on pointless struggles for power and the patronage needed to satisfy their supporters.

Indicative of the altered culture, Mississippi's political leaders did not rush to serve in the armed forces as they had done in the Mexican, Civil, and

Spanish-American Wars. The frontier ethic of individual responsibility for defending the community did not motivate political leaders to enlist, and voters remained divided on supporting the First World War. Martin Sennet "Mike" Conner, a young Speaker of the House of Representatives, used his position to avoid service. Will Percy continued the aristocratic/frontier custom by serving in the trenches, but none of the leading politicians felt the traditional urge to volunteer and earn their constituents' admiration by fighting in Europe. A romantic youth in Oxford descended from a Confederate soldier, William Faulkner joined the Canadian air force to get into the war, but never made it to the fighting. Eventually he returned to Lafayette County, renamed it Yokappatawpha, and won the Nobel Prize for literature for his efforts to understand and explain his world.

Bluesmen made a similar effort in a different medium and gave birth to American music in the process. The creative force of Mississippians, impoverished by the destruction of their land and the failure to escape the grip of cotton agriculture, amazed the world and left a legacy difficult to comprehend. Faulkner populated his fictional world with ruthless men who tamed the wilderness, mixed-race wise men who understood the mysteries of nature and the human condition, a boy initiated into those secrets by a bear and a Feist dog, and the barn-burning Snopeses, who understood nothing but procreated and prospered to conquer Faulkner's fictional county. Faulkner's mythic depiction shaped the world's understanding of Mississippi, but art demanded distortion, and the truth of the state's past is both more prosaic and more hopeful. Despite woefully inadequate political leadership, losing so much of its population, and enduring almost unimaginable hardships during the Depression, Mississippians, as Faulkner said, prevailed and eventually came to grips with modernity in a fashion.

Governor Bilbo made an impressive effort to reform state government so that it worked better for tenants and small farmers. As noted earlier, he passed a long list of legislation for which he worked sixteen-hour days and lobbied the 1916 legislature in person. He came from Pearl River County, home to many subsistence farms and almost no plantations. His father helped him to attend college out of state, but Bilbo had an affinity for downtrodden farmers and adopted their manners. He enjoyed crackers and sardines. He spoke the "redneck" language and delighted in using oratory to entertain and move his audiences. Vardaman appealed to the prejudices and emotions of the masses, but he never abandoned his aristocratic airs and pretensions. In Bilbo, the rednecks saw the qualities Faulkner identified with the Snopeses. A Baptist "lay minister" who condemned alcohol and dancing in public, Bilbo enjoyed his private drink and a reputation for sexual adventures that dogged him throughout his career. His scandalous behavior and the constant charges of corruption lowered the level of political life during the war and Depression years.

In the early years of the First World War, Mississippians and Bilbo vacillated on the war issue as cotton prices plummeted. The state attempted to sell its cotton to Denmark for transshipment to Germany and only abandoned the plan when the federal government assured state authorities that the British would seize the cotton as contraband. Timber prices fell 25 percent. Lumber mills closed, and others ran half-time shifts, but as the British and French began to buy both cotton and lumber for their war machines, Mississippi opinion shifted toward the allies. Pancho Villa's raid into the United States mobilized the Mississippi National Guard and increased patriotic emotions. President Woodrow Wilson's preparedness campaign turned Mississippi against Senator Vardaman's pleas to remain neutral, and by 1916 the state Democratic convention defeated Vardaman's supporters and issued a veiled endorsement of the president's policy heartily supported by Senator Williams. After trying to avoid the controversy, Governor Bilbo appealed for enlistments in the National Guard and eventually backed Wilson completely, breaking with his old ally Vardaman, who continued his staunch opposition to the war.

In 1917, as war propaganda stirred the public, Vardaman hung in effigy at the Clarksdale cotton exchange, and Vicksburg newspapers warned of possible German spies in the city. Williams condemned his junior colleague's opposition to the war and drew on the civic religion of the Lost Cause to justify the war. Too old to volunteer, he took pride in the fact that three of his sons did. Vardaman too recalled the Civil War but warned that it had been a "poor man's fight" as would the next war, which, he said, was created by bankers and big business. Although he voted against the declaration of war on Germany, he maintained the Mississippi military tradition and volunteered to serve after he lost the vote. He also sent two sons to war, but continuing his dissent, Vardaman opposed the draft because he believed it would fall disproportionately on the poor. He also warned that enlisting blacks would endanger white supremacy. Williams supported the draft both to ensure a successful war effort and as the best means of withdrawing equal numbers of blacks and whites from the population to maintain a continued balance between the races. Vardaman lost again opposing the draft, but his predictions proved accurate because Mississippi draft boards sent more young whites into the army from the poor white counties and exempted whites in the black counties, sometimes along with the black tenants of influential planters. The sparring in the Senate spilled over into state politics, with Williams supporting Pat Harrison's campaign to unseat Vardaman.

Pat Harrison defeated Vardaman, establishing himself as the friend of presidents and a masterful national politician who would have become majority leader in the U.S. Senate except for Bilbo's vote against him. Photo courtesy of the Southern Media Archive, Special Collections, University of Mississippi Libraries.

Harrison grew up in Crystal Springs, where his mother ran a boardinghouse after his father, a Confederate veteran, died. Harrison sold newspapers and drove a mule-drawn buggy from the train station to the city's Chautauqua Park, where he no doubt learned some of his considerable oratorical skills. Attending Ole Miss and then Louisiana State University, where he played baseball on scholarship, Harrison opted for a stint as a semiprofessional ball player in the "Old Tomato League" before he taught school in south Mississippi and passed the bar. Moving to Gulfport, he got elected district attorney and won a seat in Congress in 1910. Not particularly progressive, opposing child labor laws and rejecting woman suffrage, he took to the Chautauqua circuit with a speech entitled "Less Government in Business and More Business in Government." His performance in Congress and Williams's friendship readied him to challenge Vardaman.

Williams persuaded President Wilson to cut off Vardaman's patronage in Mississippi, and Harrison opened his campaign in Meridian, where the same man who had organized the forty yoke of oxen to haul Vardaman into town in 1911 repeated the stunt for Harrison, proclaiming that they had pulled Vardaman into office and now they would pull him out. Harrison made Vardaman's "disloyalty" his theme. Staying away from any domestic issues, Harrison touted his support for the president and the war. The rural press that published Vardaman's message for many years remained steadfast for him and reported his speeches to what they said were enthusiastic crowds. But Vardaman carefully stayed in the smaller towns and rural areas. He had probably suffered a stroke, and his massive body had shrunk, leaving him weak and unable to stand the campaign trail rigors. He played the race card, decrying the return of black soldiers who had known French women, but he had to contend with jeers of "Von Vardaman" and an occasional stage painted yellow. Harrison won handily, but Vardaman carried twenty-four counties, mostly in the northeast hills. Given the level of propaganda spewing from the national government, Wilson's letter declaring that a Vardaman victory would be a repudiation of his policy, and the fact that all of the state's large newspapers excoriated him, Vardaman's vote seemed remarkable. In wartime, 41 percent of Mississippi voters refused to support the government and braved their neighbors' disdain to support their old champion. Some observers thought Vardaman's vote would have been higher but for the intimidation of voters by war supporters.

A few Mississippians defied the draft, as some did during the Civil War. Twelve percent deserted, and in the spring of 1918 the army sent troops into three counties to round up deserters being protected by friends and family. Only two deserters resisted and died in Tippah County—a county Vardaman carried in the primary. Mississippi sent more blacks into the military than whites, inducting 19,296 whites and 24,066 African Americans. Confederate-era Mississippians, no doubt, would have been amazed at such behavior.

Bilbo sought to take advantage of Harrison's leaving his congressional seat, announcing his candidacy for the primary in 1917 even though his term as governor did not end until 1918. His attempt to continue in office offended many voters, who complained about a well-compensated official running while on the government's payroll. His opponent, Judge Paul B. Johnson, hailed from Hattiesburg and spoke, he said, for the runt hogs among the population. So Bilbo faced another populist during wartime, when the voters were distracted from class and social issues. Bilbo's association with Vardaman proved problematic. Voters favoring the war disliked Bilbo's old ties to the senator, while those who opposed the war and remained loyal to Vardaman hated Bilbo for abandoning their hero. But Bilbo discovered that his fatal mistake had been to sign a tick dipping law.

Babesiosis, or Texas fever, infected cattle in south Mississippi. Open range still existed, and small farmers had neither the time nor the inclination to round up their cattle every two weeks to dip them in vats of chemicals. The U.S. Department of Agriculture (USDA) tried voluntary dipping programs, but farmers refused to participate, so the USDA asked states to pass legislation requiring dipping in counties declared quarantine areas. Bilbo did not push the legislation, but when the legislature adopted the law, he signed it. South Mississippi farmers hated the imposition of dipping. As jacks-of-all-trades who ran free-range cattle for their own consumption,

In the 1920s Mississippi farmers declared war on the U.S. Department of Agriculture and the state when they tried to stop the enforcement of a tick dipping law for the state's cattle. Courtesy of the University of North Texas Digital Library.

they had no interest in the national cattle market that the USDA and big ranchers intended to create. The ticks did not often make their hardy animals sick, and finding the cattle and transporting them to vats over the dirt tracks that passed for roads in Mississippi required too much time and effort for no return—additionally, many of these farmers included distillation of illegal alcohol among their many jobs. Having "government boys" around their farms might have led to other problems. Primarily they resented anyone telling them to do anything. Judge Johnson promised not to send any of those refusing to obey the law to jail and defeated Bilbo handily. Bilbo cried that he had been crucified on a cross of ticks.

Bilbo's departure from the governor's office made no difference in the defiance of the tick dipping law, which turned violent. In the 1920s resistors intending to dynamite a vat 200 feet from the Amite County courthouse ran into a local "range rider" hired by the USDA to guard the vat. When the range rider killed one of the farmers attacking the vat, the district attorney prosecuted him for murder, but the range rider escaped conviction and moved to Arizona. The state had to resort to trying dynamiters in federal courts in order to convict them. The government hired more range riders, built protective barricades around the vats, and mounted machine guns to defend tick dipping facilities from farmers. The range riders always traveled in groups of three, with one man constantly alert with his weapon at the ready in order to avoid ambush. The battle over tick dipping signaled another milestone toward the end of the yeoman's independence from governmental control. While south Mississippi farmers may have been ambivalent about the war in Europe, they fought hard against government intrusion into their lives.

After suffering his humiliating defeat, Bilbo faced a hostile legislature in 1918. In 1916 Bilbo supported Mike Conner for Speaker of the House of Representatives in order to block Oscar Johnston, a Delta planter, from getting the post. The wunderkind of Mississippi politics, Conner was only twenty-five. His father, a wealthy timber baron from Seminary, sent Conner off to Ole Miss, where he thrived and finished both college and law school with straight A's. Adding another law degree from Yale, Conner returned to Seminary to practice law. An absolute teetotaler, he refused to defend moonshiners or bootleggers. He married a local schoolteacher but had the political acumen to oppose tick dipping when his constituents "instructed" him to do so. Elected Speaker, Conner promoted two other young men to assist him—Walter Sillers Jr. and Thomas Lowery Bailey. A planter from Rosedale, Sillers's father had been a power on the levee boards and behind the scenes manipulating elections. Originally from populist Webster County, Bailey was a self-made man teaching school in Madison County while attending Millsaps College. He moved to Meridian, the state's largest city, in 1912 to practice law. Three years later he was elected to the House of Representatives and rose rapidly to a leadership position. Conner disliked Lieutenant Governor Lee Russell, who ran the Senate for Bilbo, because of Russell's crusade against fraternities at Ole Miss when they were students. Russell came from the poor south end of Lafayette County, waited tables to support himself, and once had a bucket of water tossed on him from a fraternity window. As a student, he came to Jackson and lobbied to ban fraternities and led protests on campus against the privileged students in them. Despite their personal animosity, Conner and Russell served on a special committee between the 1916 and the 1918 legislative sessions with Alfred Stone, Bilbo's appointee to the new tax commission. Bringing national experts to Jackson, they sought ways to end Mississippi's chronic shortage of tax revenue, which the legislature usually had to "solve" by authorizing bond sales. Gaining experience and confidence, Conner felt able to challenge the weakened Bilbo. Conner prided himself on his dedication to fiscal responsibility, but Bilbo, who had convinced the legislators to lower taxes in 1916, came to them in 1918 with requests for increased expenditures. Conner invited national experts to speak to a joint legislative meeting, and his team launched war on Bilbo. From this legislature forward, the House of Representatives and its Speaker came to dominate Mississippi politics. The constitution granted the governor little power and the legislature much. Conner and those who followed him as Speaker became the wielders of power for the rest of the century.

In 1918 Bilbo proposed a new constitution, angering those in the northern hills and the Delta, both of which areas would lose representation to the faster-growing southern end of the state. The rumor spread that Bilbo had "bought" forty wood columns removed from the Old Capitol for a $1 bid and shipped them to Juniper Grove to install in the dream house that he planned to build. Another rumor placed Bilbo and his cronies in the state asylum using the nursing staff as a harem. Conner launched a legislative investigation. The legislators found evidence of drinking on duty at the asylum, women visiting male staff members in their rooms, and at least one abortion performed in the infirmary at the facility. The chairman of the committee declared the record so disgusting that he ordered the committee's papers burned. Yet another rumor had Bilbo involved in an affair with a nurse at Beauvoir—then an old soldiers' home. Conner and Bailey, who taught a men's Bible class at Central Methodist Church in Meridian, probably shared Percy's opinion that Bilbo was a moral leper, and they saw to it that Bilbo got none of his requests from the legislature, hoping to rid the body politic of both Bilbo and Vardaman permanently. Neither of the populists intended to abandon politics, and both endorsed Russell to follow Bilbo as governor.

As the white politicians fought one another, black Mississippians who were denied the ballot voted with their feet. Between 1900 and 1910, 35,500 blacks left the state, which totaled just slightly more than the number of whites leaving, but in the decade 1910 to 1920, 148,500 blacks escaped north, exceeding the white exodus by around 36,000. Pushed by the injustice of the segregation system and pulled by the lure of jobs in northern cities, 100,000 blacks left Mississippi in the war years (1915–1920). The war cut off the supply of European immigrants, on whom northern factory owners had grown to depend for inexpensive labor. As a remedy, industrialists began to send labor recruiters south. Mississippi and other southern states countered by passing laws to regulate the practice by registering the recruiters and levying high fees on them. Local governments and mobs employed extralegal means to chase the recruiters out of the county. Initially newspapers welcomed the departure of blacks, but they quickly changed their editorials as planters began to decry the loss of their labor force. Nothing whites did stemmed the tide. Sleeping-car porters delivered the *Chicago Defender* to Mississippi cities, and the black newspaper, full of stories of the good life waiting for migrants, passed from hand to hand. Some ministers read the tattered newspapers from the pulpit in black churches, and in some instances whole congregations left as a group. Ministers also read letters to their flocks from those who had made the journey north and reported back home that they could vote, send their children to good schools, earn a decent living, call no one "Captain," and wear their hats in anyone's presence. Mississippi policemen began to arrest blacks gathering at train stations to depart or when they tried to buy their tickets. In a few instances, policemen stopped trains and dragged black migrants out of the cars. Of course, blacks countered by buying a series of tickets to local destinations, until they found a safe ticket window in a distant town. The mayor in Meridian decreed that importation of the *Defender* constituted a crime, but he certainly could not enforce the prohibition against the paper, which porters continued to smuggle into town. The urge to escape to the North grew into a mania, and what had been a steady stream of migrants became a flood. Some white Mississippians reacted by raising wages and treating their tenants better.

Planters formed the Mississippi Welfare League to produce propaganda to dissuade blacks from migrating and to lure them back to the South. They encouraged black leaders to speak out against migration, and some such as William H. Holtzclaw and Laurence C. Jones, educators who truly believed blacks would eventually prosper in the South, did, but black ministers who tried to spread the message in return for donations from planters found themselves without a congregation or alternatively with no money in the offering plate. Southern white newspapers played up the race riots in St. Louis and Chicago in an effort to frighten potential migrants. The secretary of the Mississippi Welfare League even made a trip to Chicago in the wake of the riots to personally request former sharecroppers to return, but he failed to persuade them.

Blacks who chose to stay in Mississippi quickly took advantage of white need for laborers to press for a better deal for their race. In 1916, when Sunflower County's white newspaper invited Dr. Joseph E. Walker, a black leader, to publish a plea for blacks to stay, he did, but indicated that whites had to change their behavior in order to entice blacks to remain. Specifically, he mentioned that planters had to cease cheating their ignorant tenants. Charles Banks answered a similar plea to stem the tide of migrants by warning his white neighbors that lawlessness pushed many blacks to depart and advised whites to end lynch law. A black school principal delivered the same message to Leroy Percy when consulted about the exodus. In 1918 the Warren County Colored Ministers Association petitioned local governments for better black schools as a means of inducing more laborers to remain in the community. A black delegation visited the legislature asking it to give black students, from elementary school to college, the same educational opportunities provided to whites. Given the recent history of racial violence, even such carefully worded demands spoke loudly of the changing relationship between the races. Blacks gained some advantage as whites acknowledged their need for black labor, and black leaders worked carefully to exploit the opportunity.

Drawing on the battered Vardaman-Bilbo faction of the Democratic Party, Russell defeated four candidates, including his primary rival, Oscar Johnston, the Delta's candidate. Russell attempted to continue Bilbo's agenda, but the legislature thwarted him at each turn. His administration stumbled through a series of disasters. An insurance crisis erupted when an antitrust suit against the companies led them to cease writing policies in the state. Lack of insurance threatened to destroy cotton farmers, who needed to protect their stored bales. Russell engaged in petty battles in Oxford, where a minority continued to denounce him as common bounder, character assassin, and liar. The anti-Russell clique managed to deny him a place in the delegation to the national Democratic Party convention in 1920, delivering a stunning rebuke to a sitting governor. In retaliation, Russell, claiming a census error, removed Oxford's government officials and appointed his own city government. When students at Ole Miss hung a Russell effigy and set it ablaze, the governor stormed up to the school, personally interrogated students, expelled several, and ruled that students had to report every organization to which they belonged. He intended to smash the fraternities, which had gone underground. Many students, including William Faulkner, left school rather than comply.

The enraged university community gloated the next year when Frances Birkhead, a former secretary, charged Russell with seducing and impregnating her. In a federal lawsuit, she claimed that he forced her to have an abortion that went wrong, causing her grave injury, and she demanded $100,000 in damages. Russell alleged that Bilbo had paid Birkhead to bring the suit. The two men fell out when Bilbo criticized Russell's administration, and Russell saw the suit as Bilbo's method of eliminating him from the upcoming Senate contest. Because Russell's was a federal case, the lawsuit landed in Oxford. Russell subpoenaed Bilbo, believing that he had evidence of Bilbo's involvement in the plot.

Bilbo hid out on his Pearl River farm until a deputy sheriff found him in a barn hiding behind a heifer. Sullens editorialized that the only one involved in the affair deserving any sympathy was the heifer, implying to knowledgeable farm folks that Bilbo probably engaged in illicit sex with the animal. Hauled into the Oxford courtroom, Bilbo refused to testify, claiming attorney-client privilege, because what he knew about the case came from

Russell when he acted as Russell's attorney. Federal judge Edwin Holmes rejected Bilbo's explanation, fined him, and ordered Bilbo to jail for thirty days. The jury found Russell innocent, but the scandal ruined him. He never returned to Oxford. Bilbo held court in his Oxford jail cell, receiving visitors and reveling in the spotlight. The judge made an error in both fining and jailing him, so he revoked the fine and released Bilbo after ten days. Bilbo engineered a large audience and grandstand seats in Oxford's square for his exit from the jail, announcing from the steps that he intended to run for governor again in 1923.

Women, especially offended by Bilbo's behavior in the Russell suit, denied him a second term in 1923. Women's participation in public life increased during the early years of the twentieth century. They provided the majority of church members, created a club movement to educate themselves, gained the right to vote, softened racial oppression, built health care institutions, supported missionaries, and entered public offices. Shunted aside by their husbands and male ministers, who limited women's roles in churches during the frontier era, women battled back by carving out their own organizations, first within churches and later independent of them. For example, the Ladies Auxiliary of Oxford's First Presbyterian lapsed during the Civil War, but in 1868 the churchwomen organized the Ladies Aid Society. By sewing and selling a variety of goods from dresses to quilts, they raised money to support foreign missionaries, buy an organ, and provide general support to the church. When the male leadership blocked their efforts to build a new church, they repaired the old one and saved their money until the men suggested the need for a new building. Then they offered $1,000 for the project and furnished the structure with carpets, lamps, and furniture, proclaiming they accomplished it all on a foundation of cakes and pies sold at fundraisers. In 1900 the Oxford Presbyterian women supported the construction of a school for black children; they formed a committee to discuss work with "local negroes" in 1915; and beginning in 1919, they paid the expenses for a delegate to attend the Colored Women's Conference each year. Women's groups such as Oxford's Presbyterians existed across the state and made similar contributions to their communities.

Some of the fast-growing evangelical churches accepted women as ministers. For example, the Assemblies of God, which held its first statewide convention services at the Magnolia Springs Campground in 1899, grew through Sunday schools, healing crusades, and itinerant evangelists holding brush arbor services. By 1909 the Pentecostal group operated the School of the Prophets in Hattiesburg and admitted women. In 1929 half of new ministers admitted to Assemblies of God churches were female, making a quarter of their leadership women. Assemblies of God services preserved much of

In 1923 Nellie Nugent Somerville, a product of the Mississippi Women's Club Movement, became the first woman elected to the Mississippi legislature. Courtesy of Delta State University Archives & Museum, Lucy Somerville Howorth Collection.

frontier-era traditions with emotional shouting, foot-washing, singing, and even some biracial events. At their 1919 state meeting, the members spoke in tongues, danced, rejoiced, and prophesied, attracting increasing numbers of converts—mostly lower-class individuals and more females than males.

For middle-class white women with more education, the outlet for their skills and emotions took different paths. In Greenville, Nellie Nugent Somerville, for example, began by working in the Methodist church, but the subordination to men required in that institution infuriated her. In the 1890s she joined an invitation-only literary club named Hypatia in honor of the pagan Greek female intellectual of Alexandria murdered by a mob led by Christian monks who were outraged by her defying the conventions of the time. The club members included the Delta's female intelligentsia, who met regularly to discuss literature and history and to hear speakers before launching into their own research to share with the group. Somerville presented on sensitive issues such as a woman's right to decide if she would engage in sexual intercourse with her husband, women's legal status, and men's opposition to improving the status of women. Inspired by Frances Willard, national president of the Woman's Christian Temperance Union (WCTU), Somerville entered into the crusade to end alcohol consumption and another to gain women the right to vote.

Somerville took on the presidency of the Mississippi Woman Suffrage Association and utilized her Christian faith to press for direct political action. At the local level, she helped to establish a public library and hired the first public health nurse in Mississippi, insisting that the nurse serve both the black and white communities. Statewide, she worked with other women to install no-spitting signs in rail cars and train depots. Mississippi, like the rest of America at the turn of the century, suffered from an ocean of tobacco spat everywhere, including houses of worship, because most men then chewed tobacco rather than smoking it. Somerville campaigned against spitting as a health issue, but she probably had aesthetic motives as well. The legislature took her seriously. In 1914 she and other suffragettes spoke to a joint session of the House and Senate, but despite the support of Governors Noel and Vardaman, the legislature refused then and in 1918 to pass the constitutional amendment giving women the vote. When enough other states did pass it and Mississippi women got the vote in 1923, Somerville ran and was elected to the House of Representatives, where she chaired the committee that oversaw charitable institutions.

Belle Kearny, a Mississippi daughter of a Madison County planter, shared some of Somerville's experiences and played leadership roles in the same organizations, but she joined the national Chautauqua circuit and even went international with their crusades for prohibition and suffrage rights. In 1923 she returned home to be elected to the Mississippi Senate. She differed from Somerville and many other southern women in that she supported federal intervention in order to modernize Mississippi. She tried to ban smoking in the legislature and failed, but she did get the Senate to open its sessions with a prayer. Both Kearny and Somerville lived long as well as active lives, maintaining their places in upper-class Mississippi society despite their feminist crusades, but "modern" women who rejected more of the traditional woman's role in society fared less well.

Minnie Brewer, a younger woman who adopted the flapper lifestyle of the 1920s, ended her life in the state's insane asylum. Daughter of Governor Brewer, she grew up at the governor's mansion in Jackson and the replica of it that her father built in Clarksdale after his term in office. She attended several colleges in and out of the state, but took only the courses that interested her and never earned a degree. She wore her hair bobbed, favored short skirts, ran with a wild crowd including returned soldiers, and drank. She rejected a series of marriage proposals—one because her suitor prayed just after he delivered his request for her hand. She said that she wanted no one praying over her, especially her husband. Passionate about politics, at the age of twenty-four she founded a weekly newspaper, *Woman Voter*, using her father's money. When the money ran out, Brewer worked in a beauty parlor, dyed her hair red, and became a town eccentric. Doctors diagnosed syphilis as the cause of her insanity, but some evidence cast doubt on their conclusion.

In 1923 Minnie Brewer declared Bilbo to be a rascal and wrote that denouncing him did not constitute partisan behavior for her newspaper, simply good sense. She attacked Bilbo unmercifully, claiming that his pronouncement that he was "crazy" about women indicated the problem with him. She reminded women that they held the balance of power and should use it to send Bilbo back to his pecan farm. When Bilbo's *Free Lance* returned fire, Brewer adopted the slogan, "Bilbo says that you should not read *Woman Voter*, so subscribe today."

The 1923 primary offered voters a wide choice for governor. Conner had reached the constitutional age to run and left his more powerful post as Speaker of the House of Representatives to do so. Governor Russell supported Lester Franklin, a Vardaman backer, from the hills but then living in the Delta. A judge from Greenville, Percy Bell tossed his hat in the ring. Bilbo established a statewide newspaper after his last defeat and campaigned nonstop for years. He had intervened in the 1922 Senate race late by speaking around the state to support Vardaman's losing effort to return to Washington. After the primary, Vardaman retired to his daughter's care in Birmingham, Alabama, blaming Bilbo for his loss to the colorless Hubert D. Stephens, but leaving the Man to exploit the redneck following they had established. Henry Whitfield filled out the field.

Whitfield began as a schoolteacher, adopting his father's occupation, and seemed destined to follow the path of most of Mississippi's political leaders during this period into the legal profession, but Governor McLaurin appointed him state school superintendent before he finished his law studies. A product of Mississippi College in Clinton, Whitfield remained a dedicated Baptist his entire life. He used his superintendent's office as a bully pulpit to encourage Mississippians to improve and extend the state's educational system. A friend of Laurence C. Jones, the founder of the Piney Woods School, Whitfield often visited with Jones and shared the black educator's philosophy of mixing physical labor, intellectual improvement, and Christian teaching to mold students. After two terms as state superintendent, Whitfield followed the traditional career route of the time, accepting appointment as president of Mississippi Industrial Institute and College in Columbus in 1907 with Governor Vardaman's full support. Whitfield made a popular president of the country's first state-supported women's college. He lectured the students in chapel on duty, often using the phrase "march all the way to Appomattox"; took them on field trips to visit industries; encouraged their work in the college's model garden; and generally played the genial father figure. Chewing tobacco and smoking cigars appeared to be his only vices because he did not drink and he forbade student dancing for the first ten years of his presidency. Bowing to

Laurence C. Jones, black advocate of separate economic development for blacks and founder of the Piney Woods School. Courtesy of the Mississippi Department of Archives and History.

student requests, he changed his policy in 1917 to allow them to dance once per month as long as no men were present.

He found the college's faculty undereducated and sent them back to school. He improved the college facilities and tripled the library holdings. When he arrived the majority of the students studied in the college preparatory area, but before his departure he abolished the precollege program and admitted only college students. He brought in famous speakers to inspire students, including the Wright brothers and former president William Howard Taft. He lobbied the legislature effectively for funds and earned high social standing in Columbus, where he attended the First Baptist Church regularly with his family. He frequently preached at his church and others in surrounding communities. He attended the Baptist convention, demonstrating a strong interest in church governance. Whitfield made himself a paragon of healthy, progressive ideals, playing both golf and tennis frequently, consulting with national educational leaders, and worrying about the state's destruction of its natural resources. He enjoyed the reputation of a modernizing voice in the state, but he refused to give his support to Russell in 1919 and campaigned for his opponent. As a result, Russell fired him the next year.

The politicians offered Whitfield a position running one of the state's agricultural high schools, but he declined in order to accept a job at a boy's orphanage school operated by the Columbus Masons. He and the boys grew vegetables to feed themselves, and Whitfield delivered the surplus produce

Henry Whitfield, educator who moved into politics, defeated Bilbo, and served as a progressive governor before dying in office from cancer. Courtesy of the Mississippi Department of Archives and History.

sold to his old school, renamed Mississippi State College for Women. Dressed in overalls and a straw hat, Whitfield portrayed the perfect martyr to corrupt political infighting. He worked a network of former students who introduced him at speaking engagements across the state and provided the womanpower for his campaign.

The institutions of higher learning took on leading roles in the 1923 campaign. Joe Cook, president of the Hattiesburg teacher's college, endorsed Whitfield, who appointed the son-in-law of the university's vice chancellor as his state campaign manager. Bilbo sought similar endorsements at the state's higher education institutions and received many, including that of university chancellor Joseph Powers.

Playing up his claim as the clean candidate, Whitfield promised never to embarrass Mississippi, to reverse the antibusiness policies of the populist administrations, and to govern as a businessman's progressive, a nationally popular ideology at the time. Leroy Percy claimed that both Franklin and Bilbo belonged to the rejuvenated Ku Klux Klan, which had grown nationwide during the Red scare following the First World War and the showing of the landmark movie *Birth of a Nation* in theaters throughout Mississippi and the nation. Percy reported that Conner, Bell, and Whitfield kept free of the secret organization making inroads into many legislatures around the country. In the first primary, Bilbo went after Conner as a draft dodger, and Conner countered that Bilbo hid in the Pearl River swamps during the Spanish-American War and that all he ever gave Mississippi was a bad name. For a multiplicity of reasons, Whitfield suited the voters fatigued by the scandals, corruption, and crude rhetoric of Bilbo and other populists. After leading in the initial primary, he defeated Bilbo handily in the runoff. No doubt the new female voters made the difference in Whitfield's 16,000-vote triumph.

Whitfield lectured the audience at his inauguration, telling the state that it wasted its natural resources by "mining" the soil instead of cultivating and renewing it and by "slaughtering" its forests. Because of the state's shortsighted misuse of its patrimony, he said that the "simple life," meaning the frontier, had come to an end. He called for Mississippi to follow the example of more successful states and adopt modern, progressive ideas to attract business and industry to the state. Referring to the state's loss of population, he suggested increasing taxes on luxuries in order to lighten the burden on farmers, but he warned that he believed in strict economy and would veto unbalanced budgets.

Unfortunately, Whitfield had not served in the legislature, did not seek enough advice from those who had, alienated his supporters, and fought with Walter Sillers Jr. about the levee board. First elected to the legislature in 1915, Sillers joined Conner and Bailey to form a clique to run the House of Representatives. Conner had bequeathed the speakership to Bailey when he resigned to run for governor, and Bailey added to Sillers's list of powerful leadership posts in the legislature after becoming Speaker. Sillers and Bailey enlisted Lawrence T. Kennedy, a Natchez lawyer, and Joseph W. George, the son of James Z. George, into their clique, which became known as the Big Four. George, a lawyer from Yazoo City, served as Whitfield's advocate in the House of Representatives. He shepherded through an income tax, an inheritance tax, and some of the luxury taxes asked for by the governor. Under George's leadership, the legislature reversed Vardaman's anticapitalist laws to give corporations the right to own more land and use eminent domain to build hydroelectric facilities. In a speech concluding one debate, George said that Mississippi had been going backward because of populist legislation and losing population and manufacturing because of the state's hostile attitude toward capital. His appeal worked, but the populists condemned the session as conservative to the point of turning farmers into peons.

Whitfield asked for increased funds for higher education, but instead the legislature investigated extravagance in the state's institutions of higher learning and cut their budgets—in spite of a 33 percent increase in the student population. The legislators did increase funding for the teacher's college in Hattiesburg slightly, and Sillers got funding approved to establish a teacher's college in the Delta. The 1926 session started badly because the Bible

Crusaders of America, along with other fundamentalists, came to Jackson to lobby for an antievolution bill. The university community opposed the bill, as did Speaker Bailey and Julius Christian Zeller, a progressive education advocate from the Delta, but it passed nevertheless by a wide margin, and Whitfield signed it. According to some legislators, the state lost some fine teachers as a result, but later in the session George belittled the request to pay teachers more, saying they did not appear to be starving and that they seemed to be the best-dressed group of people around. Whitfield took up Zeller's campaign, under way since 1920, to consolidate the University of Mississippi, the Mississippi College for Women, and Mississippi A&M into a major state institution located at Jackson, but the legislature delayed his request by establishing a committee to study the idea.

Stymied in his effort to present Mississippi as a progressive state, Whitfield did improve race relations by advocating better treatment for blacks. In his inaugural address, he reminded Mississippians that blacks made up over half of the state's population and that prosperity could not be achieved without including black people. He visited black educational institutions, graciously welcomed black delegations to the governor's office, and spoke at black church conventions. He urged law and order, and lynching declined during his time in office, but he was not above a bit of humor at the expense of blacks. When a delegation came to his office to protest a lynching, he heard them out but only then indicated his surprise that a black delegation expressed so much concern about the death of a white man. The delegation mistakenly assumed the lynched man to be black, and Whitfield delayed giving them the information that he was white in order to laugh at the black protesters. Still, he treated blacks far better than the populist governors had. Whitfield stirred Bilbo to attack him by appointing a black man as a notary in Vicksburg.

Despite his good intentions, Whitfield played no role in the major educational advancement to occur during his occupation of the governor's office. In 1922 Zeller introduced legislation to allow the state's agricultural high schools to begin offering the first two years of college work if they desired. Established in 1908 to provide a high school opportunity for the state's population, the schools built dormitories and graduated an increasing number of students, but by the 1920s more towns and counties created their own nonboarding high schools closer to students' homes, leaving the state with unneeded facilities. Zeller, an independently wealthy educator, had served as the superintendent of the Bolivar County Agricultural High School and, while working on one of his degrees, had encountered the idea of junior colleges at the University of Chicago. Seeing an opportunity, Zeller got permissive legislation passed. Pearl River County Agricultural High

School, with the support of Bilbo, had offered freshman college courses in 1921 anticipating passage of the law. Hinds joined Pearl River the first year after passage of the law, and three years later two more agricultural high schools took advantage of the permission granted them.

By 1929 the number of junior colleges grew to eleven, but in 1928 Zeller got the legislature to apply birth control to the growth of new schools. The state granted a small budget for the schools and created a commission to oversee them, but each institution had its own governing board usually controlled by the county supervisors and penetrating to the beat level in county politics. The junior colleges grew their own faculty, sending high school teachers to graduate school for summer courses to prepare them to teach college classes. As with the teacher's colleges, the presidents imposed strict discipline in a highly paternal atmosphere. Students could work for their room and board to keep costs extremely low, providing a path to college for many who would have made it into higher education no other way. As a result, Mississippi developed one of the nation's earliest junior college systems, growing the schools from the grassroots with local participation and control.

Despite his ineptitude with the legislature, Whitfield tried to do good work, pressing for a state library commission, a state textbook commission, and a forestry commission. He recognized the state's needs and would have liked to have done more. The state institution for the mentally ill bears his name in recognition of his efforts that led to the construction of a decent facility. Whitfield died of cancer, suffering the amputation of a leg in an effort to save his life, and the lieutenant governor, Dennis Murphree, assumed the office in 1927. A newspaper owner from Pittsboro in Calhoun County, Murphree launched the "Know Mississippi Better Train" in 1925. With exhibit cars, a college band, and hundreds of Mississippians, including sometimes the state health officer and the state school superintendent, the train pulled into a city and disgorged the state's promoters, who marched into nearby hotels to banquet and speak about the good life in Mississippi. Although his trains continued to run for many years, the promotional effort suffered a setback when the Mississippi River flooded and the Delta remained under water for months, thousands of whites evacuated, planters with the governor's support imprisoned blacks on the levees in order to prevent them from joining the exodus north, and the Delta lost an entire year's cotton crop. Murphree hoped to win the governor's office for a full term in the next election, but he had little time to campaign because of his work dealing with the 1927 natural disaster.

As the governor struggled with the flood's aftermath, Mississippi musicians sprang their invention of American music on the country. Big

Jimmie Rodgers grew up in Meridian, where he absorbed the music of his age and invented "country music." Courtesy of the Jimmie Rodgers Museum.

Bill Broonzy, who claimed Scott as his hometown, recorded several songs documenting his family's experiences with the flood. Charley Patton from Sunflower County recorded "High Water Everywhere" for one of the record companies scouring the South for "race record" material. The competing record companies issued several "flood" songs as the nation followed the news of the disaster and sought to understand the pain and suffering visited on the Delta. In North Carolina, an itinerant white musician from Meridian encountered a Victor Talking Machine Company representative looking for hillbilly material. Jimmie Rodgers grew up near and in Meridian, where he saw entertainers passing through the Grand Opera House and other theaters of the state's largest city. He knew the railroad shops, pool halls, and black joints along Fifth Street as he roamed the alleys at night running errands for pocket money to pay for tickets to the movies and vaudeville shows. He was infected early by the desire to perform, and his father had to drag him home twice before he was thirteen because he left town heading his own traveling show. After the second traveling show episode, his father got Jimmie a job as water boy for his railroad right-of-way maintenance crew. Eventually Rodgers became a brakeman and saw the country while mingling with rail men and entertainers—black and white. After his field recording, Rodgers went to New York and convinced the Victor Company to record four songs—one of which propelled him to stardom. "T for Texas," or as the company labeled it, "Blue Yodel," was a blues song sung by a white man, and some early reviewers mistook the color of Rodgers's skin. Known today as the father of country music, Rodgers produced music reflecting the culture of his era—longing for his rural home but inhabiting the bars and riding the rails. Though his tuberculosis led him to seek a drier climate in Texas, he always recognized Meridian as home and sang frequently of missing Mississippi in his less bluesy ballads. Sharecroppers with little disposable income parted with their quarters to buy his records and jammed his shows, which he continued despite his declining health. Rodgers and the black bluesmen mixed Mississippi's black and white musical traditions, merging the frontier brush arbor church music into a new sound that conquered the world.

At the same time, Mississippi also provided the U.S. Senate with its most popular member. Pat Harrison entered the Senate in 1919, and Williams, the senior Mississippi senator, introduced him and eased his way into a leadership role quickly. A loyal party man, Harrison supported Wilson's League of Nations and the World Court, spoke against the Republicans with wit and humor, and rose to influence on the Senate Finance Committee. Back home, he headed the 1920 delegation to the presidential convention instead of Governor Russell, even though Percy declared the delegation was dominated by Klan members. When Williams retired, Harrison inherited his support, and in 1922 he sent his secretary back home to manage the campaign for the victorious Hubert D. Stephens. In 1924 Harrison served as temporary chairman of the presidential convention and gave a rousing keynote speech condemning Republican scandals. He toured the country speaking for Democratic candidates and mastered the new medium of radio. In the primary for reelection, he carried every county in the state against former governor Brewer. His only problem appeared to be Bilbo, who refused to accept political defeat.

By 1926 Bilbo had boosted circulation of his weekly *Free Lance* to 17,000, and he fanned the flames of populist discontent over the legislature's repeal of populist legislation at the behest of Whitfield. A year ahead of the 1927 primary, he activated his organization to begin the campaign for governor. Conner, along with incumbent governor Murphree, opposed him as a scourge that Mississippi needed to eradicate, but Bilbo hammered away at two proposals to improve the lives of Mississippians. First, he promised a state-run textbook factory to publish schoolchildren's texts at lower prices because book monopolies drove up the price of books and hampered the education of poor children. Second, he advocated paving Mississippi roads with brick. God gave Mississippi clay, he said, and the devil provided prisoners who could turn that clay into bricks. Waving a brick in the air, he proclaimed that Mississippians could drive for 100 years on one side of the bricks, then turn them over for a second century, and if they stood them on end, they could ride to kingdom come. The rednecks roared their approval of his antics and agreed with Conner and Murphree that Bilbo was not respectable. That was the reason they loved him so much. Bilbo missed taking the first primary by only 1 percent. Conner backed Murphree in the second round, and the Masonic Grand Master issued a letter charging that Bilbo intended to back the Catholic, antiprohibition Al Smith for president in 1928, but even with all "respectable" Mississippians against him, Bilbo denied his support of Smith and squeaked into a second term as governor without a real agenda except the books and the bricks.

The Big Four denied Bilbo his textbook factory and demolished every proposal the governor sent them. He suggested a sales tax to remedy the continuing shortfall in state revenue, and the Big Four defeated his plan. Bilbo in turn vetoed every bill they passed, leaving the state in fiscal crisis. Taking a break from battling the legislature, Bilbo broke his campaign promise and joined Harrison to support Smith for president, even speaking for Smith in forty Mississippi counties and other states. He made the main speech to a Birmingham, Alabama, rally near the end of the campaign when the Klan appeared poised to deliver Alabama to the Republicans and held the state for Smith. Balancing his act, Bilbo also used race for the first time in a political campaign, accusing Smith's opponent, Herbert Hoover, of dancing with a black woman at a social event in Washington, D.C. Back in Mississippi, Bilbo called the legislature into special session to pass his highway program of a $60 million bond issue and a new highway commission, which Bilbo would appoint. The Big Four had no intention of giving Bilbo such a massive patronage machine, and they rejected all of his proposals again. Bilbo called another special session in the summer of 1929 as the federal government announced that it would cut off funds unless the state created an acceptable highway bureaucracy. Despite an audit revealing the inadequacies of the existing commission and the federal declaration that funding required a new one, the Big Four stood firm and adjourned the special session without accomplishing anything. The next year they forced Bilbo to accept an elected three-member highway commission and a revenue plan that he detested.

Bilbo's attempt to reform Mississippi's institutions of higher learning overshadowed his other defeats. He based his plan to consolidate the white colleges and university into one school located in Jackson on a study commissioned by Whitfield. Governor Whitfield admired the progressive "Wisconsin Idea," which was to use the state university as a stimulus for agricultural reform and industrial development. Whitfield took a group of Mississippi educators, farmers, bankers, and businessmen to Wisconsin for a two-week inspection tour and then hired some Wisconsin consultants to study Mississippi's education system. Professor Michael O'Shea led the team, and their report appeared under his name in 1927. O'Shea found that Mississippi's institutions of higher learning clung to genteel traditions and resisted modernization. Mississippi educators stressed, he said, "developing character" above all else. This wording no doubt covered the frequent sermons delivered by presidents such as Whitfield and Cook. O'Shea indicated the need to train college students with a curriculum designed for scientifically oriented individuals capable of reforming agriculture and building industries.

The colleges and the university entered into the 1927 primary with their usual vigor. Mississippi State College for Women supported Murphree openly and fully. Mississippi A&M and the State Teachers College at Hattiesburg opposed Bilbo circumspectly, but some faculty members at the University of Mississippi angered Bilbo most by writing letters against him and belittling him in their classes. Spies at the university kept the Man well informed of their activities, and the chancellor refused to discipline them when Bilbo demanded it. The former chancellor, fired by Whitfield, worked in Bilbo's campaign, and everyone expected Bilbo to fire Whitfield's man and rehire his chancellor after the election. Bilbo had political motives, but he also had the O'Shea report. Bilbo possessed a good case for moving the university to Jackson. The campus had run down, as the move had been contemplated for decades. A poll of the university students supported moving their school 410 to 219. In his inaugural address, Bilbo called for the move, and, in an unusual alliance, Jackson's elite lined up behind him, but Chancellor Alfred Hume developed a strategy to appeal to the legislature based on the Lost Cause religion. He spoke to the legislature of the hallowed ground where Confederate heroes lay buried and told the legislators they could move the university but could not call it Ole Miss if they did. They voted overwhelmingly to keep it in Oxford. Two weeks later Bilbo conceded defeat but asked the legislature for a large special appropriation to improve the institution, which had recently lost accreditation for its law school. The university's two-year medical school was on probation. Students complained that books deemed disturbing to the status quo were banned from the library, and they referred to Ole Miss as "Hume's Presbyterian University" because the chancellor imposed an oppressive religious atmosphere.

Bilbo convinced the State Teachers College board to dismiss Cook as president because of similar complaints, but the central board refused to remove Hume even though he generated student protests and insisted that academic freedom did not protect a historian who questioned the validity of the Lost Cause tradition. Frustrated by the conditions at Mississippi schools and the legislature's refusal to approve any of his proposals, Bilbo decided to act decisively, using his executive authority alone. By 1930 he had appointed the majority of the central board that controlled most, but not all, of the institutions. With the backing of his board members, Bilbo dismissed Hume, some staff, and many faculty members at all of the state's institutions under the board's control, setting off a firestorm of criticism. Knowing Bilbo to be a career politician, critics assumed that he appointed political hacks as replacements, which did not prove to be the case. He rehired Powers as chancellor, but he installed Zeller as vice chancellor. In addition to being a state senator with a distinguished record on educational issues, Zeller held seven degrees and had served as president of the University of Puget Sound. Bilbo's replacement professors as a rule were younger and better qualified than the men displaced. When one of Bilbo's supporters at the university wrote to ask why he had been fired, Bilbo replied that he fired him for being lazy and not doing his job. In retrospect, Bilbo appeared to have been honestly trying to improve the state's higher education system. Few believed that analysis at the time, and Mississippi colleges and universities lost their accreditation, which would not be regained until after Bilbo left office.

Mississippi lost its last planter-statesman in the 1920s when Williams retired. Harrison and Bilbo dominated the headlines, while the Big Four controlled state politics from the House of Representatives. Harrison invested not in a plantation but in Gulf Coast real estate during the boom Whitfield helped to fuel by building a seawall and describing the Mississippi coast as another California. Bilbo bought land and planted pecan trees in Pearl River County, but despite his "Dream House," it never came close to being a functioning plantation. Harrison lost his fortune when the Gulf Coast land prices collapsed. Cotton remained the dominant crop, but only the rich Delta soils made it profitable for the big planters such as Percy and the Delta and Pine Land Company. When the Great Depression hit the state in the 1930s, most Mississippians had been experiencing hard times for a lifetime. Their career politicians became absorbed in controlling the federal money and patronage flowing into the state to relieve the suffering. Friendly to the planters and big business, Harrison represented the remaining Bourbon element without being truly one of them, while Bilbo kept alive populist dreams by becoming a loyal New Deal Democrat.

In the 1920s the price of cotton fell from forty cents a pound to nine. Sharecroppers raised most of the cotton, even on the Delta plantations, using mules. A family could work ten acres of cotton at most and, after expenses, perhaps cleared $300, meaning that no matter how hard a family worked, they could not earn a decent living in the agriculture system dominating the state. Some farmers diversified into dairy operations, and Starkville welcomed a condensed milk factory in 1926. In the denuded south of the state, L. O. Crosby extracted resins from the stumps of the downed forests in order to manufacture varnish and other products. William Mason of Laurel invented a process to turn wood chips into boards using steam and undertook mass production in the year the Depression descended on the country. Other Mississippians relied on more traditional skills, such as the residents of Kiln who produced moonshine and shipped it by rail to Al Capone's gang in Chicago. Near Crystal Springs, farmers grew tomatoes and other vegetables to ship north, but even in that new industry not everyone prospered.

Eudora Welty chose a poor black couple farming tomatoes for a white overseer to illustrate the total poverty that she observed as a Works Progress Administration (WPA) photographer during the Depression. In "The Whistle," as the couple lay trembling from the cold on a pallet of quilts in their almost bare sharecropper shack, the whistle sounded, warning them to cover their newly planted tomatoes to protect them from freezing. Taking their quilts and even their clothes for that purpose left their bodies exposed to the freezing temperature. Jason, the husband, brought the last of their firewood into the shack and built up a fire to ward off the cold, but when it burned out, he silently broke up their chairs and table, feeding them to the fire. Welty left the couple's heads bent, sitting before the dead coals listening to the whistle blowing. Welfare workers brought in by federal money reported Mississippi families clad in only one garment for each person—a pair of overalls or a dress without underwear; homes without sheets, towels, or pillow cases; and only tattered, patchwork quilts to serve for every purpose. By the Depression era, the majority of Mississippians suffered desperate poverty. In 1920 the per capita income of the average Mississippian stood at 43 percent of the American figure, but ten years later the income had declined to 32 percent of the national average. Observers from Welty to Bilbo knew the reason—sharecropping and trying to grow cotton on land not suited to it.

Mississippians sought relief from poverty and worldly cares in religion and music. Black Baptists claimed 40 percent of the state's church membership by the mid-1930s, leaving the Methodists with their requirements for educated ministers far behind. Among whites, the Southern Baptists served as the black Baptists' largest rival, with 150,000 members. Mississippians favored churches with ecstatic services and strict gospel discipline, as illustrated by the birth of the Church of Christ Holiness. Charles P. Jones served a black Baptist establishment, Mt. Helm Baptist Church, in Jackson until his teaching of a second blessing of the Holy Ghost, which he called "sanctification," disturbed some of his more conventional flock, who sued to oust him from their pulpit. The members of Mt. Helm, along with most of their white brethren in long-lived religious establishments, had adopted more of a corporate attitude about religion, eliminating the moral courts held in pre–Civil War churches to expel members for a variety of sins. Jones reinstituted the discipline, demanding that followers forego dancing, card playing, and drinking, and his new Church of Christ Holiness mushroomed, spreading to Vicksburg, then other cities and states. He founded a school, a printing press, and a magazine, *Truth*. In 1918 he joined the Great Migration, moving his headquarters to Los Angeles, but his church continued growing.

Richard Wright, who became the voice of the black Great Migration, turned his poverty-stricken early life into award-winning literature, documenting black life in Mississippi and leaving historians a clear description of both the established black church and the fundamentalist fervor of his grandmother's Seventh Day Adventist services in Jackson. The Adventist's all-night prayer meetings with images of lakes of eternal fire, multiple-headed monsters, and Armageddon moved him, as did the sermons and the hymns. He contrasted that emotion with the more staid Methodist church that his mother attended, where he found that the middle class, or aspiring-to-be middle class, raised money for good causes, gossiped, intrigued, formed clans, and practiced snobbery. The Methodists, he thought, prided themselves on abandoning the more emotional services of their neighbors. He chose neither church, but though he rejected both, he clearly preferred the emotion and music of the Adventists.

Black Pentecostal churches produced a revolution in gospel music, with congregations channeling their emotion and creativity into singing driving rhythms with percussive accompaniment as the long-established churches moved the singing out of the congregation, formed choirs, and set them behind the minister in separate seating. Bluesmen played the jukes on Saturday nights and the churches on Sunday mornings. Though churchgoers might condemn their devil music for its lyrics, gospel and blues had the same roots. Mississippi exported music along with its people and enlivened Chicago and Detroit. White gospel musicians adopted musical instruments and built their own traditions, and by the end of the 1920s gospel quartets toured churches, made records for the fast-spreading Victrola, and provided the basis for a rash of new publishing companies established to serve the white southern market.

White ministers also quickly turned to radio to spread their message. From the first station licensed in 1924, religious programming made up an important part of the broadcasts. Howard S. Williams of Hattiesburg secured the third license in the state with permission to change the location of his "station" every two weeks as he moved his revival tent around the state. In Meridian, the First Presbyterian Church received a license to operate its own station, while other churches simply acquired feeds into stations as they went live. In 1931 the Laurel station had established lines to the city's

Mary Wharton grew up playing the organ in her Port Gibson church, studied music around the country, and taught in colleges before returning to her hometown to teach in Sunday school classes in the 1950s and 1960s that segregation was wrong. Courtesy of the Mississippi Department of Archives and History.

Presbyterian, Baptist, and Methodist churches. Despite, or perhaps in part because of, the on-air services, membership in the middle-class churches declined during the Depression. Only the black Baptists, Catholics, and the white fundamentalists/Pentecostalists increased their numbers.

Hortense Powdermaker, a white anthropologist, studied Indianola in the late 1930s as if it were a foreign society and reported that both black and white societies enjoyed complete faith in the Christian creation story, a biblical definition of absolute right and wrong, and acceptance of heaven and hell. She said that most middle-class whites took part in church activities, including worship services, Sunday school classes, and prayer meetings on Wednesday nights. Younger whites, she found, went more often to movies and parties than church, tended to drink, and engaged in premarital sex. Black life revolved around churches, which represented the most important haven from oppression by whites. Powdermaker found black services more emotional than white services, with chants, shouting, and physical possession expressed frequently. She reported the major difference in the message delivered by black ministers to be an emphasis on brotherly love, even extending to the white landowners who cheated their congregations. Older whites, she believed, seldom allowed their Christian faith to soften their segregationist views, but she found younger whites to be less strident on the race question. What she saw was younger Mississippians trying to adapt to modernity straying from the religious certainties of their parents and questioning segregation slightly, while blacks sensed an impending change, which they awaited with growing impatience.

One young white woman, Mary Wharton, faced modernity and the question of race squarely by teaching her Bible class at Port Gibson First Presbyterian Church that Christians could not continue to condone racial hatred or an education system that spent $100 to educate a white child and only $12 for a black child. Born in the town to deeply religious parents in 1889, she played the organ in the church from age eight before studying music in Chicago and teaching it at colleges in North Carolina and Jackson. Never marrying, she devoted herself to teaching, her community, and her church. Because she never actively condemned segregation, her church and community accepted her social gospel and embraced her as a leader. Mississippi harbored many such individuals, especially among its female population.

With Vardaman gone from the scene and Whitfield's soothing of race relations, Mississippi politics took a breather from the vociferous, ugly racist political rhetoric that dominated the early 1900s. Bilbo did not practice racist demagoguery until late in his career because segregation appeared secure, and no politician espoused any attack on it. Therefore racial rhetoric would have provided no benefits in those years.

Bilbo did nothing to deal with the onset of the Great Depression, and by 1931 he and the legislature bankrupted the state. Bilbo ignored calls for a special session because he feared the legislature would impeach him. Voters dismissed 151 of the 189 members of the legislature, but the Big Four, who had blocked Bilbo's legislative agenda, returned. Ironically Mississippi finally elected Conner, a rich lawyer-businessman, to deal with the Depression. He found that Bilbo left the state in such poor condition that he had to write a personal check to feed the state's mental patients. Facing down mobs in his capitol office and pitching Bilbo's sales tax idea to white voters as a way to make the black population pay taxes, Conner persuaded the Big Four to adopt the tax in order to return the state to solvency. He generated a budget surplus while the population suffered, and eventually, when he asked to use some of the surplus to relieve suffering among the poor, the Big Four said no. Wedded to a business-friendly philosophy, Conner offered next to nothing to his constituency and simply relied on the federal largesse, which he tried to administer honestly.

Always in debt, Bilbo lost his "Dream House" and the farm to a creditor, his wife separated from him when he left the governor's mansion, and he had no job during the Great Depression. He applied to Harrison to find him something in the federal bureaucracy after the "respectable" state politicians maneuvered him out of running for a House of Representatives seat in a statewide race scheduled because of a delay in redistricting. Senators Harrison and Stephens had every reason to remove Bilbo from Mississippi because Stephens faced a reelection contest in 1934. The secretary of agriculture turned Harrison down when he asked for a position for Bilbo, so Harrison went to an old friend heading the Agricultural Adjustment Administration (AAA). Assuring his friend that Bilbo was a good Democrat, he requested a suitable position, and the administrator readily agreed. Turning to leave the office, Harrison stopped and indicated to his friend that Bilbo should not make any speeches because his style would embarrass the AAA. Starting out again, Harrison came back to say that Bilbo should not be allowed to handle any money. As he again turned to leave, he paused to suggest that any secretaries provided to Bilbo should be carefully chosen to prevent Bilbo from being tempted. Laughing, the friend observed that Bilbo would be a perfect civil servant if gagged, bound, and gelded. His Washington job made Bilbo a laughingstock because it consisted of clipping articles and pasting them in a scrapbook. For being called "pastemaster general," Bilbo seethed and plotted his revenge.

Meanwhile in Mississippi, Governor Conner won praise for his fiscal conservatism, traveling to New York and California to address admiring bankers and businessmen. He rehired Hume as chancellor of the University of Mississippi along with some of the fired faculty and staff members, regaining accreditation for the colleges and university. Employing Sillers as his floor leader, he got legislative cooperation and muted the populist element. Senator Hubert Stephens's seventy-eight-year-old father, who won election to the 1931 legislature thirty-six years after he first served, told a reporter that that the legislature had not changed since the days of Lamar and Walthall.

Harrison earned the same access to national leaders that Lamar had enjoyed. When Al Smith wanted to rest after his defeat in the 1928 presidential election, he visited Harrison on the Mississippi Gulf Coast. Harrison had already grown close to the governor of New York, Franklin D. Roosevelt, whom he called Frank, and Harrison supported FDR for president, helping to deliver the Mississippi delegation at the convention. Harrison spoke across the country on FDR's behalf, and as chairman of the Senate Finance Committee, Harrison played a major role in FDR's New Deal legislation.

In 1934 Bilbo resigned as "pastemaster general" and announced for Stephens's Senate seat. For the most part Harrison stayed out of the contest, although he did get Roosevelt to summon Stephens for a visit during the campaign in order to impress the voters. Bilbo ran what, for him, was a low-key race, promising a veteran's bonus, an old age pension, government-imposed wage-and-hour laws, and unemployment insurance. At his kickoff picnic, Bilbo reasoned that the poor had always supported him and since the Depression had made everyone poor, he should win in a landslide. He won by over 7,000 votes, so Harrison tried to be cordial, securing Bilbo a choice office and good committee assignments. Although Bilbo chafed at the requirement that new senators remain silent and disliked committee work, he loyally supported the president's New Deal. His constituents wanted jobs, and dirt farmers and sawmill workers felt close enough to the Man that they wrote to ask for them. Bilbo found 2,000 letters waiting for him when he arrived at his new office. He hired additional secretarial help and answered the letters as he went to work to secure control of the federal jobs created by the alphabet agencies of the New Deal back home.

Bilbo did not have the influence with the administration to control the state's federal patronage, but Harrison did, and at first Bilbo worked through him to deny it to Governor Conner, who intended to challenge Harrison for his seat in 1936. When Bilbo's followers failed to receive enough jobs, he turned on Harrison and asked for joint patronage rights. He did not get them, but his stature climbed with the administration when he took on Huey Long, the "Dictator" of Louisiana whose "Share the Wealth" plan challenged Roosevelt. Mississippi's 1935 gubernatorial election provided the battleground and Bilbo the excitement. He backed his south Mississippi neighbor Hugh White, a wealthy timber baron, who had been mayor of Columbia before heading the Mississippi WPA, and opposed Johnson, the man who defeated him for Congress in 1917. Ideologically, the lineup made no sense, but Conner backed the populist Johnson in order to prepare for his Senate race, and Bilbo backed White because White had supported him in the 1934 Senate campaign. Long entered the fight in an effort to extend his political influence and backed the Conner-Johnson faction.

Bilbo came home and drew enormous crowds to hear him speak against Long's "invasion." In Meridian, the attendance at Bilbo's rally surpassed Vardaman's and Harrison's numbers for previous years. The bleacher seats erected for the event collapsed, and when officials asked people to go home to listen to Bilbo's speech on the radio, another group appeared to fill the vacated area. Throughout the state, farmers and sharecroppers dressed in overalls or cheap Sunday suits, if they owned one, packed the courthouse squares to hear the Man. White won, and Bilbo's stock soared as he appeared to be a speaker capable of neutralizing Long for the administration. To celebrate his new status, Bilbo, who bought back his "Dream House" with his new Senate salary, issued an open invitation for all to join him on a weekend just before Christmas at his home. The food for the party included 600 cans of sardines and ten cases of crackers. Bilbo provided guests with 800 nickel cigars and fifty gallons of claret. Back on top, Bilbo reveled in his success and wanted to share it.

While Bilbo campaigned in Mississippi drawing massive audiences, Harrison slipped the nomination of Edwin R. Holmes to the Fifth Circuit

Court of Appeals past Bilbo. Holmes was the judge who sent Bilbo to the Oxford jail, but he was also the son-in-law of John Sharp Williams, to whom Harrison owed so much. Enraged, Bilbo declared political war on the senior senator and Holmes. Harrison was the most popular man in the Senate, and Bilbo only embarrassed himself and his state by opposing the nomination and bringing financial misconduct charges against Harrison. Back home, Bilbo weakened his faction by switching to support Conner for the Senate the next year in order to get his revenge on Harrison. Harrison countered by using New Deal patronage to get jobs for the likes of Murphree and by enlisting Ellen Woodward, the most powerful Mississippi woman in the administration, to purge Bilbo men from the WPA. Bilbo and Harrison crisscrossed the state trading barbed speeches, but Roosevelt lent his considerable support to Harrison. Conner's organization proved weak, and Harrison won handily, leaving the two sitting senators to battle for control of the growing federal funds and patronage in the state. Bilbo's usefulness to Roosevelt crashed with Long's assassination, and Bilbo waged an uphill fight against Harrison, but as Harrison turned against Roosevelt over his scheme to pack the Supreme Court, Bilbo began to get some cooperation from the New Dealers.

The climax of the personal feud between the Mississippi senators came when Harrison stood for election as majority leader. Bilbo hinted to an intermediary that he would vote for Harrison if Harrison would ask him in person—the two refused to speak to one another. Harrison responded that he would not speak to the son of a bitch for the presidency. Thus the division between the Bourbons and the rednecks wrecked Mississippi's opportunity to win one of the most influential offices in the national government. Harrison lost by one vote—Bilbo's.

Despite the fact that they failed to cooperate and spent a great deal of their time fighting to control the jobs generated by the New Deal, Harrison and Bilbo played a role in supporting the federal programs that remade Mississippi. In recent years historians have belittled the New Deal's contribution toward change in the South because they have concentrated on progress in race relations and societal development. Historians point to the planters' manipulation of the Agricultural Adjustment Act to rob their tenants and their use of the money to begin mechanization, leaving the tenants unemployed. It is true that the New Deal accomplished little social reform because local administrators insisted on maintaining segregation in all programs, giving only the lowest sort of work to blacks. Planters and lumber barons used federal programs to enrich themselves, but federal workers also began the restoration of the forests, dammed rivers, filled lakes, and improved the state's environment beyond measure.

At the beginning of the Great Depression, the *Clarion Ledger* estimated that nineteen million of the state's thirty million acres had been almost clear-cut and that a million of the cutover acres had been seized for delinquent taxes. No one wanted cutover land. Farmers who tried to make it productive abandoned it. Gambling timber men who lacked $5 for the poker pot threw a deed to forty acres in as a substitute. Some timber men joked among themselves to be sure that the land was not included when they purchased trees for harvest. Their methods of clear-cutting skidded logs across the land to rail sidings, and in the process logs uprooted small trees and gouged the earth. Lumbermen left treetops piled among the stumps, which fueled fires and left a wasteland where a forest had once stood. A federal forester who examined much of Mississippi's cutover land in the early 1930s described scrawny cattle feeding on scant grass while razorback hogs rooted out the weak seedlings trying to get established. Buzzards circled overhead eyeing the carcass of a cow felled by ticks and disease. Mississippi's forests, in Whitfield's words, had been "slaughtered" and its animals hunted to extinction. Farmers destroyed the Carolina parakeet because the bird ate the fruit from their orchards. Hunters killed cougars, bears, and red wolves because they posed a threat to humans and stock—and for the joy of the chase. Destruction of the forests exterminated the large ivory-billed woodpecker along with many less noticeable birds. Mississippians approached the land, forests, and animals as if they were inexhaustible, but by the 1920s much of the state's trees and animals had been harvested and land in the hills had lost its fertility.

In the fertile Delta, the state's last frontier, 60 percent of the land, which had been hardwood forests, was under the plow by 1932, and clearing continued apace. Levees, railroads, towns, and waterways comprised 4 percent of the land. The 36 percent left in forest concentrated in the swamps in the southern counties, but the remaining forests were classified as "deteriorated" as a result of the selective cutting of saw logs.

A few Mississippians understood the environmental crisis and sought government intervention to combat the destruction. The primary proponent of forest restoration and conversation was the Conservation Department of the Mississippi Federation of Women's Clubs. Working with staff from the U.S. Forest Service, the women promoted education and supported Whitfield's establishment of the Mississippi Forestry Commission. Never adequately funded, the commission nonetheless existed to work with New Deal agencies during the Depression.

Fannye A. Cook, a graduate of the women's school at Columbus who loved Mississippi wildlife, undertook, on her own initiative, to study the state's animals and spearheaded their protection, preservation, and

Fannye A. Cook, a Mississippi teacher with a love of the state's environment who carried out a one-woman campaign to protect and defend the state's natural resources. Her work led to the founding of the Department of Wildlife, Fisheries, and Parks as well as the Museum of Natural Science. Courtesy of the Mississippi Museum of Natural Science from the Mississippi Department of Wildlife, Fisheries, and Parks.

management. After teaching literature and history in Mississippi schools and then in Wyoming and the Panama Canal Zone, she returned to Mississippi in 1924 and out of sheer love of the place began a one-woman career dedicated to preserving it. She found trappers and hunters unregulated because no state agency existed to enforce the few existing laws. In 1926, at her own expense, she began traveling the state campaigning for a conservation program. She set up exhibits at fairs around the state and spoke to clubs and schools. Impressed by her biological surveys, her posters, and her talks, professors at Mississippi A&M donated office space to her. Encouraged, she founded the Mississippi Association for the Conservation of Wildlife to advocate for a state department of conservation, hunting licenses, and wildlife refuges. At the time, every state except Mississippi had such an agency. In 1932 the legislature established the State Game and Fish Commission, which Cook sought to head, but because she was a woman, she had to settle for the position of director of research and education, from which she continued to dominate the growth and development of the agency. Doing surveys of game animals, she bided her time, worked with the WPA, and supervised National Youth Administration workers until 1935, when the WPA financed her long-desired plant and animal survey of the state. Her specimen collection became the basis for the state's natural science museum. She was one of the few dedicated Mississippians who worked hard to reverse the environmental destruction, but federal money and leadership were required to tackle the massive restoration of the state's forests.

The Civilian Conservation Corps (CCC) moved onto cutover land and planted new forests. Made up of unemployed young men organized by army officers, the CCC men lived in tents and worked to restore Mississippi. Courtesy of the Mississippi Department of Archives and History.

Harrison persuaded his Senate Finance Committee to designate $50 million to fund the creation of national forests in Mississippi where not one existed. The Forest Service sent Ray M. Conarro to the state to survey the situation, purchase land, and establish national forests. Eager to unload the worthless land, timber companies sold at good prices, and Conarro refused to buy the overpriced lands touted to him by companies hoping to swindle the government. Aside from Holly Springs, where Congressman Wall Doxey promoted the purchase of many worn-out small farms, Conarro bought large tracts from big companies and corporations. Soon he created five national forests, most of which lacked trees.

The Civilian Conservation Corps (CCC) moved onto the cutover land and planted new forests. Made up of unemployed young men organized by army officers, the CCC men lived in tents and worked to restore the land. Establishing both a state nursery at Stone-Harrison Junior College and a national facility in the De Soto National Forest to produce seedlings, the CCC planted 147,000,000 trees during the Depression, replacing the devastated forests. Company 4441 at Camp F-24 near Richton, for example, began in 1935 by clearing land, constructing buildings, and making roads. In two years Company 4441 planted 6,297,108 trees, built twenty-six miles of roads, put up forty-five miles of hog-proof barbed-wire fence, installed seven bridges, created fifty miles of fire lanes, and ran ten miles of telephone line. Other camps did similar work, in addition to seeding and sodding thousands of square yards of gullies to stop erosion. They built lookout towers to help control forest fires, installed sewer systems, and sometimes just dug latrines. In addition to creating the national forests, the CCC workers made Mississippi's state parks. Before the Depression the state had no parks, but by 1940 the CCC had created ten, working with the WPA and other agencies. At the height of the New Deal programs in 1937, Mississippi hosted thirty-four CCC camps, and in nine Depression years the federal government invested $60,969,271 in Mississippi's CCC work.

In the same period, the Flood Control Act began to remake the Delta by building dams in the hills to control the waters that flooded the Yazoo basin. Congressman Will D. Whittington, a planter from Greenwood, chaired the House committee on flood control. Taking advantage of the 1927 flood, he brought his entire committee to his home on an inspection tour, convincing them to fund a comprehensive study finished in 1931. Funded in 1936, the work on the headwaters began the next year with the construction of Sardis Dam on the Little Tallahatchie. Thousands of men worked twelve-hour days, sometimes seven days a week, using mules, axes, and crosscut saws to clear fourteen miles of cutover hardwood forest to make way for the lake. A hydraulic fill machine pumped earth up to create the dam of impressive height. Faulkner had his hunter character muse on the disappearance of the "Big Bottom" where he had run deer with his mixed-race companion. Thinking of the layers of beer cans and bottle tops coming to coat the bottom of the new government lake that had swallowed their hunting ground, he understood what had vanished. Although not finished until the 1950s, the dams transformed life in the Delta by eliminating flooding and in the hills by creating lakes to draw tourists.

The New Deal also revived highway construction and helped to spread electricity to many more Mississippians. The Tennessee Valley Authority (TVA) reached into northeast Mississippi, where Congressman John Rankin proved to be one the staunchest proponents of government power. As a result, Tupelo, his hometown, became the first city to receive TVA power, and rural electrification associations spread light to farms. When a monster tornado hit Tupelo in 1936, Mississippi's politicians poured into the disaster area, bringing hundreds of CCC and WPA workers to get the city back on its feet. New Deal money and workers benefited white Mississippians, improving impoverished lives in a host of ways. The state public health service had begun to combat hookworm, pellagra, and malaria before the Depression began, but in 1928, 75 of every 1,000 babies born died before their first birthday, in part because one-third of the population possessed no sanitary facilities. Because of New Deal programs educating people to employ better health practices, and the building of 183,651 privies, in 1940 only around 53 of every 1,000 babies died in their first year, and this improvement took place in the Depression era with Mississippians fighting hunger and poverty.

The New Deal alleviated much suffering despite the fact that most of its funds went to the wealthy. Between 1938 and 1940 the WPA alone employed at least 25,000 Mississippians and often as many as 40,000. All of the alphabet agencies between 1935 and 1940 made work for almost 75,000 people in the state, which came to rely on federal funding for its operating budget. The state never matched the federal contributions as the various laws required because the federal administrators granted exceptions due to the grinding poverty in Mississippi. As a result, the state remade its fiscal base. Until the passage of the sales tax, Mississippi had relied on property taxes for 90 percent of the state's income, but thanks to the federal largesse and sales, liquor, and gasoline taxes, Governor White got the legislature to grant homestead exemptions, lowering property taxes to 6.5 percent of the budget. The Social Security Act required the state to create its first welfare establishment, replacing the county-run poorhouses that dated from antebellum times with a professionally staffed welfare agency. In 1937 Mississippi's old age pension only averaged $3.84 per month, but its existence marked progress. Mississippians appreciated their federal government and all but worshipped FDR.

Despite the New Deal, segregation remained in place. Mississippi New Dealers hired almost no blacks in the WPA or other work programs except for a few menial jobs. The state excluded blacks from the new parks entirely and did not, as some states did, create a separate park for black citizens. Even during the Depression the migration north continued.

Born in 1913, Ida Mae Brandon lived in east Mississippi between Houston and Okolona on land belonging to her father, who raised cotton and hogs until he died at age forty-three from an illness stemming from plunging into a swollen stream to rescue some of his hogs. Because he went into a diabetic coma, young Ida Mae believed that her mother and the community buried him alive. With his death, Ida Mae's tomboyish behavior became more pronounced, and she fought boys and chopped wood like a man. She matured beautifully, the boys' behavior toward her changed, and young men began to court her at church and in her mother's parlor. At sixteen, she chose a serious, silent George Gladney to be her husband. She admired his steady courtship that required walking four miles each Sunday to sit with her under her mother's gaze. With only the schooling of the one-room log schoolhouse a few miles from her home, Ida Mae knew little of the world beyond Chickasaw County. Her only trips to Okolona had been as girl with a white neighbor who employed her to gather eggs and took her to town to make deliveries. The trips ended when an egg customer criticized her white employer for bringing a "nigger" to the front door of her home. At sixteen, Ida Mae moved a few miles away with Gladney to where his extended family lived as sharecroppers on Edd Pearson's plantation near the Natchez Trace.

Ida Mae lived in a wood cabin with a leaking roof. A hard worker, George raised cotton and a garden to feed his family collards, corn, sweet potatoes, and peanuts. Mr. Edd, as they called the owner, treated them well according to the customs of the place, allowing Gladney to clear a few dollars in cash at settlement time. Ida Mae picked cotton poorly, but raised chickens well and learned to cook greens with pork fat in the manner Gladney preferred. She bore three children, but lost one to the flux. At age twenty-four, Ida Mae's life seemed settled. She had an older sister and two half-brothers who joined in the Great Migration, and the sister in Milwaukee urged Ida Mae to join her, but she stuck to Gladney. Then one night in 1937 Mr. Edd and a gang of white men beat on Ida Mae's door in the middle of the night looking for Joe Lee, one of Gladney's cousins whom the community knew to be thief. Ida Mae's neighbor raised turkeys, and most of her flock had gone missing. Worried that Mr. Edd would blame her for losing the turkeys, she had gone to him and accused Joe Lee. Joe Lee sneaked into Ida Mae's house as she slept, and the mob of white farmers flushed him out as one farmer threatened Ida Mae with a chain. Mr. Edd protected her, but the incident angered Gladney, who was away from home that night. After protesting to Mr. Edd, retrieving his cousin from jail (the wandering turkeys had returned), and soaking away the shredded clothes embedded in his cousin's battered body, Gladney made the decision to move to Milwaukee. He did not consult Ida Mae. He just announced his decision, settled with Mr. Edd, and bought the tickets at a distant station for safety's sake. He took the precaution of having relatives bring Ida Mae and the children to the station to meet him. They loaded their overstuffed bags and traveling food into the baggage racks and left Mississippi because Gladney felt his family was not safe. Knowing he could not protect them in Mississippi, he refused to accept that situation and braved migration for his growing family—Ida Mae departed Mississippi, pregnant again.

Black Mississippians had to fear not only extralegal white gangs but also the police and courts. A 1934 murder trial in Kemper County illustrated the course of whites-only justice and provided hope that change could be made.

An intruder broke into sixty-year-old Raymond Stuart's home six miles east of Scooba and bludgeoned him to death with tools stored in his house. A white mob beat several black tenants on Stuart's farm and hanged one by a rope several times, seeking to extort confessions. Subsequently the sheriff arrested Ed Brown, Stuart's most trusted tenant who often carried the dead man's keys, for the murder. Lauderdale County authorities took Henry Shields into custody in Meridian, where he had fled from the farm after a fight with his wife. Finally, a Kemper deputy arrested Arthur Ellington, the man hanged by the mob three times without confessing. The deputy, a friend of the deceased, beat all three men with a studded leather strap until they confessed—two in the Lauderdale County jail and Ellington on the journey to Meridian. In order to prevent a lynching, the Kemper sheriff sent the accused to the Lauderdale County jail. Both the Kemper and Lauderdale County sheriffs interviewed the prisoners, who repeated their confessions, fearing more torture if they refused.

Returned to Kemper County guarded by machine-gun-wielding deputies, the accused faced John C. Stennis, the young University of Virginia–educated prosecutor who presented them to a grand jury, which indicted the men quickly. The judge set a short date for trial and appointed three DeKalb lawyers to defend the trio. During the trial, John Clark, a rising politician who played a leadership role in the state senate for Governor Conner, developed a troubled conscience when his client and the others recanted their confessions and all three pointed out the scars they bore from their torture. Clark raised the question of the admissibility of the men's coerced confessions, and Stennis, who had rested his prosecution after introducing their confessions, scrambled to support the case against them. More testimony only confirmed the truth of the defendants' accusations as multiple witnesses confirmed the beatings. The judge ignored the testimony, although he instructed the jury that they must find the confessions voluntary in order to convict the defendants. The jury needed only thirty minutes to find the men guilty, and the judge sentenced them to death just one week after the murder. The Kemper sheriff built a gallows in the jail yard and prepared to carry out the sentence.

Clark conferred with the prisoners in Meridian and wrote to the National Association for the Advancement of Colored People (NAACP) seeking financial support to appeal the convictions, despite the advice of all of his legal community friends against an appeal. Clark's wife served as a national committeewoman for the Democratic Party and had a brother holding the superintendent's position at Parchman, so the well-connected couple understood the danger and audacity of what he chose to do. The NAACP sent a small check, but initially took almost no interest in the case,

Bessie C. Alford from McComb partnered with Ethel Featherstone Stevens of Jackson to run the Mississippi chapter of the Association of Southern Women for the Prevention of Lynching at Tuskegee in 1938. Courtesy of Jessie Daniel Ames Papers, Southern Historical Collection, Wilson Library, University of North Carolina at Chapel Hill.

undertaking no demonstrations or publicity campaigns. In November 1934 Clark argued his appeal before the Mississippi Supreme Court and lost, but Judge William Dozier Anderson strongly dissented, giving Clark's appeal legitimacy. Although Clark did not raise the issue, Anderson noted that the trial violated the due process clause of the Fourteenth Amendment, suggesting a basis for an appeal to the U.S. Supreme Court. Clark initially seemed to relish the prospect, but intense pressure in Kemper County led to a complete physical and mental breakdown, prompting him to inform the NAACP that he could not continue.

His wife, Matilda Clark, went to her old friend, former governor Brewer, and persuaded him to take up the appeal. Brewer took on the job gratis, got the Mississippi Supreme Court to grant an extension of the appeal date, and convinced Governor Conner to postpone the executions. He added the due process argument to his appeal to the Mississippi Supreme Court and lost, but got a second, strong dissenting opinion from Judge Virgil Griffith, who was elected to the court with controversial support from Bilbo. Expenses for an appeal to the U.S. Supreme Court required more support than the NAACP could afford. Brewer turned to Episcopal bishop Bratton, who served as the Mississippi representative on the Commission on Interracial Cooperation (CIC). Headquartered in Atlanta, the CIC formed to combat the upsurge in racial violence against returning black veterans in 1919, and it helped to encourage the formation of the Association of Southern Women for the Prevention of Lynching, led in Mississippi by Ethel Stevens. Stevens used her organization to raise money for Brewer's appeal. The CIC matched her funds and those of the NAACP, for a total of almost $2,000. An article in the *Nation* prompted wealthy liberals to send money directly to Matilda Clark, who told donors that she and her husband were engaged in a just cause combating intolerance and injustice. John Clark lost his Senate seat in 1935 as Brewer prepared the appeal to the Supreme Court.

Observers noted that Brewer made an effective presentation of the case before the Supreme Court, telling the justices that Mississippi officials had been "walking with the mob" to convict his clients. The justices ruled unanimously in his favor, marking an extension of the due process clause of the Fourteenth Amendment to apply to fair trials, but the court issued its decision upholding the constitutionality of the TVA on the same day, overshadowing Brewer's victory in the news.

The *Meridian Star*, which had approved wholeheartedly of the initial trial, had no editorial comment on the Supreme Court's decision, and most of the state press ignored it. The decision left it to Stennis either to retry the men or drop the charges. After remaining quiet through the appeals, Stennis announced that he would retry the men. When he failed to set a date, Brewer went to Hinds County court seeking a writ of habeas corpus, and the judge, former governor Longino, granted the writ. Stennis appealed to a supreme court justice to stay the writ and agreed with Brewer to change the venue for the retrial to Columbus. In a move consistent with Mississippi justice for its black citizens, Stennis and Brewer negotiated a deal under which the three men pleaded nolo contendre to manslaughter and served terms of seven-and-a-half to one-and-a-half years. Eventually, they survived to be free men again.

Rationally, the outcome made no sense. If one or all of the defendants killed Stuart, they got off far too lightly. The affair demonstrated the worst behavior on the part of law enforcement personnel, the judges, and the prosecutor, but at the same time the best on the part of Clark, Brewer, Bratton, and Stevens. In 1939 Kemper County voters sent Matilda Clark to the Mississippi House of Representatives, demonstrating perhaps that the community on reflection appreciated the family's bravery. For his skill in navigating the muddy waters of the Mississippi justice system, Governor White appointed Stennis judge of the court that convicted the trio so quickly.

Elected in 1935, Governor White brought his Balance Agriculture with Industry (BAWI) program from Columbia, where he made it work as mayor, to the state level. His plan called for governments to provide incentives such as buildings, land, and tax breaks to companies willing to locate in the state. The plan called for each community of 1,500 souls to attract small factories with low labor costs, allowing Mississippi to retain its rural nature, supplementing agriculture with light industry. Making the most of federal highway funds, he paved around half of the state's roads during his administration. Local Mississippi governments embraced BAWI as bankers initially condemned it as socialism. After the first five years, BAWI enterprises employed 14 percent of the state's industrial workers. During White's administration, cotton acreage declined while yields per acre increased. New crops such as tung oil, pecans, and sweet potatoes were grown, with Mississippi ranked fourth in the nation for sweet potato production and second for pecan production. The number and quality of cattle increased, and grains became major crops. Mississippi still suffered from the Depression, but change had begun.

In 1939 Bilbo made a treaty with Johnson, his natural ally, and they became a populist team, with Bilbo running for reelection to the Senate in 1940 and Johnson seeking the governor's office in 1939. Harrison and White backed Conner against Bilbo in the Senate race and Tom Bailey, the House Speaker, against Johnson for governor. Preparing for the contests, Bilbo could not get Harrison's man fired from the WPA state leadership post, but FDR removed him from the state temporarily in order to encourage Bilbo's men. Despite his opposition to FDR's legislative agenda and court-packing scheme, Harrison maintained support with the New Deal's operatives because Bilbo's style offended their sensibilities, whereas they found the gentlemanly Harrison, despite his conservatism, more personally appealing. In Mississippi, political scuffling around the highway commissioners grew fierce as well, because the commissioners controlled many jobs. Knowing every pig trail in the state, Bilbo shared the thousands of friends' names collected during a lifetime of running for office with Johnson, urging an all-out effort to turn out his voters. Providing populist campaign promises, Bilbo and Johnson backed a state old-age pension and a third term for FDR. When Johnson won his race, the *New York Times* headlined Bilbo and the New Deal as the victors.

Johnson proposed a "little New Deal" for Mississippi, including free textbooks, pensions for teachers and the elderly, hospital care for the poor, repeal of poll taxes, and a host of other measures. He prevented Sillers moving up to Speaker when Bailey vacated the speakership to run for governor and got his candidate elected, but Sillers formed an "economy bloc" in the legislature to defeat most of Johnson's populist agenda in the name of fiscal soundness. Bilbo easily defeated Conner with 60 percent of the vote by endorsing FDR for a third term and praising the largesse of the New Deal.

Eudora Welty, novelist, short story author, and photographer who captured and preserved Mississippi's story-telling tradition, earning a Pulitzer Prize for literature. Courtesy of the Mississippi Department of Archives and History Graphic Records Collection.

In the next presidential election, Bilbo, not Harrison, toured the country for FDR speaking from New York to Kansas, but Harrison remained the senior senator, keeping Mississippi split between the rednecks and the Bourbons.

Even though Mississippi's battling political traditions seemed often to cancel one another out, currents prepared to wash over the state during the war, altering the 100 years of stagnation imposed by the cotton kingdom. Between 1840 and 1940 Mississippi had a black majority population, and the ruling white minority became, and remained, obsessed with imposing and maintaining its rule. So many blacks escaped the state during the First World War and the Depression that whites became the majority again. The new white majority required decades to adjust to the change and accept racial equality, but the seeds for the new attitude lay waiting to germinate, as demonstrated by Clark's and Brewer's defense of the Kemper County black men beaten and forced to confess to murder.

Given that Mississippi's Bilbo turned his rhetorical genius loose on black Mississippians and the state earned a reputation for violent opposition to integration by burning churches, beating protesters, and murdering civil rights workers, observers had difficulty grasping the subtle changes occurring at the same time. But as all of the violence and hate played out, Eudora Welty grew up quietly in Jackson, ignored the pressure for religious conformity, and attended black churches and musical events while enjoying a close set of literary friends who nourished her writing ability. Observing, photographing as a WPA employee, and listening, she developed the ability to portray Mississippians in all their diversity and to bestow nobility on both races. In the same years, Faulkner mined the state's past and universalized its history, using romance and myth in an effort to understand the place for himself and others. Musicians captured the essence of the emotions and feelings born from the suffering produced by the people's poverty, pain, joy, and exuberance. Jimmie Rodgers played with black musicians and no doubt understood how much he borrowed from them to create the country music so loved by white Mississippians. Writers and musical artists conveyed a modern vision of the world to those who listened and read. A gradually growing economy outside the cotton agriculture trap that had enslaved the state brought some prosperity and increased educational opportunities for more of the population, enabling them to grasp and accept modernity.

Chapter Twelve

WORLD WAR II, ECONOMIC IMPROVEMENT, AND SOCIAL CONFUSION

When the Second World War began, Mississippi and the nation still lingered in the Depression. Mississippians earned less than half the national per capita income each year. The Balance Agriculture with Industry (BAWI) program had attracted only twelve manufacturing plants employing 2,700 people. Most farmers still sharecropped and raised cotton with mules, but signs of change abounded. Some planters saved their Agricultural Adjustment Administration (AAA) payments and bought tractors. They had used New Deal assistance programs to support their workers in slack seasons, and many of their former tenants had moved into town, where some found work as domestics or other town jobs, only returning to the fields to pick cotton. The change provided former tenants with a less secure existence, but the new wage structure eroded and weakened the "feudal" system of personal dependence between agricultural workers and plantation masters.

On the other hand, the planter's responsibility for "his people" vanished. The Great Migration continued to demonstrate Mississippians' hunger for change. Hundreds of thousands went north and west, but those who remained in the state moved too. When military bases and factories advertised jobs, thousands flocked to the sites. A few came barefoot and most lacked needed skills, but they learned what they needed to know. In one case, a dirt farmer claimed to be a carpenter and worked at Camp Shelby for two weeks before being fired for his lack of skills. Undeterred, the farmer tramped to several other construction sites, learning a little each time until he knew enough to pass for a carpenter. Black general laborers at Camp Shelby earned forty cents an hour for a ten-hour shift, which meant they made more cash in a day than many of them had seen in a month as sharecroppers. Cash meant freedom to shop where an individual chose instead of the plantation store and in a sense gained former sharecroppers their economic independence.

The infusion of federal funds revolutionized the state. The military buildup began with the New Deal alphabet agencies still in place, and for a brief period funds continued to flow from those agencies and the military. During the war, Mississippians doubled their per capita incomes, and although their incomes rose only to half the national figure by 1945, Mississippians saved or deposited almost five times the amount of money that they had in banks before the war. In addition, many Mississippians paid off mortgages on their property.

Relative economic prosperity mattered, but perhaps more important, Mississippians met new people, traveled the world, and encountered an infinite variety of cultures. More Yankees came to train at the state's thirty-six military bases than invaded the state during the Civil War. Many of them took Mississippi wives home with them, forging new ties of kinship across the country. Hundreds of thousands of Mississippians served in the armed forces dispersed to every conceivable corner of the globe, where they encountered cultures very different from their own. Japanese American soldiers trained in the state, befuddling the caste system, which usually recognized only black and white. Northern, city-raised black troops also trained in Mississippi, generating conflict and confusion. Mississippi women worked in factories building ships and manufacturing ammunition. They learned auto mechanics when the men got drafted. They acquired new skills, such as shopping. Traditionally, farm men went to the general store and brought home the family's few store-bought goods, often including the material the wife asked for to make a new dress. The war emancipated women and provided a new independence as well as loneliness at times.

Mississippians entered the Second World War with greater enthusiasm than they did the First World War. The New Deal made them feel to be an integral part of the nation, a feeling they had not experienced in 1918. The ubiquitous radio brought Franklin Delano Roosevelt into their homes along with Joe Louis's boxing matches, baseball games, and church services. Even before the United States entered the war in 1941, Mississippians raised funds to assist war victims in Europe and held church services featuring young men parading the American flag while the congregation sang "America." In Meridian, the schools began teaching skills needed for defense industry work; the American Legion met to form a home guard to replace the National Guard, which was soon to be activated; and the Veterans of Foreign Wars (VFW) followed suit. Members of the Exchange Club voted to endorse the draft and sent notification to their congressmen. The prospect of war unleashed pent-up energy. The *Meridian Star* reported 146 more marriages in 1940 than in 1939. Mississippians greeted the Second World War with patriotism, optimism, and even enthusiasm. They sensed the end of the

Depression and the possibility of more change than the state had seen since the Civil War.

The state's political leadership feared change and fought it. In January 1940 Harrison and Bilbo reconciled their political feud in a Capitol Hill elevator when Harrison asked Bilbo about his health. The elevator operator, the only witness, knew their enmity well and professed to have almost collapsed from the shock of overhearing the exchange between the two bitter enemies. Their pleasant conversation continued in the hallway just outside the elevator and focused on how to defeat an antilynching bill in the Senate. Harrison had dropped his opposition to the Roosevelt administration as the president's focus shifted from domestic social projects designed to end the Depression to readying the nation to fight the Second World War. In order to preserve his position as the most popular member of the Senate, Harrison happily allowed Bilbo to take the lead in filibustering against antilynching legislation and for the preservation of southern whites' "right" to kill blacks with impunity. When his fellow senators nominated Harrison for president pro tem, Bilbo seconded the nomination. Recognizing politics as the art of the possible deal, the two Mississippi senators united against the looming possibility of challenges to segregation and the associated social system often referred to as the "southern way of life."

Ida Mae and George Gladney found no jobs in Milwaukee, and Ida Mae, who did not trust northern hospitals, returned home to have her baby delivered by a Mississippi midwife in her mother's home. After her new daughter fattened nicely, Ida Mae rejoined George in Chicago, where he found work delivering fifty-pound blocks of ice from a horse-drawn cart to the cold-water apartments of the city's black ghetto. Though they lived in a basement apartment little if any better than their leaky, plantation log cabin back in Mississippi, George and Ida Mae found the Illinois Democratic Party solicited their votes, instructed them how to vote, and transported them to the polls if need be. Ida Mae soon became a poll worker. In the election of 1940, the votes of black migrants like her provided Roosevelt his small cushion of victory in Illinois.

That same year, Richard Wright published *Native Son* and visited Mississippi for the last time in his life. Making his way back to Natchez by train from Mexico, where he had been living with his white wife, he left her behind, knowing that he could not travel with her through the South. His expensive clothing and air of sophistication aroused suspicion from whites, but he wanted to see his father, who had deserted his family when Wright was a child; Wright also needed to find a birth certificate in order to register for the impending October draft registration. Natchez dismayed Wright, who described it as a nightmare filled with filth, poverty, lard-rich food, and

Richard Wright rejected Mississippi's segregationist role for him as a black man, left the state, and wrote autobiographical novels about his experiences, giving voice to the black diaspora. Courtesy of the Richard Wright Estate.

ignorance relieved, he said, only by sex, religion, and the scent of magnolias. Looking for the cabin where he had been born, he learned that it had burned and the site lost to local memory. Mississippi kept no birth records until 1912 so he failed to obtain a document to satisfy his New York draft board.

His father appeared to Wright to be a "creature of the earth," barely human in the modern understanding of the term. Wright described his father as bent and white-haired, with gnarled hands clutching a hoe, but the two surviving photographs from Wright's visit reveal his father's hair to have been black and his back still straight. Wright hated his native state as a child for its treatment of his race, and his distorted observation of Mississippi magnified his disdain for the place and its people. *Native Son* made Wright the spokesman for the black Mississippi diaspora and a powerful voice against segregation. His first book provided the literary world with its hottest topic of conversation in 1940, and the literati lionized Wright. Although the autobiographical *Black Boy* did not appear until 1945, white Mississippi leaders understood what Wright's challenge to segregation meant. Wright's career personified the segregationists' worst fears. While working for the Works Progress Administration (WPA) as a writer in Chicago, Wright joined the Communist Party, later married two white women from the party, and condemned segregation effectively in his books and articles.

Just as troubling to politicians, white Mississippians also questioned and condemned segregation and the "southern way of life" by 1940. Frank E.

Smith, whose father had been a deputy sheriff in Leflore County gunned down by a black hitchhiker when Smith was eight, had spent his teenage years in the 1930s engaged in a self-study "course" examining American race relations and had convinced himself that integration eventually had to replace the existing evil segregationist society. Having published his views in his Delta junior college newspaper and in articles written as he eked out a living as a freelance writer in Greenwood during the Depression, 1940 found Smith at the University of Mississippi finishing his degree in history. In the history department, Smith studied under James W. Sliver, finding Silver making the same intellectual journey toward integration. An attentive politician with his ear to the ground, Smith easily sensed such changing attitudes in Mississippi.

In 1940 Meridian's Edward Kimbrough Jr. published *From Hell to Breakfast*, a novel based on Bilbo's career, as a means of exposing the corruption of the state's political culture. Senator Gus Robertson, his Bilbo character, began his career as a revival-style, emotional preacher, but was a dedicated drinker who espoused prohibition. Married to an imposing southern woman, his best friend was a prostitute with whom Gus shared his real life. When his wife divorced him at the outset of his reelection campaign, Gus staged a public confession in order to bribe a reporter from a Jackson newspaper to rush into print a photograph of Gus on his knees in a revival tent begging forgiveness. Gus had two opponents in the Senate race: a mayor and the revolution-seeking son of one of his most important, rich supporters. Gus's daughter fell in love with the wayward son, who was involved with a former Communist working to organize Mississippi laborers. The organizer accidentally killed a black man pursued by the mayor. Gus made a deal with the former Communist, represented him in court, got an acquittal, embarrassed the mayor, and then bribed the mayor to drop out of the contest in return for Gus's support in the upcoming gubernatorial race. Only twenty-three when he published the novel, Kimbrough drew national praise but mixed state reviews because of his treatment of religious life in Mississippi.

While upset about his treatment of religion, Mississippi reviewers did not quibble over much about his parody of state politics. Mississippi's largely undistinguished congressional delegation was composed of lawyers elected to district attorney posts or educators who made their way into politics. Unlike the state's early leadership, only two congressmen had any military record. John E. Rankin served twenty-one days in officer-training school during World War I, and William Colmer rose to the rank of sergeant in the quartermaster corps during the same conflict. The Delta's Will Whittington earned respect as "Mr. Flood Control" because of his effective committee work. Ross Collins made a mark for his contribution to defense

James O. Eastland defended segregation and promoted his planter class as the rightful rulers of the South until the end of his career, when he accepted black equality without apologizing for his opposition to it. Courtesy of the Library of Congress.

issues through his congressional committee. Rankin drew the most attention nationally for his frequent condemnation of the Jewish people, using offensive anti-Semitic language. In 1941 Rankin earned universal contempt nationwide when a Jewish representative from New York died on the floor of the House of Representatives from a heart attack following his response to one of Rankin's attacks on international Jewish bankers. Jamie Whitten joined the delegation in 1941, winning a special election to launch his long tenure on the powerful Appropriations Committee, but power required decades of tenure to acquire.

Harrison died of cancer in 1941, depriving Mississippi of its one politician with a solid national reputation and power. Bilbo saw an opportunity to elect a colleague more to his liking and immediately began to promote the candidacy of Representative Wall Doxey as Harrison's replacement. Governor Johnson wanted his old friend Woods Eastland to have the Senate seat, apparently never considering that Eastland's horrific lynching of Luther and Mary Holbert in 1904 presented any impediment. Woods and his son, James O. Eastland, responded to Johnson's invitation to dinner in the governor's mansion by traveling down from the Delta. Over their meal, Johnson made the offer of the Senate seat and Woods declined, but indicated, according to James, that "the boy will do it." Woods controlled his son's life in a manner reminiscent of the pre–Civil War patriarchs, sending him to

Ole Miss, Vanderbilt, and the University of Alabama before ordering James home without a degree to learn plantation management. Johnson agreed with Woods's suggestion and so did James, although his father had failed to discuss the idea with him before announcing it to the governor.

No Deltan had served in the Senate since John Sharp Williams, and James Eastland's chances of winning a full term seemed slim. Eastland's appointment only lasted ninety days, and he promised not to run in the special election held to select a replacement senator until the election for a full six-year term in 1942. Eastland left the special election to Doxey, but he made the most of his time in office. He fought the Office of Price Administration (OPA), which tried to limit the price of cottonseed as a war measure, and he forced the OPA to rescind its price control, making other planters and himself money in the process. He defeated the OPA by accusing the administration of being prejudiced against the South and insensitive to planters' economic welfare. He followed up his success with an attack on tariffs, characterizing the national policy as "enslaving" the poor planter. Aside from the Roosevelt administration, he focused on "Communist" labor organizers threatening, he claimed, to upset the existing capitalist labor system by creating a socialist, egalitarian one.

Eastland stumbled on to a winning set of issues feeding Mississippians' fear of modernism by calling it Communism, protecting his and other planters' economic interests, and using the language of the Lost Cause civic religion to do it. Fearing another able opponent, Bilbo urged the thirty-six-year-old Eastland to join the military, and when his appeal to patriotism failed, Bilbo sought the names of the men serving on Eastland's draft board. An ally warned Bilbo that all of the draft board members were friends of Woods Eastland and Governor Johnson, so James Eastland would be granted a medical deferment. Bilbo supplied Doxey his list of supporters and contributors, including the war contractors who had been generous to him. Eastland started with an advantage over most Delta politicians because his family hailed from Forest in the Scott County hills. He began his state political career as a member of the House of Representatives there before moving to the family's 3,000-acre plantation in Sunflower County, and he opened his Senate campaign in Forest with the governor and newspaper owner T. M. Hederman on the platform with him. Fueled with big contributions, Eastland allied himself with Walter Sillers, accused Senator Doxey of being soft on the "Communistic" labor unions, and by implication of not being a true son of the South. Doxey's charge that Woods and James Eastland profited from federal farm support payments paled by comparison. Defeating Bilbo's legions, Eastland won in what a Jackson newspaper called the greatest farce in Mississippi history, but the Forest newspaper noted that the paternalism

Walter Sillers Jr., Delta lawyer-planter who thwarted Bilbo in his second term as governor and came to dominate state politics as Speaker of the House of Representatives into the 1960s. Courtesy of the Mississippi Department of Archives and History.

of the New Deal had worn thin among Mississippians. Even as Mississippians fought the Second World War and sought to improve their lives, Mississippi's political leaders maneuvered to keep their electorate focused on preserving segregation and the "southern way of life." In the wake of his victory, Sillers urged Eastland to make "White Supremacy and Southern Democracy" his themes, which he did. Because of Eastland's identification with planters and his anti–New Deal views, Bilbo refused to sponsor the new senator at his swearing-in ceremony as was the Senate custom. Bilbo opposed Eastland's antilabor legislation, and initially Bilbo and Eastland revived the Bourbon-redneck divide. In an unusual move, Doxey accepted appointment as the Senate's sergeant-at-arms, ensuring himself a job.

The last of the nineteenth-century-style populists, Governor Johnson got some of his "little New Deal" legislation enacted, such as providing textbooks to schoolchildren, but Sillers blocked other legislation in the name of fiscal responsibility. Overshadowed by the war, Johnson died in office and did not live to see the state's Democratic Party turn against Roosevelt because of FDR's efforts to promote racial equality. By the end of the war, threats to segregation forced even Bilbo to abandon his economic liberalism in order to combat such threats.

Despite the opportunities for growth, development, and change, most white Mississippians refused to accept racial equality. For example, Pascagoula experienced an incredible boom during the war because of the Ingalls ship-building company's location there. In the 1930s the town lived on shrimp fishing, oyster harvesting, and growing pecans, with a population of just under 6,000. With the building of the massive Ingalls ship works, the municipality held 30,000 souls by 1943. The city acquired new schools, post offices, hospitals, increased city services, housing, and infrastructure often paid for by the federal government. Before federal action, one woman housed thirty-two people in her attic, forcing the city to step in. Rural migrants erected tents until the government built trailer parks with common toilets and bathhouses.

The Mississippi social divide survived urbanization. The homeowners looked down on the inhabitants of the government-built housing even though the apartments had indoor toilets, refrigerators, and other amenities unknown to 90 percent of rural Mississippians. The trailer-camp dwellers lorded over the inhabitants of tents and shanties. The apartment and trailer dwellers accused the tent/shanty folk of wasting their high incomes on snuff, chewing tobacco, and moonshine. The tent/shanty element refused better quarters on the grounds that they did not expect their jobs to last and because they wanted to return home and buy land. Dormitory-style housing for single workers proved disastrous because of violence, drinking, and the spread of venereal diseases. Half-day shift schools left unattended children, who created major problems for policemen. Food shortages increased business at the post office, where patrons collected food from their country relatives and sent off their dirty laundry for cleaning. Even the government-run housing units allowed chicken pens. Workers set fish lines in the Pascagoula as they made their way to work and checked for a catch on their meal breaks and after work. When Jitney Jungle constructed a supermarket complete with a 200-car parking lot, the Ingalls's company paper ran an article explaining how a self-service store operated. Most Mississippians had been accustomed to giving a clerk in a general store a list of items, which the clerk assembled and recorded in the store ledger as a charge to the customer's account. Selecting their "own" groceries and paying at the time of purchase took some adjustment.

The wartime shortage of men required a major alteration in gender roles. Women picked up men in a new custom called "wolfing." Some women took to paying the bill on dates. Even in the male-starved community, some young girls became prostitutes in order to serve the less desirable men. Despite, or perhaps because of, these anomalies, the migrants turned to religion for comfort and as a guard against such societal ills. The Pascagoula First Baptist Church constructed a new building seating 1,000 worshippers. An empty apartment in the government-built housing project became a Bible study center. The unions kept blacks out of the skilled jobs, and all aspects of life remained segregated. The urban/industrial experience did not alter the state's core culture.

In Mississippi's largest urban center, Meridian, churches played major roles in organizing social activities, but a wider array of organizations complemented their work. The first Indiana military unit to arrive at Key field found the American Legion prepared to entertain them with a dance band provided by the WPA. The Indiana soldiers repaid the community's hospitality by providing comedy skits spoofing army life at a fund-raiser to benefit Greek war refugees. Because Sunday movies remained illegal in Mississippi, the Temple Theater donated its auditorium on that day for community programs such as a VFW-led "I Am an American" patriotic pageant. By mid-May 3,000 workers labored long hours at Key field under the direction of the Army Corps of Engineers, which was called in to oversee the quick construction of military installations across the state. Camp Shelby's medical regiment sent its choir to sing at Meridian's First Baptist Church in an interbase exchange. Housing shortages developed quickly and bedeviled officers seeking off-base accommodations, but Meridian's citizens tried to soften the hurt by taking servicemen home to "dinner" after church services on Sundays. Civic organizations and churches cooperated to open United Service Organizations (USO) for white troops, but relied on the black community to care for "colored" soldiers in less formal and less well equipped venues. Black Meridianites actively supported their men and the war effort, providing recreation centers and finally a USO for blacks late in the war. Black soldiers' wives formed an organization labeled the Soldiers-Civilian Busy Housewives Victory Club. At one point, the Red Cross complained about the white community's failure to meet its donation goal by announcing that black Meridians had already fulfilled their quota.

Only race seemed to mar relations between the mostly midwestern troops and their Meridian hosts. When a "Yankee" wrote to the *Star* complaining about the city's treatment of its black population, the letters sent in response were not friendly. Meridian reveled in the prosperity brought to the city by a large construction project and all that military pay spent in the community, but one custom illustrated the spiritual side of the population's reaction to the war even before the United States entered it. The Pilot Club asked every citizen to pray for peace once each day, and the mayor ordered the city siren at the waterworks to sound at noon as a reminder. The custom continued until the war's end as the *Star* reported the mounting number of county causalities regularly.

In the Delta, Mrs. Keith Frazier Somerville created a remarkable record of war on the Mississippi home front by writing a column for the *Bolivar Commercial* entitled "Dear Boys." Married to the son of Nellie Nugent Somerville, she came from a prominent political family in Tennessee, but lived most of her life in Cleveland, Mississippi, where she taught school after her husband lost their money in a Depression-era bank failure. She became obsessed with her column, traveling across the Delta, on school buses at times, gathering information on the whereabouts of men and women scattered around the world and communicating to them how the Delta was coping with their absence and changes brought about by the war. The most striking aspect of her column was the inclusive nature of her coverage. She traveled to Mound Bayou and visited with its independent black community to report their strong support for the war and their dreams of a prosperous American life following the conflict. She observed photographs in the food market of former Chinese employees in their army uniforms and reported that one of them had earned a Purple Heart. Stressing the service of Italian Americans and their Rome-born priest in the Delta, she assured readers of that ethnic group's loyalty and military service.

As an impoverished member of the elite, she hosted "Coke parties" only for the white wives of the men off to serve, but she provided far more recognition of blacks than was normal at the time, noting, for example, that Amzie Moore, the janitor at the post office, was stationed in Phoenix and had achieved the rank of sergeant. She stressed that blacks volunteered for military service in large numbers along with the thousands drafted, reporting their locations from Africa to the Pacific. She included Amzie Moore's leave among the white soldiers recorded as being home. Describing the mass murder of Jews in Europe enabled Somerville to publish a defense of religious and ethnic tolerance, including the observations from soldiers who expressed joy at serving with Jews and Catholics in defiance of the racist Nazi ideology. Condemning the idea of racial superiority as stupid, Somerville made every effort to depict Mississippi as a united society dedicated to equality, knowing it to be untrue but powerfully expressing a hope and vision that it could become a new reality after the war. Having lived in Washington, D.C., while her father served in the Senate, she understood political realities, but during the heady days of a war waged against fascism, she imagined that Mississippi could embrace racial equality to build a better society.

Arvarh Strickland, a ten-year-old boy when the Second World War began, remembered how the war changed his black Hattiesburg community. His alcoholic father had deserted him and his beautiful schoolteacher mother before the war, so he grew up in the home of his blacksmith grandfather and his grandmother, "Big Mama" Mamie Calloway. They lived in a bustling section of town with black-owned businesses and professionals such as doctors and dentists occupying offices scattered among the cleaners, grocery stores, shoe repair shops, and beer joints. His world revolved around St. Paul Methodist Episcopal Church, Eureka school, and the N. R. Burger Center, which became the black USO. When the boom began with the reopening

Arvarh Strickland observed the Second World War in Hattiesburg, leaving a vivid memoir after becoming a historian and college professor in Missouri. Courtesy of the Strickland family.

and enlargement of Camp Shelby, his mother quit her $20-a-month teaching job to cook at the Ritz café, earning far more money. Relations and friends from as far north as Kemper County began to ask about staying with his family when they came to work on the base. Big Mama transformed their home into a boardinghouse, cooking meals, packing the boarders a lunch, washing sheets, and generally treating the visiting workmen as her sons.

Strickland caught a sense of excitement and possibility. Lionel Hampton, among many famous celebrities, visited the USO and Strickland's school, giving concerts, speaking, and linking Mississippi to the wider world. Black troops spent their leave time in his part of the city. They showed no diffidence to the local police, and when a constable ventured into Bill Carmichael's beer hall, several patrons knocked him to the floor, forcing him to pull his pistol and fire from the floor to protect himself. Black military policemen, in deference to white sentiment, only carried nightsticks, while white ones were armed with .45 automatics. Nonetheless, blacks in Hattiesburg enjoyed white discomfiture when the city had to install partitions on buses to stop the mingling of the races and the police chief had to warn taxi drivers to cease hauling black and white passengers at the same time. The city's black leadership met at the Burger USO to organize their air-raid wardens and participated in Red Cross drives. Strickland joined the other newspaper delivery boys in collecting metal from customers along his route to help the scrap drives. When he worked part-time busing tables at the Ritz, he noticed Japanese American soldiers sitting as a separate group drinking a great deal of beer, and he wondered at their classification as "white."

The Japanese Americans training to replenish the "Purple Heart" brigade fighting in Italy came from California and Hawaii. The California unit shipped in first to build the camp for the 1,000-man 442nd, who had been shipped in from Hawaii and then in shuttered trains to Wisconsin before ending up at Camp Shelby. Confined to base at first, the army allowed them into town with instructions to use the white facilities and water fountains. The mainland Japanese and the Hawaiians got on badly because they were separated by different cultures, and they fought frequently with one another and with white troops who insulted them on the base. When they got into Hattiesburg, the whites did not allow them into the USO, and they had orders not to go to the black USO. They sometimes ignored orders not to ride in the back of the bus and sympathized with black soldiers who often had to walk the fifteen miles to town because the bus had seating for only ten blacks at a time. Once when a white bus driver literally kicked a black soldier off of a bus, a Japanese Hawaiian soldier beat the white bus driver. Congressman Rankin accused the Japanese Hawaiian recruits of committing sabotage to aid the Japanese attack on Pearl Harbor and declared that Mississippi did not want them in the state. When a Japanese wife of an American soldier drove her Buick through Meridian on her way to California, the police stopped her for questioning and summoned the Federal Bureau of Investigation (FBI), which cleared her to continue her drive across the country. Isolated in hostile Mississippi where the black/white divide failed to give them a niche, the Nisei found a friend.

Born in Ovett near Hattiesburg, Earl M. Finch had never traveled more than 100 miles from home until he got involved with the Nisei. He left school at ten because his father could not afford shoes for him, but he made a small fortune operating a clothing store, a secondhand furniture establishment, a bowling alley, and a cattle ranch. He lived with a partially paralyzed mother and an aging father, attended the First Baptist Church regularly, never dated, did not drink or smoke, and spent his leisure time with his aging parents. He volunteered for the army but could not pass the physical. One afternoon he observed a forlorn-looking Nisei looking in a drugstore window, and on an impulse, he invited him to Sunday "dinner." The soldier accepted and asked to bring a friend, which he did. Finch had invited soldiers for meals before, but the next day when he returned home he found the two soldiers had returned with a dozen roses for his mother, who enjoyed their tales about life in Hawaii. He began to invite large numbers of Nisei to his ranch,

Earl M. Finch adopted the Japanese Americans training at Camp Shelby as his friends, became their advocate as they challenged Mississippi's segregation system, and ended his life as an immigrant to Hawaii. Courtesy of the 442 Veterans Club Archives.

feeding them watermelon, taking them coon hunting, and organizing parties and rodeos. He found allies in Hattiesburg to help. The editor of the *Hattiesburg American* began to run stories of the Japanese Americans' heroics in the Italian campaign. A Methodist minister joined him in urging the community's acceptance, and the Nisei began to attend services at his church. Hawaiian relatives sent Finch money, and he organized a separate USO for his friends. He coordinated visits from Japanese women from internment camps in Arkansas. Learning about Japanese food, he began to import fish to treat the soldiers. He sponsored their baseball team, which won the Camp Shelby championship. On a trip to New Orleans, when the hotel refused to rent rooms to the Nisei, he bought out a small hotel in the French Quarter for them. Many times he journeyed to Japanese internment camps to tell a family that their son had died in battle. Some in Hattiesburg developed concerns about his one-man crusade to befriend the Japanese Americans, suspected him of homosexuality, and had the FBI question his neighbors, business associates, and fellow church members. The FBI found no one willing to speak ill of Finch. Asked by a reporter why he did it, Finch responded: "I do it because I like these boys."

It may have been that simple, or it may have been a release from the racial division that dominated his society. Everyone involved recognized the irony of the situation. Decades later Senator Daniel Inouye remembered that the first time in his life that he danced with a white woman was when

William Faulkner won the Nobel Prize for chronicling the history of Lafayette County in a series of novels and short stories that shaped the world's perception of Mississippi. Courtesy of the Cofield Collection, Special Collections, University of Mississippi Libraries.

he was in training at Camp Shelby. The war flooded Mississippians with opportunities to reconsider their racial prejudice and segregation.

A small, secret army project conducted on Cat Island just off the Mississippi coast demonstrated the extent to which racial prejudice pervaded all aspects of life in and out of the state. Obeying orders from Washington, commanders in Wisconsin selected twenty-five Nisei and flew them to the Mississippi Gulf Coast, where they boarded coast guard ships in the dark in order to reach Ship Island unseen. They lived on the island for four months and commuted each day to Cat Island, where dog handlers used them as bait for dogs. The army theorized that Japanese possessed a distinguishable odor or essence recognizable by dogs. Dogs labeled "scouts" tracked down single individuals. Killer dogs were trained to invade Japanese-held territory and kill the enemy. Given meat to entice the dogs, the Nisei climbed trees, waded swamps, and suffered attacks with inadequate protective padding, but to no avail. Once the dogs consumed the meat held by the Nisei, they lost interest in the men. As Ray Nosaka, one of the Nisei bait-trainers, observed, the dogs only smelled Americans. The army abandoned the experiment.

A few Mississippians left a record of how they wrestled with racial prejudices during the war. After Pearl Harbor, Frank Smith tried to join the navy, where his brother had been serving for a number of years, but failed the physical. The army proved less discriminating and drafted him. He applied for officer candidate school and graduated as an artillery officer, despite being overweight and averse to spit and polish. Having fallen in love, he spent the war in France writing his intended, an Alabama young woman, explaining to her what he had read and the process by which he abandoned racial prejudice and adopted hope for an integrated society. In one letter, he analyzed his home state as sharing a fascist mentality with the Germans he was fighting and in many letters urged her to shed racial prejudice and adopt his dream of an integrated society.

Few Mississippians shared such a radical opinion, but perceptive observers such as William Faulkner grappled to understand what they knew would be substantial change. The Second World War found Faulkner at his professional nadir. After looking for a commission in flight training or some other role in the national service, he returned to Hollywood, renewed an old affair, and penned movie scripts, including one about the French exile leader Charles de Gaulle. He wrote little about Mississippians coping with the war, but he struggled with his Victorian values and distrust of big government while supporting the war.

In his short story "The Tall Men," Faulkner had an old deputy marshal and a Jackson-based investigator seek to arrest two draft "evaders" named McCallum. As the men approached the McCallum farmhouse, they discovered that the "evaders'" father had almost severed his leg in an accident. As the father ordered the doctor to amputate his leg, he drank whiskey for the pain, and listened to the explanation of how his sons, the "evaders," had violated the law by not registering for the draft. Faulkner described the family's defiance of the New Deal's farm programs and their refusal to accept subsidies or governmental controls because their independence was precious to them. As McCallum recalled being wounded in France and the amputation proceeded, he ordered his sons to go to Memphis and enlist. When the draft board investigator protested that the young men could not "evade" punishment by enlisting, the marshal told him to be quiet and assured him that no one was interested in his rules. As the marshal and the investigator made their way with a lantern to the family graveyard to bury the severed leg, the marshal ruminated on government regulations and alphabet agencies taking away men's backbones. With the hole dug, he asked the investigator if he had noticed that the McCallum sons did not question their father's order and kissed him good-bye in silence, likening their behavior to their grandfather's in the Civil War. Faulkner continued to dislike big government, but supported the war.

In "Two Soldiers," he described two farm boys listening to a radio outside a neighbor's house in order to hear war news. When the older boy decided to enlist to fight the Japanese, his no-good father argued that the country had not been invaded and that his eight months in Texas after being drafted in the last war, along with an uncle wounded in France, constituted enough family contribution to the United States. The boy's mother cried and prepared food for her son's journey to Memphis for enlistment, telling him to go if he must but not to expect her to understand why. The little brother followed the enlistee to Memphis, giving Faulkner an opportunity to imagine rural Mississippians' wonderment at the larger world they would encounter as a result of the war. In "Shall Not Perish," Faulkner adopted the voice of the little brother to describe his mother's coping with the death of her son in the Pacific. The little brother accompanied his mother to Major de Spain's palatial home in Jefferson to join de Spain in his mourning for his only son, who flew a plane into a Japanese destroyer, becoming the second Yoknapatawpha native to die in the war. The boy watched his mother confront de Spain next to his son's coffin draped in a Confederate flag topped by a photograph, gun, and medal. She removed the gun and asked de Spain to weep, but instead he railed against governments and leaders who made the war, harking back to his country—the Confederacy. When she protested that their sons had been right to fight, de Spain asked her for an explanation, but she claimed not to know why. She said that she only knew that her son knew, as her brother had in the First World War and her grandfather in the Civil War. Pressed by de Spain for clarity, she could only say that whatever they knew was strong. Obviously Faulkner's reasoning remained inchoate early in the war.

His letters made clear that by the summer of 1943, Faulkner understood the change the war would bring. When his Jewish publisher's son died in the Pacific, Faulkner told his stepson that he hoped not to encounter a "hundred percent American Legionnaire" until he felt better. He noted the black air unit fighting for the United States and asked his stepson how whites would react if they lived in the Congo and had to convince their government to allow them to fight or if they were segregated out of housing and restaurants. Faulkner predicted that America had to change its society and live up to politicians' shibboleths about freedom, liberty, and human rights, or the men serving in the war would have wasted their time and many their lives. By the last year of the war, Faulkner began to work on *A Fable*, the story of a Christ figure who emerged in the First World War as a corporal and sought to end war forever, only to suffer a second crucifixion before a firing squad. Thus by 1945 Faulkner supported the war only if it remade the world.

Among southern writers, Faulkner proved a rarity because most of them wrote little about the war or its impact on the South. Mississippi's other literary giant, Eudora Welty, spent much of the war, as many Mississippians of her class did, working at the Red Cross and the USO. Her brothers and the man she loved, John Robinson, fought in the war, and her worry about their safety reduced her production of stories while she sought diversion in music, painting, and gardening. She worked some months in New York as a newspaper editor and writer while seeking an overseas journalist's assignment to get into the war, but failed to find one. Back in Mississippi, she struggled to understand the human essence of the war experience. In letters, she explained to fellow writers her unease at the evil loose in the world and her knowledge of the connectedness of all humanity to the vast universe. She examined what she termed the pagan elements of black church services featuring fruits and plants as props, and she attended black dances on Farish Street, marveling at the life on display there. She bristled at what she described as the ignorant, stupid, scatterbrained women who worked alongside her at the Red Cross and USO. Their bloodthirstiness terrified her because, she said, they had no understanding of what they wished for. When the army transferred John Robinson away from the front, Welty returned to writing in order to send him a story, which eventually grew into *Delta Wedding*. In one scene, Welty had Robinson's relative emerge nude from a river swim, break up a knife fight between two black boys, bind one's wounds, and hold both of them to him as they cried in his arms. Thus Welty answered Nazi Germany's values and denied the segregationists at home through human relationships. She told Robinson that Mississippi politicians' racism enraged her and made her "sick."

Responding to black demands in June 1941, FDR issued his first executive order, creating the Fair Employment Practices Committee (FEPC) to end employment discrimination in defense industries. Bilbo and Rankin led the fight against the FEPC, with Bilbo charging that the blacks behind the committee's creation dreamed of social equality and interracial marriages, while Rankin called the committee the thin wedge of the coming Communistic dictatorship. Eastland joined them with a four-hour speech matching Bilbo's racist rhetoric. Equally threatening to segregation between late 1943 and early 1944, the administration pushed a measure to create a federally regulated absentee voting system to ensure servicemen the opportunity to vote. A southern coalition formed to defeat the measure in the name of states' rights and to prevent black soldiers from voting. Eastland led the fight against it in the Senate and Rankin in the House of Representatives. Eastland went so far as to denigrate black servicemen's contribution to the war, stating that white troops won the war while blacks performed poorly and raped women. The *Clarion Ledger* assured its readers that white Mississippians preferred sacrificing the right to vote in a few elections to opening up the possibility of black soldiers' gaining the right to vote.

Throughout the war, whites disturbed by Eleanor Roosevelt's efforts to secure better treatment for blacks talked of "Eleanor Clubs" rumored to be arming themselves with ice picks or guns for the purpose of an immediate uprising or one delayed until black veterans returned. Generated by improved financial conditions, which made hiring black cooks, maids, and child care workers more difficult during the war, white Mississippians took the rumors seriously, and the FBI investigated the stories, but found no evidence of the alleged clubs. The *Meridian Star* reported the FBI findings, but rumors continued. Eastland's wife complained to her husband that she found it impossible to hire a black babysitter in Sunflower County. L. O. Crosby, a major Mississippi businessman, reported to Bilbo that his black maid had been found lying on the sofa smoking and listening to the radio when she should have been cleaning.

Such "troubling" behavior and fears of impending racial conflict fed by the racist rhetoric of the congressional delegation led Mike Conner and Tom Bailey, opposing one another in the 1943 gubernatorial runoff, to stress opposition to Washington's growing bureaucracy and the necessity of maintaining states' rights. The next year the states' rights forces staged a surprise coup in the Democratic state convention, denying Mississippi's support to FDR in the presidential nominating convention. The legislature had to meet in special session to overturn the coup and restore the votes to Roosevelt.

As disturbing as black challenges to segregation were to white Mississippians, the war muted black protests. Richard Wright, the exiled voice of black Mississippians, published three weeks before Pearl Harbor *12 Million Black Voices*, which effectively indicted the nation's treatment of blacks for 300 years with words and photographs, but Wright moderated his stand on the war as it progressed. In December 1941 he wailed in a letter to a Mississippi friend that blacks were being asked to die for freedom they had never had. Facing the draft and the possibility of being sent south, where his pregnant white wife would not be able to visit him and where he would again suffer the indignities of segregation, Wright looked for a government position in which he could use his writing skills to fight the Nazis and promote black support for the war. Although granted 3A status by claiming his mother and sister as dependents, Wright felt insecure and considered moving to Canada to escape the draft. By 1942 Wright convinced his wife that the Communist Party used black people for its own purposes and that they should leave it, which they did. The Brooklyn Heights draft board reclassified him 1A. He got a ninety-day appeal, friends wrote to Eleanor Roosevelt for help, and he took the Volunteer Officer Entry Exam. First the government notified him that he passed the exam, then that he had not, and the draft board changed his status to 3A again without an explanation. The FBI learned from Communist Party sources that he had quit the organization, and he never went to war, although the FBI watched his movements until he moved to France after the war.

Most Mississippians were neither intellectuals nor politicians. They struggled to earn a living and/or served their country with the certainty of Faulkner's young characters in "Two Soldiers," motivated by the strong belief that they did the right thing. Just over 237,000 Mississippians—men and women, black and white, Choctaw and Chinese—served in the armed services during the war. Four thousand one hundred and seventy-eight died in military service. Six won the Medal of Honor, including Van T. Barfoot, whose grandmother was Choctaw.

From Carthage, Barfoot enlisted just prior to the war and served in Puerto Rico and several states before being shipped to Italy, where he participated in numerous amphibious landings. In January 1944, pushing out from Anzio, Sergeant Barfoot scouted the German lines near his unit. When the attack began, he asked to lead a squad because he knew the ground, especially the location of minefields. Advancing alone to the German flank, he destroyed a machine gun position with a hand grenade. Entering the German trench, he found a second machine gun and attacked it with his Tommy gun, killing two soldiers and capturing three. The entire crew of a third machine gun emplacement surrendered to him. Later in the day, when German tanks counterattacked, Barfoot secured a bazooka and, kneeling in front of three tanks, disabled the middle tank and killed three of the escaping crew. As the remaining tanks changed direction toward the unit's flanks, Barfoot charged ahead to destroy an abandoned artillery piece with a demolition charge. Returning to his unit's position, he assisted two badly wounded men to safety along the way. Barfoot's heroism illustrated one Mississippi war story of thousands.

From his relative safety in the artillery fire direction center, Captain Frank Smith admired the infantrymen who risked more than anyone else in the war. He assured his fiancée that fighting meant living in the rain and mud and that most soldiers discussed food more than sex. Letters, Cokes, and snacks mailed from home brightened a soldier's life above all else. Smith's brother went down with his ship, inspiring Smith with determination to see the war to the end and justify his brother's sacrifice. Dale Mullen, Smith's friend from Oxford, wrote letters to Smith describing his life as a forward artillery observer and documenting his evolution from enjoying the excitement of the war to burning out in years of combat.

The war challenged ordinary people to accomplish extraordinary feats. James Rundles wanted to be a marine, but he was black, and the marines did not accept blacks until FDR issued an executive order ending the ban in 1942. At sixteen, Rundles became the first black to enlist in the marines. His segregated unit trained in North Carolina, and he rose to be a drill instructor. After a special inspection ordered by FDR, the black marines shipped

Jake W. Lindsey won the Medal of Honor and, as the one hundredth recipient during the Second World War, received the honor before a joint session of Congress from President Harry Truman. Courtesy of the McCormick Research Center and the 16th Infantry Regiment Association.

out to Iwo Jima, where they fought the Japanese in hand-to-hand combat, killing them in their caves.

In 1939 Jake W. Lindsey, a slight, wiry youth from Lucedale, quit high school and joined the army. Five years later, while fighting in Germany with a wounded leg, he repulsed an entire German company backed by several tanks. When he ran out of ammunition, he killed three Germans with his bayonet and captured three more. Because he was the 100th winner of the Medal of Honor in the Second World War, President Truman awarded Lindsey's medal before a joint session of Congress joined by the cabinet. George C. Marshal read the citation, and Truman told Lindsey that he would rather have that medal than be president. The Mississippi congressional delegation took Lindsey and his family to a catfish lunch.

American victories brought captured German and Italian prisoners to Mississippi. The training camps, whose trainees had begun to decline in numbers, became prisoner-of-war (POW) camps. The army transformed Camps McCain, near Grenada, and Shelby, Clinton, and Como, in the Delta, into POW installations. Italians went briefly to Como before being replaced by Germans, who eventually populated all the Mississippi POW installations, numbering around 20,000 at all the camps. Barracks housed approximately fifty POWs each, and a mess hall served five barracks. The military supplied more than adequate food, including cereal, toast, milk, coffee, and sugar for breakfast; roast pork and vegetables for lunch; and meat loaf or scrambled eggs with bread for dinner. The prisoners could buy beer in the canteen if they landed in a wet county. The officers housed at Clinton enjoyed even better accommodations and food. The former commanding general of the Afrika Korps rated a car and driver along with his own house.

The POWs formed sports teams and symphonies, planted flower gardens, and organized libraries. Enlisted men worked finishing construction of a lake near Shelby and building a scale model of the Mississippi River at Clinton. By 1944 the army developed fifteen branch camps, ten in the Delta and five in south Mississippi. In the Delta, the Germans worked the cotton fields and the forests in the piney woods. They weeded and picked cotton or planted seedlings and cut pulpwood. They usually escaped with ease if they desired but never got far, except for the one officer who had an affair with a planter's wife, who helped him get to Nashville before they were caught. As a rule, the local police found escaped POWs window-shopping or eating in restaurants in nearby towns. The officers dug a tunnel at Clinton, but guards stopped them a few feet from the fence. Curious Mississippians observed POWs at the camps' perimeters and on work details. Black American troops resented the fact that the white POWs sometimes used facilities denied to them.

From the beginning of the war, racial incidents plagued black military forces. Until 1943 most incidents involved whites attacking individual black soldiers, but in the spring of that year black units began to mount serious revolts. The military took precautions to stop black soldiers collecting and hiding ammunition by frequent searches with mine detectors of their barracks and surrounding areas. Most affrays involved combat soldiers who had reached their limit of tolerance with training and no prospect of combat. The most serious event in Mississippi occurred at Camp Van Dorn near Centreville. Detached from a larger unit that had been sent to Liberia, the redesignated 364th Infantry stationed in Phoenix, Arizona, refused orders and then in a second conflict shot at black military police. After transferring fifty men, the base commander provided improved recreational facilities to the unit, giving the impression of rewarding the disorderly troops. A few months later the army transferred the 364th to Van Dorn, which was isolated from towns of any size, but near Centreville, with a population of 1,200. The 364th saw their transfer as punishment, resented the lack of black facilities on the base, and boasted of their intention of "taking over" the camp, the town, and the state of Mississippi if they had to. At the black service club on base, they cursed, brought beer from the exchange in violation of rules, and refused to vacate the building at closing time. The next night the manager closed the building when the black troops became threatening. On a Saturday night, seventy-five members of the 364th visited Centreville behaving in a similar manner, leading the town's chief of police and deputized citizens to confront them with shotguns. Military police dispersed them and returned the soldiers to the base.

On Sunday the county sheriff interrupted a fight between one of the unit's members and a military policeman near the base. When the offending soldier attempted to flee, the sheriff shot him dead. News of his death sparked a near mutiny. The troops looted rifles from the supply room, and black military police fired into a crowd near the exchange. The military police required several days of searching to find the missing rifles. The commander imposed severe discipline and revoked all privileges for the regiment, but a month later the 364th initiated a near riot during a base dance at the service club. Surrounding civilians demanded the regiment's transfer, and the army obliged by sending the 364th to the Aleutian Islands, where they replaced a white unit and spent the rest of the war. The events gave rise to rumors and lingering accusations of a massive slaughter at Van Dorn, but no proof emerged.

Such incidents disquieted white Mississippians because of their racial fears and produced both dread and hope among the state's black population. A host of threats to the existing social and economic status quo signaled trouble. During the Depression, the Southern Tenant Farmers Union (STFU) tried to organize both black and white tenants into a union to bargain cooperatively with planters and farmers. Refugee tenants run out of Arkansas settled in Bolivar County and formed the Delta Cooperative Farm, supported by some of the nation's leading intellectuals such as Reinhold Niebuhr and H. L. Mitchell, executive secretary of the STFU. With its socialist economic philosophy and egalitarian ideas, the farm generated excitement and publicity in the national press. The farm appeared to prosper because of contributions flowing from out of state, and the cooperative provided the same education for blacks and whites, unlike the rest of the state. Large vegetable gardens and animals raised on the farm provided workers with a balanced diet, and the cooperative recruited both a doctor and nurse to provide health care. Quaker volunteers assisted the community, performing farm labor and construction work. While Mississippians left the farm in peace, rumors that the whites at the farm "Mistered" blacks produced murmurs of discontent. When contributions fell off with the coming of the war, the trustees sold the farm in Bolivar County and moved to "Providence," a farm near Cruger in Holmes County. War work lured cooperative members away and the draft depleted the population further, but the farm lingered on throughout the war.

Neither Kimbrough nor Faulkner, who wrote in *The Mansion* of Jefferson's (Oxford's) Communists during the war, invented their labor organizers purely from their imaginations. They existed. Probably due to its history as a rail town, workers in Meridian organized heavily before the Second World War. Rail workers struck during the war. Local 152 of the American Federation of Musicians complained about bands from Key field playing in town and depriving them of work. The Gulf Coast also suffered strikes during the war, and the new Congress of Industrial Organizations (CIO) competed with the STFU to organize cotton pickers when labor grew scarce as a result of the war. Labor unrest did not become widespread and unions did not grow to be a major force in the state, but they caused unease combined with what Mississippians considered radical ideas. Mississippi's intolerance of such activities remained far more powerful than labor unions. In 1944 Meridian's chief of police threatened to arrest workers malingering and taking unauthorized days off work. By contrast, in early 1945 the *Meridian Star* reported that Charles A. Wells, who wrote for Southern Baptist publications, presented a lecture at the First Baptist Church entitled "Religious and Racial Persecution at Home and Abroad" in which he praised labor unions and compared American racial prejudice to Nazism. The newspaper recorded no backlash, but such a message must have disturbed his audience.

Senator Eastland despised such "radical" talk, labor unions, and paying cotton pickers $3 for every 100 pounds of cotton picked in 1944. In 1940 pickers worked for $1 per 100 pounds. After his election to a full term, Eastland renewed his war on the Office of Price Administration (OPA) in order to keep cotton prices high—it had reached twenty-six cents a pound—and to depress wages while keeping pickers plentiful. Planters had friends in the U.S. Department of Agriculture (USDA) who would be sympathetic, so Eastland and other southern legislators arranged for OPA's regulatory authority over agriculture to be transferred there. When labor grew scarce in 1945 and the CIO and STFU pushed for a minimum wage of $3.50 per 100 pounds picked, Eastland appealed to federal regulators to step in and place a ceiling of $2.10 per 100 pounds, which they did. He also lobbied the federal government to supply POWs as labor on the plantations, which it did. Sunflower County, where the Eastlands farmed, got two satellite POW camps housing hundreds of workers who picked for $2.00 per 100 pounds paid to the government, undercutting free labor. At least twenty POWs worked for Eastland. They proved so valuable that Eastland and others persuaded the government to keep them in place through 1946 after the war ended.

With Eastland capably representing their interests in the Senate, the remarkable planter class that dominated Mississippi during the antebellum years reasserted control of state politics. They seized control during Redemption, and fought Vardaman and Bilbo for power during the revolt of the rednecks. Sillers and the Big Four stymied the redneck governors throughout the 1920s and 1930s, awaiting an opportunity to revive the Bourbon agenda. In Eastland, they found their new champion. He proudly remembered that both of his grandfathers fought the Republicans and carpetbaggers, whom he believed tried to destroy the white race. Eastland embraced his heritage, intending to combat change in his state to preserve the "southern way of life." When modernism and ideas of racial equality triumphed in the rest of America, Bilbo and Eastland led Mississippi in rejecting that mindset.

Yet even as Eastland brought the interests of cotton planters to the fore in Congress, cotton mattered less and to fewer Mississippians since so many had escaped the fields. The spread of electricity to rural parts of the state increased the production of other crops. The Tennessee Valley Authority (TVA) moved into the northeastern counties, and the Rural Electric Administration (REA) created cooperatives to provide electricity statewide to farmers, who produced more chickens and hogs as a result. By the end of the war, feeder pigs and chickens brought Mississippi farmers 25 percent of what cotton did. In addition, electric milking machines increased dairy herds. New Deal soil conservation programs and education through extension education workers, who insisted on the value of hairy vetch and other improvements, helped some farmers to rescue cotton-impoverished soil. Of course, not all the experts' advice proved valuable, because agronomists still pushed kudzu as a cover and feed plant. Many farmers gave up the struggle with the land. Between 1940 and 1945, 8,500 whites left the land along with 20,000 black sharecroppers. Fewer farmers competed for the land, so for the first time since the Civil War, the acreage of the average Mississippi farm began to increase.

Some farmers abandoned homes in the hills and piney woods, allowing the eroded land to return to forest. By 1942 Mississippi had no remaining first-growth trees. After the timber boom, small sawmills relying on inferior second-growth trees dotted the state and continued to harvest hardwoods left during the clear-cutting of the massive pine forests. Wartime demand encouraged woodsmen to continue overcutting and even increased the number of small mills by 500. By the end of the war, all that remained was loblolly pines for pulpwood. In 1940 the legislature changed the tax structure in a manner that encouraged tree farming. Until that date, Mississippi taxed forestland with an ad valorem tax just as it did farmland, which made tree farming, requiring twenty to thirty years to harvest a crop, unattractive. With the adoption of a severance tax falling due when the owner harvested his or her trees, landowners began to plant seedlings, reducing the state's acreage in scrub left from the early clear-cutting of the state and increasing the number of tree farmers. Tree farms required large acreage to prosper and discouraged the old sharecropper system.

Increases in size and mechanization clearly pointed to the future. In 1944, when the Hopson brothers experimented with a one-row cotton picker on their place, 2,500 spectators gathered to watch. Mules and small farms still predominated in Mississippi during the war, but many understood their days were numbered.

Howell and Richard Hopson led Mississippi farms in adopting mechanization of agriculture. Courtesy of the Mississippi Department of Archives and History from the Farm Security Administration Collection.

Excited by the influx of war "visitors," the movies, the newsreels that preceded them, and letters from sons, husbands, sisters, and daughters in distant parts of the world, Mississippians wanted to escape the poverty of the Depression and looked forward to a better tomorrow. Just before the war began, Meridian got its first drive-in theater, and the newspaper lauded the theater's individual speakers available for each automobile. When the legislature, under pressure from churches, refused to legalize Sunday movies, theater owner Lloyd Royal began showing them anyway without selling tickets. He simply left a box at the door for donations, and the police did not arrest him. Constrained by rationing of everything from sugar to hamburger, Mississippians coped without too much complaining. Wanting to be on the move, the shortage of automobile tires seemed to hurt most, and when too many people stole tires in order to keep moving, the legislature made tire theft a felony. People walked more and learned not to go to the grocery with a set menu in mind because shortages demanded flexibility. In 1944 smokers got a shock when a cigarette shortage hit the state, and they complained loudly. Mississippians grew a little tired of the war bond drives by the end of the war, and promoters resorted to allowing bond and stamp purchasers to sign bombs to be dropped on specific enemies.

Mississippians drew the line at accepting any change in segregation. The Hattiesburg schools refused to take in a Japanese boy and created a one-room schoolhouse on Hardy Street, employing his mother to teach him. When George C. Marshall ordered twelve black officers to Camp Shelby in 1943, the camp commander gave them no meaningful duties, and white officers ignored their rank, refusing to accept them. For the most part, even if "visiting" northern whites found it distasteful at times, few of them protested to Mississippians over the state's treatment of other races.

In March 1944 Bilbo decided to adopt defense of segregation as his hallmark issue as he never had in the past. He arranged to address a joint session of the legislature, where he accused the North of pushing antidiscrimination legislation with the FEPC and warned Mississippi to draw the color line tighter around the state. He told the Yankees "to go to hell." Fifteen radio stations carried his address live, and Bilbo had 50,000 copies of the speech printed. He reintroduced his "Greater Liberia" bill in the Senate and wrote to black correspondents that they should prepare to move to Africa. He began to compile his list of arguments for segregation in what would eventually be published as *Take Your Choice: Separation or Mongrelization*. Bilbo endorsed Bailey in the runoff primary for governor, but because he was undergoing gall bladder surgery at the Mayo Clinic, he missed the state Democratic convention that denied FDR the state's support for the presidential convention.

Bailey apparently agreed with Bilbo on the race issue, as did Eastland. No moderate dared contradict Bilbo. Before he died in office, Bailey introduced the first teacher retirement system; rejuvenated the BAWI program, which Johnson had allowed to lapse; and promoted a secondary highway system, which he called "farm to market" roads. He appointed the first trustees to the new board of the Mississippi Institutions of Higher Learning (IHL) written into the constitution by the legislature and approved by the voters. Bailey made a solid contribution to moving Mississippi toward modernization through industrialization, but by siding with Bilbo on the race issue, he left a contradictory legacy. After him, Mississippi governors had two discordant themes for their administration of the state—protect segregation and modernize the state by attracting industrial development.

Wright published his autobiographical *Black Boy* in 1945 and prepared to move to France for the rest of his life. Bilbo condemned the book in the Senate as obscene filth designed to plant the seeds of trouble-making in the minds of every "American Negro." Smith returned from the war, married his fiancé, tried to become a writer, and dreamed of establishing a liberal newspaper in his hometown to launch the education of his fellow Mississippians. Faulkner returned to Oxford, continued writing, and won fame after the war. In 1945 Welty voiced her fears for Mississippi privately to friends, analyzing Mississippians as being in a trance that kept them from seeing the truth. She felt Mississippi unworthy of the returning soldiers, who defeated fascism, and she reported being unable to sleep because of her raging indignation. Bilbo's declarations of racism as the theme of his upcoming campaign sickened her. The shy, retiring Welty publicly expressed outrage by writing to the *Clarion Ledger* when the anti-Semitic, Holocaust-denying Gerald L. K. Smith spoke in Jackson and the newspaper provided respectful, neutral coverage. She asked her community if it could not open its collective mind and its unseeing eyes to end its apathy. In conclusion, she denounced the politics of Bilbo and Rankin and hoped Mississippi would accept a more open society than it had in the past.

Barfoot met Welty's expectations. When he traveled to Washington to be feted for winning the Medal of Honor, the Mississippi congressional delegation flocked to be photographed with the hero. Bilbo inquired of him if they had problems with "nigras" overseas. Barfoot responded that he had found that "colored boys" fought "just as good" as white boys and that the war had changed his mind about "colored people," and he added many other southern whites felt the same. But many did not. Byron De La Beckwith, a noncommissioned officer in the marines, fought as a machine gunner during the invasions of Guadalcanal and Tarawa. Shot in the chest during the attack on the second island, Beckwith swam half a mile to a reef to survive. Returning home, he married a WAVE from Rhode Island, whom he met during the war, and settled down in Greenwood, working as a tobacco salesman. But he adopted preserving segregation as the ruling passion of his life, injecting race into every conversation at his church or meetings of the Sons of the American Revolution. Some white veterans simply reverted to their old racial habits when they returned home. Ben Fielder, a black Mississippi soldier who served in both Europe and the Pacific, remembered traveling home by train from California with a white Mississippi soldier. For days they exchanged stories of family and women left behind, shared meals, and revealed their dreams to one another, but when they reached the South, the white soldier assumed his old dominant role, telling Fielder that the war was over, they were back home, and he was just a "nigger."

Returning black veterans provided the leadership for the civil rights movement, but for the most part they did not return to Mississippi as militants. They had to be forced into revolt by hostile whites. During the war, Rieves Bell returned home to Starkville on leave in his uniform, which angry young white men objected to his wearing. When they attacked him and tried to strip if from his body, he defended himself and earned three and half years in Parchman. Henry Murphy's father met him at Camp Shelby with a set of civilian clothes in 1946 and made his son change in the car as they drove to Hattiesburg because he told his son that the police beat blacks who appeared publicly in uniform and searched their clothes for photographs of white women. If they found a photograph, he said, they killed the black man carrying it.

Former black soldiers interviewed and taped by historians did not return from the war ready to fight segregation. Black veterans reported to historians hating segregation, but being more anxious to get a job and an education in 1945. They said they wanted to earn a decent living to buy a house. What almost all black veterans told interviewers, however, was that during the war they experienced the feeling of being a man equal to any other and saw that they were capable of matching any other man when they worked or fought alongside other races. The war changed Mississippi most by instilling the certainty of equality in the minds of its black population and in those of a few of its whites.

When the Japanese surrendered, Meridian went wild. False fire alarms rang throughout the city. Citizens surged downtown by the hundreds and cried and cheered at the same time. They blew whistles, rang bells, and beat on tin cans. Confetti, scrap paper, and empty boxes rained down from the tallest buildings. In Jackson, the crowds gathered near the governor's mansion and strolled about enjoying the news and one another's company somewhat more sedately while savoring the end of the war.

Mississippians participated fully in defeating fascism. Many died in the effort while others earned medals and suffered grievous wounds. Some soldiers such as Barfoot and Smith understood the close relationship between fascism and segregation's racist ideology or just appreciated the bravery and service of their fellow black soldiers, but the majority rejected racial equality. Farsighted intellectuals such as Welty and Faulkner recognized that segregation had to end, but the state's political leadership marshaled its resources to protect segregation and prevent the emergence of an integrated society. Bilbo, who served as the voice of poor white sharecroppers throughout most of his career, abandoned the New Deal's efforts to provide economic justice for poor whites because he came to see the dangers the New Deal posed to segregation. Representing the interest of the planters, Eastland dedicated his long political career to preserving a way of life stretching back to the antebellum planters, merely substituting segregation and economic dominance for slavery. In the postwar years, the dreams of the farsighted died as Mississippi developed an increasingly oppressive, hate-filled, closed society walling itself off from the spread of integration and acceptance of racial equality.

Chapter Thirteen

A CLOSED SOCIETY'S RESPONSE TO CHALLENGE

At the end of the Second World War, Mississippians faced a dilemma. Most Mississippians wanted the new world of supermarkets, automobiles, movies, factory jobs, and suburban homes, but at the same time, whites wanted to preserve racial segregation and deny that lifestyle to blacks. Black Mississippians wanted to end segregation and to attain a standard of living equal to whites. As a minority population before the war, white Mississippians created a society devoid of public spaces. Every restaurant and railroad waiting room became a private club to which they were admitted on the basis of the color of their skin. Whites denied the black majority entrance and enjoyed membership in a closed society. In white minds, their segregated spaces became extensions of family territory, and blacks who demanded admittance to white schools or restaurants violated the sanctity of what whites considered their personal space. To the white caste, a black person wishing to attend Ole Miss would not be entering a public space, but a personal one, an extension of white homes.

Black integrationists understood restaurants, waiting rooms, and schools as public spaces such as they encountered in the North, Europe, or Asia, where humans interacted freely with at least the outward appearance of equality. Almost evenly divided between black and white in 1945, Mississippians eyed one another uncomfortably. Traditional segregation remained intact, but all knew that it had been challenged by wartime experiences. In the 1940s and early 1950s the two races maintained an uneasy truce. Fragments of personal relationships between individuals of different colors survived into the postwar world and enabled some men and women to continue to deal across the racial divide with respect and common humanity, but incidents of racial conflict multiplied, and black Mississippians reached out to a sympathetic wider world to support their demands for an end to segregation. The climax came in 1955 with the murder of Emmett Till, a black teenager from Chicago visiting his uncle in Mississippi. The publicity

Mose Wright, a minister and farmer, hosted his nephew Emmett Till, identified Till's killers in court, and fled north with his family after his court appearance. Courtesy of the Library of Congress.

and international condemnation of the state generated by the subsequent trial acquitting the murderers led white Mississippians to withdraw into their closed society, where they attempted for a decade to evade the inevitable destruction of their whites-only society.

Till's uncle, Mose Wright, typified the manner in which many blacks handled race relations in this period. Wright left home at sixteen and worked as a sharecropper raising cotton and the devil on Saturday nights until his first wife converted him to Christianity. He joined the Church of God in Christ and educated himself by reading the Bible until he began to preach. During World War I, he claimed conscientious objector status when drafted and spent thirty days in jail as a result. After his release, he became a local celebrity and his preaching career expanded. His first wife died in the influenza epidemic that swept the world at the end of the First World War, and he married Elizabeth, the light-skinned granddaughter of a white slave owner. She worked as a schoolteacher before the marriage and further increased his standing in the black community. In 1945 Wright's plantation owner of over a decade sold his land to another white man. Wright did not like the new owner because he did not consider him to be as decent and trustworthy as his longtime boss, so Wright established a new relationship with a white man whom he did trust and moved to a farm near Money, a small Delta town. Elizabeth Wright called her husband "Preacher" and urged him to move to Chicago, where they had relatives. Wright refused because he loved his native state and lived a decent life in it.

His post-1945 home had previously belonged to his new plantation owner. It had a screened-in porch across the front of the house and contained four bedrooms. Wright worked hard, rising early to care for his livestock and a large garden. He tended the plantation owner's garden, but did not work the cotton fields as his children did for day wages. With a milk cow, pigs, and chickens as well as a garden, the family ate well. They listened to the Friday night fights and the Grand Ole Opry on an electric Philco radio. Wright preached on Sunday wearing one of several suits that he owned and white shirts that he had laundered in Greenwood. He subscribed to the *Memphis Commercial Appeal*, and his children remembered him and Elizabeth spending evenings on the front porch discussing politics. By the early 1950s he owned both a Ford and a refrigerator. Sometimes he traveled to Chicago to preach funerals of congregants who had moved north. To avoid the treatment accorded to blacks in local stores, Wright bought almost all that he needed from the Sears catalog. By such measures, Wright kept his contact with white-imposed segregation to a minimum and lived the best possible life on his own terms. He chose which whites to associate with and defied others at times. When he left the untrustworthy plantation owner in 1945, the new boss sent word for Wright to move out of his tenant house, to which Wright immediately responded that he would move when he had secured a new house, which he did without further interference. Segregation continued to be a system open to negotiation.

Douglas Conner's experiences illustrated the process well. He grew up in Hattiesburg and attended Alcorn College, which he remembered as "another world"—an all-black society completely cut off from whites. Graduating in 1943, Conner headed north to Detroit, where he worked a factory job, joined the union, and enjoyed escaping the segregation system. Drafted within a year, he requested and received training at Walter Reed as a surgical technician. Mustered out at Camp Shelby in 1946, he journeyed to Starkville to reunite with his new wife, Nita. After a short stint in a Chicago steel mill, he attended Howard University Medical School funded in part by Mississippi's program designed to keep its white schools segregated by providing blacks with graduate training outside the state. Completing his medical studies and internship in 1951, Conner wanted to return to his home state, and his wife's uncle formed a community committee to facilitate his establishing a practice in Starkville. The uncle's committee checked with the town's white leadership for approval and everyone welcomed Dr. Conner to Starkville. Conner accepted white paternalism with a mental shrug, and the four white doctors in town accepted him readily. He set up an office and practiced in the segregated hospital, seeing primarily black patients. Most white nurses tolerated him, but he responded to the racist few who disliked taking his orders by being "overly kind." A few white men came to him for treatment of sexually transmitted diseases to avoid the embarrassment of treatment by a white doctor. His best ally proved to be a white doctor who insisted on seeing patients in the order of their arrival at his office regardless of their race. When whites complained about waiting for him to see blacks ahead of them, the white doctor advised the disgruntled patients "to get the hell out" of his office. He helped Conner to establish his practice by sending reluctant black patients to Conner with assurances that Conner was a good physician. Some blacks practiced a sort of racial discrimination by assuming that a white doctor would be better. Conner took his turn "on call" at the hospital along with the white doctors. If a white patient refused his services, the nurses called one of the white doctors. Most whites accepted him, demonstrating again that the seemingly strict rules of segregation embraced all manner of individual exceptions and interpretations. As always, local rules prevailed.

Despite Mississippians' increased contacts with the wider world, local communities guarded their individualism jealously. At the war's end, Mississippi had no television stations. Local news dominated the state's small communities. Radio remained the chief source of home entertainment and a good deal of national and international news. Politicians made efforts to utilize the air waves as President Roosevelt had done in his fireside chats. In 1944, when Bilbo spoke to the legislature to announce his program strengthening segregation, he assembled a "network" of radio stations to broadcast his message. Governor Wright followed a similar path when he rallied the state for segregation.

But newspapers remained the most exciting venue for shaping public opinion. Most papers supported segregation and reinforced parochial attitudes, but a few challenged the status quo, shaping communities more willing to accept change. George McLean, who bought a bankrupt biweekly in 1934, returned to Tupelo from his naval war service to resume editing his paper and used it as the vehicle to bring about community improvement based on his strong Christian social activism. Hodding Carter, identified by Bilbo as his punching bag for his reelection campaign, returned from military service to his Greenville paper to assemble an excited group of talented young reporters for the purpose of challenging the conservative segregationists in the Delta. Former captain Frank E. Smith tried graduate school in Washington, D.C., but quickly returned to the Delta when Carter recommended him to a reporter with family money seeking to establish a "liberal" newspaper in Greenwood, Smith's home town. In the aftermath of the war, such "moderates" wrote to one another disclosing their dreams of a state transformed through the power of ideas provided to the public through newspapers.

Smith's experience paralleled that of many such "moderate, "idealistic" veterans. He could not afford a car and rented a small apartment in Greenville. The *Greenwood Morning Star* paid a portion of his salary out of federal funds provided to train veterans as part of their transition to civilian life. Mississippi made the most of such federal funding. A number of Mississippi counties paid full-time advisers to reap maximum benefits from the federal government through the veterans' programs, and in some instances employers developed scams providing no training for the money they received. The colleges and law schools expanded quickly to absorb the flood of veterans going to school on the GI Bill. In Smith's case, he worked nights in Carter's printing plant to edit and print a newspaper delivered to Greenwood by jeep in the wee hours of the morning. If lucky, Smith could hitch a ride to his apartment with the jeep driver as he left town.

Smith dreamed in the mid-1940s that Mississippians could be educated to drop their racism and gradually adopt integration. A recent historical study numbers Smith among 127 white "moderates" in the state during this period. Few of them joined Smith in hoping for eventual integration of the races, but most of them, like Smith, were college educated and had seen some of the world. They included newspaper editors, writers, historians, businessmen, and ministers. They embraced the idea of changing segregation and considered it a positive good to treat black people with dignity and respect while talking about the possibility of changing the state's social system. The impressive fact was that so few existed. The overwhelming majority of whites refused to contemplate any alteration of segregation. The history of the state between the end of the Second World War and Mississippi's withdrawal behind its Magnolia curtain in 1955 was dominated by the political and social struggle to preserve segregation, but larger economic, demographic, and social forces made their resistance futile.

Between 1940 and 1950, 326,000 blacks left Mississippi compared to 108,000 whites, and this trend continued for decades, growing Mississippi's white majority. Planters saw increasing numbers of cars bearing Michigan and Illinois plates parked at their sharecroppers' houses and knew they could not stem the tide. World War II finally destroyed the antebellum plantation system based on forced labor. First slavery and then sharecropping provided planters with dependent labor, but that ended with the repatriation of German prisoners months after the war ended.

Howell and Richard Hopson pioneered the path for cotton planters on their 4,000-acre plantation in Coahoma County. On their farm, which had been in the family since 1852, they switched to tractors and wage labor during the Great Depression, phasing out mules and sharecroppers and experimenting with new crops such as soybeans, oats, barley, hay, and clover. But cotton remained their primary crop, picked during and after the war by Mexicans, war prisoners, and migratory laborers. Cooperating with International Harvester, the Hopsons experimented with and purchased early versions of mechanical pickers. In 1944 the brothers planted eighty acres and harvested it without any hand labor. They employed the latest plowing techniques, used flame "weeders" to keep down grass, and picked the crop with machines. The harvesters ran all day and then switched on their headlights to keep working after dark. Reporters covering the story described the Hopson plantation as running like a Detroit assembly line. Questioned about displacing farm laborers, Hopson declared that mechanization would make life better for those who remained on the land and that retaining an outmoded, uncompetitive farm hurt everyone.

By 1950 just over half of Mississippi farmers remained tenants, and over 75 percent of farms still raised cotton, so change took time. Over 60 percent of Mississippi's black population resided in rural farm areas in 1950, but that figure dropped by half in the next decade. As late as 1960 only 40 percent of the state's cotton was picked by machines. Yet a decade later the figure reached almost 100 percent. Mississippi poised for change in 1945, but its agricultural transformation required a quarter of a century.

In the same quarter of a century, railroads and timber companies seeking to produce pulpwood revived Mississippi's forestry industry. Attracted by the new law taxing forestland only at harvest and by the work of the Civilian Conservation Corps (CCC), International Paper and other large corporations began to buy cutover lands for reforestation. In 1945 the legislature created the Mississippi Forestry Commission (MFC) to aid the companies in their work. The MFC and the companies faced an enormous challenge because some observers in the piney woods areas of the state reported being able to see the curve of the earth looking over some denuded areas. The MFC published and distributed textbooks to schoolchildren urging tree farming and forest fire prevention. The Illinois Central railroad invented and promoted the use of a mechanical planter for pine trees. Attempts at replanting suffered most from fires deliberately set by unfriendly locals. In 1946 the Dantzler Lumber Company reported that it had done no planting for the year because it made no sense to plant until the fire hazard had been eliminated. The pulp and paper companies wanted slash or loblolly pine, so, when they replanted, they girdled the post oaks that had sprung up on the cutover pinelands. The squirrel and deer hunters took exception to the destruction of the acorns and burned the company's land in retaliation. Surveying property lines also proved unpopular. Local farmers had helped themselves to trees from the company's land for years and took exception to being told to cease their depredations. Occasionally surveying crews saw stills in the forests, and if revenue agents happened to raid a still any time afterward, the moonshiners burned the company's land in revenge. Eighty-five percent of forest fires at the time originated from the same type of individuals who fought tick dipping in an earlier era.

In 1947 an official of Gaylord Container Corporation flying from Jackson to Bogalusa reported the state was being burned clean because he counted twenty-eight fires in one evening—many on his company's lands. The MFC did little to fight forest fires and the CCC had been disbanded, so the companies had to develop their own firefighting capabilities. They introduced patrols using airplanes to direct trucks and other equipment to fires. At first the pilots dropped notes, but soon they introduced radio communication with their ground crews. By 1950 pilots had the capability, using loud speakers on their planes, to order men tending dangerous fires on the ground to extinguish them. Despite all their efforts, 1952 proved to be the worst fire season in history, but fires declined as the companies began to hire some of the men setting the fires to protect their forests. Companies also began leasing land to hunting clubs to provide incentives for locals to protect the companies' vast holdings. In 1954 Mississippians planted trees on 65,000 acres as farmers adopted the idea of tree farming. By 1955 the state led the nation in the number of private landowners using progressive forestry practices and selling their trees to the pulp and paper mills.

The politicians paid relatively little attention to the massive changes occurring in agriculture and forestry as they focused on the preservation of segregation. Walter Sillers Jr. won the speakership of the Mississippi House of Representatives in 1944 and remained in that office until he died in 1966. A lawyer-planter from Rosedale, he came from a political family. His father had served on the Levee Commission and had been a political boss for decades. Having participated in the 1875 "Redemption" of the state from blacks and white Republicans, Sillers Sr. typified the Delta planter, combining a legal profession, farming, and politics to further his fortune. He sent his family, including Sillers Jr., to various "springs" resorts during the summer to protect them from malaria and other diseases. Despairing of his son's education in Rosedale's public schools, Sillers Sr. sent him to an academy at Sewanee, Tennessee, and later to college at the University of Mississippi. Sillers Jr. returned to practice law in the family firm in Rosedale and entered the legislature in 1916. In the business progressive era of Mississippi politics, Sillers rose to become one of the Big Four in the legislature. He mastered the Mississippi legislature's operation and traditions, refusing opportunities to run for higher offices. Instead, he used his increasing political power to thwart populist or progressive reform, always citing fiscal responsibility. Sillers served as president of the Delta Council in the 1940s and supported his Delta neighbor, Eastland, in his election to the Senate, encouraging the senator's defense of the "southern way of life."

As the war ended, the nation began to focus on Bilbo and his growing expressions of racist sentiments, which constituted the keystone of the "southern way of life." The *New York Times* and the *Nation* began to call for Bilbo's removal from office because of his anti-Semitic remarks and insults to Italian Americans. Bilbo renewed his proposal to send African Americans to Liberia and suggested crowning Eleanor Roosevelt queen of the resulting nation. His statements incensed many, including Roosevelt's son, who suggested that he would like to give Bilbo and Congressman Rankin to the Republicans. Republican senator Robert Taft countered by asking for Bilbo's removal from the Senate for his outrageous and offensive remarks. Thus Bilbo initiated Mississippi's alienation from the nation sensitized against his racist rhetoric by the recent discovery of the German death camps. National media compared Bilbo to Hitler and reported that Germans asked American occupying troops about his racism.

Rumors of Bilbo's ill health encouraged some Mississippi politicians, including a member of the House of Representatives, Ross Collins, to believe that they might defeat the "Man." Bilbo suffered from cancer of the mouth caused by the cigars that he smoked constantly. Unfazed by his opponents, Bilbo requested leave from his Senate colleagues to return to Mississippi for the purpose of defeating the "peckerwoods" trying to deprive him of his seat. In the ensuing Democratic primary in the summer of 1946, Bilbo advised white Mississippians to visit blacks the night before the election to ensure that blacks did not vote, adding that if his white listeners did not understand what he meant then they were just plain dumb. Bilbo's old nemesis, Fred Sullens, wrote an editorial in the *Jackson Daily News* entitled "Don't Try It" advising blacks not to attempt to vote. When the Mississippi National Association for the Advancement of Colored People (NAACP) and the Progressive Voters League, a black organization urging black registration, protested, Bilbo said in Okolona that they should be exterminated from the earth with an atomic bomb.

Black veterans attempted to take advantage of a recently passed law exempting Mississippi veterans from paying poll taxes to vote. Etoy Fletcher went to the Rankin County courthouse to register, only to be ordered out and advised that blacks could not vote in the county. As he waited for a bus to return to Jackson, where he was in school, a car full of white men pulled up and ordered him in. The men took him to a wooded area, ordered him to strip, and beat him with a cable. He reported the beating to the NAACP, prompting the organization to appeal to the attorney general for federal troops to protect Mississippi voters during the upcoming primary. Speaking in Tishomingo County, Bilbo defied the attorney general to intervene and assured his audience that he would personally defend anyone indicted and that no jury of twelve white men would ever convict a white man for violence against black voters. Bilbo's remarks went too far even for Sullens and the Hedermans, who deplored his statements in their newspapers, warning that he might provoke federal intervention in Mississippi.

Statewide, only a few thousand blacks had successfully registered to vote and could not have influenced the outcome of the primary. Nevertheless, whites sometimes employed violence against those who attempted. In Canton, a white farmer greeted blacks trying to enter the polling station with a club and beat a well-known black businessman. In Gulfport, whites assaulted a black couple in city hall. At Prentiss, whites confiscated the ballot boxes and sent blacks to a new polling station where a watchman advised them to leave without voting. In Clarksdale, blacks voted unimpeded. In Mound Bayou, the Bolivar County sheriff challenged the townspeople's right to vote by questioning whether the residents were true Democrats. The town's election judges overruled the sheriff, but the party challenged the votes, which probably went uncounted. In McComb, a seventy-seven-year-old black man approached the polls, a white man accused him of pushing him off the sidewalk, and the police took the old man to jail. In Jackson, at a polling site located on the porch of Bilbo's former residence, sixteen blacks voted peacefully. In Decatur, Medgar and Charles Evers led a group of veterans to the polls, where a threatening mob of white men turned them back. Though the mob could not know it, Medgar Evers personified their worst nightmares. He served in France during the war and fell in love with a French woman there. He considered not returning to Mississippi, but he did with the determination to change his native state and assert his right to equality.

The NAACP orchestrated a petition to the Senate asking for an investigation of the primary vote, and a "National Committee to Oust Bilbo" attracted a host of national black leaders along with celebrities such as Albert Einstein. The defeated Collins charged Bilbo with accepting bribes from war contractors and presented his allegations to the Senate campaign committee. Worried, Bilbo sought and secured a meeting at the governor's mansion with Bailey—never a supporter—in order to win a promise that Bailey would appoint him if the Senate refused to accept his credentials. Dying of cancer, Bailey gave the pledge—if Bilbo's rejection stemmed from his speeches against black voting. The Senate campaign committee sent investigators to Mississippi, and they determined that blacks had been denied the opportunity to vote in the Mississippi Democratic primary. Subsequently the committee scheduled hearings in Jackson. Louisiana senator Allen Ellender chaired the committee and conducted the proceedings.

Three hundred blacks appeared to testify, including Etoy Fletcher and the president of the NAACP chapter at Tougaloo College. Among other charges, they reported that Bilbo had instructed circuit clerks not to register blacks. Several circuit clerks retorted in Bilbo's defense that they would not register blacks in any case and did not need or get Bilbo's advice. Ellender and the majority of the committee found for Bilbo despite the testimony.

But early in the new year, another Senate committee opened hearings into Bilbo's relationship with war contractors, eliciting testimony of construction done free on Bilbo's property, contributions to the Juniper Grove Church fund controlled by Bilbo, and a gift Cadillac. Bilbo appeared before the committee missing several front teeth removed in preparation for an operation on the cancer located in his mouth and throat. He sat with his feet on the table calmly smoking a black cigar in a mouth twisted into a demonic grin by his dental work. His grilling continued for seven days, with Bilbo dismissing the Cadillac and other gifts as examples of an old southern custom. The Senate refused to accept Bilbo's election, but negotiated a compromise. Citing the need for his salary to finance the impending operations, Bilbo asked for and got his pay without being sworn in. After an operation in New Orleans, he returned to Mississippi and invited 10,000 supporters to a barbecue at his Juniper Grove home. Toward the end of the affair, he removed the bandages from his mouth to insert a cigar. Other operations followed, but Bilbo died drugged and finally speechless in August 1947.

Early in 1946 doctors diagnosed Governor Bailey with cancer of the spine, which he had an operation to remove. Lieutenant Governor Fielding Wright served as acting governor and assumed the office when Bailey died in November 1946. Wright grew up in Rolling Fork, and his elevation to the governor's office gave the Delta control of all of the state's highest offices, including the lone senator, the Speaker of the Mississippi House of Representatives, and the governorship. A successful lawyer, Wright fought as an enlisted man in France during the First World War and then organized a National Guard unit in his hometown after the war. Achieving the rank of captain, he served with his outfit during the flood of 1927 and used his service to help launch his political career. After years in the legislature, Wright retired briefly and opened a string of law offices dealing in the burgeoning Mississippi oil business. Having ensured his fortune, he reentered politics in 1943, running for lieutenant governor. After he succeeded Bailey, the legislature passed a resolution endorsing his candidacy in the next governor's election, and Sullens endorsed him in the *Daily News*.

Following the controversy generated by Bilbo in the 1946 primary, Governor Wright called the legislature into special session to deal with the threat of blacks voting in Democratic primaries. Wright's message to the legislature made clear his belief in states' rights and, in his mind, the threat posed by the growth of federal power. Yet his instructions to the special session illustrated the dilemma Mississippians faced because he added an item to its agenda to take advantage of the federal government's offer to establish funding for a school lunch program. Wright wanted to be left to manage the state's black population without interference, but he could not resist the much-needed federal money. Backed by the Bilbo machine grateful for Wright's pledge to Bilbo (before his death) to appoint him senator if the Senate rejected his credentials, Wright won an overwhelming victory in the first primary, ensuring four more years in office. As governor, he particularly disliked the growing number of persons from outside the state who wrote and visited him in order to condemn the state's treatment of black Mississippians. The case of Willie McGee gave Wright the most trouble.

In November 1945 Willette Hawkins, a middle-aged white woman, accused McGee of breaking into her Laurel home and raping her as she lay comforting a sick baby in the early morning hours. Her husband had retired to another bedroom in the back of the house after some hours with her and the sick child. She could not identify her assailant because the electric line to the house had been severed and the attack occurred in pitch black, but she did not scream or call out to her husband during the attack. The police arrested McGee in Hattiesburg after he failed to appear for work at the wholesale grocery where he drove a truck. Coworkers placed him in the vicinity of the house. For his protection, authorities sent McGee to jail in Jackson. He returned to Laurel for trial under heavy guard, and the all-white jury required only three minutes to convict him. His trial attracted almost no notice at first, but recent court decisions invalidating convictions by juries that excluded blacks led to a prolonged series of appeals, retrials, and finally numerous appeals to the U.S. Supreme Court.

During the appeals, McGee began to claim that he had a long-standing affair with Hawkins, who was obsessed with him and who cried rape, he said, because he refused to kill her husband and continue their affair. The Civil Rights Congress (CRC), an organization shunned by the NAACP for its Communist Party connections, took up McGee's case supplying lawyers, funds, and publicity. Well into the case, Rosalee Safford from Lexington, Mississippi, claimed to be McGee's wife, corroborated his story, and made speaking tours on his behalf outside of Mississippi. The publicity that she and the CRC generated proved so effective that the world believed McGee's story, and he became a cause célèbre. Foreign governments made protests. All manner of famous individuals bombarded Wright with appeals. William Faulkner even issued a statement condemning the state's intention to execute McGee.

Investigators never discovered the truth. Hawkins sued the *Daily Worker* for libel because it published McGee's account of their "affair" and won $5,000 in damages, but on the night of his execution McGee told the prosecutor, who plied him with a bottle of whiskey, that the sex was consensual. The traveling executioner electrocuted McGee in the Laurel courthouse on May 8, 1951, despite the furor whipped up against the state. Clearly McGee fabricated much of his story, claiming a wife who was a complete fiction. Wright and others knew some of McGee's story to be untrue, but in the climate of the times created by Bilbo's speeches and the violence endemic against black people in the state, spokesmen defending Mississippi encountered a hostile, unbelieving world.

Mississippians signaled their desire to defy hostile world opinion by electing men who promised to defend segregation while using the world's condemnation of the state to their political advantage. John Bell Williams typified the sort of congressman popular with Mississippi voters in the 1940s. From Raymond, Williams attended Hinds Junior College and the Mississippi School of Law. Entering the U.S. Army Air Corps, Williams earned his wings and crashed in Guyana on his way to North Africa, losing part of his left arm and suffering horrible wounds. With a medical discharge, he returned to Raymond, and Governor Bailey appointed him as a district attorney. From that office he challenged the incumbent representative as being too weak in his opposition to the CIO and other "subversive" organizations. An effective campaigner, Williams mastered the trick of grasping a microphone at rallies with the metal devise that replaced his left hand in order to create a shrill sound reminding the voters of his war injury. Defeating his opponent handily, Williams entered Congress as a devotee of Rankin, a vociferous Bilbo defender, and a supporter of Wright's crusade against black voters.

Bilbo had collected his prejudices in *Take Your Choice: Separation or Mongrelization*, but his rant provided a poor intellectual legacy. Senator Eastland discovered a philosophy and a plan to provide the intellectual underpinning for his and Wright's political crusade to defend the "southern way of life" in Charles W. Collins's *Whither Solid South? A Study in Politics and Race Relations*. A constitutional scholar educated in Ivy League schools, Collins traced African and African American history to "prove" white supremacy, denied the legality of the Fourteenth Amendment, denounced federal legislation intended to foster racial equality, and advocated the establishment of a "forty-ninth all-black state in Africa." For the South, Collins proposed a return to the rule of a small group of educated whites qualified by "birth and intelligence." Eastland sent Wright a copy of Collins's book, which Wright happily embraced. The Deltans worried about President Harry Truman's

Fielding Wright, successful oil industry lawyer who served as governor and ran for vice president on the Dixiecrat ticket to preserve segregation. Courtesy of the Mississippi Department of Archives and History.

support of integration and sought a plan to prevent any disruption of Mississippi's segregation system.

A glimmer of worry appeared in state politics. In the 1947 primary, a group of young veterans—several still in law school—won election to the legislature. They seemed unhappy with the status quo and appeared likely to cause problems for Speaker Sillers. One of the new young state senators, Frank Smith, left his newspaper job and compounded the establishment's concern by going to work for Judge Stennis, who ran for Bilbo's seat in a special election in November. The Mississippi A&M alumni were grooming Stennis for a run at the governor's office and decided that the name recognition garnered in the Senate race would be an asset even if he could not win that office. Congressman William Colmer seemed to have an inside track in the race and positioned himself to the right of Stennis as tougher on the CIO and Communism. Smith had been drawn to Stennis because of the judge's support for the United Nations and because Stennis adopted a moderate stance on race, proclaiming that his father advised him to say nothing on the subject, which he took as his policy. Despite Stennis's role in the prosecution of the tortured blacks accused in the Kemper County murders, the leading black newspaper editor, Percy Greene, quietly supported him as the most moderate candidate. When Stennis seemed to gain strength, Congressman Will Whittington attacked him as a friend of labor forces, but Stennis stuck to a bland campaign calling for agricultural development. Winning with a plurality that required no runoff, Stennis immediately became the hope of the small band of Mississippi moderates. Smith went to Washington with Stennis as an assistant before resigning to return to his seat in the Mississippi Senate.

Anticipating President Truman's call for a civil rights bill, Wright delivered an aggressive inaugural speech in January 1948 questioning the South's continued support for the Democratic Party. Eastland, Rankin, and Williams issued strong support for the governor's position. Congressmen Whitten, Winstead, and Whittington expressed sympathy and a general agreement. Only Stennis refused to fall in line. Eastland brought Collins to Jackson for a conference with Wright, and they sent 300 copies of Collins's book to leaders across the South seeking to spark a regional revolt against the president. Wright tried to promote a southern conference at the meeting of the Southern Governors' Conference in February only to get the cold shoulder from his fellow governors. Undeterred Mississippians rallied to his crusade and backed a meeting of "true Jeffersonian Democrats" in Jackson. Speaker Sillers threw his considerable weight behind the movement. Most Mississippi newspapers, along with a host of state officials, backed the governor.

One hundred black leaders met in a Jackson church prior to the "Jeffersonian" conference in order to craft a position on demands for civil rights. Newspaper editor Greene made the key speech of the meeting, demanding the vote but denying anyone wanted intermarriage and expressing some understanding of continued social separation. But the attendees drafted a telegram to President Truman offering black Mississippians' full support for his civil rights legislation.

The "Jeffersonian" conference drew 4,000 participants, and Wright entered Jackson's city auditorium to deliver the keynote address with the building awash in Confederate flags. He accused Truman and the national Democrats of "treason" against the people and in essence asked Mississippians how far they wanted to go to preserve states' rights. Senator Stennis spoke too, urging moderation and conversations with national Democratic Party leaders. He joined Wright in condemning Truman's proposed civil rights legislation but called for cooperation with the national Democratic Party to protect states' rights. Sillers chaired a committee at the conference, which ignored Stennis's moderate ideas, and offered resolutions backing Wright's call for a third party. A few Mississippi newspapers editorialized for Stennis's position, but the vast majority backed Governor Wright.

Gatherings and conferences continued, culminating with meetings scheduled for eighty-one counties on March 20, 1948. Newspapers announced the well-publicized events on their front pages, including the fact that Governor Wright would speak via radio and loudspeakers mounted around courthouses. Local elected officials and Democratic Party leaders spoke prior to the governor's address at 3:30 P.M., and high school bands played. In his radio speech, Wright laid out Truman's plan: a civil rights section in the Justice Department; antilynching, anti–poll tax, and antisegregation legislation; and the reestablishment of the Fair Employment Practices Committee (FEPC), which Wright told the assembled white population of the state amounted to an assault on southern traditions similar to the one made by carpetbaggers and scalawags during Reconstruction. The county assemblies passed resolutions backing Wright, and the state Democratic Party organized speakers to follow up. A women's organization supported the party's activities and the governor's personal appearances around the state. Eastland and the congressional delegation added their support via telegrams from the nation's capital. A spiritualist claimed that Bilbo sent his blessing from beyond the grave.

Wright and his allies called for a second Jackson meeting in May to include representatives from across the South. On May 9, as a prelude to that conference, Wright addressed Mississippi's black population by a statewide radio network. As a lead-in, Wright issued a press release to Mississippi blacks assuring them that all the white people wearing states' rights lapel buttons had not joined an antiblack organization, and he promised to dispel blacks' misconceptions about his campaign to protect segregation, assuring blacks that he recognized their citizenship. Wright proposed a remarkable event—to speak directly and honestly to his black constituents. On May 9, Wright told blacks that social inequality would be maintained and if any blacks had "deluded" themselves into believing that they would enter white schools or patronize white hotels or cafés, they should leave the state and find a new home. Greene predicted a mass exodus after the speech, but no public protests greeted Wright's remarks. A biracial group of ministers who met with Wright shortly after the speech got no encouragement from the governor for a suggested interracial commission. Wright made his position clear and did not want to discuss it any further.

The climax of Wright's crusade came in Philadelphia, Pennsylvania, when Mississippi and other southern delegations walked out of the 1948 presidential nomination convention to protest the civil rights planks in the Democratic Party platform. Wright and his allies had hoped for a dramatic exit, but the dense crowd made a mass walkout impossible. The Dixiecrats, as they became known, reconvened in Birmingham, Alabama. Former governor White led an Ole Miss group into the convention hall under a Confederate flag, which became the symbol of the Dixiecrats and segregationists across the South. Mississippi's congressional delegation, including Stennis, turned up. Strom Thurmond of South Carolina won the presidential nomination, defeating Wright, who had to settle for the vice presidential slot on the Dixiecrat ticket.

Governor Fielding Wright mobilized Mississippi to support the Dixiecrat revolt against the Democratic Party. Photograph courtesy of Ron Wade.

As Wright campaigned to preserve states' rights and segregation, Mississippi continued to function by making adjustments in order to preserve the essence of the old system in a changing world. Parchman provided a model of how the system survived and thrived. Governor Johnson unsettled the prison farm by appointing a south Mississippi superintendent, Lowery Love, who upset the Delta nabobs by refusing to fawn and by introducing reforms. Refusing to sanction graft, Love alienated the local "contractors" accustomed to bribes. He tried to clean up prostitution and gambling, which had enlivened life in the cages scattered about the farm, and as a result the shooters and gunmen neared revolt. Fred Jones, a member of the House of Representatives from Sunflower County, home of Parchman, and Oscar Wolfe Jr., a Delta senator who helped Sillers run the legislature, took the matter in hand, working with Governor Bailey to introduce reforms in 1944. Bailey looked for a Delta farmer to restore equilibrium to the state's main tool in managing any troublesome members of society, and he settled on Marvin Wiggins.

After thirty years of farming in the Delta, Wiggins knew how to manage men and a plantation. He had the temperament of a rattlesnake and the eye of a gunfighter. Surrounding himself with competent underlings and keeping the political sycophants out, Wiggins took down the plantation great house with its Victorian embellishments and replaced it with a ranch house where his sweet, caring wife oversaw the luckiest trustees who served the family. Wiggins sold all of the farm's cotton at the best market prices, but he gave away beef from the prize herd that he built. He looked away as prostitution and gambling returned to the cages, but he invited ministers to preach and established the first education programs, raising the reading level among the inmates. The new parole board released his best shooters and took the old incentive system out of Wiggins's hands. He invented new rewards such as a two-week Christmas parole and better jobs out of the cotton fields. Buying tractors and growing an abundance of food allowed Wiggins to feed prisoners better, giving them unlimited amounts of vegetables and fruit along with enlarged portions of meat. He shipped the surplus of canned food to other state facilities. Under his management, Parchman enjoyed its golden years.

Wiggins did not believe in the need for psychiatrists and other professionals, but he welcomed them along with the white guards hired to replace the diminishing number of trustee shooters. They enlarged his empire and provided needed employment as well as patronage. He maintained a personal dictatorship tempered with human mercy by maintaining spies in the cages so that he knew everything. He seemed to favor black inmates, believing he understood them. When a black shooter turned "rabbit" and tried to escape, Wiggins heard that he did it to reach his dying mother and had the man brought to his office. After checking and finding the story true, Wiggins ordered the man cleaned up, gave a staff member money out of his pocket to buy flowers, and told the staff member to drive the man home to sit with his mother until she died. On the other hand, Wiggins still used the famous leather strap, Black Annie, to impose discipline. He provided the model of a farmer and administrator maintaining the personal, patriarchal methods inherited from the plantation in the midst of professionalization and reform movements.

Faulkner, Mississippi's most famous chronicler of the state's tortured past, returned from Hollywood in 1945 as his family members came back from the war. Writing, editing, and rewriting *A Fable*—his comment on war—produced no income, all of his novels except *Sanctuary* had gone out of print, and he needed money. Growing fame abroad prompted publication of a collection of his earlier works in *The Portable Faulkner*, beginning his climb to financial security. Eyeing the economic and social changes around him, Faulkner decried the subdivisions, the cars, and women smoking in Oxford's supermarkets. He longed for a quieter time before car radios created a din on the square. Finally in 1948, in the midst of Wright's crusade, he decided to lay aside *A Fable* in order to comment on Mississippi's race relations in a short novel set in his mythical Jefferson. He chose to revive one of his old ideas—a detective story in which he first intended for a black descendent of a union between a planter and a slave to solve the mystery from the jail cell where he had been thrown for the murder. Instead, Faulkner decided to have Lucas Beauchamp, his noble black character, rely on a young white boy, who owed him a debt for saving his life, to symbolically unearth the body of the murdered man (and the state's past) to prove Beauchamp's innocence. Despite the fact that Faulkner had turned polemicist, he could not produce a clear analysis of the state's problem. His muddled message emerged as: the North should leave the South to solve its own problem, which Faulkner admitted the South did not seem capable of doing. Segregationists attacked him for suggesting change, while integrationists condemned him as deluded in his thinking.

Despite the fact that *Intruder in the Dust* was a bad novel, the timing proved right. It sold better than anything that he had ever written, and Hollywood picked it up. Early in 1949 the director arrived in Oxford to scout out locations. Many in town disliked the idea of a movie about a lynching being made in their midst, but business sense prevailed. The Chamber of Commerce and forty merchants published their approval in the *Eagle*. Locals solved the problem of housing the movie's black actors—there was no hotel for blacks—by recruiting Oxford's leading black citizens to take them into their homes. Faulkner got into the act by helping the director to find locations. When the director began casting locals for the film, interest and excitement heated up. Faulkner read the script and pronounced it near perfect. His family prevailed on Faulkner to take them to the set to watch the filming, and he took some of the cast sailing on Sardis Lake. When the family had the movie's cast out to Rowan Oak for a party, the Faulkners did not invite the black Puerto Rican playing Beauchamp because they could not have him without inviting the black family housing him, and they refused to breach the segregationist custom to entertain a local black family in their home.

The movie premiered at the Lyric in Oxford with spotlight and hype. The family prevailed on Faulkner to attend, and he bowed twice to thunderous applause. Both the townspeople and Faulkner liked the movie. The University of Mississippi faculty voted not to grant him an honorary degree, but in 1949 the Nobel committee in Stockholm awarded Faulkner its prize for literature. Yet he never came to grips with the revolution threatening his state. He condemned federal intervention in the economy speaking to the Delta Council and weighed in against the execution of Willie McGee, but like most Mississippians, Faulkner seemed bewildered by it all.

Eudora Welty defended Faulkner when some reviewers criticized *Intruder in the Dust*, but in 1948 she considered the Mississippi legislators a "collection of morons" and wrote a friend that she thought of burning the *Clarion Ledger* building every morning when she read the paper. When some members of the legislature proposed giving anyone who wanted to leave the state a free ticket, she expressed a willingness to be first in line. She made no analysis of the state's racial problems during the postwar years, restricting her stories to searching for the heart of human existence and avoiding Faulkner's slide into didacticism. She went sailing with Faulkner on Sardis Lake, but they never discussed writing. Welty traveled to San Francisco, New York, and Europe, where she violated Mississippi's restrictions against dining with black people. She returned to Mississippi and appreciated how her sense of place informed her writing without feeling the need to make public statements, which she had the sagacity to know Mississippians would not heed.

Lacking any encouragement even from the few white intellectuals in the state, black Mississippians continued to press cautiously for legal, economic, and political rights. Schools constituted one of the most glaring inequities in Mississippi. Black schools in inadequate structures held sessions two months shorter than white ones and paid their teachers less than half of what white teachers received. The state did not provide any transportation for black students and often gave them worn-out old textbooks salvaged from white schools' castoffs. At Alcorn College, conditions deteriorated to the point that some students began relieving themselves in the woods in order to avoid the institutions' restrooms. The white state agent for "Negro Education" expressed his disdain for blacks openly and attempted to discourage principals from buying dictionaries or encyclopedias for their students because the agent did not believe black students would use them.

In 1948 Gladys Noel Bates, a science teacher at Smith Robinson High School in Jackson, decided to file suit against the city school board on behalf of herself and her fellow black teachers, asking the court to equalize their salaries with those of white teachers. Unlike the majority of black teachers, Bates had graduated from college and had done graduate work out of state.

Her father worked as a railroad mail clerk, providing the family income outside of local white control, and he had long been a member of the NAACP, which agreed to provide legal representation. Bates's case illustrated the obstacles slowing black civil rights activism. The NAACP lawyers in New York needed a Mississippi attorney of record, and Bates asked S. D. Redmond to take on that role. One of the wealthiest men in the state with both law and medical degrees and known to be interested in improving the status of his people, Redmond agreed for what Bates considered an inflated fee. The Mississippi Teachers Association (MTA), the black teachers' organization, called Redmond's bluff by providing the money that he asked for. Redmond then refused Bates any assistance, citing some business deals that such a role would endanger. After unsuccessfully approaching several white attorneys, Bates found an unlicensed black "counsel" in Meridian who agreed to take her case. When she filed the suit, the Jackson public schools fired her and her husband, and then argued that as an ex-employee, she had no status to continue the proceedings. A principal at Lanier High School identified one of his teachers who was about to be fired to step in as the interim plaintiff, and the MTA paid his expenses also. Maneuvering kept the case tied up in courts until 1949, when a similar case in Georgia went against the black teachers there and gave the Mississippi federal judge an excuse to dismiss it.

Perhaps spurred by the suit and rumblings of discontent, Governor Wright addressed the annual meeting of the MTA at Lanier. He repeated the message delivered earlier by radio, which the thousand black teachers met with frowns and motionless postures. Unnerved by the obviously hostile atmosphere, Wright began to ramble. Noting that he had been accused of uttering the word "nigger" fifty-seven times in his radio address, the governor rejected the charge, insisting that he enunciated "Negro" perfectly each time. When Wright sat down, the president of the MTA, W. Milan Davis, who headed a private junior college in Okolona, rose to reply. He used the popular song "Open the Door Richard," which grew out of a vaudeville routine featuring an intoxicated man in rags moving a ladder across a stage and constantly knocking on a series of imaginary doors. The national civil rights movement picked up the phrase and used it on banners and in speeches. After each sentence demanding equal treatment for Mississippi blacks, Davis intoned, "Open the Door Richard." In conclusion, he told Wright that he would clean himself if the governor hated him for being dirty. He would educate himself if the governor hated him for being ignorant. But if the governor hated him for being black, he only could commend the governor to the God who made him. Not noted for his sweet temper, Wright undoubtedly experienced extreme embarrassment and discomfort before he could retreat across town to the governor's mansion.

Some white Mississippians wished to soften Wright's outspoken hostility to blacks. William F. Winter, who commanded a black unit at the end of the Second World War, and Frank Smith, the secret integrationist, served in the legislature that Welty called a bunch of morons. Despite Wright's inaugural address, they and other new members harbored hope for progress. The House of Representatives welcomed 78 new legislators to the body of 140. Many of the first-termers had recently returned from the war, and fifty-seven were under the age of forty. They tried attacking the state's blue laws as an impetus to reform and managed to get a workman's compensation act passed over the governor's objection—making Mississippi the last state to adopt such a law. But on the whole, the new representatives and senators kept their heads down. Smith reported his only act of defiance consisted of not wearing the ubiquitous states' rights lapel button sported by almost every member of the legislature.

A few Mississippians defied Wright and the states' righters to join Welty in supporting Truman in 1948. From his perch in Stennis's Washington office, Smith secretly prompted his old friend Philip Mullen of the *Eagle* and professor Jim Silver to organize a Mississippi slate of electors for Truman. Several law students joined the effort, for which they earned the enmity of their peers, and a few had to leave the state after graduation in order to practice. Mullen reported being lampooned at Ole Miss sporting events and generally made a laughingstock because of his involvement. The state's few moderates began to go underground, faced with overwhelming support for Wright and segregation. Eastland encouraged their decision to keep quiet by speaking of "mongrels" among them when he addressed the legislature to decry integration. The rhetoric tended to excesses unheard since the secession era. John Bell Williams accused the president of stabbing southerners in the back with a political dagger and seeking to drink "our blood" from the wound.

The president withheld patronage from Mississippi's congressmen because of the Dixiecrat revolt, but the congressmen retained their seniority and moved into leadership posts. Eastland chaired the Senate Judiciary Committee's subcommittee on civil rights. Colmer moved up to a leadership spot on the Ways and Means Committee in the House of Representatives, which controlled the flow of legislation to the House. In 1949 Wright hosted another Dixiecrat convention in Jackson, but Thurmond did not attend. Other southern states recognized Truman's victory as a signal to drop the Dixiecrat revolt, but Mississippi persisted with a third convention in 1950, making the state a bastion of states' rights.

Prodded by federal courts' trend toward integration decisions, in 1950 Governor Wright proposed and the legislature passed a large school equalization law in an effort to protect segregation, but it failed to be implemented because of provisions calling for local school districts to match state funding. Black Mississippians enjoyed a growing sense of empowerment even as they failed to get relief.

Representative Will Whittington created the only major Mississippi political contest in 1950 by choosing to retire. Frank Smith and another young veteran challenged the old guard by running against Oscar Wolfe Jr., Sillers's candidate. Though "Mr. Speaker" had no wish to leave the state for Washington, D.C., he desired a reliable ally to look after the planters' interests in the House of Representatives. He wanted Wolfe, a fellow planter and legislative partner, to have the seat, so Smith and the other young veteran had an uphill fight. Smith won the right to face Wolfe in the runoff primarily because he came from Greenwood, one of the Delta's few pockets of white population and thus voters. Smith lied about his racial views, backed segregation, and relied on the southern code not to discuss race issues if possible—as Stennis had. Still, the Delta contained few whites, and many of them remembered Smith's junior college days and the editorials he wrote as a young man questioning segregation. Sillers knew him to be unsafe on the race issue and pulled out all of the stops to defeat him. Sillers appeared on the stump for Wolfe to tell voters that segregation would be safer in his friend's hands. The night before the primary Sillers spoke via a Delta-wide radio network telling voters that Wolfe was the segregationist candidate. Associating Smith with Hodding Carter, Sillers alleged that Carter had made himself unfit to live in white society by addressing a group of black voters in Greenville the previous evening. Nevertheless, Smith won by around 2,000 votes, leading Carter to editorialize that Smith's victory made him, and by inference the Delta, part of "the American hope" rather than the "feudalism" represented by Sillers.

Smith's election provided a glimmer of hope to the 127 moderates in the state, but Smith knew that the decline in Mississippi's population meant that the state would lose a congressman after the 1950 census. His only hope of remaining in office was to convince Sillers not to redistrict him into a new district with a sitting opponent possessing a large white constituency. Smith provided what Sillers called the best "service" that he had ever gotten from anyone in Washington. Smith approved the execution of Willie McGee in his congressional newsletter and appealed to Sillers to keep his Delta district, which Sillers did. Assured of some security for a decade, Smith dropped his slavish adherence to pleasing Sillers after redistricting, but could not openly defy the segregationists.

In 1951 Wright continued to urge a third party approach, but former governor Hugh White replaced him in the governor's mansion. A strong supporter of the Dixiecrat revolt, White campaigned as the strongest advocate of states' rights and segregation as well as being the "greatest proponent of industrialization" in Mississippi history. As a business "progressive" in the Whitfield tradition, White worked hard to get equalization of the state's dual school system in order to protect segregation, asking the legislature to fund large improvements and reorganization of the antiquated, decrepit system. A legislative recess committee in 1953 recommended consolidating school districts—whites had 849 and blacks 1,239. Governor White called a special session of the legislature to address the committee's report, but the session failed to act. In the 1954 regular session, the legislature passed a bill to increase school funding, but knowing a U.S. Supreme Court decision was coming, delayed spending the bulk of the money until the decision was issued. White undertook a charm campaign with black Mississippians, speaking frequently at black educational institutions and conventions with a tone and message that were conciliatory compared to Wright's confrontational style.

Some blacks cooperated with him. John Dewy Boyd, president of the MTA, endorsed White's efforts to equalize the segregated schools, as did Harry Henry Humes, one of the leading black Baptist ministers in Mississippi. Editor Percy Greene favored concentrating on voting rights, leaving desegregation for a later time when blacks enjoyed more political clout, so black leadership remained divided on the question of demanding immediate desegregation.

In the early 1950s Theodore Roosevelt Mason Howard reigned as one of the most prominent black leaders in the state, and he seemed to lean toward the old Booker T. Washington model of earning economic independence first. Born in Kentucky to a poor family, Howard added Mason to his in name to honor the white doctor who sponsored his medical education in Seven Day Adventists' schools across the nation. After studying and working from Alabama to California, Howard landed in Mound Bayou in 1942 as the chief surgeon in a hospital built by the Knights and Daughters of Tabor, the state's leading black fraternal organization. Howard prospered, operated a large plantation, ran an insurance company, and acquired a restaurant with a beer garden, a construction company, and a zoo. He drove about the Delta in an air-conditioned Cadillac. When the Tabors tried to fire him, he established his own hospital across the street from them and challenged the black establishment by founding the Regional Council of Negro Leadership (RCNL).

The RCNL neglected the black ministers, usually included among the black elite, and attracted businessmen such as Amzie Moore, who returned from the war to open a gas station along with other businesses, and a pharmacist, Aaron Henry. In 1952 Howard hired Medgar Evers—fresh out of

Alcorn—and his wife, Myrlie, to work for his insurance company. While selling insurance, Evers also worked for the NAACP and joined Howard and others in a campaign to force gas stations to provide restrooms for black patrons. Many white station owners built only "white toilets," so the RCNL advised its members not to buy gas where they could not use the restroom. Their tactic worked, and new "black toilets" began to appear at stations. The RCNL leadership met with the commissioner of the Mississippi Highway Safety Patrol to complain about incidents when troopers abused black motorists and won a news release from the commissioner promising action to ensure against such behavior on the part of his officers. Howard imported a black congressman from Chicago to address the annual meeting of the RCNL in 1952, causing a media frenzy and raising expectations. Frustrated by the legislature's failure to supply adequate funding for segregated schools, Howard, Moore, and Evers met with Sillers in the summer of 1953 to discuss the state of black education. The Speaker kept his back turned on the other three men and refused to make eye contact with them while offering only vague promises of new building appropriations. The following November Howard issued his first public condemnation of "separate but equal" and soon began to call Boyd and Humes spineless Uncle Toms for supporting Governor White's education initiative. Greene stormed out of an RCNL leadership meeting, cursing Howard for his new stance in favor of integration.

In January 1954 the RCNL and the NAACP joined forces to support Evers's application to the law school at the University of Mississippi. While the university pondered its decision for almost a year, Evers continued selling policies for Magnolia Life Insurance. In the spring Howard threw the biggest annual event in the RNCL's history, with six high school bands and one college band following him and Thurgood Marshall, special counsel of the NAACP, as they waved from the back of a convertible making its way through Mound Bayou. The meeting concentrated on exposing Mississippi's restrictions on black voting as everyone awaited the Supreme Court's decision on integrating public schools. Howard and Marshall urged RNCL members to contribute money to a fund to be used to file local suits to implement the expected decision against "separate but equal." Marshall held a workshop to train attorneys on court procedures. NAACP chapters multiplied around Mississippi as black leaders anticipated challenging the segregation system.

In the two years leading up to the Supreme Court's decision in *Brown v. Board of Education*, white politicians had not united behind one course of action. Governor White abandoned Wright's third party strategy and led a delegation to the 1952 Democratic Party national convention in Chicago hoping to delete civil rights from the platform and to nominate a conservative southerner as the presidential candidate. In the end the Mississippi

John C. Stennis replaced Bilbo in the U.S. Senate and built a reputation as the conscience of that body, accepting integration in his old age and earning black support in his last election. From the Mississippi Official and Statistical Register, 1968–1972.

party stayed loyal to the national ticket headed by Adlai Stevenson with Alabama senator John Sparkman as his running mate. Sillers did not join the congressional delegation in supporting Stevenson, turning to Dwight Eisenhower instead. He created a group called Democrats for Eisenhower, earned control of federal patronage in the state as a reward when Eisenhower won, and initiated the migration of Mississippi segregationists toward the Republican Party. White pressed on with his plan to build a more equal segregated school system, while Sillers promoted the idea of abolishing the public school system in order to allow whites to build a private option for their children.

On May 17, 1954, the Supreme Court issued the *Brown* decision, declaring "separate but equal" illegal. Initially white Mississippians responded with a variety of voices. Eastland, who had been using his office to link the civil rights movement to Communism, declared that Mississippi would never obey what he called a political court and called for Mississippians to take any steps necessary to preserve segregation and "Americanism." Stennis asked his state not to panic, indicating there would be years to craft a solution to the problem. Moderate journalists agreed with him. A few ministers asked their church members to accept the court's authority. Governor White forged ahead with his plan to create better black schools and honestly hoped to persuade black Mississippians to voluntarily continue in a separate school system. In July White met with the black college presidents, Humes, and Greene, all of whom assured the governor of blacks' support. White followed up with a plan for a larger conference, inviting around ninety black leaders to Jackson. Among those he asked was Emmett J. Stringer, a young Columbus dentist who headed the NAACP. Stringer used his network to identify the other participants and called them to a meeting the night before the governor's conference. Humes and Howard

Robert "Tut" Patterson, Delta plantation manager and founder of the White Citizens Council as the defender of segregation. Courtesy of the Mississippi Department of Archives and History.

almost came to blows, but the integrationists won a commitment to present a united front to the governor. The next day in a state office building, the blacks confronted the governor and the Speaker, stating their united support for the Supreme Court's decision. Howard told the governor and Speaker that Mississippi blacks would not participate in any scheme to undermine the court's "just and humane decision." In desperation, Sillers turned to Humes, who opined that for too long black children had studied the earth through the floors of their schools and the stars through the roofs, and it was time for change. Shaken, White adjourned the conference and admitted to waiting reporters that he was stunned.

That same month Herman Moore, president of the Indianola Bank; Arthur Clark Jr., a lawyer; and Robert "Tut" Patterson, plantation manager, founded the White Citizens Council for the purpose of suppressing dissenting white voices and removing black integrationists from their community. They planned to use social and economic tools to protect segregation while eschewing Ku Klux Klan–type violence. Circuit Judge Thomas Brady spoke to the Greenwood chapter of the Sons of the American Revolution on the *Brown* decision and used Congressman John Bell William's terminology to describe the *Brown* "event" as Black Monday. Brady's message consisted of the argument that black people were biologically inferior to whites, that blacks had made no significant historical contributions to advancing civilization, and that integration led to amalgamation. He concluded that Americans had a patriotic duty to resist the *Brown* decision because it was a part of an international conspiracy to destroy the United States. Members of his Greenwood audience urged Brady to publish his talk as a book. In June 1955 he did as a ninety-two-page, "single-syllable" refutation of the *Brown* decision designed to appeal to confirmed racists. The Citizens Council adopted it as its text, sold it, and encouraged its duplication. One member of the Sons of the American Revolution, Byron De La Beckwith, sold it on street corners in Greenwood, and it appeared on countless restaurant counters near the cash registers across the South.

White Mississippians fought the desegregation of Mississippi's public schools with every weapon at their disposal. In December 1954 they voted two to one approving a constitutional amendment abolishing the state schools system if it integrated. Federal judges in the state consistently upheld clearly illegal efforts to thwart the Supreme Court's decision only to have their rulings overturned by appeals courts. Some blacks, benefiting from the state's effort to improve black schools, supported their existing schools. Significant integration of the public schools did not take place for sixteen years after the *Brown* decision and then only because of the efforts of dedicated black parents who prodded the federal government to implement the Supreme Court's decision.

In September 1954 the state replied to Evers's application for law school admission by summoning Evers to an interview with Attorney General J. P. Coleman. The attorney general seemed to urge Evers to accept Mississippi's support for an out-of-state education, but Evers insisted that he wanted to study in the state where he intended to practice. When Coleman asked Evers if he intended to live and eat on campus, Evers answered yes, but that he was clean and his brown skin color would not rub off. The university denied him admission, but the NAACP offered Evers employment as a full-time field secretary. He accepted because he wanted action. Evers admired Jomo Kenyatta and the Mau Mau fighting British imperialism in Kenya and named his son Kenyatta. He considered the possibility of taking up arms in rebellion against the oppression and poverty that he saw among the sharecroppers to whom he sold insurance policies in the Delta. Instead, he traveled the state enrolling black Mississippians for an organization dedicated to using the legal system to end segregation.

Citizens Councils spread quickly across the state, and any white refusing to join suffered ostracism. Any black who dared seek enforcement of the *Brown* decision experienced a complete economic meltdown. When the Yazoo City NAACP undertook to use the courts to require integration, the local Citizens Council bought ad space to list all fifty-three of the parents joining in the suit on the front page of the town's newspaper. Whites fired all of those plaintiffs who were working for them and boycotted any independent blacks such as plumbers or businessmen. As a result all fifty-three either removed their names from the suit or left town. Stunned blacks left the NAACP in large numbers while the Yazoo City Citizens Council grew from 16 members to 1,500. Similar trends followed across the state as the Eisenhower administration declined to intervene to enforce the Supreme Court's decision.

Blacks seeking to register to vote encountered the same sort of treatment, but sometimes more violence. The Belzoni Citizens Council forced Gus Counts, who owned a grocery store, to resign the presidency of the town's NAACP, and when his friend George W. Lee, a minister and printer, continued to urge blacks to vote, someone drove alongside his car and shot him to death. Lee had attended Howard's 1955 Mound Bayou rally just before his death, and Howard contacted Congressman Charles Diggs of Michigan, who had also taken part in the rally, for support. Diggs got the Federal Bureau of Investigation (FBI) to do a precursory investigation, but it produced no results. Another person unknown gunned down Counts, who survived but fled to Chicago to recover. In Brookhaven, an unknown assassin gunned down Lamar Smith, a sixty-three-year-old black veteran, among a Saturday crowd of bystanders on the courthouse lawn for urging blacks to vote in the Democratic primary. The sheriff admitted seeing a white man leaving the scene covered in blood, but no witness came forward to identify the killer, who walked free.

These horrific murders did not shock the nation or Mississippi into soul-searching, but the brutal murder of Emmett Till did. Moses Wright went to Chicago to preach the funeral of a departed congregant who had migrated to that city, and he returned to Money with three young men who wanted to visit relatives in Mississippi. Two stayed at Wright's house on Dark Fear Road, and one went to his family in Greenwood. Wright's son, Simeon, who was twelve, looked forward to Bobo's visit (he did not learn Till's first name until after his death) because, at fourteen, Till could describe life in the big city. Till looked different because he dressed in khaki trousers and penny loafers, appearing to the Wright boys as if he were always on his way to a party. He tried picking cotton with them, but only lasted one day before hanging up his sack. In the evenings, Till roamed the neighborhood with his cousins, impressing them with comedy routines that he had memorized from stars such as George Gobel and bragging about how, in Chicago, teenagers refused to be intimidated by bullies. One evening, Maurice, Simeon's older brother, drove his dad's 1946 Ford to a watermelon patch where they stole melons to eat on the bank of the Tallahatchie River. On Wednesday, August 24, 1955, Maurice drove the boys to Bryant's store in Money. As they milled around outside, Till, who always had pocket money, went in with one of the boys, who came out quickly, leaving Till alone in the grocery with Carolyn Bryant. Maurice sent Simeon inside as soon as he noticed because the boys knew that they had to protect the Chicago boy who did not understand the complex rules of segregation. Simeon's memory is that Till had no time or opportunity to commit any breach of racial etiquette, but after they exited the store, Bryant came through the door walking toward her car. Till then wolf-whistled at the attractive storekeeper. Frightened, the boys scrambled into the Ford and left town.

They kept Till's indiscretion a secret, but they soon heard from neighbors that the whistle story had spread, and the gossip held that the Bryants would exact revenge. On Saturday the boys ventured to Greenwood for movies and girl watching, arriving home after midnight. In the early hours of Sunday morning, three men called Wright onto his porch demanding the fat boy from Chicago. Wright saw Roy Bryant, his half-brother J. W. Milam, and a black man he could not identify. With a gun in one hand and a flashlight in the other, the two white men invaded Wright's home and ordered Till to dress. Wright's wife pleaded with the men not to take Till, but Wright told his son that they took him to their waiting vehicle, where a woman's voice identified him as the one. As they departed, Elizabeth Wright ran next door, seeking help from their white neighbors. They refused assistance, and she demanded that her husband get her out of the house. He took her twenty-five miles north to her brother's house, and she never set foot in her home again.

After dropping off his wife, Wright drove around looking for Till. After having no success, he got the other visiting teenager out of his house and to a relative in Duck Hill in order to catch a train back to Chicago. He notified the Leflore County sheriff of the abduction and then called to tell Till's mother the bad news. He sent his sons to stay with neighbors and slept that night in his church.

As the half-brothers later told the story, they only intended to whip Till, but he defied them. Milam asked Till if he considered himself equal to whites. He answered "yes." Milam asked if he "had" white women. Till replied "yes." Even as they beat him savagely, he refused to grovel, and so they decided to make an example of him. Eventually they shot him to death and dumped his body into the Tallahatchie tied to a gin fan. Three days later, a fisherman found Till's mutilated body. Wright's wife accompanied her nephew's body to Chicago and never returned. Neighbors urged Wright to flee, but he refused. The sheriff arrested Milam and Bryant.

Initially Mississippi newspapers demanded justice for Till's murder, calling the brothers white trash. Robert "Tut" Patterson, executive secretary of the Association of Citizens Councils, proclaimed regret for the murder and claimed that the councils had been founded to prevent just such violence by maintaining segregation. But Till's mother announced from Chicago that the entire state would pay for her son's death. She held an open casket visitation and funeral. The world's press and television news departments flooded their front pages and screens with the story, condemning Mississippi as a savage cesspool of violence and racial hatred. From Rome, Faulkner observed that if we murder children, we do not deserve to survive.

Then the state's newspapers shifted focus, playing up Carlyon Bryant's beauty and running photographs of Till making him appear older and more sinister. The *Greenwood Commonwealth* countered the negative publicity with a story of a white girl risking her life to save her black nurse from drowning in the Tallahatchie. Instead of referring to the murderers as white trash, papers began to run photographs of them in their dress military uniforms. From Greenwood, one of Congressman Smith's relatives wrote that she felt sick watching the community rally behind the despicable brothers.

As the brothers' trial approached in Sumner, seat of Tallahatchie County, the *Clarion Ledger* reported the funeral of Kid Townsend, a local black victim of a heart attack, whose widow received generous support from the white community. Whites attended the funeral in some numbers, occupying a separate seating area in the black church. Visiting newspaper and television reporters shocked by the small town ventured the opinion that Faulkner now seemed to them to be more a reporter than a writer of fiction.

Wright's testimony provided the most dramatic moment of the trial before a white judge and all-white jury. Asked to identify the murderer, he rose, pointed his finger, and said there he is. At least one of the gaggle of black and white reporters in the courtroom reported that Wright said "Thar he." Simeon, who was also in the courtroom, denied the account, noting his father's education and public speaking experience. The trial lasted longer than usual because Howard and Evers found black witnesses who received a hearing, but in the end the sheriff had to tell the jurors to make it good by not coming in too quickly with the inevitable not guilty verdict.

Fallout from the verdict reverberated for years. News reports had Wright fleeing Mississippi to avoid being murdered. The murderers sold their story to *Look*, which ran their confessions with photographs of the smiling men hugging their wives and enjoying large victory cigars after their acquittal. To counter the negative publicity, Senators Eastland and Stennis gained access to Till's father's military record and revealed that he had been executed for raping two Italian women and murdering a third. Mississippi papers used the story to justify young Till's murder and the killers' acquittal, poisoning the already volatile atmosphere.

Roy Bryant and his half-brother J. W. Milam celebrating their acquittal for the murder of Emmett Till. Photograph courtesy Corbis Images.

Wright did not flee the state after abandoning his vehicle at the train station, as some reported. He went to his house, gathered his sons, returned his new refrigerator to the store, and packed what he could transport on the train. He left his dog, as some reported, probably doubting it would like Chicago. When Tallahatchie County tried Milam and Bryant for kidnapping Till, Wright returned to testify against them, but to no avail. The NAACP sent him on a three-month speaking tour before he found a job as a janitor in a nightclub.

On Saturday, December 3, 1955, Milam went hunting and drinking with his friend Elmer Kimball. Afterward Milam loaned his Chevrolet to Kimball, who drove to Glendora where he pulled into a gas station. Clinton Melton, a black father of four, filled the tank. When Kimball came out of the station, he blew up, insisting that he only ordered $2 worth of gasoline. He threatened to come back with a gun and kill Melton. Later he returned with a shotgun and fired two rounds into Melton's head. Melton had no friends or near relatives in Chicago, the NAACP did not intervene, and the press did not cover Kimball's trial. The white Lions Club of Glendora did issue a letter condemning Melton's murder as an outrage not only against him but against Glendora, Mississippi, and the human family. The Lions regretted the damage done to the relationship between the races and expressed

Famed novelist Walker Percy, observing the state where his uncle William Alexander Percy raised him, from his more tranquil Louisiana home in the 1960s, pronounced Mississippi insane. Photograph © by John R. Kemp.

sympathy for Melton's widow and children. They confessed repentance and offered themselves as agents of God's will to create his justice and peace for "human society." Melton's widow died in a car accident rumored to have been caused by someone running her off the road to prevent her participation in Kimball's trial. Tried in the same courtroom as his friend Milam, Kimball went free too.

Many white Mississippians felt as the Glendora Lions did, but the state's leaders encouraged a siege mentality, and the Citizens Councils punished any sign of independent thought. Eastland had held subcommittee investigative hearings to establish Communist connections to moderate whites willing to consider cooperating with blacks seeking their civil and political rights. Eastland publicly urged whites to join the Citizens Councils to protect segregation, and Citizens Councils practiced thought control. In Holmes County, the Citizens Council ostracized Hazel Brannon Smith because she criticized the white male power structure. Although as an Alabaman she supported segregation, the council's actions eventually bred doubts in her mind, and the council organized a boycott of her paper to crush her when she hinted at dissent. Historian David Donald, teaching at Columbia University, tried to explain his native state, noting that Mississippians lived in a self-contained world, read only the state's newspapers edited by locals, studied at Mississippi colleges taught by Mississippians, and thus knew nothing of the world beyond their borders. Donald's friend at the University of Mississippi, Jim Silver, later called his account of Mississippi's integration crisis *The Closed Society.* From 1955 through the integration of the University of Mississippi in 1962, the state earned the reputation of being a world apart from the rest of America. From his home in Louisiana, William Alexander Percy's nephew, physician-novelist Walker Percy, analyzed Mississippians' misunderstanding over private and public spaces, diagnosed the state's society, and declared it insane.

Chapter Fourteen

THE CIVIL RIGHTS MOVEMENT AND WHITE DEFIANCE

In the 1950s and 1960s Mississippi music rocked the planet as the world watched Mississippians engage in bloody, violent battles over black equality. Sharecropping disappeared as chemicals and machines industrialized agriculture, forcing laborers and small farmers off the land. Towns and rural neighborhoods shriveled and died as general stores closed, automobiles multiplied, and television antennas graced homes sometimes even before the tenants moved their toilet indoors. By 1960, 15.7 percent of the white population air-conditioned their homes, while only 1.5 percent of blacks enjoyed the blessing of a refuge from heat and humidity. African Americans continued to flee the state with the encouragement of the planters who no longer needed their services. The most vulnerable children paid a terrible price for the transition during this period of "leave or starve." In 1946 Mississippi had lowered black infant mortality to 40.8 per 1,000 live births, but by 1965 the number increased to 55.1, making Mississippi the only state in the nation to experience such a rise during the boom years of postwar economic growth.

Bulldozed fields and dredged canals exterminated alligators. DDT eliminated eagles and a variety of other animals, but deer and turkey revived with game management, hunting laws, and the growth of commercial pine forests. The physical alteration of the landscape and the gradual whitening of the state's population coincided with spiritual anguish among its people. While many whites continued to profess belief in the curse of Ham—that God made "colored people" inferior—most whites may have doubted that segregation enjoyed divine sanction. Many grieved deeply as they watched white Mississippians beat children trying to integrate a school or whites screaming obscenities at African Americans seeking to register to vote. Mississippi's Methodist women endorsed a progressive plan for race relations twice in the 1950s and upgraded it in the mid-1960s despite crosses burned on their lawns and abusive telephone calls. Just as the fire-eaters forced Mississippians into the Civil War, 100 years later the segregationist Citizens

Arthur Crudup worked as a farmhand and lumberman, bootlegged moonshine, did migrant labor, and sang in juke joints. He made some records but never made the big time. Elvis Presley sang Crudup's "That's All Right."

Councils and the politicians who established the Sovereignty Commission coerced white Mississippians into a racist conformity that encouraged the worst elements of society to commit what today would be labeled crimes against humanity.

Despite the upheaval, or perhaps because of it, Mississippians revolutionized the world's music by creating a hybrid of blues, gospel, and country called rock 'n' roll. Jimmie Rodgers pointed the way in the 1920s, and Muddy Waters and a host of other bluesmen spread their sound across the country as they fled Mississippi. Memphis proved to be the epicenter for rock 'n' roll after World War II as rural Mississippians and other southerners escaped or were pushed off declining small cotton farms to a city where both races mingled and made music. Arthur Crudup from Forest earned the title of father of rock 'n' roll because Elvis Presley used Crudup's songs to make his breakthrough to fame. Crudup worked as a farmhand and lumberman, bootlegged moonshine, did migrant labor, and sang in juke joints. Whites defied segregation custom to hear him sing in black bars, and Crudup landed a recording contract in Chicago when an RCA representative found him living on the streets in 1941. He had hit records, but lacking an education, he fell victim to cheats and never received the royalties due him. In 1954 a poor white migrant from Tupelo, Elvis Presley, sang Crudup's "That's All Right" in Sam Phillips's Memphis recording studio clowning with friends. Phillips heard him and got him to record it, then persuaded a friend from a black-run radio station, WDIA, to play it, creating an immediate sensation. The flip side of Elvis's first hit was Bill Monroe's "Blue Moon of Kentucky,"

The Red Tops, headquartered in Vicksburg where the black band members all had day jobs, won the hearts of white fans with a mix of blues, jazz, and pop while wearing red jackets and colonel ties. Courtesy of Archives and Special Collections, J. D. Williams Library, University of Mississippi.

illustrating the merger of black and white music. Listeners could not discern Elvis's race on the radio, and to most it did not matter.

Music transcended all racial, class, and ideological boundaries. The Red Tops earned the reputation of being the Mississippi Delta's favorite band of the period. Headquartered in Vicksburg where the black players all had day jobs, the ten Red Tops wore matching red jackets and colonel ties; played a mix of blues, jazz, and pop; and used disciplined business practices, booking dates a year in advance. Their 1958 record "Suwanee River Rock" used horns to produce a big band, soft-rock sound, and Rufus McKay, the lead singer, always included a rendition of "Danny Boy," which stopped dancers and brought them to the edge of the stage to pause in admiration. On request, the Red Tops would play "Dixie." Working both black and white venues, the band created a devoted fan base of young whites who traveled across the Delta wearing the band's uniform (red jackets and colonel ties) each weekend to hear their favorite band.

Such behavior worried segregationists. Robert "Tut" Patterson, founder of the Citizens Council, attended a performance of Louis Armstrong's band

Elvis Presley absorbed Mississippi music in Tupelo and then moved to Memphis, Tennessee, where he recorded black musicians' numbers, which gave birth to rock 'n' roll. Courtesy of the Library of Congress.

at Ole Miss in 1955 and wrote to a friend complaining about the interracial makeup of the group and Armstrong hugging white members of the band as he called them by their first names, but the coeds screaming for the black musicians upset Patterson the most. He enjoyed the music, but worried about white women responding so emotionally to black men. Playing a high school fraternity party in Meridian, Chuck Berry had a close encounter when, according to his memory, a young white woman came to the stage and kissed him. Her date called out to his friends that Berry had "asked her for a date," which sent Berry running for the exit. The Meridian police and a sympathetic fraternity member got Berry to jail for his safety, where the jailer relieved him of several hundred dollars as a "fine" before releasing him the next day. Black men sometimes felt jealous of their women too. In 1956 Elvis attended a black music festival sponsored by WDIA featuring artists such as B. B. King, Ray Charles, and the Five Blind Boys, and as he listened in the wings, Elvis got pushed on stage. The black teenage girls exploded in a crescendo of screams and rushed the stage, requiring several policemen to restrain them. A black disc jockey observing the teenagers' behavior groused that they showed no such affection for King while going wild for a "Memphis white boy." Muddy Waters returned to Mississippi to play at an Ole Miss dance in 1960, and he was amazed to see the coeds twisting so furiously in their short skirts that he

Father Nathaniel (Robert Machesky) came to Greenwood as a missionary to serve the black population and after the invading civil rights workers left, organized the local religious leaders to demand equality. Here he is shown with the first communion class of 1955. Courtesy of St. Francis of Assisi Parish.

saw their panties. The university staff panicked, turned out the lights, and sent Waters's band outside to wait for their pay in the rain.

Sandra Scarborough, one of those dancing coeds, grew up in Meadville and traveled to Natchez, where her boyfriend took her to the Black Cat to hear black bands on Saturday nights. Then she remembered going to her Baptist church on Sundays, being taught Jesus loves the little children—"red, yellow, black, and white"—and feeling that he did. She recalled her fellow students groaning when they entered a dance venue on campus and saw a white band. The power of music seemed to be tearing away at the walls of segregation, but the segregationists moved to stop the trend. A Red Tops fan looked forward to enjoying his favorite band during his senior year (1958/1959) at Delta State only to learn that the Tops would not be allowed on campus that year because their presence violated "some rule" of segregation.

As music challenged segregation, so did a few religious efforts tolerated by white Mississippians. For example, Father Nathaniel, born Robert

Machesky in Detroit, came to Greenwood as a Franciscan missionary in 1950, remodeled an old nightclub on twelve acres at the edge of town, and turned it into a school for black youngsters as a way to attract their parents to his church. He supped, played golf, and visited with the white elite of the town as well, and in the process attracted a widow, Kate Foote Jordon, to convert from the Episcopal Church to Catholicism. A member of a prominent Greenville family, "Miss Kate" recruited other pious women and founded Pax Christi, which she called a secular institute, whose members lived like nuns, wore light blue uniforms, took annual vows of poverty and chastity, and swore to serve the poor.

Working for poor blacks, Miss Kate opened the St. Francis Information Center, where she and the women provided a clinic, a used-clothing store, Girl and Boy Scout troops, music lessons, after-school tutoring, and evening classes for adults. Father Nathaniel organized a cooperative and a credit union, which whites in Greenwood accepted even as they joined the Citizens Council and provided that organization its national headquarters. Merchants continued to donate to the Catholics because Miss Kate and Father Nathaniel stayed clear of politics and only quietly challenged segregation by their service to the black community.

The Catholic missionaries shared Greenwood not only with the Citizens Council but also with R. C. Colvin, a Carroll County native who flew for the Royal Air Force during World War II and who started a crop-dusting service in 1945. Colvin did not worry about the toxic effects of the chemicals that he sprayed on Delta fields, sharing, with most of the public, the opinion that the government would not allow dangerous products to be sold. He noticed no illness himself, nor did he observe it among the workers who loaded his planes or the flagmen who marked his passes over the fields that he sprayed. He knew that before the war, crop dusters had used a mixture of nicotine and calcium arsenic, which killed as many mules and cattle as bugs, but DDT and other synthetic insecticides seemed safe to him.

By the 1950s Mississippians, especially in the Delta, lived in a toxic soup of chemicals used to kill weeds and bugs in the state's fields. Agribusiness, the federal Agriculture Research Service, and the U.S. Department of Agriculture encouraged Colvin and the public to believe in the safety of pesticides by combining to cover up the dangers of the chemicals and the studies revealing residues found in milk, beef, and baby food. Mississippians used DDT liberally, even spraying it in homes to kill insects.

By the mid-1950s many began to notice poisoning incidents. Dr. Mary Elizabeth Hogan, a Starkville native who practiced medicine in Glen Allan, observed that her mostly poor black patients' visits to her office increased from 25 or 30 per day to 125 each day when planters started spraying parathion. Poison mists hung over Lake Washington and the entire countryside in the evenings. Her patients presented with high fevers, confusion, and coughing up blood; many lay on the ground around her office awaiting admittance because they were too weak to stand. She diagnosed chemical pneumonia and treated them with atropine, advising them to stay away from fields during spraying. A public health officer touring the Delta contradicted her opinion and declared Asian flu to be the culprit, but Hogan, whose clinic was surrounded by cotton fields, had parathion drifting through her window screens and fell victim herself. She had to abandon her clinic and the Delta to recover from the same symptoms that she diagnosed in her patients.

Charles Lawler's poisoning and the subsequent response to his lawsuit against the crop duster and planters responsible illustrated the methods used to protect agribusiness's use of chemicals. Lawler managed a cotton gin in Sunflower County repairing and constructing other gins during slack seasons. On August 16, 1956, he and a black helper were welding on a concrete slab next to the Marie gin when the renter of the adjacent field stopped to tell Lawler that a crop duster would spray later that day. Lawler, not wanting to be exposed to the poison, asked the planter to delay until he finished welding. The planter failed to pass along the request, and just before lunch, as Lawler hunched over his welding, a crop duster flew under a power line from his rear and dumped a mixture of malathion, endrin, and a solvent xylene directly on Lawler. His helper yelled a warning and retreated under a shed, but the poisons drenched Lawler, and his welding mask filled with the liquid. He fell ill immediately and went into a coma the next morning. In the hospital, Lawler learned from the planter that his insurance did not cover exposure to those chemicals and that Lawler could expect no financial help. Though he could no longer perform manual labor, Lawler continued to manage the gin for a year with the help of his wife. After inadequate treatment and bad advice from a lawyer about workmen's compensation, Lawler sought Hogan's help and found Pascol Townsend, a Drew lawyer who took his case seriously, launching a suit against the crop duster, the renting planter, and the landowner. The powerful Delta establishment recognized that a Lawler victory would open a floodgate of legal actions against agribusiness, so they engaged Forrest Cooper, a politically astute, aggressive attorney. B. F. Smith, head of the Delta Council, lined up the Mississippi Farm Bureau Federation and expert witnesses from the state and federal governments, as well as industry scientists, to support Cooper. At trial, Lawler's first doctor offered suspect testimony denying that he initially treated Lawler for chemical poisoning, and the jury found for the planters and crop duster. Townsend persuaded the Mississippi Supreme Court to overturn the verdict because medical records contradicted the doctor's version of events, but after years of litigation Lawler settled for $4,599, and spraying continued unabated.

Eventually even the planters admitted quietly that spraying chemicals degraded their environment. In 1963 Speaker Sillers complained to the head of the Mississippi state board of health that many observers thought agricultural poisons harmed people as much as they did insects. Sillers noted that riding through the countryside during spraying season affected his eyes, ears, and throat. Conceding the value of spraying to farmers, Sillers asked the administrator to be discreet in his investigation, but indicated finally that human and animal welfare had to be protected.

Despite his ability to make a moral choice on the environment, Sillers never did the same on the question of black equality, and neither did many of his fellow Mississippians. Following the *Brown* decision, the Southern Baptist Convention, the Methodist Council of Bishops, and the Southern Presbyterian General Assembly issued statements favoring desegregation. However, former governor White spoke for the majority of Mississippi church members when he threatened to find another place to worship if his Presbyterian church "observed" the Supreme Court's decision. The Sovereignty Commission enlisted ministers such as Belhaven College's president emeritus G. T. Gillespie to write pamphlets defending segregation. In *A Christian View of Segregation*, Gillespie revived James Smylie's curse of Ham. D. M. Nelson, president of Mississippi College, signed on to the Sovereignty Commission's speakers' bureau as well as writing tracts for the agency.

Millsaps College stood out as a proponent of furthering better race relations because faculty members there cooperated with Ernst Borinski, a Tougaloo College professor and refugee from Nazi Germany, to conduct interracial forums on racial issues for many years. Borinski said more than once that segregation violated Christian principles, but after a forum in 1958, the segregationists pressured Millsap's board of trustees, which released a statement endorsing segregation. Academic freedom stood no chance of survival in post-*Brown* Mississippi hysteria. Will Campbell, a native Mississippi Methodist who directed religious life at the University of Mississippi, tried to bring in an Episcopal priest to speak for "religious emphasis week," but when it became known that the priest had donated to the National Association for the Advancement of Colored People (NAACP), the administration forced Campbell to cancel the invitation. After Duncan Gray Jr., an Episcopal priest who was the son of the state's bishop, told a group in a Starkville church that he believed segregation to be "incompatible with" the Christian faith, Mississippi State University canceled his invitation to speak on campus.

Ernst Borinski, a Jewish refugee from Nazi Germany, taught at Tougaloo College and promoted interracial dialogue among Mississippi students and college faculty members. Courtesy of the Mississippi Department of Archives and History from the Tougaloo Collection.

Even in churches that were not vocal in their support of segregation, segregationists made their point of view heard. For example, Archibald Stinson Coody IV belonged to the First Christian Church of Jackson, where the minister asked his congregation to avoid racial prejudices and narrow provincial ideas dividing humanity. Coody taught the opposite philosophy in a Sunday school class named for him within the church. His teaching revolved around the idea that God created differently colored human beings as unequal—mentally, physically, and morally—that it was God's will for distinct races to be treated differently, and that God intended for people of European descent to rule the world. Equally prejudiced against Jews, Coody openly defended Adolph Hitler's war aims in his Sunday lessons. Convinced that southern whites confronted a Communist conspiracy allied with the U.S. Supreme Court, the president, the NAACP, the National Council of Churches, and the United Nations, Coody proudly admitted his membership in the Ku Klux Klan. In a letter to his son, Coody endorsed violence to make clear Mississippians' intention to resist the conspiracy.

Neither Coody's class members nor Mississippi's society at large dismissed him as a crank. Senator Bilbo ordered copies of Coody's pamphlet, entitled *The Race Question*, to distribute to friends. The first head of the Sovereignty Commission wrote Coody a supportive letter and ordered 500 copies of his publication for distribution in support of the state's segregationist policies. The president of Mississippi College, Congressman John Bell Williams, and Speaker Sillers also wrote admiringly to Coody, although his ideas harked back to antebellum ministers who supported slavery. Educated in the state's public schools and a pharmacy school in Atlanta, Coody read law on his own and made his way into politics supporting Vardaman and Bilbo. He worked for the Mississippi State Tax Commission for thirty-six years and became a respected member of the capital city's society.

Segregationist church members organized to combat the more liberal national, regional, and state leaders within their denominations. Presbyterians, for example, formed the Mississippi Presbyterian Laymen's Association, and Methodists joined the Mississippi Association of Methodist Ministers and Laymen (MAMML). Baptists had more direct control of their institutions and did not need additional organizations to contest with their governing bodies. The state attempted to assist the segregationists not only through the Sovereignty Commission but also through changes in the law. The Senate considered an act to require integrated churches to pay taxes. Though some denounced it as an attack on the Catholic Church, which at the time was the only church allowing integrated services, it passed the Senate unanimously, only to die in the House of Representatives. In 1960 MAMML and the Citizens Councils got the legislature to enact a law giving two-thirds of a church's membership the authority to remove church property from the control of a denomination. They meant this law to enable the state's segregationist Methodists to claim their church property, which legally belonged to the larger Methodist Church. Some legislators proposed abolishing the Methodist Church in Mississippi because of the national organization's stance favoring integration.

The Citizens Councils conducted a steady campaign questioning ministers' loyalty to segregation and accused ministers of Communist affiliations. Some local Citizens Council members solicited information through Congressman John Bell Williams, who had access to the House Un-American Activities Committee (HUAC) reports about ministers in their area. The hysterical atmosphere of fear and distrust neutralized the clergy, except for rare individuals such as Gray, who stated his opposition to segregation and remained in the state. Most ministers feared to even suggest moderation to their congregations and suffered expulsion if they did.

With the clergy rendered mute, secular intellectuals felt an obligation to fill the void. James W. Silver, historian at the University of Mississippi, spoke to civic groups and noted the parallels between the post-*Brown* activities of the Citizens Council and the fire-eaters 100 years earlier. He drew closer to Faulkner, and the two men cooperated to appeal for moderation. As the state's leading writer, Faulkner felt a responsibility to advise his fellow Mississippians to bridle their ugly racism. He published his award-winning but disappointing antiwar novel *A Fable* in 1954 and undertook a role as the spokesman for the nation, visiting foreign countries at the behest of the State Department. In the mid-1950s he wrote letters to the editor seeming to endorse integration, and he told a Japanese audience that the United States needed to practice democracy itself by ending discrimination. Yet when Silver persuaded Faulkner to read a paper at a meeting of the Southern Historical Association in Memphis, the novelist sounded a more moderate note, doubting that blacks wanted integration and emphasizing that the economic system supporting segregation needed to be addressed first. In 1956, reacting to an attempt to integrate the University of Alabama, Faulkner wrote "A Letter to the North," advising integrationists to go slow. Then while drinking heavily, Faulkner gave an interview to a reporter in which he said he wanted a "middle road," but that if it came to fighting, he would make the same decision Robert E. Lee had made. He would fight for Mississippi and shoot "Negroes" in the street. Later he wrote letters trying to hedge his remarks, saying no sober man would make such a statement.

Silver introduced Faulkner to P. D. East, a homegrown Mississippi integrationist who edited the *Petal Paper*, and the three men agreed to produce the *Southern Reposure* as a vehicle for Mississippi moderates, but because they lampooned racists such as Senator Eastland, they did so under the name Nathan Bedford Coolose and not their own. Faulkner ventured to write "A Letter to the Leaders of the Negro Race" advising them to adopt Gandhi's methods and attitudes. By 1957 Faulkner began to spend more time in Virginia where his daughter lived and where the university offered him employment. He ceased offering advice, and his few statements on race relations grew more conservative. He said that he liked Virginia because its people were snobbish and he liked snobs. As with his efforts to deal with war, his message on race grew muddled and provided no aid to Mississippians dealing with the upheaval of integration.

Mississippi's other leading intellectual, Welty, wished to leave Mississippi to escape the violence and ugly racism around her, but caring for an ill mother kept her in Jackson. She quietly made her position clear in 1958 after Millsaps issued its endorsement of segregation by going to Tougaloo to speak at Borinski's forum established to provide a model for integration. No doubt she knew that the Sovereignty Commission maintained a watch on whites who visited the black campus. She refused to speak to the press when they asked for comments, telling friends that she was a coward and that it would not help. At other times she feared for the treatment that her mother might receive in a nursing home if she gave public voice to her feelings. She did not believe that a writer was required to crusade, and when she did write two short stories addressing the violence of the times, they both provided understanding, not condemnation—even of a murderer.

Deprived of leadership from the state's spiritual leaders and intellectuals, Mississippians looked to newspapers and television for their news and ideas. Unfortunately, as a whole, Mississippi's newspapers proved to be the weakest in the nation in their coverage of the civil rights movement, according to the *Columbia Journalism Review*. The arch segregationist Hederman family owned the papers with the highest circulation in Jackson and Hattiesburg. Their headlines and locally written news stories dehumanized the "mixers," as they called integrationists, referring to them as human freaks and abnormal mammals. Readers who got past the headlines into the text of wire service reports got more balanced information because the editors did not rewrite wire reports.

Between 1954 and 1962 people in Jackson enjoyed access to a rival paper, the *State Times*, funded by businessmen disgusted with the monopolistic practices and advertising charges imposed by the Hedermans. Norman Bradley, a respected Mississippi native who edited a Chattanooga paper, returned home to found the *State Times*, but returned to Tennessee two years later, turning it over to J. Oliver Emmerich from McComb. Emmerich, a confirmed states' rights advocate who walked out of the Democratic convention in 1948 to protest the civil rights plank in the Democratic platform, gradually came to support better treatment of blacks. In his *Enterprise-Journal*, he carried news from the black community and used courtesy titles for blacks, explaining that not to do so denied blacks their dignity. His example, however, did not spread to most Mississippi papers.

The hard-charging Hodding Carter of Greenville proved to be the state's most famous newspaper maverick by advising moderation on race and writing for national publications to explain the South to the nation. He retired to Maine in May 1960 before the height of the civil rights movement and turned the newspaper over to his son, Hodding Carter III. Young Hodding hired well-educated reporters, some of whom dated the civil rights workers in Greenville and yet according to critics provided fair and balanced accounts of the movement to their subscribers. In Tupelo, George McLean did not support integration, but neither did he inflame emotions as too many did. Moderation and balanced coverage helped where it existed. Greenville's

Hazel Brannon Smith owned small newspapers in Mississippi and somewhat reluctantly came to support the opposition to segregation, winning the Pulitzer Prize for editorial writing in 1964. Courtesy of the Mississippi Press Association Records, Special Collections Department, Mitchell Memorial Library, Mississippi State University.

police chief during the civil rights era gave credit to Carter's *Delta Democrat Times* for the lack of violence in that community. A few other editors braved ostracism in their communities and opposed segregation. Hazel Brannon Smith in Lexington and Ira B. Harkey Jr. in Pascagoula won Pulitzer Prizes for their editorials opposing segregation. Harkey sold his paper the year that he won the prize, and it immediately slid back into the racist mode common in most of the state's papers. Harkey and Smith suffered gunshots at their offices, crosses burned on their lawns, and fires in their buildings. Carter carried a gun and gave his reporters permission to fight back when racists threatened them. One of his journalists became especially well known for beating supposedly tough racists in fistfights. Most communities did not have newspapers capable of overcoming the massive resistance mounted by the state, and on the whole the state's newspapers fed the flames of emotional resistance to integration.

Newspapers played a significant role, both positive and negative, but television shaped Mississippians' minds with programming originating in New York, well beyond the Hedermans' control, although the Hedermans did own one of the Jackson stations. The other television station in the capital belonged to the Lamar Life Insurance Company, which hired Fred L. Beard, an outspoken member of the Citizens Council, as general manager. He aired the Citizens Council's *Forum* as a public affairs program and disrupted his station's signal when a black person appeared on screen. Black Mississippians liked the novelty of seeing black professional people and entertainers on screen. When one appeared, shouts brought an entire household to the set, but black viewers recognized that poor reception often followed a black person's appearance as the segregationist technicians disrupted the signal. In some instances stations simply blocked transmission entirely and broadcast a "network trouble" sign. Black Mississippians relied on network news shows as their main source of information, but those too got censored. Sometimes local television cameramen shot footage of protest events and shipped the film to New York, only to have it blacked out in Jackson. Inconsistency proved the norm. The Jackson stations refused to carry Nat King Cole's show, but Meridian and Hattiesburg stations did. When the stars of *Bonanza* cancelled an appearance in Jackson because their audience would have been segregated, the mayor called for a boycott of the highest-rated program in the nation. Although the press, along with a host of prominent citizens, supported him, the NBC affiliate continued to air the show and local advertisers still bought ads. Preachers railed against *Bonanza* and the Citizens Council fumed, but Mississippians could not be persuaded to abandon their Sunday night horse opera. Despite the clumsy efforts by segregationists to censor news and integrated programming, Mississippians and the rest of America watched the battle for civil rights on television and formed their opinions based on the images provided by the news organizations of the national networks.

Until 1960 Governor J. P. Coleman held Mississippi's worst racist elements in check and kept Mississippi off the nation's television screens by using the legal system and personal intervention to prevent integration. Descended from substantial slaveholders but growing up in a family of modest means, Coleman continued a family tradition of being polite racists and maintained a strong bent for law and order. As attorney general, he opposed clemency for Willie McGee but fought the states' rights forces of Sillers, Wright, and Eastland. He rode in an automobile to the 1952 Democratic presidential convention with Stennis and headed the Mississippi party's successful effort to be seated after party members walked out of the last convention. On the other hand, he sold out William Winter when Winter challenged Sillers for the speakership on behalf of the moderates in the legislature. In the 1955 primary election for governor, Coleman left the Citizens

Council support to Paul Johnson Jr. and staked his claim to office on an appeal for law and order, choosing to make gamblers and bootleggers his opponents in order to appeal to the public. In the runoff between the two men, Coleman convinced the electorate that he could defend segregation and prevent school integration in the courts to win the election. When the legislature passed a resolution claiming interposition (the right of a state to declare federal actions unconstitutional) as the legal remedy, Coleman called it poppycock and enlisted Professor Silver's assistance to marshal historical precedents to prove it. He signed the law creating the Mississippi Sovereignty Commission but defeated the Citizens Council's effort to send a states' rights delegation to the 1956 Democratic Party national convention. He supported the party's nominee, Adlai Stevenson, and the next year he hosted John F. Kennedy at the governor's mansion when the aspiring presidential candidate visited Jackson to speak to the Young Democrats of Mississippi. Unfortunately for Coleman, the Little Rock, Arkansas, integration crisis occurred during the visit, and Kennedy, while in Jackson, had to endorse school integration. That same year Coleman had to decide to either kill the construction of a veterans' hospital or accept an integrated facility. Defying the legislature and the Citizens Council, Coleman signed a deed granting the land to the Veterans Administration for an integrated institution. Trying to balance his record, Coleman signed a 1958 law to close the state's public schools if the federal courts made continued segregation impossible. He also oversaw the rejection of Clennon King Jr.'s attempt to integrate the University of Mississippi.

King, a native of Georgia, preached in Mississippi's African Methodist Episcopal churches and taught history at Alcorn College, where he caused students to boycott his classes by criticizing the NAACP and questioning integration as the best course for African Americans. After being fired by Alcorn, the erratic King applied to the University of Mississippi for admission as a doctoral candidate in history—a degree that the university did not offer at the time. White supporters during his episode at Alcorn probably convinced King, who held unconventional, unrealistic views, that he would be allowed to attend the university. He explained to Ole Miss alumni in Harrison County, whose endorsement he needed for a successful application, that he have would preferred a black school, but that he needed to attend the University of Mississippi, and knowing southerners to be the "Negro's best friend," he expected them to understand.

Coleman watched King's movements closely, conferring with E. R. Jobe, the administrator of the board of trustees of the Mississippi Institutions of Higher Learning (IHL), at length after Jobe's meeting with King. The governor gathered police reports from Georgia and had the Sovereignty

Theodore Roosevelt Mason Howard, Mound Bayou physician and businessman who promoted equal rights and trained movement leader Medgar Evers. Courtesy of Special Collections, University of Memphis Libraries.

Commission investigate. When King took a bus to Oxford, Coleman had a plainclothes state trooper ride along and an unmarked car tail the bus. The governor stationed himself in Batesville twenty miles from campus, but placed fifty uniformed and plainclothes highway patrolmen around the lyceum and at the entrances to campus. Detailed plans involving the state's leadership and school officials included where King could use "colored restrooms" provided for menial black staff members.

University personnel took King to a meeting room and examined his application, which contained alumni endorsements apparently forged by King. When the Ole Miss representatives informed King that his application was not acceptable for a number of reasons, he refused to leave the room. After considerable delay, Coleman ordered patrolmen to remove King, who panicked, screamed, and resisted. Taken to Jackson patrol headquarters, the governor had him committed to Whitfield for psychological testing. Twelve days later the state released King and told the court that it found no evidence of mental disorder. King returned to his Gulfport church and got involved in attempts to integrate the city's public schools before leaving Mississippi a few months later to wander the world continuing his bizarre behavior.

Despite his erratic behavior, King frightened state officials, who took his threat to segregation seriously and mobilized many of the state's resources

Clyde Kennard, a veteran, returned to south Mississippi to care for his mother on the farm that he had purchased for her and tried to enter the segregated state teacher's college in Hattiesburg, leading to his incarceration at Parchman. Courtesy of the McCain Library and Archives, University of Southern Mississippi.

to control him. Since the *Brown* decision, not one school or other facility had been desegregated. School boards ignored their black parents' petitions to integrate schools. Local newspapers published the parents' names, and whites applied economic pressure by firing the petitioners, calling in their loans, and canceling work for independent black contractors. Mound Bayou's T. R. M. Howard left for Chicago saying he could do more there than from a weedy grave in Mississippi. The number of blacks registered to vote plunged from 22,000 in 1954 to 12,000 in 1955 thanks to more onerous voting requirements passed by the legislature. As a result of the massive economic pressure and the threat of violence, most middle-class blacks refused to participate in civil rights activities and retreated into the Jim Crow system.

In the mid-1950s Medgar Evers continued to promote integration for the NAACP, but he raged against uncooperative middle-class blacks and expressed frustration about the lack of progress. The most serious threats to segregation came not from the "movement" but from a few strong-willed individuals such as Clyde Kennard. Born in Hattiesburg, Kennard left at age twelve to get a better education in Chicago. Joining the army, he served in Germany, where he taught a de-Nazification course, and in Korea. After leaving the military, he bought a twenty-acre farm for his mother and stepfather in Etonville, but he remained in Chicago and had almost finished a degree in political science at the University of Chicago when his stepfather died. Returning to run the farm for his mother, Kennard wanted to continue his education at Mississippi Southern College (later the University of Southern Mississippi) located fifteen minutes from his farm.

Although he belonged to the NAACP, Kennard did not act on the organization's behalf, but alone. He first applied in 1955, but had to concede his inability to provide references from five alumni. The new college president, William D. McCain, talked with Kennard and refused to supply him a list of college alumni in order to prevent Kennard from searching for five rare white individuals willing to recommend him. McCain reported to the Sovereignty Commission that Kennard's grades from Chicago were above average and that he met all other requirements for admission. Kennard continued to manage his chicken farm, but in December 1958 he wrote an eloquent letter to the *Hattiesburg American*, which for some reason the Hedermans' editor chose to publish. Kennard explained that he did not wish to mix socially with whites, preferring to remain in the black community, but he desired equal opportunities to better himself and for that reason announced that he planned to attend Mississippi Southern in January.

Coleman ordered the Sovereignty Commission to investigate Kennard, but the investigator found little negative to report. The college registrar formed a grudging respect for the intelligent, courteous, polite young man who played the organ in church and had an outstanding reputation in the community. Dudley Conner, an attorney who headed the local Citizens Council, offered to force Kennard out of the community or kill him, but neither the investigator nor the commission requested him to follow through with that threat. The commission arranged instead for a committee of black educators to call on Kennard. The committee included N. R. Burger, principal of a Hattiesburg high school; another principal of a school near Kennard's farm; and J. H. White, president of Mississippi Valley, who subtly tried to trade their cooperation for the establishment of a black junior college in Hattiesburg. Kennard turned down the black educators, so Coleman invited Kennard to meet with him in the governor's office in 1959 shortly after the New Year.

No record exists of what was said, but the rumor among NAACP members in Hattiesburg held that Coleman offered Kennard admission after the 1959 gubernatorial primary in return for Kennard's withdrawal. Coleman backed Carroll Gartin, more of a racial moderate, against Ross Barnett, who ran with the full backing of the Citizens Council. Both the governor and Kennard knew that Kennard's application would strengthen Barnett's campaign. Whatever was agreed, Kennard renewed his application immediately after Barnett's victory in the primary. By 1959 Kennard become more active in the local civil rights movement, asking the college registrar for additional application forms for others in his community, accompanying other blacks to the courthouse when they tried to register to vote, and protesting the closure of a school on whose board he served. His community had unusually large numbers of aggressive, light skinned, highly educated individuals rumored to be descended from an intermingling of whites (who refused to fight in the Civil War) and blacks. Kennard probably began to receive encouragement from the Etonville community.

In September 1959 he wrote a long letter to the college registrar demolishing the arguments used to defend segregation and cannily pointing out that a little integration would prevent federal intervention. Neither McCain nor another black educator's delegation dissuaded Kennard, but when he came to see McCain, two local constables arrested him for speeding to campus and planted liquor in his car. The Sovereignty Commission played no role in the frame-up, but reported it to Coleman, who ordered that Kennard be told only that his application was not in order, but the law-and-order governor took no action against the constables. Convicted by the local court, with the assistance of the NAACP Kennard appealed all the way to the U.S. Supreme Court and continued to write letters arguing his wider case with appeals to American history and the philosophies of John Locke, John Stuart Mill, and Jean-Jacques Rousseau.

While Kennard worked to enter college, Mississippi suffered its last old-fashioned lynching, and Coleman brought the Federal Bureau of Investigation (FBI) into the case in an effort to maintain law and order, which ensured Barnett's victory in the primary. On the evening of February 23, 1959, Jimmy and June Walters's car broke down on Highway 11 between Poplarville and Lumberton, and Jimmy walked for help, leaving June and their daughter in the car beside the highway. Mack Charles Parker drove past the car and saw Jimmy walking away. After dropping off a carload of friends, Parker returned and raped June. She identified her rapist in a lineup, but Jimmy refused the police's offer of a gun to kill Parker because he did not believe in violence and because he and June wanted the rapist tried for his crime. The circuit judge who heard the case, Sebe Dale, belonged to the Citizens Council and sat on the Sovereignty Commission after losing a race for lieutenant governor in 1955 to Gartin. Supported by recent precedents, Parker's lawyer argued that his client could not get a fair trial because voter registration excluded blacks, who therefore could not serve on Parker's jury. Dale, a virulent racist, threw out all the lawyers' motions as J. P. Walker watched from the back of the courtroom.

Walker, son of a former Pearl River County sheriff, served in the army before World War II, but after deserting and reenlisting under another name, the army discharged him as being psychologically unfit to serve. He joined the National Guard to fight in Korea and returned home to work as a deputy sheriff, although he regularly frequented bars and poolrooms and had a reputation for abusing prisoners. He lost a race for sheriff in 1955 and had announced his intention to run again in 1959. Meanwhile he made a living with an automobile body shop. Walker disliked Parker's demeanor in court, finding it cocky, and he saw an issue to ensure his election as sheriff, so he began to talk up the idea of lynching Parker.

Recruiting a Baptist preacher and part of his congregation from Gumpond, Walker's group sent representatives to ask Jimmy Walters to join them, but despite considerable pressure from his family and his band leader, Jimmy Swann, Walters declined. His brother did join the lynch party, which met on a farm in full moonlight to plan the lynching. Securing access to the keys from the jailer made entrance easy. Parker's resistance made removing him bloody, difficult, and noisy, but no one interfered with the lynch mob, who drove Parker to the Pearl River, killed him, wrapped his body in chains, and dumped him off the bridge into the river. Osborne Moody, sheriff of Pearl River County and a member of one of the area's most wealthy families, searched for the mob and Parker without finding them. He, Dale, and Governor Coleman worried that they might be criticized for not bringing in the National Guard as had been customary in the past. Coleman quickly called for the FBI to intervene in an effort to deflect as much press criticism as possible. J. Edgar Hoover responded with sixty agents, and the press descended on Poplarville in a frenzy. Governor Coleman announced that members of the mob would be charged with premeditated murder, which carried the death penalty. As locals tried to ignore the attention thrust upon them, not one of the seven ministers preaching in the town's white churches the day after the lynching mentioned the event.

Ten days after the lynching, Parker's body escaped its chains and surfaced, catching in a logjam where a highway patrolman and FBI agent spotted it. The ensuing press coverage painted a poor portrait of the state, leading Radio Moscow to feature the story to bolster its criticisms of the United States. After Parker's burial, the news surfaced that he had been dishonorably discharged from the military, and white veterans' groups began to demand that Parker's mother return the flag provided for the funeral. The FBI leaned heavily on locals to reveal the identities of the mob members, generating resentment, especially when two recently questioned individuals attempted suicide. Coleman demanded an investigation of the FBI and sent Attorney General Joseph Patterson to Poplarville to mediate between the FBI and local officials. In the maelstrom of press stories and the gubernatorial primary, Roy Wilkins appeared in Jackson to speak to 1,200 NAACP supporters on the fifth anniversary of the *Brown* decision. The Citizens Council obtained warrants to arrest Wilkins and state NAACP field secretary Evers for conspiring to overthrow segregation, an action outlawed by the legislature in 1954. Getting wind that Hinds County sheriff's deputies intended to enforce the warrants, Governor Coleman ordered the attorney general to withdraw the warrants, prompting Wilkins to praise Coleman for his devotion to law and order.

Deputy Chief J. L. Ray (right) arrests Roy Wilkins (left), executive secretary of the NAACP, and Medgar Evers, (center) NAACP field secretary, who are picketing outside of a Woolworth's department store in Jackson, Mississippi. Courtesy of Corbis Images.

Wilkins's endorsement did not help Coleman's efforts to assist Gartin's campaign, which had been transformed into a referendum on Coleman's moderate approach to opposing integration. Gartin had run against Eastland for the Senate, ensuring Eastland's support for Ross Barnett, who represented the Citizens Council. Barnett condemned Coleman and Gartin as weak-kneed and cited Coleman's bringing the FBI into Pearl River County as the most recent example of their "moderation"—an adjective assumed to be linked with Communism in Mississippi at the time. Votes for lesser candidates denied anyone a majority and forced Barnett and Gartin into a runoff, which Barnett won by a close margin.

Walker ran for sheriff and lost his runoff by a slight margin. The FBI delivered its report to Coleman in May, naming Walker as the leader of the lynch mob, but the governor sat on it until after the election. After the primary, Coleman sent it to the district attorney, who refused to present it to a grand jury. Walker ran for sheriff again in 1963 and won. The Veterans Administration forced Parker's mother to return the flag used to bury her son. An attempted federal charge for violation of Parker's civil rights failed, and June Walters, who recanted her identification of Parker, was harassed by the federal grand jurors to the point that she fled the room in tears.

Barnett told the FBI to stay out of Mississippi's business and demonstrated his handling of civil rights protestors by his treatment of Kennard, who continued his application for admission to Mississippi Southern. The Sovereignty Commission presented the new governor with a thick file on Kennard, and the veteran published another letter in the *Hattiesburg American,* which

Ross Barnett, elected governor as agent for the White Citizens Council, bungled the integration crisis at the University of Mississippi. Courtesy of the Mississippi Department of Archives and History from the Governors of Mississippi Collection.

increased Barnett's concern. Kennard paid off a judgment won against his farm by the Forrest County Cooperative, which supplied his chicken operation, and rumor had Kennard working for a black insurance company in Hattiesburg, which might limit the economic pressure whites could exert on him. All the white officials knew that if he went to the courts as he now threatened to do, it would be almost impossible to prevent his admission.

Although records do not exist to prove who orchestrated Kennard's arrest, it would be difficult to imagine that Barnett did not order the quick solution to end Kennard's threat to segregation. In September 1960 the Forrest County Cooperative charged that one of its employees stole five bags of chicken feed worth approximately $25. The employee alleged that Kennard planned the theft, which was a felony under Mississippi law. Colleges barred felons from admission, and an all-white jury took just ten minutes in November to convict Kennard, whom the judge sentenced to seven years of hard labor at Parchman. Kennard worked the prison's cotton fields created to break the will of black men, but incredibly kept his spirits up in part by teaching other prisoners on Sundays how to read. When colon cancer struck him, Kennard's doctors at the University of Mississippi Medical Center recommended that the governor grant Kennard early parole because they estimated he would live only five years at most. Barnett sent Kennard back to the fields, and when Kennard grew too weak to walk to the fields, guards carried him and made him work until he collapsed. The governor released Kennard only when it seemed that he would soon die, because Barnett wanted to avoid the negative publicity that would result if he died at Parchman. Kennard died in Chicago following surgery, but true to his Christian

Gilbert Mason, a Biloxi physician, challenged the segregation policy denying him the right to use the public beaches on the Gulf Coast, leading to bloody confrontations with segregationists. Courtesy of the McCain Library and Archives, University of Southern Mississippi.

beliefs told a friend before his death that there were a few good white people in the state, and he wanted them to be recognized.

Dr. Gilbert Mason, an Eagle Scout who grew up in Jackson and took advantage of the Mississippi program that paid for blacks' education out-of-state in order to maintain segregation, launched the state's first civil rights' protest in Biloxi, where he established a medical practice. Mason worked patiently within the segregation system between 1955, when he moved to Biloxi, and 1959, when he went for a swim at the whites-only beach. For example, he accepted a "scientific" membership in the Coast Counties Medical Society, which meant that he had to wait while the white doctors ate lunch before he could join them for the speaker who followed the meal. In 1959 he turned up at the end of the white doctors' meal only to be told that Rubel Phillips, the Republican candidate for governor, had insisted that he would not speak to an integrated audience. The executive committee asked him to leave, but four of the organization's white members protested until the argument grew so heated that all five left. Mason sensed a change coming and wanted be part of it.

Mason decided to challenge Mississippi's segregated beaches on his own after his local NAACP chapter refused to get involved with his project. He simply gathered some friends and a few of his Boy Scouts and went to the beach. A traffic accident near them attracted the police, who ordered his group off the beach, and when Mason argued with them, the police told him to follow them to city hall. When no one could explain to him why the beach was segregated, the police asked him to return the next day to discuss it with the mayor, which Mason did with no better results. He hired a white attorney to research the legal precedents of the restriction. Not satisfied with inaction, Mason appealed to his fellow church members on Easter morning, 1960, to join him on the beach again. Greensboro students in North Carolina had set an example that swept the nation by "sitting-in" at a Woolworth's lunch counter in February, and Mason hoped for similar support; however, none of his fellow church members came to the beach. Mason parked his car near the Biloxi lighthouse and entered the water alone. Ten minutes later a motorcycle police officer spotted him and ordered the "boy" out of the water. When the officer recognized Dr. Mason, they began to argue about his right to swim. Telling Mason that he was under arrest, the officer ordered him to follow in his car to the station, where Mason posted bond. A small group of blacks on Gulfport's beach the same day were not arrested, but hundreds of protestors turned out for Mason's trial, and he organized a well-publicized wade-in for the next Sunday. Approximately 125 waders assembled and marched to the beach, where a white mob armed with baseball bats, chains, pipes, and bricks attacked the protesters, beating them badly. Law enforcement officers watched the attack and then arrested the black protesters, allowing the white mob to escape. They let Dr. Mason sew up his friends before he turned himself in.

White violence against random blacks continued for a week, culminating in the murder of a young black man with a mental disability in front of Beauvoir. Mason received protection from Black Angry Men (BAM) friends, who watched his house and shot at whites in passing cars trying to attack him. Medgar Evers came to Mason's aid on the Monday after the wade-in, promising NAACP legal assistance. During this period, Mason remembered a white doctor suddenly asking him one evening to go out for a drink together. Mason reluctantly declined, knowing that no place existed where they could share a drink without having to fight other whites, which his colleague expressed his willingness to do. Mason appreciated the sentiment and encouragement engendered in the invitation and the offer to fight alongside him for their right to drink together. Kennard's attempt to attend Mississippi Southern and Mason's wade-in contradicted the segregationists' claim that outside agitators caused the racial strife in the state. Evers had been actively challenging segregation since the 1940s. Tougaloo College students sat in at the Jackson public library in March 1961, and Jackson College students protested the arrest of the "Tougaloo Nine" as Barnett reviewed 3,000 men marching past the governor's mansion to celebrate the secession of the state 100 years earlier. The trial of the "Tougaloo Nine" the next day attracted a crowd of black observers, and when the defendants arrived at the courthouse, the black crowd broke into applause. Twenty-five Jackson policemen using two German shepherds attacked the blacks, beating

Freedom Riders challenged the segregation of black patrons on interstate buses, were arrested in a deal with the federal government, and landed in Parchman, where their treatment forged the leadership for the civil rights movement. Courtesy of the Mississippi Department of Archives and History.

them with pistols and clubs. A flurry of protests followed at the Jackson zoo, swimming pools, and movie theaters across the state.

The Freedom Riders raised the stakes and introduced a more radical, nonnative element into the movement for civil rights. The Congress of Racial Equality (CORE), a group originating in Chicago in the early 1940s and basing its philosophy on Christian pacifism, the writings of Henry David Thoreau, and the tactics of Mahatma Gandhi, organized a freedom ride to force integration of interstate bus travel. Attacked in Alabama, beaten by white mobs, and having their bus burned, the CORE group abandoned bus travel and flew to New Orleans. The Student Nonviolent Coordinating Committee (SNCC) mounted another freedom ride out of Nashville to challenge Mississippi. SNCC grew out of student sit-ins in North Carolina and based its activities on grassroots democracy, spending extended periods of time in a community to empower local people and to fight against the existing social, economic, and political establishment. The Alabama incidents forced the Kennedy administration to protect the lives of the SNCC Freedom Riders. Robert Kennedy, the attorney general, did not trust Barnett and worked instead with Coleman, Eastland, and Jackson mayor Allen Thompson to broker a deal. First the Alabama National Guard and then the Mississippi National Guard ensured that no attackers got to the bus as it made its way to Jackson, but then Jackson police arrested the Freedom Riders with Kennedy's consent. Neither the federal nor state officials expected SNCC's next move, which was to refuse to pay their fines or to post bail, delivering themselves instead into the hands of Mississippi jailers. CORE and SNCC called for volunteers to fill Mississippi jails, and they came throughout the rest of the summer, numbering 328 by fall.

Barnett decided to send the riders to Parchman, but because of the glare of publicity, he ordered guards to break their spirit but not their bones. Isolated from the general population, the riders exercised, debated philosophy and religion, and sang freedom songs. For ignoring commands to cease singing, the guards took the riders' mattresses, and when they continued to sing the guards sprayed them with fire hoses, then chilled them with fans at night, and closed the unit's windows in the day to roast the singers. Released after thirty-nine days, the Parchman veterans became the shock troops of the Mississippi civil rights movement. Barnett seriously miscalculated because Parchman's system did not work without extreme physical violence, and by simply mistreating the riders, Barnett only increased their determination.

Robert (Bob) Moses became the most influential nonnative leader in the state. Raised in Harlem, Moses proved to be a brilliant student who studied philosophy at Harvard and taught math in a prestigious New York high school. Traveling the world, he came under the influence of Albert Camus's neo-existentialism. His belief that his actions defined him led Moses to join SNCC in an effort to end segregation by empowering Mississippi's black population. He came to the Delta recruiting for SNCC, met Amzie Moore, and took the older activist's advice to concentrate on voter registration as the best means of beginning to change the state. When Moses completed his teaching contract in New York and returned to work with Moore in the summer of 1961, Moore judged the Delta unready for such a campaign, so he sent Moses to McComb. Moses worked to establish credibility with locals, but whites attacked blacks when they attempted to register. On September 25, 1961, at a cotton gin near Liberty, E. H. Hurst, a member of the state legislature, shot to death one of the local vote-drive workers, Herbert Lee, and went free because witnesses feared the same fate if they testified. When McComb's high school students began to demonstrate and get arrested, their parents turned against SNCC. Although McComb provided Moses and his colleagues valuable lessons, it did nothing for the local population, who rejected SNCC's leadership.

In Jackson, Moses shaped the Council of Federated Organizations (COFO) into an effective coalition of civil rights groups working in the state,

Amzie Moore, black veteran with a secure federal job and independent businesses, provided guidance and advice to civil rights workers entering Mississippi. Courtesy of Estuary Press.

including CORE, SNCC, and the NAACP. Aaron Henry headed COFO, with Moses and David (Dave) Dennis of CORE running the organization. SNCC dominated COFO, but ceded the Fourth Congressional District to CORE as its territory. The majority of the black middle class continued to ignore the movement, fearing for their teaching jobs or their church's safety. Independent farmers such as Vernon Dahmer and Hartman Turnbow or businessmen such as Moore played key roles, but much of the support for the movement came from the fringes of society, such as the young prostitute Ida Mae Holland or the sharecropper Fannie Lou Hamer. Mississippi blacks taught the outside agitators the facts of Mississippi life—how to treat chiggers, for example. While the outsiders taught pacifism, the Mississippians armed themselves and stood guard at times to protect themselves and the naive agitators from white violence. Most of the outsiders were secular in their worldview and found the faith of their Mississippi allies troubling and inspiring at the same time.

Hamer said that she had never known that blacks could vote until the SNCC organizers told her. Holding a strong Christian faith, possessing a good singing voice, enjoying the ability to size up other people, and blessed with a strong storytelling talent, she developed into a star of the civil rights movement. Hamer's grandfather had been a slave; her parents sharecropped with twenty children to feed. She dropped out of school at age twelve to work in the fields and later married Perry "Pap" Hamer, also a sharecropper.

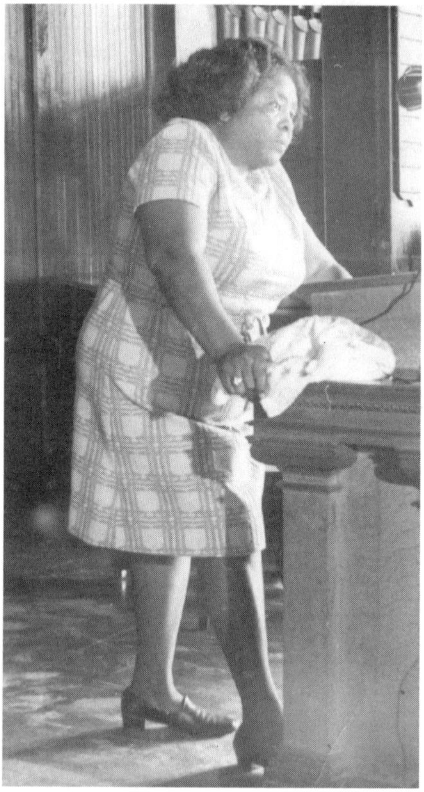

Fannie Lou Hamer with her husband, Perry. Hamer grew to be the mother figure to the Mississippi civil rights movement, and her husband quietly supported her activities. Courtesy of MS Department of Archives and History.

For eighteen years she and Pap worked on B. D. Marlowe's Sunflower County plantation, with Hamer becoming Marlow's timekeeper. A neighbor who provided housing for the SNCC organizers invited Hamer to accompany her to a "mass" meeting hosted in a nearby church on August 27, 1962. Pap agreed that Hamer could go if she picked enough cotton first. The freedom songs based on hymns and spirituals inspired Hamer, and when the minister asked for volunteers to accompany the SNCC workers to the courthouse in Indianola to register to vote, Hamer raised her hand high. She failed to interpret the Mississippi Constitution to the satisfaction of the white registrar, and as the group left town a policeman arrested them because their bus too closely resembled a school bus. By the time she returned home that evening, concerned whites had pressured Marlow into confronting her with the option of withdrawing from her registration effort or leaving the plantation. She left that night and stayed with friends, but night riders shot into the house. The threat of violence kept her and Pap moving for months, until Pap found a black landowner to rent them a house. Unemployable because of the white pressure, Hamer accepted Moses's invitation to travel to Fisk

University for workshops training organizers. Back in Ruleville, she studied the constitution and registered to vote. Soon she began teaching, canvassing for potential voters, and helping to sign people up for a federal program dispensing food, referred to as commodities. SNCC employed her as its oldest field secretary, and she received an irregular $10-per-week salary along with a few other grants. Pap supported her, and the young SNCC workers idolized her as an authentic voice of the South.

Hamer shared Sunflower County with Eastland, whose power increased with seniority and his increasing tenure as chair of the Senate Judiciary Committee. President Kennedy had worked with Eastland when he was in the Senate, and Robert Kennedy depended on him to handle the confirmation of judges. They turned to Eastland for the deal on the Freedom Riders, knowing that Eastland's word could be depended upon. Eastland also developed close ties with J. Edgar Hoover, who supplied him information, which he passed on to his old friend Earle Johnston at the Sovereignty Commission. Eastland concentrated on labeling the civil rights workers as Communists and convincing northerners that they misunderstood southern support for segregation. He used the recently integrated Washington, D.C., to prove his point, as whites fled to the suburbs and resegregated the schools in the nation's capital.

White Mississippians' opposition to integration continued to be massive, but political maneuvering exposed differences of opinion. Barnett brought members of the Citizens Council into his administration and used the Sovereignty Commission to funnel the state's money into the council, financing the production of *Forum*, for example. The Sovereignty Commission undertook a publicity campaign sending speakers around the country and making films touting the wonderful life made possible in the state by a segregated society. The commission and its allies such as the Paul Revere Ladies flooded the state with anti-Communist speakers. Jackson appearances brought out the state's leaders, from the governor to the Speaker.

In May 1962 Earle Johnston delivered a graduation address at Grenada high school condemning the NAACP and the Citizens Council, referring to council members as "extremists" prone to threats and intimidation causing friction and bitterness between the races. He called for practical segregation without hysteria, noting the need for cooperation between the races to deal with problems. Only William Winter, whom Coleman had appointed state tax collector as a peace offering after selling him out to Sillers, commented positively on Johnston's speech, calling it a realistic assessment of the situation. Johnston followed up with an editorial in his *Scott County Times* accusing the Citizens Council of seeking to turn the state's whites against one another. He accused Citizens Council leader William J. Simmons of favoring the swinging club and cracking whip and of sowing strife, confusion, and violence. He told a *Delta Democrat-Times* reporter that no one in the state felt comfortable about making a move without consulting the "rajah of race." Simmons called for Johnston's head. The governor delayed the Sovereignty Commission's scheduled June meeting, but the next month in a contentious session the commission members debated the dispute and arranged for Johnston's resignation by November; they also approved a secret resolution adopting his policy of cooperation with "Negroes" to maintain segregation. Speaker Sillers offered the resolution, indicating that the establishment believed the Citizens Council had overreached and that white violence had to be curbed to restore law and order. Patterson, the attorney general and a member of the Sovereignty Commission, opposed the transfer of state funds to the Citizens Council and expressed similar sentiments about law and order. The rank-and-file members of the legislature ignored the signal to moderate their rhetoric and increased funding for the Sovereignty Commission, accusing the brave four souls who voted against transferring state money to the Citizens Council of being integrationists.

In June 1962 the Fifth Circuit Court of Appeals in New Orleans ruled that the University of Mississippi had denied James Meredith admission to the University of Mississippi solely on the basis of his race, which all knew meant that the confrontation avoided since the 1954 *Brown* decision was imminent. Meredith came from an independent land-owning family in Attala County just outside Kosciusko. His father, called Cap—short for Captain—bought eighty-four acres while working in a cottonseed oil mill. Cap walked four miles to work six days a week, farmed his land without borrowing money, and built a fence alongside the one erected by his white neighbor in order to eliminate any possibility of a dispute. Even whites called Meredith's father Cap, a title usually used by blacks addressing white men. Meredith's family taught him pride and self-respect, isolating the family as much as possible from whites. Cap sent his children to school in town to ensure they got a better education. After walking to work all of those years, he sold timber to buy a truck, which they drove to school. In 1950 Meredith moved to Florida in order to finish high school, and after graduation he joined the air force because he lacked the money for college. During his eight years of service, he was stationed in Japan as well as stateside, studied Russian, bought land back home, and married. In 1960, with the money carefully saved over the years, he bought the family farm from his ailing father to enable him to retire.

As the date for his separation from the air force neared, Meredith suffered from separation anxiety severe enough to require psychological evaluation. He intended to return home and enter the civil rights movement as a soldier to defeat segregation. He recalled being inspired by a colonel from

James Meredith, a veteran, integrated the University of Mississippi, sparking a riot by segregationists and U.S. military intervention. Courtesy of the Southern Media Archive, Special Collections, University of Mississippi Libraries.

Mississippi who discussed the movement and the key role that men such as Meredith would play in it during a promotion review. Back in Mississippi, Meredith attended Jackson State College to work on his degree begun in the air force. Meredith decided to apply for admission to the University of Mississippi because he said it was the best school in the state and he wanted the best.

He contacted both Evers and the U.S. Department of Justice to announce his intention to apply. Evers connected him to the NAACP's Legal Defense Fund, and William L. Higgs, a white Ole Miss and Harvard graduate practicing law in Jackson, called Burke Marshall, an acquaintance who headed the Justice Department's Office on Civil Rights, in order to introduce the two men. Meredith knew the fates of King and Kennard, and he intended to survive and protect his family. As soon as his application became public, the Sovereignty Commission began investigating, and cars filled with white men began to appear in the parking lot of his apartment building in a black Jackson neighborhood. The court battles raged through Meridian, Biloxi, Jackson, New Orleans, and then Washington, D.C., to the inevitable conclusion.

U.S. Supreme Court Justice Hugo Black, a former Ku Klux Klan (KKK) member from Alabama, finally ordered Meredith's admission. Meredith telegraphed Barnett asking him to use both the delegated powers and the

"Christian influence" of his office for a peaceful transition. Barnett did not respond directly, but he still sought to prevent Meredith's admission. The son of a Civil War veteran from Leake County, Barnett worked his way through Mississippi College at a variety of jobs, including selling cookware. After graduating from Ole Miss, he became a highly successful damage suit lawyer in Jackson, where he entered politics in 1951 running the first time for governor. After winning the office in 1959, Barnett concentrated on industrial development, but his administration failed due to corruption and inept management. He appointed cronies to every state agency, and when he undertook a crusade against vice among the bars and gambling dens along the Gulf Coast, he angered some former supporters, one of whom threatened to kill him. In an effort to appease the disgruntled contributor, the governor sent a highway patrolman to return the donor's money. Installing a "gold-plated" bathroom in the governor's mansion grabbed headlines, and Ole Miss fans booed Barnett at a football game in 1960.

Surrounded by Citizens Council advisers, Barnett spoke to the state via television and radio declaring that no school would be integrated while he was governor and that he would go to jail rather than obey the courts. He issued a proclamation invoking interposition and in doing so made defiance of the law respectable. Nearly all state and local officeholders applauded his stance. The entire congressional delegation, except Frank E. Smith, communicated their support of Barnett's hopeless defiance of the federal government. Smith, a closet integrationist, had been redistricted into an unwinnable race because of his support for the Kennedy administration, and although he still occupied his seat in the House of Representative, Kennedy had named him to the Tennessee Valley Authority's governing board. Smith issued a statement declaring that Barnett was leading Mississippi down a blind alley despite passionate pleas from supporters back home to remain mum. Smith received a torrent of profane abuse and the labels of quisling and scalawag. Told that he would not be safe on the streets of Greenwood, Smith left Congress despised in his home state, and the Mississippi delegation declined to sponsor the traditional farewell in the House of Representatives.

The Kennedy administration did not offer support to the civil rights movement and had to be coerced to make any intervention such as the one with the Freedom Riders. The Kennedys preferred to rely on state and local governments, but Justice Black had involved the Justice Department when he handed down his order leading to the deployment of U.S. marshals, who made discreet trips to Ole Miss to scout out the terrain.

Ole Miss served as the finishing school for Mississippi's elite and the training institution for the lawyers who ran the state. The university did not have a high academic reputation but was famous for beautiful women and winning football teams. Between 1948 and 1961 an Ole Miss student gained the Miss America title eight times while the football teams won the conference championships perennially. In 1960 Ole Miss was national football champion. Colonel Reb ruled as the school's mascot, and football fans waved the Confederate battle flag by the thousands. A black man forcing his way into the institution violated the segregationists' sense of propriety as no other act could. Symbolically, integration of Ole Miss signaled the end of the segregated world. Faulkner did not live to see it. Back in Mississippi for some time at Rowan Oak, Faulkner died just weeks before Meredith arrived on campus.

Two days after his defiant speech, Barnett opened negotiations with Robert Kennedy to arrange Meredith's registration, discussing the details of when, where, and how. Barnett stalled, suggesting that arrangements would take a year. The IHL board divided over a course of action, but no one consulted the chancellor. The legislature, in session to redistrict the state, gave Barnett a hero's welcome, and his public popularity soared. Barnett expanded the legislature's special session purview to include the integration crisis, and the state filed legal charges against Meredith, hoping to convict him of a felony as it had done with Kennard. In Memphis, Meredith made an optimistic forecast that Mississippi would protect him and that he would probably not need marshals.

The federal courts cut through the state's legal maneuvers and ordered Barnett to admit Meredith. Barnett twice refused in person—once in Oxford and the second time in the Woolfolk State Office Building in Jackson. Barnett continued to talk secretly with Robert Kennedy, insisting that he preferred jail to admitting Meredith. Bowing to Kennedy's pressure, Barnett agreed to a time for Meredith to arrive at the university, but then pleaded again for Kennedy to keep him away. The conversations degenerated into ridiculous appeals from Barnett for marshals to draw their guns on him in order for him to salvage some pride. He missed the last confrontation at the university entrance because his plane could not fly, and Lieutenant Governor Paul Johnson engaged in a shoving match with marshals in his stead. The court found Barnett in contempt and levied a $10,000 per day fine, giving him until the next week to admit Meredith or go to jail. Meanwhile Robert Kennedy mobilized marshals and the army to enforce the court's order.

As the weekend approached, armed men representing the KKK and other right-wing groups planned to converge on Oxford, and Mississippians celebrated their victories in repulsing Meredith. Cars festooned with Confederate flags raced across the state, and radio stations played "Dixie" over and over again. Two crosses burned on the Ole Miss campus. On Friday night, CBS aired a half-hour special report on the crisis, concluding that Mississippi had pushed it to the ultimate limit. The court found Johnson in contempt for his shoving match, fined him, and gave him the same deadline as the governor.

The president talked to Barnett for the first time on Saturday, and in the midst of the discussion Barnett thanked him for his interest in the state's poultry industry. Barnett expressed doubt that he could maintain law and order; however, he sent a Jackson lawyer to Washington for direct negotiations but then backed out of every deal. Barnett proved too mercurial and would not keep his word. Oxford emptied on Saturday to attend the football game against Kentucky in Jackson, and Barnett left the negotiations to appear in the stadium. At halftime, in response to chants of "We want Ross," Barnett went to midfield with a fist held high and said: "My fellow Mississippians, I love Mississippi. I love her people, our customs. I love and respect our heritage." The stadium erupted into rebel yells, and the Confederate flags waved furiously as the Ole Miss band played "Dixie." The erratic, foolish governor doomed the state to disaster.

Most Mississippians had the good sense not to follow their governor into the abyss. Sunday morning orders reached Mississippi calling out the Mississippi National Guard to ensure Meredith's admission. Barnett's son and his son-in-law reported as instructed, as did Senator Stennis's son, eleven members of the legislature, and Charles Sullivan, former gubernatorial candidate.

Barnett did not return to Oxford to face Meredith again, knowing that he would have to step aside. He ordered the highway patrol to clear the campus of non-university persons and to secure the campus's entrances. He sent four "personal representatives," including the president pro tem of the Senate and one of Siller's lieutenants in the House of Representatives. No one bothered to tell the chancellor that Meredith was arriving Sunday night, and the chancellor began to plan for a Monday morning registration only to be interrupted by Assistant Attorney General Marshall with the news that Meredith would soon be on campus. The chancellor went to the campus radio station to tape an appeal to students to remain calm and behave.

As the chancellor had warned Marshall, the returning students, buoyed by Barnett's speech, gathered to challenge the marshals gathered around the Lyceum. The crowd became a mob when they heard Meredith was on campus. Highway patrolmen watched, sympathized with the rowdy students, and did nothing to aid the marshals. One of the governor's representatives ordered the highway patrol home, but a flurry of calls got Barnett to countermand the order. At 7:30 P.M. Barnett went on television to try and justify his surrender to the superior power of the United States while maintaining that his "principles" remained unchanged. He accused the federal government of destroying the Constitution and declared he would continue to fight in the courts. His pathetic effort accomplished nothing. Molotov cocktails and tear gas exploded across the Ole Miss campus. Students and segregationist sympathizers, including a right-wing retired general from Texas, fought the marshals using, at one point, a stolen bulldozer. The colonel of the local National Guard unit, Faulkner's nephew, led the first troops into the battle, suffering a broken arm from a brick thrown through the window of his jeep. It required reinforcements from regular army troops to secure the campus at 6:16 Monday morning.

Meredith went to bed at 10:00 P.M. in a dormitory guarded by marshals and slept through the night. As he moved around campus after the riot, students reacted courteously most of the time. Students who dined with him had their rooms vandalized and Meredith heard taunts and catcalls on occasion, but mostly students refused to see him and ignored his presence. Silver began to eat with Meredith in the cafeteria, and some faculty members' wives joined them, breaking Meredith's complete isolation on campus. Meredith encountered some academic difficulties in the fall semester, but he ended speculation that he might not return for the spring at a press conference in which he described Ole Miss students as "basically good people."

Someone blasted Meredith's parents' house with a shotgun, and in Greenwood, where SNCC ran a voter registration program, the county supervisors of Leflore County decided in November 1962 to drop their participation in the federal surplus food program as a means of starving local blacks who supported the voter drive. Sunflower County followed suit, restricting its commodity program as well. SNCC workers, such as Sam Block, who had been a student at Mississippi Valley, initiated a national appeal for food and clothing. The first responders, two black students from Michigan State University, had their truckload of supplies confiscated in Clarksdale, where they spent eleven days in jail for possession of narcotics—the aspirin and vitamins in their truck. Harry Belafonte and Dick Gregory mounted fundraisers, and tons of supplies poured in, allowing SNCC to enlist more people into their protests. By March 1963 SNCC transferred all forty of its Mississippi employees to Greenwood. Local black ministers began to finally open their churches to the protestors. Bloody confrontations between marchers and Greenwood police reached the point that the Kennedy administration filed for a federal injunction, but Robert Kennedy also negotiated with Gray Evans, an ex-aide to Frank E. Smith who lived in Greenwood. Evans told Kennedy that if the federal government suspended city, county, and state police powers, the locals could not be responsible for anything that happened. Senators Stennis and Eastland condemned SNCC and rejected federal intervention, indicating they would use their considerable power against the administration if it continued to interfere in Mississippi. Visions of sending the army to occupy the Delta brought the Kennedys up short, and they withdrew their request for an injunction. Moses and the other SNCC workers saw their dream of federal protection vanish. Despite their support for the black community, Father Nathaniel and Miss Kate refused to associate with SNCC workers, whose personal behavior they considered immoral. For all of the pain and suffering, SNCC registered only a handful of voters and accomplished little else in Greenwood.

Early in 1963 Dean W. Colvard, the first non-Mississippian to be appointed president of Mississippi State University (MSU), struck a blow against segregation by challenging the unwritten rule that Mississippi's sports teams did not play against opponents with black players. Jones Junior College was the last Mississippi school to dare to violate the ban when its football team played for the national championship in 1955. Colvard managed his violation of the rule masterfully. After MSU's basketball teams won the Southeastern Conference championships in 1961 and 1962, they did not get to play in the National Collegiate Athletic Association (NCAA) tournament because of the rule, and Colvard said nothing, but in 1963 when MSU won a third Southeastern Conference (SEC) championship, Colvard, whom the Sovereignty Commission watched closely, carefully contacted his school's supporters for their opinions. With fanfare, he accepted a petition for the team to play in the tournament from a leading businessman, Owen Cooper.

He did not tell Barnett his intentions, but he called Stennis, who gave his secret blessing and regretted that he could not go public because Barnett might run against him in the next Senate race. Colvard waited until fifteen minutes before MSU's last game of the season against Ole Miss to make his announcement. Called a carpetbagger and subjected to increased Sovereignty Commission attention, Colvard waited for the IHL or the governor to fire him. Barnett left the decision to the IHL, which supported Colvard by a vote of nine to two. The segregationists got a court injunction to stop the team's departure for the tournament, but Colvard drove to Birmingham and spent the night there to prevent being served with the papers. He believed that his actions made a significant impact on the state's leadership and encouraged moderates to take hope.

Newsworthy civil rights movement activities shifted to Jackson, where an NAACP group tried to mount a boycott against white merchants in opposition to the wishes of the national office and the other COFO organizations. At the end of May 1963, three Tougaloo students sat down at Jackson's Woolworth's lunch counter, and as a crowd gathered, John Salter, a white Tougaloo professor, joined them. Soon a mob of over 200 whites began to beat the protestors and to pour salt and pepper on their wounds while the police watched through the store windows. Reacting to the white mob's attack, protests by blacks multiplied, and Wilkins rushed to town with much of his NAACP staff. Wilkins replaced Salter with more conservative local black leaders and thwarted Evers's support for direct action. But black leaders had been complaining to the Federal Communications Commission (FCC) about Jackson's television stations unbalanced news coverage and denial of airtime to blacks. After Mayor Thompson went on air to reject the NAACP's request for a meeting with him, Evers asked for comparable airtime. Worried about losing their stations' license, the stations granted it to him. On May 20, 1963, Evers appeared for the only time in his life on local television. He bluntly announced that what the "Negro" wanted was the end of segregation and that change was coming whether the state liked it or not. His appearance on screen disturbed some of his friends, who realized that before the appearance on television, he had only been a name in a newspaper, but now he had become the face of the movement.

Evers withdrew from the fighting generated by the NAACP's moves to stifle the street protests. On June 11, as President Kennedy went on national television to announce he would introduce civil rights legislation, Evers attended a "mass meeting" with disappointing attendance at a Baptist church. When he pulled into his driveway just after midnight, Byron De La Beckwith crouched in a honeysuckle thicket across the street and shot him in the back. Evers's neighbor came out firing a pistol in the air and frightened Beckwith into abandoning his rifle in the honeysuckle. Evers died en route to the hospital.

Hamer learned of Evers's murder as she emerged from jail in Winona, where the local police made black prisoners beat her for being a member of the NAACP. Arrested at a bus station during a rest stop on a trip back from South Carolina where the group attended a workshop, all of the participants were beaten. Sent to jail because of the boycott he organized in Clarksdale, Aaron Henry, president of the Mississippi NAACP, spent part of his jail time working on a garbage truck. Moses analyzed the lack of progress and recognized that Mississippi segregationists had broken the back of the movement so he altered tactics. COFO launched the "Freedom Ballot Campaign," asking blacks who could not get registered to vote in mock elections held in the black community.

Aaron Henry ran for governor, and Ed King, a white native of Vicksburg who worked at Tougaloo, accepted the designation of candidate for lieutenant governor. Henry enjoyed the stump, once observing to an audience that the segregationists seemed to be very concerned about blacks "fooling"

Aaron Henry, pharmacist and civil rights leader, broke with the radical elements in the movement in order to work with whites willing to accept integration. Courtesy of the McCain Library and Archives, University of Southern Mississippi.

with white women. He said he just wished white men were as satisfied with their women as black men were with theirs. With a goal of 200,000 voters, COFO only produced 83,000, mostly from the Delta. A few white student volunteers worked during the mock campaign, and the idea of bringing in white workers for the coming summer produced much dissension among the black SNCC staff. Moses overrode their objections and set in motion what would be called Freedom Summer.

In the 1963 Democratic primary, which determined the election of all the state's elected officials, Coleman, who had returned to the legislature as a member of the House of Representatives when he left the governor's office, ran again for election as governor against Charles Sullivan and Lieutenant Governor Johnson. Coleman and Johnson faced off in the runoff, with the "moderate" Coleman tarred as a friend of the Kennedys and Johnson claiming his glory for blocking Meredith's entrance into Ole Miss. Predictably his "Stand Tall With Paul" slogan saw him into office as the toughest segregationist in the race.

The unusual aspect of the political year was that Johnson faced a serious Republican opponent in the fall. Divided into the Black and Tans from Reconstruction days and the Lily Whites who had unsuccessfully sought in the early twentieth century to take control of the Republican Party, the state party remained a shell operation until 1956, when a young insurance executive named Wirt Yerger took over both remnants and began to build a real organization. Drawing from former Democrats for Eisenhower who deserted the Democratic Party and were rewarded with the Republican administration's patronage administered by Speaker Sillers, Yerger recruited a former member of the Mississippi Public Service Commission, Rubel L. Phillips, to carry the standard in 1963. Phillips made a creditable showing with 38 percent of the vote.

Governor-elect Johnson learned of President Kennedy's assassination when he was speaking to a Mississippi Economic Council meeting, and he stopped to request a moment of silence. He learned later of the cheers from white students around the state when they heard the news. Perhaps that helped Johnson decide to change the direction of state government. He broke with the Citizens Council and never addressed another council meeting as governor. He went to New York and secretly met with television and print media executives, answering their questions and explaining Mississippi's view of the civil rights movement. Tom Brady, the author of *Black Monday*, whom Barnett had appointed to the supreme court, administered the oath of office to Johnson, who ended his inaugural address by asking his audience to recognize that, like it or not, Mississippi was part of the world and that they were Americans as well as Mississippians. He promised not to fight a rearguard action or to be led by hate, prejudice, or ignorance and concluded by asking for God's blessing on all Mississippians, both black and white.

Johnson struggled to restore law and order, beefing up the highway patrol and using it against the growing Klans. After the integration of Ole Miss, the Citizens Council lost support because its tactic of legal challenges and economic pressure had not worked. Until 1963 the Klans had almost no presence in the state, but various versions of Klan organization grew quickly and added to the violence. Responding to the breakdown of law and order, state business groups also deserted the Citizens Council and refocused on saving the state from chaos.

The trend became clear in the prosecution of Beckwith for the murder of Medgar Evers. Beckwith received support from the Greenwood Citizens Council and monetary donations that enabled him to employ a team of lawyers, including one from Governor Barnett's firm. Buoyed by his success, Beckwith wrote Louisiana supporters, before his trial, that he would win "with honor." Housed in the Rankin County jail, Beckwith kept his gun collection in his cell, and women vied for the privilege of supplying him with food. The business community, however, encouraged an aggressive prosecution, and William Waller, the Hinds County district attorney, maneuvered through a minefield of social customs trying to convict him.

For example, when Myrlie Evers testified about her husband's death, Waller could not address her as Mrs. Evers or he would lose the white segregationists on the jury. She had let it be known that she would not answer to Myrlie, which convention required Waller to use. In order to get her testimony and keep the jury sympathetic to him, Waller avoided using her name at all. In the courtroom, Beckwith slapped Waller on the back and offered him cigars. On the stand, Beckwith sighted his rifle over the jury's heads and as much as admitted his guilt by his demeanor. Barnett dropped by the courtroom to shake Beckwith's hand and chat. But in his summary to the jury, John Fox III, Waller's assistant, depicted Evers as a family man shot in the back by a coward who had run from the scene. To Beckwith's dismay, the jury deadlocked. In his hastily arranged retrial, Beckwith appeared a beaten man. Waller asked the jury how they could live with honor if they acquitted a man who admitted his guilt by his demeanor, but the second jury failed again to reach a verdict, leaving Beckwith free but stripped of the honor he sought.

The KKK supported Beckwith at his second trial, and membership in the KKK grew rapidly, even among law enforcement officers around the state. Violence increased even as the new governor and the business community sought to combat it because Barnett had weakened respect for law and order. In March 1964 COFO moved to displace the Mississippi Democratic Party by forming the Mississippi Freedom Democratic Party (MFDP). Barnett had withdrawn Mississippi from the Democratic Party, and the state elected unpledged electors in 1960 presidential contest. COFO believed an opportunity existed to claim Mississippi's place within the national party organization, but its immediate priority in the summer months was to train and deploy student volunteers to staff Freedom Schools and voter registration drives.

Training took place on a college campus in Oxford, Ohio, where the mostly black SNCC workers attempted to prepare the largely white volunteers for what they would encounter in Mississippi. When the affluent students laughed at the appearance of poor blacks in a television documentary being used for orientation, the SNCC trainers lost their tempers, and harsh words flowed. It required singing freedom songs to smooth over the disagreement and restore good relations. The Sovereignty Commission had a mole among the handful of black volunteers in Oxford and another in COFO headquarters in Jackson. The Ohio spy reported that interracial sexual encounters among the workers and volunteers began during the training period—not helpful behavior for a successful operation.

As the seminars continued in Ohio, the White Knights of the KKK beat the board members of the Mount Zion Methodist Church in Longdale as they emerged from a meeting, and the Klansmen returned later that night to

Michael Schwerner, Andrew Goodman, and James Chaney, two white civil rights volunteers and a black Mississippian murdered in Neshoba County.

burn the church to the ground because the board had agreed to allow CORE to use the church as a Freedom School. Most of the northern volunteers rode to Mississippi on buses, but Andrew Goodman got a ride with Michael Schwerner and James Chaney, who had driven from Meridian, where Schwerner and his wife, Rita, had established a CORE office. Schwerner had recruited Goodman to join them for the summer. After an all-night drive, they agreed to travel the next day—a Sunday—to Neshoba County to see the members of the burned church and discuss how to establish the proposed school. Sam Bowers, the leader of the White Knights, had issued an order to kill Schwerner, so a deputy sheriff, Cecil Price, arrested the three men and held them in the Neshoba County jail until the Klansmen got organized to take custody of them. That night, the deputy released them, and the Klansmen murdered the three men before burying them in an earthen dam.

The missing civil rights workers created intense national publicity and political pressure on everyone from the president to local law enforcement officers. President Johnson called Mississippi's two senators about the murders. Eastland assured Johnson that it was a trick on the part of the civil rights groups to garner publicity, while Stennis told the president that the men were certainly dead. The Federal Bureau of Investigation (FBI) entered the case twenty-four hours after the murders and called in navy men from Meridian Naval Air Station to comb the swamps and woods looking for the bodies. J. Edgar Hoover came to Jackson to initiate the establishment of the largest FBI office in the country and to deliver to the governor in person the names of KKK members among the state's highway patrolmen. Rita Schwerner flew to Jackson and found Governor Johnson along with Alabama's George Wallace shaking hands in a reception line formed outside the governor's mansion. She got close enough to hear Johnson joke that only he and Wallace knew the location of the three missing men, and they were not telling. When Schwerner reached the governors, she grasped his hand and demanded to know where her husband was, and the governors fled into the mansion, quickly closing the door behind them.

Despite the murders, the volunteers arrived in Mississippi even as the news media covered the search for the bodies of Schwerner, Chaney, and Goodman. The volunteers found a warm welcome in black communities, where their hosts greeted them with open arms and southern cooked food. Blacks liked hosting white visitors in their homes. The novelty created a sense of adventure and the possibility of a new world opening up for all of them. Children sometimes asked to touch the white strangers, who called their parents Mr. and Mrs. in contravention of segregationist custom. When the volunteers discovered chiggers, their new Mississippi friends instructed them in the use of kerosene as a home remedy. The nonviolent whites reacted with sighs of relief when their hosts mounted armed guards at night. SNCC members debated arming themselves but decided against it: however, they accepted that local blacks would and should carry guns because it was a central part of the culture and it provided necessary protection. In a strange twist of fate the students from America's elite universities enamored of Gandhi's teachings gladly accepted the armed protection of Mississippi's black men from the threat of the Klansmen and other white night riders.

"Freedom Riders," as the black population referred to the volunteers, went out in pairs with clip boards in hand to visit black homes and ask people to register to vote, or they taught black students in schools established in black churches or sometimes under oak trees when necessary. Policemen arrested the volunteers for all manner of infractions, even speed walking on occasion. Some whites entertained the young volunteers. Hazel Brannon Smith, wearing her accustomed pearls, invited them to Hazelwood, her white-pillared southern mansion. Red Heffner and his wife had some workers over to their home for dinner, and despite the fact that his daughter was Miss Mississippi and that they had deep roots in McComb, their neighbors ran him and his family out of the state. The police and abusive whites almost always seemed fixated on the possibility of interracial sex, asking the white workers about their sex lives in graphic language in many confrontations.

During the summer of 1964, the police made 1,000 arrests—most of them of civil rights workers, while white terrorists bombed or burned sixty-five buildings, including thirty-five black churches. They also beat eighty civil rights workers and murdered six, including the Neshoba County trio.

The civil rights workers established fifty Freedom Schools and served 2,500 students of all ages. The school planners established a curriculum designed to elicit discussion and encourage two-way learning. Black history proved to be the most popular subject in the schools. The Mississippi state curriculum purposefully deleted black accomplishments and distorted the story of the past in order to support segregation, and students reported finding a more accurate account revolutionary. Voter registration accomplished less, and some volunteers proved to be "ugly Americans" in their attitudes, attempting to take command from the experienced black leadership, and some angered both SNCC and the local community by engaging in interracial sex. SNCC tried to screen out those applicants who expressed a desire for such behavior and instructed volunteers to avoid it, but a minority of the white females engaged in a series of affairs, damaging the entire Freedom Summer project.

Governor Johnson turned over the search for the missing Neshoba County trio to the FBI, but when the Civil Rights Act became law on July 2, 1964, Johnson advised Mississippians not to obey it. He refused to meet with the former governors of Tennessee and Florida when they visited Mississippi to monitor enforcement of the law. Near the recent murder scene at the Neshoba County Fair on July 5, Johnson stated his support for segregation as the best system to maintain good race relations and said that it was the federal government's job to enforce the new law and that Mississippi would not do so. Even that statement did not go far enough for his audience, who gave more applause to a John Birch Society speaker offering more radical rhetoric.

The Jackson Chamber of Commerce called on its members to comply with the new law, and on July 5 an NAACP delegation flew to Jackson and registered at the Heidelberg Hotel without incident. The manager greeted them with a smile, and a white bellhop took their bags to their rooms. They integrated the dining room and then drove in a caravan to visit other Mississippi cities. Philadelphia crowds forced an early exit, but in other towns from the Gulf Coast to the Delta, they found accommodations and restaurants willing to serve them. In Greenwood, a local black man, Silas McGhee, tried to sit in the white section of the movie theater and was beaten by whites. When he reported the assault to the police, they wanted to know who "put him up" to going to the theater and expressed no interest in the men who beat him.

Klan informants finally breached the wall of silence surrounding the murders, and on August 5, 1964, the FBI dug the Neshoba trio out of a dam on the "old Jolly Place." At Chaney's funeral in Meridian, CORE's leader, Dave Dennis, delivered a powerful eulogy expressing the movement's frustrations with the lack of progress. For the first hour with television cameras and bright lights disrupting the service, local ministers spoke as if Chaney had died in some routine accident. Dennis rose to place the blame for Chaney's death on everyone from the president and the governor down to those who pulled the trigger. Dennis said he did not grieve for Chaney because Chaney had led a full life and had his freedom. Admitting to having vengeance in his heart, Dennis invited the congregation to join him in his anger and told them that if they continued to take what whites were doing without fighting back, then "God Damn your souls."

In August COFO switched from voter registration drives to a full-court press to select a delegation of the MFDP to travel to the national Democratic Party convention in order to challenge the regular Mississippi Democrats for the state's seats in the convention. COFO leaders rigged the selection process to keep the moderate black middle class out and to include many rural poor blacks such as the Turnbows. Hartman and "Sweets" Turnbow from Holmes County had sheltered the volunteers on their land and mounted guard to protect them. "Sweets" carried her pistol to the convention in a brown paper bag, keeping it close even as she addressed other state delegations seeking recognition for the MFDP.

President Johnson wanted the Atlantic City convention to crown his nomination without disruptions and sought to thwart MFDP's plan for recognition. Governor Johnson had chosen a group of regular Democratic delegates designed to keep a low profile. None of Mississippi's congressional heavyweights took part, choosing to stay at a safe distance from the controversy, but they approved his plan to reconvene the state Democratic convention after the national meeting to deal with developments. COFO members hired an experienced labor lawyer to present their case, and they had some hopes of success given the national publicity condemning the state. Testifying before the credentials committee, Fannie Lou Hamer turned in the star performance of the MFDP. She described the beating administered to her in Winona and ended with "I question America." So powerful was her speech that the president called a press conference in the White House Rose Garden to deflect the news cameras, but his plan backfired when all of the networks ran long segments of her testimony on their evening news shows.

The president sent Hubert Humphrey, his vice-president-to-be, with a compromise offer of two seats for Aaron Henry and Ed King. Despite heavy pressure, the delegation voted to refuse and left the convention feeling angry and deprived of what they felt was justice. The Democratic Party's denial of the seats proved to be a watershed in the movement, which split, with leaders such as Henry joining the moderates and the SNCC members moving toward Black Power.

Freedom Summer enjoyed some successes. In Panola County, where the segregationist sheriff maintained law and order without abusing the

Freedom Summer brought white volunteers into Mississippi, established fifty Freedom Schools, and served 2,500 students of all ages, but registered relatively few new black voters. Courtesy of the McCain Library and Archives, University of Southern Mississippi. Courtesy of McCain Library and Archives, University of Southern Mississippi. © Herbert Randall.

civil rights workers, SNCC registered hundreds of black voters. The Citizens Council continued to publish their names in the county paper, but there were too many for all to be targeted. Even the black high school principal registered. Pap Hamer, Fannie Lou's hard-drinking husband, summed it up when a white policeman asked how he liked having those white boys staying at his house. Pap, who supported Fannie without becoming an activist, answered that they made him feel like a man because they treated him like one.

When most of the volunteers went home in order to return to college, the violence got worse in the KKK areas of the state. By the end of September, blacks had begun to fight back, not relying on white law officers. President Johnson ordered the military to prepare to occupy McComb, which suffered a string of bombings. Informed of the plan, Governor Johnson drove to McComb with the head of the highway patrol, met with local leaders, and told them that he intended to send in the National Guard before the president acted. Asking for forty-eight hours, city and county authorities arrested eleven KKK members, got them to plead guilty to relatively minor charges, and released them on probation. McComb quieted down when local law enforcement officers, under threat of military occupation, restored a semblance of law and order, but the city also reverted to segregation in public areas when the news cameras left town.

In Natchez, blacks armed themselves after a car bomb almost killed the leader of the city's NAACP. George Metcalfe housed SNCC workers when they first arrived in town and openly cooperated with them in their voter registration drive. He worked at Armstrong Tire and Rubber, which also employed many KKK members and where racial tensions simmered. Charles Evers had made himself state field secretary for the NAACP, whose leaders did not like him but felt compelled, by the sympathy and fame earned by his brother, to accept him. Evers did not consult headquarters and went his own way, carving out the section of southwest Mississippi as his stronghold. A small-time gangster in Chicago, Charles Evers ran numbers and pimped prostitutes while managing nightclubs where Mississippi bluesmen played. He initially brought members of a black motorcycle gang back to Mississippi with him to provide security. In a speech to a large crowd after the Metcalfe bombing, Evers threatened that if the KKK perpetuated any more violence, blacks would counterattack. He claimed that blacks were armed and were not going to take it. Armed men patrolled the streets in the black sections of town. Evers organized a boycott and developed a list of demands for the city council. The council responded by passing a 10:00 P.M. curfew enforced only against blacks. Faced with a race war, Governor Johnson ordered in 650 National Guard troops. Evers canceled a planned march but continued the boycott. The boycott worked, and Martin Luther King Jr.'s Southern Christian Leadership Conference (SCLC) moved in to take command. Evers undermined their plans, played all the other civil rights organizations against one another, and started to cooperate with his own NAACP headquarters. He also bought a grocery store in order to benefit from the boycott of white businesses.

In the midst of the assault on Mississippi's segregationist society, the Atomic Energy Commission (AEC) detonated an atomic bomb in a salt dome twenty-eight miles southwest of Hattiesburg on October 22, 1964. The editor of the *Hattiesburg American* reported that his newspaper building swayed for three minutes from the blast. Homes closer to the Tatum Salt dome suffered major damage, wells went dry, and creeks turned black with silt for days. Drilling into the salt dome after the explosion brought contaminated water and soil to the surface, causing long-lasting clean-up problems. Residents interviewed by the *Hattiesburg American* resented being subjected to the nuclear test, but the newspaper editorialized that readers should support the testing because the security of the United States required it.

As blacks and whites fought in the streets across the state, Mississippi politicians stumbled toward adjusting to the new social and political system imposed in this second Reconstruction. In the presidential election, white Mississippians demonstrated their rejection of the new reality by voting overwhelmingly for Barry Goldwater, the Republican candidate, because he had voted against the Civil Rights Act. They even elected their first Republican congressman since Reconstruction—Prentiss Walker, a chicken farmer from Smith County. The MFDP continued its political fight by challenging the seating of the state's congressional delegation, using a law from the first Reconstruction. The MFDP put up candidates against all of the state's congressmen. Fannie Lou Hamer ran against Jamie Whitten and went to Washington to enjoy watching the Mississippi members of the House of Representatives have to stand aside because of the challenge while other members took the oath of office. The Democratic members from Mississippi pooled their resources to hire a lawyer to handle the challenge, but Walker had to hire his own. Almost a third of the House voted to sustain the challenge, shocking the Mississippi delegation and making the point again of Mississippi's isolation.

Governor Johnson attended President Johnson's inauguration and returned home determined to refocus his administration. In December 1964 Governor Johnson addressed the state via radio touting the creation of the Mississippi Research and Development Council, which he intended to use to support his efforts to industrialize the state. He placed economic development as his first priority and dedicated the state to cooperation with the FBI to preserve law and order. In 1965 he called former governor White, father of the Balance Agriculture with Industry (BAWI) program, to the capital in order to celebrate the achievement of balancing industry with agriculture in Mississippi. Johnson kept Johnston at the Sovereignty Commission and used him to spread the message that Mississippi had accepted the Civil Rights Act and would abide by the law. Johnston spoke to the Mississippi sheriffs' association along those lines, and the sheriffs responded with a resolution condemning the Klans and endorsing the governor. The governor followed up with a half-million-dollar publicity campaign announcing Mississippi's new policy. The manufacturing association followed the Mississippi Economic Council in asking for compliance with the Civil Rights Act, along with the associations of county supervisors, county clerks, and even voting registrars. The governor told a friendly newspaper columnist that he sensed the majority of white Mississippians backed a more moderate course by 1965. From his seat on the Mississippi Supreme Court, Tom Brady upheld the legality of the Civil Rights Act.

In May 1965 Johnson refused to attend the Citizens Council's annual meeting in order to fly to Washington and to Europe on an economic development venture. Eastland, Sillers, Gartin, and the rest of the establishment appeared at the Citizens Council event, but desegregation continued apace. Ole Miss hired its first black faculty member at the medical center, and Mississippi State admitted its first black student with little publicity. Richard Holmes, the adopted son of Dr. Conner, finished high school in Starkville and then went to college in Texas, but he returned home for the summer in 1965 and wanted to take two classes. In order to be at home, he applied to Mississippi State. Colvard called the governor when he learned of Holmes's application, and the governor responded that everyone would have to work together to handle the matter. Only the Starkville paper carried the story, and Colvard kept it low key. Conner drove Holmes to campus and let him out of the car near the registration building alone, and Holmes registered without incident, only reading a brief statement to the press asking to be left alone. Conner collected Holmes, and they went home, where later that evening 200 white students and probably some others, whom Conner called riffraff, vocally vented their disapproval. Conner waited for some time before calling the police because the demonstrators seemed to pose no threat. The crowd left before the police arrived. At school, students ignored Holmes, vacated tables in the library when he sat down, and made catcalls from a distance, but no student ever confronted him directly. Although the atmosphere proved unpleasant, Holmes decided to enroll for the fall semester to finish his college degree and encountered no opposition.

In the summer of 1965 Congress passed the Voting Rights Act, to which Governor Johnson responded by calling a special session of the legislature ostensibly to bring Mississippi into compliance, but in reality to seek a means of barring federal registrars from the state. At the Neshoba County Fair, Johnson argued against "blind defiance" and fiery language, advising white Mississippians to take advantage of the looser franchise requirements to register and vote. In August 1965 Mississippi voters approved constitutional amendments enacting provisions to thwart black voter registration by almost three to one. The state did not welcome new black voters. With Stennis's full support, Patterson, the attorney general, tried unsuccessfully to use the state courts to prevent federal registered voters being added to the rolls.

That same summer Congress passed LBJ's Great Society and "War on Poverty" programs, establishing the Office of Economic Opportunity (OEO) and sending a shower of money on the Magnolia State intended to end poverty and raise living standards for the poor. The "War on Poverty" pitted the revolutionaries in SNCC and CORE against Eastland, Stennis, and the Mississippi establishment. The NAACP withdrew from COFO in 1965, criticizing SNCC for having ties to Chinese Communism. Eastland had all of the FBI reports on the civil rights workers and knew that, although there were almost no Communist Party members among them, many held radical ideas to the left of the old Soviet-style party. An American Civil Liberties Union (ACLU) lawyer familiar with SNCC wished that the organization contained some Communists because, he said, they would be a moderating influence. The heart of the struggle centered on Head Start. The movement personnel formed the Child Development Group of Mississippi (CDGM) to receive the millions of dollars intended to provide education, medical care, and food to Mississippi's poor children. Headquartered at Mount Beulah College in rural Hinds County with the MFDP, the same people who had run Freedom Summer received the federal largesse and intended to use it as a political tool.

Eastland and Stennis mobilized all of their considerable power to stop funding for the CDGM, and Eastland went public, accusing the CDGM of being more dangerous than Cuban or Vietnamese guerrillas. Enjoying federal funding, CDGM leaders saw no problem with using the federal government to overturn the Mississippi establishment, which to their minds created poverty and starved poor blacks as a matter of normal policy. In response to the senators' criticism, the OEO created Mississippi Action for Progress (MAP), made up of upper-class whites such as Hodding Carter III and planter LeRoy Percy and black leaders like Aaron Henry. Intended to replace the CDMG as the recipient of federal poverty dollars, MAP excluded the radicalized lower-class blacks such as Hamer in favor the middle class, who had often failed to respond to the movement. By 1966 Johnston began to use the Sovereignty Commission to persuade whites to get involved with the Great Society's poverty programs.

White Mississippians who chose to endorse integration did so at a cost to themselves, their families, and their associates. In 1965 Frank E. Smith, former congressman and Tennessee Valley Authority (TVA) director, accepted an invitation to address the Mississippi Council on Human Relations. The council included Tougaloo College professor Ernst Borinski and the new Catholic bishop, Joseph Brunini, along with leading businessmen, but it promoted integration, and by making the talk Smith labeled himself an integrationist. His supporters and even some family members had rationalized his condemnation of Barnett during the Ole Miss crisis as a political necessity required by his appointment to the TVA board, and they forgave him accordingly. Gray Evans, his former assistant, contacted Smith's mother, asking her to persuade Smith not to make the address, and when she declined, Evans wrote to Smith from Greenwood pleading with him to cancel his trip to Jackson. Evans explained that Smith's views on civil rights hurt him, his wife, Smith's family, and all of those who had supported him for office. Evans said his business had suffered, as it had for Smith's other allies. At one point Smith felt that the pressure on his mother had become intolerable, and he cancelled his planned speech; however, his mother told him that she could take it and he should make the talk. Smith told Evans that he realized that speaking out amounted to only a "drop in the bucket," but someone had to begin to "twist the faucet." Not unsympathetic, Evans responded that he did not have the strength to go against family and friends, but admired Smith for his determination.

As individuals struggled with personal decisions about race relations, the battle to control federal funds progressed, as did the race war over voter registration and school integration. In January 1966 Vernon Dahmer, who had been urging his neighbors to register to vote, suffered a Klan raid on his store and comfortable ranch house located on his 400-acre farm. While burning his store, the Klansmen fired into his house. Dahmer fired back, but a firebomb thrown at his house so severely burned his lungs that he died the next day. While federal voter registration continued, so also did the violent opposition. Technically, Mississippi schools complied with the Civil Rights Act using "freedom of choice," which admitted 2 percent of black students into white schools, achieving token integration in some districts.

Into the swirl of contention stepped James Meredith again. After graduating from Ole Miss, he dropped out of Mississippians' sight, traveling to Africa and then entering law school at Columbia University, but again without consulting anyone, he decided to march "against fear" from Memphis across the state to demonstrate that blacks could feel free to register to vote. On the second day of his march, a Memphis man attacked him with a shotgun, sending him to the hospital. Representatives of all of the civil rights groups came to his bedside asking for his blessing to finish the march, which he gave.

Martin Luther King Jr. and Stokely Carmichael shared the spotlight as the large group marched south protected by twenty highway patrol cars. Encouraged by the governor not to make trouble, Grenada allowed 1,300 blacks to register to vote and ignored insults to the town's Confederate monument, but the governor cut the number of protective cars to four in the daytime while ignoring the black armed guards who protected the marchers' camp at night. In Greenwood, Carmichael went to jail for ignoring orders not to erect tents on a school ground. Speaking to a crowd after his release, Carmichael uttered the words that made him famous—"We want black power"—along with suggesting that all of Mississippi's courthouses should be burned. King detoured to Philadelphia, where he spoke with the murderers of Schwerner, Chaney, and Goodman standing behind him, and a white mob attacked the marchers. At Canton, highway patrol troopers assaulted 2,500 marchers trying to raise their tents for the night. The troopers used tear gas and waded into the choking marchers with gun butts and nightsticks. The march finished at the capitol, where 15,000 heard King declare the demonstration the greatest in Mississippi's history. In fact, the out-of-state organizations created turmoil and left local blacks to try and find a way to live with their white neighbors.

Impressed by the success in Grenada during the march, King's SCLC moved into town to establish its only long-term Mississippi project. When Carmichael tried to horn in, SCLC ran him out of town, but local whites decided that their cooperative behavior during the march was a mistake not to be repeated. Marches and boycotts disrupted the community, registered some voters, and desegregated the library. A federal judge ordered a freedom of choice plan for all twelve school grades to take effect in the fall of 1966, leading to one of the most revolting episodes in the history of the race war. On the first day of school, 150 black children entered into the school early in the day, but a white mob assembled and prevented forty others from reaching the school door. When the black students emerged at the end of the half-day session, white men armed with pipes, chains, and ax handles beat thirty of the black boys and girls breaking limbs and bloodying their bodies while local law enforcement and the FBI looked on. Seventy-five whites participated in the assaults, but 400 others cheered them on, including screaming women.

In 1966 SNCC expelled all whites in keeping with its Black Power theme, and Hamer resigned in protest. CORE ceased to function in Mississippi as the NAACP strengthened its power base. Charles Evers emerged as the most effective leader left in the state, conducting successful boycotts in the southwestern portion of the state. Changes in social, political, and economic spheres evolved in the later 1960s.

Governor Johnson appealed to the legislature in 1966 to approve a referendum allowing voters to legalize liquor sales. He pointed out that the fifty-eight-year ban had been amended when the state began taxing bootleg spirits across its borders, before the alcohol was shipped to Mississippi bootleggers. The system, Johnson said, made Mississippi the laughingstock of the nation for its hypocrisy. Three nights after his speech to the legislature, the governor went to the Jackson country club for a nightcap following the Junior League carnival ball only to find that Hinds County deputies had smashed open the liquor cabinet and confiscated the club's entire supply. The legislature voted for a referendum, and the voters approved. Seventy percent of the state's counties went wet within a year.

Although Johnson did not stress corruption and improving law enforcement as a part of his drive to legalize alcohol, legalization of liquor sales had that result. Sheriffs often benefited from bootlegging and lowered public respect for the law. Following legalization, sheriffs persuaded the legislature to allow them to serve multiple consecutive terms, which led to more professional training and more honest administration.

In the summer of 1966 Johnson realized his dream of bringing a major manufacturer to the state when he sold Ingalls on investing in its Pascagoula shipyard as the site for future expansion. Ingalls's existing shipbuilding facilities, constructed in 1938, were outdated and inadequate, and the company had proposed to move out of state. Johnson pursued Ingalls hard, arranging private jets and utilizing his newly created Research and Development Center fully. He called all of Mississippi's political candidates to the mansion and taped their commitments to support the project. With assurance of their backing and the tapes to prove it, he called the legislature into special session and asked for bond money along with laws needed to smooth the way for expansion without any local governmental roadblocks. By 1969 Ingalls employed 25,000 people, making it the largest employer in the state. Such economic investment might change the state over time, but political change seemed to take longer than economic progress.

The number of black voters soared thanks to federal registrars, but in the first test of black electoral influence in the 1967 elections, the results proved modest and sorely disappointed the activists. The ardent segregationist John Bell Williams lost his seniority in the House of Representatives for his open support of Goldwater in 1964 and decided to leave Congress and run for governor. William Winter, a moderate, had kept in touch with Frank E. Smith at his TVA post, sending reports on the progress of integration and plotting as part of what they called in their letters the "Mississippi underground" to preserve a moderate presence within the Mississippi Democratic Party. Smith counseled Winter to skip the 1967 race because Smith considered Williams unbeatable, but Winter, who had won office as state tax collector and treasurer, ran anyway. Barnett made an effort to return to office in 1967, and the Coleman group in the Democratic Party backed Williams in order to block the former governor, which deprived Winter of some natural support. In the thick of the fight, Winter brought his moderate credentials into question by stressing his family's ties to the Confederate States of American (CSA) and appealing to segregationists, but Williams won handily by promising to refuse federal financial assistance and to maintain segregation.

Symbolic of the fate of the political reform movement across the state was the mayor's election in Sunflower, a town of 700 residents located eight miles south of Eastland's plantation. Blacks made up 70 percent of the town's population, and Hamer conducted an all-out crusade to take the mayor's office from the white incumbent. The previous year her twenty-two-year-old daughter began to hemorrhage during childbirth, and two local hospitals refused her admission because of her race. She died as Hamer drove her toward Memphis. Suffering from that loss and years of working in the civil rights movement without a solid victory to show for her efforts, Hamer saw the mayoral election as an opportunity to gain a concrete victory at long last. She and her friends from the movement backed Otis Brown, a twenty-one-year-old former Freedom School teacher, for mayor and ran a complete slate of aldermen. She poured her heart into the campaign fund-raising in the North and canvassing door to door in town. The incumbent, W. L. Patterson, broke tradition and campaigned for black votes—a necessity because they made up the majority. He paved roads and erected signs in the black community, which Brown was promising to do. But on election day whites also employed intimidation at the polls, menacing new black voters. Only four of the town's voters failed to turn out, but Patterson got 60 percent of the vote, and not one MFDP alderman won a seat. Hamer and her allies blamed the loss on intimidation alone and refused to contemplate that some black voters for a variety of reasons may have preferred the white candidates. Patterson thanked his black supporters and took encouragement from the victory, realizing that whites could still function in an integrated electoral environment.

Defying political change, whites reelected Eastland in 1966, chose Williams for governor in 1967, and voted for George Wallace for president the next year. Twenty-one blacks won local offices in 1967, and Holmes County sent Robert G. Clark, grandson of a slave, (and great-grandson of a white planter and a Creek) to the Mississippi House of Representatives, making him the first "black" legislator since Reconstruction. No one would sit with Clark in the legislature or at official banquets. Clark joked for years that he gained a great deal of weight because he sat alone at tables set for half a dozen and could not resist all of the extra deserts at his lonely table.

Evers challenged Governor Williams's congressional assistant Charles Griffin for a House of Representatives seat in a contest devoid of racial appeals by either candidate. Obviously Mississippians grappled with finding a new civility to replace the hate-filled rhetoric of the recent past. Mississippi's Young Democrats led by Hodding Carter III challenged the regular Democrats led by Governor Williams. When the MFDP attempted to take over the organization, Carter walked out and appealed to the national Young Democrats for recognition, which they granted, creating a splinter of the Mississippi Democratic Party loyal to the national Democrats. This small group worked with the NAACP to create a "moderate" challenge to the regulars for control of the delegation to the presidential nominating convention in 1968. The moderates invited Vice President Hubert Humphrey to speak at Ole Miss before a gathering of elected officials from around the state.

Smith, who had not often been back to Mississippi since his speech to the Human Relations Council, attended the event to hear Humphrey in the spring of 1968 and reported his delight and amazement to an old newspaper editor friend. The night before the event, Smith went to a party hosted by the Sunflower County Board of Supervisors in the alumni house, which had the designation of being legally off campus, allowing liquor to be served. In the hospitality room, the former president of the Indianola Citizens Council cordially received, in normal convention-style fellowship, Aaron Henry and Charles Evers. At breakfast the next morning, Smith met many of the civil rights leaders whose names he knew from his work in Atlanta with the Voter Education Project, which had financed their voter registration campaigns. Governor Williams refused to appear, but Lieutenant Governor Charles Sullivan and William Winter listened to R. L. T. Smith, a black political activist, deliver the invocation at lunch. The all-white Leflore County delegation waved Smith to their table, where he sat with some individuals who would have made it unsafe for him to walk the streets of Greenwood during the Ole Miss crisis. Humphrey gave what Smith called a "brotherhood of man" talk and encouraged Mississippi to send an integrated delegation to the 1968 convention.

Williams blocked efforts among the regulars to heed Humphrey's call, and the MFDP decided to join with the Young Democrats and other moderates in an effort to overcome Williams and the regulars. They elected Carter and Henry as cochairs and went to the disastrous Chicago convention, where they displaced the regulars and were awarded all of the seats by the convention.

Before the convention, President Johnson decided not to seek a second full term because of the unpopularity of the war in Vietnam, and the street battles in Chicago sealed the fate of the national Democratic Party. Mississippians supported the war more than the nation as a whole, but the war added to the division between the races. Members of the MFDP called on blacks not to fight for what they considered an imperialist war, and some charged that all-white draft boards sent more blacks than whites to war. Middle-class whites joined the National Guard to avoid serving in Vietnam, and at one point in the war only one black man served in the 10,000-man Mississippi National Guard. Few protests interfered with the state's substantial contribution to the war effort. Pilots and ground forces trained at the many bases in the state, and the senators along with Congressman G. V. "Sonny" Montgomery supported the war fully. Montgomery made twelve fact-finding trips to Vietnam seeking to encourage and care for the fighting men. Mississippians displayed little sympathy with the antiwar sentiment widespread in the rest of the nation. When a few students objected to compulsory Reserve Officers' Training Corps (ROTC) at Ole Miss and tried to harass participants, the university sent three of them home. The university got a court order to prevent a Quaker antiwar activist speaking to a class, shutting off his talk in midsentence when a federal marshal served him the papers.

In the midst of the war, sweeping political change, and a revolution in social relationships, Mississippians made thousands of local adjustments to interracial relationships, and gradually the people of the state adapted to an integrated society. In Greenwood, the bravery, dedication, and sacrifice of civil rights workers such as Sam Block and Ida Mae Holland accomplished little of substance because of determined white resistance. As the SNCC workers drifted away to work in Head Start and other Great Society programs, an integrated movement replaced them and finally won meaningful concessions from the white-controlled government. Freed by the arrival of Bishop Brunini, who favored integration, Father Nathaniel met with Greenwood's segregationist mayor Charles E. Sampson to ask for a few small concessions for the black community. The Franciscan had remained on the sidelines during the SNCC years, but his time in the community and his witness of the violence generated by the movement caused him to write an editorial in *Center Light*, his church's little newspaper, calling for a black organization to make a revolution in Greenwood. Shortly after his editorial appeared, he joined with Melvin J. Black and William Wallace, two black ministers who had also avoided the SNCC-led movement, to form the "Greenwood Movement." They identified their goals as being jobs and respectful treatment from the business community. They mounted a boycott of the city's merchants who depended on black consumers for their profits.

Launched on December 6, 1967, as the Christmas season neared, the boycott enjoyed a small, immediate success as a few stores hired blacks into responsible positions, but then when the organizers published an exemption from the boycott of those stores and Christmas drew close, the boycott fell apart. Martin Luther King Jr. made a visit to Greenwood in March 1968, stopped at the Catholic school, and spoke to a mass meeting at a Christian Methodist Episcopal (CME) church. Three weeks later an assassin gunned him down in Memphis. In Greenwood, the National Guard watched over the resulting march conducted to express the black community's grief and outrage. Because of King's murder, the boycott resumed. Father Nathaniel worried about the safety of his school, Miss Kate's center, and his colleagues because Beckwith, Evers's murderer, roamed free in the city with like-minded Klansmen.

The trio of two ministers and a priest tried to bargain with the mayor, but he refused to meet, causing them to draft a long list of demands, including employment opportunities and a fair share of governmental services. Espousing belief in King's policy of nonviolence, those in the Greenwood Movement made clear that their movement did not belong to any larger organization and that it was homegrown. They formed committees for varied activities and appointed colonels and captains to oversee assigned districts with an office at the St. Francis Information Center. They kept daily pickets marching the sidewalks in front of stores in a well-disciplined maneuver. To white Greenwood, the greatest shock was the presence of the Pax Christi women among the black protestors. On occasion, white women said to the Pax Christi members: "You should be ashamed" or "You know better than this." The Catholic women only smiled and marched on.

The Greenwood Movement differed from the SNCC effort in significant ways. The white people of Greenwood knew these protestors. The Pax Christi women came from the Delta—some even from leading families. Father Nathaniel had been a resident for many years and played bridge and golf with the leading white families before he founded the protest movement. Afterward whites ceased to keep his company, but they knew him. They disliked his protests, but they also disliked the gunmen who shot into his church and his car. Some of the priests had to take up arms to protect church members' lives and property. Father Nathaniel answered the door one day to find a stranger who asked for him. When Father Nathaniel identified himself, the man said that the KKK had paid him $10,000 to kill the priest. Father Nathaniel invited him in for coffee. A month later the man returned to say that he had given the money back because he could not kill the bravest man he ever saw.

As the boycott threatened the livelihood of the merchants, they asked a young Catholic among them to negotiate, but the merchants could not get the mayor to accept any concessions. In 1969, when the mayor sought a fourth term in office, a former mayor employed by a local gasoline company, Thurman Henry, announced as an opponent with the slogan "A Time for Change." Sampson won small majorities in white areas of the city, but the black section swept Henry into office. A few weeks after he entered his office, Henry hired the city's first black police officers. The leaders called off the boycott on December 10, 1969.

A Delta newspaperman observed that money seemed to be accomplishing what protests and preaching brotherly love had not. As Great Society funding provided middle-class jobs for blacks, their willingness to cooperate with whites increased. Hamer complained of the same trend as she continued to seek a better life. Revolutionized by her SNCC training and a visit to Africa, she hoped to create a better world by building a socialist community. As the black population left the Delta in huge numbers seeking work, she turned back to the land, establishing Freedom Farm with donations from the North.

Beginning with a "pig bank" provided by the National Council of Negro Women, Hamer raised the funds to buy land. Pascol Townshend, Charles Lawler's lawyer and city attorney for Drew, did much of the farm's legal work because he was the only lawyer Hamer trusted. In one of those ironic Mississippi twists of human relationships, Townshend objected loudly to Freedom Summer, but later befriended Hamer and assisted her farming venture. The farm evolved into a social service agency, building seventy homes with affordable mortgages. The farm's labor-intensive, hand-picked cotton could not compete with industrialized agriculture. Most people only wanted to work in the vegetable fields at harvest time, and by 1971 Hamer's socialist dream appeared to be on the verge of collapse.

Hamer's neighbor, Senator Eastland, by contrast, continued to enlarge his plantation to almost 6,000 acres, making him one of the wealthiest men in the Senate. As Hamer tried to establish her small cooperative farm, the federal government paid the 340 farmers in Sunflower County $6.8 million to limit their cotton acreage. Eastland received $170,000 of that total, and when Congress reformed the system to limit payments to any one planter to $55,000, he evaded the limit by creating six partners—his wife and four children—to each get the maximum. To his credit, Eastland continued to house his workers even when he no longer needed their services. As with planters of the past, he looked after "his people," and they responded with loyalty.

Of the historically deprived peoples in Mississippi, the Choctaw fared better than any other group during the War on Poverty by gaining control of their government and using it to build a new economy. Phillip Martin stepped down as chief in 1966 to run the Choctaw's Community Action Program (CAP) and then resumed his role as leader in 1971 when CAP funding expired. Martin grew up around the Bureau of Indian Affairs (BIA) headquarters, where his father worked. Martin believed that a white man burned the family home at the BIA headquarters because the arsonist resented an American Indian living so well. His comfortable life changed after his father died in an accident, and he experienced hard times before joining the military. Service in Europe, where he saw French poverty and German recovery, convinced him that his people could work their way to prosperity in Mississippi. Marrying and returning to Meridian in 1957, Martin looked for a job, but to no avail. He ignored the whites-only signs on restrooms and in restaurants without being challenged, but in spite of his military background he had great difficulty finding work. His wife took a position with the BIA, so they moved to Tucker, living with her mother. Martin used his G.I. Bill to study at community colleges, and finally he

Phillip Martin, Choctaw veteran who could not find work near his home, became the leader of the Mississippi band and developed economic opportunities for his people. Photo courtesy of Bob Ferguson.

became a refrigeration repairman at the Meridian Naval Air Station. Meanwhile, he also had become active in the Choctaw Tribal Council. In 1963 he went to work full time as administrator under a white superintendent (superintendents had always been non-Choctaws). Martin intended to challenge the BIA and begin economic development for the Choctaw, who suffered around an 80 percent unemployment rate.

Beginning with $100,000 derived from timber sales, which the superintendent had neglected to tell the council that the tribe controlled, Martin started to wrest power from the BIA by visiting Washington, D.C., and lobbying the bureaucrats directly. Martin became proficient at grant writing and obtained funds from the War on Poverty to establish Choctaw-controlled economic development projects. He persuaded the BIA to hire a Choctaw as superintendent, which aided his progress, and by the 1970s Martin had laid the groundwork for a Choctaw economic miracle to match what he witnessed in Germany.

In the late 1960s school integration became the central political issue for Mississippians. Eastland and Stennis cajoled the federal bureaucracy into accepting freedom of choice plans for token desegregation of the state's schools. Because of the state's poverty, the federal government provided Mississippi the highest proportion of funding in the country—$38 million of a $200 million budget. Lauderdale County typified the system. Meridian denied James Chaney's younger brother admission to the white school in the year after the Neshoba murders. In 1966 only thirty-five black students attended what had been all-white schools in the county. Mississippi used federal money to support segregation by hiring more black teachers to bring down the student/teacher ratio in black schools and making other improvements. Prior to 1969, only two Mississippi school districts voluntarily integrated, and those districts had small black populations. Many districts remained completely segregated because whites continued to intimidate and threaten black parents for choosing to send their children to white schools. Black children in white schools encountered cruel treatment such as name-calling, spitballs, and teachers spraying deodorant on them. Some teachers segregated blacks in the classroom and referred to them as "niggers," but most black students reported that teachers maintained control of the classroom, disciplined whites who wanted to abuse them, and showed a real interest in their work.

Integration of Mississippi schools truly did not begin until 1970, when the federal courts ordered an end to freedom of choice. In heavily black counties such as Tunica, whites immediately abandoned public schools, looting them to establish segregated academies in churches and other hastily arranged buildings. In Tunica, white teachers, including the school superintendent's wife still being paid by the county, taught white students in the church-housed schools using the county's textbooks that students had been told to take home at Christmas break. In many counties, whites stole desks and sports equipment from the public schools for their new private academies. In Jackson, 40 percent of the white students dropped out of the public school system, but statewide only 8 percent of whites left the public schools. In an odd development, some white parents adopted the methods of the civil rights movement, marching in protest, sitting in at school libraries, and picketing city hall. Some systems tried internal segregation. Kemper County housed black and white students in separate wings of the building, changed classes to separate bells, and fed black and white students at different times.

Senator Stennis used his considerable power to pressure President Nixon to continue freedom of choice policies, which enabled Mississippi to maintain de facto segregation of its public schools, but in October 1969 the Supreme Court, in *Alexander v. Holmes*, ruled that the evasion of its 1954 decision must end. Governor Williams went on television to rail against the *Alexander* decision requiring an end to freedom of choice, but he refused to close the schools, just as he had broken his campaign promise to reject federal monies. Instead, he established a bureaucracy in his office to receive and disburse them. He joined with Senator Stennis to support former Jackson mayor Thompson's organization called Freedom of Choice in the United States (FOCUS). Williams told a FOCUS rally of 4,000 in Jackson that they would continue to fight integration even though all legal efforts had failed in the courts. In a strange move, the state attorney general urged Mississippi lawyers to go north and west filing suits to get the courts to "destroy" school systems outside the South. He reasoned that this would persuade the rest of the country to overturn the courts' actions.

Hurricane Camille split Ship Island with 200-mile-per-hour winds and pushed a wall of water more than twenty-two feet high over the state's coastline. Approximately 150 people died in Mississippi. Photograph by Fred Hutchings.

Recalling the conflicts of the 1960s, the amazing fact was that integration of the schools took place without violence. Whites did move to eliminate black teachers and administrators or to render them powerless. Black principals remaining in the school systems found themselves demoted to assistant principals with no duties. Some carved out new roles for themselves, attending education seminars gaining expertise and becoming grant writers and consultants. Many black parents quickly questioned the value of having their children instructed by unsympathetic white teachers and losing the more nurturing atmosphere of the old black schools. Some soon called integration the worst thing ever to happen to their children.

Just as Mississippians faced school integration in August 1969, a category five hurricane, Camille, split Ship Island with 200-mile-per-hour winds and pushed a wall of water more than twenty-two feet high over the state's coastline. Approximately 150 people died in Mississippi, and the Gulf Coast suffered enormous property damage. John Bell Williams, the last openly racist governor of Mississippi, earned high praise for his handling of the disaster by getting to the scene quickly and mobilizing federal and state resources.

Violence of another sort erupted at Jackson State in the spring of 1970 when a police riot killed two and injured twelve. President Richard Nixon had just widened the Vietnam War into Cambodia, causing an outbreak of

At Jackson State in the spring of 1970, a police riot killed two and injured twelve when officers fired 460 rounds at a dormitory filled with students. Photograph courtesy Corbis Images.

demonstrations, including one at Kent State in Ohio, which resulted in the death of four students. Jackson State students heard a rumor that Charles Evers and his wife had been killed on the evening of May 14, which caused some students to congregate on campus. A busy thoroughfare—Lynch Street—bisected the campus. Whites drove through, flinging insults and objects at students on occasion, and that night some students began to throw rocks and bottles from dormitory roofs onto passing white-driven automobiles. Rioters overturned a dump truck in the middle of the street and set several fires. The National Guard, highway patrol, and city police responded to the scene. The guardsmen remained down the street while seventy-five patrolmen and police confronted the crowd and protected firemen extinguishing the flaming dump truck. The patrolmen and police marched up the street in a line toward a women's dormitory facing approximately 100 people. Bottles and debris came from the dorm, striking one officer, and when either a breaking bottle or a gunshot sounded just after midnight, the patrolmen and perhaps the police opened fire with shotguns, submachine guns, and pistols. They killed one college student and a high school student who paused to watch the action on his way home from his job at a nearby grocery store. Four hundred and sixty rounds hit the dorm. The officers picked up their shell casings before calling ambulances for the wounded and hysterical students, who tried to flee into the dorm during the attack. No charges were ever brought against the officers for what was in effect a police riot.

Racism and the emotions it generated died hard. In 1970 Mississippi became the last state east of the Mississippi River to establish a public broadcasting network. Soon the network got pressured to remove the popular, nationally produced children's show *Sesame Street* because of its integrated cast, who spread the idea of brotherly love among all peoples. When powerful politicians leaned on the network, *Sesame Street* vanished from Mississippi Educational Television for twenty-two days. As with the earlier attempt to boycott *Bonanza*, however, the racists failed in their attempt to control television. Mississippi children rejoined the rest of the nation learning their numbers and racial tolerance from *Sesame Street*. Ironically the show owed much to Jim Henson, a native of Greenville.

The 1971 governor's race did much to mark the end of overt racism in the public life of the state. Longtime politician Lieutenant Governor Charles Sullivan ran on the slogan "It's Charlie's Time." He began as the front runner with the backing of the Hedermans and all but two of the daily papers in the state, while his opponent, William (Bill) Waller, who had energetically prosecuted Beckwith for murdering Evers, started as a dark horse. Neither Sullivan nor Waller voiced the racist rhetoric so common in the past, leaving that role to the musician and radio man from Hattiesburg, Jimmy Swan. Waller engaged an up-and-coming media consultant, Deloss Walker, who helped use television to the best advantage by having Waller campaign against the "Capital Street Gang" with the slogan, "It's Time for a Change." In the first primary Sullivan led Waller by 60,000 votes, and Swan polled about half what the two leaders got. As Waller prepared for the runoff, Eastland, the leader of the Capital Street Gang, joined the Waller camp, providing access to his donors and his advice. Eastland disliked Sullivan personally and saw him as threat to his power base in the Delta. Waller upset Sullivan and earned the label of Mississippi's New South governor. William Winter, member of the Mississippi underground, also won the office of lieutenant governor.

Charles Evers ran against Waller in the fall election, and although they avoided any references to race, the Republicans chose not to contest the election in order not to split the white vote and deliver the office to Evers. Hodding Carter refused to endorse a candidate, saying that either would make a good governor and praised both for running the cleanest election in the state's history with race only a muted issue. On election night, Evers tracked the victorious Waller down at a television studio, where Waller had made a victory statement, in order to shake hands and congratulate him on his win. Such a cordial scene would have been impossible in the past. Mississippians had slowly begun to bridge the chasm dividing the two races throughout its history.

When the Jackson State killings occurred, New Stage Theater near Welty's home was preparing a production of *The Ponder Heart* based on her 1952 novel. Florence Roach, a Jackson State student who was living with a white roommate—another member of the cast—announced that she would continue in the play despite the deaths on campus. The director wrote an article for the *Jackson Daily News* praising Roach's decision. Welty clipped the article and sent it to a friend along with a letter saying that it demonstrated what so many people in the South felt: "the knowledge and intimacy and understanding between the races that is still, amazingly still, undestroyed." Thus in 1970, one of the most perceptive observers of the Mississippi scene believed it possible to salvage some of the human understanding between the races that cropped up through the layers of racism and hatred that had weighted the state down throughout its history.

Chapter Fifteen

MISSISSIPPI AND THE MODERN WORLD

In the last three decades of the twentieth century and the opening years of the twenty-first, Mississippians struggled to remake their society; to construct a two-party political system; to build schools, libraries, museums, and other cultural institutions; and to understand their past. While accepting and nurturing a large gambling and tourist business, they sought and obtained impressive industrial assets and yet maintained a largely rural landscape fostering a preindustrial social mindset. The Americanization of the state continued apace, but Mississippians learned to cherish their uniqueness and seemed determined to preserve their much-vaunted sense of place.

Elvis Presley provided the musical theme for Mississippi in the 1970s with his performance of "American Trilogy," combining the southern anthem "Dixie" with the Yankee crusading Civil War song "Battle Hymn of the Republic" along with fragments of the slave spiritual "All My Trials." Dressed in his white polyester outfits complete with cape, Elvis visually transcended his redneck origins, pointing his fans toward a modernism far removed from his working-class roots in Tupelo and Parchman, where his father served time. But in the 1970s, Elvis, living with his mother and father in Graceland, watched Rex Humbolt, a transplanted southerner, who pioneered televised evangelical preaching. While not a traditional Christian, Elvis remained loyal to his birth-state's culture, retaining at least remnants of the religion of his youth. In country music, the favorite genre of most white Mississippians, Charley Pride won the Country Music Award's entertainer of the year in 1971 and male vocalist of the year for both 1971 and 1972. Born in Sledge to a poor sharecropping family, Pride pitched in the Negro Baseball League until he won a recording contract in Nashville and became the first black superstar of country music. His success in country music signaled to white Mississippi racists, perhaps even more starkly than the newly integrated schools did, that their segregated world had vanished.

To fight back, white Mississippians rejected modernism and turned to more conservative religious denominations, eventually embracing politically active ministers and lay leaders espousing the union of politics and religion. In January 1970 the legislature debated a bill to repeal the state's antievolution law, which made it illegal for teachers to teach evolution in the public schools. At a time when every other state in the nation had legalized such teaching, the overwhelming majority of Mississippi legislators agreed to maintain the outdated statute because they saw its repeal as an attack on what one legislator called "a Christian state." In 1971, 51 percent of Mississippians worshipped in 4,382 churches. Twenty years later the percentage climbed to 70 percent in 5,433 churches. While the number of Southern Baptists grew, the United Methodists, tied to national campaigns for integration, stagnated, but the greatest increases occurred in white churches such as Church of God Prophecy and the Pentecostal Church of God. White Mississippians sought to regain the certainty of their vanished rural-dominated, segregated society through religious faith that rejected modernism and ignored integration. Although churches that had resisted integration nominally opened their doors to all races during the 1970s, Sunday morning church service time remained the most segregated hour across the state.

Acceptance of racial equality played out in millions of individual decisions. While racists conceded defeat, resentment surfaced constantly. Governor Waller set an example by integrating the Mississippi Highway Safety Patrol, hiring black aides, and appointing large numbers of blacks to state boards and commissions. His black appointees for the most part experienced southern hospitality as relieved white members accepted their black colleagues with a sense of gratification that they could drop the old segregationist conventions. Still, resentment roiled beneath the amenable veneer, perhaps more against whites who favored integration early than against blacks who demanded civil rights. In her memoir, Norma Watkins captured some of the spirit of the times when she returned to Jackson for her mother's funeral in 1970. Daughter of the attorney who represented Governor Barnett in his negotiations to integrate the University of Mississippi, she earned her college degree at Millsaps during the civil rights movement thanks to a black maid who cared for her house and children, and she had an affair with one of the out-of-state lawyers volunteering to represent civil rights workers. Disillusioned with the racism of her family, including her husband, she left him and her children to escape the state with her lawyer-lover. After four years of outward family acceptance during visits home, she found at the family reading of the will that her mother had disinherited her for rejecting, she said, the life of church bazaars and the Junior League. In 1972 Jim Silver, who had been run out of the state by the board of the Institutions of Higher

Learning for his radicalism, returned to Oxford on a visit, and the student president of the University of Mississippi's history honor society invited Silver to dine at the society's annual banquet, which coincided with his evening in town. The lone segregationist faculty member in the Ole Miss history department never spoke to the student president again. Mississippians spent the decade of the 1970s groping for comfort in the new integrated society.

Mississippians had erected mental walls to allow themselves to ignore criticism from the rest of the world, and even as they began to integrate, they often struggled to come to terms with the past and only gradually would they accept condemnation of the racists who ran the state. One incident that illustrated the state's inability to cope with national critics occurred in 1971 when the American Association of University Professors (AAUP) and the American Historical Association (AHA) concluded a three-year-long investigation into allegations of plagiarism against University of Southern Mississippi (USM) president William D. McCain. A historian, McCain stole from a young woman's master's thesis for an article he published in the *Journal of Mississippi History*—a publication he founded as director of the Mississippi Department of Archives and History. Although the AAUP and the AHA found McCain guilty and condemned him as a plagiarist in their publications, no Mississippi institution moved to sanction or punish him. He had served the segregationists well in the Kennard incident and supported the Citizens Council's work loyally, which seemed to ensure his unmolested tenure at the university. In any other state, McCain would have been censured and probably fired for committing the ultimate academic crime, but Mississippi's institutions had not made the transition from the closed society and ignored the condemnation of respected national organizations with few qualms. When McCain retired a few years later, USM named the graduate library in his honor.

Everyone struggled to make sense out of what they had experienced in the 1960s and how to function in the altered society. At the end of 1972, William F. Buckley Jr. tricked Walker Percy and Eudora Welty into appearing on his public television show, *Firing Line*, by promising to discuss literature and not politics with them. Displaying his arrogance as a northern intellectual, he broke his promise and asked the Mississippi authors how a sensitive southern writer could possibly live in a segregated society. Both writers rejected the idea that morality required them to leave the South. They tried to explain that staying and looking deeply into human relationships contributed far more than self-imposed exile. Welty told Buckley that her whole body of work dealt with injustice as a human characteristic, and she admitted that during her many trips to New York, northern ignorance of the South and, by implication, northerners' assumed moral superiority,

Josephine Haxton adopted the pen name Ellen Douglas in order to write about Mississippians struggling to leave segregation behind for an integrated society. Photo courtesy of Kay Holloway.

enraged her as much or more than the southern segregationists did. In the 1970s Welty struggled to write a nuanced story depicting a black man's rape of a white schoolteacher, but she never finished the story and turned instead to the past with publication of her Works Progress Administration (WPA) photographs and an autobiography in which she captured the cozy, comfortable world that she had experienced as a child in Jackson. Spending much of her time being honored for her life's work, Welty abandoned any effort to dissect and reflect on the new realty.

Under the pen name Ellen Douglas, Josephine Haxton tried in her novel *The Rock Cried Out* to do what Welty would not. As her voice, she chose Alan, a young man descended from a plantation owner. Alan rejected racism in the 1960s and service in the Vietnam War by becoming a conscientious objector. In 1971 she had him leave Boston, where he worked in a factory and wrote poetry, to return to the rundown family plantation, where Noah, an old black man descended from Alan's ancestors' slaves, linked Alan to the distant past and where Alan uncovered several "truths" about his family. His aunt, for example, had an affair with Noah's son and then punished the son for rejecting her by leasing Noah's land, given to him by her grandfather, to the government for a satellite-tracking station.

Haxton portrayed Alan's cousins Lee and Dallas Boykin as on two paths taken by Mississippians. Lee became a marijuana-smoking hippie supporting integration and making a living as a photographer, while Dallas served in Vietnam, lived in a trailer, and cut pulpwood for a living. Creating Dallas's wife, Lorene, allowed Haxton to describe the charismatic religious scene in the state, while Dallas's desperate desire to achieve the bliss his wife enjoyed gave Haxton a tool to reveal Dallas's murder in 1964 of another female cousin loved by Dallas and Alan. Along the way, Lee and Alan decided to collect oral histories in order to write about Chickasaw Ridge, where they lived, and in doing so, they learned from a college-educated octoroon neighbor that Lee's mother had been orphaned when her father died at the hands of rednecks who objected to his religious teaching including integration and labor organizing. Lee's mother exposed the area's Ku Klux Klan (KKK) members and their activities to the Federal Bureau of Investigation (FBI) in a letter but died before receiving the reward check, which her KKK-member husband used to escape to Texas and achieve prosperity.

In the end, Alan became a welder, wrote the record of his experiences (Haxton's novel), and lived alongside the descendants of his family's slaves. Haxton had Alan's in-law, a J. C. Penney manager, warn Alan about the family's eccentricities, which, he said, kept them from achieving economic security and wasted the land by not exploiting its potential for development as an efficiently run business.

In 2003 a literary critic praised Haxton's novel for repudiating Faulkner's treatment of race and substituting race as a "cultural construction." References to Faulkner pepper the novel, and Alan, through the course of the novel, evolved a new position on race. Initially he rejected responsibility for his family's sins as slave owners and sharecropper masters. Early in the book, Alan asked Noah not to make him feel bad by mentioning how Noah had been cheated by the family, but in the end Alan created an accurate record of his evolution containing all the characters' points of view. Allen concluded his history of Mississippi in the 1970s with a promise to listen to Noah's stories in order to learn all that he could from the old man.

Haxton's fiction reflected reality in the 1970s because such plantations existed. For example, the Finley plantation in Marshall County, Strawberry Plains, had a widowed relative living in the old plantation house without electricity and with only black sharecroppers of long service and a shepherd-mix dog for company. No passable road to the house existed, and visitors parked in a field and crossed a treacherous bridge to walk a sunken road to the house. In the early 1970s Margaret Finley Shackelford, who owned the 2,500 acres with her sister, retired back home after a career in public health service in Oklahoma with her physician husband to restore the country mansion. Her sister, Ruth Finley, occupied the family's town house. Ruth never married and ran the plantation with her father, Thomas Finley, until he died. Finley made money for the family, but in a conservative manner as benefited a staunch Presbyterian. He never raised a tenant's rent once he let a piece of land. In 1976 the sisters deeded some of their land to a black church, making good on a promise made by their father to the congregation in 1921. After her father died, Ruth returned more of the land to nature, refusing to destroy a beaver dam when it flooded fields and forbidding hunting on the property. In 1975 Margaret and her husband moved into the restored antebellum plantation house and filled it with antique furniture, but the two sisters determined to leave the land to a conservation organization. In 1982 they willed the plantation and town house to the Audubon Society as an education center and preserve.

Outside of fiction, perhaps Parchman offered the best place to begin the analysis of basic change in Mississippi because the prison symbolized the old society as the institution established by Vardaman to enforce segregation in an openly brutal fashion. As late as 1971, rural white sergeants or guards still selected killers as armed trustees to intimidate and ultimately kill those who bucked the system. Roy Haber, a Jewish lawyer from New York who worked out of a Farish Street office as a civil rights volunteer, began to investigate the prison. His inmate informants braved beating and torture to meet with him to tell their stories, and within a few weeks Haber amassed a fifty-page, single-spaced document listing murders, rapes, beatings, and torture committed over the past two years. As word of his work spread, Danny Bennett, who had been a promising white football player before being sent to prison, died after he collapsed on the long line in a Parchman field. Shocked with cattle prods and beaten with ax handles, Bennett died in the back of an open truck where his assailants threw him. Despite the physical evidence of his torture, the prison doctor recorded his death as resulting from heat stroke. A committee of the Mississippi legislature investigated and condemned Bennett's death as resulting from the brutal system employed by Parchman, warning that reforms had to be addressed before the federal government intervened.

In the wake of the report, Haber filed his suit in federal court on behalf of four inmates, claiming that Parchman's system violated several amendments to the U.S. Constitution. William Keady, federal judge for the Northern District of Mississippi, received the case. Son of an Irish saloon keeper,

Keady became an outstanding student and attended Washington University law school in St. Louis on a scholarship before enjoying a successful practice at William Alexander Percy's law firm in Greenville. Although steeped in the traditional segregationist culture, Keady possessed a keen sense of fair play and a strong desire to dispense even-handed justice, and thus he determined that Haber's case qualified as a class action suit covering all inmates, to which Keady added a subclass of black convicts. Keady visited the prison several times, viewing the inhumane conditions and listening to inmate tales of horror. The U.S. Justice Department filed a brief in support of the convicts, and in October 1972 Governor Waller refused to defend the institution, admitting the state's failure to meet its constitutional obligations. As a result, Keady issued a strong, passionate finding for the plaintiffs and in effect took control of Parchman, ordering massive changes to restore prisoners' human dignity. His ruling ended the last vestiges of slavery in Mississippi.

In the 1972 elections, the Mississippi Republican Party began its ascent to dominate the state. The electorate bestowed 78 percent of their votes on the incumbent, Richard Nixon. A young teacher in Vardaman confessed in class to supporting the Democratic candidate, George McGovern, and her students called her a Communist. The white Mississippi Democrats in office dared not support their national party, the Mississippi Freedom Democratic Party (MFDP) had ceased to be an important force, and Charles Evers survived as the strongest black leader in the state. Since 1968, Mississippi supported two Democratic parties, the old regulars and a biracial "loyalist" group founded by men such as Aaron Henry and Hodding Carter III. They recruited middle-class blacks such as Starkville's Dr. Conner, who had been ignored by the MFDP, and refugees from the MFDP such as Pat Derian, who came to Mississippi in order to work for school integration and stayed. Waller made an effort to merge the two factions but failed.

Eastland, who was president pro tempore of the U.S. Senate as well as chair of the Judiciary Committee, enjoyed enormous power in Washington, D.C., and Mississippi with a network of supporters buoyed by patronage and a dedication to preserving the old "southern way of life." Eastland made it plain to his campaign manager that he would not make the usual speeches to service clubs and campaign rallies to win reelection, so his manager organized "Eastland Appreciation Dinners" around the state. Once as Eastland left the new Gulfport banana terminal after a brief tour of the facility, a crowd of longshoremen insisted on shaking hands and chatting for an hour. The perspiring Eastland issued orders never to let that happen again. His favorite method of campaigning consisted of inviting important supporters into his air-conditioned vehicle for a whiskey and a brief chat. As Eastland coasted effortlessly toward reelection,

James Meredith threw the political system into disarray by qualifying to run against Eastland as a Republican. The Republican Party had no intention of challenging Eastland, who harbored not a shred of sympathy with his national Democratic Party, but the Republicans could not allow the man who integrated Ole Miss to claim membership in their all-white party. Party leaders persuaded Gil Carmichael to run against Meredith in the primary by buying Carmichael a plane and supplying funds to finance his campaign. Naturally he defeated Meredith, but then to the dismay of the party leadership, he ran an active race against Eastland in the general election. Nixon and the Republicans openly supported Eastland, earning Carmichael press support as an underdog abused by the system. Eastland's supporters injected large amounts of money to prevent an upset by Carmichael, who further angered his fellow Republicans by making clear his sympathy with the black population.

Fannie Lou Hamer considered another quixotic run against Eastland in 1972, but she suffered a nervous breakdown in January. The failure of the Freedom Farm and mounting poverty in the Delta depressed her spirit, and deteriorating health problems rendered her helpless.

State congressional contests illustrated the direction of Mississippi's politics better than the Senate contest. In the Fourth Congressional District, Ellis Bodron, a member of the old guard with twenty-four years of service in the legislature, ran as a regular Democrat, but he had made an enemy of Charles Evers, who as mayor of Fayette and a businessman wanted to build a nursing home in his town. Bodron owned nursing homes and blocked Evers's operation permit in the legislature. Evers retaliated by supporting Eddie McBride, a black candidate, against Bodron. Black voters made up 30 percent of the electorate and delivered the victory by a plurality to Thad Cochran, the Republican candidate. In the Second Congressional District, which included much of the Delta and a heavier black vote, no African American ran. A regular Democrat, David Bowen, who had dispensed federal funds to both black and white recipients for Governor Williams, defeated, among others, Frank E. Smith, who hoped to benefit from his support for black rights since leaving office and serving at the Tennessee Valley Authority (TVA). Smith quipped that the white voters remembered him and the black ones did not. On the Gulf Coast, Democratic congressman Colmer called it quits and supported his aide, Trent Lott, who ran as a Republican, to replace him. With a smaller black constituency, Lott carried the district handily for his new party, demonstrating the white voters' shift to the Republicans, who represented postsegregation conservatism better than the regular Democrats tainted by their liberal national party and the biracial "loyalist" organization.

Thad Cochran won seats in Congress thanks to divisions between the black and white wings of the Democratic Party and became the moderate face of the state's Republican Party. Courtesy of the Mississippi Department of Archives and History.

At the local level, whites calling themselves Democrats but denying any ties to the national party continued to dominate politics, serving on public school boards, for example, after the schools transitioned to a black majority. The white school officials sent their own children to segregated academies while continuing as top administrators in the public schools and while relegating the principals of the former black system to assistant positions without duties. Depending on the proportion of black students, some white parents sent their daughters to segregated academies and allowed their sons to attend integrated public schools. In Starkville, Dr. Conner's experience proved fairly typical. His wife, who taught in the city schools, resigned when the white principal tried to force her to raise the grade of a white student whose parents played a prominent role in the community. Dr. Conner ran unsuccessfully for office three times and organized a boycott of town businesses to force merchants to hire black workers. When the boycott failed, the merchants hired blacks who had refused to support the boycott. Behind the scenes, both state and federal authorities began to consult with Conner, and Mississippi State University (MSU) appointed him to serve on the selection committee charged to hire a new football coach. One of the town's banks named him to its board of directors. Though publicly supportive of the Democratic Party, he voted for Carmichael and against Eastland, but he did support the reelection of Senator Stennis in 1982 after Stennis announced his intention to vote for the renewal of the 1965 Voting Rights Act.

Not much had changed in the structure of state government since Sillers and a small group of legislators had taken control from Governor Bilbo.

Avery Wood (standing second from left) served as head of the Mississippi Game and Fish Commission and played a major role in preserving the Pascagoula River as the longest free-flowing river in the lower forty-eight states.

Limited to one term, Mississippi's governor lacked much power because the other fifteen members of the executive branch won popular elections along with him. Power resided in the legislature and the 150 boards and commissions created by the legislators, who also held key positions on most of the boards and commissions. The legislators appropriated the boards' and commissions' budgets, hired the employees staffing the bureaucracies, and oversaw their administration. Any legislator of any substance controlled his or her own fiefdom. Progress could be made but not without understanding and operating within the complex, highly personalized system.

The legislation preserving the Pascagoula River area demonstrated the operation of the system at its best. The Pascagoula Hardwood Company owned 42,000 acres of cypress-tupelo swamps, bottomland forests, and pine ridges. A group of four families scattered from Laurel to New York owned the company, which they simply allowed to lie dormant because they did not need the money its sale would bring. Knowing that in time its value would increase, they practiced patient inactivity, which had made their holdings one of the few remaining wilderness areas in the state.

Waller appointed one of his Greenwood supporters, Avery Wood, to head the Game and Fish Commission after asking him to shave off his mustache because he might be mistaken for a hippie. Wood grew up hunting and fishing in the Delta and then served in the navy. When he returned to the Delta in 1956, the destruction of his hunting sites by industrialized agriculture distressed him. An avid duck hunter, he joined Ducks Unlimited and learned of the national destruction of wildlife habitat. In his new political office, he assigned his assistant, Bill Quisenberry, to gather the figures on losses in Mississippi, and what he read on the chalkboard in his office appalled him. Since 1965 Mississippi's industrial farmers had converted almost a million new acres into cropland and a quarter million more into pasture. Industrialists and real-estate developers took tens of thousands of acres for their projects, and together the developers and farmers channelized 2,500 miles of rivers and streams. In the hills, the increasing pine plantations created ecological deserts, decreasing the rabbit and quail populations precipitously. Wood understood that hunting constituted a major component of Mississippi culture. His agency sold 600,000 licenses to hunters and fishermen each year, and the state only contained around two million citizens. Woods wanted to preserve something of his boyhood experience of hunting and fishing in the Delta, but his agency controlled only 21,000 acres purchased with license-generated funds.

Graham Wisner's family moved north from Mississippi, and he grew up in Washington, D.C.'s historic Georgetown neighborhood while his father worked for the Central Intelligence Agency (CIA). Wisner adopted an antiestablishment mentality and became a member of the era's counterculture. On a school project, he came south to make a movie about offshore oil workers and began spending weekends in an old family camp on the Pascagoula River, where he made friends with the game warden, who doubled as the Pascagoula Hardwood Company's caretaker. Often accompanied only by a mongrel dog, Wisner came to love the wilderness and eventually sought advice from one of his father's retired CIA colleagues on how to preserve the forested Pascagoula area. His father's friend connected him to the Nature Conservancy, an organization dedicated to preservation headquartered in Boston.

Eventually the conversancy sent its representative, Dave Morine, to Jackson, and he partnered with Wood to save the Pascagoula from clear cutting and development. Wood worked with the legislature to establish the Wildlife Heritage Committee and got the right members of the legislature to serve on it. Ivy League to the hilt, Morine dismissed the cigar-smoking legislators as colorful hicks, but when he lost his composure in one meeting and berated the legislators for failing to protect "a way of life" that he had seen vanish in his New England, they invited him back for another meeting. When he got down to facts and figures for the acquisition of the property, Morine altered his opinion of the legislators, who demonstrated deep knowledge and understanding of the complicated financing and political maneuvering necessary to accomplish the deal.

Charlie Deaton, representative from Greenwood who knew Wood from their boyhood days, handled the matter in the House of Representatives. Wood asked Quisenberry, his quiet, self-effacing, devoted Christian assistant, to sell the deal to the public. Despite the fact that he drove at a maddeningly slow pace and got airsick in planes, Quisenberry traveled the state speaking to hundreds of groups because he became a believer in the mission. When Wood deemed the support sufficient to overcome the opposition from the hunting club that had rented the rights to the Pascagoula Hardwood Company's lands, he signaled Deaton to introduce the legislation. In the midst of legislative activity, Governor Waller blocked International Paper's attempt to make a bid on the land with a telephone call to the company's CEO. Lieutenant Governor William Winter assigned the bill to a friendly committee in the state senate in order to block an opponent determined to punish Waller for not hiring the senator's people into the welfare department. The bill passed when Ellis Bodron, a member of the Heritage Committee, diverted the calendar by slipping the Pascagoula bill just under the cutoff clock in the Senate.

With the bill enacted, Morine handled the negotiations with the four families, which proved contentious. The leading negotiator for the families took exception to Waller's blocking International Paper's offer and made it clear that the families could continue to wait for the best offer regardless of the state's desire to preserve the Pascagoula. They did not like the publicity that the legislation turned on them, and they demanded tax savings so complex that Morine had to sell the deal to the Internal Revenue Service (IRS) using all the conservancy's contacts. Eventually Morine had to sacrifice a quarter of the company's land, excluding the pine ridges from the deal, but the conservancy bought the Pascagoula Hardwood Company, dissolved it, and sold it to the state, preserving the longest undammed river in the lower forty-eight states thanks to the largest donation to conservation in the nation's history.

Saving the Pascagoula from development illustrated a new Mississippi attitude—seeking to avoid some of the mistakes made in more industrialized states. Having shed its greatest evil with the end of segregation, some Mississippians sought to preserve the best of a still preindustrial society based on direct human relationships with and connections to the land. Seeking institutions to help with understanding and preserving what they considered a unique place, Mississippians built a much stronger library system. Not blessed with many bookstores in 1970, Mississippians bought comparatively few books, but Welty reported having admirers frequently tell her that they had their name on the list to check out her latest book at the library. Mississippi's counties had begun to overcome the paucity of libraries by organizing regional units serving several counties. Fifteen such organizations provided books to forty-nine counties in 1971. For example, the pine forest regional library joined Covington, Lamar, Perry, Stone, and Greene Counties in a library pool. Prior to the consortium, libraries had existed only through the work of women's clubs and the Works Progress Administration (WPA), but in the 1970s Sumrall, Lumberton, and Purvis got new buildings designed as libraries—a pattern replicated across the state.

As the state added public libraries, its junior colleges created branch campuses to respond to Mississippians' educational needs, and provided an example of how Mississippi institutions responded to the postsegregation era. In 1972 Mississippi had thirteen junior college districts based on the old agricultural high school organization, in which counties joined together to support a school. The state also had generated three anomalies among its two-year schools. Meridian grew out of the city's municipal school system and lacked the multicounty support system, as did the two black junior colleges, which answered to boards of supervisors. Men led all of these institutions with the support of a board in each district; only 2.7 percent of the trustees were women, and none were black. Supervisors appointed the trustees with roots reaching to the county beat level, and they served long terms. The presidents controlled their institutions and the system by working their way through the state's public schools serving as teachers, coaches, and principals in high schools before being tapped to lead the junior colleges. They operated by gentlemen's agreement trusting one another and respecting each president's absolute control of his institution. They created the Junior College Association, where they met to discuss and decide policy for the state system. Legally the state had a Junior College Commission, with university presidents appointed to oversee the system and George Moody, a former teacher and administrator from Pearl River Junior College, as director, who also served as the association's secretary. The commission always deferred to the association, and Moody carried out the decisions of the junior college presidents.

As the Department of Health, Education, and Welfare (HEW) sought to integrate Mississippi schools, the agency contacted the IHL and the Mississippi state superintendent of education, demanding a desegregation plan for the junior colleges. Both bureaucracies responded that each junior college had its own governing board of trustees. The national government never found a means of imposing a plan similar to the one imposed on the state's colleges, universities, and public schools, but the junior colleges gradually and quietly integrated because a portion of their funds came from federal support for vocational education. Schools accepting those funds had to end racial discrimination, which the junior colleges did first in vocational and then in academic programs quietly and without fanfare or court orders.

Beginning with Gulf Coast Junior College in Perkinston, the schools opened branch campuses in growing urban areas, which often grew to dwarf the home campuses, but the new branches became community colleges lacking the sports teams and other collegelike aspects of the mother campuses. The presidents protected the rural mother campuses by refusing for years to change the system's funding formula to provide the new community college branches full credit for the part-time students, and by keeping funding weighted to full-time day students. By the end of the decade as the state provided more of the institutions' funding, the legislature began to press for reform, but change came slowly during the 1980s, with the system evolving and retaining much of its original structure.

On the whole, the junior and community colleges prospered compared to the state's universities, which suffered from the publicity generated by the integration crisis and then operated under the cloud generated by the suit initiated in 1975 by Jake Ayers Sr. on behalf of his son, a student at Jackson State University. The suit sought damages for Mississippi's three black institutions of higher learning, charging that segregation denied them adequate funding and stunted their development. Litigation to decide the issue continued for over thirty years.

Governor Waller supported the junior and community colleges but clashed with the university presidents and took on the domination of the system by the big three, Ole Miss, MSU, and USM. He appointed the first black and the first Mississippi University for Women (MUW) "representative" to the IHL as well as a Delta State person. As an antidote to domination of the big three schools, Waller supported legislation elevating five of the colleges to university status and the creation of professional schools in dentistry, veterinary medicine, and architecture in order to stem the brain drain created by such students leaving the state for professional and postgraduate training. Waller enjoyed emphasizing his break with the past by unusual acts such as attending Mississippi Valley State College's homecoming football game.

Waller and his wife, Carol, worked through most of his administration to save the governor's mansion, which Governor Williams abandoned after the state building commission declared it unsafe for habitation. The Wallers raised money and worked to have the mansion declared a National Historic Landmark by the secretary of the interior. Carol Waller personally researched the history of the mansion and worked closely with architects, gardeners, and design experts to carry out a restoration of the building and grounds, completing the work and reopening the mansion in 1975.

Cliff Finch ran for governor that year, building on Waller's legacy as an outsider and making a populist appeal by working at a series of jobs such as bagging groceries and driving a bulldozer, bringing along a lunchbox, which became his campaign symbol. He defeated Eastland's candidate, Maurice Dantin, and Lieutenant Governor William Winter in the Democratic primary and Republican Gil Carmichael in the general election. The Republicans expected to win and blamed Carmichael's loss on his progressive ideas, such as registering handguns and writing a new constitution.

The white-haired Finch became the first Mississippi governor to address the state National Association for the Advancement of Colored People (NAACP) convention. He did so at the Holiday Inn near the governor's mansion with a glass wall behind him and lightning illuminating him in dramatic fashion. Finch owed his election to an alliance of rural whites, who voted with blacks to give him the victory, which enabled him to unite the Regulars and Loyalists by creating joint chairs—black and white—to run the united Democratic Party. Dr. Conner of Starkville served alongside a George Wallace supporter on an important committee and reported it difficult, but looking back on the experience, he found they could work together despite their differences and in the end found it interesting to get to know his "enemy" as a person. In 1976 Wallace won the Mississippi presidential caucuses as a Democrat—not as an independent—and then supported Jimmy Carter after Carter won the presidential nomination. Wallace's example persuaded many Mississippi Regulars to stay in the party and work with black Democrats. The Democrats in the Mississippi congressional delegation also finally favored the union of the two factions of the Democratic Party in order to protect their seniority. Williams's loss of his congressional seniority had made an impression. In addition, the Mississippi Republicans divided into angry camps, one supporting President Gerald Ford and the other Ronald Reagan, which eased the pressure on their opponents. Eastland and Stennis accompanied Carter to campaign in the state, helping the Southern Baptist candidate—who proclaimed himself a born-again Christian—to carry the state, which provided him the necessary electoral votes to win the presidency.

During Finch's administration, the legislature overcame the state savings and loan disaster, rescued the banks, and forced them to qualify for federal depositor insurance, but Finch proved to be a poor administrator. Small Toyota pickups clustered around the mansion most days as Finch huddled with the good ole boys and his dealings quickly grew murky. Rumor held that Finch's wife shot him over an extramarital affair, but the official version claimed that he was rushed to the medical center for appendicitis. The carefully selected furnishings for the restored mansion suffered heavy wear by the Finches and guests, driving the caretakers from the Mississippi Department of Archives and History to distraction.

As Eastland's reelection neared in 1978, the senator had a tearful meeting with Aaron Henry, hired a black assistant, and won Henry's endorsement. Henry enlisted Charles Evers to help, and at the 1977 Mississippi Democratic Jefferson-Jackson Day dinner, Eastland broke bread with black party members at their table. Veteran news reporter Bill Minor expressed amazement in his column, recalling all of the White Citizens Council's banquets that Eastland had graced and opined that anything seemed possible after witnessing Eastland's conversion to integration. Despite Eastland's support for Waller in his gubernatorial race, Waller announced his intention to challenge the incumbent senator. Unable to face making a traditional appeal to the voters, Eastland withdrew. Finch, along with a host of other Democrats, announced he would oppose Waller. Dantin won the primary despite political ads depicting a smoking cigar in an ashtray next to a glass of whiskey tying him to Eastland.

Thad Cochran went to Eastland in 1976 shortly after his reelection to the House of Representatives to tell the senator that he intended to run for the Senate only if Eastland retired. Eastland confided that he would not run, giving the Republican two years to quietly prepare. Obviously Eastland changed his mind when the race drew near, but he nonetheless encouraged a Republican to be prepared. Charles Evers threw the election to Cochran. By 1978 Evers had become a Republican, but he ran as an independent to negate the black-white Democratic coalition that elected Waller, Finch, and Carter. An unashamed capitalist, Evers claimed that he despised his old Democratic friends for providing a welfare state that ruined black life. Cochran won the Senate seat, as he had the one in the House, with a plurality, not a majority, of the votes cast.

Finch served out the remainder of his term as governor under a cloud of corruption. During his last year in office, the major topic of conversation among his staff and appointees was "has the FBI talked to you yet?" In part to stave off indictment, Finch ran for president, riding cross country with long-haul truckers who were protesting high fuel prices. He appeared in the newspaper wearing only bubbles in a heart-shaped bathtub during a stop in Arizona.

Senator Eastland retired to his plantation, and while he refused to apologize for his segregationist past, he made sizable contributions to the NAACP and maintained a close friendship with Aaron Henry. He enjoyed his return to country life, maintained housing for former black employees in their retirement, and thanked Henry for helping him to understand the "whole picture."

His neighbor, Fannie Lou Hamer, died in 1977, broke and having suffered physically at the end, but her funeral served as a celebration of the victory of the civil rights movement. United Nations ambassador Andrew Young, who had bailed Hamer out of jail in Winona, flew into Indianola on a government jet accompanied by Assistant Secretary of State Hodding Carter. Stokely Carmichael, the originator of the Black Power slogan, and Ella Baker, the teacher of nonviolent protest philosophy, attended, along with congressmen and other dignitaries. After the Tougaloo College Choir sang, Young spoke movingly of Hamer's bravery and credited her with shifting the foundation of the nation, observing that it was the black votes that her leadership produced that made Carter president.

The year after Hamer died, an English professor and a geographer convened a conference at USM entitled "A Sense of Place and the Americanization of Mississippi" at which a mixture of scholars, writers, and public intellectuals probed to understand what made Mississippi "different." Willie Morris provided the introduction to the conference, recalling a New York bar rant by a friend from New Orleans who overheard a group of writers discussing change in Mississippi. His friend declared that Mississippi had produced the world's best writers from a "haunted landscape" populated by people born of more miscegenation than in Brazil. Mississippians, he said, spoke in a manner that would make a drunken Irishman envious and regularly produced a sense of the histrionic that made the Old Testament pale by comparison. He suggested erecting large green signs at every state entrance reading "Posted No Trespassing." While Morris sympathized with the sentiment, he went on to declare that he had witnessed the Americanization of Mississippi. He remembered watching with friends in New York an Ole Miss–Alabama game played in Jackson. They marveled at the sea of Confederate flags and the band playing "Dixie" every five minutes while black and white cheerleaders and ball players on both teams embraced and high-fived. His friends asked: "What the hell is going on down there?"

Morris wondered too, noting that the Jackson skyline from Interstate 55 could have been Cleveland, Ohio; that his grandparents' Jackson home had been demolished to build a shopping center; and that Mississippi seemed to be disappearing in a rush to build franchise stores, pizza parlors, and chain motels. William Faulkner's niece, Dean Faulkner Wells, complained to Morris that the new MacDonald's in Oxford had placed a poster advertising a quarter-pound cheeseburger next to her uncle's portrait chosen to decorate the restaurant.

The black voice at the conference noted that he found it difficult to see the "New Mississippi" described by so many white observers because he still saw Klansmen flaunting their symbols of hate, segregated academies, and a 33 percent unemployment rate among the state's young black population. He believed that too many white Mississippians cherished the "old way" and concluded not with a plea for preservation but for more change.

Ida Mae Brandon lived in east Mississippi as a sharecropper until her husband took her to Chicago as part of the Great Migration. She never lost her Mississippi accent or her country values in the city. Courtesy of New Albertson's, Inc.

Meanwhile that same year at Ole Miss, the history department inaugurated the Chancellor's History Symposium by inviting the nation's leading historians to reconsider the historical treatment of slavery. The administration reined in the excited history faculty a bit by vetoing their first choice of a poster for the event, which depicted a clenched black fist with chains falling away. The Black Power symbolism proved too much for the chancellor.

In Chicago, Ida Mae Gladney had re-created an extended Mississippi family on the south side of the city even as her neighborhood turned into a ghetto. Her husband, George, died of a heart attack, but she, her children, and her grandchildren lived in adjoining apartments, insulating themselves from the decay surrounding them. In 1977 Chicago's Jewel supermarket chain chose Ida Mae and her family to represent the idealized family at Thanksgiving. Ida Mae never cut her Mississippi roots, held on to her family values, raised admirable children, and still baked the best sweet potato pies. She spoke all her life with her Mississippi country accent and maintained what her biographer called her spiritual being. The Jewel advertisement photograph caught her in the center—matriarch of the family—wearing polyester and big goggle glasses, smiling, unburdened, and holding a platter of salad. She never returned to the "New Mississippi" but instead took the old one to Chicago.

Back in Mississippi, church membership increased, and religion fused with politics. Black and white Mississippi Baptists moved to cooperate in 1975, forming the Cooperative Ministers Program without seeking to merge their congregations. Both black and white Baptists agreed that they wanted to continue worshipping separately for cultural reasons. In 1979 they launched "Good News Mississippi," which began with a state convention bringing black and white Baptist women together to explore their common pilgrimages of faith. Although both races expressed a desire to unite in faith, real biracial services rarely developed. The only biracial Southern Baptist church was in a Jackson neighborhood transitioning from a white to a black population, but it failed to flourish. An African American, John Perkins, became the leading prominent spokesman for racial cooperation. Perkins fled the state for California after a policeman killed his brother in 1946. After becoming a successful businessman, he experienced a religious conversion, which led him to return to Mississippi on a religious mission. He founded Voice of Calvary Ministries (VOC), worked in the civil rights movement, received a brutal beating from the police, and persevered to create a church dedicated to community betterment. His VOC achieved remarkable success with urban renewal in Jackson and a literacy program among many outreach efforts. Other black ministers, such as Luke Edwards in Meridian and Phillip Coleman in Jackson, followed the same path, combining religion and self-help economic development ministries.

White Mississippi ministers' work fell under the shadow of religious-political activists in the state. Roy McMillan of Kosciusko, who claimed to have been abandoned naked in a shoebox shortly after birth, made protesting abortion his life's work. He met his wife, Dr. Beverly McMillan, in church after she abandoned her practice in an abortion clinic, and together they earned a national reputation for picketing and other protests against abortion. Their Christian Action Group garnered massive contributions to finance their activities and earned them national reputations.

Tupelo's Donald E. Wildmon made more of a sensation by attacking the media with his National Federation for Decency, later known as the American Family Association. Wildmon grew up in Ripley's First United Methodist Church playing school sports and achieving honors as a Boy Scout. His college experiences at MSU and Millsaps proved disappointing, but he shone at Emory University's school of divinity. He remained in the United Methodist Church, serving as pastor in Tupelo and Southhaven until one

Tupelo's Donald E. Wildmon garnered national headlines by attacking the media with his National Federation for Decency, later known as the American Family Association. Photograph courtesy of the American Family Association.

evening in 1978, while watching television with his family, he grew disgusted with the sex, violence, and profanity on the screen and turned it off. Resigning from his church post, he launched a boycott against Sears for sponsoring programs that he disapproved of, and Sears canceled its advertisements for those shows. His success earned him an alliance with Jerry Falwell, the Virginia-based leader of the Moral Majority, which had developed major political muscle nationwide. Their alliance racked up even larger memberships, donations, and victories, forcing such giants as Proctor & Gamble to withdraw advertising from shows identified by Wildmon as offensive. The Wildmon-Falwell partnership ended quickly, but Wildmon continued his crusade, targeting Holiday Inn for "pornographic" movies in its motels, 7-Eleven for selling *Penthouse* and *Playboy*, and CBS for what Wildmon said was a scene in a Mighty Mouse cartoon where the rodent-hero sniffed cocaine. His national fame did not seem to earn him respect in Tupelo, where he ran for the state house of representatives and came in third in a four-person field. The North Mississippi United Methodist Annual Conference declined to endorse Wildmon's Coalition for Better Television, but his high profile in the national media gave the nation the impression that he represented religious sentiment in Mississippi.

The Huff brothers' experiences illustrated the path of many young Mississippians tempted away from their rural, traditional religious roots only to find their way back through mystical, miraculous versions of Christian

David and the Giants, the Huff brothers, and Keith Thibodeaux became a regional rock 'n' roll success in the 1970s before turning to evangelical religion and Christian rock later in their careers.

belief. David Huff and his twin brothers, Clayborn and Rayborn, grew up in Raleigh, Mississippi, in the heart of Sullivan's Hollow. Their father, who worked as a logger and later as an oil-rig worker, loved country music and bought his children instruments so they could play. Their family attended a Baptist church regularly, but the boys found more inspiration in music than religion, although David did the expected baptism at age twelve. David Huff began performing country music on a local Saturday radio show and by age thirteen moved into bars and honky-tonks. Rayborn and Clayborn fell under the influence of the Beatles and formed a high school band, playing for local dances imitating their British heroes. David moved to Laurel to attend nearby Jones Junior College, formed a rock band called the Twisters, and worked the rough joints around town. The brothers united as David and the Giants, and when they got gigs on the Gulf Coast, they brought in a drummer, Keith Thibodeaux, who had worked in Hollywood as a child actor in *I Love Lucy*. His parents split, and he moved back home to Louisiana with his mother, where he became addicted to drugs. The Huffs neither drank nor used drugs until Thibodeaux introduced them to both. Sex, drugs, and rock 'n' roll became their lifestyle, along with big heads of hair and bell-bottom pants. With a couple of regional hits, the band members enjoyed the female groupies in motels and in a rural frame house in the Mississippi woods at the end of a long dirt road.

In a drug-altered state, Thibodeaux experienced the presence of the devil in the band's rented house, sending him back to his family's traditional Catholic church for mass and confession. Fear of death from the band's lifestyle sent Thibodeaux back to his mother in Louisiana, where she introduced him to a charismatic prayer meeting, which included miracle healing, music, and speaking in tongues. He sensed the love of God in the meetings, and when a priest laid his hands on him, Thibodeaux collapsed in what he learned to call being "slain in the spirit." Then he saw Jesus in a light hovering about him, felt Jesus's empathy, and accepted Jesus's forgiveness for his many sins. He returned to the only job that he had—with the band—and slipped back into old habits, but took up reading the Bible and praying. He tried manual labor to escape the band life, but returned to rock 'n' roll. He met Kathy Denton while playing in a supper club on the Ross Barnett reservoir, dated her, and convinced her to marry him by asking God if they should marry with a Bible upright in her lap, which fell open on an appropriate page in the Book of Ruth. After their marriage, during a visit to California Thibodeaux watched the *700 Club*, heard "contemporary Christian music," and began to consider a new career.

Meanwhile, with Thibodeaux's encouragement, the Huff brothers began to read the Bible between gigs. The twins had been reduced to living in their Volkswagen van until David took them into his apartment, where the three of them conducted Bible-study classes. They dropped out of music for a while, but in 1977 they recorded their first contemporary Christian album and another each year for the next two years. The twins cut their hair and began to play in churches, usually for "love offerings." They reconstituted David and the Giants as a Christian rock band, inviting Thibodeaux to rejoin the group. Thibodeaux's wife, Kathy, had their first child and returned to ballet dancing. In July 1979, during a Giants concert in Laurel, she answered the band's call for conversions at the end of the concert. She continued to dance but after her conversion experience did it as a tribute to God. She became the principal dancer for Jackson Ballet Company and won the silver medal at the international ballet competition in Jackson dancing to "We Shall Behold Him," a song glorifying Jesus.

The Giants went international with a tour in England, where the band once baptized converted motorcycle punkers in a mass ceremony in the Thames lighted by the punkers' bikes' headlights. Near the end of his term as governor, Cliff Finch sent a document to the Giants proclaiming the band "Goodwill Ambassadors for Cliff Finch and the State of Mississippi." Kathy eventually left the Jackson Ballet and started her own Christian ballet company, Ballet Magnificat, and Keith left touring to become manager of the company, which ran several programs sending dancers to schools, nursing homes, day care centers, and churches. The Huffs continued their

Christian music careers, competing with more conventional groups such as the Southernaires, a black gospel group formed in Jackson in 1940 and touring through the 1980s. Both the Giants and the Southernaires insisted that their music be considered a form of ministry, and while they made their living from their sacred music, they used it as a means of spreading their religious beliefs. They and the churches raised the numbers in church membership almost 20 percent between 1970 and 1990, with the evangelical churches growing faster than even the Baptists.

While ordination of women as priests split the Mississippi Episcopal Church, the Southern Baptists rejected women ministers, and most fundamentalist churches never considered it. The Equal Rights Amendment, sent to the states by Congress in 1972, generated heated opposition in the Mississippi legislature, which annually refused to ratify it. The International Women's Year (IWY) state conference was held to select delegates to attend the national conference, which culminated in the mobilization of the Christian Right and turned an unfavorable spotlight on Mississippians' unprogressive attitudes toward women's rights. Both the Ford and Carter administrations supported the United Nation's request to participate in what would eventually be an international conference to promote women's rights. Congress appropriated money to fund the IWY, and although feminists dominated the organization, a sizable number of Mississippians supported it as well, including contingents at the state's universities and in the larger urban areas. Evelyn Gandy, the lieutenant governor, even lent her careful endorsement, but ministers around the state condemned the IWY as a front for Communism and Godless humanism.

The conservative churches planned the takeover of the state IWY conference held at Hinds Community College. Several Pentecostal ministers bused in congregations. The crowds overwhelmed the organizers, who expected far fewer attendees. Compressed crowds led to short tempers and physical confrontations, which some conference-goers tried to quell by singing patriotic songs. The technique worked well until some of the civil rights veterans tried to sing "We Shall Overcome," only to be drowned out by angry responses from the church groups. Men wielding hand-held radios barked orders and herded the conservative women around the building instructing them how to vote. Dallas Higgins, wife of the George Higgins, Grand Dragon of one of the state's Klans, played a prominent role in the conference, as did Richard Barrett, a transplanted northern lawyer who came to Mississippi and established himself as spokesman for "white rights." The religious conservatives elected an all-white delegation to attend the national conference with one token black woman who later resigned. Several males served in the delegation, and the conference adopted resolutions condemning sin as

Rea Hederman, member of the family controlling Mississippi's leading newspapers and educated at the country's best school of journalism, revolutionized the family's papers into a force for reform. Courtesy of the *Clarion-Ledger*.

defined in the Bible, singling homosexuality out for special condemnation. The conservatives endorsed education only after deleting a call for public kindergartens, believing that children should remain at home with their mothers as long as possible.

Newspaper columnist Bill Minor, who covered the civil rights movement in Mississippi, wrote that the IWY conference demonstrated the nature of the new Mississippi conservatism that replaced the old antiblack militancy. Although claiming not to be racist, the religious conservatism grew out of a reactionary backlash against the defeat of segregation. The Religious Right replaced the black man with liberalism of any sort as the new threat. Minor predicted that the legislators would react by moving in the same direction.

The culture wars of the period engulfed families as well as churches and other institutions. The Hederman newspapers quieted their strident racism by the early 1970s with the defeat of segregation, but in 1973 Rea Hederman took control of the *Clarion Ledger*. Hederman studied journalism at the University of Missouri, home to one of the country's best schools of journalism, and he hired like-minded young writers from around the nation, including the paper's first black reporters. He published a young white columnist who reflected on his generation's experiences growing up during the civil rights movement, explaining how he wrestled with accepting black equality. Hederman hired investigators and went after corruption in the state, turning what had been considered the worst newspaper in the country into an award-winning paper with a social conscience. Death threats did not deter him, and he waged daily battles with an extended network of relatives who disliked what he published. When the family tried to starve the paper by

Lemuria and Square Books demonstrated the destruction of the Magnolia curtain and the creation of a society open to new ideas. Photograph of Lemuria courtesy of Ken Murphy. Photograph of Square Books courtesy of Adam Brady.

denying him funding, Hederman commissioned books, which he sold along with collections of southern recipes and football calendars to raise cash. When he had an affair with the paper's style editor, the family fired him and sold all of its newspapers to Gannett. Hederman abandoned Mississippi, moved to New York, and used his share from the sale of the paper to buy the *New York Review of Books.*

Local television relented in its biased coverage of black issues when WLBT in Jackson lost its license. The United Church of Christ, which supported Tougaloo College, appealed to the Federal Communications Commission (FCC) to revoke the station's broadcast license because it did not serve the interests of its black viewers. After WLBT's management repeatedly ignored warnings to change, the FCC awarded the license to a biracial group that promised to operate the station in a manner promoting tolerance under new management. WLBT became the only television station in the nation permanently to lose its license for such behavior.

As the wall of resistance to outside influences and ideas began to collapse, quality bookstores began to open across the state. Lemuria began in 1975 with a few books in a converted apartment in the Quarter on Lakeland Drive in Jackson. In two years it grew into a small bookshop in Highland Village, and by the 1980s it occupied a large space in Banner Hall. Staffed with people who read books, it became famous for book signings by major authors. Square Books in Oxford filled a void in the university town in 1976 with an upstairs shop on the town square. A book lover with strong family ties to the community, Richard Howorth began with the mission of featuring southern literature and history. Soon after he opened his store, Ellen Douglas did a reading from *The Rock Cried Out* and signed copies for customers. When the university opened the Center for the Study of Southern Culture and added the likes of Morris and Barry Hannah as writers in residence, more and more authors dropped in to visit. Soon Lemuria and Square Books had reputations of being among the best local bookstores in the country.

In 1979, as the inept Finch administration drew mercifully to a close, Mississippians seemed prepared to quit their habit of electing clownish populists to the governor's office and turned instead toward candidates more suited to the changing culture of the state. Lieutenant Governor Evelyn Gandy seemed to be the most likely candidate to win the governor's office. She graduated from Ole Miss law school in 1943, the only woman in her class, and won election to the Mississippi House of Representatives in 1947. She served as state treasurer and insurance commissioner before being elected lieutenant governor in 1976. As lieutenant governor, she broke a tie vote in the Senate to remove control of sixteenth-section lands from the county supervisors, who too often made sweetheart deals that produced inadequate funding for schools. The resulting new law gave control of the lands to school boards as agencies more likely to demand fair market rent to benefit education, and the act provided her progressive credentials.

William Winter, twice defeated for governor, hesitated to make a third run at the office, but some heavyweights who had supported Finch begged to make amends for a bad decision by providing financing, and polling indicated that the majority of Mississippians seemed unlikely to vote for a woman. Winter counted on defeating the other men in the race and winning the runoff against Gandy, which he did with television ads featuring tanks and Winter firing a pistol at the highway patrol firing range.

Gil Carmichael ran again against Finch's record in an "I told you so" mode. Billy Mounger, one of the Mississippi Republican Party founders, believed that the party would suffer more with a Carmichael administration that it would by losing to Winter, so he listened to former governor John Bell Williams's advice to recruit a Delta planter, Leon Bramlett, who had worked in Williams's administration, to block Carmichael. Bramlett and Carmichael fought a brutal primary campaign, which Carmichael ultimately won, resulting in Mississippians having the choice in November 1979 between two candidates dedicated to reform and favoring good race relations. The conservative Republicans despised their party's candidate for his reform-mindedness and positive attitude toward the black community, and the regular Democrats had condemned Winter for decades as a known "moderate" who timidly espoused compromise during the darkest period of segregationist rhetoric. Old battles, however, sometimes appeared to have been forgotten. Walter Sillers's wife, Lena, invited Winter to lunch at Rosedale and assembled family members to pledge their support for his campaign. Mounger voted for Winter, who won by almost 150,000 votes.

Winter opted for an inaugural seminar, rather than a ball, entitling the seminar "Mississippi and the Nation 1980." Eudora Welty, the black author Margaret Walker Alexander, and some participants from the civil rights movement spoke, heralding a new era in state history. Held in the Old Capitol, the event set the tone for an administration dedicated to reform. Winter installed former congressman Frank E. Smith as his idea man, but filled his administration with young men dubbed by the press as the "boys of spring." Winter showcased Mississippi's rich culture with a series of dinners at the mansion coordinated by Smith for the purpose of encouraging Mississippians to embrace a rainbow of ideas and people. They chose early to honor opera star Leontyne Price as one of the most outstanding black women proud to claim her Mississippi roots. Following her performance, they produced a discussion of Mississippi culture featuring Bill Ferris, the director

William F. Winter led the few progressive Democrats during the era of massive resistance to integration and finally won the governor's office in 1980, making education reform the cornerstone of his administration. Courtesy of the Mississippi Department of Archives and History.

of the Center for the Study of Southern Culture at Ole Miss. On another evening, Winter brought his old history professor, the exiled Jim Silver, back to lecture. Writers such as Welty, Walker Percy, Willie Morris, and Alexander read their works and discussed the reasons for Mississippi's plethora of gifted writers. The governor invited former secretary of state Dean Rusk to talk about foreign affairs and the Chinese ambassador to introduce his country to Mississippi. Jerry Clower came and also spoke about a changing world in his unique manner. The Winters honored Muddy Waters, who recalled working on a plantation until he fled north. They capped their entertaining by hosting President Jimmy Carter.

Politically, Winter stumbled at the outset of his administration by suggesting that the time for cochairs—black and white—had ended and that the Democratic Party should elect a white chair. The national party leaders stepped in and quickly forced a compromise, but Ronald Reagan, who visited the Neshoba County Fair, appealed to white Mississippians with his humorous Carter put-downs. To the delight of the crowd, Reagan asked fairgoers how they ever conducted such an event without federal support. The selection of the venue—the county where the famous civil rights workers were murdered—communicated to Mississippians that Republicans had forgiven and forgotten the dark past and that Mississippi values provided a model for the country. With both candidates campaigning in the state, Reagan won Mississippi in 1980 by a tiny margin, as Carter had done four years earlier.

In the 1980 general election, Jon Hinson's congressional campaign demonstrated that Mississippi's Democrats required the functioning of their black-white Democratic coalition in order to defeat Republicans. Hinson, an aide to Cochran, succeeded his old boss in the Fourth District congressional seat, but during the preparation for his first reelection in 1980, Hinson warned his fellow Republicans that he had been arrested in Washington in circumstances implicating him in homosexual activities. The former marine denied that he had ever engaged in a homosexual act, but the Jackson newspapers pursued the story, which proved ever more damning. The Democrats, running a young lawyer, should have had a great opportunity to capture Hinson's seat, but Leslie McLemore, a black political science professor at Jackson State University, entered the race in response to Winter's bungled attempt to end the cochair arrangement in the Democratic Party. McLemore wanted to make the point that white Democrats could not take black voters for granted. Hinson won with only 39 percent of the votes.

In February 1981 capitol police arrested Hinson after observing him committing a sex act in an isolated restroom that they had under surveillance because of complaints about such activities. A press account quoted a Tylertown shopper as saying that he had voted for Hinson despite believing him to be gay because "a gay was better than a Democrat," which indicated the strong emotions engendered in the political battles of the 1980s.

The special election to choose a replacement for Hinson, who resigned a month after his last arrest, took on special significance as a test of the Democratic black and white coalition and of the Republican strength coming so soon after Reagan's victory. The Republicans demonstrated discipline by sending only one man into the contest while the Democrats, with their usual lack of discipline, sent three into the fray, although all were white. One of them, Wayne Dowdy, mayor of McComb, endorsed the renewal of the 1965 Voting Rights Act, which would come up for a congressional vote in 1982. His promise solidified the black and white coalition, and although he got far fewer votes than the Republican front-runner in the first round, he won the runoff by 912 votes.

Two years into his four-year tenure, Governor Winter decided to challenge the Mississippi establishment as he had in 1955 when he ran against Sillers for the House of Representatives speakership. Winter won in 1982 because the Supreme Court decision for one man one vote had finally begun to reshape the Mississippi legislature. In 1979 an old Mississippi Freedom Democratic Party–initiated case forced the legislature to adopt single-member districts for themselves. Until 1979 members of the Mississippi House of Representatives came from multiple-member districts, which insulated them from public scrutiny. Weak press coverage had meant that the public knew almost nothing about what their representatives did in Jackson, but the new *Clarion Ledger* exposed their records to public scrutiny.

Despite the beginning of change in the legislature, Winter faced a tough fight for education reform because C. B. "Buddie" Newman controlled the House and Brad Dye presided in the Senate. Newman, a cotton and soybean

Buddie Newman reigned as the last of the all-powerful Speakers of the Mississippi House of Representatives until his "veto" of kindergartens led to his political demise. From the Mississippi Official and Statistical Register, 1984–1988.

farmer from Issaquena County, represented the long-powerful planter tradition. He served continuously in the legislature from 1948 to 1988. Sponsored and shepherded by Walter Sillers, Newman helped Sillers end Winter's challenge in 1955. As reward for his faithful service, Newman chaired the House of Representative Ways and Means Committee, rose to be speaker pro tempore, and in 1976 earned the speakership, ruling—as his mentor had—with an iron hand. Outside the legislature, Newman served on the Mississippi Budget Commission and the Board of Economic Development. Dye, a member of the Eastland organization, had served in the legislature, in the Williams administration, and as the state treasurer before being elected lieutenant governor in 1979. The presiding officers in each house referred all bills to the committee of their choice and as a rule had the power to defeat any measure they chose. The chair of each committee enjoyed the same power. If the chair chose not to meet, the committee had no recourse. If the chair decided not to bring up a bill for consideration, the bill died. If the chair brought up a bill for committee consideration and did not wish to recognize a member asking to the address the bill, the member got no opportunity to speak. Overcoming the entrenched leadership and the tradition of legislative domination looked all but impossible.

The 1981 legislature ignored the recommendations of a bipartisan committee appointed by Winter and chaired by Jack Reed, a progressive

Robert Clark, elected as the first post-Reconstruction black member of the Mississippi legislature, served as chairman of the education committee and later as speaker pro tempore. © 2002 J. D. Schwalm.

Republican from Tupelo—a city known to be the home of a fine public school system. At the opening of the 1982 regular session, Winter warned the legislators that it was "boat rocking time." The focus of debate came down to kindergartens, which every other state had and Mississippi did not. The common refrain heard in the legislature and around the state called kindergartens "babysitting services for blacks," reflecting profound ignorance and lingering hostility toward the black community growing out of the hostility toward the state's Head Start program. Robert Clark, the first black man since Reconstruction to serve in the legislature, chaired the education committee because he had supported Newman at a key point in Newman's rise to the speakership. Clark supported education reform and kindergartens and tried to get recognition to bring a bill before the House of Representatives for a vote, but Newman refused to recognize him. Ignoring what appeared to be a majority of the House members, Newman adjourned the House after a dramatic confrontation, believing that members wished to publicly speak for the bill while privately they desired not to have to vote for it. The next day education supporters criticized Newman's handling and demanded a vote. But the rules required that two-thirds of the House members vote for the bill because it had missed the previous day's deadline. Supporters could not muster the votes of two-thirds of the chamber.

The Winter team contacted an ABC producer for the news show *20/20* and offered the story of Newman's killing the education bill. Subsequently *20/20* aired a segment portraying Newman as the symbol of all that held Mississippi in poverty and darkness. The show emphasized that Mississippi remained the only state without kindergartens because of a political system managed by a few powerful men retarding progress. The Gannett-owned newspapers took up where Rea Hederman left off and reinforced the story told by national television.

Winter and the "boys of spring" organized a political campaign to garner public support for their reform package in advance of a special session of the legislature, which Winter intended to call. Through the spring and summer, Winter and his staff talked to every group in the state willing to listen, gathering over 40,000 cards with supporters' contact information. The campaign culminated with a series of education forums or rallies to impress the members of the legislature. Winter scheduled the first one in Oxford, expecting perhaps 500 attendees; 3,000 turned out at Oxford High School, leading some legislators to believe that Winter had created an atmosphere of mass panic by the end of his campaign.

Education supporters placed a constitutional amendment on the November ballot to abolish the election of the state superintendent of education and replace the old board of elected officials with an appointed superintendent and a board of education made up of interested citizens. The amendment passed by a slim margin, but despite the close vote, Winter called the special session to meet in December. Winter met with key committee chairmen from the legislature and dropped his long-standing demand for an oil and gas severance tax to fund the reform, telling the chairmen that he would leave it to them to identify the funds. Winter wrote to his 40,000 supporters asking them to demand action from their legislators. The *Clarion Ledger* flooded the capitol with reporters digging into all committee meetings and creating a "Hall of Shame" for those blocking progress on passage. The paper won a Pulitzer Prize for its coverage of the special session, and the legislators bowed to the pressure. Dye intervened with a defiant chairman in the Senate and Newman supported Clark in the House. Winter got his reform bill, including kindergartens, four days before Christmas, and in doing so he altered the legislature, starting it on the road to reforming itself.

In 1981 Attorney General Bill Allain provided the other impetus for reform by notifying thirty-six legislators serving on executive branch boards that they were violating the state constitution, which forbade such service. Believing they were a law unto themselves, legislators had simply ignored the constitution for decades and took no notice of Allain's communication. In April, after the passage of the education reform, the legislators and Allain asked the courts to decide the issue. A Hinds County judge ordered the legislators off the executive commissions, and the Mississippi Supreme Court unanimously upheld the lower court. Reluctantly, the legislators passed legislation bringing their branch into compliance with the court's decision, diminishing their power and handing more to the governor. The infighting involved politicians, still nominally all Democrats, within the system.

Meanwhile the Democrat versus Republican battles continued. A thirty-four-year-old Republican, Haley Barbour, challenged eighty-one-year-old Stennis for his Senate seat in 1982, but Stennis endorsed the extension of the 1965 Voting Rights Act as Dowdy did, and blacks held their noses to vote for the old segregationist. Barbour tried to use the age issue, but Stennis replied that Mississippians should not send a boy to do a man's job. Of course, Mississippians also knew that Stennis brought home the bacon with his seniority and wanted to complete construction of projects such as the Tennessee-Tombigbee Waterway in northeast Mississippi. Stennis won handily, but in 1984, the Democratic presidential candidate, Walter Mondale, did not stand a chance against Reagan, who benefited from the new Christian conservative movement. Campaigning in northeast Mississippi, Mondale faced a forum attendee who asked how he could claim to be a Christian when his platform endorsed abortion and gay rights. Winter challenged Cochran in the Senate race that year, but Cochran rode Reagan's coattails to a landslide victory over the governor.

Dirty politics as a part of the Republican-Democratic contest for power reached its nadir in the 1983 gubernatorial race. Bramlett easily secured the Republican nomination and Allain the Democratic slot. Republican leaders got wind of rumors that Allain engaged in sexual relations with black male transvestites and hired a detective agency to "prove" the allegations, which they proceeded to accomplish to their satisfaction. Bramlett considered the story too disgusting to believe and refused to endorse its release to the public, but Republican Party leaders charged ahead without their banner carrier's support. Allain denied the charges and went to Louisiana to take a polygraph examination, which he passed. His former wife made an ad supporting her ex-husband, and Governor Winter rallied the Democratic Party behind Allain. Despite television interviews with the transvestites, Allain won the election with 55 percent of the votes, demonstrating again the strength of the black and white Democratic coalition.

Ray Mabus, one of the "boys of spring," surveyed the political landscape toward the end of the Winter administration and settled on the office of state auditor as the launching pad for his gubernatorial aspirations. From Ackerman, where his family owned a hardware store, gins, and timberlands, Mabus attended Ole Miss, but then went to Johns Hopkins for a master's degree and to Harvard law school, earning academic honors at each institution. Widely traveled with his father and as a student, Mabus served on a guided-missile cruiser during the Vietnam War and then as law clerk to the Fifth Circuit Court of Appeals. When Winter offered him a job, Mabus worked for a subcommittee of the House Agriculture Committee as legal counsel. Active in Winter's education reform campaign, Mabus discovered the sorry state of

Ray Mabus entered politics as one of Governor Winter's "boys of spring," served as state auditor, and then won the governorship promising reforms that he failed to deliver because of an obstinate legislature. Later he served as ambassador to the Kingdom of Saudi Arabia and as secretary of the navy. Courtesy of the U.S. Department of Defense.

the auditor's office while doing some routine legal work for the governor. Reading about the powers of the auditor's office, Mabus saw the potential in a position that allowed him to investigate every official in the state.

In the late 1970s William G. "Bill" Burgin Jr., the longtime chairman of the Senate Appropriations Committee, went to prison for profiting from contracts with the Mississippi Department of Public Welfare, lending credence to a public perception of rampant corruption in state and local governments. The segregationists' defiance of the law had bred an atmosphere of lawlessness in Mississippi, and the legislature, in order to protect those defending segregation, even passed a law providing that conviction of a federal offense did not require a Mississippi official to resign his or her state office. The Mississippi system of government invited corruption. Most counties, for example, allowed supervisors to operate road repair and most other services at the beat level, making each supervisor ruler of his or her little fiefdom, where he or she ordered materials and paid for them without oversight. Voters expected graft, asking their supervisors to gravel their drives and dig their loved ones' graves with the county's backhoe. Most of the public knew that local public servants took bribes, but rationalized that their pay was too low and that they were good ole boys still. Mississippians had grown accustomed to graft, and while they knew it to be illegal, they did not consider it to be wrong.

Seventy-three-year-old Hamp King chose not to run for auditor again in 1983, having held the office since 1964, but adhering to custom, he arranged for an underling to have the position, with each department employee contributing 2 percent of his or her salary to finance the campaign. In the 1983 race, Mabus charged incompetence in the auditor's office and promised reforms. The voters did not buy King's defense of the old system, and Mabus won easily. When Mabus moved into his new office, he found a shoebox full of uncashed checks totaling $330,000 sent to King as payment from local governments for services provided by state auditors. The department had fallen years behind in its audits and had no filing system. Mabus got the legislature to fund private certified public accountant (CPA) firms to catch up on audits and assist his department in overhauling the system. Mabus waded into the political swamp, addressing the supervisors at their annual meeting and warning them that he would enforce the law strictly, allowing no gravel or culvert installation on private property or opening of graves with county labor and equipment. He followed up his speech with visits to each county and established a technical assistance unit to help supervisors wishing to operate within the law. One supervisor in Warren County began carrying a plastic sandwich bag filled with gravel in his jacket pocket, and when asked for gravel, he produced it for his constituent, explaining that the bag was all the gravel that he could provide. Many did not adjust so readily to Mabus's new regime.

Howls of fury greeted Mabus's reforms, and pundits predicted that the legislature would rein in the young upstart. However, as soon as lawmakers heard from constituents approving of the changes in the corrupt system, they backed off. Many county supervisors admitted grudgingly that Mabus had done them a favor by restricting the demands on county resources. One estimated that the man hours and gravel saved totaled millions of dollars in the first eight months of the crackdown, but the entrenched culture of corruption continued.

The FBI began to investigate county governments when agents questioned John Burgess, a Pentecostal minister and businessman who invested in a concrete manufacturing business that went bankrupt. Burgess learned that supervisors routinely required a 10 percent bribe to buy his company's pipes. He contacted the FBI with the information and heard nothing, but when his company went bankrupt, the FBI came to interview him about hidden assets, and he again told the agents about the bribes. The agents recognized a golden opportunity and persuaded him to open a front for them named Mid-State Pipe Company across from his building supply company in Carthage. The FBI named the undercover operation "Pretense," which was an acronym for "Preacher's Ten-Percent Supervisor's Expense."

Burgess wore wires and taped transactions with supervisors, but later "sold" the company to his "sales force" composed of FBI agents, who continued taping, selling pipes, and paying bribes across the state. After three years of investigation, the FBI charged 57 of the 410 county supervisors in the state with crimes, including bribery, extortion, accepting kickbacks, rigging bids, and billing counties for goods never delivered. They also indicted fourteen vendors and salesmen along with two of the state's three highway commissioners. Mabus, who had cooperated with the FBI operation, announced his candidacy for governor just after the news of the indictments broke.

The Republicans nominated Jack Reed, a Tupelo department store owner who served on the new state board of education. Mississippi voters had to choose between two progressive candidates whose policies would probably differ little. Reed cut into the Democrats' rural white votes, while Mabus encroached on the Republicans' urban white voters thanks to his anticorruption record. In the end, Mabus won by just over 3 percent of the vote thanks to loyal black Democrats and took office as the youngest governor in the nation.

Clearly Mississippi had changed since the troubled 1960s. Two political parties competed in most of the statewide elections. The state established a public radio network in 1984 with transmitters covering the entire state to deliver classical music, outstanding news shows, blues, and bluegrass on Saturday nights. The Mississippi Supreme Court got its first female justice in 1983 and its first black justice two years later. The black out-migration reversed in the 1970s as blacks began to return to Mississippi and other southern states. Newspapers painted a rosy picture. The *San Francisco Chronicle*, for example, quoted Etta Willis, who left California for Mount Olive, Mississippi, as finding less racism in Mississippi than she did in San Francisco. In the city, the racism was subtle, she said, while in the South it was direct and in your face, but she reported experiencing none. Earnest Smith, who left Mississippi for Chicago in 1944, returned to Mississippi in 1970 and told *Ebony* that he found an amazingly hospitable environment where white folks stopped him on the street to say hello and addressed his wife as "Miss Smith," called him "Sir," and answered "yes ma'am" and "no ma'am" to his wife. He noted the contrast to how he had been treated in 1944 and seemed astonished by the difference. Elijah Davis moved back to Jackson after twenty years in Gary, Indiana, because in Jackson he could walk the streets without fearing for his life.

As with the out-migration, the return resulted from both a push and a pull. As northern cities became increasingly undesirable and unsafe habitations, the end of segregation and the decline of the KKK made Mississippi more appealing. Black migrants to the North maintained family ties, and parents often sent their children to live with grandparents in order to attend Jackson State University or Mississippi Valley State. If a child of a migrant got into trouble with the authorities in Chicago or New York, his or her parents shipped him or her to Vardaman or Belzoni to escape city life and learn some old-fashioned values in the country. The first generation of migrants still felt the pull of place. Some worked hard and invested their money in a brick ranch house, which their parents occupied until the migrant retired back home. For those migrants who had established themselves in good-paying factory jobs or professional occupations with good pensions, the return produced a good life, but others sank back into the poverty they had sought to escape.

Dorothy Mae Scott grew up on a plantation in Sunflower County and married a blacksmith, Ruffin Scott, from the Will Dockery plantation. He called her Gypsy because of her light skin and straight hair. They had a rocky marriage, and at her mother's urging, Dorothy took a practical nursing course and fled to Chicago, where she worked as a private live-in nurse. Periodically Dorothy returned to Mississippi and lived with her husband long enough to produce a house full of children, but she always went back to Chicago to earn more money, which she saved to buy land in the Delta. She fixated on the idea of owning her piece of Mississippi and farming it as an ideal existence. Gradually, in three transactions over the years, she accumulated almost fifty acres, and after witnessing gang youths murder two other young men and wound a third, she left Chicago for good, seeking refuge from city violence on her land outside Ruleville. She bought a tractor and a harvester, hoping that some of her children would join her in farming. They refused, the equipment rusted, Dorothy slid back into poverty, and eventually a drug addict murdered her in her home while stealing $60 from her.

By the 1980s Mississippians who stayed at home worked out postsegregation relationships that amazed many observers. Willie Morris depicted the new society by writing about a talented football player named Marcus Dupree, who played for Philadelphia High School. At the first football game Morris attended in Philadelphia, he noted the black minister praying before the game and the manner in which blacks and whites alike cheered their team, composed almost equally of white and black players. He encountered the occasional white racist during his travels between Oxford and Philadelphia, but on the whole Mississippians seemed to have accepted integration. Cecil Price Jr. and Marcus Dupree played on the same team, had gone to school together since the first grade, and visited in one another's homes. Cecil Jr. had been born about the time his father, as deputy sheriff, had participated in the infamous murder of the three civil rights workers. When Cecil Sr. returned from serving his prison term he had to make a decision

Marcus Dupree and Cecil Price Jr. played on Philadelphia High School's football team and were longtime friends despite the elder Price's involvement in the Neshoba County murders. Courtesy of the Philadelphia Public School District.

about his son's education, and he decided that because his son would have to live in an integrated society, it would be best for him to attend the public schools. Cecil Jr. played little football because he was too small, but he helped his friend Dupree don his many tear-away jerseys during games and sat next to him on the bench. Cecil Sr. watched and cheered the team from the stands. When Morris asked Dupree about his friendship with Cecil Jr., Dupree expressed no animosity toward Cecil Sr. and indicated the past played no role in his school-born relationship with the son.

The good race relations in Philadelphia extended to the Choctaw as well. Morris attended what he called the "Choctaw Bowl," where Philadelphia played Union at Choctaw Central High School football stadium. Many Choctaw attended in traditional clothing and mingled with blacks and whites. He watched black, white, and Choctaw boys playing their own version of football on the sidelines as Choctaw Boy Scouts in uniforms topped by red berets escorted the American flag along the sideline in the opening ceremony. As Morris waited for the game to begin, he chatted with an Ole Miss scout sent in the forlorn hope that Dupree might be persuaded to attend the University of Mississippi rather than one of the host of national powerhouse teams recruiting him.

Federally mandated integration of schools, restaurants, and motels played an enormous part in bringing about the social change Morris chronicled, but creating the public space noted lacking by Walker Percy in the 1960s also contributed. A retail revolution put an end to the old general stores and department stores, where blacks often suffered discrimination from clerks and managers. The new public retail spaces originated from a revolution in marketing. For example, in 1947 two sons of Lebanese immigrants launched the Fred's retail chain with a Good Luck store in Coldwater, Mississippi. By 1953 the family had fifty-three stores located mostly in small towns, where they sold discounted merchandise appealing equally to black and white customers who shopped side by side. In 1974 Wal-Mart entered the Mississippi market, targeting, at first, the same small towns favored by Fred's. By the 1980s Wal-Mart outgrew all of its competitors in Mississippi and around the world. Open twenty-four hours a day and attracting everyone with low prices that doomed the more traditional retail merchants, the corporation created the ultimate public space where all mingled equally. The Wal-Mart-less communities lost sales, tax revenue, and even population. Sam's Clubs and Super Centers magnified the effect and homogenized Mississippians' shopping experience, making it indistinguishable from that of other Americans and reinforcing the integration brought about by federal laws and courts.

Pockets of segregation still existed in the 1980s. Store clerks almost invariably told white travelers stopping for gas at a convenience store in the Delta to use "private" facilities to relieve themselves. At the Pig Stand on Highway 49 outside Belzoni, a hungry black wayfarer who happened to stop would be served, but local blacks never went to the Pig Stand, preferring the more hospitable atmosphere at Wimp's barbecue house across the tracks. Few out-of-state visitors to the Pig Stand, black or white, would have guessed that the men dressed in cotton work clothes perching on swivel stools sipping their coffee pulled in incomes in the tens of millions of dollars.

The Pig Stand in the 1980s served as the nerve center of Mississippi's major new industry—catfish farming. Delta farmers continued to be gamblers. After World War II, they diversified into soybeans and rice, grew larger, and bought more mechanized equipment. Delta Pine and Land, once the Delta's largest plantation, eventually sold all of its land and concentrated solely on seed development. Dedicated entrepreneurs, planters followed the money. Investment flowed into farming, which prospered in the 1970s. Bankers ventured into farm fields seeking to loan money, bringing prepared loan papers and writing checks in the farmers' truck cabs until the bust in the 1980s. In 1979 Mississippi row crops reached a value of $737 million, but four years later they had fallen to $181 million. Some of the Delta farmers who could borrow more money dug catfish ponds and generated a new industry in order to survive.

Larry Cochran, a third-generation planter on a piece of land near Isola, began experimenting with catfish in 1978, and when the price of row crops plummeted, he shifted from 1,000 acres of cotton and soybeans to growing two million pounds of catfish in thirty-three ponds. To pay, catfish farming

In the 1980s, when row crops declined in value, some Delta farmers who could borrow money dug catfish ponds and generated a new industry in order to survive. Courtesy of the Catfish Institute.

had to be done on a large scale. Cochran's fish ate twenty tons of feed per day, and the ponds required constant monitoring because the fish died if the temperature got too high without oxygen being introduced by aerating the ponds or if algae got out of control.

Planters such as Cochran took the unfertile clay "buckshot" land, the plentiful water, and the native catfish and combined them to build a major new agricultural industry. Major food processors moved in quickly to prepare the catfish for market, but in 1981 the planters established Delta Pride to process much of their crop. They established an institute to market their product and strictly controlled quality by hiring a taster to screen out any off-flavor fish. A farmer ready to harvest a pond brought a sample to the taster, and if the taster detected any hint of problem with the taste, the farmer kept feeding the fish tons of feed until the taste improved. Eventually the Delta farmers could produce their own feed and control the industry completely.

Delta Pride's treatment of its mostly black female workers made unfavorable headlines. On the factory fish line, the header, who sliced off the fish's head with a band saw, had to cut fifteen per minute, while the filet cutter was required to produce 800 pounds per day. The workers got one closely timed five-minute bathroom break in the morning and one fifteen-minute coffee break. Workers soon developed carpal tunnel syndrome, for which the company would pay the medical expenses, only to fire the worker when she tried to return to the job. Unions moved to organize the workers and succeeded after nasty strikes. The farmers fought back by importing Mexican laborers who refused to join the union.

Mississippi gained another ethnic minority through a somewhat similar importation of labor. In 1977 Richard Gollott, who owned Golden Gulf Seafood on Biloxi's Back Bay, needed oyster shuckers, and he heard of Vietnamese shucking oysters in New Orleans. He drove to the Crescent City in

Vietnamese refugees discovered the Mississippi Gulf Coast, established themselves as fishermen, and came to dominate the industry. Courtesy of Barry Yeoman.

a van, returned with temporary help, and persuaded one family to move to Mississippi. Others followed, building a community of strong family units working in the factories and then acquiring boats and moving out to sea, where their different methods—pushing their nets instead of pulling them and fishing north to south instead of east to west as American fishermen did—led to violent confrontations at times. Strained relations resulted as pressured American fishermen heard rumors that the government bought boats for the Vietnamese, who worked the fishing waters too often and too hard. The Vietnamese refused to report slashed nets or shots fired, not wishing to stir up more trouble. Gradually the Coast Guard translated rule books into Vietnamese, and community discussions ironed out some of the problems. The Catholic Church helped with priests, nuns, and a social support center. The Covacevich family, descendants of the Slovak immigrants who had earlier dominated the Biloxi seafood industry, rented the Vietnamese space in their boat yard. Soon the Vietnamese opened grocery stores, marine supply establishments, and restaurants. The Buddhists among them built a temple, adding to Mississippi's limited religious diversity.

In the 1980s Jackson contained only approximately fifty Indian families, but they built a Hindu temple in Rankin County and formed an Indian

A relatively small Indian population concentrated in the Jackson area built an impressive Hindu temple. Courtesy Hindu Temple, Brandon, Mississippi.

Association to promote and preserve their culture for their children. Several Indian doctors worked at the university medical center, and more taught in the state's universities. Travelers encountered Indian-run motels across the state, a practice made famous by *Mississippi Masala*, a movie made in Greenwood depicting Denzel Washington falling in love with the Indian daughter of a motel owner expelled from Uganda by the dictator Idi Amin. Natives of India could shop at an Indian-owned grocery in Jackson, rent Indian movies, and dine in Indian-run restaurants, making the state's capital more cosmopolitan.

Mississippi politicians experienced difficulty adjusting to the state's changing society. In the 1980s the Democratic Party attempted to solidify its black and white coalition, while the Republicans continued their inroads into the white majority. In an effort to maintain the black and white Democratic coalition, the legislature created a majority-black congressional district in the Delta and backed Robert Clark, who had earned a leadership post in the legislature, but the Republicans defeated him twice with a candidate who made blatant appeals with white racist images. Finally, in 1986 Mike Espy, a member of a black family whose wealth derived from a string of funeral homes and whose wealthy relatives in Chicago backed his run for the office, won the congressional seat by drawing a share of the white vote. Ruben Anderson, the first black Mississippi Supreme Court justice, won his election after being appointed to the court. Young rebels in the legislature forced Newman to retire and elected Tim Ford Speaker of the House of Representatives while reforming the House rules in an effort to make the legislature more democratic. Symbolically, the American Civil Liberties Union (ACLU) won a federal suit in 1986 forcing the state to stop illuminating a cross though the windows of the Walter Sillers State Office Building at Christmas.

In 1987 the eighty-six-year-old Senator Stennis announced his retirement, having altered his opinions on race considerably since prosecuting three Dekalb County black men on dubious murder charges. Since he was famed as the conscience of the Senate, President Nixon tried to turn to him as the arbiter in the infamous case of the missing minutes in the Watergate tapes because everyone would accept Stennis's honesty. When President Reagan nominated Robert Bork to the Supreme Court, Stennis voted against him, telling a confidant that he feared Bork might overturn the landmark civil rights cases, reopening civil rights conflicts. Stennis said that the civil rights battle had been lost and that too much had been spent fighting for segregation. He considered integration settled and wanted to move on. In the 1988 elections, white Mississippi voters flowed into the Republican Party. Congressman Lott ran against former congressman Dowdy, who, like Stennis, had accepted integration as settled. George H. W. Bush, Reagan's vice president, faced Michael Dukakis, the ultimate eastern establishment liberal. Mississippians associated Dukakis with arrogance and disdain for their way of life, while Bush told them that he respected Mississippi values, lifestyles, and culture. Political consultant Dick Morris ran Lott's campaign and softened the hard Republican position on social issues with ads featuring a young woman for whom Lott had secured a wheelchair. By compiling an overwhelming vote in his congressional district, Lott defeated Dowdy, whose white voters gave him only a slight majority in his old congressional district.

In 1987 Mabus had campaigned on the slogan "Mississippi will never be last again," and at the time of his inauguration, Welty penned an introduction to a book chronicling his entry into the governor's office. She spoke of pride and jubilation at having another "serious human being" like Governor Winter to continue moving Mississippi into the "wider world" where it belonged. In other words, she believed Mississippi had at long last joined the "modern" world to which governors such as Bilbo, whom she despised, had denied the state admittance. But Mabus's Johns Hopkins and Harvard degrees tainted his credentials as a Mississippian, and he found it impossible to lead Mississippi toward the modernity envisioned by Welty. As governor, Mabus tried to reform the corrupt county governments unmasked by the Pretense operation, but even with the support of the Mississippi Economic Council, the task proved contentious and won few political friends. The Mississippi Association of Supervisors persuaded the legislature to pass a pay raise for their members in preparation for adopting the unit system, which Mabus and other reformers touted as necessary to end corruption and improve efficiency. Mabus vetoed the raise and forced adoption of legislation requiring counties to vote the unit system up or down. Sensing the groundswell of opposition to the reform, newly elected state auditor Pete Johnson refused to endorse the unit system, resulting in a split decision. The urban counties voted for the unit system while the rural counties kept their beat systems, leaving the issue unresolved until the next administration. Mabus won a pay raise for Mississippi teachers and managed to have the legislature pass his education reform package, but it died because he insisted on funding it with a lottery as some other southern states did. A Mississippi lottery required a constitutional amendment that the legislature declined to adopt. Mabus did not grasp the necessity to compromise and to recognize the popularity of illogical but entrenched traditions. For example, he closed three charity hospitals established in Laurel, Meridian, and Vicksburg during the state's more populist era. Closure saved $7 million, which Mabus used to leverage $21 million in Medicaid funds. His policy made sense, but hospital closures enraged the affected communities. Perhaps due to his youth and inexperience, never having served in the legislature, Mabus did not understand how to work effectively with Mississippi's established leaders.

By contrast, H. L. "Sonny" Meredith demonstrated his mastery of the existing system by enacting legislation to legalize casino gambling in heavily Baptist, antigambling Mississippi. The impetus for gambling came from the Gulf Coast counties, which had not recovered from Hurricane Camille or Senator Estes Kefauver's 1951 investigation of illegal gambling. During World War II and the construction of Keesler Air Force Base, more than 300 nightclubs, hotels, and gambling dens offered illegal slot machines and table games to armed forces personnel and tourists. Kefauver's spotlight led to periodic local law enforcement crackdowns, and then the hurricane and the construction of the interstate to the north of the coastal highway devastated tourism. In December 1987 the *Europa Star*, a Panamanian-registered casino ship, docked at Biloxi and offered cruises to nowhere so that gamblers could indulge themselves beyond the three-mile limit as the *Star* cruised in the Mississippi sound. Just as Biloxi began to enjoy increased tourism, the attorney general issued an opinion that international waters did not begin until ships passed beyond Mississippi's barrier islands. The distance to the islands made the *Star*'s voyages uneconomical and burst the expanding bubble of prosperity.

The legislature considered a bill legalizing cruises to nowhere as a routine local matter, and therefore it failed to rouse the full fury of the fundamentalist churches, whose members had always considered the Gulf Coast a different, decadent section of the state. Meredith kept the legislation low key in the House and worked with the Senate, where hill-county senators, who represented church congregations that strongly disapproved of gambling, agreed to take a walk—that is, absent themselves from the Senate during the vote in deference to their Gulf Coast colleagues. Impressed by the success of the Gulf Coast and eyeing Iowa's legalization of riverboat gambling, Delta legislators, including Meredith, who represented Greenville, conceived the idea of legalizing gambling on the Mississippi River. Thus the two regions formed an alliance in the legislature.

Fearful of the tricky navigation required in the Mississippi River and wishing to maximize the gambling boats' appeal to investors, Meredith slipped out the legal term requiring boats to be "underway making way" and passed it quietly through the House. His allies in the Senate feared that when their colleagues realized they were voting to allow docked barges, boats, and ships to house gambling operations, it would never pass. The sponsoring senators brought up their bill for a vote at the end of the day when senators were tired and hungry and preceded it with a bill establishing rules for cruise vessels on the Gulf Coast. Having cleared the hill-county senators from the chamber so as not to taint them with the passage of a gambling law, the allies brought up their bill. The remaining senators cried for a quick vote in order to get to dinner, resulting in passage by a vote of twenty-two to twenty with only two or three senators aware they had just legalized dockside gambling. The unlikely legalization of casino gambling launched a major tourism industry in Mississippi, but Mabus never got his lottery to fund education improvements.

During the second year of Mabus's administration, 1989 marked the twenty-fifth anniversary of the Neshoba County murders and a turning point in how Mississippians remembered their past. The Neshoba County community, led by an interracial group of whites, blacks, and Choctaw, decided to end the sullen silence maintained by their community about the 1964 deaths. A local steering committee chose a marker dedicated to the dead trio at the rebuilt Mt. Zion Church as the appropriate means of expressing community contrition. The families of Chaney, Schwerner, and Goodman attended, along with Governor Mabus, former governor Winter, and Philadelphia native Secretary of State Molpus, who spoke for the steering committee at the ceremony. Molpus addressed the families, directly expressing the community's regret at the young men's death and the wish of every "decent" person in Philadelphia, Neshoba County, and the state to restore them to life if the community had the means. He assured the audience that most Mississippians were decent people willing to pay tribute to the sacrifice of the trio, and he invited the families to recognize the altered nature of the state around them, giving credit to the dead civil rights workers for the better society of the 1980s, where fear "of the unknown" and "of each other" had waned. Such sentiments uttered with the endorsement of the former and sitting governors helped the state turn a corner, and even the surviving segregationists voiced no public condemnation of the ceremony or the apology proffered.

The 1989 movie *Mississippi Burning* perverted historical fact but galvanized and energized Mississippians' memories, stimulating debate about the horrors of the 1960s as never before. The editor of the *Neshoba Democrat* interviewed Andrew Goodman's mother and captured her memories of her son to present Goodman to the *Democrat*'s readership as a fleshed-out human being. Jerry Mitchell, a reporter for the *Clarion Ledger*, began a career dedicated to exposing the dark secrets of Mississippi's past. Governor Mabus reacted negatively to *Mississippi Burning* and the revival of suppressed memories by hiring a public relations firm to combat the negative image created by the violence depicted in the film. He rushed to Washington, D.C., to lecture reporters on the inaccuracy of the movie's history. His storyline had been that the bad old days were behind and that the state looked to a bright future. Instead, Mitchell and others began to demand that perpetrators of 1960s violent hate crimes be prosecuted. Mitchell obtained FBI files on the Neshoba murders and published names. A federal judge, William Barbour, ordered the Sovereignty Commission's files, closed by the legislature for fifty years, opened to the public. Mitchell revealed that Sovereignty Commission agents tampered with the jury pool in Beckwith's trial for murdering Medgar Evers, and the Hinds County district attorney called a grand jury to indict Beckwith a third time for the murder. Most Mississippians had forgotten Beckwith, who served a sentence in a Louisiana prison, lived quietly in rural Holmes County, remarried, and moved to the Tennessee Mountains, where he continued to spew racist ideas like a ghost from the past. The 1980s ended with the state being called to confront the past, and for the next decade Mississippi led the nation in the number of trials seeking to convict racist criminals responsible for the violence endemic during the 1960s.

The failure of Mabus's education reform package and the accumulation of political enemies caused by his reforms in county government, along with the dismissive language that he employed against entrenched power brokers, caused a coalition of Democrats to challenge him for the nomination in 1991. The alteration of the constitution in the Allain administration made it possible for Mabus to succeed himself, but he had moved too quickly and angered too many, causing the dissidents in his own party to try to take advantage of Mississippians' unease about adapting to the "modern world." Former congressman Dowdy opposed Mabus in the primary, losing but weakening the party. Pete Johnson, grandson of one governor and nephew of another, switched from the Democrat to the Republican Party during his tenure in the state auditor's office, expecting to have the Republicans welcome him as their hope for finally taking the governor's office.

Kirk Fordice, a longtime Republican activist who owned a construction company in Vicksburg, challenged Johnson in the primary, outworked him, and defeated the former Democrat while winning the support of Republican Party managers. Fordice entered the general election with momentum from the primary, but he had to cut into Mabus's rural white votes to defeat him, because Mabus could win with only 38 percent of the white vote combined with his assured black support. To win the conservative, rural white votes, Fordice lashed out at Mabus's proposed lottery as immoral and attacked Mabus for vetoing an antiabortion bill that would have required licensing of clinics and waiting periods for patients requesting the procedure. In his effort to appeal to the church vote, Fordice decried Mabus's support for Dukakis and identified Mabus and Dukakis as fellow Harvard graduates, which, by association, made them members of the eastern liberal establishment. Fordice's strategy worked because he rejected the "modernism" ushered in by Mabus and appealed to residual racism among white voters. He won, for example, the heavily white, rural northeastern portion of the state, despite the fact that it was Mabus's home region. Securing enough of the rural white votes enabled the Republican to win narrowly.

Despite his victory making him the first Republican governor elected since Reconstruction, Fordice refused to become an adroit politician and spent his two terms quarrelling with the legislature. In the 1992 session, both houses voted to support education with a one-cent hike in the sales tax, which Fordice vetoed, only to see his decision overridden by massive majorities in both houses of the legislature. Fordice made headlines, but the real power during his administration resided where it traditionally had—in the legislature.

Since Newman's retirement, the House of Representatives had been in flux because the reformers, who ditched him, had adopted a term limit for the Speaker and installed the least objectionable and not terribly popular candidate—Tim Ford. Ford, a product of the Ole Miss law school, where he had led the student body, faced three contentious factions: the old guard, the progressives who toppled Newman, and the black caucus. The 1992 redistricting contest brought the factional fighting to a head after the legislature's redistricting plans failed to receive approval from the Justice Department under the Voting Rights Act. To end the impasse, Ford cut a deal with Ed Blackmon, leader of the black caucus, and at the same time allied himself with the old guard, who joined Ford to end the unruliness prevailing since Newman's retirement. Ford sacrificed the white progressives, who had first placed him in office, and named Robert Clark as his speaker pro tem. After defeating Ed Perry, who had been backed by the reformers and elements of the old guard for the speakership, Ford nominated Perry for clerk of the House in an effort to soothe all factions. Ford did not organize the House along party lines and instead continued appointing Republicans to chair committees. By adopting an inclusive style and always allowing members to have their say, Ford protected the institution of the House of Representatives and garnered plaudits for being one of the strongest Speakers in the nation. After a few years his reputation led Harvard to invite Ford to train incoming Speakers from around the nation for their new posts. The Mississippi House of Representatives rescinded the term limit imposed on the Mississippi Speaker, and Ford settled into the traditional Speaker's role as the most powerful politician in the state—but without the iron hand wielded by Sillers.

Perhaps Christopher Epps's rise to leadership in the Mississippi Department of Corrections (MDOC) best illustrated the changes in Mississippi society and politics. A native Mississippian, Epps attended Mississippi Valley State University, where he majored in education. After graduation, he taught in the public schools at Drew and took a second job at Parchman guarding prisoners. Initially he found having a college degree a hardship because his sergeant became suspicious and felt intimidated when Epps asked to read the "green books," as the prison's policy manuals were called. Applying for promotion, Epps had supervisors tell him to step aside, even though he was better qualified, because another candidate with political connections wanted a post. According to Epps, he avoided being derailed for promotion by remaining loyal to his superiors and by exploiting every opportunity through professional organizations to increase his knowledge of penology. Epps kept both his teaching and prison jobs until 1985, when he made the decision to devote his entire career to prison work. In 1988 Governor Mabus promoted Epps to second in command at Parchman, dismaying many white administrators. But Epps believed that he had proved himself and deflected their concern through hard work, claiming to have accumulated the most compensatory hours in the state's payroll system. Governor Fordice refused to allow Epps to remain at Parchman, where he had grown comfortable living in inexpensive housing and walking across the street to work. Fordice forced him to move to Jackson, where the governor insisted he was needed

Christopher Epps started with the Mississippi Department of Corrections as a part-time guard, but gave up teaching to make corrections his career, rising to head the department and helping to rebuild the state's prison system. Courtesy of the Mississippi Department of Corrections.

at the MDOC headquarters. The next governor made Epps commissioner and the first black man to run the state prison system, including the infamous Parchman once designed to keep men such as Epps confined to agricultural labor.

Fordice's promotion of Epps demonstrated the governor's strength as an administrator. Although Fordice never understood the legislative process and constantly suffered the embarrassment of having his vetoes overridden, he tried to select the best people in making all of his appointments. For example, faced with the task of administering the gambling industry (which he condemned as an immoral blight on the state), Fordice selected three older white men who were independently wealthy and agreed with his opinion of the casinos. He rejected anyone seeking membership on the Mississippi Gambling Commission, looked for complete integrity, and never interfered with the commissioners' decisions once they were in office.

Fordice took donations from the casinos throughout his tenure as governor without any hint of scandal. The political establishment rallied to provide protection and security for the casinos multiplying along the Mississippi River and the Gulf Coast. Speaker Ford had worked with Meredith on passage of the legislation, and they understood the necessity of assuring stability to Mississippi's large new industry. Efforts by inland counties to spread casinos across the state or raid the taxes generated by casinos went down to defeat in the legislature. In return, the Mississippi Gambling Commission required casinos to build hotels and restaurants on land to ensure that the industry put down roots and invested substantial sums of money in the state. By 2002 casino taxes funded 10 percent of the state budget, and casinos employed thousands of Mississippians.

In 1995 Fordice defeated another of the "boys of spring," Dick Molpus, in the governor's race to win a second term. As secretary of state, Molpus had rescued sixteenth-section land from county supervisors, but he suffered, as Mabus had, from association with modernism. As a strong advocate of public schools, Molpus by implication supported integration, while Fordice vetoed minority set-asides in state construction projects and threatened to call out the National Guard should the federal courts order Mississippi to raise taxes in order to fund the Ayers settlement, requiring compensation to Mississippi's historically black institutions of higher learning. Fordice criticized Molpus for his apology to the murdered civil rights workers' families, claiming that it did no good to drag up the state's past because Mississippi had the country's best race relations.

Fordice and Molpus met in a historic debate at the Neshoba County Fair and laid bare both their personal and political differences. Fordice called for a reduction of income taxes to benefit the upper and middle classes, while Molpus, who had supported the sales tax increase to fund education, advocated reducing the sales tax on food as a means of benefiting the poor and lower classes. Fordice armed his followers with flip-flops to wave at Molpus as he spoke about his tax plan, and offstage they threatened one another with ass-whippings. With an increased share of white votes, Fordice won handily, but the same voters rejected Republican Eddie Briggs's effort to retain the lieutenant governor's office and instead elected Democrat Ronnie Musgrove.

Presiding over the Senate, Musgrove appointed a record number of black committee chairmen in an effort to support the Democratic black and white coalition that had begun to fray. Briggs had won his first race for lieutenant governor because a black candidate siphoned off 9 percent of the black votes from the Democrats, throwing the election into the House of Representatives, where the overwhelmingly Democratic House ignored party loyalties and elected Briggs. One black senator referred to Musgrove's appointments as "history making." Former governor William Winter encouraged Democratic senators to organize their chamber along party lines, but they failed to follow through.

Musgrove used his office to prepare for the 1999 race for governor. Not associated with the Winter administration or the "boys of spring," he opposed abortion and positioned himself as a social conservative. The Republicans turned to a funeral home operator elected to Congress as a

Democrat before switching parties. Mike Parker proved to be a weak candidate unwilling to work the long hours required to win, but still he essentially tied the election with a popular vote only slightly less than Musgrove's. The Mississippi electoral college tied as well, sending the election to the House of Representatives, where Democrats voted as a party to give Musgrove the victory. Musgrove faced two major issues during his administration—a new flag and tort reform.

In the first year of his administration, the Mississippi Supreme Court decided a long-litigated case brought by the state NAACP asking the court to prohibit the display of the state flag because it contained a miniature of the Confederate battle flag in the corner. The court volunteered a history of the state flag, holding that no legally adopted flag existed, which opened the way to choosing a new state symbol. Black Mississippians remembered the Confederate flag as the segregationist symbol from the 1950s and 1960s and, by extension, recalled its Confederate States of America (CSA) heritage as representing a defense of slavery. Whites glossed over the recent segregationist use of the flag and denied that the flag or the Civil War had much to do with slavery, conjuring up images of bravery in battle and strong Victorian ideas of honor and virtue. Musgrove adopted the usual political dodge of appointing a commission to recommend a course of action. Former governor Winter took on the thankless task of chairing the commission, holding hearings around the state and absorbing vehement condemnation from enraged white defenders of the old flag. Religious leadership groups endorsed changing the flag as an act of brotherly love, while the universities, business leaders, and most of the professional historians in the state asked for an alteration of the flag for practical and historical reasons. The commission recommended a new flag and a referendum, which the legislature quickly voted to hold. Held on April 17, 2001, the votes confirmed the division between blacks and whites in the state, with 90 percent of the white voters supporting the 1894 flag and 95 percent of the black voters opposing it. The state retained its old flag with all of its symbolism by a vote of 494,323 to 273,359. Out of over 1,300 majority-white precincts in the state, only 43 around Jackson and in university towns voted for the new flag. Overwhelmingly, white Mississippians reacted to the civil rights revolution fought in Mississippi by ignoring both the verdict of history and their black neighbors' feelings.

Throughout the 1990s and into the twenty-first century, trials conducted to provide delayed justice to Klansmen kept the past alive. Beckwith's retrial required years, and when prosecutors asked prospective jurors if they knew the defendant, the overwhelming majority replied no. Mississippians had banished Beckwith from their collective memory. The judge moved jury

Byron De La Beckwith evaded conviction for the murder of Medgar Evers until 1994, when a Mississippi jury finally declared him guilty. Courtesy of the *Clarion-Ledger*.

selection from Jackson to Batesville, where the lawyers finally found eight black and four white jurors willing to take on the duty of reaching a verdict. Eight of them had been infants at the time of the crime. The trial with an imported jury took place in Jackson, with most of the "testimony" consisting of reading the transcripts from previous trials. Beckwith removed his hearing devices throughout most of his third trial, and in the end the jury decided, in the words of the prosecutor, "to do the right thing," sentencing Beckwith in 1994 to life in prison. Sam Bowers, a Klan leader, went to prison four years later for ordering the murder of Dahmer, and in 1999 the state convicted three Klansmen for the 1970 murder of a one-armed sharecropper. Other convictions followed in 2003, and Edgar Ray "Preacher" Killen finally lost his freedom for the Neshoba murders in 2005.

Mississippians did not, however, spend the first years of the new century obsessed with the state's old racial conflicts. Fordice had been right. Most people wanted to forget and move on. The general public took more interest in Musgrove's economic development efforts that culminated in Nissan building a major production facility outside Canton, which opened in 2003. Mississippians had worked in the low-paying garment factories created under the old Balance Agriculture with Industry (BAWI) policies, reaching a peak of 240,000 factory workers in 1978, when those jobs began disappearing into foreign lands, where workers accepted even lower wages.

By 2000 Mississippi reclaimed the same number of manufacturing jobs held in 1978, but in more high-tech industries, such as Peavey Electronics in Meridian, which makes amplifiers, speakers, and musical instruments, or at Stennis Space Center testing rocket motors. The number of farm laborers continued to plummet, with only 4 percent of the population still working the land in 2000. Outside the Delta, farms continued to return to forest until tree farms, timber company lands, and national parks covered well over half the state. "Small" Delta farmers tilling only a few thousand acres relied on Roundup Ready seeds to allow spraying Roundup on cotton to kill the weeds in their fields. They employed entomologists to advise them about dispensing poisons for the insects. A loose chain guard on a cotton picker might cost them $15,000, and they spent much of their time servicing and repairing machinery. Finding dependable workers to drive their machinery at the right time of the year proved to be the greatest headache for farmers. Many farmers and gin operators turned to Mexicans as the solution, causing Yazoo City supermarkets, as a result, to carry several varieties of chili and Mexican restaurants to offer wire money transfers, but many more farmers employed black workers part-time and cussed the "unreliability" of their longtime neighbors as their fathers and grandfathers had.

Pursuing Nissan, Musgrove spent relatively little time on agricultural issues and much more trying to curb the growing problem that the *Clarion Ledger* labeled "jackpot justice." Mike Moore and Dickie Scruggs played major roles in making Mississippi's lawyers the most successful in the nation while bringing the state's justice system into question. Both from the Gulf Coast and longtime friends, Scruggs and Moore both attended Ole Miss law school. After graduation, Moore earned a reputation as a crusader, fighting crime on the coast as a district attorney, while the former navy fighter pilot Scruggs returned home to enter private practice. Scruggs took up the already lucrative business of suing companies such as Ingalls for damages based on workers' exposure to asbestos, and Moore won the state attorney general's office in 1988. Moore enlisted his friend as "special assistant attorney general" to prosecute the asbestos industry on behalf of the state, for which Scruggs collected massive contingency fees. In the summer of 1992 Moore got wind of a plan being hatched by Steve Patterson, the state auditor, and Ed Peters, the Hinds County district attorney, to charge that the Moore-Scruggs arrangement broke the law. Scruggs, the brother-in-law of Senator Lott, got a call from P. L. Blake, a shadowy operator who had been connected to the late Senator Eastland, summoning Scruggs to a meeting at Blake's Greenwood home. Scruggs flew up to Greenwood in his private plane and met with Patterson in Blake's living room, where Patterson agreed to desist his investigation of Scruggs and Moore and to write a letter praising their

Nissan built a major production facility outside Canton in 2003, and Toyota opened its Blue Springs plant in 2011. Courtesy of Nissan North America, Inc.

work on behalf of the state. Then Scruggs, Blake, and Patterson celebrated the pact by dining at Luscos, a Greenwood landmark restaurant.

Keeping product liability cases in state courts where populist-leaning juries handed out millions in damages, Scruggs grew rich and used his money to finance an attack on the biggest prize of all—the tobacco companies. Moore and Scruggs designed an end run around the tobacco company's claim of personal liability as a defense by suing to recover the state's cost in Medicare expenses incurred by Mississippi smokers. Republican governor Fordice sued Moore in an attempt to block his campaign against tobacco companies but failed. Moore and Scruggs enlisted other states and in 1997 negotiated a settlement with the tobacco industry that awarded Mississippi $3.67 billion along with additional concessions requiring the companies to finance antismoking campaigns. The *National Law Journal* named Moore lawyer of the year, and Scruggs bought yachts and planes, stationing them around the world. Moore appeared in a 1999 movie starring Al Pacino and Russell Crowe depicting the intrigue leading to the settlement.

Success bred powerful enemies. The U.S. Chamber of Commerce intervened to oppose Mississippi trial lawyers who had been financing state politicians' and judges' campaigns as well as winning massive damage claims. The newspapers and the Chamber of Commerce focused on doctors' complaints about lawsuits, and insurance companies threatened to stop writing medical coverage without tort reform. As a result, Musgrove called a special session and the legislature passed legislation to rein in the trial lawyers and limit malpractice and product liability suits.

In the 2003 elections, Mississippi Republicans ignored the legislation, and Haley Barbour ran against Musgrove, the Democrats, and the trial lawyers as one and the same, calling for tort reform as if the special session never happened. After running against Stennis, Barbour had landed in the Reagan White House, headed the national Republican Party, and run a highly successful Washington lobbying firm. His gubernatorial campaign strategy called for mobilizing white suburban voters as Republicans had done nationally and linking Musgrove to the national Democratic Party image. The Democrats aided his cause by nominating Barbara Blackmon, a black woman, for lieutenant governor. When she raised the question of Amy Tuck, the lieutenant governor who had changed parties, having had an abortion, the uproar allowed the Republicans to link Musgrove to a black running mate who favored abortion rights. Mississippi cities and adjoining Memphis had been experiencing white flight as the rest of the country did, creating large population centers in suburban areas ready to support the Republican Party wrapped symbolically in the Mississippi state flag that Musgrove had questioned. Barbour defeated the incumbent Democrat handily.

With his election, Barbour signaled the creation of a two-party system in the legislature. Working with Tuck, Barbour ran the Senate, leaving only the House of Representatives under Democratic control. William J. (Billy) McCoy won the speakership when Ford resigned. A former vocational agricultural teacher, loan officer for the Farmers Home Administration, and school auditor for the Mississippi State Department of Audit, McCoy represented a House district in Prentiss County. Identifying himself as a farmer, McCoy represented the traditional Mississippi brand of populism familiar to the likes of Bilbo. A stern leader, he took a dim view of lobbyists' gifts to legislators, opposed abortion and gay rights, but supported education, Medicare, and other government services. He had been one of the old guard leaders who supported Ford as a means of restoring order to the House of Representatives. In 2003 a well-funded Republican physician challenged him in a district he had held since 1979, and after the election, he found Barbour trying to organize Republican House members against him in the legislature. He turned to an alliance with the black caucus and named their leaders to important chairmanships, endowing black members with far more power than the window dressing conceded by Ford. Many of his fellow white Democrats found the black and white coalition problematic in their districts, but McCoy recognized the common interests of poor blacks and whites and won more generous funding for education and Medicare than the Republicans wanted approved.

Politics took a breather in 2005 when Hurricane Katrina visited the worst storm destruction in the nation's history on Mississippi and surrounding states. With 125-mile-an-hour winds and a storm surge thirty feet high, Katrina devastated the Gulf Coast, wiping the town of Waveland out of existence, sending casino barges crashing down on historic houses, and killing over 225 Mississippians. Katrina finally weakened to a tropical storm just northwest of Meridian after damaging the southern half of the state. In

Hurricane Katrina visited the worst storm destruction in the nation's history on Mississippi and surrounding states, with 125-mile-per-hour winds and a storm surge thirty feet high. Photo courtesy of Pat Sullivan.

an odd sense, Mississippi benefited from the publicity generated by massive television coverage of the aftermath. Barbour struck a positive pose, Mississippians mounted an impressive self-help response with volunteers wielding chainsaws, and a nationally televised fund-raising event broadcast from Ole Miss featured Morgan Freeman giving a positive image of race relations and the depth of entertainers native to the state. Barbour reported that business leaders cited the images following the storm as convincing them to build factories in the state because they wanted the resourceful people they saw on television working for them. In order to ensure continued investment in casinos and tourism income, Barbour and the legislature passed laws moving casinos on land, and the casinos reopened relatively quickly while general recovery proceeded slowly.

Barbour worked hard to secure a Toyota factory to cap industrial development during his first term. Nine months before the 2007 election, he landed the big one, with an announcement of a Toyota plant to employ 2,000 workers near Tupelo at Blue Springs. As a result, Barbour lost only five majority-white counties in a walkover to retain the governorship. The Republicans left Jim Hood, the attorney general, as the sole surviving Democrat elected to a statewide office. They went after McCoy, but he retained the speakership by one vote and without a single Republican supporting him. McCoy made the two-party system official by failing to name one Republican to a House of Representatives chairmanship.

Scandals plagued Mississippi's leadership. Both Fordice and Musgrove conducted extramarital affairs that ended their marriages while in office. Rising star Congressman Chip Pickering suffered the same fate. Mike Espy became the first black secretary of agriculture under President Clinton, but had to resign for accepting too many gifts from lobbyists. Lott resigned from the Senate only a year after his reelection and a few weeks before a federal grand jury indicted his brother-in-law, Scruggs. Scruggs, his son, and a number of high-flying lawyers went to jail for bribing state judges. Beckwith's successful prosecutor, Bobby DeLaughter, who became a judge, went to jail, and his mentor, Ed Peters, avoided incarceration but surrendered his law license. Former attorney general Moore went into private practice and adopted a low profile. P. L. Blake moved to Birmingham. Lott opened a Washington, D.C., lobbying firm.

Mississippi resembled the rest of America far more in the twenty-first century than it did in the twentieth, but remained distinctive. Polls found it to be the most religious state in the nation. When Gallup asked Mississippians, "Is religion an important part of your daily life?" 85 percent answered yes. Separating whites and blacks did not affect the percentage because blacks and whites shared a common faith. But as Richard Wright observed during his last visit home, religion mixed with high sexual activity. Mississippians deliver over half of their children as unmarried teenagers. In 2009 they divorced one another at high rates, with Mississippi women ranking sixth in the nation and men eleventh. Among all the states, only Utahans accessed more pornography on the Internet, but then twice as many Utahans were connected to the Internet as were Mississippians. Utah and Mississippi also ranked among the most generous states for giving to charities. Mississippi ranked highest in infant mortality and lowest in per capita income. Fewer Mississippians had college degrees than did citizens in other states, but they owned their homes more often than the average American in part because a house cost only half what other Americans paid for one. There were twenty-four fewer Mississippians per square mile than the national average, meaning that the state remained rural and that Mississippians continued to relate to one another in more direct, personal ways.

In 2007, when Harry Maclean came from Colorado to Mississippi to write about James Ford Seale's trial for the 1964 murders of Charles Moore and Henry Dee, two black men whose bodies turned up in the Mississippi River during the massive search for the missing Neshoba County civil rights workers, he noticed the difference between Mississippi and much of the rest of the nation immediately. When he admired the music playing in a Jackson deli, the owner burned a CD for him on the spot. When he asked a stranger for directions, the stranger walked him to his destination, engaging in conversation along the way. When he was a dollar short on a bill, the clerk told him to pay it next time. He found the Jackson blues clubs "authentic" and noted that the players—whether young, old, black, or white—mixed and mingled as if family telling one another stories that illustrated they sprang from the same roots. They understood one another without explanation, Maclean said. He commented frequently on the pervasiveness of religion, noting, for example, the white businesswoman called to jury duty who explained that she belonged to Transformation Jackson, a group dedicated to redemption through prayer, and that she had attended the Killen trial in Neshoba County to pray for justice. By the time that Charles Edwards, one of the Klansmen who murdered the two young men, confessed and asked the murdered men's families for forgiveness from the witness stand, Maclean recorded no surprise when the families readily granted it. Despite noting Jackson's crime rate, he labeled the city "the best" of the South.

Mississippians have worked to better race relations both individually and through organized activities. Cecil Price Sr., perhaps motivated by his son's friendships with blacks, professed a change of heart in 2000, took a lie detector test, and offered to testify against Killen in the Neshoba County case before dying in an accident. Seale disowned a grandson for marrying a black woman. A more distant relative, Shirley Seale, who attended KKK meetings with Seale as a child, adopted his race hatred until she began to attend a black church, where she became a pastor and advocate for racial equality.

Universities joined other institutions in making amends for refusing black applicants. In 1991, prompted by a Jerry Mitchell story in the

Clarion Ledger exposing the fraud used to send Clyde Kennard to prison for attempting to enroll at Mississippi Southern College, the USM African-American Student Organization (AASO) designated a Clyde Kennard Day and invited James Meredith and a member of Kennard's family to speak. Following the occasion, the AASO requested USM to remember Kennard with a fitting memorial. During Black History Month the next year, USM named the student services building in honor of Kennard and Walter Washington, USM's first black doctoral graduate. USM president Aubrey K. Lucas, who served in the admissions office that denied Kennard entrance, apologized for the "indignities" Kennard suffered, and Washington marveled at the revolution since his days on campus. Ole Miss required another fifteen years and considerably more controversy to honor Meredith, but in 2006 the University of Mississippi dedicated a life-size statue of Meredith striding toward a seventeen-foot-tall limestone portal carrying the words "courage, perseverance, opportunity, and knowledge." Though he was present, university officials did not invite the mercurial Meredith to speak. He posed for photographs alongside former governor William Winter in front of his monument.

Winter established an institute for racial reconciliation bearing his name at the University of Mississippi in 1999. The institute's director, Susan Glisson, who earned degrees in religion and history, helped interracial communities around the state come to agreements on how to remember the past and work together in the present. She took part in the Neshoba County committee's project that led to Killen's conviction and in the Sumner community's ceremony to remember Emmett Till.

Sumner's courthouse for Tallahatchie County needed restoration, and three whites joined six blacks on a committee seeking to use the famous trial of Till's killers as the means of raising funds for the courthouse. Gradually the committee's work evolved into planning a ceremony and plaque commemorating Till's death and another apology for the state's most infamous murder. The committee grew to twelve evenly divided (by counting a Chinese Mississippian as white) who met for long hours, shed tears, grew angry, and became remorseful before inviting Glisson to help. Betty Pearson of the planter class worked with Jerome Little, a black county supervisor, to keep the group together. Pearson campaigned hard with the black men on the committee to convince them to call her by her first name as she did in addressing them, and finally she got one of the black men to call her Betty at the negotiating table, but not Little. His habit of addressing her was too ingrained. Toward the end of the planning sessions, a white male planter committee member balked at the word "apology" in the commission's statement to be read at the ceremony and substituted "regret" instead. After consulting his dictionary, Little and the Till family accepted the substitute, but apologies flowed freely in remarks at the ceremony.

Simeon Wright, along with other family members, returned to help unveil the Emmett Till memorial sign donated by Morgan Freeman's foundation. Few whites attended, but former governor Winter came, and Glisson brought some students. Little did not mind local whites' absence, and the white planter raised no objections to the use of "apology" at the ceremony, which he missed because of church activities. The negotiations and ceremony illustrated the pace of change in 2007 and seemed to indicate that progress would require more work.

Mississippi's history has made race central to its story. The state and nation got another reminder in 2011 when *The Help,* which had topped the best-seller list in 2009, became a big box office movie. Kathryn Stockett, who grew up in Jackson before leaving for the University of Alabama and New York, professed to have been inspired to write the book by her love for the black maid Demetrie (Stockett never used her last name), who comforted and cared for her until the maid's death when Stockett was sixteen. The autobiographical novel featured a Stockett character who returns to Jackson from Ole Miss in the 1960s, empathizes with her friends' black maids, and convinces them to write an exposé of the white families for whom they work. Stockett told the story from three perspectives—her own, that of an older maid full of folk wisdom, and that of a more militant, angry maid. All of Stockett's characters are stereotypes, with the worst being her white society friends and the poor white trash character who "society" shunned. Strong performances by black actresses playing the maids inspired long lines at theaters around the nation, and some Mississippians went to see the movie multiple times during opening week. Stockett had the leader of the white society women eat a shit pie baked by her fired maid in a less than subtle condemnation of Mississippi's 1960s racism. Her politically correct but exploitive and simple-minded depiction of Mississippi's recent past illustrates the danger that Mississippians, apparently hungry to understand their history, will be seduced by such distorted "memoirs" into continuing to misunderstand the complexity of the place.

Stockett's brother's maid, Alelene Cooper, sued Stockett for using her life story for the main character in the novel—"Aibileen." Stockett's brother supported his maid rather than his sister. Cooper's image and voice were captured by the press as she left the Jackson courthouse after the dismissal of her suit on technical grounds, screaming: "She's a liar. She did it. She knows she did it." Cooper's condemnation of what she considered the exploitation of her life story marred the reception of a feel-good account of Mississippi in the 1960s and reinforced the perception that racial exploitation continued.

In 2011 Governor Barbour attempted to change that image by apologizing to the Freedom Riders who returned to Jackson that summer in order to commemorate the fiftieth anniversary of their rides, arrests, and imprisonment. Barbour also supported the passage of a bond issue to build a Mississippi museum dedicated to preserving the memory of the civil rights movement. The Mississippi Economic Council's (MEC's) "Blueprint 2011" called for the cultivation of racial diversity in the workforce and in management through training and membership in national and global business networks. The MEC endorsed the Mississippi Arts Commission's report, generated with the Mississippi Development Authority, which asked communities to preserve the state's culture and history as engines for economic development, encouraging vibrant and creative forces among the state's population as a means of growing and retaining talented Mississippians. On the whole, the MEC's plan for development stressed the growth of human capital, recognizing the centrality of education, health care, and racial reconciliation as imperative for achieving solid economic growth. The civil rights movement freed all Mississippians—black and white—from an oppressive system that kept both races on the bottom of almost every national yardstick of progress. It required decades for most white Mississippians to accept that fact, and some still doubted it in 2011. The state's leaders, however, accepted it and pointed the way to a more just and prosperous future.

Further Reading

Chapter One. Rise and Fall of Indian Culture

James F. Barnett Jr., *Mississippi's American Indians* (Jackson: University Press of Mississippi, 2012), and *The Natchez Indians: A History to 1735* (Jackson: University Press of Mississippi, 2007); James Taylor Carson, *Native Americans, the Market Revolution, and Culture Change: The Choctaw Cattle Economy, 1690–1830* (Norman: University of Oklahoma Press, 2008), and *Searching for the Bright Path: The Mississippi Choctaws from Prehistory to Removal* (Lincoln: University of Nebraska Press, 2003); Michelene E. Pesantubbee, *Choctaw Women in a Chaotic World: The Clash of Cultures in the Colonial Southeast* (Albuquerque: University of New Mexico Press, 2005); Charles Hudson and Carmen Chaves Tesser, eds., *The Forgotten Centuries: Indians and Europeans in the American South, 1521–1704* (Athens: University of Georgia Press, 1994); Gregg O'Brien, ed., *Pre-Removal Choctaw History: Exploring New Paths* (Norman: University of Oklahoma Press, 2008); Richard White, *The Roots of Dependency: Subsistence, Environment, and Social Change among the Choctaws, Pawnees, and Navajos* (Lincoln: University of Nebraska Press, 1983); Daniel H. Usner Jr., *Indians, Settlers, and Slaves in a Frontier Exchange Economy: Lower Mississippi Valley before 1783* (Chapel Hill: University of North Carolina Press, 1992).

Marion Barnwell, *A Place Called Mississippi: Collected Narratives* (Jackson: University Press of Mississippi, 1997), contains an excerpt from the De Soto Chronicles by the gentleman from Elvas, a Portuguese companion of the Spanish conquistador. Elvas describes the contacts with the Chicaca. The book also contains Henry de Tonty's account of the Natchez, which can be compared to Le Page du Pratz's later description (3–15) and to Father Le Petit's report on Natchez religion (231–235).

Bradley G. Bond, *Mississippi: A Documentary History* (Jackson: University Press of Mississippi, 2003), duplicates the Elvas excerpt, but also has a selection from Iberville's diary as well as a piece from one of his lieutenants, Jean Sauvole, on life on the Gulf Coast in the 1600s. There are a number of short selections from a variety of Frenchmen describing the lives of the Africans, Europeans, and American Indians through the 1740s (4–40).

Chapter Two. Frontier and Borderland

The best document covering white settlement for this period is John Q. Anderson, "The Narrative of John Hutchins," *Journal of Mississippi History* (January 1958): 1–29. Robert V.

Haynes, *The Mississippi Territory and the Southwest Frontier, 1795–1817* (Lexington: University Press of Kentucky, 2010), provides a complete narrative. See also Gideon Lincecum, *Pushmataha: A Choctaw Leader and His People* (Tuscaloosa: University of Alabama Press, 2004); Lois Wood Burkhalter, *Gideon Lincecum, 1793–1874: A Biography* (Austin: University of Texas Press, 1965); Richard White, *The Roots of Dependency: Subsistence, Environment, and Social Change among the Choctaws, Pawnees, and Navajos* (Lincoln: University of Nebraska Press, 1983); Jack D. L. Holmes, *Gayoso: The Life of a Spanish Governor in the Mississippi Valley 1789–1799* (Gloucester, Mass.: Peter Smith, 1968).

Barnwell, *A Place Called Mississippi*, provides excerpts from Gideon Lincecum's "Life of Apushimataha" (16–23) and a selection of historian Terry Alford's "Prince among Slaves" (381–386).

Chapter Three. Mississippi Territory

Many of the books cited for the first two chapters apply to this chapter as well. John Carroll Eudy, "The Political Intrigues of Thomas Rodney: Territorial Politics, 1807–1809," *Journal of Mississippi History* 40 (1978): 329–339, provides a quick insight to the politics of the period. Clara Sue Kidwell, *Choctaws and Missionaries in Mississippi, 1818–1918* (Norman: University of Oklahoma Press, 1995), covers cultural conflict and integration among the Choctaw. See also Christopher Morris, *Becoming Southern: The Evolution of a Way of Life, Warren County and Vicksburg, Mississippi, 1770–1860* (Oxford: Oxford University Press, 1995); Janet Sharp Herman, *Joseph E. Davis: Pioneer Patriarch* (Jackson: University Press of Mississippi, 1990). Because Poindexter is so important to the period, it is worth locating and securing Suanna Smith's "George Poindexter: A Political Biography" (Ph.D. diss., University of Southern Mississippi, 1980). The same is true of Frances Elizabeth Melton's "The Public Career of David Holmes 1809–1820" (Master's thesis, Mississippi State College for Women, 1966).

John J. Audubon, who taught briefly at Jefferson College, left an account of a cougar hunt with squatters in the swamps on the border dividing the Choctaw and Chickasaw nations that gives a flavor of life in the Mississippi Territory. See Barnwell, *A Place Called Mississippi* (65–70).

Bond, *Mississippi*, provides Carter family letters describing their migration and settlement in the piney woods during the early 1800s (42–47).

Chapter Four. Frontier Democracy to Slave Society

Many of the books cited for the first three chapters are also important for this chapter. Dallas C. Dickey, *Seargent S. Prentiss: Whig Orator of the Old South* (Baton Rouge: Louisiana State University Press, 1945), chronicles the life of the leading Whig. John Edmond Gonzales, *The Public Career of Henry Stuart Foote (1804–1880)* (Chapel Hill: University of North Carolina Press, 1957), covers a leading Democrat. James P. Shenton, *Robert John Walker: A*

Politician from Jackson to Lincoln (New York: Columbia University Press, 1961), portrays a shadowy but significant operator. Bertram Wyatt-Brown, *Southern Honor: Ethics and Behavior in the Old South* (Oxford: Oxford University Press, 1982), explains the new sense of honor in the planter class. Randy J. Sparks, *Religion in Mississippi* (Jackson: University Press of Mississippi, 2001), demonstrates the changing nature of religion in the state.

Barnwell, *A Place Called Mississippi*, presents an 1837 excerpt from William Johnson's "Antebellum Diary of a Free Negro," providing a sense of the everyday violence of the time and a glimpse of the different monies in circulation (28–30).

Bond, *Mississippi*, provides a detailed description of a log home and its furnishing from the early 1840s written by Benjamin Lafayette Smith of Lowndes County (47–48) and a summary of Mississippi antebellum slave laws (66–70).

Chapter Five. Cotton Kingdom

Most important are John Hebron Moore, *Agriculture in Ante-Bellum Mississippi* (New York: Octagon Books, 1971), and *The Emergence of the Cotton Kingdom in the Old Southwest: Mississippi, 1770–1860* (Baton Rouge: Louisiana State University Press, 1988), which describe the planters' revolution of the cotton industry. Otherwise, biographies dominate: Martha Jane Brazy, *An American Planter: Stephen Duncan of Antebellum Natchez and New York* (Baton Rouge: Louisiana State University Press, 2006); James Byrne Ranck, *Albert Gallatin Brown, Radical Southern Nationalist* (New York: D. Appleton-Century, 1937); William J. Cooper Jr., *Jefferson Davis, American* (New York: Vintage Civil War Library, 2000); Reuben Davis, *Recollections of Mississippi and Mississippians* (Boston: Houghton Mifflin, 1890); Robert E. May, *John A. Quitman: Old South Crusader* (Baton Rouge: Louisiana State University Press, 1985); Fred Darbis Jr., "Alexander Keith McClung," *Journal of Mississippi History* 40 (1978): 289–296 (for an obscure but instructive character); Minor Ferris Buchanan, *Holt Collier: His Life, His Roosevelt Hunts, and the Origins of the Teddy Bear* (Jackson: Centennial Press of Mississippi, 2002); Edwin Adams Davis and William Ransom Hogan, *The Barber of Natchez* (Baton Rouge: Louisiana State University Press, 1954).

Barnwell, *A Place Called Mississippi*, offers a host of excerpts from memoirs and literature for the antebellum period: "Life and Confessions of the Noted Outlaw James Copeland," as the title suggests, provides a firsthand look at outlaws' lives before the Civil War (24–27). Excerpts from Susan Dabney Smedes's *Memorials of a Southern Planter* try to describe slavery in a benign fashion (37–46). A snippet from "Mississippi Scenes" gives the reader a taste of southwestern humor (71–73). Frederick Law Olmstead's account of his trip through the antebellum South may be the most cited observations of the era. This is a sampling (74–85). As an antidote to the Yankees' view, J. F. H. Claiborne provides a native's an account of travels in the piney woods (86–91).

Bond, *Mississippi*, delivers a wide range of documents to illustrate many of the topics covered in this chapter: Joseph B. Lightsey's diary entry of 1852 consisting of an imaginary dialogue conveys attitudes about education current in antebellum Mississippi (48–53). Amanda D. Worthington's letters cover a variety of topics, including education for a planter family (53–57). Martin W. Phillips's journal for the year 1840 gives a sense of the life of this noted agricultural reformer and the hardships imposed by the depression years (57–64). Excerpts from a number of slave narratives collected by Works Progress Administration (WPA) workers during the Great Depression give the reader one of the few eyewitness accounts of slavery. Just these few selections communicate the variety of slave experiences (70–78). Jesse Mabry's letter conveys a white man's concern about the "planned" slave rebellion in Madison County in 1835 (78–83). James Wesson's letter illustrates how slavery affected all aspects of life, as Wesson tries to sell his Bankston factory as a means of employing whites in a nonslave-type of manual labor (83–84). An entire chapter contains documents offering various views on secession, but the most important is "A Declaration of Independence" from the 1861 Secession Convention stating the reason for secession—slavery (85–105).

Chapter Six. Civil War: Disaster and Freedom

Michael B. Ballard, *Civil War Mississippi: A Guide* (Jackson: University Press of Mississippi, 2000), and *The Civil War in Mississippi: Major Campaigns and Battles* (Jackson: University Press of Mississippi for the Mississippi Historical Society, 2011), cover the military story. Timothy B. Smith, *Mississippi in the Civil War: The Home Front* (Jackson: University Press of Mississippi, 2010), covers nonwar topics, but readers will profit from primary sources collected in John K. Bettersworth, *Confederate Mississippi: The People and Politics of a Cotton State in Wartime* (Philadelphia: Porcupine Press, 1978), and *Mississippi in the Confederacy as They Saw It* (New York: Kraus Reprint, 1970), as well as James W. Silver and John K. Bettersworth, *Mississippi in the Confederacy as Seen in Retrospect* (Baton Rouge: Louisiana State University Press, 1961), and Sally Jenkins and John Stauffer, *The State of Jones: The Small County That Seceded from the Confederacy* (New York: Doubleday, 2009). For an interesting sidelight, see Herbert H. Lang, "J. F. H. Claiborne at Laurel Wood Plantation," *Journal of Mississippi History* 18 (1956): 1–17; and Andrew Brown, "Sol Street, Confederate Partisan Leader," *Journal of Mississippi History* 21 (1959): 155–173.

Barnwell, *A Place Called Mississippi*, has a small Civil War section, ranging from diaries to a selection from Shelby Foote's famous *Civil War: A Narrative*, as well as excerpts from Belle Edmondson's diary telling how she smuggled for the southern cause (144–146); a Union soldier's account of the Battle of Corinth (147–151); Foote's account of Pemberton's surrendering Vicksburg (152–156); and Jefferson Davis's account of his capture as he fled after Richmond's fall (157–158).

Bond's choices in his chapter titled "Wartime Mississippi" convey the less-covered topics of war on the home front: Matthew Dunn served in the Mississippi militia during the war, and his letters give the reader a sense of mundane military life as well as an idea of the revivals going on during the war (107–111); dying note of one of the University Greys wounded at

Gettysburg (111–112); and three women's letters and diaries dealing with aspects of the war ranging from hunger during the Vicksburg siege to a female smuggler demanding that the governor have her wagon returned (112–124).

Chapter Seven. Reconstruction: War by Other Means

Eric Foner, *Reconstruction: America's Unfinished Revolution, 1863–1877* (New York: Harper & Row, 1988); William C. Harris, *Presidential Reconstruction in Mississippi* (Baton Rouge: Louisiana State University Press, 1967), and *Republican Reconstruction in Mississippi: The Day of the Carpet-bagger* (Baton Rouge: Louisiana State University Press, 1979); James B. Murphy, *L. Q. C. Lamar: Pragmatic Patriot* (Baton Rouge: Louisiana State University Press, 1973); Nicholas Lemann, *Redemption: The Last Battle of the Civil War* (New York: Farrar, Straus and Giroux, 2006); Timothy B. Smith, *James Z. George: Mississippi's Great Commoner* (Jackson: University Press of Mississippi, 2012); Nancy Bercaw, *Gendered Freedoms: Race, Rights, and the Politics of Household in the Delta, 1861–1875* (Gainesville: University Press of Florida, 2003); Allen W. Trelease, *White Terror: The Ku Klux Klan Conspiracy and Southern Reconstruction* (New York: Harper & Row, 1971); Lillian A. Pereyra, *James Lusk Alcorn: Persistent Whig* (Baton Rouge: Louisiana State University Press, 1966).

Bond, *Mississippi*, offers a good interpretative introduction to the Reconstruction period (125–126) and: an 1866 labor contract between a freedman and a plantation owner (127); a plantation mistress's letters to her out-of-state son describing her reaction to freedmen during the early Reconstruction period (127–129); the testimony of a carpetbagger whom Klansmen whipped (129–134); and a district attorney's letter describing the Redeemers' methods used to steal elections (135–139).

Barnwell, *A Place Called Mississippi*, provides some glimpses with excerpts from autobiographies: James Lucas, a freedman, gave an interview to a white WPA interviewer in the 1930s, but it must be read with skepticism because of the context of a white Mississippian interviewing a black man (57–62). A quick view of journalist Ida B. Wells's childhood gives a glimpse into the attitudes of former slaves toward their old owners (159–161). John R. Lynch's excerpt provides a peek into the black elite's view of the period (162–168).

Chapter Eight. Redemption and Black Subjection

Stephen Edward Cresswell, *Multiparty Politics in Mississippi, 1877–1902* (Jackson: University Press of Mississippi, 1995), and *Rednecks, Redeemers, and Race: Mississippi after Reconstruction, 1877–1917* (Jackson: University Press of Mississippi for the Mississippi Historical Society, 2006); Deanne Stephens Nuwer, *Plague among the Magnolias: The 1987 Yellow Fever Epidemic in Mississippi* (Tuscaloosa: University of Alabama Press, 2009); Ronald L. F. Davis, *Good and Faithful Labor: From Slavery to Sharecropping in the Natchez District, 1860–1890* (Westport, Conn.: Greenwood Press, 1982); Melvin I. Urofsky, "Blanche K. Bruce: United

States Senator, 1875–1881," *Journal of Mississippi History* 29 (1967): 118–141; William J. Harris, "Etiquette, Lynching, and Racial Boundaries in Southern History: A Mississippi Example," *American Historical Review* 100 (1995): 387–410; Willie D. Halsell, "James R. Chalmers and (Mahoneism) in Mississippi," *Journal of Southern History* 10 (1944): 37–58; William W. White, "Marriage Insurance: The Mississippi Bubble of 1882," *Journal of Mississippi History* 46 (1984): 108–119.

Bond, *Mississippi*, provides an introductory essay titled "Reforming Mississippi" outlining Bourbon attempts to attract industry, farmers' revolts, and the temperance movement. The documents cited include: a grand jury report assessing the lack of political liberty in the state (139–140); a Republican's account of Democratic intimidation in Holmes County (140–143); letters from an anonymous "Negro" to Governor John Stone complaining about the treatment of freedmen in the state (143–145); a Grange meeting report (148–150); and the Farmers' Alliance plan to bust the jute trust (150–153). In "Suffrage for Some," Bond opens with a short historical essay on voting and follows with a host of documents covering the 1890 constitutional convention (167–179).

Barnwell, *A Place Called Mississippi*, offers only one traveler's narrative fitting this time period. Ernst von Hesse-Wartegg did not have much good to say about his train journey across the state and an overnight stay in Meridian (92–97).

Chapter Nine. Attempted Revolt of the Rednecks

Albert D. Kirwan, *Revolt of the Rednecks; Mississippi Politics: 1876–1925* (Gloucester, Mass.: Peter Smith, 1964); William F. Holmes, *The White Chief James Kimble Vardaman* (Baton Rouge: Louisiana State University Press, 1970); A. Wigfall Green, *The Man Bilbo* (Baton Rouge: Louisiana State University Press, 1963); Chester M. Morgan, *Redneck Liberal: Theodore G. Bilbo and the New Deal* (Baton Rouge: Louisiana State University Press, 1985), and *Treasured Past, Golden Future: The Centennial History of the University of Southern Mississippi* (Jackson: University of Southern Mississippi, 2010); Nollie Hickman, *Mississippi Harvest: Lumbering in the Longleaf Pine Belt 1840–1915* (Oxford: University of Mississippi, 1962); Randolph H. Boehm, "Mary Grace Quackenbos and the Federal Campaign against Peonage: The Case of Sunnyside Plantation," *Arkansas Historical Quarterly* 50 (1991): 40–59; Clyde J. Faries, "Redneck Rhetoric and the Last of the Redeemers: The 1899 McLaurin-Allen Campaign," *Journal of Mississippi History* 33 (1971): 282–298; Daphne A. Roe, *A Plague of Corn: The Social History of Pellagra* (Ithaca, N.Y.: Cornell University Press, 1973); Lewis Baker, *The Percys of Mississippi: Politics and Literature in the New South* (Baton Rouge: Louisiana State University Press, 1983); George Coleman Osborn, *John Sharp Williams: Planter-Statesman of the Deep South* (Baton Rouge: Louisiana State University Press, 1943).

Bond, *Mississippi*, includes documents from several reformers: Frank Burkitt's explanation of why he joined the Populists (153); a prohibitionist's explanation of her opposition to alcohol consumption (154); and an excerpt from a state board of health pamphlet on hookworms (154–159).

Barnwell, *A Place Called Mississippi*, presents two entertaining, if not very pertinent, biographical pieces: Mary Hamilton's account of life in the Delta at the turn of the century (46–50), and Wild Bill Sullivan stories (51–56).

Chapter Ten. Segregation: Red, Yellow, Black, and White

Neil R. McMillen, *Dark Journey: Black Mississippians in the Age of Jim Crow* (Urbana: University of Illinois Press, 1989); David M. Oshinsky, *Worse Than Slavery: Parchman Farm and the Ordeal of Jim Crow Justice* (New York: Free Press, 1996); William Banks Taylor, *Down on Parchman Farm: The Great Prison in the Mississippi Delta* (Columbus: Ohio State University Press, 1999); Pete Daniel, *The Shadow of Slavery: Peonage in the South 1901–1969* (Urbana: University of Illinois Press, 1972); George C. Rable, "The South and the Politics of Antilynching Legislation, 1920–1940," *Journal of Southern History* 51 (1985): 201–220; John M. Barry, *Rising Tide: The Great Mississippi Flood of 1927 and How It Changed America* (New York: Simon and Schuster, 1997); Katherine M. B. Osburn, "Southern Cultures: Mississippi Choctaws and Racial Politics," *Southern Cultures* 14 (2008): 32–54; James W. Loewen, *The Mississippi Chinese: Between Black and White* (Prospect Heights, Ill.: Waveland Press, 1988); Paul A. Cimbala and Barton C. Shaw, *Making a New South: Race, Leadership, and Community after the Civil War* (Gainesville: University Press of Florida, 2007); L. Moody Simms Jr., "Theodore DuBose Bratton, Christian Principles and the Race Question," *Journal of Mississippi History* 38 (1976): 47–52.

Bond, *Mississippi*, provides an entire chapter of documents entitled "The Jim Crow World," with an introduction. The selections range from Charles Bank's letter about segregated railroad accommodations to an NAACP condemnation of the Mississippi legislature's attempt to censor discussion of democracy out of textbooks used in black schools and the infamous blowtorch lynching in Duck Hill (189–208).

Barnwell, *A Place Called Mississippi*, has a mix of pieces: the historian Pete Daniels's description of the 1927 flood in Greenville (127–130); a light account of Theodore Dubose Bratton's building cabins for his children at his summer place on the Mississippi Gulf Coast (245–252); and a selection from Richard Wright's *Black Boy* (409–416).

Chapter Eleven. War, Depression, and Environmental Restoration

Isabel Wilkerson, *The Warmth of Other Suns: The Epic Story of America's Great Migration* (New York: Random House, 2010); Claire Strom, *Making Catfish Bait Out of Government Boys* (Athens: University of Georgia Press, 2009) (provides a history of federally imposed resistance to tick dipping); Martha H. Swain, *Pat Harrison: The New Deal Years* (Jackson: University Press of Mississippi, 1978); Bill R. Baker, *The Life of Henry L. Whitfield* (Jackson: University Press of Mississippi, 1974); Martha Mitchell Bigelow, "Mississippi Progressivism," *Journal of Mississippi History* 29 (1967): 202–209; James E. Fickle, *Mississippi Forests and Forestry* (Jackson: University Press of Mississippi, 2001); Gavin Wright, "The New Deal and the

Modernization of the South," *Federal History* 2 (2010): 58–73; Roger D. Tate, "Easing the Burden: The Era of Depression and New Deal in Mississippi" (Ph.D. diss., University of Tennessee, 1978); Justin C. Eaddy, "Mississippi State Parks: The New Deal's Mixed Legacy," *Journal of Mississippi History* 65 (2003) 147–168; Robert Springer, ed., *Nobody Knows Where the Blues Come From* (Jackson: University Press of Mississippi, 2006); Martha H. Swain, Elizabeth Anne Payne, and Marjorie Julian Spruill, eds., *Mississippi Women: Their Histories, Their Lives* (Athens: University of Georgia Press, 2003).

Bond, *Mississippi*, includes an entire chapter of documents covering the Great Depression and the New Deal, including letters from the down-and-out, farmers' petitions, a description of a beating administered to a union member in Macon, and a report on the value of the TVA to Tupelo. The chapter concludes with several documents on the passage of a wage-and-hour labor law (209–228).

Barnwell, *A Place Called Mississippi*, contains a rich variety of offerings on an array of topics: Nellie Somerville's speech to the Hypatia Club (171–174); a WPA researcher's description of sacred harp singing near Meridian in 1936 (261–262); a description of George E. Ohr, the mad potter of Biloxi, and some insight into an artist's life in the early twentieth century (293–296); W. C. Handy's description of encountering the blues for the first time in the Delta (297–302); Carrie Rodgers's description of her husband, Jimmie (313–316); Big Bill Broonzy on Mississippi (317–321); Walker Percy on bourbon (366–370); William Alexander Percy on the Delta (395–403); and Eudora Welty on growing up in Jackson (417–423).

Chapter Twelve. World War II, Economic Improvement, and Social Confusion

John R. Skates Jr., "World War II as a Watershed in Mississippi History," *Journal of Mississippi History* 37 (1975): 131–142; Neil R. McMillen, ed., *Remaking Dixie: The Impact of World War II on the American South* (Jackson: University Press of Mississippi, 1997); Scott Holzer, "Boomtown: The Social Transformation of Pascagoula, Mississippi, 1940–1943" (Master's thesis, University of Mississippi, 1988) (provides good insight into wartime social change); Mrs. Keith F. Somerville, *Dear Boys: World War II Letters from a Woman Back Home*, ed. Judy Barrett Litoff and David C. Smith (Jackson: University Press of Mississippi, 1991) (supplies a good record through the writing of Keith Frazier Somerville about her neighbors); Chris Myers Asch, *The Senator and the Sharecropper: The Freedom Struggles of James O. Eastland and Fannie Lou Hamer* (New York: New Press, 2008); Suzanne Marrs, *Eudora Welty: A Biography* (New York: Harcourt, 2005); Joseph Blotner, *Faulkner: A Biography* (Jackson: University Press of Mississippi, 2005); Hazel Rowley, *Richard Wright: The Life and Times* (New York: Henry Holt, 2001).

Barnwell, *A Place Called Mississippi*, offers an excerpt on attending a black church of the period in Clifton Taulbert's *Once Upon a Time When We Were Colored* (263–266); a 1940s entry from Walter Anderson's *From the Logbooks* describing his musing on Horn Island (333–334); and B. B. King's wartime experiences as a sharecropper and tractor driver from Charles Sawyer's *The Arrival of B. B. King* (338–343).

Chapter Thirteen. A Closed Society's Response to Challenge

Glenn Feldman, *Before Brown: Civil Rights and White Backlash in the Modern South* (Tuscaloosa: University of Alabama Press, 2004); John Egerton, *Speak Now against the Day: The Generation before the Civil Rights Movement in the South* (New York: Alfred A. Knopf, 1994); Charles Wallace Collins, *Whither Solid South? A Study in Politics and Race Relations* (New Orleans: Pelican, 1947) (provides the best statement of the segregationist ideology); George Lewis, *Massive Resistance: The White Response to the Civil Rights Movement* (New York: Oxford University Press, 2006); Dennis J. Mitchell, *Mississippi Liberal: A Biography of Frank E. Smith* (Jackson: University Press of Mississippi, 2001); Ann Walderson, *Hodding Carter: The Reconstruction of a Racist* (Chapel Hill, N.C.: Algonquin Books, 1993); Alex Heard, *The Eyes of Willie McGee: A Tragedy of Race, Sex, and Secrets in the Jim Crow South* (New York: Harper Collins, 2010); Michael Vinson Williams, *Medgar Evers: Mississippi Martyr* (Fayetteville: University of Arkansas Press, 2011); Simeon Wright and Herb Boyd, *Simeon's Story: An Eyewitness Account of the Kidnapping of Emmett Till* (Chicago: Lawrence Hill, 2010); Douglas L. Conner and John F. Marszalek, *A Black Physician's Story: Bringing Hope in Mississippi* (Jackson: University Press of Mississippi, 1985); Davis W. Houck and Matthew A. Grindy, *Emmett Till and the Mississippi Press* (Jackson: University Press of Mississippi, 2008).

Barnwell, *A Place Called Mississippi*, contains an excerpt from P. D. East's *The Magnolia Jungle* documenting his attempt with William Faulkner to promote Mississippi moderates, with excerpts from a paper on which the two collaborated (183–192). She also includes an excerpt from William Faulkner's nonfiction article from 1954 providing his view of Mississippi's history (103–124). An excerpt from Leontyne Price's *I Dream a World* reveals that extraordinarily talented black people made their way in many occupations during this period (349–351). A selection from Peter Guralnick's *Last Train to Memphis* describes Tupelo's musical influences shaping Elvis Presley (371–374). In "My Mother, in Memory," writer Richard Ford presents a child's view of a family's life in Jackson during this period (451–455). Walker Percy's "Mississippi: The Fallen Paradise" analyzes the public and private spaces in the state (213–224).

Bond, *Mississippi*, contains a chapter on reactions to the *Brown* decision, including: a portion of Tom Brady's *Black Monday*; Faulkner's letter to the editor on schools; a speech by T. R. M. Howard; and a letter written by J. H. White, president of Mississippi Vocational College (now Mississippi Valley State University) (227–251).

Chapter Fourteen. The Civil Rights Movement and White Defiance

Timothy J. Minchin and John A. Salmond, "The Saddest Story of the Whole Movement: The Clyde Kennard Case and the Search for Racial Reconciliation in Mississippi, 1955–2007," *Journal of Mississippi History* 71 (2009): 191–234; Charles M. Payne, *I've Got the Light of Freedom: The Organizing Tradition and the Mississippi Freedom Struggle* (Berkeley: University of California Press, 1995); Paul T. Murray, "Father Nathaniel and the Greenwood Movement," *Journal of Mississippi History* 72 (2010): 277–313; Gilbert R. Mason and James Patterson

Smith, *Beaches, Blood, and Ballots: A Black Doctor's Civil Rights Struggle* (Jackson: University Press of Mississippi, 2000); Douglas L. Conner and John F. Marszalek, *A Black Physician's Story: Bringing Hope in Mississippi* (Jackson: University Press of Mississippi, 1985); Aaron Henry, *The Fire Ever Burning* (Jackson: University Press of Mississippi, 2000); Kay Mills, *Changing Channels: The Civil Rights Case That Transformed Television* (Jackson: University Press of Mississippi, 2004), and *This Little Light of Mine: The Life of Fannie Lou Hamer* (New York: Dutton, 1993); Howard Smead, *Blood Justice: The Lynching of Mack Charles Parker* (New York: Oxford University Press, 1986); Bruce Watson, *Freedom Summer: The Savage Season That Made Mississippi Burn and Made America a Democracy* (New York: Penguin Group, 2010); Reid Stoner Derr, "The Triumph of Progressivism: Governor Paul B. Johnson, Jr., and Mississippi in the 1960s" (Ph.D. diss., University of Southern Mississippi, 1994); Charles W. Eagles, *The Price of Defiance: James Meredith and Integration of Ole Miss* (Chapel Hill: University of North Carolina Press, 2009); Pete Daniel, *Toxic Drift: Pesticides and Health in the Post–World War II South* (Baton Rouge: Louisiana State University Press, 2005).

Bond, *Mississippi*, provides two chapters of documents from this era: one on the reaction to the *Brown* decision and another on the Freedom Summer. Readers will find the following especially enlightening: a letter from a Natchez woman to a federal judge that summarizes many of the white attitudes common during the period (236–239); Faulkner's letter to the editor on the foolishness of Mississippi's segregated schools (239–240); R. N. Burger's statement of why, as black men, they supported segregation (246–251); Dave Dennis's eulogy for James Chaney (254–259); an interview with a Methodist Freedom School teacher (259–265); Freedom School children's description of Jim Crow (267–269); Hamer's testimony at the Democratic Convention (271–274); Governor Paul Johnson Jr.'s economic plan (277–283).

Barnwell, *A Place Called Mississippi*, contains several writers' observations of the era: excerpts from Florence Mars's *Witness in Philadelphia* (198); excerpts from Anne Moody's *Coming of Age in Mississippi* (203–207); Hodding Carter's description of the Heffners' dinner that led to their being run out of town from *So the Heffners Left McComb* (208–212); Tammy Wynette's memory of picking cotton in Itawamba County (375–378); and Eudora Welty's account of her family life in Jackson (417–423).

Chapter Fifteen. Mississippi and the Modern World

Charles Reagan Wilson, *Judgment and Grace in Dixie: Southern Faiths from Faulkner to Elvis* (Athens: University of Georgia Press, 1995); Bradley G. Bond, "'Unmitigated Thievery': The Case against William David McCain," *Journal of Mississippi History* 72 (2010): 163–197; Ellen Douglas, *The Rock Cried Out* (New York: Harcourt Brace Jovanovich, 1979); Donald G. Schueler, *Preserving the Pascagoula* (Jackson: University Press of Mississippi, 1980); Jere Nash and Andy Taggart, *Mississippi Politics: The Struggle for Power, 1976–2008* (Jackson: University Press of Mississippi, 2009); Bill Waller, *Straight Ahead: The Memoirs of a Mississippi Governor* (Brandon, Miss.: Quail Ridge Press, 2007); Charles C. Bolton, "William F.

Winter and the Politics of Racial Moderation in Mississippi," *Journal of Mississippi History* 70 (2008): 335–382; Peggy W. Prenshaw and Jesse O. Mckee, *Sense of Place Mississippi* (Jackson: University Press of Mississippi, 1979); Richard Schweid, *Catfish and the Delta* (Berkeley, Calif.: Ten Speed Press, 1992); Keith Thibodeaux with Audrey T. Hingley, *Life After Lucy: The True Story of Keith Thibodeaux—"I Love Lucy's" Little Ricky* (Green Forest, Ark.: New Leaf Press, 1994); James R. Crockett, *The FBI's Sting Operation on County Corruption: Pretense in Mississippi* (Jackson: University Press of Mississippi, 2003); Maryanne Vollers, *Ghosts of Mississippi: The Murder of Medgar Evers, the Trials of Byron De La Beckwith, and the Haunting of the New South* (Boston: Little, Brown, 1995); Curtis Wilkie, *The Fall of the House of Zeus: The Rise and Ruin of America's Most Powerful Trial Lawyer* (New York: Crown, 2010).

Bond, *Mississippi*, includes two chapters: "Economic Development" and "Battle Over the Flag." Paul B. Johnson Jr.'s call for Mississippians to focus on economic development (277–283), from his inaugural address, sets the scene. Two documents juxtapose the catfish industry and its workers' complaints (283–288). The final document provides a sense of the casinos' impact on the state's economy (294–296).

Barnwell, *A Place Called Mississippi*, offers quick glimpses into some of Mississippi's modern writers: Eudora Welty (417–423); Will D. Campbell (426–429); Willie Morris (432–438); Larry Brown (445–450); Ellen Douglas (456–457); and Barry Hannah (271–275).

Bibliography

Books

Abbott, Dorothy, ed. *Mississippi Writers: Reflections of Childhood and Youth*. Vol. 1, *Fiction*. Jackson: University Press of Mississippi, 1985.

———. *Mississippi Writers: Reflections of Childhood and Youth*. Vol. 2, *Nonfiction*. Jackson: University Press of Mississippi, 1986.

Alford, Terry. *Prince among Slaves*. New York: Oxford University Press, 1977.

Ames, Blanche. *Adelbert Ames, 1835–1933*. New York: Argosy-Antiquarian, 1964.

Arkush, Elizabeth N. *The Archaeology of Warfare: Prehistories of Raiding and Conquest*. Gainesville: University Press of Florida, 2008.

Asch, Chris Myers. *The Senator and the Sharecropper: The Freedom Struggles of James O. Eastland and Fannie Lou Hamer*. New York: New Press, 2008.

Ball, Howard. *Justice in Mississippi: The Murder Trial of Edgar Ray Killen*. Lawrence: University Press of Kansas, 2006.

Baker, Bill R. *The Life of Henry L. Whitfield*. Jackson: University Press of Mississippi, 1974.

Baker, Lewis. *The Percys of Mississippi: Politics and Literature in the New South*. Baton Rouge: Louisiana State University Press, 1983.

Ballard, Michael B. *The Civil War in Mississippi: Major Campaigns and Battles*. Jackson: University Press of Mississippi for the Mississippi Historical Society, 2011.

———. *Civil War Mississippi: A Guide*. Jackson: University Press of Mississippi, 2000.

———. *Maroon and White: Mississippi State University, 1878–2003*. Jackson: University Press of Mississippi, 2008.

———. *Vicksburg: The Campaign That Opened the Mississippi*. Chapel Hill: University of North Carolina Press, 2004.

Barnett, James F., Jr. *Mississippi's American Indians*. Jackson: University Press of Mississippi, 2012.

———. *The Natchez Indians: A History to 1735*. Jackson: University Press of Mississippi, 2007.

Barney, William L. *The Secessionist Impulse: Alabama and Mississippi in 1860*. Princeton, N.J.: Princeton University Press, 1974.

Barnwell, Marion. *A Place Called Mississippi: Collected Narratives*. Jackson: University Press of Mississippi, 1997.

Barry, John M. *Rising Tide: The Great Mississippi Flood of 1927 and How It Changed America*. New York: Simon and Schuster, 1997.

Bercaw, Nancy. *Gendered Freedoms: Race, Rights, and the Politics of Household in the Delta, 1861–1875*. Gainesville: University Press of Florida, 2003.

Berlin, Ira, and Phillip D. Morgan. *Cultivation and Culture: Labor and the Shaping of Slave Life in the Americas*. Charlottesville: University Press of Virginia, 1993.

Bettersworth, John K. *Confederate Mississippi: The People and Politics of a Cotton State in Wartime*. Philadelphia: Porcupine Press, 1978.

———. *Mississippi in the Confederacy as They Saw It*. New York: Kraus Reprint, 1970.

———. *The People's University: The Centennial History of Mississippi State*. Jackson: University Press of Mississippi, 1980.

Black, Earl. *Southern Governors and Civil Rights: Racial Segregation as a Campaign Issue in the Second Reconstruction*. Cambridge, Mass.: Harvard University Press, 1976.

Black, Patti Carr. *Art in Mississippi, 1720–1980*. Jackson: University Press of Mississippi in association with the Mississippi Historical Society and the Mississippi Department of Archives and History, 1998.

Blain, William T. *Education in the Old Southwest: A History of Jefferson College*. Washington, Miss.: Friends of Jefferson College, 1976.

Blotner, Joseph. *Faulkner: A Biography*. Jackson: University Press of Mississippi, 2005.

Bolton, Charles C. *The Hardest Deal of All: The Battle over School Integration in Mississippi, 1870–1980*. Jackson: University Press of Mississippi, 2005.

———. *Poor Whites of the Antebellum South: Tenants and Laborers in Central North Carolina and Northeast Mississippi*. Durham, N.C.: Duke University Press, 1994.

Bond, Bradley G. *Mississippi: A Documentary History*. Jackson: University Press of Mississippi, 2003.

———. *Political Culture in the Nineteenth-Century South Mississippi, 1830–1900*. Baton Rouge: Louisiana State University Press, 1995.

Brandfon, Robert L. *Cotton Kingdom of the New South: A History of the Yazoo Mississippi Delta from Reconstruction to the Twentieth Century*. Cambridge, Mass.: Harvard University Press, 1967.

Brazy, Martha Jane. *An American Planter: Stephen Duncan of Antebellum Natchez and New York*. Baton Rouge: Louisiana State University Press, 2006.

Brinson, Carroll. *Our Time Has Come: Mississippi Embraces Its Future*. Jackson, Miss.: Oakdale Press, 1988.

Brown, Bertram Wyatt. *Southern Honor: Ethics and Behavior in the Old South*. Oxford: Oxford University Press, 1982.

Brown, Richmond F., ed., *Coastal Encounters: The Transformation of the Gulf South in the Eighteenth Century*. Lincoln: University of Nebraska Press, 2007.

Buchanan, Minor Ferris. *Holt Collier: His Life, His Roosevelt Hunts, and the Origin of the Teddy Bear*. Jackson: Centennial Press of Mississippi, 2002.

Burkhalter, Lois Wood. *Gideon Lincecum, 1793–1874: A Biography*. Austin: University of Texas Press, 1965.

Bynum, Victoria E. *The Free State of Jones: Mississippi's Longest Civil War*. Chapel Hill: University of North Carolina Press, 2001.

Cabaniss, James Allen. *A History of the University of Mississippi*. University: University of Mississippi, 1949.

Campbell, Will D. *Providence*. Atlanta: Longstreet Press, 1992.

———. *Robert G. Clark's Journey to the House*. Jackson: University Press of Mississippi, 2003.

Carson, James Taylor. *Native Americans, the Market Revolution, and Culture Change: The Choctaw Cattle Economy, 1690–1830*. Norman: University of Oklahoma Press, 2008.

———. *Searching for the Bright Path: The Mississippi Choctaws from Prehistory to Removal*. Lincoln: University of Nebraska Press, 2003.

Cash, William M., and Lucy Somerville Howorth. *My Dear Nellie: The Civil War Letters of Williams L. Nugent to Eleanor Smith Nugent*. Jackson: University Press of Mississippi, 1977.

Cate, Wirt Armistead. *Lucius Q. C. Lamar: Secession and Reunion*. New York: Russell & Russell, 1935.

Chang, Thelma. *"I Can Never Forget": Men of the 100th/442nd*. Honolulu: Sigi Productions, 1991.

Cimbala, Paul A., and Barton C. Shaw. *Making a New South: Race, Leadership, and Community after the Civil War*. Gainesville: University Press of Florida, 2007.

Claiborne, J. F. H. The *Life and Correspondence of John A. Quitman, Major-General, U.S.A., and Governor of the State of Mississippi*. New York: Harpers & Brothers, 1860.

———. *Life and Times of Gen. Sam Dale: The Mississippi Partisan*. Spartanburg, S.C.: Reprint Company, 1976.

Classen, Steven D. *Watching Jim Crow: The Struggles Over Mississippi TV, 1955–1969*. Durham, N.C.: Duke University Press, 2004.

Cobb, James C. *The Mississippi Delta and the World: The Memoirs of David L. Cohn*. Baton Rouge: Louisiana State University Press, 1995.

———. *The Most Southern Place on Earth: The Mississippi Delta and the Roots of Regional Identity*. New York: Oxford University Press, 1992.

Collins, Charles Wallace. *Whither Solid South? A Study in Politics and Race Relations*. New Orleans: Pelican, 1947.

Collins, Donald E. *The Death and Resurrection of Jefferson Davis*. Lanham, Md.: Rowman and Littlefield, 2005.

Conner, Douglas L., and John F. Marszalek. *A Black Physician's Story: Bringing Hope in Mississippi*. Jackson: University Press of Mississippi, 1985.

Cooper, William J., Jr. *Jefferson Davis, American*. New York: Vintage Civil War Library, 2000.

Cortner, Richard C. *A "Scottsboro" Case in Mississippi: The Supreme Court and Brown vs. Mississippi*. Jackson: University Press of Mississippi, 1986.

Cozzens, Peter. *The Darkest Days of the War: The Battles of Iuka and Corinth*. Chapel Hill: University of North Carolina Press, 1997.

Crespino, Joseph. *In Search of Another Country: Mississippi and the Conservative Counterrevolution*. Princeton, N.J.: Princeton University Press, 2007.

Cresswell, Stephen Edward. *Mormons and Cowboys, Moonshiners and Klansmen: Federal Law Enforcement in the South and West*. Tuscaloosa: University of Alabama Press, 1991.

———. *Multiparty Politics in Mississippi, 1877–1902*. Jackson: University Press of Mississippi, 1995.

———. *Rednecks, Redeemers, and Race: Mississippi after Reconstruction, 1877–1917*. Jackson: University Press of Mississippi for the Mississippi Historical Society, 2006.

Crockett, James R. *The FBI's Sting Operation on County Corruption: Pretense in Mississippi*. Jackson: University Press of Mississippi, 2003.

———. *Hands in the Till: Embezzlement of Public Monies in Mississippi*. Jackson: University Press of Mississippi, 2007.

Crosby, Emilye. *A Little Taste of Freedom: The Black Freedom Struggle in Claiborne County, Mississippi*. Chapel Hill: University of North Carolina Press, 2005.

Current, Richard Nelson. *Those Terrible Carpetbaggers*. New York: Oxford University Press, 1988.

Currie, James T. *Enclave: Vicksburg and Her Plantations, 1863–1870*. Jackson: University Press of Mississippi, 1980.

Curry, Constance. *Silver Rights*. Chapel Hill, N.C.: Algonquin Books, 1995.

Daniel, Pete. *Lost Revolution: The South in the 1950s*. Washington, D.C.: Smithsonian Intuition, 2010.

———. *The Shadow of Slavery: Peonage in the South 1901–1969*. Urbana: University of Illinois Press, 1972.

———. *Toxic Drift: Pesticides and Health in the Post–World War II South*. Baton Rouge: Louisiana State University Press, 2005.

Daugherity, Brian J., and Charles C. Bolton. *With All Deliberate Speed: Implementing Brown v. Board of Education*. Fayetteville: University of Arkansas Press, 2008.

Davis, Edwin Adams, and William Ransom Hogan. *The Barber of Natchez*. Baton Rouge: Louisiana State University Press, 1954.

Davis, Reuben. *Recollections of Mississippi and Mississippians*. Boston: Houghton Mifflin, 1890.

Davis, Ronald L. F. *Good and Faithful Labor: From Slavery to Sharecropping in the Natchez District, 1860–1890*. Westport, Conn.: Greenwood Press, 1982.

Davis, William C. *A Way through the Wilderness: The Natchez Trace and the Civilization of the Southern Frontier*. New York: Harper Collins, 1995.

DeLaughter, Bobby. *Never Too Late: A Prosecutor's Story of Justice in the Medgar Evers Case*. New York: Simon and Schuster, 2001.

DeRosier, Arthur H., Jr. *The Removal of the Choctaw Indians*. Knoxville: University of Tennessee Press, 1970.

Dick, Everett. *The Dixie Frontier: A Social History of the Southern Frontier from the First Transmontane Beginnings to the Civil War*. New York: Octagon Books, 1974.

Dickerson, James. *Mojo Triangle: Birthplace of Country, Blues, Jazz and Rock 'n' Roll*. New York: Schirmer Trade Books, 2005.

Dickey, Dallas C. *Seargent S. Prentiss: Whig Orator of the Old South*. Baton Rouge: Louisiana State University Press, 1945.

Dickson, Harris. *An Old-Fashioned Senator: A Story-Biography of John Sharp Williams*. New York: Fredrick A. Stokes, 1925.

Dimond, E. Grey, and Herman Hattaway. *Letters from Forrest Place: A Plantation Family's Correspondence 1846–1881*. Jackson: University Press of Mississippi, 1993.

Din, Gilbert C. *Spaniards, Planters, and Slaves: The Spanish Regulation of Slavery in Louisiana, 1763–1803*. College Station: Texas A&M University Press, 1999.

Dittmer, John. *Local People: The Struggle for Civil Rights in Mississippi*. Urbana: University of Illinois Press, 1994.

Dollard, John. *Caste and Class in a Southern Town*. New York: Double Day Anchor, 1949.

Douglas, Ellen. *The Rock Cried Out*. New York: Harcourt Brace Jovanovich, 1979.

Doyle, Don H. *Faulkner's County: The Historical Roots of Yoknapatawpha*. Chapel Hill: University of North Carolina Press, 2001.

Doyle, William. *An American Insurrection: The Battle of Oxford, Mississippi, 1962*. New York: Doubleday, 2001.

Dray, Philip. *Capitol Men: The Epic Story of Reconstruction through the Lives of the First Black Congressmen*. New York: Houghton Mifflin, 2008.

Dubay, Robert W. *John Jones Pettus, Mississippi Fire-Eater: His Life and Times 1813–1867*. Jackson: University Press of Mississippi, 1975.

Duren, William Larkin. *Charles Betts Galloway: Orator, Preacher, and Prince of Christian Chivalry*. Emory University, Ga.: Banner Press, 1932.

Eagles, Charles W. *The Price of Defiance: James Meredith and Integration of Ole Miss*. Chapel Hill: University of North Carolina Press, 2009.

Edmiston, Fred W. *Meridian, Mississippi, At War: People and Events during World War II (1939–1945)*. Meridian, Miss.: self-published [Lauderdale County Meridian Public Library], 2006.

Egerton, John. *Speak Now against the Day: The Generation before the Civil Rights Movement in the South*. New York: Alfred A. Knopf, 1994.

Ellis, Marion A. *Dean W. Colvard: Quiet Leader*. Charlotte: University of North Carolina at Charlotte, 2004.

Ellis, Mary H. *Cannonballs and Courage: The Story of Port Gibson*. Virginia Beach, Va.: Donning, 2003.

Etheridge, Elizabeth W. *The Butterfly Caste: A Social History of Pellagra in the South*. Westport, Conn.: Greenwood Press, 1972.

Evans, Eli N. *The Lonely Days Were Sundays: Reflections of a Jewish Southerner*. Jackson: University Press of Mississippi, 1993.

Fairly, Laura Nan, and James T. Dawson. *Paths to the Past: An Overview History of Lauderdale County, Mississippi*. Meridian, Miss.: Lauderdale County Department of Archives and History, 1988.

Faulkner, William. *Collected Stories of William Faulkner*. New York: Vintage Books, 1977.

———. *Faulkner Novels 1930–1935*. New York: Literary Classics of the United States, 1985.

———. *The Faulkner Reader*. New York: Random House, 1930.

Feldman, Glenn. *Before Brown: Civil Rights and White Backlash in the Modern South*. Tuscaloosa: University of Alabama Press, 2004.

Felton, Ralph Almon. *These My Brethren: A Study of 570 Negro Churches and 1542 Negro Homes in the Rural South*. Madison, N.J.: Department of the Rural Church, Drew Theological Seminary, 1950.

Fickle, James E. *Mississippi Forests and Forestry*. Jackson: University Press of Mississippi, 2001.

Fitzgerald, Michael W. *Splendid Failure: Postwar Reconstruction in the American South*. Chicago: Ivan R. Dee, 2007.

Foner, Eric. *Reconstruction: America's Unfinished Revolution, 1863–1877*. New York: Harper & Row, 1988.

Foote, Henry S. *Casket of Reminiscences*. San Francisco: Chronicle, 1874.

Foreman, Grant. *Indian Removal: The Emigration of the Five Civilized Tribes of Indians*. Norman: University of Oklahoma Press, 1932.

Foster, Buck T. *Sherman's Mississippi Campaign*. Tuscaloosa: University of Alabama Press, 2006.

Frankel, Noralee. *Freedom's Women: Black Women and Families in Civil War Era Mississippi*. Bloomington: Indiana University Press, 1999.

Frederickson, Kari. *The Dixiecrat Revolt and the End of the Solid South 1932–1968*. Chapel Hill: University of North Carolina Press, 2001.

Friend, Craig Thompson, and Lorri Glover. *Southern Manhood: Perspectives on Masculinity in the Old South*. Athens: University of Georgia Press, 2004.

Gallay, Alan. *The Indian Slave Trade: The Rise of the English Empire in the American South, 1670–1717*. New Haven, Conn.: Yale University Press, 2002.

Garner, Alfred William. *The Public Services of E. C. Walthall*. [located in Department of Special Collections, Mississippi State University].

Garner, James Wilford. *Reconstruction in Mississippi*. Gloucester, Mass.: Peter Smith, 1964.

Gibson, Arrell M. *The Chickasaws*. Norman: University of Oklahoma Press, 1971.

Giddings, Paula J. *IDA: A Sword Among Lions*. New York: Harper Collins, 2008.

Gonzales, John Edmond. *The Public Career of Henry Stuart Foote (1804–1880)*. Chapel Hill: University of North Carolina Press, 1957.

Gray, Richard. *The Life of William Faulkner: A Critical Biography*. Cambridge: Blackwell, 1996.

Green, A. Wigfall. *The Man Bilbo*. Baton Rouge: Louisiana State University Press, 1963.

Green, Fletcher Melvin. *Democracy in the Old South and Other Essays*. Nashville, Tenn.: Vanderbilt University Press, 1969.

Guice, John D. W. *Face to Face in Mississippi Territory, 1798–1817*. Jackson: University Press of Mississippi, 1985.

Hamilton, Charles Granville. *Mississippi, Mirror of the 1920's*. Fulton, Miss.: Itawamba County Times, 1979.

Hamilton, William Baskerville. *Anglo-American Law on the Frontier: Thomas Rodney and His Territorial Cases*. Durham, N.C.: Duke University Press, 1953.

Harris, William C. *Presidential Reconstruction in Mississippi*. Baton Rouge: Louisiana State University Press, 1967.

———. *Republican Reconstruction in Mississippi: The Day of the Carpet-bagger*. Baton Rouge: Louisiana State University Press, 1979.

Harrison, Alferdteen. *Black Exodus: The Great Migration from the American South*. Jackson: University Press of Mississippi, 1991.

———. *Piney Woods School: An Oral History*. Jackson: University Press of Mississippi, 1982.

Harwell, David Horace. *Walker Percy Remembered: A Portrait in the Words of Those Who Knew Him*. Chapel Hill: University of North Carolina Press, 2006.

Hattaway, Herman. *General Stephen D. Lee*. Jackson: University Press of Mississippi, 1976.

Havard, William C. *The Changing Politics of the South*. Baton Rouge: Louisiana State University Press, 1972.

Haynes, Robert V. *The Mississippi Territory and the Southwest Frontier, 1795–1817*. Lexington: University Press of Kentucky, 2010.

Heard, Alex. *The Eyes of Willie McGee: A Tragedy of Race, Sex, and Secrets in the Jim Crow South*. New York: Harper Collins, 2010.

Helferich, Gerard. *High Cotton: Four Seasons in the Mississippi Delta*. New York: Counterpoint, 2007.

Herman, Janet Sharp. *Joseph E. Davis: Pioneer Patriarch*. Jackson: University Press of Mississippi, 1990.

Henry, Aaron. *The Fire Ever Burning*. Jackson: University Press of Mississippi, 2000.

Hesseltine, William B. *Confederate Leaders in the New South*. Baton Rouge: Louisiana State University Press, 1950.

Hickman, Nollie. *Mississippi Harvest: Lumbering in the Longleaf Pine Belt 1840–1915*. Oxford: University of Mississippi, 1962.

Hill, Samuel S. *Religion in the Southern States: A Historical Study*. Macon, Ga.: Mercer University Press, 1983.

Hogan, Wesley C. *Many Minds, One Heart: SNCC'S Dream for a New America*. Chapel Hill: University of North Carolina Press, 2007.

Holder, Ray. *Williams Winans: Methodist Leader in Antebellum Mississippi*. Jackson: University Press of Mississippi, 1977.

Holland, Endesha Ida Mae. *From the Mississippi Delta: A Memoir*. New York: Simon and Schuster, 1997.

Hollandsworth, James G., Jr. *Portrait of a Scientific Racist*. Baton Rouge: Louisiana State University Press, 2008.

Holley, Donald. *The Second Great Emancipation: The Mechanical Cotton Picker, Black Migration, and How They Shaped the Modern South*. Fayetteville: University of Arkansas Press, 2000.

Holmes, Jack D. L. *Gayoso: The Life of a Spanish Governor in the Mississippi Valley 1789–1799*. Gloucester, Mass.: Peter Smith, 1968.

Holmes, William F. *The White Chief James Kimble Vardaman*. Baton Rouge: Louisiana State University Press, 1970.

Hooker, Charles E. *Confederate Military History of Mississippi: Mississippi during the Civil War, 1861–1865*. Ed. Clements A. Evans. eBooksOnDisk.com, 2003.

Houck, Davis W., and Matthew A. Grindy. *Emmett Till and the Mississippi Press*. Jackson: University Press of Mississippi, 2008.

Howard, Hugh. *Natchez: The Houses and History of the Jewel of the Mississippi*. New York: Rizzoli International, 2003.

Howard, John. *Concentration Camps on the Home Front: Japanese Americans in the House of Jim Crow*. Chicago: University of Chicago Press, 2008.

Hudson, Charles. *Knights of Spain, Warriors of the Sun: Hernando de Soto of Spain, and the South's Ancient Chiefdoms*. Athens: University of Georgia Press, 1997.

Hudson, Charles, and Carmen Chaves Tesser, eds. *The Forgotten Centuries: Indians and Europeans in the American South, 1521–1704*. Athens: University of Georgia Press, 1994.

Hudson, Winson, and Constance Curry. *Mississippi Harmony: Memoirs of a Freedom Fighter*. New York: Palgrave Macmillan, 2002.

James, D. Clayton. *Antebellum Natchez*. Baton Rouge: Louisiana State University Press, 1968.

Jenkins, Sally, and John Stauffer. *The State of Jones: The Small County That Seceded from the Confederacy*. New York: Doubleday, 2009.

Jewett, Clayton E., and John O Allen. *Slavery in the South: A State-by-State History*. Westport, Conn.: Greenwood Press, 2004.

Johnston, Erle. *Mississippi's Defiant Years 1953–1973: An Interpretive Documentary with Personal Experiences*. Forest, Miss.: Lake Harbor, 1990.

Jordan, Winthrop D. *Tumult and Silence at Second Creek: An Inquiry into a Civil War Slave Conspiracy*. Baton Rouge: Louisiana State University Press, 1993.

Katagiri, Yasuhiro. *The Mississippi State Sovereignty Commission: Civil Rights and States' Rights*. Jackson: University Press of Mississippi, 2001.

Keating, Bern. *A History of Washington County, Mississippi*. Greenville, Miss.: Greenville Junior Auxiliary, 1976.

Key, V. O., Jr. *Southern Politics*. New York: Vintage Books, 1949.

Kidwell, Clara Sue. *Choctaws and Missionaries in Mississippi, 1818–1918*. Norman: University of Oklahoma Press, 1995.

Kimbrough, Edward. *From Hell to Breakfast*. Philadelphia: J. B. Lippincott, 1941.

Kirby, Jack Temple. *Mockingbird Song: Ecological Landscapes of the South*. Chapel Hill: University North Carolina Press, 2006.

Kirwan, Albert D. *Revolt of the Rednecks; Mississippi Politics: 1876–1925*. Gloucester, Mass.: Peter Smith, 1964.

Kousser, J. Morgan, and James M. McPherson. *Region Race and Reconstruction: Essays in Honor of C. Vann Woodward*. New York: Oxford University Press, 1982.

Krane, Dale, and Stephen D. Shaffer. *Mississippi Government and Politics: Modernizers versus Traditionalist*. Lincoln: University of Nebraska Press, 1992.

Krech, Shepard, III. *Spirits of the Air: Birds and American Indians in the South*. Athens: University of Georgia Press, 2009.

Lalicki, Tom. *Grierson's Raid: A Daring Cavalry Strike through the Heart of the Confederacy*. New York: Farrar, Straus and Giroux, 2004.

Lemann, Nicholas. *Redemption: The Last Battle of the Civil War*. New York: Farrar, Straus and Giroux, 2006.

Lewis, George. *Massive Resistance: The White Response to the Civil Rights Movement*. New York: Oxford University Press, 2006.

Lewis, Oscar. *Anthropological Essays*. New York: Random House, 1946.

Libby, David J. *Slavery and Frontier Mississippi, 1720–1835*. Jackson: University Press of Mississippi, 2004.

Lincecum, Gideon. *Pushmataha: A Choctaw Leader and His People*. Tuscaloosa: University of Alabama Press, 2004.

Litwack, Leon, and August Meier. *Black Leaders of the Nineteenth Century*. Urbana: University of Illinois Press, 1988.

Lloyd, James B., ed. *Lives of Mississippi Authors, 1817–1967*. Jackson: University Press of Mississippi, 1981.

Loewen, James W. *The Mississippi Chinese: Between Black and White*. Prospect Heights, Ill.: Waveland Press, 1988.

Logue, Cal M., and Howard Dorgan. *The Oratory of Southern Demagogues*. Baton Rouge: Louisiana State University Press, 1981.

Lord, Walter. *A Time to Stand*. New York: Harper & Brothers, 1961.

Lynch, John R. *The Facts of Reconstruction*. Indianapolis: Bobbs-Merrill, 1970.

Maclean, Harry N. *The Past Is Never Dead: The Trial of James Ford Seale and Mississippi's Struggle for Redemption*. New York: Basic Civitas, 2009.

Marrs, Suzanne. *Eudora Welty: A Biography*. New York: Harcourt, 2005.

Martin, Chief Phillip, Lynne Jeter, and Kendall Blanchard. *Chief: The Autobiography of Chief Phillip Martin, Longtime Tribal Leader, Mississippi Band of Choctaw Indians*. Brandon, Miss.: Quail Ridge Press, 2009.

Mason, Gilbert R., and James Patterson Smith. *Beaches, Blood, and Ballots: A Black Doctor's Civil Rights Struggle*. Jackson: University Press of Mississippi, 2000.

May, Robert E. *John A. Quitman: Old South Crusader*. Baton Rouge: Louisiana State University Press, 1985.

———. *The Southern Dream of a Caribbean Empire, 1854–1861*. Athens: University of Georgia Press, 1989.

McAlexander, Hubert H. *Strawberry Plains Audubon Center: Four Centuries of a Mississippi Landscape*. Jackson: University Press of Mississippi, 2008.

McBee, May Wilson. *The Life and Times of David Smith: Patriot, Pioneer and Indian Fighter*. Kansas City: E. L. Mendenhall, Printers, 1959.

McDonald, Archie P. *Travis*. Austin, Tex.: Jenkins Publishing and the Pemberton Press, 1976.

McLemore, Richard Aubrey, ed. *A History of Mississippi*. Vol. 1. Hattiesburg: University and College Press of Mississippi, 1973.

———. *A History of Mississippi*. Vol. 2. Jackson: University and College Press of Mississippi, 1973.

McMillen, Neil R. *The Citizens Council: Organized Resistance to the Second Reconstruction 1954–64*. Urbana: University of Illinois Press, 1971.

———. *Dark Journey: Black Mississippians in the Age of Jim Crow*. Urbana: University of Illinois Press, 1989.

———, ed. *Remaking Dixie: The Impact of World War II on the American South*. Jackson: University Press of Mississippi, 1997.

Miles, Edwin Arthur. *Jacksonian Democracy in Mississippi*. Chapel Hill: University of North Carolina Press, 1960.

Miller, Steven F. *Plantation Labor Organization and Slave Life on the Cotton Frontier: The Alabama-Mississippi Black Belt, 1815–1840*. Charlottesville: University Press of Virginia, 1993.

Mills, Kay. *Changing Channels: The Civil Rights Case That Transformed Television*. Jackson: University Press of Mississippi, 2004.

———. *This Little Light of Mine: The Life of Fannie Lou Hamer*. New York: Dutton, 1993.

Minor, Bill. *Eyes on Mississippi: A Fifty-Year Chronicle of Change*. Jackson, Miss.: J. Prichard Morris Books, 2001.

Mitchell, Dennis J. *Mississippi Liberal: A Biography of Frank E. Smith*. Jackson: University Press of Mississippi, 2001.

———. *A Rich Past—A Vibrant Future: The History and Renovation of the Marks Rothenberg and Grand Opera House Buildings*. Meridian: Mississippi State University, 2006.

Moore, John Hebron. *Agriculture in Ante-Bellum Mississippi*. New York: Octagon Books, 1971.

———. *The Emergence of the Cotton Kingdom in the Old Southwest: Mississippi, 1770–1860*. Baton Rouge: Louisiana State University Press, 1988.

Morgan, Albert T. *Yazoo; or, On The Picket Line of Freedom in the South, A Personal Narrative*. Columbia: University of South Carolina Press, 2000.

Morgan, Chester M. *Redneck Liberal: Theodore G. Bilbo and the New Deal*. Baton Rouge: Louisiana State University Press, 1985.

———. *Treasured Past, Golden Future: The Centennial History of the University of Southern Mississippi*. Jackson: University of Southern Mississippi, 2010.

Morris, Christopher. *Becoming Southern: The Evolution of a Way of Life, Warren County and Vicksburg, Mississippi, 1770–1860*. Oxford: Oxford University Press, 1995.

Morris, Willie. *The Courting of Marcus Dupree*. Garden City, N.Y.: Doubleday, 1983.

Moye, Todd J. *Let the People Decide: Black Freedom and White Resistance Movements in Sunflower County, Mississippi, 1945–1986*. Chapel Hill: University of North Carolina Press, 2004.

Mullins, Andrew P., Jr. *Building Consensus: A History of the Passage of the Mississippi Education Reform Act of 1982*. Self-published, 1992.

Murphy, James B. *L. Q. C. Lamar: Pragmatic Patriot*. Baton Rouge: Louisiana State University Press, 1973.

Nash, Jere, and Andy Taggart. *Mississippi Politics: The Struggle for Power, 1976–2008*. Jackson: University Press of Mississippi, 2009.

Nelson, Michael, and John Lyman Mason. *How the South Joined the Gambling Nation: The Politics of State Policy Innovation*. Baton Rouge: Louisiana State University Press, 2007.

Newton, Michael. *The Ku Klux Klan in Mississippi: A History*. Jefferson, N.C.: McFarland, 2010.

Nossiter, Adam. *Of Long Memory: Mississippi and the Murder of Medgar Evers*. Reading, Mass.: Addison-Wesley, 1994.

Nuwer, Deanne Stephens. *Plague among the Magnolias: The 1987 Yellow Fever Epidemic in Mississippi*. Tuscaloosa: University of Alabama Press, 2009.

O'Brien, Greg, ed. *Pre-Removal Choctaw History: Exploring New Paths*. Norman: University of Oklahoma Press, 2008.

Okihiro, Gary. *Whispered Silences: Japanese Americans and World War II*. Seattle: University of Washington Press, 1996.

Olsen, Christopher J. *Political Culture and Secession in Mississippi: Masculinity, Honor, and the Antiparty Tradition, 1830–1860*. Oxford: Oxford University Press, 2000.

Olsen, Otto H. *Reconstruction and Redemption in the South*. Baton Rouge: Louisiana State University Press, 1980.

Osborn, George Coleman. *John Sharp Williams: Planter-Statesman of the Deep South*. Baton Rouge: Louisiana State University Press, 1943.

Oshinsky, David M. *Worse Than Slavery: Parchman Farm and the Ordeal of Jim Crow Justice*. New York: Free Press, 1996.

Otto, John Solomon. *The Final Frontiers, 1880–1930: Settling the Southern Bottomlands.* Westport, Conn.: Greenwood Press, 1999.

Overdyke, W. Darrell. *The Know-Nothing Party in the South.* Baton Rouge: Louisiana State University Press, 1950.

Owsley, Frank Lawrence. *Plain Folk of the Old South.* Baton Rouge: Louisiana State University Press, 2008.

Payne, Charles M. *I've Got the Light of Freedom: The Organizing Tradition and the Mississippi Freedom Struggle.* Berkeley: University of California Press, 1995.

Pegg, Bruce. *Brown Eyed Handsome Man: The Life and Hard Times of Chuck Berry.* New York: Routledge, 2002.

Percy, William Alexander. *Lanterns on the Levee: Recollections of a Planter's Son.* New York: Alfred A. Knopf, 1964.

Pereyra, Lillian A. *James Lusk Alcorn: Persistent Whig.* Baton Rouge: Louisiana State University Press, 1966.

Pesantubbee, Michelene E. *Choctaw Women in a Chaotic World: The Clash of Cultures in the Colonial Southeast.* Albuquerque: University of New Mexico Press, 2005.

Polk, Noel. *A Human Perspective: Mississippi's Piney Woods.* Jackson: University Press of Mississippi, 1986.

Prenshaw, Peggy W., and Jesse O. Mckee. *Sense of Place Mississippi.* Jackson: University Press of Mississippi, 1979.

Prichard, Jo G. *Making Things Grow: The Story of Mississippi Chemical Corporation.* Yazoo, Miss.: Mississippi Chemical Corporation, 1998.

Quan, Robert Seto. *Lotus among the Magnolias: The Mississippi Chinese.* Jackson: University Press of Mississippi, 1982.

Quinn, Janis. *Promises Kept: The University of Mississippi Medical Center.* Jackson: University of Mississippi Medical Center, 2005.

Rabinowitz, Howard N. *Southern Black Leaders of the Reconstruction Era.* Urbana: University of Illinois Press, 1982.

Rable, George C. *But There Was No Peace: The Role of Violence in the Politics of Reconstruction.* Athens: University of Georgia Press, 1984.

Rafferty, Janet, and Evan Peacock. *Time's River: Archaeological Syntheses from the Lower Mississippi River Valley.* Tuscaloosa: University of Alabama Press, 2008.

Rainwater, Percy Lee. *Mississippi Storm Center of Secession, 1856–1861.* Baton Rouge, La.: Otto Claitor, 1938.

Ranck, James Byrne. *Albert Gallatin Brown, Radical Southern Nationalist.* New York: D. Appleton-Century, 1937.

Rand, Clayton. *Men of Spine in Mississippi.* Gulfport, Miss.: Dixie Press, 1940.

Ransom, Roger L. *One Kind of Freedom: The Economic Consequences of Emancipation.* Cambridge: Cambridge University Press, 2001.

Robinson, Armstead L. *Bitter Fruits of Bondage: The Demise of Slavery and the Collapse of the Confederacy, 1861–1865.* Charlottesville: University of Virginia Press, 2005.

Roe, Daphne A. *A Plague of Corn: The Social History of Pellagra.* Ithaca, N.Y.: Cornell University Press, 1973.

Rohrbough, Malcolm J. *The Trans-Appalachian Frontier: People, Societies, and Institutions 1775–1850*. New York: Oxford University Press, 1978.

Rowley, Hazel. *Richard Wright: The Life and Times*. New York: Henry Holt, 2001.

Saikku, Mikko. *This Delta, This Land: An Environmental History of the Yazoo-Mississippi Floodplain*. Athens: University Press of Georgia, 2005.

Samway, Patrick, ed. *Walker Percy: Signposts in a Strange Land*. New York: Farrar, Straus and Giroux, 1991.

Sansing, David G. *Making Haste Slowly: The Troubled History of Higher Education in Mississippi*. Jackson: University Press of Mississippi, 1990.

Scarborough, William Kauffman. *The Overseer: Plantation Management in the Old South*. Baton Rouge: Louisiana State University Press, 1966.

Scarry, John F. *Political Structure and Change in the Prehistoric Southeastern United States*. Gainesville: University Press of Florida, 1996.

Schueler, Donald G. *Preserving the Pascagoula*. Jackson: University Press of Mississippi, 1980.

Schweid, Richard. *Catfish and the Delta*. Berkeley, Calif.: Ten Speed Press, 1992.

Scott, Anne Firor. *The Southern Lady: From Pedestal to Politics 1830–1930*. Chicago: University of Chicago Press, 1970.

Sewell, George Alexander, and Margaret L. Dewight. *Mississippi Black History Makers*. Jackson: University Press of Mississippi, 1984.

Shanks, Jack. *Meridian: The Queen with a Past*. Vol. 1. Meridian, Miss.: Brown Printing, 1995.

———. *The Queen with a Past*. Vol. 3. Meridian, Miss.: Southeastern Printing, 1987.

Sharp, James Roger. *The Jacksonians versus the Banks: Politics in the States after the Panic of 1837*. New York: Columbia University Press, 1970.

Shenton, James P. *Robert John Walker: A Politician from Jackson to Lincoln*. New York: Columbia University Press, 1961.

Silver, James W. *Edmund Pendleton Gaines: Frontier General*. Baton Rouge: Louisiana State University Press, 1949.

———. *Running Scared: Silver in Mississippi*. Jackson: University Press of Mississippi, 1984.

Silver, James W., and John K. Bettersworth. *Mississippi in the Confederacy as Seen in Retrospect*. Baton Rouge: Louisiana State University Press, 1961.

Skates, John Ray. *Mississippi: A History*. New York: W. W. Norton, 1979.

Slade, Peter. *Open Friendship in a Closed Society: Mission Mississippi and a Theology of Friendship*. New York: Oxford University Press, 2009.

Slotkin, Richard. *Gunfighter Nation: The Myth of the Frontier in Twentieth-Century America*. New York: Harper Perennial, 1969.

Smead, Howard. *Blood Justice: The Lynching of Mack Charles Parker*. New York: Oxford University Press, 1986.

Smith, Bruce, ed. *The Mississippian Emergence*. Tuscaloosa: University of Alabama Press, 1990.

Smith, Dale Edwyna. *The Slaves of Liberty: Freedom in Amite County, Mississippi, 1820–1868*. New York: Garland, 1999.

Smith, Frank E., and Audrey Warren. *Mississippians All*. New Orleans: Pelican, 1968.

———. *Congressman from Mississippi*. New York: Pantheon, 1964.

Smith, James Patterson. *Hurricane Katrina: The Mississippi Story*. Jackson: University Press of Mississippi, 2012.

Smith, John David. *Black Soldiers in Blue: African American Troops in the Civil War Era*. Chapel Hill: University of North Carolina Press, 2002.

Smith, Samuel Denny. *The Negro in Congress 1870–1901*. Chapel Hill: University of North Carolina Press, 1940.

Smith, Timothy B. *James Z. George: Mississippi's Great Commoner*. Jackson: University Press of Mississippi, 2012.

———. *Mississippi in the Civil War: The Home Front*. Jackson: University Press of Mississippi, 2010.

Somerville, Mrs. Keith F. *Dear Boys: World War II Letters from a Woman Back Home*. Ed. Judy B. Litoff and David C. Smith. Jackson: University Press of Mississippi, 1991.

Sosna, Morton. *In Search of the Silent South: Southern Liberals and the Race Issue*. New York: Columbia University Press, 1977.

Span, Christopher M. *From Cotton Field to Schoolhouse: African American Education in Mississippi, 1862–1875*. Chapel Hill: University of North Carolina Press, 2009.

Sparks, Randy J. *Religion in Mississippi*. Jackson: University Press of Mississippi, 2001.

Springer, Robert, ed. *Nobody Knows Where the Blues Come From*. Jackson: University Press of Mississippi, 2006.

Stockett, Kathryn. *The Help*. New York: Berkley Book, 2009.

Stover, John F. *The Railroads of the South 1865–1900: A Study in Finance and Control*. Chapel Hill: University of North Carolina Press, 1955.

Strom, Claire. *Making Catfish Bait Out of Government Boys*. Athens: University of Georgia Press, 2009.

Sullivan, Charles L. *Mississippi Gulf Coast Community College: A History*. Perkinston: Mississippi Gulf Coast Community College Press, 2002.

Swain, Martha H. *Pat Harrison: The New Deal Years*. Jackson: University Press of Mississippi, 1978.

Swain, Martha H., Elizabeth Anne Payne, and Marjorie Julian Spruill, eds. *Mississippi Women: Their Histories, Their Lives*. Athens: University of Georgia Press, 2003.

Syndor, Charles S. *A Gentleman of the Old Natchez Region: Benjamin L. C. Wailes*. Durham, N.C.: Duke University Press, 1938.

———. *Slavery in Mississippi*. Gloucester, Mass.: American Historical Association, 1933.

Taylor, William Banks. *Brokered Justice: Race, Politics, and Mississippi Prisons, 1798–1992*. Columbus: Ohio State University Press, 1993.

———. *Down on Parchman Farm: The Great Prison in the Mississippi Delta*. Columbus: Ohio State University Press, 1999.

Thibodeaux, Keith, with Audrey T. Hingley. *Life After Lucy: The True Story of Keith Thibodeaux—"I Love Lucy's" Little Ricky*. Green Forest, Ark.: New Leaf Press, 1994.

Trelease, Allen W. *White Terror: The Ku Klux Klan Conspiracy and Southern Reconstruction*. New York: Harper & Row, 1971.

Turcotte, William H., and David L Watts. *Birds of Mississippi*. Jackson: University Press of Mississippi, 1999.

Underwood, Felix J., and R. N. Whitfield. *Public Health and Medical Licensure in the State of Mississippi 1798–1937*. Jackson, Miss.: Tucker, 1938.

Usner, Daniel H., Jr. *Indians, Settlers, and Slaves in a Frontier Exchange Economy: Lower Mississippi Valley before 1783*. Chapel Hill: University of North Carolina Press, 1992.

Vance, Sandra S., and Roy V. Scott. *Wal-Mart: A History of Sam Walton's Retail Phenomenon*. New York: Twayne, 1994.

Vaughan, George B. *The Community College Story: A Tale of American Innovation*. Washington, D.C.: American Association of Community Colleges, National Center for Higher Education, 1995.

Vollers, Maryanne. *Ghosts of Mississippi: The Murder of Medgar Evers, the Trials of Byron De La Beckwith, and the Haunting of the New South*. Boston: Little, Brown, 1995.

Von Herrmann, Denise. *Resorting to Casinos: The Mississippi Gambling Industry*. Jackson: University Press of Mississippi, 2006.

Walderson, Ann. *Hodding Carter: The Reconstruction of a Racist*. Chapel Hill, N.C.: Algonquin Books, 1993.

Walker, Margaret. *Richard Wright, Daemonic Genius: A Portrait of the Man, A Critical Look at His Work*. New York: Warner Books, 1988.

Waller, Bill. *Straight Ahead: The Memoirs of a Mississippi Governo*r. Brandon, Miss.: Quail Ridge Press, 2007.

Walther, Eric H. *The Fire-Eaters*. Baton Rouge: Louisiana State University Press, 1992.

Ward, Brian. *Radio and the Struggle for Civil Rights in the South*. Gainesville: University Press of Florida, 2004.

Watkins, Norma. *The Last Resort: Taking the Mississippi Cure*. Jackson: University Press of Mississippi, 2011.

Watson, Bruce. *Freedom Summer: The Savage Season That Made Mississippi Burn and Made America a Democracy*. New York: Penguin Group, 2010.

Watts, Trent. *White Masculinity in the Recent South*. Baton Rouge: Louisiana State University Press, 2008.

Wayne, Michael. *The Reshaping of Plantation Society: The Natchez District, 1860–80*. Urbana: University of Illinois Press, 1990.

Webb, Elizabeth Lyon. *The Education of a Mississippian: The Early Life of E. Wilson Lyon*. San Francisco: Arion Press, 2009.

Wells, James M. *The Chisolm Massacre: A Picture of "Home Rule" in Mississippi*. New York: Negro University Press, 1969.

Welty, Eudora. *Selected Stories of Eudora Welty*. New York: Modern Library, 1936.

———. *Stories, Essays, and Memoir: A Curtain of Green, The Wide Net, The Golden Apples, The Bride of the Innisfallen, Selected Essays, One Writer's Beginnings*. New York: Literary Classics of the United States, 1998.

Whalen, John A. *Maverick among the Magnolias: The Hazel Brannon Smith Story*. Minneapolis: Xlibris, 2000.

Wharton, Vernon Lane. *The Negro in Mississippi 1865–1890*. Westport, Conn.: Greenwood Press, 1947.

White, Richard. *The Roots of Dependency: Subsistence, Environment, and Social Change among the Choctaws, Pawnees, and Navajos*. Lincoln: University of Nebraska Press, 1983.

Wilkie, Curtis. *The Fall of the House of Zeus: The Rise and Ruin of America's Most Powerful Trial Lawyer*. New York: Crown, 2010.

Wilkerson, Isabel. *The Warmth of Other Suns: The Epic Story of America's Great Migration*. New York: Random House, 2010.

Williams, Michael Vinson. *Medgar Evers: Mississippi Martyr*. Fayetteville: University of Arkansas Press, 2011.

Willis, John C. *Forgotten Time: The Yazoo-Mississippi Delta after the Civil War*. Charlottesville: University Press of Virginia, 2000.

Wilson, Charles Reagan. *Baptized in Blood: The Religion of the Lost Cause, 1865–1920*. Athens: University of Georgia Press, 1980.

———. *Judgment and Grace in Dixie: Southern Faiths from Faulkner to Elvis*. Athens: University of Georgia Press, 1995.

Wilson, Charles Reagan, and William Ferris, eds. *Encyclopedia of Southern Culture*. Chapel Hill: University of North Carolina Press, 1989.

Wilson, Harold S. *Confederate Industry: Manufacturers and Quartermasters in the Civil War*. Jackson: University Press of Mississippi, 2002.

Winter, William F. *The Measure of Our Days*. Oxford, Miss.: William Winter Institute for Racial Reconciliation, 2006.

Wirt, Frederick M. *Politics of Southern Equality: Law and Social Change in a Mississippi County*. Chicago: Aldine, 1970.

———. *"We Ain't What We Was": Civil Rights in the New South*. Durham, N.C.: Duke University Press, 1997.

Wood, Peter H., George A. Waselkov, and Thomas M. Hatley, eds. *Powhatan's Mantle: Indians in the Colonial Southeast*. Lincoln: University of Nebraska Press, 1989.

Woodruff, Nan Elizabeth. *American Congo: The African American Freedom Struggle in the Delta*. Cambridge, Mass.: Harvard University Press, 2003.

Woods, Jeff. *Black Struggle, Red Scare: Segregation and Anti-Communism in the South, 1948–1968*. Baton Rouge: Louisiana State University Press, 2004.

Wright, Simeon, and Herb Boyd. *Simeon's Story: An Eyewitness Account of the Kidnapping of Emmett Till*. Chicago: Lawrence Hill, 2010.

Wyatt-Brown, Bertram. *Southern Honor: Ethics and Behavior in the Old South*. Oxford: Oxford University Press, 1982.

Wynne, Ben. *Mississippi's Civil War: A Narrative History*. Macon, Ga.: Mercer University Press, 2006.

Young, James B., and James M. Ewing. *The Mississippi Public Junior College Story: The First Fifty Years 1922–1972*. Jackson: University Press of Mississippi, 1978.

Young, Mary Elizabeth. *Redskins, Ruffleshirts, and Rednecks: Indian Allotments in Alabama and Mississippi, 1830–1860*. Norman: University of Oklahoma Press, 1961.

Articles

Abbot, Martin. "Indian Policy and Management in the Mississippi Territory, 1798–1817." *Journal of Mississippi History* 14 (1952): 153–169.

Aiken, Charles S. "Faulkner's Yoknapatawpha County Geographical Fact into Fiction." *Geographical Review* 67 (1977): 1–21.

Alexander, Florence O. "The Education of Negroes in Mississippi." *Journal of Negro Education* 16 (1947): 375–380.

Alford, Terry L. "Slavery and Christian Conscience: The Case of Edward Brett Randolph of Mississippi." *Northeast Mississippi Historical Journal* 3 (1969): 10–13.

Anderson, John Q. "Dr. James Green Carson." *Journal of Mississippi History* 18 (1956): 243–267.

———. "The Narrative of John Hutchins." *Journal of Mississippi History* 20 (1958): 1–29.

Arsenault, Raymond. "The End of the Long Hot Summer: The Air Conditioner and Southern Culture." *Journal of Southern History* 50 (1984): 597–628.

Atkinson, James R. "A Narrative Based on an Interview with Malcolm McGee by Lyman C. Draper." *Journal of Mississippi History* 66 (2004): 37–74.

Bailey, Ben. "Music in Slave Era Mississippi." *Journal of Mississippi History* 54 (1992): 29–58.

———. "The Red Tops: The Orchestra That Covered the Delta." *Black Perspective in Music* 16 (1988): 177–190.

Bailey, Robert. "Theodore G. Bilbo and the Senatorial Election of 1934." *Southern Quarterly* 10 (1971): 91–105.

Baker, Henry E. "The Negro in the Field of Invention." *Journal of Negro History* 2 (1917): 21–36.

Bearss, Edwin C., comp. "Calendar of Events in Mississippi, 1861–1865." *Journal of Mississippi History* 21 (1959): 85–112.

Beasley, Jonathan. "Black—Slaves and Free—Vicksburg 1850–1860." *Journal of Mississippi History* 38 (1976): 1–32.

Berry, Trey. "A History of Women's Education in Mississippi 1819–1882." *Journal of Mississippi History* 53 (1991): 303–319.

Berthoff, Rowland T. "Attitudes toward Immigration, 1865–1914." *Journal of Southern History* 17 (August 1951): 328–360.

Bigelow, Martha Mitchell. "Mississippi Progressivism." *Journal of Mississippi History* 29 (1967): 202–209.

———. "Vicksburg: Experiment in Freedom." *Journal of Mississippi History* 26 (1964): 28–44.

Blain, William T. "Challenge to the Lawless: The Mississippi Secret Service." *Journal of Mississippi History* 40 (1978): 119–131.

Bloom, Jo Tice. "Mississippi's Territorial Delegates." *Journal of Mississippi History* 37 (1975): 327–357.

Boehm, Randolph H. "Mary Grace Quackenbos and the Federal Campaign against Peonage: The Case of Sunnyside Plantation." *Arkansas Historical Quarterly* 50 (1991): 40–59.

Bolton, Charles C. "William F. Winter and the Politics of Racial Moderation in Mississippi." *Journal of Mississippi History* 70 (2008): 335–382.

Boman, Martha. "A City of the Old South: Jackson, Mississippi, 1850–1860." *Journal of Mississippi History* 15 (1953): 1–12.

Bond, Bradley G. "Habits of Foodstuff and Market Production: A Look at Mississippi." *Journal of Mississippi History* 56 (1994): 211–231.

———. "'Unmitigated Thievery': The Case against William David McCain." *Journal of Mississippi History* 72 (2010): 163–197.

Braden, Guy B. "A Jeffersonian Village: Washington, Mississippi." *Journal of Mississippi History* 30 (1968): 135–142.

Breen William J. "Black Women and the Great War: Mobilization and Reform in the South." *Journal of Southern History* 44 (1978): 421–440.

Brent, Robert G. "Mississippi and the Mexican War." *Journal of Mississippi History* 31 (1969): 202–214.

Briceland, Alan V. "The Mississippi Territorial Land Board West of the Pearl River 1804." *Alabama Review* 32 (1979): 38–68.

Bridgeforth, Lucie R. "Medicine in Antebellum Mississippi." *Journal of Mississippi History* 46 (1984): 82–107.

Brock, Euline W. "Thomas W. Cardozo: Fallible Black Reconstruction Leader." *Journal of Southern History* 47 (1981): 183–206.

Brown, Andrew. "Sol Street, Confederate Partisan Leader." *Journal of Mississippi History* 21 (1959): 155–173.

Brunson, G. H., "The Beginning of a New Period in Mississippi." *Publications of the Mississippi Historical Society* 11 (1910): 317–324.

Carson, James Taylor. "State Rights and Indian Removal in Mississippi, 1817–1835." *Journal of Mississippi History* 57 (1995): 25–41.

Clark, Thomas D. "The Country Newspaper: A Factor in Southern Opinion." *Journal of Southern History* 14 (1948): 3–33.

———. "The Furnishing and Supply System in Southern Agriculture since 1865." *Journal of Southern History* 12 (1946): 24–44.

Cockrell, Thomas D. "United States Senators and Representatives from Mississippi, 1828–1836: An Introduction." *Journal of Mississippi History* 49 (1987): 35–48.

Coker, William S. "Pat Harrison: The Formative Years." *Journal of Mississippi History* 25 (1963): 251–278.

———. "Pat Harrison—Strategy for Victory." *Journal of Mississippi History* 28 (1966): 267–285.

———. "Peter Bryan Bruin of Bath: Soldier, Judge and Frontiersman." *West Virginia History* 30 (1969): 579–585.

———. "Ralph Humphreys: Patriarch of the Mississippi Humphreyses." *Journal of Mississippi History* 37 (1975): 67–85.

Cresswell, Stephen. "Red Mississippi: The State's Socialist Party, 1904–1920." *Journal of Mississippi History* 50 (1988): 153–171.

Crowther, Edward R. "Mississippi Baptists, Slavery, and Secession, 1806–1861." *Journal of Mississippi History* 56 (1994): 129–148.

Currie, James T. "The Beginnings of Congressional Reconstruction in Mississippi." *Journal of Mississippi History* 35 (1973): 267–286.

Dana, Donald. "Mississippi Power Company during World War II." *Journal of Mississippi History* 57 (1994): 325–339.

Darbis, Fred, Jr. "Alexander Keith McClung." *Journal of Mississippi History* 40 (1978): 289–296.

Davis, Rebecca Miller. "The Three R's—Reading, 'Riting, and Race: The Evolution of Race in Mississippi History Textbooks, 1900–1995." *Journal of Mississippi History* 72 (2010): 1–45.

DeRosier, Arthur H., Jr. "Andrew Jackson and Negotiations for the Removal of the Choctaw Indians." *Historian* 29 (1967): 343–362.

———. "The Choctaw Removal of 1831: A Civilian Effort." *Journal of the West* 6 (1967): 237–247.

———. "Cyrus Kingsbury—Missionary to the Choctaws." *Journal of Presbyterian History* 50 (1972): 267–287.

———. "Pioneers with Conflicting Ideals: Christianity and Slavery in the Choctaw Nation." *Journal of Mississippi History* 21 (1959): 174–189.

Dolensky, Suzanne T. "The Daughters of Jefferson Davis: A Study in Contrast." *Journal of Mississippi History* 51 (1989): 313–340.

Donald, David H. "The Scalawag in Mississippi Reconstruction." *Journal of Southern History* 10 (1944): 447–460.

Drabble, John. "The FBI, COINTELPRO–WHITE HATE, and the Decline of the Ku Klux Klan Organization in Mississippi, 1964–1971." *Journal of Mississippi History* 66 (2004): 353–401.

Eaddy, Justin C. "Mississippi State Parks: The New Deal's Mixed Legacy." *Journal of Mississippi History* 65 (2003): 147–168.

Edmundson, Ben G. "Pat Harrison and Mississippi in the Presidential Elections of 1924 and 1928". *Journal of Mississippi History* 33 (1971): 333–350.

Ellem, Warren A. "The Overthrow of Reconstruction in Mississippi." *Journal of Mississippi History* 54 (1992): 175–201.

Eudy, John Carroll. "The Political Intrigues of Thomas Rodney: Territorial Politics, 1807–1809." *Journal of Mississippi History* 40 (1978): 329–339.

Faries, Clyde J. "Redneck Rhetoric and the Last of the Redeemers: The 1899 McLaurin-Allen Campaign." *Journal of Mississippi History* 33 (1971): 282–298.

Ferguson, James S. "Co-operative Activity of the Grange in Mississippi." *Journal of Mississippi History* 4 (1942): 3–19.

———. "The Grange and Farmer Education in Mississippi." *Journal of Southern History* 8 (1942): 497–512.

Fickle, James E. "Management Looks at the 'Labor Problem': The Southern Pine Industry during World War I and the Postwar Era." *Journal of Southern History* 40 (1974): 61–76.

Fike, Claude E. "The Gubernatorial Administrations of Gerard Chittocque Brandon, 1825–1832." *Journal of Mississippi History* 35 (1973): 237–265.

Flynt, Wayne. "A Vignette in Southern Labor Politics: The 1936 Mississippi Senatorial Primary." *Mississippi Quarterly* 26 (1972–1973): 89–99.

Galloway, Patricia. "Archives, Power, and History: Dunbar Rowland and the Beginning of the State Archives of Mississippi." *American Archivist* 69 (2006): 70–116.

———. "The Prehistoric Population of Mississippi." *Mississippi Archaeology* 29 (1994): 44–72.

Garner, James Wilford. "The State Government of Mississippi during the Civil War." *Political Science Quarterly* 16 (1901): 283–302.

Gillesse, Neal G. "Ole Miss: A New Look at Her First President." *Journal of Mississippi History* 30 (1968): 275–290.

Giroux, Vincent A., Jr. "The Rise of Theodore G. Bilbo (1908–1932)." *Journal of Mississippi History* 43 (1981): 180–209.

Gordon, Lawrence. "A Brief Look at Blacks in Depression Mississippi, 1929–1934: Eyewitness Accounts." *Journal of Negro History* 64 (1979): 377–390.

Gradner, Bettye. "William H. Foote and Yazoo County Politics, 1866–1883." *Southern Studies* 1 (1982): 398–407.

Grant, Philip A., Jr. "The Mississippi Congressional Delegation and the Formation of the Conservative Coalition, 1937–1940." *Journal of Mississippi History* 50 (1988): 21–28.

———. "Ten Mississippians Who Served in Congress, 1931–1937." *Journal of Mississippi History* 39 (1977): 205–212.

Griffiths, John D. M. "A State of Servitude Worse than Slavery." *Journal of Mississippi History* 55 (1993): 1–18.

Guice, John W. "Cattle Raisers of the Old Southwest: A Reinterpretation." *Western Historical Quarterly* 8 (1977): 167–187.

Hall, L. Marshall. "William Sharkey and Reconstruction, 1866–1873." *Journal of Mississippi History* 27 (1965): 1–17.

Halsell, Willie D. "The Bourbon Period in Mississippi Politics, 1875–1890." *Journal of Southern History* 11 (1945): 519–537.

———. "Democratic Discussions in Mississippi, 1870–1882." *Journal of Mississippi History* 2 (1940): 123–135.

———. "The Friendship of L. Q. C. Lamar and Jefferson Davis." *Journal of Mississippi History* 6 (1944): 131–144.

———. "James R. Chalmers and (Mahoneism) in Mississippi." *Journal of Southern History* 10 (1944): 37–58.

Hamilton, W. B. "Mississippi 1817: A Sociological and Economic Analysis." *Journal of Mississippi History* 29 (1967): 270–292.

Hardeman, Martin J. "Frontier and Community: Pike County, Mississippi 1815–1861." *Journal of Mississippi History* 59 (1997): 339–354.

Harden, Paul D. "The Early Life of Edward Cary Walthall." *Journal of Mississippi History* 6 (1944): 30–38.

Harris, William C. "The Creed of the Carpetbaggers: The Case of Mississippi." *Journal of Southern History* 40 (1974): 199–224.

———. "Formulation of the First Mississippi Plan." *Journal of Mississippi History* 29 (1967): 181–201.

Harris, William J. "Etiquette, Lynching, and Racial Boundaries in Southern History: A Mississippi Example." *American Historical Review* 100 (1995): 387–410.

Harrison, Bobby. "McCoy's Biracial Coalition Held Together in the House." *Meridian Star*, June 11, 2011.

Hataway, Marsha Perry. "The Development of the Mississippi State Highway System." *Journal of Mississippi History* 28 (1966): 286–303.

Haynes, Robert V. "The Revolution of 1800 in Mississippi." *Journal of Mississippi History* 19 (1957): 234–251.

———. "The Tragic Tenure of Territorial Governor Robert Williams." *Journal of Mississippi History* 71 (2009): 139–166.

Herring, Todd A. "Kidnapped and Sold in Natchez." *Journal of Mississippi History* 60 (1998): 341–353.

Hesseltine, William B., and Larry Gara. "Mississippi's Confederate Leaders after the War." *Journal of Mississippi History* 13 (1951): 88–100.

Hickman, Nollie W. "Logging and Rafting Timber in South Mississippi, 1840–1910." *Journal of Mississippi History* 19 (1957): 154–172.

Holder, Ray. "The Brown-Winans Canvass for Congress, 1849." *Journal of Mississippi History* 40 (1978): 353–373.

Holmes, Jack D. "Anne White Hutchins—Anthony's Better Half?" *Journal of Mississippi History* 37 (1975): 203–208.

———. "Choctaws in 1795." *Alabama Historical Quarterly* 30 (1968): 33–49.

Holmes, Williams F. "The Leflore County Massacre and the Demise of the Colored Farmers' Alliance." *Phylon* 34 (1973): 267–274.

Hospodor, Gregory. "Bound by All the Ties of Honor: Southern Honor, the Mississippians and the Mexican War." *Journal of Mississippi History* 61 (1999): 1–28.

Howell, Elmo. "Governor Alexander G. McNutt of Mississippi: Humorist of the Old Southwest." *Journal of Mississippi History* 35 (1973): 153–165.

Howell, George W. "The Buttahatchie Settlers." *Journal of Mississippi History* 34 (1972): 57–72.

Irwin, James R. "Where Have All the Sharecroppers Gone? Black Occupations in Postbellum Mississippi." *Agricultural History* 72 (1998): 280–297.

James, Newton Haskin. "Josiah Hinds: Versatile Pioneer of the Old Southwest." *Journal of Mississippi History* 2 (1940): 22–33.

Jeltz, Wyatt F. "The Relations of Negroes and Choctaw and Chickasaw Indians." *Journal of Negro History* 33 (1948): 24–37.

Jenkins, Robert L. "The Development of Black Higher Education in Mississippi, 1865–1920." *Journal of Mississippi History* 45 (1983): 272–286.

Johnson, Christopher S. "Poor Relief in Antebellum Mississippi." *Journal of Mississippi History* 49 (1987): 1–21.

Jones, Ruth Frene. "Antebellum Watering Places of the Mississippi Gulf Coast." *Journal of Mississippi History* 18 (1956): 268–301.

Jordan, Daniel P. "Mississippi Antebellum Congressmen: A Collective Biography." *Journal of Mississippi History* 38 (1976): 157–182.

Keller, Marle A. "Horse Racing Madness." *Journal of Mississippi History* 47 (1985): 165–185.

Kelley, Donald Brooks. "Harper's Ferry: Prelude to Crises in Mississippi." *Journal of Mississippi History* 27 (1965): 351–372.

———. "Intellectual Isolation: Gateway to Secession in Mississippi." *Journal of Mississippi History* 36 (1974): 17–37.

Kerr, Norwood Allen. "The Mississippi Colonization Society, 1831–1860." *Journal of Mississippi History* 43 (1981): 1–30.

King, J. Crawford, Jr. "The Closing of the Southern Range: An Exploratory Study." *Journal of Southern History* 43 (1982): 53–70.

Kolchin, Peter. "Reevaluating the Antebellum Slave Community: A Comparative Perspective." *Journal of American History* 70 (1983): 579–601.

Kondert, Nancy T. "The Romance and Reality of Defeat: Southern Women in 1865." *Journal of Mississippi History* 35 (1973): 141–152.

Kott, Elien, William Warren Rogers, and Robert David Ward. "Oscar Wilde in Vicksburg, at Beauvoir, and other Southern Stops." *Journal of Mississippi History* 59 (1997): 183–210.

Knight, Lawrence Edward. "The State Is on Trial: Governor Edmund F. Noel and the Defense of Mississippi's Legal Institutions against Mob Violence." *Journal of Mississippi History* 60 (1998): 191–222.

Ladner, Heber. "James Kimble Vardaman, Governor of Mississippi, 1904–1908." *Journal of Mississippi History* 2 (1940): 175–205.

Lang, Herbert H. "J. F. H. Claiborne at Laurel Wood Plantation." *Journal of Mississippi History* 18 (1956): 1–17.

Lowery, Charles D. "The Great Migration to the Mississippi Territory, 1789–1819." *Journal of Mississippi History* 30 (1968): 173–192.

Mabry, William Alexander. "Disfranchisement of the Negro in Mississippi." *Journal of Southern History* 4 (1938): 318–333.

Matthews, Linda. "A Brief History of the Lamar County Library System." *Mississippi Libraries* 73 (2009): 99–103.

May, Robert E. "Southern Elite Women, Sectional Extension, and the Male Political Sphere: The Case of John A. Quitman's Wife and Female Descendants, 1847–1931." *Journal of Mississippi History* 50 (1988): 251–285.

McAlexander, Hubert H. "The Saga of a Mixed-Blood Dynasty." *Journal of Mississippi History* 50 (1987): 289–300.

McCorkle, James L., Jr. "Mississippi from Neutrality to War (1914–1917)." *Journal of Mississippi History* 43 (1981): 85–125.

———. "Nineteenth-Century Beginnings of the Commercial Vegetable Industry in Mississippi." *Journal of Mississippi History* 30 (1968): 260–274.

McDonald, Forrest, and Grady McWhiney. "The Antebellum Southern Herdsman: A Reinterpretation." *Journal of Southern History* 41 (1975): 147–166.

McKee, James W., Jr. "Will Barksdale and the Congressman Election of 1853 in Mississippi." *Journal of Mississippi History* 34 (1972): 129–158.

McKibben, Davidson Burns. "Negro Slave Insurrections in Mississippi, 1800–1865." *Journal of Negro History* 34 (1949): 73–90.

Milani, Ernesto R. "Peonage at Sunnyside and the Reaction of the Italian Government." *Arkansas Historical Quarterly* 50 (1991): 30–39.

Miles, Edwin A. "The Mississippi Press in the Jackson Era, 1824–1841." *Journal of Mississippi History* 19 (1957): 1–20.

———. "The Mississippi Slave Insurrection Scare of 1835." *Journal of Negro History* 42 (1957): 48–60.

Mills, Gary B. "New Life for the River of Death: Development of the Yazoo River Basin, 1873–1977." *Journal of Mississippi History* 41 (1979): 287–300.

Minchin, Timothy J., and John A. Salmond. "The Saddest Story of the Whole Movement: The Clyde Kennard Case and the Search for Racial Reconciliation in Mississippi, 1955–2007." *Journal of Mississippi History* 71 (2009): 191–234.

"Mississippi Delta Worse Off Than It Was before Gov. Barbour." *Mississippi Business Journal*, September 12, 2011.

Mitchell, Dennis J. "The County Histories of the Mississippi Federal Writers Project: Their Value as a Historical Source." *Researcher* 10.1 (1982): 1–10.

———. "Mississippi Community Colleges 1972–2000." *Journal of Mississippi History* 76 (2007): 33–62.

Mitchell, Jerry. "'The Help' Puts up Big Box Office Numbers across U.S." *Clarion-Ledger*, September 13, 2011.

Mollison, Irvin C. "Negro Lawyers in Mississippi." *Journal of Negro History* 15 (1930): 38–71.

Moore, John Hebron. "Local and State Governments of Antebellum Mississippi." *Journal of Mississippi History* 44 (1982): 104–134.

———. "Railroads of Antebellum Mississippi." *Journal of Mississippi History* 41 (1979): 53–81.

Moore, Margaret DesChamps. "Protestantism in the Mississippi Territory." *Journal of Mississippi History* 29 (1967): 358–370.

Morgan, Chester M. "At the Crossroads: World War II, Delta Agriculture, and Modernization." *Journal of Mississippi History* 57 (1995): 353–371.

Murray, Paul T. "Father Nathaniel and the Greenwood Movement." *Journal of Mississippi History* 72 (2010): 277–313.

Nash, Jere, and Andy Taggart. "William Winter and His Campaigns for Governor: 1967, 1975, and 1979." *Journal of Mississippi History* 70 (2008): 383–402.

Nelson, Lawrence J. "Oscar Johnston, the New Deal, and the Cotton Subsidy Payments Controversy, 1936–1937." *Journal of Southern History* 40 (1974): 399–416.

———. "Welfare Capitalism on a Mississippi Plantation in the Great Depression." *Journal of Southern History* 50 (1984): 225–250.

Newell, Samuel H. "Dr. Jeremiah Chamberlain and Oakland College." *Journal of Mississippi History* 26 (1964): 322–326.

Newman, Mark. "Hazel Brannon Smith and Holmes County, Mississippi, 1936–1964: The Making of a Pulitzer Prize Winner." *Journal of Mississippi History* 54 (1992): 59–89.

O'Brien, Greg. "The Conqueror Meets the Unconquered: Negotiating Cultural Boundaries on the Post-Revolutionary Southern Frontier." *Journal of Southern History* 67 (2001): 39–72.

Onkst, David H. "First a Negro, Incidentally a Veteran: Black World War II Veterans and the G.I. Bill of Rights in the Deep South, 1944–1948." *Journal of Social History* 31 (1998): 517–544.

Osborn, George C. "The Life of a Southern Plantation Owner during Reconstruction as Revealed in the Clay Sharkey Papers." *Journal of Mississippi History* 6 (1944): 103–112.

Osburn, Katherine M. B. "Southern Cultures: Mississippi Choctaws and Racial Politics." *Southern Cultures* 14 (2008): 32–54.

Phelps, Dawson A. "The Chickasaw Agency." *Journal of Mississippi History* 14 (1952): 119–137.

———. "Stands and Travel Accommodations on the Natchez Trace." *Journal of Mississippi History* 11 (1949): 1–54.

———. "Tockshish." *Journal of Mississippi History* 13 (1951): 138–145.

Powell, Lawrence N. "Correcting for Fraud: A Quantitative Reassessment of the Mississippi Ratification Election of 1868." *Journal of Southern History* 55 (1989): 633–658.

Price, Beulah M. D' Olive. "The Mississippi-Louisiana Career of Colonel Edmund Richardson." *Journal of Mississippi History* 40 (1978): 183–190.

Pritchett, Merrill R., and William L. Shea. "The Enemy in Mississippi." *Journal of Mississippi History* 41 (1979): 351–371.

Pyburn, Rita. "Public Schools in Mississippi before 1860." *Journal of Mississippi History* 21 (1959): 113–130.

Quinn, Yancey M., Jr. "Jackson's Military Road." *Journal of Mississippi History* 41 (1979): 335–350.

Rable, George C. "The South and the Politics of Antilynching Legislation, 1920–1940." *Journal of Southern History* 51 (1985): 201–220.

Rawson, Donald M. "Democratic Resurgence in Mississippi 1852–1853." *Journal of Mississippi History* 26 (1964): 1–27.

Ringgold, May Spencer. "James Lusk Alcorn." *Journal of Mississippi History* 44 (1982): 227–234.

Robs, Cecil. "Charles D. Fontaine: A Mississippi Know-Nothing Leader." *Journal of Mississippi History* 48 (1986): 105–118.

Rutledge, Wilmuth Saunders. "The John J. Henry–Theodore G. Bilbo Encounter 1911." *Journal of Mississippi History* 34 (1972): 357–372.

Santoki, Mark. "One Man U.S.O.: The Earl Finch Story Part I." *Hawaii Herald*, September 17, 1999.

———. "One Man U.S.O.: The Earl Finch Story Part II." *Hawaii Herald*, October 1, 1999.

———. "One Man U.S.O.: The Earl Finch Story Part III." *Hawaii Herald*, October 15, 1999.

———. "One Man U.S.O.: The Earl Finch Story Part IV." *Hawaii Herald*, November 5, 1999.

Schmidt, William. "The Impact of Camp Shelby in World War II on Hattiesburg, Mississippi." *Journal of Mississippi History* 39 (1977): 41–50.

Silver, James W. "The Hardwood Producers Come of Age." *Journal of Southern History* 23 (1957): 427–453.

———. "Land Speculation Profits in the Chickasaw Cession." *Journal of Southern History* 10 (1944): 84–92.

Simms, L. Moody, Jr. "Theodore DuBose Bratton, Christian Principles and the Race Question." *Journal of Mississippi History* 38 (1976): 47–52.

Skates, John R., Jr. "From Enchantment to Disillusionment: A Southern Editor Views the New Deal." *Southern Quarterly* 5 (1967): 363–380.

———. "Journalist vs. Politician: Fred Sullens and Theodore G. Bilbo." *Southern Quarterly* 8 (1970): 273–285.

———. "World War II as a Watershed in Mississippi History." *Journal of Mississippi History* 37 (1975): 131–142.

Sledge, James L., III. "The Chisholm Massacre: Politics and Violence in East Mississippi." *Journal of Mississippi History* 55 (1993): 203–215.

Smith, Suanna. "Washington, Mississippi: Antebellum Elysium." *Journal of Mississippi History* 40 (1978): 143–165.

Sparks, Randy J. "The White People's Arms Are Longer Than Ours: Blacks, Education and the American Missionary Association in Reconstruction." *Journal of Mississippi History* 54 (1992): 1–27.

Steponaitis, Vincas P. "Prehistoric Archaeology in the Southeastern United States, 1970–1985." *Annual Review of Anthropology* 15 (1986): 363–404.

Swain, Martha. "The Mississippi Delta Goes to War, 1941–1942." *Journal of Mississippi History* 57 (1995): 335–352.

———. "A New Deal for Mississippi Women, 1933–1943." *Journal of Mississippi History* 42 (1984): 191–212.

Swearingen, Mack. "George Poindexter." *Journal of Mississippi History* 29 (1967): 348–357.

Sydnor, Charles S. "Historical Activities in Mississippi in the Nineteenth Century." *Journal of Southern History* 3 (1937): 139–160.

Thompson, Don Harris. "Senator John Cornelius Stennis, Mississippi Statesman: The Early Years." *Journal of Mississippi History* 70 (2003): 125–146.

Urofsky, Melvin I. "Blanche K. Bruce: United State Senator, 1875–1881." *Journal of Mississippi History* 29 (1967): 118–141.

Usner, Daniel H., Jr. "American Indians on the Cotton Frontier: Changing Economic Relations with Citizens and Slaves in the Mississippi Territory." *Journal of American History* 72 (1985): 297–317.

Waldrep, Christopher. "Substituting Law for the Lash: Emancipation and Legal Formalism in a Mississippi County." *Journal of American History* 82 (1996): 1425–1451.

Wells, Valerie. "News Wars: The Rise and Fall of the *Clarion-Ledger*." *Jackson Free Press*, September 11, 2011.

Whatley, Larry F. "The Works Progress Administration in Mississippi" *Journal of Mississippi History* 30 (1968): 35–50.

White, William W. "Marriage Insurance: The Mississippi Bubble of 1882." *Journal of Mississippi History* 46 (1984): 108–119.

Winbourne, Magruder Drake. "The Mississippi Reconstruction Convention of 1865." *Journal of Mississippi History* 21 (1959): 225–256.

Winter, William F. "Mississippi's Civil War Governors." *Journal of Mississippi History* 51 (1989): 77–88.

Wiseman, Marty. "McCoy's Retirement as Speaker: Extinction of Legislative Species." *Mississippi Business Journal*, June 5, 2011.

Wong, Vivan Wu. "Somewhere Between White and Black: The Chinese in Mississippi." *OAH Magazine of History* 10 (1996): 33–36.

Wright, Gavin. "The New Deal and the Modernization of the South." *Federal History* 2 (2010): 58–73.

Wyatt, Lee T., III "William S. Barry—Advocate of Secession 1821–1868." *Journal of Mississippi History* 39 (1977): 330–355.

Web Sources

Altman, Alex. "The History of Sesame Street." *Time*, December 29, 2008. http://www.time.com/time/printout/0,8816,1868862,00.html.

"Ancient Architects of the Mississippi." http://www.nps.gov/archeology/feature/riverlif.htm.

"Arthur 'Big Boy' Crudup." http://www.msbluestrail.org/_webapp_2187825/Arthur_Crudup.

"Articles on Choctaw Medicine: Medicine Made from Plants and Roots by Choctaws of Long Ago." *Bishinik*. 1994. http://www.tc.umn.edu/~mboucher/mikebouchweb/choctaw/chocmed.htm.

"The Association of Religion Data Archives." http://www.thearda.com/mapsReports/reports/state/28_compare80.asp.

Bates, Toby G. "The Vietnam War and Mississippi." *Mississippi History Now*. http://mshistory.k12.ms.us/articles/323/the-vietnam-war-and-mississippi.

Binder, David. "Jamie Whitten, Who Served 53 Years in House, Dies at 85." *New York Times*, September 10, 1995. http://query.nytimes.com/gst/fullpage.html?res=990CE3DE143FF933A2575AC0A9639582.

Bolton, Charles C. "The Last Stand of Massive Resistance: Mississippi Public School Integration, 1970." *Mississippi History Now*. http://mshistory.k12.ms.us/articles/305/the-last-stand-of-massive-resistance-1970.

Boykin, Deborah. "Choctaw Indians in the 21st Century." http://mshistory.k12.ms.us/articles/10/choctaw-indians-in-the-21st-century.

Brain, Jeffery P. "On the Tunica Trail." 1994. http://www.crt.louisiana.gov/archaeology/tunica/tunica.htm.

Brookes, Samuel. "Prehistoric Mississippi: Some New Perspectives." *Mississippi History Now*. http://mshistory.k12.ms.us/articles/255/prehistoric-mississippi-some-new-perspectives.

Brown, Robert N., and John Cromartie. "Black Homeplace Migration to the Yazoo-Mississippi Delta: Ambiguous Journeys, Uncertain Outcomes." USDA National Agricultural Library, November 2006. http://ddr.nal.usda.gov/handle/10113/36738.

Brown, Ron. "Mississippi's First African American Marine." *Mississippi Public Broadcasting*, November 12, 2009. http://www.mpbonline.org/news/story/missippis-first-african-american-marine.

———. "Prairie Women: Unsung Heroes of World War II." *Mississippi Public Broadcasting*, November 19, 2009. http://www.mpbonline.org/news/story/prairie-women-unsung-heroes-world-war-two.

Byrd, Shelia. "Traditional Hindu Temple Dedicated in Mississippi." Taiwan News Online, June 27, 2010. http://www.taiwannews.com.tw/etn/print.php.

Carson, James Taylor. "Ethnohistory of Colonial and Early National America." http://www.queensu.ca/history/People/Faculty/Carson.htm.

"Charley Pride Biography." http://www.cmt.com/artists/as/pride_charley?bio.jhtml.

"Cherokee Clothing and Adornment." 2000. http://www.thepeoplespath.net/Cherokee/WendellCochran/CCNotes-ClothingandAdornment.

"Chicago Defender Blues Advertisements: 1927 Flood." http://sundayblues.org/archives/212.

"Choctaw Food." *Bishinik*. 2002. http://marciesalaskaweb.com/choctawFood.htm.

"Church Asks Supreme Court to Halt Malpractice Lawsuit." http://www.freedomforum.org/templates/document.asp?documentID-15864.

"Civil Rights: A Little Abnormal." *Time*, July 5, 1963. http://www.time.com/time/printout/0,8816,875008,00.html.

"The Civil Rights Movement in Mississippi." Chancellor's History Symposium. February 2010. http://olemiss.edu/depts/history/symposium/Events_Symposium_previous.htm.

Clancey, Patrick. "U.S. Naval Activities, World War II, by State [Mississippi]." http://www.ibiblio.org/hyperwar/USN/ref/USN-Act/MS.html.

Collum, Danny Duncan. "The Tupelo Miracle." October 2004. http://www.sojo.net/index.cfm?action=magazine.article&issue=soj0410&article=041022.

"Colmer, William Meyers." *Biographical Directory of the United States Congress (1890–1980)*. http://bioguide.Congress.gov/scrips/biodisplay.pl?index=C000645.

"Commercial Catfish Production." http://msucares.com/aquaculture/catfish/index.html.

Cox, Kyndall. "One Mississippi Moving Forward." The DMonline, March 2011. http://www.thedmonline.com/article/one-mississippi-moving-forward.

Cresswell, Stephen. "Nuclear Blasts in Mississippi." 2008. http://mshistory.k12.ms.us/articles/293/nuclear-blasts-in-mississippi.

———. "Was Mississippi a Part of Progressivism?" *Mississippi History Now*. http://mshistory.k12.ms.us/articles/249/was-mississippi-a-part-of-progressivism.

Damms, Richard V. "World War I: Loyalty and Dissent in Mississippi during the Great War, 1917–1918." 2005. http://mshistory.k12.ms.us/articles/237/World-War-I-the-great-war-1917-1918-loyalty-and-dissent-in-mississippi.

Davies, David R. "Mississippi Journalists, the Civil Rights Movement, and the Closed Society, 1960–1964." Presented at the 1994 convention of the American Journalism Historians Association. http://ocean.otr.usm.edu/~w304644/missjourn.html.

Dufresne, Marcel. "Exposing the Secrets of Mississippi Racism." *American Journal Review* (October 1991). http://www.ajr.org/article.asp?id=1311.

"East (P. D.) Collection." 1998. http://www.lib.usm.edu/legacy/archives/m324text.htm.

Elliott, Jack D., Jr. "The Buried City: A Meditation on History and Place." http://www.newpantagruel.com/issues/1.4/the_buried_city_a_meditation_print.php.

Emmett Till Memorial Commission. http://www.etmctallahatchie.com/pages/resolution.htm.

Farrell, Sean. "Not Just Farms Anymore: The Effects of World War II on Mississippi's Economy." *Mississippi History Now*. http://mshistory.k12.ms.us/articles/247/the-effects-of-world-war-II-on-mississippis-economy.

"Fast Facts 2009–2010: State Institutions of Higher Learning." www.MISSISSIPPI.edu/research/stats.html.

Faussett, Richard. "Real-life Maid's 'Help' Lawsuit Tossed by Mississippi Judge." *Los Angeles Times*, August 17, 2011. http://latimesblogs.latimes.com//nationnow/2011/08/help-lawsuit-tossed.html.

Ferguson, Barbara. "Mabus Divorce Turns Messy When Ex-Wife Sues Over 'Secret' Recordings." *Arab News*, July 7, 2002. http://archive.arabnews.com/?page=4&section=0&article=16668&d=7&m=7&y=2002.

Fleeger, Robert L. "Theodore G. Bilbo and the Decline of Public Racism, 1938–1947." http://mdah.state.ms.us/pubs/bilbo.pdf.

"Former Attorney General of Mississippi." http://www.stennis.gob/about-the-center/board-ofo-trustees/16-mike-moore.

"Former Miss. Lt. Gov. Evelyn Gandy Dies." *USA Today*, December 24, 2007. http://www.usatoday.com/news/nation/2007-12-24-gandy-obit_N.htm.

Fowler, C. "Use of Fire by Prehistoric Native American Cultures." 1991. http://www.forestencyclopedia.net/p/p847.

"Fred's, Inc." http://www.fundinguniverse.com/company-histories/freds-Inc-Company-History.html.

Garrison, Tim Alan. Review of *Choctaw Genesis: 1500–1700*. *Mississippi Quarterly*. http://findarticles.com/p/articles/mi_hb3524/is_4_51/ai_n28721091/.

George McLean Collection, Archives and Special Collections, J. D. Williams Library, University of Mississippi. http://www.olemiss.edu/depts/general_library/archives/finding_aids/MUM00291.html#useinfolink.

Gibson, Jon L. "Poverty Point: A Terminal Archaic Culture of the Lower Mississippi Valley." 1996. http://www.crt.state.la.us/archaeology/POVERPOI/popo.htm.

Giesen, James C. "The Truth About the Boll Weevil: The Nature of Planter Power in the Mississippi Delta," *Environmental History* 14 (2009). http://www.historycooperative.org/journals/eh/14.4/giesen.ftml.

Givens, Thomas. "Ahhh, Rufus, How We Loved You!" http://www.usadeepsouth.com/article1022.html.

Gong Lum v. Rice. http://www.brownat50.org/browncases/prebrowncases/gonglumvrice1927.html.

Gray, Joe. "Red Tops Main Man, Rufus McKay, Wows Crowd!" http://usads.ms11.net/rufus.html.

Gray, Lloyd. "Lloyd Gray: Billy McCoy's Career Refutes the Caricature." *NEMS Daily Journal*, June 2011. http://nems360.com/view/full_story/13486779/article-LLOYD-GRAY--Billy-McCoy%E2%80%99s-career-refutes-the-caricature?instance=secondary_stories_left_column.

Gurwitt, Rob. "Good Old Boy, circa 2011." *Governing Magazine*, May 2001. http://www.lexisnexis.com/lnacui2api/delivery/PrintDoc.do?jobhandle=1828%3a30862.

———. "Richard Howorth: Bibilocrat." August 2001. http://www.governing.com/topics/politics/Richard-Howorth-Bibliocrat.html.

Harris, Gardiner. "Out-of-Wedlock Birthrates Are Soaring, U.S. Reports." *New York Times*, May 13, 2009. http://www.nytimes.com/2009/05/13/health/13mothers.html?pagewanted=print.

Harrison, Bobby [Billy McCoy]. *Northeast Mississippi Daily Journal*, June 8, 2011. http://ehis.ebscohost.com/eds/delivery?sid=f79189c8-d3d9-4850-90ae-blae3b223440%40.

Harrison, Suzan. "Repudiating Faulkner: Race and Responsibility in Ellen Douglas's *The Rock Cried Out*." *Southern Literary Journal*. Project MUSE, 2003. http://muse.jhu.edu/login?uri=/journals/southern_literary_journal/v036/36.1harrison.pdf.

Hartfield, Libby, and Alan Huffman. "Fannye A. Cook, Pioneer Conservationist and Scientist, 1889–1964." *Mississippi History Now*. 2009. http://www.mshistory.k12.ms.us/articles/313/fannye-cook-pioneer-conservatist.

Haynes, Robert V. "Mississippi Under British Rule—British West Florida." 2000. http://mshistory.k12.ms.us/articles/66/mississippi-under-british-rule-british-west-florida.

"A History of Square Books." http://www.squarebooks.com/history.

Holmes, Linda. "'The Help' Spawns a Lawsuit and a Question: How Much Borrowing Is Fair?" Monkey See. 2011. http://www.npr.org/blogs/monkeys/2011/02/24/134022783/the-help-spawns-a-lawsuit-tossed.html.

"Households Wired for the Information Superhighway." MERIC. http://www.missourieconomy.org/community/socioecon/households_wired.stm.

Howard, John. "An Excerpt from Concentration Camps on the Home Front—Japanese Americans in the House of Jim Crow." 2008. http://www.press.uchicago.edu/Misc?Chicago/354767.html.

Howe, LeAnne. "Betsy Love and the Mississippi Married Women's Property Act of 1839." *Mississippi History Now*. 2005. http://mshistory.k12.ms.us/articles/6/betsy-love-and-the-mississippi-married-womens-property-act-of-1839.

Huff, David. "David Huff Biography." http://www.davidhuff.com/biopage/html.

"Hurricane Katrina: Mississippi Gulf Coast Making Comeback." http://www.mississippibeyondkatrina.xom/backgroud/.

Indian Mounds of Mississippi. http://www.nps.gov/nr/travel/mounds/builders.htm.

"An Interview with Christopher B. Epps." March 2, 2009. http://www.voteforchrisepps.com/interview.htm.

Jackson State May 1970. http://www.may41970.com/Jackson%20State/jackson_state_may_1970.htm.

Jamie Whitten Obituary. http://www.nytimes.com/1995/09/10/obituaries/jamie-whitten-who-served-53-years-in-house-dies-at-85.html.

"Kathy Thibodeaux." http://aportraitofjacksonwomen.wordpress.com/2010/05/12/kathy-thibodeaux/.

Lee, Ulysses. "United States Army in World War II, Special Studies, The Employment of Negro Troops." http://www.history.army.mil/books/wwii/11-4/index.htm.

Lester, Connie. "Economic Development in the 1920s: Balance Agriculture with Industry." *Mississippi History Now*. 2004. http://mshistory.k12.ms.us/articles/224/economic-development-in-the-1930s-balance-agriculture-with-industry.

"Let a Book Traveler Guide You to Some of the Coolest Hangouts in America's Great Literary Terrain: Mississippi." http://www.squidoo.com/Mississippi-Bookstores.

Lynch, Adam. "Inmate Abuse." November 2011. http://www.jacksonfreepress.com/index.php/site/comments/protesters_demand_epps_stop_inmate_abuse_110609/.

Mara, Thalia. "About Thalia Mara." http://www.thaliamara.org/about.html.

Marszalek, John F., and Clay Williams. "Mississippi Soldiers in the Civil War." *Mississippi History Now*. 2000–2010. http://mshistory.k12.ms.us/articles/175/mississippi-soldiers-in-the-civil-war.

McCarthy, Colleen. "Miss. Continues to Rank Last in Child Welfare Stats." *Starkville Daily News*, August 22, 2011. http://www.starkvilledailynews.com/print/6965.

McCarty, Kenneth. "Depression and Hard Times in Mississippi: Letters from the William M. Colmer Papers." *Mississippi History Now*. http://mshistory.k12.ms.us/articles/221/depression-and-hard-times-in-mississippi-letters-from-the-william-m-colmer-papers.

"McGee, Daniel Rayford." *Biographical Directory of the United States Congress (1883–1962)*. http://bioguide.Congress.gov/scripts/biodisplay.pl?index=M000446.

"Mike Moore, Big Tobacco's Nemesis: Billions from a Novel and Untested Legal Strategy." http://www.governing.com/poy/mike-moore.html.

"Mike Moore: Former Attorney General of Mississippi." http://www.stennis.gov/about-the-center/board-of-trustess/16-mike-moore.

Minchin, Timothy J., and John A. Salmond. "Clyde Kennard: A Little-Known Civil Rights Pioneer." *Mississippi History Now*. http://mshistory.k12.ms.us/articles/349/clyde-kennard-a-little-known-civil-rights-pioneer.

"Mississippi: Bourbon Borealis." *Time*, February 11, 1966. http://www.time.com/time/printout/0,8816,842449,00.html.

"Mississippi, Timeline of State History–SHG Resources." http://www.shgresources.com/ms/timeline/.

"Mississippi Community Impact: Walmart Stores." http://walmartstores.com/pressroom/StateByState/State.aspx?st=MS.

Mississippi Department of Corrections. http://www.mdoc.state.ms.us/Brief_History.htm.

"Mississippi House of Representatives: William J. McCoy." http://billstatus.ls.state.ms.us/members/house/McCoy.xml.

"Mississippi Indian Tribes." 2004–2008. http://www.accessgenealogy.com/native/mississippi/index.htm.

"Mississippi Most Religious State, Vermont the Least." January 31, 2009. http://www.freerepublic.com/focus/f-news/2175715/posts.

"Mississippi Primary Polarized by Race." http://www.huffingtonpost.com/2008/03/06/mississippi-primary-lates_n_90260.html.

"Mississippi QuickFacts from the US Census Bureau." http://quickfacts.census.gov/qfd/states/28000.html.

"Mississippi's Compliance with the Ayers Settlement Agreement." Mississippi Legislature. http://www.peer.state.ms.us/524.html.

Mitchell, Jerry. "Jerry Mitchell's Entry and Biography." *Clarion-Ledger*, October 2011. http://www.clarionledger.com/fdcp/?unique=1314386209203.

Moen, Jon. "Still Playing Catch-up: Mississippi and the South." www.winterinstitute.org/documents/econo-study1.pdf.

Morgan, David. "Archaeology and Prehistoric Mississippi." *Mississippi History Now*. 2002. http://mshistory.k12.ms.us/articles/74/archaeology-and-prehistoric-mississippi.

Morris, Sara E. "Rural Electrification in Northeast Mississippi (working title)." *Mississippi History Now*. http://mshistory.k12.ms.us/articles/376/the-rural-electrification-of-northeast-mississippi.

Morrison, James D. "Articles on Choctaw Life: Tribal Rainmakers . . . Fact or Fiction?" 1987. http://www/tc/umn.edu/~mboucher/mikebouchweb/choctaw/choclife.htm.

Musgrove, Ronnie. "A Proclamation." http://mdah.state.ms.us/arrec/digital_archives/musgrove/pdfs/164.pdf.

"National: Speaker Ford Honored." http://www.washingtonpost.com/wp-dyn/content/article/2006/10/01/AR2006100100804.html.

"Nearly 600 Detained in Mississippi Immigration Raid." *USA Today*, August 26, 2008. http://www.usatoday.com/news/nations/2008-08-26-raid-miss_N.htm.

"Newman (C. B. 'Buddie') Papers." http://mdah.state.ms.us./manuscripts/z1829.html.

Nelson, Stanley. "Magical Waters of Second Creek: Indian Tom Leads Hutchins to White Apple." 2009. http://www.theconcordiasentinel.com/news.php?id=3014.

———. "Natchez Country Pioneers during British Days in 1770s: Venison/Potato Casserole." 2009. http://www.concordiasentinel.com/news.php?id=3153.

———. "Stories of Early Natchez from a Slave Named Toney: His Role in Revolt of the 1781." 2009. http://www.theconcordiasentinel.com/news.php?id=3183.

———. "Trouble at Hutchins Farm on Natchez Frontier—Kentucky John Wants a Blanket." 2009. http://www.concordiasentinel.com/news.php?id=3114.

Nuwer, Deanne Stephens. "The Importance of Wearing Shoes: Hookworm Disease in Mississippi." *Mississippi History Now*. http://mshistory.k12.ms.us/articles/241/hookworm-disease-in-mississippi:-the-importance-of-wearing-shoes.

———. "The Seafood Industry in Biloxi: Its Early History, 1848–1930." *Mississippi History Now*. http://mshistory.k12.ms.us/articles/209/the-seafood-industry-in-biloxi-its-early-history-1848.

O'Brien, Greg. "Choctaws in a Revolutionary Age: Indians of the Southeast, 1750–1830." http://www.historycooperative.org/journals/wm/60.4/br_4.html.

———. "Pushmataha: Choctaw Warrior, Diplomat, and Chief." *Mississippi History Now*. 2001. http://mshistory.k12.ms.us/articles/14/pushmataha-choctaw-warrior-diplomat-and-chief.

"Ole Miss Marks Integration Anniversary." *Washington Post*, October 1, 2006. http://www.washingtonpost.com/wp-dyn/content/article/2006/10/01/AR2006100100804.html.

Olmstead, Alan L., and Paul W. Rhode. "Wait a Cotton Pickin' Minute! A New View of Slave Productivity." 2005. http://www.unc.edu/~prhode/cotton_pickin.pdf.

Pettus, Gray. "Divorce Rates in Miss. among Highest in U.S." ClarionLedger. http://jacksonclarion.ms.newsmemory.com/eebrowser/frame/check.6246/php-script/fullpage.html.

"The Philadelphia Coalition: Uniting for Justice." http://ww.neshabajustice.com/pages/molpus899.htm.

"Phillip Martin Dies at 83: Choctaw Chief Lifted Tribe Out of Poverty." http://www.latimes.com/news/obituaries/la-me-phillip-martin6-2010feb06,0,6192733.story.

"Pierre LeMoyne Sieur d'Iberville and the Establishment of Biloxi." 1995–1996. http://www.datasync.com/~davidg59/biloxi1.html.

Plummer, William. "A New Benchmark for Mississippi—Reuben Anderson Is That State's First Black Supreme Court Justice." May 20, 1985. http://www.peoplec.com/people/archive/article/0,,20090739,00.html.

"Population, Income, Education, Employment, and Federal Funds." USDA. http:www.ers.usda.gov/StateFacts/MS.HTM.

"The Press: Revolt in Mississippi." *Time*, November 8, 1954. http://www.time.com/time/printout/0,8816,857653,00.html.

Prichard, Jo G., III. "Owen Cooper (1908–1986): Business Leader and Humanitarian." *Mississippi History Now*. http://mshistory.k12.ms.us/articles/239/owen-cooper-1908-1986-business-leader-and-humanitarian.

Primitive Eocene Whales. http://www.intersurf.com/~chalcedony/Basilosaurus1.html.

"Rankin, John Elliot." *Biographical Directory of the United States Congress (1882–1960)*. http://bioguide.Congress.gov/scrips/biodisplay.pl?index=R000056.

"Red Tops–Vicksburg." http://www.msbluestrail.org/_webapp_1827047/Red_Tops.

Reed, Branson. "Ford Drives Mississippi State Legislatures." July 2002. http://ehis. ebscohost.com/eds/delivery?sid=f79189c8-d3d9-4850-90ae-blae-3b223440%40.

"Resolution Presented to Emmett Till's Family." 2007. http://www.etmctallahatchie.com/pages/resolution.htm.

"Return Migration to the South." http://www.inmotionaame.org/migrations/landing.cfm;jsessionid=f830785691319555671245?migration=11&bhcp=1.

Robertson, Campbell. "A Maid Sees Herself in a Novel, and Objects." *New York Times*, February 17, 2011. http://www.nytimes.com/2011/02/18/books/18help.html?_r=1&pagewanted=print.

"Rod Paige, U.S. Secretary of Education—Biography." http://www2.ed.gov/news/staff/bios/paige.html.

Rucker, LaReeca. "$4M Hindu Temple Opens in Rankin." http://www.lareecarucker.com/pages/hindutemple.htm.

Russell, Charlsie. "Patriots of the American Revolution—The American Revolution in the Old Southwest: The James Willing Raid." 1995. http://www.patriotsar.com/oldsouthwest.html.

Sabo, George III. "Tunica and Koroa Indians." 2007. http://arkarcheology.uark.edu/indiansofarkansas/index.html?pageName=Tunica%20and%.

Sansing, David G. "David Holmes: First and Fifth Governor of Mississippi: 1817–1820; 1826." *Mississippi History Now*. http://mshistory.k12.ms.us/articles/265/index.php?s=extra&id=109.

———. "Ray Mabus: Sixtieth Governor of Mississippi: 1988–1992." *Mississippi History Now*. http://mshistory.k12.ms.us/articles/265/index.php?s=extra&id=157.

"Savings and Loan Run." http://www.time.com/time/magazine/article/0.9171.914296.00.html#ixzzotgVtnXJ8.

"Secret Mission: Dog Training." The Hawaii Nisei Story: Americans of Japanese Ancestry during WWII. http://nisie.hawaii.edu/object/io_1153256967265.html.

Sharkey, Betsy. "Movie Review: *The Help*." *Los Angeles Times*, August 10, 2011. Http://articles.latimes.com//print/2011/aug/10/entertainment/la-et-the-help-20110810.

Shiffman, Dan. "Richard Wright's 12 Million Black Voices and World War II-Era Civic Nationalism." *African American Review* (Fall 2007). http://findarticles.com/p/articles/mi_m2838/is_3_41/ai_n26672689.

Skates, John R. "German Prisoners of War in Mississippi, 1942–1946." *Mississippi History Now*. 2001. http://mshistory.k12.ms.us/index.php?id=233.

Sloan, Stephen. "Voices of Katrina." http://mshistory.k12.ms.us/articles/253/voices-of-katrina.

Smith, Fred C. "Cooperative Farming in Mississippi." *Mississippi History Now*. http://mshistory.k12.ms.us/articles/219/cooperative-farming-in-mississippi.

Sovereignty Commission Online. Mississippi Department of Archives and History. http://mdah.state.ms.us/arrec/digital_archives/sovcom/.

Sperry, Benjamin O. "Walter Sillers and His Fifty Years Inside Mississippi Politics." *Mississippi History Now*. 2010. http://mshistory.k12.ms.us/articles/356/walter-sillers-and-his-fifty-years-inside-mississippi-politics.

Spillane, Edward. "Jean-Baptiste Le Moyne, Sieur de Bienville." http://www.newadvent.org/cathen/02560b.htm.

Stone, Kenneth E., Georgeanne Artz, and Albert Myles. "The Economic Impact of Wal-Mart Supercenters on Existing Businesses in Mississippi." http://www2.econ.iastate.edu/faculty/stone/mssupercenterstudy.pdf.

Stout, Davide. "Byron De La Beckwith Dies; Killer of Medgar Evers Was 80." *New York Times*, January 23, 2001. http://Query.mytimes.com/gst/fullpage.html?res=9B02EED9103CF930A15752C0A96779C8.

Swain, Martha H. "Women's Work Relief in the Great Depression." *Mississippi History Now*. 2004. http://www.mshistory.k12.ms.us/articles/251/womens-work-relief-in-the-great-depression.

Thomas, Danielle. "Biloxi Vietnamese Say Poor Economy Equals Local Population Rise." May 10, 2009. http://www.wlox.com/Global/story.asp?S-10336767.

Time. http://www.time.com/time/magazine/article/0,9171,914296,00.htm#ixzzotgVtnXJ8.

"Top Ten Songs of Each Year (1970–1979)." http://www.digitaldreamdoor.com/pages/best_songs70-79.html.

Trice, Dawn Turner. "Immigration Issues Redefine Catfish Industry in Mississippi Delta." http://www.floridafarmes.org/news/articles/Immigrationissuesredefinecatfish.htm.

"U.S. Census Bureau." http://www.census.gov.

"Wall Doxey Sergeant at Arms, 1943–1947." U.S. Senate: Art & History Home. http://www.senate.gov/artandhistory/history.common/generic/SAA_Wall_Doxey.htm.

"Whitten, Jamie Lloyd." *Biographical Directory of the United States Congress (1910–1995)*. http://bioguide.Congress.gov/scripts/biodisplay.pl?index=W000428.

"Whittington, William Madison." *Biographical Directory of the United States Congress (1878–1962)*. http://bioguide.Congress.gov/scripts/biodisplay.pl?index=W00 0430.

"The William Winter Institute for Racial Reconciliation." http://www.winterinstitute.org/pages/aboutus.htm.

"Winstead, William Arthur." *Biographical Directory of the United States Congress (1940–1995)*. http://bioguide.Congress.gov/scripts/biodisplay.pl?index= W000641.

Theses and Dissertations

Armstrong, Margaret. "James Zachariah George: Champion of White Supremacy." Ph.D. diss., University of Alabama, 1938.

Bailey, Robert J. "Theodore G. Bilbo: Prelude to a Senate Career, 1932–1934." Master's thesis, University of Southern Mississippi, 1971.

Balsamo, Larry T. "Theodore G. Bilbo and Mississippi Politics, 1877–1932." Ph.D. diss., University of Missouri, 1967.

Bassett, Mary Jane H. "The Moral and Social Attitudes of Baptists in Antebellum Mississippi." Master's thesis, Mississippi State University, 1972.

Behel, Sandra K. "The Mississippi Home Front during World War II: Tradition and Change." Ph.D. diss., Mississippi State University, 1989.

Boothe, David F. "The Negro and Religion in Antebellum Mississippi." Master's thesis, Mississippi State University, 1965.

Boschert, Thomas. "A Family Affair: Mississippi Politics, 1882–1932." Ph.D. diss., University of Mississippi 1995.

Brady, Hugh G. "Voting, Class and Demography in Antebellum Mississippi." Ph.D. diss., Northern Illinois University, 1977.

Brazy, Martha J. "An American Planter: Slavery, Entrepreneurship, and Identity in the Life of Stephen Duncan, 1787–1867." Ph.D. diss., Duke University, 1998.

Brown, Robert L. "A Revival of Conservatism in Mississippi Politics: The Administration of Henry L. Whitfield, 1924–1927." Master's thesis, University of Mississippi, 1960.

Cameron, Mary Effie. "The Summer of 1835 in Mississippi History." Master's thesis, University of Mississippi, 1931.

Cammack, Abner Sam. "Emmett Lloyd Ross: Soldier, Editor and Politician." Master's thesis, Mississippi State University, 1965.

Cartledge, Connie Lynette. "James P. Coleman: Moderate Politician in an Age of Racial Strife, 1950–1965." Master's thesis, Mississippi State University, 1984.

Chance, Russell J. "Alexander Melvourne Jackson: Mississippi Lawyer, Editor, Soldier, and Politician, 1823–1857." Ph.D. diss., Mississippi State University, 1970.

Clay, Mary Harrison. "Gideon Lincecum, Southern Pioneer, 1793–1874." Master's thesis, Mississippi State University, 1953.

Cockrell, Thomas D. "Mississippi's Congressional Delegation and National Politics, 1828–1836." Ph.D. diss., Mississippi State University, 1981.

Cranford, Sammy O. "The Fernwood, Columbia and Gulf: A Railroad in the Piney Woods of South Mississippi." Ph.D. diss., Mississippi State University, 1983.

Davis, William Graham. "Attacking 'The Matchless Evil': Temperance and Prohibition in Mississippi, 1817–1908." Ph.D. diss., Mississippi State University, 1975.

Derr, Reid Stoner. "The Triumph of Progressivism: Governor Paul B. Johnson, Jr., and Mississippi in the 1960s." Ph.D. diss., University of Southern Mississippi, 1994.

Dodson, Leslie Weldon. "The Mississippi Sharecropper in Fact and Fiction." Master's thesis, Mississippi State College, 1952.

Ethridge, Richard C. "Mississippi's Role in the Dixiecrat Movement." Ph.D. diss., Mississippi State College, 1971.

Fox, Lisa Ann. "Cracking the Closed Society: James W. Silver and the Civil Rights Movement in Mississippi." Master's thesis, University of North Texas, 2010.

Gibson, Nola Kay Pearson. "A Biography of William F. Winter with Special Emphasis on his Contribution to Improving Education in Mississippi." Ph.D. diss., University of Mississippi, 1993.

Gleeson, David T. "The Mississippi Irish, 1700–1865." Ph.D. diss., Mississippi State University, 1993.

Gonzales, John Edmond. "The Public Career of Henry Stuart Foote, 1804–1880." Ph.D. diss., University of North Carolina, 1957.

Gregg, William B. "The Agrarian Movement in Grenada County." Master's thesis, Mississippi State College, 1953.

Hamilton, Charles. "Mississippi Politicians in the Progressive Era 1904–1920." Ph.D. diss., Vanderbilt University, 1958.

Hamilton, William Baskervill. "Holly Springs, Mississippi, to the Year 1878." Master's thesis, University of Mississippi, 1931.

Helms, Douglas. "Just Lookin' for a Home: The Cotton Boll Weevil and the South." Ph.D. diss., Florida State University, 1977.

Herring, Todd Ashley. "Natchez, 1795–1830: Life and Death on the Slavery Frontier." Ph.D. diss., Mississippi State University, 2000.

———. "Saloons and Drinking in Mississippi from the Colonial Era to Prohibition." Master's thesis, Mississippi State University, 1991.

Hillard, Elbert Riley. "A Biography of Fielding Wright: Mississippi's Mr. State Rights." Master's thesis, Mississippi State College, 1959.

Holzer, Scott. "Boomtown: The Social Transformation of Pascagoula, Mississippi, 1940–1943." Master's thesis, University of Mississippi, 1988.

Jackson, Annie Kate Hollingsworth. "The Political Rise of Martin Sennett Conner." Master's thesis, Mississippi State College, 1950.

Jordan, Amy Kearny. "Citizenship, Welfare Rights and the Politics of Respectability in Rural and Urban Mississippi 1900–1980." Ph.D. diss., University of Michigan, 2003.

Latham, Robert C. "The Dirt Farmer in Politics: A Study of Webster County, Mississippi, during the Rise of Democratic Factionalism, 1880–1910." Master's thesis, Mississippi State College, 1951.

Lucas, Sue T. "Edmond F. Noel: Progressive." Master's thesis, Mississippi College, 1965.

Luckett Jr., Robert E. "Yapping Dogs: Joe T. Patterson and the Limits of Massive Resistance." Ph.D. diss., University of Georgia, 1999.

Lundy, James W. "Alexander G. McNutt: A Biography." Master's thesis, Mississippi State University, 1965.

McCutchen, Samuel Proctor. "The Political Career of Albert Gallatin Brown." Ph.D. diss., University of Chicago, 1930.

Melton, Frances Elizabeth. "The Public Career of David Holmes 1809–1820." Master's thesis, Mississippi State College for Women, 1966.

Melton, Thomas R. "Mr. Speaker: A Biography of Walter Sillers." Master's thesis, University of Mississippi, 1972.

Mills, Gwen Ann. "A Social History of Jackson, Mississippi, 1920–1929." Master's thesis, University of Mississippi, 1965.

Montgomery, Joe Pressly. "Union Sentiment in the Tombigbee Prairie of Mississippi, 1851–1861." Master's thesis, Mississippi State College, 1971.

Mounger, Dwyn M. "Lynching in Mississippi, 1830–1930." Master's thesis, Mississippi State University, 1961.

Neal, Lamar Brown. "Chronicles of the Fire-Eaters: A Contemporary Account of the Secession Controversy in Mississippi, 1849–1853." Master's thesis, Mississippi State University, 1956.

Oldham, Dorothy Zellieoffer. "Life of Jacob Thompson." Master's thesis, University of Mississippi, 1930.

O'Neal, Stella Anne. "The Legislative Leadership of Governors Bilbo and Conner." Master's thesis, University of Mississippi, 1944.

Peck, Lucy Bryant. "The Life and Times of James Z. George." Master's thesis, Mississippi State University, 1964.

Quinnelly, Charles M. "The Mississippi Justice of the Peace." Master's thesis, Mississippi State University, 1957.

Rees, Gary L. "The Birth of a Legend: John A. Murrell's Connection to the 1835 Mississippi Insurrection Hysteria." Master's thesis, University of Southern Mississippi, 1982.

Rodabough, John E. "A History of the Negroes of Aberdeen and Monroe County, Mississippi, 1790–1916." Master's thesis, Mississippi State University, 1964.

Sallis, William Charles. "A Study of the Life and Times of LeRoy Percy." Master's thesis, Mississippi State College, 1957.

Saucier, Bobby W. "The Public Career of Theodore G. Bilbo." Ph.D. diss., Tulane University, 1971.

Smith, Charles P. "Theodore G. Bilbo's Senatorial Career: The Final Years: 1941–1947" Ph.D. diss., University of Southern Mississippi, 1983.

Smith, Suanna. "George Poindexter: A Political Biography." Ph.D. diss., University of Southern Mississippi, 1980.

Smith, Susan L. "Sick and Tired of Being Sick and Tired: Black Women and the National Health Movement, 1915–1950." Ph.D. diss., University of Wisconsin, 1991.

Sperry, Benjamin O. "Caught Between Our Moral and Material Selves: Mississippi's Elite White 'Moderates' and Their Role in Changing Race Relations, 1945–1956." Ph.D. diss., Case Western Reserve University, 2010.

Sumners, Mary Floyd. "Edgar Stewart Wilson: The Mississippi Eagle, Journalist of the New South." Ph.D. diss., Mississippi State University, 1962.

Tate, Roger D. "Easing the Burden: The Era of Depression and New Deal in Mississippi." Ph.D. diss., University of Tennessee, 1978.

Vance, Sandra Stringer. "The Congressional Career of John Bell Williams, 1947–1967." Ph.D. diss., Mississippi State University, 1976.

Vargis, Salli. "History of the Mississippi Federation of Business and Professional Women's Clubs 1924–1995." Ph.D. diss., Mississippi State University, 2004.

Vickers, Kenneth W. "John Rankin: Democrat and Demagogue." Master's thesis, Mississippi State, 1993.

Washburn, William Neil. "Progressive Educational Reform in Mississippi during the First Bilbo Administration, 1916–1920." Master's thesis, University of Mississippi, 1962.

White, Jesse Lamar, Jr. "Mississippi Electoral Politics, 1902–1976: The Emerging Modernization Consensus." Ph.D. diss., Massachusetts Institute of Technology, 1979.

Williams, Kenneth H. "Mississippi and Civil Rights, 1945–1954." Ph.D. diss., Mississippi State University. 1985.

Woods, William Leon. "The Travail of Freedom: Mississippi Blacks, 1862–1870." Ph.D. diss., Princeton University, 1979.

Wylie, Roxanne. "The Home Front in Faulkner's War Fiction." Master's thesis, Tennessee Technological University, 2009.

Zhang, Kemin. "Why They Fought? An Analysis of the Motives of Nonslaveholding Whites Toward the Civil War." Master's thesis, University of Southern Mississippi, 1993.

Miscellaneous

Brewer Papers. Mississippi Department of Archives and History. Z348 Box 1.

Clipping, University of Southern Mississippi, University Libraries. Maurice Zolotow, "The Man Who Astonished Hattiesburg," *Saturday Evening Post*, November 10, 1945.

Dye, David H., and Ronald C. Brister. *The Protohistoric Period in the Mid-South: 1500–1700: Proceedings of the 1983 Mid-South Archaeological Conference*. Jackson: Mississippi Department of Archives and History, 1986.

Kennedy, Lawrence T. Subject File. Judge George W. Armstrong Library, Natchez, Miss.

Mitchell, Dennis J. "Trial for Honor." In *Mississippi Mindscape*. Jackson: Mississippi Committee for the Humanities, 1986.

Report to the Mississippi Legislature: Review of the Mississippi Community College Foundation. Jackson, Miss.: PEER Committee, 1995.

Index